THIRD EDITION

EDUCATIONAL COMPUTING FOUNDATIONS

MICHAEL R. SIMONSON

Iowa State University

ANN THOMPSON

Iowa State University

Merrill,
an imprint of Prentice Hall
Upper Saddle River, New Jersey   Columbus, Ohio

Library of Congress Cataloging-in-Publication Data

Simonson, Michael R.
    Educational computing foundations / Michael R. Simonson, Ann Thompson.—3rd ed.
      p. cm.
    Includes bibliographical references and index.
    ISBN 0-13-375262-3
    1. Educational—Data processing—Study and teaching (Higher) 2. Computers—Study and teaching (Higher) 3. Computer-assisted instruction.   I. Thompson, Ann (Ann D.) II. Title.
LB1028.43.S57   1997
   370'.285—dc20   96-7075
                                   CIP

Cover art: ©Peter A. Simon/The Stock Market
Editor: Debra A. Stollenwerk
Production Editor: Louise N. Sette
Design Coordinator: Julia Zonneveld Van Hook
Text Designer: Susan E. Frankenberry
Cover Designer: Rod Harris
Production Manager: Pamela D. Bennett
Electronic Text Management: Marilyn Wilson Phelps, Matthew Williams, Karen L. Bretz, Tracey Ward

This book was set in Goudy Old Style and Avant Garde by Prentice Hall and was printed and bound by R.R. Donnelley & Sons Company. The cover was printed by Phoenix Color Corp.

© 1997 by Prentice-Hall, Inc.
Simon & Schuster/A Viacom Company
Upper Saddle River, New Jersey 07458

Earlier editions © 1994, 1992 by Macmillan College Publishing Company.

Printed in the United States of America

10 9 8 7 6 5 4 3 2 1

ISBN: 0-13-375262-3

Prentice-Hall International (UK) Limited, *London*
Prentice-Hall of Australia Pty. Limited, *Sydney*
Prentice-Hall of Canada, Inc., *Toronto*
Prentice-Hall Hispanoamericana, S. A., *Mexico*
Prentice-Hall of India Private Limited, *New Delhi*
Prentice-Hall of Japan, Inc., *Tokyo*
Simon & Schuster Asia Pte. Ltd., *Singapore*
Editora Prentice-Hall do Brasil, Ltda., *Rio de Janeiro*

Educational Computing Foundations, Third Edition, is written for use in an introductory instructional computing course for preservice or in-service teachers. It provides readers with the basic information they need to use computers professionally. A now-famous quote, known as "The Law of the Hammer," by an anonymous computer user best explains the philosophy behind this book.

> Give a 2-year-old a hammer, and suddenly a lot of things need hammering.

The teacher who uses this book will be able to distinguish between appropriate uses of computers in education and uses best met by other techniques. The computer is a powerful tool with incredible potential, but is not the only tool or technique available to the teacher. The educator who thinks the computer is the machine that will solve all learning problems is as naive about the potential of this technology as is the teacher who believes the computer has no place in the classroom.

The chapters are divided into two parts. Part One, Foundations of Educational Computing, provides the reader with the background information needed by computer users. The goal of these chapters is to provide the reader with a foundation of information to draw on in Part Two, Applications of Educational Computing. The assumption is that computer use in education is more than the application of the computer to the tasks of the teacher. Rather, effective educational computing is based on fundamental concepts that provide long-term direction to specific computing activities.

Chapter 1 is a new chapter in this edition. It presents information about how technology is transforming schools. Chapter 2 presents the computer's use in society and school, emphasizing the relationship between school uses and general uses outside the school. Theories and research that support the use of computers in teaching are presented in Chapter 3. If computers are to have a significant, long-term effect on education, there must be a theoretical rationale for their use that is based on research. Chapter 3 presents the beginnings of that rationale. Chapter 4 covers the technical information required by the teacher who uses computers. This information is presented early in the text so later chapters can refer to it. General programming techniques are also presented in Chapter 4. The fundamental organizational procedures followed when traditional languages such as BASIC are used to design instruction are included in this chapter.

Chapter 5 explains how computer-based learning affects the school curriculum. Specifically, it presents the rationale and techniques for teaching with computers. Chapter 6 concentrates on teaching about computers in the school, discussing curriculum topics such as keyboarding, computer literacy, computer programming, and computer science. Chapter 7 focuses on the equity issues in the use of computers and related technology.

Part Two, Applications of Educational Computing deals with the primary applications of computers for educators, such as word processing, data management, spreadsheet use, and computer communications. Chapters 8 through 11 discuss each of these important "tool applications" of computers. Each technique is explained, and examples of its relevance to teachers are given in each chapter. Chapter 11 has been extensively revised and includes a lengthy discussion of the Internet, the World Wide Web, and the potential of telecommunications.

Chapter 12, "Managing Computers: Selecting Software and Hardware," reviews the process of locating, evaluating, purchasing, and distributing computer lessons and machines. This chapter focuses on selecting items that complement and support the school's curriculum.

Computer languages are important tools that teachers also use. Although languages often are not considered applications, they often are used as such by teachers. Visualization and animation with computers using languages such as LOGO are discussed in Chapter 13. Because of its unique approach, LOGO is a computer language of considerable interest to teachers of all grades and subjects.

Recently, new "languages," such as hypermedia, have become available that differ significantly from other computer programming languages. Chapter 14 presents information on hypermedia. Two hypermedia authoring systems, Apple's HyperCard and IBM's LinkWay Live!, are also discussed in detail because they are used often by teachers and students to develop computer-based instruction. Interactive computer and video systems are also explained in Chapter 14. Chapters 13 and 14 are overviews. The reader therefore can intelligently select "second-level" courses in one of the languages, or can begin studying the syntax of a language, using one of the many individualized tutorials that are available.

Part Two concludes with Chapter 15, which forecasts the role of the computer in education and the future effect of computer systems on the teaching and learning process.

Educational Computing Foundations concludes with four appendixes, a comprehensive glossary, and a detailed index.

RESEARCH-LITERATURE REPORTS

Educational Computing Foundations contains numerous notes from the literature of the educational computing field. These short summaries of pertinent research results and reports from the professional literature are located in appropriate sections of chapters to support the narrative of the text. Notes From the Literature are included because educational computing, as a course of study, is of sufficient importance and sophistication that the user should be sensitive to the research and theory-building that provide a foundation for the effective use of computers in the schools.

TERMINOLOGY

Many terms are used to describe the use of computers in the school: computer-assisted instruction (CAI) and computer-managed instruction (CMI) are the oldest. Unfortunately, these terms sometimes give readers the wrong impression about the role of the computer in the school, especially CAI, which connotes a relatively insignificant purpose for the computer. *Computer-based instruction* (CBI) and *computer-based learning* (CBL) are often used to replace CAI because they more accurately describe the computer's important place in the teaching and learning process. In this text, CBI and CBL are used whenever possible.

In summary, this book is a text for teachers. Its purpose is to give a broad, yet detailed, explanation of how computers work (systems), how they are used (applications), and how instruction is designed for them (authoring). The computer is viewed as a multidimensional tool just beginning to be correctly applied in education. Teachers who use this book to learn about computers will contribute to the continued understanding of this powerful technological device.

WHAT'S NEW IN THE THIRD EDITION?

The third edition of *Educational Computing Foundations* differs from the second in these ways:

1. More than 100 new photographs and drawings have been added.
2. All chapters have been significantly revised and updated.
3. A new chapter on how schools are being restructured around technology has been added.
4. New sections of chapters on statistical software and IBM's LinkWay have been added.

5. More information on hypermedia environments has been added.

6. An expanded chapter 11 discusses the Internet, World Wide Web, and the increased importance of computer communications.

We believe these changes keep *Educational Computing Foundations* current and useful.

ACKNOWLEDGMENTS

We appreciate the helpful suggestions of the following reviewers: Pedro L. Cartagena, University of Puerto Rico; Richard A. Couch, Clarion University; Daniel C. Orey, California State University–Sacramento; and Donald J. Winiecki, Texas Tech University.

BRIEF CONTENTS

CONTENTS

3

Research on Computers in Education   35

4

Computer Systems: What Teachers Need to Know   59

5

Teaching with Computers: An Overview of Computer-Based Learning   93

CONTENTS

9

Managing Information: Data Managers   183

10

Managing Numbers: Spreadsheets and Statistical Analysis   201

11

Managing Information: Telecommunications and the Internet   225

12

Managing Computers: Selecting Software and Hardware   257

13

LOGO: A Visualization Language for Learners   275

14

Hypermedia and Multimedia With HyperCard and LinkWay   303

15

Computers in Education: Past, Present, and Future   327

APPENDIX A:

Computer Systems   347

PART ONE

FOUNDATIONS OF EDUCATIONAL COMPUTING

CHAPTER ONE

TECHNOLOGY AND SCHOOL TRANSFORMATION

GOAL

This chapter introduces the concept of school transformation and ideas about how technology can be used to facilitate school transformation.

OBJECTIVES

The reader will be able to do the following:

1. Cite specific ways that roles of learners are changing in schools.
2. Cite specific ways that roles of teachers are changing in schools.
3. List five major goals for schools of the future.
4. Define *metacognition.*
5. Describe the two major educational reform efforts of the past two decades.
6. Describe what is meant by *active learning.*
7. Describe a specific example of a constructivist learning environment.
8. Explain the relationship of the computer and progressive education.
9. Define *metacognition.*
10. Summarize Sheingold and Hadley's findings on changes taking place in technologically enriched classrooms.
11. Summarize Becker's findings on trends in K–12 computer use.
12. Summarize the major findings from the ACOT project.

We are at a point in the history of education when radical change is possible, and the possibility for that change is directly tied to the impact of the computer.

Papert (1980)

It is important to note at the beginning of your study of computers in education that technology alone will not change or improve education. In fact, most uses of computers in school up to this point have been to do what we were already doing in schools, but in a slightly different way. Although educators agree that computers can be used to engage students in new and more productive types of work, most current computer use in schools still focuses on learning about the computer, using the computer as an "electronic worksheet," or using the computer in activities that are isolated from the rest of the curriculum.

ABOUT THE CHAPTER

You will begin your study of computer use in education with an introduction to how computers can be used to expand and enhance what happens in classrooms. Throughout this text, emphasis will be placed on using computers and technology to change schools for learners. Thus, this chapter will include a discussion of the changing roles of schools, learners, and teachers as well as a discussion of the role technology can play in these changes.

The chapter begins with a discussion of transforming schools and then moves to the potential role of technology in this transformation process. There is much discussion in the education community about both restructuring and transforming schools. In this chapter, the terms school *restructuring* and *transformation* are used interchangeably.

The information in this chapter will be the basis and rationale for the more specific topics presented in the chapters that follow.

INTRODUCTION TO SCHOOL TRANSFORMATION

Living in a technologically based information society has created new expectations regarding the education of students. These changing societal expectations, along with new research on how children learn, have challenged the traditional model of schooling. No longer is the teacher-centered, delivery-of-information mode of instruction considered adequate for preparing students for the future. Educators and policy makers nationwide recognize the critical need for restructuring the teaching and learning process, and for helping students become independent thinkers, explore complex problems, and apply what they learn in real-life situations.

In this chapter, restructuring and transforming schools will refer to changing both what and how students learn in school. We will suggest that schools are in the process of changing the types of subjects and skills taught to students, as well as the ways in which these things are taught.

Many proponents of school restructuring efforts (David, 1991; Collins, 1991; Sheingold, 1991) have identified technology as a critical ingredient that can support the new recommendations for schools. The new information and communication technologies are heralded by many educators as exciting new conceptual tools that can promote students' active learning (Barron & Golman, 1994). The potential of technology to support the teaching–learning process has created important implications for educators.

HISTORICAL BACKGROUND

In the last two decades the educational reform movement has focused its efforts on two major but divergent directions. During the late 1970s and early 1980s, reformers responded with a "back-to-basics" approach as a reaction against a perceived growing liberalism and permissiveness among educational practices. Assuming that the problems in education were caused by teachers and administrators, professionals and lay activists translated their demands for academic excellence into more required subjects, into increased teacher regulation, a longer school year, more homework, and higher test scores (Cuban, 1990; Muffoleto, 1994).

The current wave of educational reform is founded on a more radical assumption that the whole system needs to be restructured to achieve the kinds of learning now seen as important for students (Sheingold, 1991). Teachers and students are now considered part of the solution to the problems, and not the problem (Muffoleto, 1994). It is suggested that the new reform must begin with new and shared understandings of how students learn. David (1991) comments that the scope of current restructuring efforts "goes well beyond that

FIGURE 1.1
Technology can help teachers assume the role of facilitator.
Photograph courtesy of Apple Computer, Inc.

of any previous reforms by identifying the many levels and pieces of the system that must change in order to transform the learning process" (p. 39). Changes in the way schools are organized and the way individual roles are defined are called for to create more challenging and appropriate learning environments for students.

THEORETICAL BASE FOR THE NEW EDUCATIONAL DIRECTIONS

The idea of active learning advocated by the restructuring movement is not new. John Dewey, at the beginning of the century, talked about the need for experiential and student-centered learning. In the past, however, approaches that placed students in the center of the learning experience "were seen as important for only selected groups of students" (Lauren, 1987, cited in Sheingold, 1991). Today, Sheingold (1991) argues, active learning is a priority for *all* students. The growing body of research and learning theory that supports these learning goals "both demands and makes credible a broader commitment to this approach than has thus far been attempted" (p. 18).

The theoretical base for restructuring has its roots in cognitive psychology and constructivist theory (Collins, 1991; McDaniel, McInerney, & Armstrong, 1993). Cognitive psychologists believe the essence of any act of learning is the active role played by the learner in transforming the message of instruction into the learner's own cognitive structures. The underlying idea is that "concepts which are integrated into the cognitive schema(ta), are constructed rather than borrowed" (McDaniel, McInerney, & Armstrong, 1993, p. 74).

Constructivists believe learning occurs when learners become agents of their own knowledge. Rather than absorbing information delivered by the teacher, learners in a constructivist environment develop their own understanding and meaning of the world through experimentation and active engagement in challenging tasks. Through interaction with and support from the world of people, objects, and technologies, the learners' experiences are expanded and their understanding is modified in light of the new data (Sheingold, 1991; Strommen & Lincoln, 1992). Whereas more traditional models of learning emphasized teachers delivering information to students, constructivist models emphasize students constructing their own knowledge.

New Learning Environments

A constructive learning environment should engage learners in real-world activities and provide them with the metacognitive skills required to function in those authentic activities. In these environments the instructor is a facilitator who guides and supports students in establishing and monitoring their goals and strategies. Students engage in complex tasks and a rich variety of experiences that enable them to approach and evaluate new concepts from multiple perspectives. Higher-order activities will help them understand the relationships among new concepts and promote a deeper, more critical role in learning.

Figure 1.2 compares traditional school environments and constructivist environments. It should be noted that almost all the characteristics associated with constructivist classrooms tend to be learner-centered rather than teacher-centered.

Changing Views of Learning, Learners

The traditional views of learners and learning have emphasized a static view of the learner. In these views, the learner is a vessel to be filled with knowledge. Correspondingly, learning is viewed as collecting pieces of information or filling up the vessel. The job of the teacher is to fill the learner with knowledge and information and the job of the learner is to receive this information.

New views of learners and learning tend to emphasize the dynamic nature of the learning process. The learner is viewed more as a lamp to be lit and learning is viewed more as making connections, solving problems, and constructing knowledge. This active view of the learner also suggests a different view of teachers. The teacher is a facilitator of student learning, with classroom emphasis on the activity of the students.

FIGURE 1.2
A look at school environments

Traditional Classrooms	Constructivist Classrooms
Curriculum is presented part to whole, with emphasis on basic skills.	Curriculum is presented whole to part with emphasis on big concepts.
Strict adherence to fixed curriculum is highly valued.	Pursuit of student questions is highly valued.
Curricular activities rely heavily on textbooks and workbooks.	Curricular activities rely heavily on primary sources of data and manipulative materials.
Students are viewed as "blank slates" onto which information is etched by the teacher.	Students are viewed as thinkers with emerging theories about the world.
Teachers generally behave in a didactic manner, disseminating information to students.	Teachers generally behave in an interactive manner, mediating the environment for students.
Teachers seek the correct answer to validate student learning.	Teachers seek the students' points of view to understand students' current conceptions for use in subsequent lessons.
Assessment of student learning is viewed as separate from teaching and occurs almost entirely through testing.	Assessment of student learning is interwoven with teaching and occurs through teacher observations of students at work and through student exhibitions and portfolios.
Students primarily work alone.	Students primarily work in groups.

What Students Learn

Along with new views of students and teachers have emerged new ideas of what should be taught in schools. Although educators may differ some on the specifics, most agree that the following five areas are the most important curricular areas for children who will live their professional lives in the Information Age:

1. Problem solving and critical thinking
2. Information handling skills
   - Accessing
   - Manipulating
   - Synthesizing
   - Evaluating
3. Global awareness
4. Technology skills
5. Ability to collaborate and cooperate with others

It should be noted that all five of these areas tend to encourage students' learning process skills rather than learning discrete facts. Given the large amounts of information that students will be asked to work with in their professional lives, experts agree that learning to handle information efficiently is more important than memorizing that information.

Following the new educational directions, however, is not easy. Changing what and how students learn and how teachers teach are difficult tasks to accomplish. As David (1991) states, "these changes do not happen by fiat or rhetoric" (p. 40). In fact, these changes have been suggested for more than 30 years. If one looks carefully into the history of U.S. education, one will find that progressive, learner-centered education has been advocated and attempted several times in the past. Although many of the early experiments with progressive education were successful, most schools have returned to traditional models of education. Some have suggested that technology may be the critical missing piece that will make progressive, learner-centered education possible in U.S. schools. The following discussion will focus on how well-integrated technology can be a critical ingredient that can support the new educational directions.

HOW TECHNOLOGY CAN HELP

Proponents of restructuring with technology argue that today's technologies have the potential to transform the relationships between students and teachers and to change how schools operate (Bagley & Hunter 1992;

Notes From the Literature

"What is curious about these earlier technologies [film, radio, instructional television] and their cycles of optimism and pessimism is that none (was) associated with national reform movements. If there is any pattern in the movements to reform schools since the mid-nineteenth century, it is that none (was) dependent on instructional technologies beyond teacher, blackboard, textbook, pen and paper."

Cuban, L. (1993). Computers meet classroom: Who wins? Teachers College Record, 95, 185–210.

David, 1991; Collins, 1991; Sheingold, 1991). The underlying assumption of these claims is that the computer-related technologies—unlike older forms of media, like televisions and film projectors—are *learning* devices rather than *teaching* devices (Thomas & Boysen, 1984). According to the same authors, the computer's capability to interact with students and react to their individual needs has the potential to provide the context for student-centered learning and to assist students in learning to educate themselves.

Papert (1993) argues that the computer, in all its manifestations, offers progressive educators the tools that can bring and shape qualitative changes in education. One reason early designers of experiments in progressive education failed to bring change, Papert believes, is that they lacked the *tools* to create new methods in a reliable and systematic manner.

> When educators tried to craft schools based on the ideas of visionaries it was as if Leonardo (da Vinci) had tried to make an airplane out of oak and power it with a mule. Most practitioners who tried to follow the seminal thinkers in education were forced to compromise so deeply that the original intent was lost. (pp. 15–16)

The literature that interrelates technology and restructuring, although not extensive, shows evidence that technology can provide the tools for advancing the new educational goals. The following discussion will focus on the potential of technology to address some of the goals for restructured schools.

Metacognitive Skills

Perhaps one of the most promising benefits that computer-related technologies offer is the possibility of helping students develop metacognitive skills. Metacog-

nition, a major field of cognitive and developmental psychology, refers to one's self-awareness of knowledge and control of cognitive strategies during problem solving (Montaque, 1992).

In one sense, students using metacognitive strategies become self-conscious about their learning and problem solving. They are aware of the strategies they are using for problem solving; they monitor and regulate their own strategies. Clements (1987) found that students working with LOGO improved in both comprehension monitoring and realizing when they did not understand something. Lehrer and Randle (1987) conducted a study in which one group of first graders used LOGO and one other used a commercially available problem solving software. Findings indicated that both environments enhanced problem solving performance, but LOGO was reported as most facilitative for "learning to learn."

Another example of a computer environment that promotes metacognitive thinking is the Jasper Series, developed by the Cognition and Technology Group at Vanderbilt, which provides a variety of video disk adventures of a person named Jasper Woodbury. In one of Jasper's adventures, for instance, students have to help Jasper get home without running out of gasoline. The purpose of this activity is to encourage students to use their cognitive and metacognitive skills to solve the problem. Possible outcomes could be that students develop a problem solving strategy—for example, identify Jasper's major goal (to get home before sunset without running out of gasoline), generate the subproblems that represent obstacles to this goal (e.g., running out of gasoline), and devise strategies to deal with the various subgoals (The Cognition and Technology Group at Vanderbilt, 1990).

Higher-Order Thinking

Another potential for computers in a restructuring learning environment is the encouragement of higher-order thinking. Computers can easily perform lower-lever mechanical tasks, while the students are immersed in higher-order cognition. For example, word processors can handle the mechanical part of the writing process, while students focus on elaborating and expanding their ideas. In the same sense, the ability of data bases to store, manage, and sort facts and details leaves students free to engage in more complex tasks, such as analyzing, evaluating, organizing, and applying information. The encouragement of testing and refining of hypotheses is one possible outcome when working with data bases (Hunter, 1985). For example, students could be asked

FIGURE 1.3
Technology can help facilitate the learning of problem solving skills.
Photograph courtesy of Apple Computer, Inc.

to examine the hypothesis that "good electrical conductors are also good heat conductors." In this case students could search a data base that includes information about various elements to find all the elements that meet each of the above criteria separately, and then both of the criteria combined. Then students could test the hypothesis they originally formulated and later try a different hypothesis (Hunter, 1985).

Christopher Dede suggests that the words *intelligence amplification,* or IA, describe the role of the computer in promoting higher-order thinking in students. In Dede's model, the computer does what it does best (generally lower-order menial calculation and organizational activities) while the human user does what he/she does best (higher-order thinking and problem solving). Given this relationship, the human and the computer are "smarter" together than either would be on its own and the product is generally of much higher quality. Dede's ideas about computer use in schools are discussed further in Chapter 5.

Notes From the Literature

We feel that the greatest potential for computer applications is in the area of retrieval, manipulation, and exchange of information. Full utilization of the capabilities means an escape from '2 X 4 learning'—that is, learning bounded by the two covers of the book and the four walls of the classroom.

McDaniel, E., McInerney, W., & Armstrong, P. (1993). Computers and school reform. Educational Research Technology and Development, 41(1), 73–78.

INFORMATION LITERACY AND COMMUNICATION SKILLS

Information literacy and communication skills are also important goals of restructuring schools. Being able to read and write is no longer adequate for the Information Age. To communicate effectively, a person must also be able to understand the author's intent, evaluate the message, and apply the acquired knowledge in a meaningful way. The computer, which is at its basis a communication tool, provides fertile ground on which information literacy skills can be nurtured. Ready access to large data bases and electronic networks makes it easier for students to examine topics of their interest using whatever information is available, then to analyze it, organize it, and share findings that are unique to each student (McDaniel, McInerney, & Armstrong, 1993).

Telecommunication technologies can also extend learning beyond the classroom. For example, Pearlman (1989) reported a project in which 200 schools throughout the country worked in teams to measure the acid level of their local water, communicated their results via National Geographic Kids Network, consulted experts in the area, and compared their findings with current scientific analyses.

At Iowa State University (ISU) many telecommunication projects are going on, in which preservice teachers communicate with public school students through the Internet and the fiber-optic Iowa Communication Network. In a recent project, elementary students in Seattle solved mathematical problems online with the help of preservice teachers at ISU (Poole, 1995).

Cooperative Social Structure

Rather than isolating the students and the teacher, computer-related technologies tend to promote a cooperative social structure. Because these technologies require the use of new complex skills, users frequently consult one another to use them successfully (Ray, 1991). For example, a Rochester, New York, middle school project has helped students learn about their environment through collaborative problem solving processes. Student teams gather material and communicate their understandings via a multimedia computer exhibit.

Student-Centered Learning

When carefully designed and implemented, computer-related technologies also have the potential of providing student-centered learning, one of the most critical educational directions of the restructuring movement. The Archeotype project at Dalton School in New York, for example, involves sixth-grade students in a simulated archaeological dig in ancient Greece (Hawkins, 1993). Groups of students dig simulated classical sites, classify the artifacts they uncover, and consult a variety of sources on a common data base. When they complete their exploration, they come up with an overall interpretation and produce reports about their investigations. In this learning environment students learn many historical inquiry skills by doing history rather than by just reading about history. Making the same point, Shanker states, ". . . for most of us, the best way of learning is by doing, by making and unmaking something, solving problems and investigating for ourselves the questions we are made to care about" (Shanker, cited in Pearlman, 1989, p. 14).

Currently, many model projects and schools around the country are experimenting with using technology combined with new structures, schedules, and spaces to promote active student learning. The Rochester, New York, project mentioned earlier has middle school students working in team-taught grade-level clusters in a project called Discover Rochester (Sheingold, 1991). The project is an interdisciplinary effort designed to develop thinking and problem solving skills. Students, working in groups, collect information about the Rochester environment from a scientific, mathematical, historical, cultural, and literary perspective. Students communicate their work through text, audio, graphics, music, and maps on Macintosh computers. One entire day each week is devoted to student project work. Student multimedia projects are displayed at the

FIGURE 1.4
Students engaged in learning activity.
Photograph courtesy of Apple Computer, Inc.

Rochester Museum and Science Center. Preliminary results from the project are encouraging. Students and teachers are enthusiastic about the project, and the quality of student work has improved. Student attendance has also improved.

Changing Teacher Roles

In addition to changing the roles of students in the learning process, computer-related technologies have the potential of changing the role of the teacher in the classroom. Successful integration of technology, although not widespread in schools, is happening in some places. Held, Newsom, and Peiffer (1991), reporting on their experiences from the integration of technology into their restructuring classrooms, state that the computers helped them adopt a "Guide on the Side" philosophy that allowed children to work more independently and gave them more time to spend with small groups of students. LOGO, a key piece of their classroom environment, provided their students opportunities to explore microworlds in mathematics. More importantly, it gave the teachers a window into their students' thinking processes as they observed their work.

Sheingold and Hadley (1990) reported three major changes taking place in technologically enriched classrooms: (1) teachers expect more of their students and can present more complex material, (2) teachers have greater opportunities for individualization, and (3) integrating the computer in the instruction changes the roles of teachers and students such that classrooms are more student-centered and teachers act more as coaches and facilitators. They also found that computer-using teachers devote considerable time and effort to teaching with computers in their classroom, and that they are supported in their efforts.

In a study of telecommunication use in schools, Honey and Henriquez (1993) found similar effects for telecommunications use on teacher style. Teachers who use telecommunications tended to assign more independent, project-based work, and spend less time lecturing and more time with individual students. Moreover, computers can empower teachers by breaking the isolation of individual teachers from the confinement of their own classroom walls. Telecommunications give teachers the tools to develop and sustain conversations with experts and peers and to exchange and discuss well-developed materials and examples of good practice (Hawkins, 1993).

Notes From the Literature

A theoretical base for redesigning classrooms exists in the work of cognitive psychologists who are emphasizing the importance of mental activity in transforming information into larger concepts, perceptions, and beliefs.

McDaniel, E., McInerney, W., & Armstrong, P. (1993). Computers and school reform. Educational Research Technology and Development, 41(1), 73–78.

FIGURE 1.5
Newer views of learning focus on active learners.

Photograph courtesy of Apple Computer, Inc.

Evidence from Apple Classrooms of Tomorrow

In the mid-1980s, Apple Computer funded several schools around the country so that the schools could provide computers and technology to every student at certain grade levels. Funded classrooms were called Apple Classrooms of Tomorrow (ACOT). These classrooms provided computers for every child and every teacher and, in some cases, home computers for the students. As part of the ACOT project, researchers have studied both children and teachers in these computer-enriched classrooms to help provide insight into the possible effects of technologically enriched environments.

The research on ACOT schools has evolved over the decade that the project has been in operation. Early in the project, results shattered some of the preconceived notions against using technology in classrooms. It was found that in these technologically enriched classrooms:

- Teachers were not helpless technical illiterates.
- Children did not become social isolates.
- Children's interest in and engagement with the technology did not decline with routine use.

- Children, even very young ones, did not find the keyboard a barrier to fluid use of the computer (Dwyer, 1994).

In more recent years, technology use in ACOT classrooms has accompanied major changes in how teachers teach and how children learn. "Simply put, an array of tools for acquiring information and for thinking and expression allows more children more ways to enter the learning enterprise successfully. These same experi-

> ### Notes From the Literature
>
> Schools equipped with telecommunications networks become schools without walls, where learning can continue after the bell and in spite of the buses. Teachers equipped with computers at home and school can create, preserve, revise, and convey their instructions in forms hitherto denied them. They gain access to resources both within and outside the school.
>
> *Thomas, D. W. (1994). Technology's next phase is ready to fly: Are we? The Education Digest, 59(9), 13–20.*

ences provide the skills that will enable students to live productive lives in the global, digital, information-based future they all face" (Dwyer, 1994, p. 9).

Researchers from the ACOT project say technology encourages change in classrooms in the following ways:

- Technology encourages fundamentally different forms of interactions among students and between students and teachers.
- Technology engages students systematically in higher-order cognitive tasks.
- Technology prompts teachers to question old assumptions about instruction and learning (Dwyer, 1994, p. 9).

Certainly the data from the ACOT schools look quite promising as we consider the potential of technology to help facilitate change in schools. Visiting an ACOT school, an observer will immediately notice the ease with which students turn to the computer as a tool. Students tend to use the computers with the same ease that students in traditional schools use pencils, paper, and chalk. Student projects in the ACOT schools show evidence of a variety of computer applications, from using telecommunications to obtain information to using a graphics program to draw graphics to illustrate a project.

Although the results from the ACOT schools help demonstrate the potential of the computer in the transformation of schools, it should be noted that the situation in the majority of U.S. schools is still quite different from that in the ACOT schools. In the next section, the current state of computer use in schools will be summarized.

CURRENT TECHNOLOGY USE IN SCHOOLS

Although technology, tied to the goals of the restructuring movement, can change the roles of students and teachers, it is not being used to its full potential. Research findings suggest, in fact, that computers are generally still used to accomplish traditional tasks in schools, rather than to support new directions for teachers and students (Becker, 1994; Honey & Henriquez, 1993).

K–12 Schools

In a recent analysis of the trends of K–12 school use of the new information technologies, Becker (1994) reported the following:

- Similar to the focus of computer use in schools during the past decade, the largest portion of computer use today remains focused on computer education classes in secondary schools and drill-and-practice exercises in elementary schools.
- The major use of computers is not to expand the curriculum but to provide information to students and teach basic skills.
- The amount of hardware available in U.S. schools continues to increase, although outdated hardware still dominates both the installed base and the acquisitions of school computers.
- Computers in schools are primarily located in computer labs.
- In spite of the changes that computers have brought to schools, only a small minority of teachers can be said to be major computer users.

Honey and Henriquez (1993) reported similar findings in a study investigating the trends in telecommunications. They found that most teachers and students do not use technology to expand and enhance the curriculum, and that the available hardware is insufficient. They suggested that more time for telecommunications should be allowed for teachers and students and that more attention should be paid to the education of the teachers.

Many reasons have been cited for the lack of influence of technology in the school arena. The most frequently cited reasons include the lack of awareness of appropriate uses of technology, limited budgets, lack of adequate time and support, absence of new forms of assessment, difficulty in disturbing the school system, as well as teacher education priorities (Becker, 1994; Collins, 1991; Strommen & Lincoln, 1992). Whatever the reasons, it is clear that technology has not yet come close to its potential for changing schools.

Teachers suggest that time is the biggest reason for the lack of powerful applications of computers in schools. Teachers need time to learn how to use computers and computer-related technologies, and how to effectively integrate these technologies into their teaching. Unfortunately, most schools and districts put money into hardware and software, but fail to allocate sufficient funding to support teacher time for learning about its most valuable uses.

Teacher Education

Given the need for more time for teachers to learn about technology, it seems natural that teacher education institutions would include technology as an impor-

Technology is not central to the teacher preparation experience in most colleges of education. Consequently, most teachers graduate from teacher preparation institutions with limited knowledge of the ways technology can be used in their professional practice. (Office of Technology and Assessment, 1995, p. 165)

The authors of the report cite several specific examples of current projects modeling uses of technology that can help transform teacher education. Similar to K–12 education, technology can help faculty create classrooms that are more learner-oriented and less focused on lecture methods. In one college of education, students use CD-ROM materials that simulate classroom management situations; the materials create real-life classroom situations that students are asked to solve and discuss. In another college, preservice teacher education students use telecommunications to communicate with fifth-grade students about solving mathematics problems created by the teacher education students. In both cases, computers are helping teacher education students become more actively involved in the real world of the classroom.

Many authors argue that for teachers to use computers to change and improve classrooms, they must have had powerful learning experiences with computers themselves. It appears that preservice teacher education is a natural starting place for this important process.

tant component of preservice teacher education. Clearly, spending time working with preservice teachers to help them learn to use technology and to develop a vision of how to use technology in teaching is a sound investment in the future.

Although there are teacher education institutions around the country that are integrating technology into their instruction, many institutions face some of the same difficulties as K–12 institutions in terms of technology use. Much of the current use of technology in teacher education is still in a separate course that is "about technology" rather than in the entire teacher education curriculum. To integrate technology into the teacher education curriculum, education faculty must learn to use technology and also learn to teach with technology. A report from the Office of Technology Assessment (1995) stated:

SUMMARY

It seems clear that computers and computer-related technologies can be used to help facilitate major changes in the way teachers teach and the way students learn. Computers can be used to help teachers focus on student-centered activities and to help students produce authentic products. In reality, however, computers have been used to do what we already do in school, just in a slightly different way.

For schools and teachers to take full advantage of the potential of computer-related technologies, more time must be allotted for teachers to learn to use the technologies. In addition, teachers must be provided help in learning to integrate technologies into their teaching.

The information in this textbook will focus on using computers and computer-related technologies to expand and enhance the activities of both students and teachers. We believe these technologies can help facilitate transformation of schools and will present specific information with this goal in mind.

SELF-TEST QUESTIONS

1. The idea of learner-centered classrooms is a relatively new one in education.
   a. True
   b. False
2. Describe what is meant by constructivism.
3. List five major goals for schools today.
4. Students in ACOT schools tend to work individually on computer projects.
   a. True
   b. False
5. Describe the traditional view of the role of learners in school.
6. Describe the traditional view of the role of teachers in school.
7. Becker found that most schools in the '90s use computers to help students develop problem solving skills.
   a. True
   b. False
8. Teachers indicate that lack of available computers is the major barrier to using computers in classrooms.
   a. True
   b. False
9. Teachers indicate that time is the major barrier to their ability to use computers effectively in classrooms.
   a. True
   b. False
10. Describe three of several ways computers can contribute to school transformation.
11. Which of the following computer uses are most common in schools today?
    a. Problem solving
    b. Tool software
    c. Drill and practice
12. Most computers in school are located in individual classrooms.
    a. True
    b. False

ANSWERS TO SELF-TEST QUESTIONS

1. b. False. For years, educators have been advocating learner-centered classrooms. Efforts to achieve this goal, however, have failed and schools have returned to traditional, teacher-centered environments.
2. Constructivism is a philosophy of learning that suggests learners construct their own knowledge and meaning. Constructivist learning practices encourage the learner to relate new information and experiences to previous experience and thus to create meaning.
3. Five major goals for schools today usually include:
   1. Problem solving and critical thinking
   2. Information handling skills
      Accessing
      Manipulating
      Synthesizing
      Evaluating
   3. Global awareness
   4. Technology skills
   5. Ability to collaborate and cooperate with others
4. b. False. Studies in ACOT schools have shown a movement toward a cooperative social structure; students tend to work together to produce complex projects.
5. Traditionally, students in school have been viewed as vessels to be filled with information. More recent views of learners, however, emphasize the role of learners as active participants in their learning.
6. Traditionally, teachers in schools have been viewed as deliverers of knowledge and information. In traditional classrooms, the teacher has been the center of attention. In transformed schools, however, the teacher assumes the role of facilitator for active student learning.
7. b. False. Becker's results indicate that schools are still using computers for drill and practice and for learning about computers.
8. b. False. Although availability of computers is cited as a problem by teachers, teachers indicate that having time to learn about using the computers and develop approaches to using computers is their biggest barrier in using computers in classrooms.
9. a. True.
10. Technology can be used to help students develop metacognitive skills. Technology can be used to help students develop problem-solving skills. Technology can facilitate the use of cooperative social structures. Technology can help the teacher focus on student-centered learning activities. Technology can help the teacher become more of a facilitator in the classroom.

11. c.   Schools are beginning to use computers as tools and for problem solving, but drill and practice remains the most common use.
12. b.   False. In most schools, computers are located in centralized laboratories.

REFERENCES

Bagley, C., & Hunter, B. (1992). Restructuring, constructivism, and technology: Forging a new relationship. *Educational Technology, 32*(7), 22–27.

Barron, L. C., & Golman, E. S. (1994). Integrating technology with teacher preparation. In B. Means (Ed.), *Technology and educational reform: The reality behind the promise.* San Francisco: Jossey-Bass Publishers.

Becker, H. J. (1994). *Analysis and trends of school use of new information technologies.* Prepared for the Office of Technology Assessment, U.S. Congress (Contract: No. K3-0666.0). Irvine, CA: University of California, Department of Education.

Clements, D. H. (1987). Longitudinal study of the effects of Logo programming on cognitive abilities and achievement. *Journal of Educational Computing Research, 3*(1), 73–94.

Collins, A. (1991). The role of computer technology in restructuring schools. *Phi Delta Kappan, 73,* 28–36.

Cognition and Technology Group at Vanderbilt. (1990). Anchored instruction and its relationship to situated cognition. *Educational Researcher, 19*(6), 2–10.

Cuban, L. (1990). Reforming again, again, and again. *Educational Researcher, 19*(1), 3–12.

David, J. (1991). Restructuring and technology: Partners in change. *Phi Delta Kappan, 73,* 37–40, 78–82.

Dede, C. (1987). Empowering environments, hypermedia, and microworlds. *The Computing Teacher, 14*(3), 20–24.

Hawkins, J. (1993). *Technology and the organization of schooling* (Tech. Rep. No. 28). New York: Bank Street College of Education, Center for Technology in Education.

Held, C., Newsom, J., & Peiffer, M. (1991). The integrated technology classroom: An experiment in restructuring elementary school instruction. *The Computing Teacher, 18*(6), 21–23.

Honey, M., & Henriquez, A. (1993). *Telecommunications and K–12 educators: Findings from a national survey.* New York: Bank Street College of Education, Center for Technology in Education.

Hunter, B. (1985, May). Problem solving with data bases. *The Computing Teacher,* 20–27.

Lehrer, R., & Randle, R. (1987). Problem solving, metacognition and composition: The effects of interactive software for first-grade children. *Journal of Educational Computing Research, 3,* 409–427.

McDaniel, E., McInerney, W., & Armstrong, P. (1993). Computers and school reform. *ETR&D, 41*(1), 73–78.

Montaque, M. (1992). The effects of cognitive and metacognitive strategy instruction on the mathematical problem solving of middle school students with learning disabilities. *Journal of Learning Disabilities, 25*(4), 230–248.

Muffoleto, R. (1994, February). Technology and restructuring education: Constructing a context. *Educational Technology,* 24–28.

Office of Technology Assessment. (1995). *Teachers & technology: Making the connection.* Washington, DC: U.S. Congress.

Papert, S. (1993). *The children's machine: Rethinking school in the age of the computer.* New York: Basic Books.

Papert, S. (1980). *Mindstorms.* New York: Basic Books.

Pearlman, R. (1989). Technology's role in restructuring schools. *Electronic Learning, 8*(8), 8–9, 12, 14–45, 56.

Poole, D. (in press). Making mathematics real for preservice teachers: Using the Internet. In D. Carey, R. Carey, D. A. Willis, & J. Willis (Eds.), *Technology and Teacher Education Annual 1995.* Greenville, SC: East Carolina University.

Ray, D. (1991). Technology and restructuring part I: New educational directions. *The Computing Teacher, 18*(6), 9–20.

Sheingold, K. (1991). Restructuring for learning with technology: The potential for synergy. *Phi Delta Kappan, 73,* 17–27.

Sheingold, K., & Hadley, M. (1990, September). *Accomplished teachers: Integrating computers into classroom practice.* New York: Bank Street College of Education, Center for Technology in Education.

Strommen, E. F., & Lincoln. (1992). Constructivism, technology, and the future of classroom learning. *Education and Urban Society, 24*(4), 466–476.

Thomas, R. A., & Boysen, J. P. (1984, May/June). A taxonomy for the instructional use of computers. *Monitor, 26,* 15–17.

REFERENCES FOR ADDITIONAL STUDY

Becker, H. J. (1991). When powerful tools meet conventional beliefs and instructional constraints. *The Computing Teacher, 18*(8), 6–9.

Brooks, D., & Kopp, T. (1989). Technology in teacher education. *Journal of Teacher Education, 40*(4), 2–8.

Brooks, J. G., & Brooks, M. G. (1993). *The case for constructivist classrooms.* Association for Supervision and Curriculum Development.

Bruder, I. (1989). Future teachers: Are they prepared? *Electronic Learning, 8*(4), 32–29.

Elmore, R. F. (1992). Why restructuring alone won't improve teaching. *Educational Leadership, 49*(7), 74–78.

Goodlad, J. I. (1994). *Educational renewal: Better teachers, better schools*. San Francisco: Jossey-Bass Publishers.

Handler, M. G. (1993). Preparing new teachers to use computer technology: Perceptions and suggestions for teacher educators. *Computers and Education, 20*(2), 147–156.

Honebein, P. C., Duffy, P. C., & Fishman, B. J. (1993). Constructivism and the design of learning environments: Context and authentic activities for learning. In T. M. Duffy, J. Lowyck, D. H. Jonassen (Eds.), *Designing environments for constructive learning*. New York: Springer-Verlag.

Ingram, J. M. (1992). Who's teaching the teacher: Elementary education and the computer. *Journal of Computing in Teacher Education, 8*, 17–19.

Novak, D. I., & Berger, C. F. (1991). Integrating technology into preservice education: Michigan's response. *Computers in the Schools, 8*(1/2/3), 89–10.

Simonson, M. R., & Thompson, A. (1994). *Educational Computing Foundations* (2nd ed.). Upper Saddle River, NJ: Merrill/Prentice Hall.

Solomon, M. B. (1994, February). What's wrong with multimedia in higher education? *T.H.E. Journal.*

Thompson, A., & Schmidt, D. (1994). A three-year plan to infuse technology throughout a teacher education program: Year 3 update. In D. Carey, R. Carey, D. A. Willis, & J. Willis (Eds.), *Technology and Teacher Education Annual 1994* (pp. 358–360). Greenville, SC: East Carolina University.

Thompson, A., Schmidt, D., & Topp, N. (1993). The development and implementation of an instructional computing program for preservice teachers. In D. Carey, R. Carey, D. A. Willis, & J. Willis (Eds.), *Technology and Teacher Education Annual 1993* (pp. 130–132). Greenville, SC: East Carolina University.

Wetzel, K. (1993). Teacher educators' uses of computers in teaching. *Journal of Technology and Teacher Education, 1*(4), 335–352.

CHAPTER TWO

COMPUTER APPLICATIONS AND IMPACT

GOAL

This chapter provides an overview of the potential of the computer.

OBJECTIVES

The reader will be able to do the following:

1. Discuss why it is important to determine the unique applications of computers.
2. Explain the relationships among applications of the computers in the school, in the home, and in business.
3. List the most common locations where computers are used in schools.
4. List the categories of applications for computers in the home, and give examples of each.
5. List the categories of applications of computers in businesses, and give examples of each.
6. Explain the potential for the computer in artificial intelligence systems and robotics.

THE STIRRUP

An Innovation that Changed the World

The acceptance or rejection of an invention, or the extent to which its implications are realized if it is accepted, depends quite as much on the condition of society, and on the imagination of its leadership, as on the nature of the technological item itself. . . . The Anglo-Saxons used the stirrup, but did not comprehend it; and for this they paid a fearful price. . . . It was the Franks alone—presumably led by Charles Martel's genius—who fully grasped the possibilities inherent in the stirrup and created in terms of it a new type of warfare supported by a novel structure of a society which we call feudalism. . . . For a thousand years feudal institutions bore the marks of their birth from the new military technology of the eighth century.

White, 1962, pp. 28–29

Many believe our society is in the midst of a technological revolution, the essence of which is change. Technological change and innovation have occurred continuously during human development. Scholars consider the invention of the printing press a technological breakthrough that changed and reshaped society. The printing press made books widely available and greatly expanded access to information. Today we talk of the computer in similar terms.

However, as White (1962) noted in his discussion of a simple innovation, the stirrup, it is not the invention itself, or even its use, that alters society. Rather, change occurs because of people who fully grasp the possibilities inherent in the innovation and have the ability to effectively act on their insights.

It is possible to examine the computer in this context. Certainly the computer is a great technological invention with considerable potential. Increasingly, computers are being used in various settings—from the office, to the school, to the home. Thousands of books, articles, and monographs have been written about the applications of the computer, and some research data indicate that computer use is significantly changing education. Yet, has anyone really demonstrated an understanding of what makes the computer a unique innovation? Most often, computers are being used to improve productivity in traditional ways, such as word processing instead of typing, but they are not changing how teaching and learning occur. Certainly, increased efficiency is desired, but many wonder if the true effect of the computer is yet to be discovered.

In this text, several potentially significant uses of computers will be presented. For example, Seymour Papert's work with LOGO, artificial intelligence, and new applications of multimedia and hypermedia are potentially unique applications of computers. Most uses of the computer, however, merely do more of what we have always done, only faster.

Students and educators should keep in mind that merely learning how to operate a computer is not the ultimate goal of this book. Developing skill at computer operation may be an immediate objective, but there is a much more important goal: to find the unique contribution the computer can make to education and to the individual educator.

Merely using a potentially significant idea or device does not change either the individual or the society. The Anglo-Saxons—the dominating enemy of Martel's Franks—used the stirrup but did not understand its implications for warfare. The stirrup made possible the emergence of a warrior called the knight, who knew that the stirrup enabled the rider not only to keep his seat while protected with nearly impregnable armor but also to deliver a blow with a lance that had the combined weight of the rider and the charging horse. This simple concept permitted the Franks to conquer the Anglo-Saxons and changed the face of Western Civilization. A feudal society that lasted for a thousand years was created, and chivalry was born, all to support the knight. Martel had the vision to seize the idea and use it. Many believe the computer is an innovation that, when combined with the right idea, will change education for the better.

White concludes his landmark historical work about Charles Martel, knights, and knighthood with a famous quote, "It was impossible to be chivalrous without a horse" (White, 1962, p. 29). In the future, it may be impossible to educate without computer technology. The ultimate purpose of this book is to provide the instructional computing student with the competence required to understand the computer's potential and to use the computer correctly to change each learner's education for the better.

ABOUT THE CHAPTER

The computer is a powerful tool for the teacher. However, it is also a tool used in business and in the home. This chapter begins examining the computer's potential by looking at how the computer is used, both inside and outside school settings. This chapter will briefly review the broad categories of computer applications so that in subsequent chapters these applications can be compared with the important educational, in-school uses of computers. Also included are explanations of artificial intelligence and expert systems.

A TOOL FOR THE TEACHER

Educators have access to a vast array of new and established technologies. Some have hypothesized that education has changed positively because of the availability of machines such as television sets, motion picture projectors, and microcomputers. Others have lamented that education is the worse because of this infusion of technology.

Technology, however, has always played a role in education. For example, in 1468, Johannes Gutenberg, a small-town blacksmith, invented the printing press, and the printed word became widely available (Figure 2.1). Many historians consider this the watershed event that intellectually separated the Middle Ages from the modern era. Certainly, society and formal education changed significantly.

Even this important invention may have seemed threatening to some, just as computers seem threatening to certain people today. The Amalgamated Union of Scribes, if there had been such a group, might have organized picket lines around the printing press "factory" because the profession of copying books by hand was in jeopardy; similarly, the people who manufactured quill pens might have been upset. A larger and more influential group might have been even more concerned: University professors may have believed their job of "professing," or presenting information orally for students to copy, was threatened. Students could now have access to information in printed books, information that had previously been the exclusive territory of professors. Many may have thought that no one would go to lectures because printed books would contain all one needed to know.

Quite the opposite happened, however, because professors and other teachers found that the new technology provided more effective methods of communicating. Students seemed better prepared. They formulated questions before coming to class, and more discussions about the meaning of key ideas resulted. Students learned more because of the availability of books, but professors were still needed to clarify concepts and to

FIGURE 2.1
Gutenberg's printing press was a technology that changed not only teaching but also society in general.

teach, rather than profess. The printing press did not replace teaching; rather, it facilitated the entire process of communication, and society benefited.

Technology continued to be applied to education after the 15th century. Progress was slow by today's standards, but still there were changes. Graphs and charts became available. Slate boards were introduced, and the formal training of educators in the methods of teaching became the norm.

By the beginning of the 20th century, the application of technological devices and processes to education began to occur more rapidly. During the 1920s, school museums were being used in a number of cities. Motion pictures, invented by Thomas Edison late in the 19th century for schools, became available. During the 1930s and '40s, photography, displays, radio, handouts, and programmed instruction were introduced into U.S. schools.

Television receivers became widely available in the 1950s and '60s, to the point that they were commonplace. During the 1970s, videotape recorders were added to televisions, and the use of prerecorded programs became a major educational activity. In the late 1970s and early '80s, the microcomputer began to appear in schools. Today, according to several published national surveys, computers are more prevalent than television receivers in classrooms and are becoming the most widely available type of instructional technology.

In short, some form of technology has always been found in the school. But recently, many dramatic, powerful technological devices and processes have become available. While rapid change can be unsettling, it is obviously the logical and desirable consequence of the growth of a sophisticated society. In short, microcomputers are merely the most recent in a long process of modification and refinement inherent in dynamic institutions. The infusion of technology will continue to make available to the teacher new innovations. Possibly, the teacher's "pet" of the 21st century will be a robot possessing sophisticated artificial intelligence. One way to examine the current effect of computers on education is to identify their uses.

Three categories of educational applications for microcomputers have been identified: (1) teaching, (2) managing the school or classroom, and (3) improving other activities. These topics are discussed in detail throughout this text. To support these applications, most schools locate microcomputers in one of three settings: special laboratories, media centers, and classrooms.

Notes From the Literature

After citing six common myths concerning classroom computing (e.g. "Kids love to use computers-so they must be learning"), Woronov describes five promising truths about educational technology:

1. New standards in math and science call for active, inquiry-based, hands-on learning, which can be facilitated by computer-based laboratories and simulations.
2. A few highly technologically literate schools around the country are beginning to produce their own educational materials and distribute them to others.
3. More than 40 states have organizations to provide telecommunication links or technology support to school districts.
4. Technology has enabled students with a wide range of disabilities to participate fully in mainstream classes and develop skills previously considered beyond them.
5. Extending the learning community beyond the classroom walls through the use of electronic mail and the Internet.

Woronov, T. (1994, September/October). Myths about the magic of technology in schools. The Harvard Education Letter, 10, 1–3.

COMPUTERS IN THE SCHOOL

Computer Labs

To teach class-size groups of students how to use computers, many schools have microcomputer laboratories. These labs have from 15 to 30 stations that are used individually or by pairs of students. Research studies on lab use of computers have found that two students can share one microcomputer during class without a reduction in effectiveness, even though one student per computer is considered optimum. When more than two students are required to share a terminal, at least one student becomes a passive observer of instruction, and learning is adversely affected (Klinkefus, 1988).

Usually, labs are used for three activities: 1) instruction in computer literacy; 2) a specific unit by a class that ordinarily would meet in another room, such as for a unit in word processing in a business education course; and 3) for homework or study by students during and after school.

A classroom full of computers has many advantages: A relatively large number of students can be taught computer concepts quickly and efficiently. Distribution of software is facilitated because computer-based lessons can be stored in one location and conveniently checked in and out. Supervision and security are also easier.

Unfortunately, there are disadvantages to collecting a school's microcomputers in a laboratory. First, access by individual students is limited to those times when lab classes are not in session. Second, most educators agree that proximity to materials promotes their use. In other words, if the language arts teacher has a classroom on the opposite end of the school building from the microcomputer laboratory, this teacher is unlikely to use microcomputers very often. Last, labs tend to promote the mystification of the microcomputer. When devices are put in a "special" location that is monitored by "special" people, some tend to think that those devices are also "special" and are not for everyone to routinely use.

The solution is to assign computers to the school's media center and to individual classrooms, as well as to laboratories. In short, computers should be found throughout the school.

Computers in Media Centers

Media centers have long been the place where technologies are made available to teachers and students. Because the media center is a place where students go to study and to complete class assignments, it makes sense to locate computers there. As a matter of fact, the media center is where a school's first computers are often located. Then, as more are purchased, laboratories are established, and microcomputers are assigned to individual classrooms (Figure 2.2).

Media center microcenters can be used to prepare term papers or other projects. They can be used by students to complete computer-based assignments. They can be used for searches of the media center catalog and other data sources via the Internet. Increasingly, school media centers are using microcomputers to access national data bases such as Dialog's "The Magazine Index" (Figures 2.3 and 2.4).

Computers in Classrooms

The most appropriate location for computers is the individual teacher's classroom. Placing computers in classrooms offers the greatest benefit to education from

FIGURE 2.2
Centralizing computer hardware in labs makes software checkout simple. Students check out computer lessons and are assigned to a computer at the same time.

FIGURE 2.3
Computer labs can be more efficient and effective learning environments when the computers are linked in a network and when the teacher's computer is connected to an overhead projector and liquid-crystal display unit.

computers. A cluster of computers in the classroom can be used by the teacher for small-group instruction, for interest and learning centers, or for remediation when students fall behind regular class instruction. Many schools have adopted the concept of the computer-rich curriculum built around the use of computer-based instruction in all classes and subjects. Obviously, this approach to computer use requires the availability of computer hardware in classrooms.

One interesting consequence of using computer-based instruction for remediation is the enthusiasm students show when they are assigned to the computer.

FIGURE 2.4
Students using microcomputers in the school media center have easy access to information.
Photograph courtesy of International Business Machines Corporation.

Many educators believe the stigma that students often associate with remediation is not nearly as negative when the computer is used to deliver review material. Many students consider using the computer a privilege rather than a penalty.

COMPUTER APPLICATIONS IN THE HOME

While many call the microcomputer the "home" computer, it is in the home where they have most failed to meet expectations. During the 1980s, computer companies advertised their machines in much the same way they promoted other consumer products such as microwave ovens, stereo systems, and videocassette recorders. The famous Apple Computer ad stating "in the future there will be two kinds of people, people who use computers, and people who use Apples," was an example of how advertising agencies pushed the computer as a basic household appliance. Unfortunately, this potential has not yet been widely realized. Computer use in the home is increasing, however; and as it does, the teacher will find it easier to assign computer projects because the computer will be a device familiar and available to many, even most, students (Figure 2.5).

Six categories of applications of microcomputers in the home are gaming, record keeping, word processing, instruction for self-improvement, access to information, and hobbies.

Gaming

The computer game market was initially one of the primary promotional techniques used to sell microcomputers. This is not to imply that using computers for game playing was not, and is not, an important application. Game playing is one of the most effective methods for introducing computers to new users, and many thousands of games exist. It is obvious, however, that using a $2,000 multipurpose microcomputer for game playing is not very cost-effective. So, although using a home computer to play games is widely practiced, it is apparent to most computer owners that the computer in the home needs to be used for more than this.

Record Keeping

Another of the often-discussed, but seldom practiced, applications of microcomputers is the keeping of household records. While in theory this seems a logical use of the microcomputer, with the exception of financial records, most homes do not have records complex or varied enough to warrant computerization.

Telephone numbers are probably easier to find using a telephone book or personal address book. Recipes can probably be found more easily in a cookbook or in a card file rather than in a computer. Generally, home record keeping is simple enough to be handled manually.

One notable exception to this is the use of a spreadsheet program, such as Excel or Lotus 1-2-3, to keep financial records. The automation of budget keeping

FIGURE 2.5
A computer in the home can benefit both student and parent. In addition to its more obvious uses as word processor and statistical tool, the computer can be used as a communications device and for data retrieval from local, regional, or national networks.
Photograph courtesy of International Business Machines Corporation.

allows immediate updating of a family's finances and projections of money requirements to pay for family needs, such as a home repair, a new car, or a vacation.

Record keeping with a home computer holds great promise for the future, however. As national data bases become more widespread, less expensive, and more consumer oriented, the home computer will increasingly be used to access records and to collect information for the home user.

Word Processing

Along with gaming, the use of the computer as a word processor to replace the typewriter initially attracts more users to the computer than any other application. The ease of preparing letters and reports is an important application for many people. Most who decide to use a home computer for word processing have learned this skill at school or the office and want to have the same benefits for their personal correspondence.

Unfortunately, most home users of microcomputers do not write enough letters to warrant the purchase of more than $2,000 worth of computer hardware and software, and a letter to Mom or Dad that is printed on a dot-matrix printer does not have the same personal touch as a handwritten note. Certainly, professionals who complete office work at home can rationalize the purchase of computer equipment, but word processing alone may not be a cost-effective reason to purchase a computer for the home.

Self-Instruction

Home computers are also used for individual teaching at home—and not just by children doing homework. Programs are available that can provide instruction in everything from buying stocks intelligently, maintaining an automobile, and picking the winners of football games, to learning a foreign language. In other words, the computer is being used in much the same way that self-help books and videos have been used previously. In the opinion of many, this use of the home computer, especially when networks of computers become more prevalent, is the most exciting.

Access to Information

One accessory to the home computer is the modem, which is used to connect users to information utilities such as America Online, Prodigy, CompuServe, Dialog, the local public library, and even the local school's net-

work. Homeowners use their computers to check stock prices, read movie summaries, find airline schedules, check out books, and review the agenda for the next parent-teacher meeting.

Hobbies

It is probably the computer hobbyist who can most easily rationalize the purchase of a home computer. Because of the virtually unlimited potential of the personal computer, there is almost no end to what the hobbyist can accomplish, given enough time and money. For example, hobbyists have built computer systems that automatically turn house lights on and off at preset times. Others have built computer systems connected to video cameras that monitor children's rooms and set off warning signals if problems occur. The computer-controlled home, "rigged" by today's hobbyist, previews the standard home of the next decade.

Future Uses for the Home Computer

Three home uses of microcomputers will probably have greater significance in the immediate future, and all have been mentioned. First, the use of the home computer for data retrieval from local, regional, or national networks will increase in importance. Whether the user wants to find a certain book at the public library, read the school lunch menu, or review the qualifications of candidates for the school board, the computer will be an invaluable tool for accessing information stored in public data bases.

Next, the home computer will increasingly be important as a communications tool. The telephone will not be replaced by the computer but rather will be used *with* the computer. Invitations to a dinner party can be sent simultaneously to the home computers of all those on the invitation list. Mail-order companies will make it possible not only to order products with a computer but also to find the current status and availability of products, as a supplement to printed catalogs.

Last, computers will be used to efficiently manage and control increasingly more complex homes. What today is the domain of the computer hobbyist will soon become the standard. Initial studies indicate that computer-managed environmental controls for the home can reduce heating and cooling costs by 10% to 40%. As stated earlier, it is quite possible that computers will become standard, built-in appliances.

In summary, there are many applications for computers in the home. Whether these uses are widely accepted

Notes From the Literature

A meta-analysis of 36 independent studies showed that computer applications had a positive effective on students' academic achievement from elementary school to college. The average effect size was .38 standard deviations. Effect sizes were higher in situations where LOGO programming was the computer application used. The authors said "overall, this review study indicates that the instructional use of the computer increases student's academic achievement." However, it is possible that there was confounding of the results in many of the studies reviewed, similar to the criticism by Richard Clark of Kulik's meta-analyses.

Khalili, A., & Shashaani, L. (1994). The effectiveness of computer applications: A meta-analysis. Journal of Research on Computing in Education, 27(1), 48–61.

including word processing; 3) instruction; 4) automation of design and production; and 5) artificial intelligence (Figure 2.6).

Record Keeping

Usually, a pressing need to control records or finances motivates a business to computerize. Financial success is closely related to keeping track of the "things" of business, and as a successful business grows it becomes nearly impossible for people to manually manage critical information such as inventory, accounts, payrolls, and supplies. Therefore, both private and public institutions have eagerly accepted computers as basic tools for organizational management.

General ledgers are financial record-keeping systems that in their simplest form are income and expense statements that show profit or loss during a specific time period. More complex general ledgers allow for projecting into the future and for determining the financial "what if" regarding certain proposals. For example, a company going through labor negotiations might wonder what a $5 across-the-board hourly raise to all employees would do to the company's profitability if all other factors remained the same. Electronic general ledgers make this kind of analysis relatively simple.

Inventory control and its counterpart, *production control*, were among the first manufacturing functions to be automated. In one common example of an inventory control system, a sales forecast is entered into a computer. Next, a projection of the maximum inventory levels of raw and finished goods is made. This pro-

and considered cost-effective is difficult to determine. It does seem apparent, however, that the home computer will at some point be considered a necessity.

BUSINESS APPLICATIONS OF COMPUTERS

Computers have been the most widely used and accepted in the business community. Five categories of applications of computers in business and industry will be discussed: 1) record keeping; 2) communication,

FIGURE 2.6
The computer has all but eliminated the typewriter in offices. But whereas typewriters were largely confined to the desks of secretaries, the computer is used by employees at all levels of the business hierarchy.
Photo courtesy of International Business Machines Corporation.

Notes From the Literature

American schools steadily increased their stock of microcomputers during the latter half of the 1980s. Early in the decade, computers were seen as motivating devices, were used to enrich the curriculum, and were used for computer literacy skills. Later in the decade, these uses still dominated, but the range of activities using computers increased dramatically. An increased use of computers for word processing was an indication of interest in using the computer as an information and resource tool. Unfortunately, in many schools, learning how to word process consumed more student time than word processing itself. During the decade, the number of microcomputers available increased nearly 50-fold from fewer than 50,000 to more than 2.4 million.

Becker, H. (1991). How computers are used in the U.S. schools: Basic data from the 1989 I.E.A. computers in education survey. Journal of Computing Research, 7(4), 385–406.

jection is based on the rate at which goods are used and the delivery time required to obtain more. Production capacity is then determined, and as the manufacturing process continues, the system monitors production rates and recalculates manufacturing schedules and order processing.

Another example of an inventory control system is used by many supermarkets with optical bar code checkout stations. Once desired quantities of products are obtained, the inventory control system takes over. As goods are sold, a central computer connected to the store's cash registers keeps track of the rate of sales. When inventories reach a certain level, a command is issued to order more. This directive can be processed automatically or can just be a prompt to the supermarket's manager that bean soup, for example, needs to be reordered.

Simple inventory systems are commonly used by businesses of all sizes to keep track of machinery and nonexpendable goods such as vehicles in the motor pool or hand tools in a machine shop. Generally, these inventories are lists of items in some order, such as an inventory control number. These lists are easy to update as new equipment is purchased and reorganize as items are assigned to different departments. Depreciation rates for tax purposes are also easy to track.

Product information is another business use of computers. Companies develop computer-based lists of

their products for use by their own staff and for use by potential customers. For example, a mail-order clothing company might have its entire inventory of clothing listed in a computer file. When orders are received, either through the mail or by telephone, the order clerk accesses this file to determine if the size and style of clothing requested by the customer are available. When the order is confirmed, the clerk generates a work order with just a few keystrokes that alerts stock handlers in the warehouse to fill the order. The computer might even generate a mailing label and a bill.

Many companies make their entire computer catalog accessible by customers. For example, public libraries are rapidly abandoning the traditional card catalog in favor of a computer catalog that lists the availability of books and other materials. Patrons can find out which Isaac Asimov books the library has by entering his name at a computer terminal rather than by scanning a card catalog. The computer file tells the patron which Asimov books the library owns, whether any of them are checked out, and when they will be available. Many catalogs are accessible at home using a modem and communication software.

Communication and Word Processing

Businesses have used dedicated word processing systems for decades. These systems were expensive, but they offered the power and flexibility of computer technology to the tedious task of preparing written communication. In today's businesses, the microcomputer with sophisticated word processing software is a standard item on desks. Many of these computers are networked so correspondence can be transmitted electronically instead of by paper.

The most impressive growth in the use of computers in businesses is in the coupling of the computer to traditional communication systems, such as telephones. Obviously, computers can replace telephone operators to control call routing and switching. Computers are also being used to manage other complex telephone routing needs.

The most interesting changes have occurred in the area of data transmission. Sometimes called "electronic mail" systems, the sending of computer-generated data over telephone lines has revolutionized business communication.

The most obvious characteristic of computers—speed—is the primary reason for the popularity of computer communication. Telephone conversations require minutes or even hours. Mail services can send more complex messages, but days or weeks are required. However, when computer-generated data are transmitted, complex documents and records can be sent and received in seconds or fractions of seconds. The entire content of this textbook, for example, could be transmitted coast to coast in minutes.

Another important use of computer technology for communication is in the transfer of information within the organization through a local area network. Interoffice memoranda are sent by computer from the office of one division of a company to the office of another division. Individual employees also can exchange messages by computer. One commonly used method is to assign each employee an electronic mailbox. Other employees then send messages instantly to that mailbox. Of course, the person the message is sent to may not read it immediately, but at least the delivery time for messages is virtually eliminated.

Although this may seem to be an unnecessary duplication of traditional telephone communication—and for general and informal discussions it would be—the delivery of longer, more complex, or more detailed messages with graphics is facilitated. Also, messages may be sent at any time, even when the person the message is being sent to is not in the office, or when that person is busy on another call.

Many companies have also found that it is cost-effective to send messages electronically between branch offices in different cities, either using a leased telephone line or by accessing the Internet. For example, when the branch manager of the Los Angeles offices of XYZ Corporation arrives at work at 8 am, the morning's work from the New York branch can be waiting in an electronic mailbox.

Computer-assisted communication promises to continue to be a significant application in the foreseeable future, especially in business and industry. Additionally, computers increasingly will be used for personal and educational communication systems.

Instruction

On-the-job training is taking on a more formal appearance. The concept of apprenticeships is being supplemented by training programs using instructors, media, tests, and even graduation ceremonies. Training programs have been established by unions, manufacturers, financial institutions, and real estate agencies. Obviously, the increased complexity of the

workplace and the sophistication of office and plant machinery make it necessary for companies not only to train new employees but also to continually retrain experienced staff members.

The increased numbers of private companies that offer formal education experiences to their employees is an interesting and important trend to be dealt with in the future by professional educators. The eager adaptation of technology, including the computer, is a characteristic of private-sector training programs that traditional education systems are examining and modeling.

Computers are important tools for job training in many of the same ways they are for education. Simulations, tutorials, and problem-solving lessons are especially applicable and are widely used.

Automation of Design and Production

Today, two applications of the computer experiencing considerable growth are computer-aided design (CAD), and computer-aided manufacturing (CAM). CAD is the use of computer technology in the design of new products to simulate their production so they can be tested before their manufacture. CAM, of which robotics is an important component, involves the use of computer-controlled machines to automate the production of things or materials once they have been designed. Both concepts are a logical progression in the application of technology to the development of new materials and devices, and both are viewed by many as the inevitable next step in production and manufacturing. While not universal, and just recently approaching wide use, these applications of computers are receiving more attention and interest than some other applications with greater immediate utility, such as record-keeping systems and computer-based communication systems.

Although the initial entry of a design into the computer's memory is time-consuming, all subsequent revisions, including size changes, flip-side views, and three-dimensional imaging, are accomplished by using the computer's capabilities. The initial design process is similar to the traditional approach, but once information is contained in the computer's memory, the process of modification and revision occurs electronically, and design changes can be completed in seconds rather than days.

The most positive consequences of the use of CAD are quicker and more precise new product development, fewer models and mock-ups, and lower costs. It has been estimated that more than 50% of major manufacturing revisions now occur with some assistance from CAD systems.

CAM involves the use of numerically controlled machines, industrial robots, and artificial intelligence systems. Numerically controlled machines have been used in manufacturing since Jacquard's looms in the 19th century. Not until the early 1950s, however, did modern techniques for controlling machines with computerlike devices come into widespread use. At that time, certain manufacturing processes involving complex devices, such as milling machines and drill presses, began to be precisely controlled by a punched tape with instructions that were repeated for each part manufactured by the machine.

This process entered the computer age with the development of a small computerlike device that not only issued commands to the machine to conduct some step in the manufacturing process but also received information from the machine about how the process was proceeding. Information such as tool precision, sharpness of cutting blades, and machine working temperatures was relayed to the computer and used by it to control the manufacturing process.

The benefits of computerized manufacturing are numerous. Repetitive tasks are completed without boredom affecting the worker. Assembly speed can often be increased, precision can be exactly monitored, and working environments that would be dangerous to human beings can be tolerated by machines. Also, it is generally simple—depending on the design of the numerically controlled machine—to change specifications, tolerances, or other design characteristics, such as when a new car model is introduced.

Robots are the direct result of improving the design of numerically controlled machines. A robot is a reprogrammable, multifunctional manipulator designed to move material, parts, tools, or specialized devices through variable programmed motions to perform a variety of tasks. Robots are often parts of larger, numerically controlled machines, and ordinarily, only their "arms" move.

Robot "arms" and "hands" are currently the most important components used in manufacturing. The "hands" can pick up objects, rotate them, move them, and replace them during manufacturing. "Arms" allow the machine that controls them to reach and retrieve objects, such as a rod in the core of a nuclear reactor.

Currently, more than 100 companies manufacture industrial robots and tens of thousands of robots are in use. Most are used in industrial applications such as spot welding, spray painting, and loading. They do the dangerous, dirty, and monotonous jobs that are difficult for human beings. Robots are also effective at tasks that require extreme precision and reliability, such as testing computer circuits, assembling oddly shaped parts on printed circuit boards, and even performing microsurgery on human beings.

One of the primary reasons industrial robots are cost-effective is that they can be used in developing small quantities of products that are similar yet slightly different, such as versions of a basic electric motor. Robots' capabilities certainly will improve dramatically, especially when they are combined with expert systems that use artificial intelligence concepts (Figure 2.7).

Although the robots of Isaac Asimov are not likely to be seen in the immediate future, and Arnold Schwarzenegger's *Terminator* robots or Sigourney Weaver's humanoid helper robots from *Alien* probably will not be seen in school hallways, many theorists believe computer technology will make one of its greatest contributions in the area of robots and intelligent systems.

Artificial Intelligence

Because of its potential, artificial intelligence is an important topic for the educator to be familiar with. Artificial intelligence is defined as the use of a computer to perform tasks that a person might assume require intelligence. *Intelligence* is the ability to think, reason, know, and most important, learn. It is important to deal with an often-stated concern expressed about computers and artificial intelligence. Can machines "think"? If they can, then are humans no better than machines? These philosophical concerns trouble many people.

It is interesting to compare this level of concern with previously expressed ideas that seemed to threaten people. When Copernicus stated that the Earth was not the center of the universe, and when Darwin demonstrated that human beings were part of the biological world, people were shaken, and many feared that these theories would devalue human worth and adversely affect human existence. Of course, this knowledge did just the opposite. Scientific advancement based on research and theory provides humanity with a better and more meaningful existence. The same is true for the study of intelligence. Theories on how humans think are not immutable, any more than are theories on our place in the universe. Rather, they help us all to understand ourselves better.

FIGURE 2.7
Robots and robotics are important tools used by manufacturers.
Photo courtesy of Fischer America, Inc.

Scientists say there are three major problems of science: 1) the origin of the cosmos, 2) the origin of life, and 3) the nature of intelligence. It is the study of each that gives science meaning, and it is a better understanding of intelligence that possibly is the greatest contribution of computers to science. The development of intelligent systems, based on concepts of artificial intelligence, may be one of the unique applications of computers, similar to Charles Martel's application of the stirrup to warfare discussed at the beginning of this chapter.

The concept of artificial intelligence was born during a 1956 conference at Dartmouth University. Since then, more than 30,000 people working in more than 500 locations have made contributions to what some call "The Second Computer Age." Artificial intelligence is based on knowledge engineering, which in turn is used to develop expert systems. Low-level expert systems are called *knowledge systems*. An expert system is a computer system that demonstrates expert reasoning. It allows for the rapid analysis of large amounts of information according to some predetermined plan.

Examples of expert systems are those used in the medical profession to help diagnose illnesses based on an analysis of a medical examination. One system helps physicians analyze symptoms and prescribe antibiotic treatment for bacterial blood infections. It engages in a dialogue with the physician, asking for information on the patient's history and symptoms and the results of laboratory tests. It gradually narrows down the possibilities, based on information provided to it, and ultimately recommends a treatment. The knowledge base of the computer system MYCIN is the knowledge that a specialist in blood diseases would have. It is used as a tool by the physician, not to replace the doctor's judgment. Similarly, other expert systems are used to assist in decision making, not to replace the human decision-making process.

An expert system, and also a knowledge system, consist of three parts: 1) a knowledge base, 2) an influence system, and 3) a human–machine interface that often uses a human language dialogue between the expert system and the user.

The knowledge base of an expert system is a data base that consists of facts and other information, but it also includes heuristics. *Heuristics* are the rules of thumb and experiential knowledge used to select, apply, and understand factual information used during problem solving.

The *inference engine component* of an expert system refers to the logic that is applied during problem solving. Logic deals with how the system "thinks through" a problem. Two different but parallel approaches to "thinking" by expert systems are being studied. The first involves the study of how human beings solve problems so computer programs can be written to use similar strategies. This technique is based on psychological theories and has helped promote the study of human intelligence. The second procedure being examined emphasizes mathematical procedures as the basis for machine techniques. The aim is to develop "thinking" without drawing heavily on human or animal psychology.

The perspectives offered by these two procedures for developing a system of machine logic are not mutually exclusive. Rather, they complement each other. Both concern solving problems when a precise definition of a procedure to be followed is not possible but when intelligence is needed.

Of the three components of an expert system, those studying the inference engine component have the most difficult problems. The essence of intelligent behavior is the thinking through of a problem. It involves the application of facts and experience but also requires hard-to-define intuitive behaviors.

The third component of an expert system is the human–machine interface. Most efforts in this area are focused on speech recognition and speech production by the computer. While it is possible to use traditional interface tools such as the keyboard when using expert systems, it is believed that the more an expert system emulates human behavior, the more readily it will be accepted.

Application and Value of Expert Systems.

Artificial intelligence systems, including expert systems, have many current applications and hold considerable promise for the future. Currently, expert systems are being used to diagnose and correct human diseases and machine malfunctions. For example, the MYCIN system described earlier allows physicians to easily access information that they might not otherwise be aware of. Corrective action, however, is the responsibility of the doctor who actually prescribes the medicines and other treatment for the patient.

Expert systems are also being used to diagnose problems in machines. In these situations, an expert system might be connected to a series of machines used to manufacture some item. Sensors are included in critical components of the machinery, and if stress of some kind, such as overheating, or extraordinary wear, is sensed, then this information is sent back to the expert system, where displays indicate the problem. This kind of sensing system is not dramatically different from the warning lights for oil pressure found in automobile dashboards.

In the expert system, however, the problem is often repaired or corrected automatically. This might be accomplished by adding oil to a hot bearing or by switching to a backup conveyor if the primary conveyor shows an impending malfunction. Theoretically, industrial robots then repair the primary conveyor without affecting the manufacturing process. Probably, however, a human technician is dispatched to complete the repair.

Situational analysis is another application of artificial intelligence. Complex problems, such as military maneuvers or economic conditions, can be analyzed by expert systems. Masses of information about all the variables related to the situation are either automatically, or manually, input to an expert system, which then provides indications of success for various alternatives.

Star Trek fans will remember Captain James T. Kirk's frequent inquiries to Mr. Spock, who in turn queried the ship's computer, about the likelihood of success of solutions to problems the U.S.S. Enterprise had encountered. After a rapid analysis, the computer responded with the probability of success of a specific solution to the problem. In these situations, the ship's computer was acting as an expert system.

Software development is another use of expert systems. Increasingly, computer software is becoming so complex and intricate that development of new programs takes thousands of person-hours. Several companies are beginning to use expert systems to design software. Humans set the framework, or algorithm, for the project, and evaluate the results, rather than work on the tedious job of writing codes. Error checking is another contribution to software development being made by expert systems.

Expert systems have many educational applications. Research questions and hypotheses can be tested. Expert systems generate a design, analyze collected data, compute statistics, and draw conclusions. In other words, the computer acts as the research assistant, and the educator makes decisions based on the recommendations provided.

Several researchers are exploring the concept of "brain-compatible teaching," which takes into account the psychological characteristics of each learner when methods of teaching are prescribed (Dunn, Beaudry, & Klavas, 1989; Gregorc, 1986). Specifically, the expert system's knowledge base would contain exhaustive information about the topic being taught. Additionally, the computer would contain considerable data on how this information might best be presented to students with various learning styles.

When information about a student—such as background knowledge, IQ, brain hemisphere dominance, and style of information processing—is analyzed, the expert system may diagnose, prescribe, and even deliver the correct kind of information, in the best sequence, using the most appropriate method for that individual student, very similar to how an expert tutor might teach. While these kinds of systems are exciting, because of the complexity of the teaching and learning process, they currently show more promise than results.

Artificial intelligence is of value for several obvious reasons:

- Artificial intelligence systems allow for capturing, refining, and distributing human expertise.
- Expert systems can be used to find solutions to problems too complex or too time-consuming for human solution.
- Artificial intelligence brings together, or fuses, the expertise of a number of disciplines.
- Expert systems become the "memory" for an organization, so that when a human expert leaves or retires, the knowledge acquired by that person remains.

Artificial intelligence systems will continue to grow in number and effect because of the increased speed of computers, the growing availability of inexpensive computer memory, and the improved understanding of machines, problem-solving procedures, and programming.

The potential for "machine learning" is, as yet, unrealized. In other words, computers have not yet been developed that can dramatically improve their ability to solve problems, as they solve problems. Rather, artificial intelligence and expert systems are tools, as the printing press is a tool. When printing became more readily available, memorization became less important. Instead, the use of the mind was concentrated on more "meaningful problems." Most believe artificial intelligence will cause similar results.

Notes From the Literature

A survey of more than 1,200 teachers who were considered accomplished at integrating computers into their teaching were asked about how they used computers in the classroom. The results indicated the following:

1. They are comfortable with computer technology, devote their own time to learning about computers, and receive local support for using computers.
2. They work in schools averaging more than twice the number of computers than other schools.
3. They use computers for many purposes, such as demonstrating an idea, instruction, word processing, and promoting student-generated projects.
4. They expect more from their students, are able to present more complex material, and foster independence in the classroom.

Sheingold, K., & Hadley, M. (1990). Accomplished teachers: Integrating computers in classroom practice. New York: Center for Technology in Education, Bank Street College of Education.

SUMMARY

Computers, like most other technologies, are used widely throughout society. Schools and teachers, if they are to be relevant to society, should understand the variety of applications of computers. This chapter presents an overview of these current and future uses.

The first section of this chapter presented the ways computers are used in the school to support the learning process. Second, teacher uses and computer locations in schools were presented. The categories of home applications for computers were discussed: gaming, record keeping, word processing, self-instruction, access to information, and hobbies, as well as future applications. Last, the five categories of applications for computers in the business sector were presented. Record keeping, communication, word processing, instruction, and computer-automated design and manufacturing were discussed, followed by an overview of what may prove to be the truly unique application of computer technology: artificial intelligence.

The next chapter discusses computer research. As computer use becomes widespread, it is important to base implementation decisions on more than trial and error. Theory, based on research, gives the information necessary for effective decision making. Chapter 3 summarizes this kind of information.

SELF-TEST QUESTIONS

1. Relate the effect of historical innovations, such as the stirrup, to the potential of the computer.
2. What is generally considered the maximum number of students who can simultaneously use a single computer without reducing what is learned?
3. List disadvantages of using computers in a school laboratory.
4. What is one important reason that using computers for remediation in the school may be a good idea?
5. What are the six categories of applications for computers in the home?
6. EXCEL is an example of a spreadsheet software package. What is a spreadsheet?
7. Define *computer-aided design (CAD)*.
8. Give one reason that robots can be cost-effective when used in manufacturing.
9. Define *artificial intelligence*.
10. What is an expert system?

ANSWERS TO SELF-TEST QUESTIONS

1. The Franks discovered the uniqueness of the stirrup. They realized that a horseman could carry a lance and that the stirrup enhanced the effectiveness of the lance during battle. The Anglo-Saxons, on the other hand, did not see the implications of the stirrup. Many believe the uniqueness of the computer is yet to be discovered. Artificial intelligence efforts, or robotics research, may have the greatest promise for identifying what computers can do that cannot be done as well, or even at all, any other way.
2. Two is usually recognized as the maximum number of students who can use a computer at one time during a class. The optimum is one, but achievement does not seem to be influenced adversely if two students work together.
3. a. Access is limited to times when classes are not scheduled in the lab.

b. Teachers who have offices or classrooms that are far from the laboratory are not likely to use it.
   c. Putting things such as computers in special locations tends to make people think these things are special, and this tends to "mystify" the computer.
4. Because many students think using a computer is a privilege, they do not have the same negative feelings about being assigned projects on the computer as they often feel about noncomputer remediation assignments. In other words, because many students think using the computer is a good thing, they often view what they have to do on the computer positively, too.
5. a. Gaming
   b. Record keeping
   c. Word processing
   d. Self-improvement instruction
   e. Access to information
   f. Hobbies
6. A spreadsheet, or income/expense package, permits keeping track of money received as income and money spent as expenses. Projections that deal with a budget, such as the purchase of a new automobile, are also possible because the computer-based general ledger system computes all figures automatically.
7. Computer-aided design is the use of computer technology during the design of new products to simulate their production so they can be tested and experimented with before their manufacture.
8. Robots are often cost-effective to use during manufacture because they can be easily reprogrammed to make small numbers of items that differ slightly from each other. For example, a robot can be used to manufacture wood screws that are ½" long, ¾" long, and 1" long by changing only a few commands in the program that controls the robot.
9. *Artificial intelligence* is defined as the use of a computer to perform tasks that a person might assume requires intelligence or intelligent behavior. Intelligence is the ability to think, reason, know, and most important, learn.
10. An expert system is a computer system that demonstrates expert-level reasoning. An expert system consists of a knowledge base, an influence system (logic), and a human–machine interface, usually speech.

REFERENCES

Dunn, R., Beaudry, J., & Klavas, A. (1989). Survey of research on learning styles. *Educational Leadership, 46*(4), 50–58.

Gregorc, A. (1986). Styles of the mind: What you should know—part 1. *Gifted Children Monthly, 7*(1), 1–3, 6–7.

Klinkefus, M. (1988). *Paired versus individualized learning when using computer-assisted instruction.* Unpublished master's thesis. Ames, IA: Iowa State University.

White, L., Jr. (1962). *Medieval technology and social change.* London: Oxford at the Clarendon Press.

REFERENCES FOR ADDITIONAL STUDY

Becker, H. (1991). How computers are used in United States schools: Basic data from the 1989 I.E.A. computers in education survey. *Journal of Educational Computing Research, 7*(4), 385–406.

Carrington, B. (1990). Expert systems: Power to the experts. *Database, 13*(2), 47–50.

Connel, S., & Galbraith, I. A. (1982). *Electronic mail: A revolution in business communications.* White Plains, NY: Knowledge Industries Publications.

Duffy, T. (1992). *Computing concepts* (2nd ed.). Belmont, CA: Wadsworth.

Ernst, M. L. (1982). The mechanization of commerce. *Scientific American, 247*(3), 132.

Froelich, L. (1981, January). Robots to the rescue? *Datamation,* 85–96.

Gunn, T. G. (1982). The mechanization of design and manufacturing. *Scientific American, 247*(3), 115.

Harmon, P., & King, D. (1985). *Expert systems: Artificial intelligence in business.* New York: Wiley.

Hock, S. (1989). *Computers and computing.* Boston: Houghton Mifflin.

Kinnucan, P. (1984, January). Computers that think like experts. *High Technology,* 30–42.

Lieberman, M. A., et al. (1982). *Office automation: A manager's guide for improved productivity.* New York: Wiley.

Lillie, D. L., Hannum, W. H., & Stuck, G. B. (1989). *Computers and effective instruction.* New York: Longman.

Lucas, H. (1982). *Information systems concepts for management.* New York: McGraw-Hill.

Mandron, T. W. (1982). *Microcomputers in large organizations.* Englewood Cliffs, NJ: Prentice-Hall.

Nillson, N. J. (1980). *Principles of artificial intelligence.* Palo Alto, CA: Tioga.

Vockell, E., & Schwartz, E. (1992). *The computer in the classroom* (2nd ed.). Watsonville, CA: Mitchell McGraw-Hill.

Wessells, M. (1990). *Computer, self and society.* Englewood Cliffs, NJ: Prentice-Hall.

Waltz, D. L. (1982). Artificial intelligence. *Scientific American, 274*(4), 118–133.

Wilson, H., & Burford, A. (1990). Artificial intelligence and expert systems. *Journal of Education for Business, 65*(6), 75–79.

CHAPTER THREE

RESEARCH ON COMPUTERS IN EDUCATION

GOAL

The purpose of this chapter is to present the theories and research that support the design and use of computers in education.

OBJECTIVES

The reader will be able to do the following:

1. Explain behaviorism, systems theory, cognitive theory, constructivism, and situated cognition—and describe how they relate to computer-based learning.
2. Summarize and interpret the results of research on computer-based learning, and review explanations provided by researchers about what these results mean.
3. Describe research on the use of computer "tool software."
4. Explain research about effective instruction using computers.

Finally, the most fundamental and most important characteristic of a profession is that the skills involved are founded on a body of intellectual theory and research. Furthermore, this systematic theory is constantly being expanded by research and thinking within the profession. . . . The practice of a profession cannot be disjoined from its theoretical understandings, and vice versa . . . the antithesis to a profession is an avocation based upon customary activities and modified by the trial and error of individual practice. Such an avocation is a craft . . . the difference between the bricklayer and the architect lies right here.

Finn, 1953, p. 8

Most teachers consider themselves professionals, and most consider teaching a profession. However, educators often make decisions about what is effective and appropriate based on intuition rather than on clearly stated theoretical principles supported by research. Many believe that until educators routinely base instructional decisions on scientifically established evidence, rather than trial and error, education will be more akin to the craft of bricklaying than to the profession of architecture.

The theories and research explained in this chapter are an attempt to provide teachers with scientifically supportable reasons why computers are effective in education. We will also examine instances when computers and computer-based instruction (CBI) are not effective and should not be used.

THEORIES SUPPORTING COMPUTER USE IN EDUCATION

Several theories have been the basis for investigating the effect of computers in the teaching and learning process. Most of the techniques applied to the design and use of CBI can be traced to one of these theories. Behaviorism, systems theory, and cognitive theory will be discussed with an emphasis on how each provides direction to the design, use, or effect of computers in education. Additionally, constructivism and situated cognition will be related to uses of interactive multimedia systems and hypermedia lessons.

Behaviorism

Of the theories supporting computer use in education, behaviorism has historically had the greatest influence. Behaviorism was used as the basis for designing early CBI and was also the impetus behind many related teaching strategies, such as the use of teaching machines and programmed texts. Thorndike's connectionism, Pavlov's classical conditioning, and Skinner's operant conditioning were theories that directed early researchers who examined the effect of CBI on behavior (Skinner, 1954; Thorndike, 1969).

Applications of behaviorism in education are based on the principle that instruction should be designed to produce observable and quantifiable behaviors in the learner. Behaviorists consider the mental state of a learner to be merely a predisposition to behave. Because mental states cannot be observed, behaviorists do not believe teaching should be directed toward strengthening the mind, a common goal of educators of the early 20th century, but should be aimed at producing desirable behaviors in students. In other words, behaviorists expect any effective instructional activity, such as a computer-based tutorial, to change the student in some obvious and measurable way. After completing a lesson, students should be able to do something that they could not do, or could not do as well, before the lesson.

Using behavioral objectives is one technique advocated by behaviorists that many educators have found to be very effective. Behavioral objectives are easy to develop and have been related to improvement in student achievement.

The rationale of the behaviorist may be better understood by examining the work of several theorists. Edward Thorndike was born in Massachusetts in 1874 and wrote about psychology and education in the early decades of the 20th century. This work was so influential that for more than 50 years his ideas dominated thinking in both professions.

Thorndike's connectionism theory stated that learning was based on a series of associations, or connections, between the problems of a particular situation and what had been accomplished previously. Complex ideas, such as balancing a chemical equation, which is an application-level activity (remember Bloom's Taxonomy?), should be broken down into related concepts that need to be applied (e.g., the use of the Periodic Chart of the Elements) and understanding what happens during chemical reactions, which are lower-level knowledge and comprehension activities in Bloom's Taxonomy. If students are positively reinforced as they learn these prerequisite concepts, then they will be able to correctly apply them to more complex, higher-level learning activities, such as the balancing of a chemical equation.

While connectionism is not considered a behaviorist theory, it does closely parallel the work of behaviorists, and it gave direction to behavioral theorists such as B. F. Skinner. Connectionism also provided impetus to the programmed instruction movement. Developers of programmed instruction tried to organize their lessons so that information provided early would be linked to topics presented later.

The Law of Effect is a main contribution of Thorndike's connectionism. It states that when a modifiable connection between a situation and a response is made and is accompanied or followed by a satisfying state of affairs, then that connection's strength is increased. An ice skater who receives praise and notoriety will be more likely to be a good in-line roller blader than if no praise had been given. In this case, skills necessary for ice skating are transferred to the similar techniques of roller blading. Conversely, when the connection is followed by an annoying state of affairs, its strength is decreased.

Amplifications and extensions of connectionism were used to support many changes in education during the first half of the century. First, specific goals for education, such as the ability to read at a certain level, became the focus of the school curriculum, rather than teaching subjects to strengthen the mind. Second, the measurement of educational outcomes was promoted. Thorndike is credited for having said, "If something truly exists, then it can be measured." The corollary to this is that if something cannot be measured, then how can one know if it exists? Last, connectionism encouraged teachers to break down complex tasks into simpler ones and to reward practice to build up bonds or connections between instructional situations and desired behaviors.

The establishment of specific goals for teaching, the expectation that goal-related changes could be measured, and the idea that large tasks should be subdivided into simpler ones became basic concepts of behaviorist thought. These ideas are also used extensively in the design of CBI.

Thorndike's ideas became one of the two major areas of interest for those attempting to establish a theory of learning in the first half of the 20th century. His ideas were the basis for those researchers who concentrated on the detailed analysis of reinforcement and the effect of reinforcement on behavior. Skinner's work, discussed later in this chapter, was based on Thorndike's work. Some even say that newer theoretical models, such as connectionism and situated cognition, draw upon Thorndike's ideas.

Ivan Pavlov's (1927) research was the second area of interest for learning theorists in the first half of the 20th century. Pavlov was born in Russia in 1849 and won the Nobel prize in physiology in 1904. His research was not on the psychology of learning but rather on the function of the nervous system in digestion. His discovery of the conditioned reflex was the result of serendipity rather than planned effort.

Most college students are familiar with Pavlov's classic experiments with dogs. He observed that after a short time, dogs who were about to be fed began to salivate. He produced this salivation by ringing a bell before food was placed in a dog's mouth, and after a short time he observed salivation when the bell was rung, even if the dogs did not receive food. He called this phenomenon a "psychic stimulus." This technique became known as *classical conditioning.*

Specifically, Pavlov theorized that by starting with a reflex and its stimulus it is possible to arrange a situation so that another stimulus occurs before the original reflex. Over time, the new stimulus will produce the response, even if the original stimulus is removed.

The classic example of this was the ringing of the bell before the food was given to the dog. The unconditioned reflex, or result, was salivation in the dog's mouth when food was placed in it. The conditioned response was salivation when the bell was rung, but food was not received. Pavlov used this principle as the building block for studying more complex behavior, such as learning.

Higher-order conditioning is the result of building complex chains of stimuli that control behaviors. The most important educational and computer-based learning (CBL) consequence of Pavlov's work was that it served as the basis for attempts to promote the idea that the learning process should be organized from very simple to very complex events.

Also affecting CBI is research on ways to use stimuli to produce desired behaviors in students. Classical conditioning is possibly responsible for producing negative feelings about computers in students. Beeping by the computer when the wrong computer keys are struck, cryptic messages such as SYNTAX ERROR, and the propensity of programs to "crash" and stop running are all thought to classically condition some students to have negative attitudes and high levels of anxiety.

While some consider Pavlov's work to be of only peripheral importance to behaviorist thinking, it did a great deal to gain recognition for behaviorism.

The theorist most closely associated with behavioral theory is B. F. Skinner. He did more to popularize this theory than anyone else, primarily because of his interesting research, but also because of his flair for publicity.

Skinner viewed the study of learning as a science, and he looked to the same model for investigating events that Pavlov used. He was said to have stated that other learning psychologists gave no glimpse of experimental method but that Pavlov did. Pavlov controlled the environment so he could see order in behavior. Because of this orientation, Skinner viewed learning as the change in behavior that was observed under properly controlled situations.

Skinner believed there were two types of learning. The first was Pavlov's classical conditioning, where a stimulus was applied to an organism to produce a response. Learning would occur when there was a transfer of stimulus control for a response from one stimulus to another stimulus.

The second kind of learning, and the category most often associated with Skinner, is called *operant conditioning.* This approach for producing behavior change uses no identifiable stimulus before a response, but rather uses reinforcers that follow a response or that are produced by a response. These reinforcers are responsible for a behavior change. Operant conditioning involves the use of reinforcement to promote desirable changes in behavior, and this reinforcement occurs following desired actions.

For example, a science teacher might have students participate in a series of organized laboratory exercises. The first few activities might be computer lessons that permit little student variation but that praise the student for correct answers. These computer lessons would give cues to students to ensure success. Later, as students become more knowledgeable and confident, the cues would be gradually removed so that in later laboratory exercises students could work on their own.

In this case, the science students would be conditioned to correctly complete sequential science procedures by the reinforcement contained in the computer lessons so that eventually they would complete these procedures without the need for prompting.

Skinner's contributions to educational practice, and to CBI, are numerous. They include the following techniques:

- Stating objectives in terms of desired outcome behaviors.
- Assessing a student's previously acquired behaviors before any instruction.
- Placing learners in a sequence of instruction where they can achieve at the 90% level, but before new instructional activities where they would not be this successful.
- Using teaching machines to reinforce and to strengthen desired behaviors.
- Recording a learner's progress through a lesson to gain feedback for revising the lesson.

Skinner was a vocal advocate of behaviorist principles and the use of machines to teach. As late as the mid-1980s he reiterated his belief that behaviorism was a critical theory for educators to understand and apply. He also has advocated the use of computers in education because he believed that when computers were correctly programmed, they became ideal teaching machines.

Behaviorism has had considerable effect on education in general and on CBI specifically. First, and most important, is the principle that all instruction should be designed to produce observable and measurable outcomes in students. Instruction should be based on objectives that state clearly what is expected of the learner.

Next, behaviorist thought promotes the use of preassessment of students so they can be placed in an instructional sequence at the point where they can achieve at a 90% level. Following preassessment, students are expected to continue participating in learning activities until they demonstrate how well new information has been learned at a 90% level of proficiency. This 90% principle is one of the basic tenets of the mastery learning movement, a subcategory of behaviorist thought.

Behaviorism tells instructional developers that cues should be used to prepare students for information that follows. Small "chunks" of information should be presented by computer lessons, and students should be reinforced positively when success at learning is demonstrated. This means that interactive learning between the student and the computer is critical. Additionally, instruction based on behaviorist principles should allow for the collection of information from students as they learn. For example, if a student in a tutorial dealing with the Pythagorean Theorem constantly has problems with the algebra involved, then the lesson should route the student to a sublesson that reteaches basic mathematics. This information, a type of feedback, should be used to modify the lesson and to monitor the student's progress. Last, student learning should be measured, and students who do not "measure up" should be rerouted through the same or a similar lesson until their competency level meets minimum expectations.

To some, there is much about behaviorism that is unattractive. Because of its emphasis on outcomes, behaviorism is criticized as dehumanizing the teaching and learning process. Behaviorists counter this argument by saying that the emphasis on behaviors need not be to the exclusion of the affective dimension of education, and in fact, behaviorists have developed taxonomies and behavioral objectives for attitudes. At any rate, CBL owes a great deal to the principles advocated by Skinner and other behaviorists.

Systems Theory

In its broadest conceptualization, systems theory concerns the organization and structure of entire organisms. A biologist, Otto von Bertalanffy (1968), is credited with stating the theoretical foundation of systems theory. This foundation is based on the scientific exploration of "wholes" and "wholeness" and on the study of their structure and stability. Systems theorists state that events should be studied in relationship to other events. These relationships should be identified and their effect measured.

Environmentalists believe that the whole Earth is a closed system and that events in one country influence the environment in all other areas: Oil well fires in Kuwait will ultimately influence not only the ecology there, but also to a lesser extent the rest of the world; gaps in the ozone in the atmosphere above Antarctica have consequences elsewhere. Advocates of systems theory believe that it is possible to describe phenomena in the world accurately and to predict future events based on observations (Romiszowski, 1981).

Systems theory was developed in the first third of the 20th century as a direct consequence of the increased importance and acceptance of science and the scientific method. As scientists began to solve problems effectively, their methods were widely studied and applied to new areas of concern. Systems theory was an attempt to clearly state a procedure for describing how real-world events interacted. It was hypothesized that systems principles would be usable in a variety of situations, not just those involving scientific research or technology development.

The scientific method requires controlling for all potential variations in events except two, the variable being studied and one variable thought to influence it.

In this way the scientist can observe phenomena and comment on how they are influenced. If a teacher presents information to one class using CBI and lectures to another to see if student learning is better in one situation than in another, the teacher is practicing a kind of scientific inquiry advocated by systems theorists.

Two related theoretical movements paralleled and complemented the development of systems theory. First was the critical analysis of traditional Newtonian mechanics and the subsequent shift of focus in this discipline to the study of quantum physics and its examination of the notion of "organized complexity." Physicists believed the nature of the universe was dictated by laws that could be discovered, understood, and used to explain events. This reexamination of physics was based on the study of wholes, the same approach as systems theory.

Communication theory was also being developed at about the same time that general systems theory was emerging. Communication theory is based on scientific studies that examine all the components influencing communication. In other words, it attempts to explain and account for all the phenomena related to and influencing communication. Communication theorists based their effort on von Bertalanffy's systems theory. They contributed to his work by expanding on the understanding of the role of feedback in systems. The introduction of the term *cybernetics* to explain the effect of feedback on systems provided support to the growth of systems thinking.

In education, systems theory was made practical by the development of the systems approach. This technique was a translation of the principles of general systems theory into a procedure for the applied field of teaching. The systems approach is a kind of "cookbook" of procedures for designing instruction. The systems approach is based on the following ideas:

- The systems approach applies to learning a method of logical problem solving similar to the scientific method.
- Instruction designed using the systems approach is self-correcting and uses logical methods of decision making.
- Instruction developed using the systems approach applies rational procedures for designing instructional programs that ensure the attainment of specific behavioral objectives.
- The systems approach incorporates ways of looking at complex organizational problems that take into account contingencies.

The systems approach is intended to be prescriptive rather than explanatory. It gives instructional planners a rational procedure to follow when instruction is designed and developed. The systems approach is based on one important principle: a belief in the natural order and rationality of the world. Systems planners are scientific realists who hold the view that natural laws, combined in closed systems, can be used to solve problems.

It rains because of evaporation from large bodies of water and because of the effect of the sun's heat on the atmosphere. Students learn because they receive stimuli from the environment, and if these stimuli are appropriate to their level of maturation and experience, learning occurs. Students process information and decode clues that allow them to understand. How learners process stimuli is predictable and can be understood. The systems approach gives educators a procedure for using what is known about learners and learning in the design of instruction. This approach was based on the ideas of objectivity and causality. Objectivity implies that a person can observe and accurately describe the physical world. Because the world is considered orderly, predictable, and generalizable, it is possible to observe events and use this information to predict what is likely to happen in the future.

The belief in causality of events is closely related to the belief in the objectivity of scientific observation. Specifically, *causality* implies that effects can be planned for and predicted. In other words, systems theorists say there is a natural order to things, and the rules that govern this natural order can be determined and used to explain the causality of events.

One of the earliest and most widespread applications of the systems approach is the technique advocated by proponents of the Michigan State University instructional development model, which is a three-part, nine-step procedure for designing instruction. It was developed at Michigan State University in the 1960s (Figure 3.1).

The systems approach to instructional development is actually a series of steps that guide the developer of instruction, including CBI, in the design of learning activities. Stage I in this model is called *system definition*. This stage refers to the start-up activities that must be planned and organized before the development of instructional materials occurs. First, the instructional problem in terms of a broad goal is identified. Next, the setting, or instructional situation, is analyzed. Information about students, such as background knowledge, learning styles, and motivation, is matched to instructional resources and teaching strategies. Last, the procedures used to manage the instructional activities are organized.

Stage II is termed the *system development* stage. Here, specific performance standards, materials specifications, and design limits are stated. Precise behavioral objectives are written, teaching methods are identified, materials are chosen or developed, and the entire instructional procedure is designed. This instructional plan is called a *prototype* because it is tested and revised in stage III of the systems approach.

Stage III identifies evaluation procedures. At this stage, instructional materials and techniques called *prototypes* are evaluated and revised. This revision process continues until the validity of the new instructional system is determined. Feedback lines connect all stages in the process. In the context of the systems approach, *feedback* refers to information that is used to make adjustments to the instructional materials and procedures.

Each stage of the instructional development model contains three substeps or functions. These functions provide the instructional developer with additional procedures to follow when CBI is designed (Figure 3.2).

The systems approach for instructional design is behaviorally oriented. It strongly advocates the application of behaviorist principles such as preassessment of the target audience, use of objectives stated in terms of expected outcomes, and use of feedback. One important planning tool of the instructional designer is the flowchart. Flowcharting will be discussed later.

Systems theory, the systems approach, and the instructional development model give considerable

FIGURE 3.1

Three-part instructional development model, developed at Michigan State University

Barson, J. (1967). *Instructional systems development. A demonstration and evaluation project.* U.S. Office of Education, Title III-B, Project OE-3-16-025, Michigan State University.

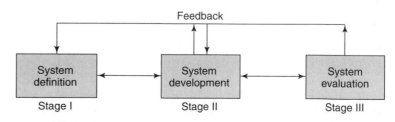

Feedback

| System definition | System development | System evaluation |
| Stage I | Stage II | Stage III |

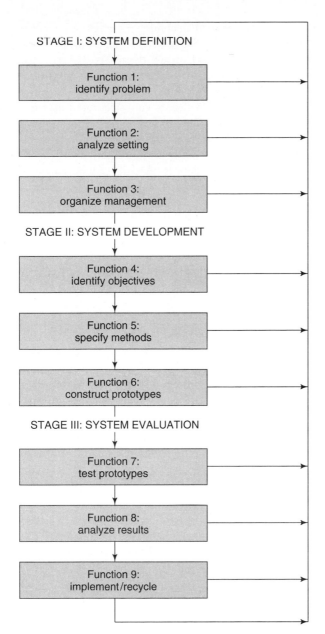

STAGE I: SYSTEM DEFINITION

Function 1:
identify problem

Function 2:
analyze setting

Function 3:
organize management

STAGE II: SYSTEM DEVELOPMENT

Function 4:
identify objectives

Function 5:
specify methods

Function 6:
construct prototypes

STAGE III: SYSTEM EVALUATION

Function 7:
test prototypes

Function 8:
analyze results

Function 9:
implement/recycle

FIGURE 3.2
Steps within the three-part instructional model, developed at Michigan State University

Barson, J. (1967). *Instructional systems development. A demonstration and evaluation project.* U.S. Office of Education, Title III-B, Project OE-3-16-025, Michigan State University.

been derived from systems theory that are routinely used to develop CBI. Systems theory gives educators a prescription for designing effective computer lessons, and although not universally applicable, it does provide considerable direction to educators interested in differentiating between ineffective materials and techniques and those likely to be more successful.

Cognitive Theory

Educational psychologists and learning theorists are moving away from the behaviorist approach and have advocated a closer look at the internal processes that occur in learners during instruction. Behavioral psychologists generally ignore the cognitive changes that mentally occur during teaching and maintain that it is impossible to design instruction on changes in a learner's brain because these changes are not observable, not measurable, and are impossible to predict. On the other hand, cognitive psychologists, a common name for advocates of cognitive theory, attribute a greater degree of autonomy and initiative to the learner (Bruner, 1960; Carey, 1986, Hilgard & Bower, 1975).

Cognitive theory concentrates on the conceptualization of students' learning processes. It focuses on the exploration of the way information is received, organized, retained, and used by the brain. Proponents of cognitive theory believe instructional design should take into account the cognitive structure of the learner, and of groups of learners. Several people have been influential in advocating the cognitive approach, including Jerome Bruner, Jean Piaget, and Seymour Papert.

Many consider Bruner (1960) the primary early advocate of cognitive theory. He has proposed that much of behavior depends on how we structure knowledge about ourselves and the world around us. Cognitive theorists believe instruction must be based on a student's existing state of mental organization, or schema. How knowledge is internally structured or organized by a student has considerable effect on whether new learning will occur. Some have hypothesized that students with a dominant left hemisphere of the brain process information more sequentially and logically than do students who have a dominant right-brain hemisphere (Carey, 1986). In other words, CBI needs to be organized and delivered in a way that complements the cognitive structure and level of sophistication of the learner. Where behaviorists were concerned with the outcomes of instruction, cognitive scientists are more interested in the content of instruction.

guidance to educators interested in designing or evaluating CBI (Dick & Carey, 1990). Preplanning, audience assessment, feedback, interaction between elements of the system (student and lesson), and use of performance-based objectives are techniques that have

Hypermedia, a computer-based instruction approach that is nonlinear and nonsequential, is a powerful tool being used by cognitive scientists to examine how students interact with instruction during the process of learning. The way students use hypermedia gives insights into the structure of thinking and how learning occurs.

Bruner and other cognitive theorists focus on several concepts: (1) how knowledge is organized and structured, (2) readiness for learning, (3) intuition. By intuition, Bruner means the intellectual techniques used for arriving at plausible but tentative conclusions without going through a series of analytical steps. In other words, the value of the "educated guess" is recognized. Last, the importance of motivation, or desire to learn, is identified. Specifically, cognitive scientists accept the importance of students having positive attitudes toward learning.

Cognitive theory gives educators interested in designing or evaluating CBI several guidelines:

1.   Predisposition to learning is important. Instruction needs something to get it started, something to keep it going, and something to keep it from being random. Bruner (1960) would call this activation, maintenance, and direction.

2.   The structure and form of knowledge must be considered. Specifically, the body of material to be learned should be organized in some optimal way. Cognitive theory is partially based on the concept that children are first able to understand concrete operations, then graphic representations of reality, and finally abstract verbal and numerical symbols. Dale (1946) formalized this concept with his Cone of Experience, which organized experiences in 12 levels of increasing abstraction. Dale stated that before learners can understand abstract experiences they require a sufficient depth and breadth of more realistic experiences. Children cannot understand a computer-generated drawing of a flower unless they have first experienced real flowers.

3.   Sequencing of instructional material is important. Cognitive theory is based in part on the idea that there is an optimal sequence for presenting educational experiences. Sequencing must take into account the limited capabilities of learners to process information. Because a child's cognitive style may partially determine success in learning activities, many educators in recent years have begun to attempt to identify cognitive styles of learners, such as their brain hemisphere dominance,

their level of field dependence, and their level of visual processing. Students with different dominant learning styles respond better to instruction sequenced according to their needs. As was stated earlier, left-brain dominant students may respond best to instruction that is very structured and in a logical, easy to follow order. Right-brain dominant children might learn more from instruction that first shows them what they are expected to learn and then fills in the details. A correctly constructed interactive multimedia lesson permits students with different cognitive styles to learn according to the way that is best for them.

4.   The form and pacing of reinforcement must be considered. Learning depends a great deal on knowledge of results at a time and place when that information can be used. For example, compound sentences should not be taught before simple sentence structure is learned. Feedback should be directed toward what is appropriate, not what is inappropriate. For example, a language student should be told that the subject and verb in a simple sentence should agree and that for the sentence to be more correct the direct object of the sentence should be corrected.

5.   Discovery learning is one important technique that incorporates much of cognitive theory. Discovery learning consists of inserting learners into educational situations without telling the student what is already known about that situation. The assumption is that with minimal help from the teacher the student will learn more by discovering the lesson found in the situation. Papert's (1980) LOGO language is an excellent example of a computer-based tool often used to teach problem solving by discovery learning. Hypermedia is an example of computer-based instruction that gives students the opportunity to explore a lesson in a way that is most appropriate for them.

In summary, cognitive theory provides educators with a missing piece of the puzzle. Where behaviorists look at outcomes, and systems theorists look at the factors that affect entire entities or systems, cognitive scientists look at learners. Certainly, there is considerable common ground to be found. All approaches advocate feedback, and all approaches are interested in how experiences are sequenced. As research continues, components of many theories likely will emerge to become parts of procedures used to design effective instruction.

Constructivism and Situated Cognition

Recently, constructivism and situated cognition have captured the attention of teachers and computer education specialists. Most consider these two models directly related to cognitive theory, but they have interesting implications for the design and use of computer-based instruction. Constructivism is founded on the belief that there is a real world that is experienced but that meaning and understanding of the world are imposed by the person.

There are many ways to structure the world, and many perspectives for an event or concept. Learners construct their own meaning from instructional activities. Meaning is rooted in and indexed by experience. Each experience with an idea—and the environment of the idea—becomes part of the meaning of that idea. The experience in which an idea is embedded is critical to the individual's understanding of and ability to use the idea. Most constructivists believe the experience with concepts and ideas in school is quite different from the experience with those concepts in the real world. Constructivists emphasize situating cognitive experiences in authentic activities.

Situated cognition, or situated learning, occurs when students work on "authentic tasks" in a real-world setting. It does not occur when students are taught decontextualized knowledge and skills (Brown, Collins, & Duguid, 1989). This implies that effective instruction should be based on authentic tasks that permit the student to construct a learning environment meaningful to them. Students do not discover knowledge, they construct it in authentic settings.

Constructivist and situated cognition principles are causing educators to rethink computer-based learning. First, learner control and use of authentic information are critical to effectiveness. The lesson must be flexible and rich in content, so students can draw on many stimuli to construct knowledge. Second, use of multimedia that includes still visuals, graphics, motion segments, visual mnemonics, and sound is important. Computer-based instruction should allow students to receive stimuli from a variety of sources and in many different ways.

Finally, it seems obvious that hypermedia and interactive multimedia systems that use laser disks, compact disks, digitized graphics and visuals, and sound, and that are controlled by a flexible authoring system such as hypercard, LinkWay Live, or Hyperstudio on a powerful computer platform, will be the educational computing system of the future.

Currently, there is more theorizing about constructivism and situated cognition by computer educators than actual application. This almost certainly will change as design models become more sophisticated and as powerful multimedia computers become more widely available.

Implications of Theories

A theory base has two important purposes. First, theories provide a direction to research. Theories are based on research results, but they are not static. They continue to evolve as new research findings are reported. In other words, theories are used as guides for researchers who continue to examine what the theories imply in an attempt to clarify them. Ultimately, scientists strive for the development of laws that can be accurately and widely applied to solve problems.

Second, theories provide direction to the practice of a profession. Specifically, behaviorism, systems theory, cognitive theory, constructivism, and situated cognition guide developers of CBI. They also give teachers a sound basis for evaluating materials developed by others. Traditionally, behaviorism and systems theory have been the primary theories used to support the application of computers to learning. Increasingly, however, cognitive science with its many subcategories and adaptations such as schema theory, constructivism, and situated cognition has demonstrated relevance to those who study CBI.

Even a superficial examination of behaviorism, systems theory, and cognitive theory reveals commonalities. Most obvious is the importance of feedback to all three theories. A behaviorist would advocate the use of feedback to modify behavior. Systems theorists advocate the use of feedback to monitor and alter the functioning of the system, and cognitive theorists recognize the importance of correctly timed, positive feedback as a mechanism for supporting correct mental functioning, and for giving students input about decisions they have made.

Another area of common ground is the importance of the assessment of learners so they can be assigned to instruction appropriate for them. Cognitive theory advocates the importance of determining as much as possible about the learner, and the structure used by the learner to process information, so that instruction can be matched to their schema. In situated learning activities, students often need specific prerequisite skills to function effectively.

Behaviorists have different reasons for advocating the importance of preassessing students, specifically to determine if they are ready for a lesson, and by doing so they recognize this technique as important. Similarly, systems theorists mandate examining input so it can be correctly processed by the system.

Another similarity is the importance of individualized instruction. Individualization seems to be the most logical method of instruction, based on what these three theories say. Group instruction can be designed based on any or all of these theories, but individual instruction seems to be a powerful method of teaching. Certainly CBI, which usually is individualized, is the most logical method for differentially applying to students the techniques advocated by these three theories. Only individual tutoring by a teacher would be more effective. Recently, however, collaborative learning advocates have proposed a redesign of some kinds of computer-based instruction so students work in learning groups and collaborate with others, even when using computers.

In summary, many specific techniques are supported by these theories:

- The level of competence required to successfully begin the lesson should be clearly stated.
- The materials should provide for timely, individualized, and positive feedback.
- Outcomes of instruction should be clearly stated, probably in terms of student performance.
- The lesson should individualize both the rate and the route of teaching. Progress through the lesson should be based on the needs of the student who is being taught.

Notes From the Literature

Most children prefer to work at the computer with another individual rather than alone, indicating that a one-to-one computer/student ratio may not be the ideal classroom configuration. The use of the computer encourages interaction among students.

Rosengren, K. S., Gross, D., Abrams, A. F., & Perlmutter, M. (1985, September). An observational study of preschool children's computing activity. Paper presented at Perspectives on the Young Child and the Computer, Austin, TX. (ERIC Document Reproduction Service No. ED 264 953)

- There should be mechanisms to provide for multiple contingencies that might affect the successful completion of the lesson. Specifically, the ultimate CBI system should be an intelligent system that "learns" as it is used.
- Instruction should be motivating to the learner, both cognitively and affectively. It should be both informative and interesting.
- Active involvement by the learner is important. Intellectual, psychomotor, and affective involvement should be required of the learner.
- The learner should be assessed continuously. Students should know how well they are doing on lessons they are taking, not only at the end of lessons but also during lessons.
- The sequence of lessons should be logical and based on the needs of the learner. The rate and route taken by a student during instruction should not be left merely to the discretion of the learner. At the very least, a framework for learning should be provided.
- Some instruction should give students the opportunity to demonstrate their intuitive abilities.
- In many classrooms students should not have their own computer. Rather, they should be taught to collaborate when using computers. Learning groups of three to five each may be optimum. More research is needed in this area.
- Instruction that is authentic and based on real-world events will sometimes be very effective.
- Extremely flexible instruction, hypermedia instruction, that permits the construction of knowledge may be a worthwhile goal for newly designed CBI.

Certainly, these guidelines are only general explanations of what is implied by behaviorism, systems theory, and cognitive theory. Some educators would even consider it improper to try to identify similarities between these three theories.

Understanding the implications of these theories to the practice of CBI is most important. One simple, yet fairly accurate, way to relate these three theories to one another is to apply each to something familiar, such as getting a good picture on a color television set. In other words, compare quality learning to a quality TV picture:

- *Behaviorists* would be content with adjusting the knobs and controls on the television. They work with the situation at hand and manipulate it to get results. Getting the best picture possible would be their major concern.

- *Systems theorists* would examine more of the situation. They would want to check the antenna, the location of the set in the room, and the distance from the broadcast tower to be sure that the signal was the best possible. Controlling the television viewing environment would be a primary concern of the systems theorist. The incoming signal, the quality of the television, and the viewing room would need to be examined and controlled.
- *Cognitive scientists* would use special scopes and monitoring devices to examine every tube and transistor inside the television. They would try to examine the video signal to be sure it was being correctly processed by the television's electronic parts. Faulty or weak components would be identified and replaced. How the television's electronic components manipulated the signal would be of paramount importance to the cognitive scientist. Probably the right approach to achieving a quality TV picture would be to use all three sets of processes.

In a teaching situation, the behaviorist wants to take the learner and produce the desired behaviors by controlling the learning environment. Manipulating the learner and learning situation to produce the desired outcome would be most important to the behaviorist. The systems theorist, on the other hand, would want to evaluate all input and output variables in the learning situation to produce learning. The cognitive psychologist would want to study the brain and its functioning to see how learning occurs. This information would then be used to facilitate learning in students. Probably the most successful learning situation would apply techniques from more than one theoretical approach.

Behaviorism is considered by many to be the most practical, easily applied theory. It is probably the least sophisticated. Systems theory is more complex and likely to work, but in many teaching–learning situations it is impossible to effectively apply, even though its principles are sound. Cognitive science is the most sophisticated approach, but unfortunately not all of the "scopes and monitors" needed to study thinking are available to the educator. Ultimately, constructivism may offer a great deal to teachers and developers of instructional materials. In today's classroom, however, constructivist principles are difficult to apply.

SUMMARIES OF RESEARCH ON INSTRUCTIONAL USES OF COMPUTERS

> The best current evidence is that media are mere vehicles that deliver instruction but do not influence student achievement any more than the truck that delivers our groceries causes changes in nutrition. . . . Only the content of the vehicle can influence achievement. (Clark, 1983)

This quote has caused considerable furor among educational researchers since it was published in 1983. Clark's hypothesis that media do not influence achievement went against the thinking of many who believed that media, including computers, would produce significantly better learning when used in almost any situation. Clark (1983) substantiated his argument by reanalyzing several decades of media research.

Also of interest is a different position taken by several others who argue that important learning outcomes

Notes From the Literature

Media are delivery vehicles for instruction and do not directly influence learning.

Clark, R. E. (1983). Reconsidering research on learning from media. Review of Educational Research, 53(4), 445–459.

Any resulting changes in student learning or performance may be attributed to the uncontrolled effects of different instructional methods, content, and/or novelty.

Clark, R. E. (1985). Evidence for confounding in computer-based instruction studies: Analyzing the meta-analyses. Educational Communications and Technology Journal, 33(4), 249–262.

In reply to Clark (1983), Kulik and Kulik (1987) found from a meta-analysis of more than 200 studies that students using computer-based instruction had better exam scores, better attitudes toward instruction, better attitudes toward computers, and required less instructional time than students receiving traditional instruction.

Kulik, J. A., & Kulik, C. C. (1987). Computer-based instruction: What 200 evaluations say. In Simonson, M. R., & Zvacek, S. M. (Eds.). Proceedings of selected research presentations (pp. 17–24). Atlanta: Association for Educational Communications and Technology.

are directly attributable to the use of computers. Both positions will be discussed, but first a historical overview of research related to computers is needed (Kulik, Bangert, & Williams, 1983; Kulik, Kulik, & Bangert-Drowns, 1984, 1985; Kulik, Kulik, & Cohen, 1980).

Clark (1994) reiterated his position in an article with the provocative title *Media Will Never Influence Learning*. In this article, which Clark later defended during a debate, he made the following statement:

> Whenever you have found a medium or set of media attributes which you believe will cause learning for some learners on a given task, ask yourself if another (similar) set of attributes would lead to the same learning result. If you suspect that there may be an alternative set or mix of media that would give similar results, ask yourself what is causing these similar results. It is likely that when different media treatments of the same informational content to the same students yield similar learning results, the cause of the results can be found in a method which the two treatments share in common.... Give up your enthusiasm for the belief that media attributes cause learning. (p. 28)

A number of researchers and theorists have also written to this issue. Kozma (1994) stated that the profession should move to the study of ways we can use the capabilities of media to influence learning for particular students, tasks, and situations. He also proposed an interesting counter-analogy to Clark's "delivery trucks" statement. Kozma compared media, especially computer-based systems, to buildings in which various activities could take place. Depending on the configuration of the building, such as its size, some activities would be possible and others not. The building is a venue for athletic events, just as the computer may be a vessel for learning events.

Notes From the Literature

When compared with conventional instruction, computer instruction raises achievement scores .45 standard deviations for elementary students and .32 standard deviations for secondary education.

Kulik, C., et al. (1984). Effects of computer-based education on elementary school pupils. Paper presented at the annual meeting of the American Educational Research Association, New Orleans.

Kulik, J., Bangert, R., & Williams, G. (1983). Effects of computer-based teaching on secondary school students. Journal of Educational Psychology, 75, 19–26.

Research on Programmed Instruction

The beginnings of instructional computing research can be found in research on programmed instruction and teaching machines. Although most of this research was conducted more than 30 years ago, it is still relevant because it provides a foundation for today's research on computers (Ofiesh & Meierhenry, 1964).

Programmed instruction techniques were developed as a direct consequence of the application of behaviorism and systems theory to education. Programmed instruction is the delivery of teaching using a systematic technique that has been adequately validated before use, involves the learner by requiring feedback, and expects the learner to obtain specific behaviorally stated objectives. Instruction usually is delivered in small steps or chunks of information. Programmed instruction traditionally is delivered by teaching machines and programmed texts.

Because programmed instruction is based on behaviorism, and behaviorists believe in the need for scientific validation, it has been examined as a technique by researchers in many studies (Ofiesh & Meierhenry, 1964). The results of these studies demonstrated several things. First, researchers found that programmed instruction worked and that programmed texts were as effective as teaching machines, but that neither mechanical machines nor printed texts produced generally better results than more traditional methods of teaching. As a matter of fact, most research on programmed instruction showed little support for its use other than as an alternative to conventional instruction, such as in correspondence education or remedial instruction. It was also reported that students did not like to learn from programmed materials. They considered them boring and simplistic.

Educators had an explanation for this lack of support for programmed instruction. Many thought the procedures used to deliver programmed information—specifically, the programmed text and the teaching machine—were at fault, but that the applicability of programming techniques to education was sound. At any rate, the programmed instruction movement declined in importance during the 1960s and '70s.

During this time the computer was becoming an important force in society. While computers had only a minor effect on education—except for administrative uses—until the 1980s, many researchers began to examine the use of the computer as a teaching tool. One of the first of these scientists was Patrick Suppes, who explored the use of the computer to deliver math drill and practice lessons (Suppes & Morningstar, 1969).

Suppes used teletypewriter terminals attached to a mainframe computer to deliver lessons to mathematics students. Generally, he found that students improved their math skills, and they enjoyed the experience of working on the computer. Because of the expense, however, and the inaccessibility of mainframe computers, Suppes's approach to teaching mathematics was not widely adopted. His work did provide a foundation for future efforts and bridged the gap between early programmed instruction applications and today's procedures that use the computer as the delivery medium.

Meta-Analysis and Instructional Computing Research

Meta-analysis is a statistical technique for summarizing the results of a large number of research studies to identify general, or cumulative, effects. Kulik and his colleagues at the University of Michigan conducted a number of meta-analyses of studies that dealt with the effect of CBI on learning (Kulik, Bangert, & Williams, 1983; Kulik, Kulik, & Bangert-Drowns, 1984, 1985; Kulik, Kulik, & Cohen, 1980).

Kulik's investigations produced some interesting results concerning the effectiveness of CBI and computer-managed instruction (CMI). Kulik found that when the results of 175 studies were summarized using meta-analysis procedures, students who were taught using computers scored about .29 standard deviations higher on achievement tests than students taught using methods not involving computers. This translates as an increase in achievement scores from the 50th to the 61st percentile. It can also be translated as a gain in grade-equivalent scores of about three months.

Kulik's analyses showed that CBI produced varying results, depending on the grade level of the students involved, their ability level, and the type of instruction presented. For example, Kulik reported that drills and tutorials, the simplest kind of instruction similar to the use of flash cards, were almost always successful when they were used in elementary schools. Student scores were raised on average about .47 standard deviations.

However, using computers to manage instruction, or to keep track of how elementary students were doing and to prescribe what they needed to do next

Notes From the Literature

Well-designed computer-aided instruction (CAI) can be an effective means of maintaining high levels of task engagement during independent practice while increasing spelling achievement for students with learning disabilities.

MacArthur, C. A., et al. (1987). Computer assisted instruction with learning disabled students. Achievement, engagement, and other factors related to achievement. Paper presented at the annual meeting of the American Educational Research Association, Washington, DC.

was not as successful as teaching with computers. Achievement scores for students who had instruction managed by computer were only .07 standard deviations higher than other students' scores. On the other hand, Kulik reported that CMI contributed a great deal to instructional effectiveness for high school and college students. High school students who were involved in studies of CMI were reported to have achieved an average of .40 standard deviations better than other students. College students had scores .35 standard deviations higher.

Based on the results of these meta-analyses, Kulik concluded the following:

- Computer-based education has had positive effects on student learning.
- Computer-based education was not uniformly successful for all uses or at all levels. Elementary students benefited most from drills and tutorials and less from computer-managed instruction systems. High school students seemed to be positively influenced by both computer-assisted and computer-managed instruction, and college students seemed to benefit only moderately from computer-based education.

In short, Kulik's reports seem to indicate a rosy picture about the use of computers in teaching. Others, such as Richard Clark, however, present a different summary of the research on CBI.

Alternative Interpretation of Meta-Analysis Results

Clark (1983), the author of the "mere vehicles" explanation of the role of media and computers on student achievement, states that computers are not the powerful instructional tools that Kulik's results indicate. According to Clark, the studies included in Kulik's reviews suffer from two critical problems. First, many were poorly designed—correct research procedures were not followed. Second, students in the CBI classes tended to receive enhanced instruction, either in the form of more time learning the skill in question or in the form of better prepared instruction. Clark supports his claims by reexamining a random sample of the studies Kulik had also investigated. He reports the following conclusions based on this analysis:

- In 75 of the studies, serious design flaws were found.
- In more than 50 of the studies, there were obvious failures to control the amount of instruction received by the computer and the traditional instruction groups. Students who received computer instruction usually received either more or better teaching.
- In 40 of the studies where the same teacher taught both the computer and the traditional students, the improvement in effect size for CBI was only .09 standard deviations.
- Instructional method was not controlled in half the studies. When it was, there was no difference between achievement scores for computer students when compared with traditionally taught students.

Clark summarizes his critique of Kulik's meta-analyses by reporting that the achievement gains attributed to the computer mode were probably due to the method of teaching used by the software—specifically, the difference between the way the teacher taught and the way the computer program presented the instruction. Clark (1985) reiterates his more general statement about media by directing it specifically to computers:

> Computers make no more contribution to learning than the truck that delivers groceries to the market contributes to improved nutrition in a community. Purchasing a truck will not improve nutrition just as purchasing a computer will not improve student achievement. Nutrition gains come from getting the correct "groceries" to the people who need them. Similarly, achievement gains result from matching the correct teaching method to the student who needs it. (p. 259)

Kozma's (1994) interesting metaphor about computers being like buildings in which many events might occur is another interpretation of the role of technol-

ogy. Certainly the conflicting interpretations of the research data leave the teacher in a bit of a fix about what to believe. Obviously, proponents of the two sides of the argument are not attempting to mislead; rather, both Kulik and Clark explain the information according to different sets of rules. Generally, Kulik's work liberally summarizes the results of several generations of research on the effect of computers. Clark takes a more conservative approach. Probably neither is absolutely correct. As researchers are prone to say, "More research is needed."

In the meantime, educators should probably not make grandiose claims about the power of the computer to improve student achievement in all situations. Similarly, researchers should probably not attempt to compare CBI with traditional "teacher-centered" teaching. Instead, the advantages of using computers in specific situations and for teaching specific topics should be the focus of research efforts.

Just because a school building or district purchases computers, or develops a computer literacy program, is no guarantee that students in that district will score higher on the Standardized Achievement Test or be more likely to go to college. Or on a smaller scale, there should be no expectations that sophomores will write clearer term papers because they are using word processing, or that juniors will complete more geometry proofs because a computer lab is across the hall. Computers are only as good as the programs used in them, and programs are only useful if the teacher who assigns them realizes how they contribute to an entire curriculum plan. In short, computers are not a general solution to the problems of education in the 21st century. Rather, they are a powerful tool in the teacher's repertoire of tools and techniques. This is one generalization that both theory and research support.

EFFECTIVE COMPUTER-BASED INSTRUCTION: WHAT THE RESEARCH SAYS

Since the 1970s, many research studies have been conducted on the effect of computers in the schools. One category of studies included those reviewed by Kulik (Kulik, Bangert, & Williams, 1983; Kulik, Kulik, & Bangert-Drowns, 1984, 1985; Kulik, Kulik, & Cohen, 1980). These studies essentially compared two groups of students with each other. One group received CBI while the other group received comparable instruction by some other method, usually live teaching. Certainly, this kind of research is interesting and could be important if it were possible to demonstrate that computers were a consistently better delivery system than other media. Unfortunately, this kind of "bottom-line" research is controversial, and while studies such as Kulik's have produced generalizable results, some conclusions from this research are considered suspect.

There also has been a shift in how computers are used that has not been adequately tested by researchers. Increasingly, educators are designing computer environments where learners interact with instructional events. Students are allowed to construct their learning activities based on their own interpretation of what is needed. They are not presented with information; rather they are expected to interact and even cause changes to the information made available by the computer-based system.

Luckily, other approaches to research tend to produce more consistent findings. This research concentrates on part of the question at one time, rather than on more comprehensive investigations. For example, a researcher might want to explore the concept of *branching* or *linking* the variety of possible routes that a student can take through a lesson, to determine how many remedial sessions work best in tutorial lessons. Another researcher might be interested in the question of equity and computer use. Do girls and women use computers more or less than boys and men? Do members of different ethnic groups demonstrate higher or lower levels of computer anxiety? Do students from poorer families demonstrate higher or lower levels of motivation toward learning from computers? These questions are just as interesting as the research asking, "Are computers generally better than teachers?" and are probably much more meaningful.

Notes From the Literature

Feedback during computer-assisted instruction helps promote retention of material presented.

Chanond, K. (1988). The effects of feedback, correctness of response and response confidence on learner's retention in CAI. In Simonson, M. (Ed.), Proceedings of selected research paper presentations (pp. 134–146). New Orleans: Association for Educational Communications and Technology Individualization.

The following section will present summaries of research in two categories. Included will be discussions of research on the design of computer lessons and research on computer use.

Design of Computer-Based Instruction

Programmed instruction research, and more recent research on microcomputer use, have produced several generalizable conclusions about how CBI should be designed. Naturally, any summaries such as these should be taken as general recommendations, not hard-and-fast rules.

KCR: Knowledge of Correct Results.

Knowledge of correct results (KCR) is one technique identified by both research and theory as important. Students should have correct responses reinforced in some positive manner. It is also effective to give students clues when incorrect answers are given. In a lesson on vocabulary, students who spell a name incorrectly but close to the correct spelling should be told they have made a spelling error rather than that their answer is incorrect. Clues and prompts should positively reinforce what was right about the response and should give students directions about how to correct what was wrong with the answer. In a drill or tutorial lesson a rule of thumb is to allow two or three incorrect answers before students are given the correct response.

Feedback.

Students should be given information about their progress through a lesson, both during the lesson and at the end of the lesson. Games are popular with students partly because they usually give students immediate feedback. This not only reinforces the correct response, it also makes the activity more interesting and motivating.

When a lesson is concluded, students should be given feedback on their progress. While a simple score, such as 8 problems solved out of 10, is feedback, a more complete diagnosis of student progress is much more effective. Recommendations for additional instructional activities are also appropriate. For example, a computer lesson on balancing chemical equations could give the student information on how many problems were solved correctly, on what kinds of problems the student seemed to do well, and on what kinds of topics the student did not do well. Additionally, the

Notes From the Literature

After computer lessons, especially simulations, students should be allowed to participate in a discussion of what they learned, and their reactions to the lesson. This debriefing increases understanding, improves problem-solving ability, exposes misunderstandings, increases recall, and improves motivation.

Gray, B. (1988). Enhancing learning through debriefing. The Computing Teacher, 15(9), 19–21.

lesson might recommend that the student brush up on the periodic chart by taking a drill lesson on the symbols for the elements before attempting more equation balancing. In other words, the closer the feedback from a computer lesson matches what a live tutor would say to a student, the more effective the feedback will be.

Feedback in an interactive multimedia environment would be different. Certainly, a test could be given to quantitatively assess a student's learning. Also, an assessment of how the student used the lesson might provide further feedback. Information about how many branches were used, or which nodes in the lesson were visited, might help the students analyze their learning. Probably new types of assessment and feedback will be necessary for new types of computer-based instruction.

Branching.   Branching, the route a student takes through a lesson, is directly related to KCR and feedback. Usually, branches that students take through a lesson depend on their responses to questions. For example, a student who misses a self-test question on the effect of the Union's blockade of the South during the U.S. Civil War might be branched to a review section of the lesson that deals with the economic condition of the Confederacy in 1861.

Another kind of lesson branch is initiated by the student. For example, in a writing tutorial, a student who is unclear about how to respond to a requirement to diagnose a short paragraph may elect a help option to review the correct use of prepositional phrases. When ready, the student would "branch back" to the main lesson to complete the diagnosis. Linking in a hypermedia lesson is another example of student-controlled branching.

Assessment.   Another characteristic of effective CBI is assessment. Students should be assessed during and at the conclusion of lessons. Obviously, assessment is closely related to both KCR and feedback. Testing gives the student information about how well the lesson is being completed.

Less obtrusive, or obvious, assessment also can be given. Student response times can be monitored to determine if information is clearly understood or if students must figure things out before answering. For example, in a drill, the amount of time an elementary student takes to complete short division problems is probably related to ability. Students who take longer probably need more practice.

Computer-based lessons also can diagnose a student during a lesson, much as a competent teacher "gets a feeling" for how well a student is doing. Obviously, this kind of assessment is much more difficult, but as CBI continues to improve, it will become easier. Most important, the research indicates that this kind of "intuitive" assessment is important.

Advance Organizers.   Lessons that indicate to students where they are going and what is expected of them generally produce higher achievement levels than lessons without this kind of simple advance organizer. Behaviorally stated objectives that are shown to the student at the beginning of a lesson act as organizers and have been found to enhance student achievement.

More subtle advance organizers that preview subsequent information and prepare the learner for what is expected of them can, and should, be used throughout lessons. Just as a good teacher previews the next day's lesson, an effective computer lesson can indicate the relationship between what is learned first (e.g., the importance of raw materials to a manufacturing economy) with what will be learned later (e.g., the restriction of access to raw materials because of naval blockades during wartime).

Prompts.   Effective teachers prompt or give clues to students to help them reach correct conclusions. Good CBI should do the same. Prompts can be as simple as "You're close, try spelling the name of the state differently," to something as sophisticated as "Think about the problem differently. What could you say to be more descriptive instead of 80 feet high? Is there any structure in your home town that is about that tall?" Prompts guide student responses. They help students understand and are an important characteristic of effective teaching. Prompts can also be used to provide structure to an interactive multimedia lesson and help students stay on task.

Pacing.   There was a time when variable pacing was considered the major contribution to teaching that individualized instruction had to offer. Advocates of mastery learning principles have demonstrated something called the "90/90 rule." This rule states that 90% of students can learn 90% of what is important about any topic, given adequate time. Interestingly enough, research has supported this idea, and one of the major forces behind the push to individualize instruction is the belief that one important reason some children achieve more than others is that they learn faster, not more. The idea of "fastness of learning" was considered an inadequate reason for labeling some as less intelligent.

One important characteristic of CBI is that it tends to be individualized. Students proceed through learning activities by themselves, at their own pace. In classrooms with one teacher and 30 students, a uniform pace must be set. This pace is too fast for some and too slow for others, and advocates of mastery learning principles would claim this is largely why some children achieve better than others. Computer-based individualized instruction eliminates this problem. Certainly, learners do not have infinite time. Well-designed lessons assist the student to use their time well and wisely.

Screen Design.   As microcomputers have proliferated, so has concern over how information is presented on the multitude of screens in use. Recently, considerable research on screen design has been reported, and more is under way. This is an area of continuing interest to computer educators. As early as 1973, James Martin wrote, "As yet, no acknowledged sense of style has developed for Computer Assisted Instruction (CAI). . . . In the meantime, however, some singularly unstylish CAI programs are being written" (in Heines, 1984, p. 130).

Screen style is still an issue. Resolution of the screen should be the first style consideration when CBI is designed. The screens used with some microcomputers have very low resolution, meaning that they do not produce high-quality images. In general, anything written or drawn on a computer screen will be of lower quality, or resolution, than it would be if it were written on paper. When screens are designed, and when teachers evaluate a lesson's screens, three areas should be considered: the kind of information presented, the screen components, and the readability of the information shown.

Also, the use of visual metaphors have been found to be useful. Visual metaphors are as simple as the icons used to depict files, folders, and trash. They can

be as sophisticated as visual mnemonics that help learners remember sophisticated ideas. The "It is not how hard you work, it is how much you get done" visual of the farmer taking pigs to market printed in chapter 10 is an example of a visual metaphor.

Screen Information.   Words, graphics, and space are the three kinds of "information" on a computer screen. Generally, all are used in effective screen design. Graphics should be designed according to the level of realism required by the sophistication of the students who will use the lesson. Dale's Cone of Experience (Dale, 1946) is a guide here. Abstract symbols will not be understood by students who have not had sufficient realistic experiences with the content of the symbol. In other words, line drawings, outlines, and diagrams may not be effective. The kinds of visual information presented by a computer lesson must be evaluated in terms of not only the lesson's content but also the learner's experience level. Other information presented on the screen must be evaluated in the same manner.

Usually, it is best if one idea or topic is presented on one screen at a time. Simple is usually better than complex. Multiple ideas shown on one screen tend to confuse the student. On the other hand, if topics are closely related, it may be necessary to retain portions of one screen when a new topic is presented. A compromise would be to give the student the option of reviewing screens shown previously.

When graphics or drawings are shown to students, they tend to look at them in a clockwise sequence. Usually, the eye first looks at the upper left quadrant of the screen and moves clockwise around the screen. Prompts such as arrows or directions can be used to reinforce or alter this natural viewing pattern.

Screen Components.   The way the computer screen is organized should give the student a feeling of control. No learners enjoy being placed in a situation where they have no say in what is happening. First, the screen should provide orientation information to the student. This might include statements about where the student is in the sequence of the lesson, analogous to page numbering in a book. Some call this information the lesson's "cognitive map." Because it is hypothetically easy to get lost in a lesson (lost in hyperspace), especially a hypermedia lesson, it is important that students know where they are. A lesson's cognitive map gives such orientation information.

Students also need to know how to move through the lesson. A "navigation system" can help. Simple page turning or screen changing is a kind of navigation system, but more sophisticated lessons have easy-to-use ways of "jumping around" in a lesson, such as to the beginning of a section, or back to the lesson's start. Effective CBI lessons have cognitive maps and navigation systems. Lesson section titles can be used, as can visual symbols that indicate where the student is within the lesson (Figures 3.3, 3.4, 3.5, and 3.6).

Directions should be clearly given to students about what they are expected to do. These directions can be as simple as "Read this and press RETURN" or as sophisticated as "Solve this problem, and type in your answer using this form, $a+by+cx = 0$." Also important is information about the student's response: What the student types at the keyboard should be shown on the screen. Unbelievably, some programs do not even provide this minimal response information.

Error messages should be clear and easy to understand and should give the student directions about what to do next. Messages that say "Break in 2333," "Abort, Retry, Fail?", or a bomb icon with an error number will quickly sour students on CBI.

Options should be given to the student, too. For example, what keys to press to get help, to skip this page, or to go back and review are important components of effectively designed screens. Again, a well-designed screen gives the student the feeling of being in control, not of being controlled. There always should be clear directions for how a student can return to a major subsection of a lesson. "Safe-havens" for learners can be the home page, a table of contents page, or a section start-up page. Effective lessons even use bookmarks within computer-based instruction so the learner can easily return to the spot they left off.

Readability. Because the resolution of a computer screen is generally lower than for a page of a book, extreme care must be taken to ensure that what is written can be read. First, writing should be simple. Long, complex prose is not meant to be read from a computer screen. Next, upper- and lower-case lettering should be used because it is easier to read. Third, justified right margins should be avoided. Ragged right margins show up better on more computer screens. Fourth, shorter rather than longer lines are best. Eighty-column text displays should be avoided, if possible. Forty columns of text is the standard. Last, one letter size should be used for all text.

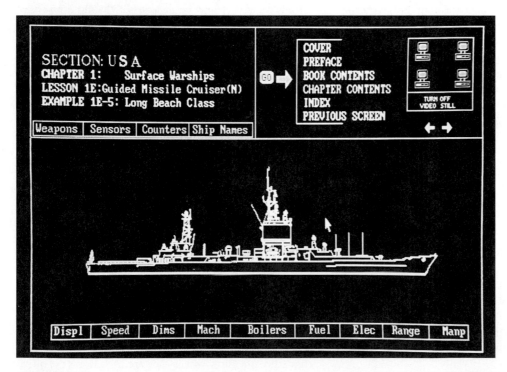

FIGURE 3.3
A page from the U.S. Navy's "Threat Matrix" hypermedia lesson designed using IBM's LinkWay program

FIGURE 3.4
A cognitive map indicates the location of the page within the lesson. This helps prevent the learner from becoming lost in what is sometimes called "hyperspace."

Larger titles can be used, but the use of three or four type sizes for the main textual portion of a lesson is distracting to the reader.

Readability and legibility can sometimes be improved by the use of underlining, reverse printing, and blinking words. Although effective in many situations, overuse of these techniques can be distracting and detrimental to learning. World Wide Web systems have begun to standardize on the use of reverse printed words and characters as indicators of linking points. In other words, when a browser using the World Wide Web wants to move to another section of the Web they click their mouse button on a reverse printed word.

Screen design is a critical component of a computer lesson. If design is haphazard, learning will be affected. The kind of information presented, the components

FIGURE 3.5
Navigation buttons allow movement through the lesson. Video buttons activate images from a laser disk.

FIGURE 3.6
The U.S. Navy's "Threat Matrix" lesson requires an MS-DOS type computer with monitor and a second monitor on which to display images from a laser disk player.

found in each screen, and the readability of the text must all be considered when CBI is designed or evaluated. The research shows that it makes a difference.

SUMMARY

The method of teaching with computers is directly related to student achievement. Computers, like any tool, can be used either correctly or incorrectly. Teachers should attempt to maximize the positive effect computers can have and minimize potential negative influences.

Individualization.   CBI is an individualized approach to teaching. Students should be allowed to work at their own rate. Several researchers have reported that two students can work together on a les-

son with no apparent loss of effectiveness. However, when more than two students work on one computer at a time, some students' learning likely will be adversely affected (Klinkefus, 1988), unless the lesson is designed to be a collaborative one. Increasingly, individualized instruction means that the computer does not always deliver instruction while the learner receives it. Rather, students interact with a computer-controlled learning environment and construct meaning while participating in learning activities.

Learner Control.   When teachers direct instructional activities, they control pace and direction. When computers are used to deliver instruction, the focus of control changes. Originally, most CBI allowed the student considerable flexibility in controlling the pace and route of the lesson. Recent research demonstrates that this may not always be a good idea. Students might not review when review is needed, might not follow remediation directions when they are suggested, or might not read all information presented when they have complete control over the program. Increasingly, CBI is being designed so the computer has some ability to regulate a student's progress.

Attitude Change.   Lessons that present new information, require both physical and intellectual involvement, and present relevant information are most likely to be favorably received and to produce positive attitudes. These positive attitudes would be directed toward both the content of the lesson and the use of the computer. In other words, it is possible to design CBI so that students' attitudes can be changed both toward the topic being taught and toward the importance of CBI.

Notes From the Literature

The microcomputer environment is "intrinsically motivating" to young children because it allows moderate control of the learning situation and provides immediate feedback—a critical factor in producing and maintaining performance gains.

Armour-Thomas, E., White, M. A., & Boehm, A. (1987, April). The motivational effects of types of computer feedback on children's learning and retention of relational concepts. Paper presented at the annual meeting of the American Educational Research Association, Washington, DC. (ERIC Document Reproduction Service No. ED 287 446)

Computer Anxiety. Computer anxiety, the fear felt by people when using computers, or when computer use is anticipated, is a documented problem for certain individuals. A significant proportion of any group of computer users will be considerably more anxious than others in the same group, and this anxiety has been shown to be related to problems these people have when they use computers. There is also growing evidence that there is a gender difference related to computer anxiety. Girls and women tend to be more anxious than boys and men. Researchers have indicated that students should be diagnosed for anxiety, and those students with high levels of computer anxiety should be given individual attention to reduce their apprehension. Currently, most evidence indicates that individual attention from a trained and sensitive tutor is the best way to reduce a student's anxiety level. Merely requiring anxious students to work on the computer to overcome their fears will not reduce anxiety. As a matter of fact, this kind of "throwing them in the deep end" remediation produces more anxiety and is likely to produce computer hatred (Maurer & Simonson, 1994).

Computer Labs. Accessibility is strongly related to use. Teachers and students who have easy access to computers are most likely to use them. The more roadblocks that are placed between the user and the computer, the less likely it is that computers will be used. If use is to be promoted, then computers should be distributed throughout the school in classrooms and small labs. Centralizing computers in laboratories, or media centers, may have many management advantages, but it may reduce use.

Because of the relative newness of CBI, much of the information about use is not adequately documented. Anecdotal information abounds, but scientific evidence is somewhat scarce. Educators should proceed cautiously when making decisions about how CBI is implemented. Local field testing of procedures is a must.

Educators should not forget, however, that techniques proposed by theory, and supported by research, form the foundation for effective CBI. In subsequent chapters, procedures for use of CBI will be presented. At the root of these recommendations will be the information discussed or implied in this chapter on theory and research. Teaching is a profession. Decisions should be "founded upon a body of intellectual theory and research. The practice of a profession cannot be disjoined from its theoretical understandings" (Finn, 1953, p. 8).

SELF-TEST QUESTIONS

1. Match the name to the theory.
   Theories
   A. Behaviorism
   B. Systems theory
   C. Cognitive theory
   Names
   a. von Bertalanffy
   b. Seymour Papert
   c. Jerome Bruner
   d. B. F. Skinner
   e. Patrick Suppes
2. Which of the following techniques, or concepts, would not be used by a behaviorist when instruction is designed?
   A. Feedback
   B. Cognitive style
   C. KCR
   D. Performance
   E. Post-test measurement
3. Match the technique to the theory:
   Theories
   A. Behaviorism
   B. Systems theory
   C. Cognitive theory
   Techniques
   a. Feedback
   b. Performance objectives
   c. Schema
   d. Input
   e. KCR
   f. Discovery learning
   g. Advance organizer
   h. 90/90 rule
4. Should the learner have control over the pace and route of individualized instruction? Why or why not?
5. Of the three theories examined, which is considered the easiest to apply in the classroom?
6. What did Richard Clark say was the role of the computer in computer-based instruction?
7. Define *constructivism.*
8. Define *situated cognition.*

ANSWERS TO SELF-TEST QUESTIONS

1. a. B
   b. C

c. C
d. A
e. A
2. B
3. a. A, B
   b. A
   c. C
   d. B
   e. A
   f. C
   g. C
   h. A
4. No, students should not always be allowed to have complete control over the rate and route of their computer-based instruction for the following reasons:
   a. They may not take remediation when it is needed.
   b. They may skip parts of lessons.
   c. They may not read all that is presented.
5. Behaviorism.
6. Clark called computers, and all media, "mere vehicles" that store and deliver instructions but that do not influence the learning that occurs.
7. *Constructivism* holds that there is a real world that is experienced. However, meaning is placed on the world independently by us rather than existing in the world independently. There are many ways to structure the world, and there are many meanings or perspectives for any event or concept. Students construct meaning during the learning process.
8. *Situated cognition* is also referred to as situated learning. This approach implies that knowledge is situated as it is partly a product of the activity, context, and culture in which it is used. Knowledge is situated and not constant.

REFERENCES

Bertalanffy, L., von. (1955). *General systems theory: Foundations, development, applications.* New York: George Braziller.

Brown, J., Collins, A., & Duguid, P. (1989). Situated cognition and the culture of learning. *Educational Researcher, 18*(1), 32–42.

Bruner, J. (1960). *The process of education.* New York: Random House.

Carey, S. (1986). Cognitive science and science education. *American Psychologist, 41*(10), 1123–1130.

Clark, R. (1983). Reconsidering research on learning from media. *Review of Educational Research, 53*(4), 445–459.

Clark, R. (1985). Confounding in educational computing research. *Journal of Educational Computing Research, 1*(2), 137–148.

Clark, R. (1994). Media will never influence learning. *Educational Technology Research and Development, 42*(2), 21-29.

Dale, E. (1946). *Audio-visual methods in teaching.* New York: Dryden Press.

Dick, W., & Carey, L. (1990). *The systematic design of instruction* (3rd ed.). Glenview, IL: Scott, Foresman.

Finn, J. (1953). Professionalizing the audiovisual field. *Audio-Visual Communication Review, 1*(1) 6–17.

Heines, J. (1984). *Screen design strategies for computer assisted instruction.* Bedford, MA: Digital Press.

Hilgard, E. R., & Bower, G. H. (1975). *Theories of learning.* Englewood Cliffs, NJ: Prentice Hall.

Klinkefus, M. (1988). *Paired versus individual learning when using computer assisted instruction.* Unpublished master's thesis. Ames, IA: Iowa State University.

Kozma, R. (1994). Will media influence learning? Reframing the debate. *Educational Technology Research and Development, 42*(2), 7–19.

Kulik, J., Bangert, R., & Williams, G. (1983). Effects of computer-based teaching on secondary students. *Journal of Educational Psychology, 75*(1), 19–26.

Kulik, J., Kulik, C., & Bangert-Drowns, R. (1984). Effectiveness of computer-based education in elementary schools. *Computers in Human Behavior, 1*(1), 59–74.

Kulik, J., Kulik, C., & Bangert-Drowns, R. (1985). The importance of outcome studies: A reply to Clark. *Journal of Educational Computing Research, 1*(4), 381–387.

Kulik, J., Kulik, C., & Cohen, P. (1980). Effectiveness of computer-based college teaching: A meta-analysis of findings. *Review of Educational Research, 2*(2), 525–544.

Maurer, M., & Simonson, M. (1994). The reduction of computer anxiety. *Journal of Research on Computing in Education, 26*(2), 205–219.

Ofiesh, G., & Meierhenry, W. (Eds.). (1964). Trends in programmed instruction. *Papers of the first annual convention of the National Society for Programmed Instruction.* Washington, DC: Department of Audiovisual Instruction of the National Education Association.

Pavlov, I. (1927). *Conditioned reflexes.* London: Oxford University Press.

Romiszowski, A. (1981). *Designing instructional systems.* London: Kogan Page.

Rosen, L. D., Sears, D. C., & Weil, M. M. (1987). Computerphobia. *Behavior Research Methods, Instruments, and Computers, 19*(2), 167–179.

Skinner, B. (1954). The science of learning and the art of teaching. *Harvard Educational Review, 24,* 86–97.

Suppes, P., & Morningstar, M. (1969). Computer assisted instruction. *Science, 166,* 343–350.

Thorndike, E. (1969). *Educational Psychology.* New York: Arno Press.

REFERENCES FOR ADDITIONAL STUDY

Alessi, M., & Trolipp, S. (1985). *Computer based instruction: Methods and development*. Englewood Cliffs, NJ: Prentice-Hall.

Banathy, B. (1973). *Developing a systems view of education: A systems model approach*. Belmont, CA: Fearon Press.

Bangert-Drowns, R., Kulik, C., Kulik J., & Morgan, M. (1991). The instructional effect of feedback in test-like events. *Review of Educational Research, 61*(2), 213–238.

Barson, J. (1967). *Instructional systems development: A demonstration and evaluation project*. U.S. Office of Education, Title III-B Project OE 3-16-025, Michigan State University.

Bertalanffy, L., von. (1968). *General systems theory* (rev. ed.). New York: George Braziller.

Clark, R. (1992). Media use in education. In M. Aiken (Ed.), *Encyclopedia of educational research* (pp. 805–814). Upper Saddle River, NJ: Prentice Hall.

Clark, R. (1989). Current progress and future directions for research in instructional technology. *Educational Technology Research and Development, 37*(1), 57–66.

Clark, R. (1985). Evidence for confounding in computer-based instruction studies: Analyzing the meta-analyses. *Educational Communications and Technology Journal, 33*(4), 249–262.

Clark, R. (1983). Reconsidering research on learning from media. *Review of Educational Research, 53*(4), 445–459.

Clark, R., & Salomon, G. (1986). Media in teaching. In M. Wittrock (Ed.), *Handbook of research on teaching* (Vol. 3). Upper Saddle River, NJ: Prentice Hall.

Duffy, T., & Jonassen, D. (1992). Constructivism and the technology of instruction: A conversation. Hillsdale, NJ: Earlbaum.

Gagne, R., & Briggs, L. (1979). *Principles of instructional design* (2nd ed.). New York: Holt, Rinehart, & Winston.

Gagne, R., Wager, W., & Rojas, A. (1981). Planning and authoring computer-assisted-instruction lessons. *Educational Technology, 21*(9), 17–26.

Hannafin, M., & Peck, K. (1988). *The design, development, and evaluation of instructional software*. Upper Saddle River, NJ: Prentice Hall.

Hooper, S. (1992). Cooperative learning and computer-based instruction. *Educational Technology Research and Development, 40*(3), 21–38.

Kulik, J., Kulik, C., & Schwab, B. (1986). The effectiveness of computer based adult education: A meta-analysis. *Journal of Educational Computing Research, 2*(2), 235–252.

Mory, E. (1992). The use of informational feedback in instruction: Implications for future research. *Educational Technology Research and Development, 40*(3), 5–20.

Papert, S. (1980). Teaching children thinking. In R. Taylor (Ed.), *The computer in the school: Tutor, tool, tutee* (pp. 161–176). New York: The Teachers College Press.

Petkovich, M., & Tennyson, R. (1984). Clark's "Learning from media": A critique. *Educational Communications and Technology Journal, 32*(4), 233–241.

Reigeluth, C. (Ed.). (1983). *Instructional design theories and models*. Hillsdale, NJ: Lawrence Earlbaum.

Simonson, M., Clark, R., Kulik, R., Tennyson, R., & Winn, W. (1987). What the research says by those doing the saying: A summary of media research. In *Proceedings of selected research paper presentations* (pp. 1–66). Convention of the Association for Educational Communications and Technology, Atlanta, GA.

Simonson, M., Maurer, M., Montag-Torardi, M., & Whitaker, M. (1987). Development of a standardized test of computer literacy and a computer anxiety index. *Journal of Educational Computing Research, 3*(2), 231–247.

Skinner, B. (1971). Toward a psychology of science. *American Psychologist, 26*, 1010–1015.

Smith, B. (1951). *Readings in the social aspects of education*. Danville, IL: Interstate Printers.

Snelbecker, G. F. (1974). *Learning theory, instructional theory, and psychoeducational design*. New York: McGraw-Hill.

Thomas, R. M. (1979). *Comparing theories of child development*. Belmont, CA: Wadsworth.

Thompson, A., & Simonson, M. (1992). *Educational technology: A review of the research*. Washington, DC: Association for Educational Communications and Technology.

Walker, D., & Hess, R. (1984). *Instructional software: Principles and perspectives for design and use*. Belmont, CA: Wadsworth.

Winn, W. (1993). Instructional design and situated learning: Paradox or partnership? *Educational Technology, 33*(3), 16–21.

CHAPTER FOUR

COMPUTER SYSTEMS

What Teachers Need to Know

GOAL

The purpose of this chapter is to present the terminology for computer hardware and software and to describe how computer hardware and software are organized into systems.

OBJECTIVES

The reader will achieve the following:

1. Explain the relationships among the categories of computers.
2. Define the terms used to describe the components and functions of computers.
3. Explain how data are stored in digital computers in bits and bytes.
4. Explain the system for organizing computer terminology.
5. Explain the $\frac{1}{10}$–10 relationship.

The chief merit of language is clearness. . . . We know that nothing detracts so much from this as do unfamiliar terms.

Galen, 129 to 199 A.D.

In the past several years, a new set of terms has emerged among members of the professional education community. Although these terms have long been familiar to computer scientists and engineers, until recently, they were of little interest to most educators. During the first few years when computers were beginning to be used in schools, the "jargon-wise" often intimidated the uninitiated with their use of the many terms and acronyms of the computer industry. Many teachers perceived this computer-speak as an indication of the technically complex nature of computers. Nothing was further from the truth. Conceptually, computers are relatively simple machines. Just as certainly, however, users of computers must possess an understanding of terminology so that the goal of "clearness of language" that Galen praised nearly 2,000 years ago can be obtained.

Today's computers are simple to operate and use. They are consumer products similar in sophistication to the videocassette recorder or automobile. Computer users probably do not need to know about CPUs, RAM, or ROM any more than VCR users need to know about helical scanning or motorists need to know about fuel injectors. On the other hand, understanding basic concepts about computers, VCRs, and automobiles helps those people be better able to use these categories of devices.

The information in this chapter will concentrate on the basic skills about computers that will help the teacher become a better computer consumer. This information will help answer questions such as "How much memory do I really need? Which word processor is best for me? Will a CD work with my computer? How do I know if a computer lesson is teaching what it is supposed to?"

This chapter will present the important terms describing computer hardware and software, and will concentrate on those general and basic concepts that will continue in use as computers evolve. Also, an organizational structure will be presented that places specific terms in relationship to each other. The relationship between hardware and software will be explained; categories of computers will be defined; and the four components of all computers will be identified.

Terms that relate to these four components of computers will be presented, and techniques for data transmission will be explained. This will be followed by a discussion of computer systems, and the chapter will conclude with the usual self-test questions and references for additional information.

HARDWARE AND SOFTWARE

Hardware and *software* are widely used terms that originated in the computer industry. Simply defined, hardware means machines, and software means information to control machines. Computer hardware is directed to perform actions by software. Stated another way, hardware means physical, real devices that when used with software are able to accomplish tasks. A videocassette player is nothing more than a machine with buttons and lights until a prerecorded videocassette is inserted in it and played. An overhead projector is merely a spotlight until a transparency is placed on its projection

---

Notes From the Literature

Becker (1992) studied teachers in 31 schools in 16 states who provided substantial computer-based learning activities to one of their classes. Each class had a computer for every two students, used the computer for at least one hour per week in mathematics, and had a comparison class of similarly achieving students, usually taught by the same teacher, using only "traditional" media. After an academic year of instruction, students experiencing traditional media were compared with those having computer-based instruction. The outcomes on five mathematics achievement tests indicated little difference between students. The results suggest that "teachers and schools that provide students with substantial computer experiences will implement a fairly traditional program of instruction that will not be greatly different from the curriculum that the students would have followed without the computer" (p. 8).

Becker continues to argue that "the way that teachers teach is a product of their own schooling, training, and experiences as teachers" (p. 8). Putting computers into the schools will not increase the chances that changes in education will occur.

Becker, H. J. (1991). When powerful tools meet conventional beliefs and institutional constraints. The Computing Teacher, 18(8), 6–9.

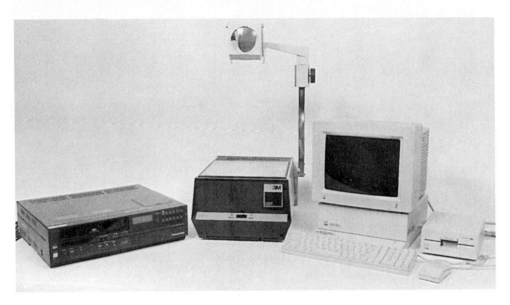

FIGURE 4.1
Videocassette recorders, overhead projectors, and microcomputers are hardware used
by teachers.

platform. And a computer is nothing more than a complex connection of switches, resisters, and transistors until it is programmed by software. Videocassette players, overhead projectors, and computers are hardware (Figure 4.1). Videocassettes, transparencies, and programs are software (Figure 4.2).

This simple dichotomy is complicated somewhat when the two terms are examined in greater detail. For example, a blank videocassette is software, but obviously a videocassette with a feature-length film recorded on it is significantly different from when it was blank. Both the videocassette and the program

FIGURE 4.2
Videocassettes, transparencies, and floppy disks are software.

recorded on it are software. More precisely, the videocassette is the medium used to store the message so it can be delivered and retrieved to a different location or at a different time by a videocassette player.

The same distinction is made for computer software. The primary media used to store computer programs are the floppy disk, hard disk, and compact disk. A set of directions to order a computer to accomplish a task can be stored on any of these media. Both the directions, or program, and the media are called *software*.

Defining hardware involves a similar set of distinctions. Obviously, the machine we call *the computer* is an example of hardware, but what about the boards that are inserted into it, or the chips that are placed in the computer's board? Are they hardware, too? Some computer scientists use the term *firmware* to more precisely explain these objects. It would be correct, however, to label chips, boards, and other internal components of computers as hardware (Figures 4.3 and 4.4) because

they have little utility in themselves unless they are controlled by software, even if the controlling software is a permanent part of the object, as with read-only memory (ROM) chips. The chip is hardware, the directions/program stored in its circuits are software. That is the most important distinction between the two terms: software gives directions to hardware. Machines are hardware, and programs are software.

THE MAINFRAME, THE MINICOMPUTER, AND THE MICROCOMPUTER

1/10–10 Relationship

Computer users often label the machines they use with the terms *mainframe*, *mini*, and *micro*. These terms are relatively straightforward, yet they imply subtleties,

FIGURE 4.3
Computer chips are wonders of miniaturization. This 4 million-bit memory chip can store the equivalent of 400 pages of typewritten text.
Photograph courtesy of International Business Machines Corporation.

FIGURE 4.4
Cards, also called *firmware,* are added to computers to enhance their capabilities. This
is an ethernet card from an IBM-compatible computer.

also. In the early 1980s, when most people thought about computers, they usually thought about mainframes. Mainframes got their name from the way they were constructed. The original computer's parts were attached to a large metal or wood framework.

Mainframe computers are characterized by their large size, usually enough to fill a good-size room. Mainframe computers are multipurpose, multiuser (used simultaneously by dozens or even hundreds of users) machines that are the fastest, most powerful computers widely available (Figure 4.5). A new category of super mainframe computer has emerged since the mid-1980s. These supercomputers are about 10 times as powerful as the average mainframe computer.

Minicomputers, the second category of computers, were introduced in the 1960s because many users did

FIGURE 4.5
A mainframe computer is the largest of the three categories. Mainframes are expensive, require trained operators, and are used by multiple users in a time-sharing system.
Photograph courtesy of International Business Machines Corporation.

not require the power of the mainframe. Generally, minicomputers occupy about as much space as a five-drawer filing cabinet. Minicomputers are less powerful, have less memory, and do not compute as rapidly as mainframes.

In the 1970s, a further reduction in the size of computers occurred with the introduction of the microcomputer. The microcomputer is generally about the size of a typewriter with a small monitor on top. Micros are usually meant to support only one user's needs at a time, and usually have only a small number of input and output devices. They are slower and have less memory than minicomputers. Microcomputers, also called *personal computers (PCs)* or *desktop computers*, brought about the computer revolution in schools (Figure 4.6).

Although defining the three categories of computers by their physical size may be convenient, it is probably the least important distinction between them. To help explain the differences between the categories of computers, the concept of the 1/10–10 relationship was developed. The 1/10–10 relationship states:

> If the three categories of computers—mainframes, minis, and micros—are placed on a continuum, the magnitude of difference between each category for any characteristic of computers is either a multiple of 1/10 or 10.

For example, mainframe computers are roughly 10 times more expensive than minicomputers, and minis are about 10 times more expensive than the average microcomputer. Mainframes usually have about 10 times more memory than do minis, and minis have about 10 times more memory than micros. As the three categories of computers are compared, many of their characteristics vary in about the same ratio.

The 1/10–10 relationship guideline is also helpful in understanding the less obvious characteristics of com-

(A)

FIGURE 4.6

A. Minicomputers bridge the gap between mainframe computers and microcomputers. Although less powerful than mainframes, they can be used by multiple users, at much lower cost. B. Microcomputers are the smallest computers. They are meant to be used by one person at a time. Microcomputers are the most commonly used type for computer-based instruction. When they were introduced in 1994, the Macintosh PowerPC computers were the highest performance and most expandable computers Apple had ever produced. C. The Zenith Z-Select PT is a DOS-compatible microcomputer.

A. Photograph courtesy of International Business Machines Corporation. B. Photograph courtesy of Apple Computer, Inc. C. Photograph courtesy of Zenith Data Systems.

FIGURE 4.6
(continued)

(B)

(C)

puters. Because computers are changing almost daily, the capabilities of today's microcomputers rival those of the mainframe of a few decades ago. This is a corollary to the 1/10–10 relationship:

> Every 10 years the capabilities of any category of computer improve by a multiple of 10.

In other words, today's microcomputers rival the minicomputers of a decade ago, and in 10 years, microcomputers will be as powerful as today's minicomputers. As innovations are made, computers improve. Large computers do not necessarily get any larger; rather, they improve their capabilities. The same is true for medium-size computers and for small, personal ones.

Specifically, when we look at the 1/10–10 relationship guideline, we are most interested in speed and memory size. Speed refers generally to how many computations a computer can handle in a period of time. For example, many microcomputers can handle 1 million instructions per second, while a mainframe might easily handle 100 million instructions per second. An instruction might be a direction to add two numbers together.

Memory size also differentiates computer categories. Many personal computers can store 8 million characters (letters, numbers, or symbols) in memory. Large mainframes might have storage memory for 500 million or 1 billion characters.

While we assign labels to certain computers to better understand and explain them, it is important to remember that the computers we are labeling will change. The average personal computer of the near future will probably be as powerful as today's mainframe.

DATA STORAGE IN DIGITAL COMPUTERS: BINARY CODE

Inside computers, data are stored electronically. Electrical impulses are used in special circuits to represent information. Specifically, switches are used to either turn electrical current on or off. This means two values can be represented in a specific location in a computer's memory, zero or one. The basic unit for data storage in a computer's memory is an off or on—zero or one—value. This unit is called a *bit* of information. Bit is derived from the two words *Binary digIT*.

Because a single bit can represent only one of two values, by itself the bit is not very useful. It cannot be used to represent numbers, letters, or characters. Bits therefore are grouped to form a collection or series of binary digits. These groups of bits are called *bytes* and normally are in multiples of two, such as 4, 8, 16, or 32. Eight bits is a common byte size used in microcomputers.

The concept of bits and bytes can be clarified by thinking about the light switches in a classroom. Many rooms have three or four switches that control different lights. If a classroom has three switches, there will be eight (two to the third power) different combinations of on and off positions.

off off off
off off on
off on on
on on on
on off off
on off on
off on off
on on off

In other words, groups of switches are used to store information, and these groups are called *bytes*. Bytes are areas of computer memory that are used to store alphanumeric characters, or special symbols. In microcomputers, eight bits make up a byte, so in memory, eight adjacent switches (bits) make up one character (byte) (Table 4.1).

Binary code is a system for storing information that uses the bit as its basic component. One of the most widely used coding systems for representing data in main computer memory is the American Standard Code for Information Interchange (ASCII Code; Table 4.2). When a character, number, or symbol is entered at the keyboard, the computer interprets the character and stores it in memory in a combination of bits that are either on or off, depending on the character. ASCII (pronounced "ask-key") code uses the seven rightmost bits of the eight to represent characters. This means there are 128 (two to the seventh power) unique combinations of zeros and ones possi-

TABLE 4.1
Six-bit binary-coded decimal code

1	000001	A	110001	N	100101
2	000010	B	110010	O	100110
3	000011	C	110011	P	100111
4	000100	D	110100	Q	101000
5	000101	E	110101	R	101001
6	000110	F	110110	S	010010
7	000111	G	110111	T	010011
8	001000	H	111000	U	010100
9	001001	I	111001	V	010101
0	001010	J	100001	W	010110
		K	100010	X	010111
		L	100011	Y	011000
		M	100100	Z	011001

TABLE 4.2
Microcomputers use ASCII code. ASCII is an abbreviation for American Standard Code for Information Interchange and is pronounced "ask-key."

ASCII											
ASCII Character	Binary	Decimal	ASCII Character	Binary	Decimal	ASCII Character	Binary	Decimal
---	---	---	---	---	---	---	---	---
0	0011 0000	48	C	0100 0011	67	O	0100 1111	79
1	0011 0001	49	D	0100 0100	68	P	0101 0000	80
2	0011 0010	50	E	0100 0101	69	Q	0101 0001	81
3	0011 0011	51	F	0100 0110	70	R	0101 0010	82
4	0011 0100	52	G	0100 0111	71	S	0101 0011	83
5	0011 0101	53	H	0100 1000	72	T	0101 0100	84
6	0011 0110	54	I	0100 1001	73	U	0101 0101	85
7	0011 0111	55	J	0100 1010	74	V	0101 0110	86
8	0011 1000	56	K	0100 1011	75	W	0101 0111	87
9	0011 1001	57	L	0100 1100	76	X	0101 1000	88
A	0100 0001	65	M	0100 1101	77	Y	0101 1001	89
B	0100 0010	66	N	0100 1110	78	Z	0101 1010	90

ble using these seven binary digits, so 128 different characters can be represented using this coding system. The leftmost bit is not used to represent characters in the ASCII system. For fun, try writing your name in binary code.

COMPUTER MEMORY SIZE

The computer's main memory is made up of thousands of circuits organized into byte-sized groupings. Each byte can be used to store one character. Usually, the size of the computer's main memory is expressed in terms of thousands or millions of storage locations. The metric term *kilo,* abbreviated K, is used to indicate a thousand bytes of storage, and the metric term *mega,* abbreviated meg, is used to indicate 1 million storage spots in computer memory.

For example, a 640-kilobyte-sized memory, abbreviated 640K, would be able to store 640,000 characters, and an 8-meg memory could store 8 million characters. Actually, the real size of 1 kilobyte of memory is not 1,000 but 1,024 (2 to the 10th power), so a 640K computer would really have 640 times 1,024 bytes, or 655,360 bytes. Similarly, an 8-megabyte memory could store 8,000 times 1,024, or 8,192,000 characters. In terms of computer memory at least, bigger is better.

COMPUTER COMPONENTS

There are four components common to all computers: input devices, output devices, computation devices, and memory devices. An additional collection of items is necessary when computers are used. They are the connectors and cables used to attach components to one another. Cables and connectors are used to transfer information or power between pieces of hardware or between internal components of a machine. Terms related to each of these computer components will be discussed next.

Input and Output Components

Because there is considerable overlap, input and output devices will be discussed together. There are three categories of input–output devices. There are those only for the input of information, such as keyboards; those only for the output of information, such as printers; and devices that can both input and output information, such as disk drives (Table 4.3).

Input-Only Devices. Keyboards are typewriterlike devices used to enter characters into the computer's memory. When a person types information into a computer, the process is called *keyboarding.* This

TABLE 4.3
Computer input–output devices

Input–Only Devices	Input–Output Devices	Output–Only Devices
• CD–ROM players	• Disk drives	• Printers
• Keyboards	Floppy (e.g., 3½ and 5¼)	Thermal
• Light pens	Hard	Dot-matrix
• Microphones	• Magnetic tape drives	Daisy wheel
• Card readers	• Modems	Ink-jet
• Optical character	External	Laser
readers (OCR)	Internal	Chain
• Scanners	Acoustic	• Video (CRTs)
• Touch screens		Monitors
• Mouse		Receivers
• Game paddles		Monitor/receivers
• Joy sticks		Plasma displays
• Touch pads		Liquid crystal displays
		• Pen plotters
		• Electrostatic plotters
		• Voice synthesizers

differs from regular typing in part because of the multiple keying requirements (holding down one key while typing another) of computers. The keyboard is the most important input device.

Light pens are also input-only devices. Light pens scan light reflected from some printed impression and translate the reflection into computer input. Bar codes are one kind of information read from documents by light pens (Figure 4.7).

Research is improving the quality of light pen devices so that it is simple to scan printed documents to input text. One light pen-like device most of us are familiar

FIGURE 4.7
Using a barcode reader, such as this cordless model, the user of a laser disk player can move to predetermined places in a disk almost instantly.

with is the optical reader used to input price and product information from merchandise in the supermarket. Since these readers were introduced in the mid-1970s, checkout lanes at supermarkets have moved more quickly, and data entry errors have been virtually eliminated.

Voice-recognition devices use a microphone to translate sound waves into electrical signals that a computer understands. Voice-recognition systems permit the computer user to speak to enter data into the computer's memory. While many technical problems still must be resolved, voice-recognition input holds considerable promise for the future. Researchers in robotics and artificial intelligence are especially interested in voice- or sound-recognition input devices.

Scanners are popular input devices that do almost the same thing as optical character recognition devices, except they are primarily used for inputting, or digitizing, graphics. These days, even high-quality color scanners can be found for relatively little money.

In the 1980s, card readers were important input-only devices. Card readers made it possible to enter information that had been previously keypunched into, or marked onto, a computer card. Optical scan sheets, such as those used in test taking, and hole punch cards are the two primary kinds of software used by card readers. Readers that sense, or "read," pencil marks on a test sheet are called optical character readers (OCRs).

A collection of devices automatically enters data into a computer's memory. These devices are often called *analog input devices* because they translate analog information, such as time and temperature, into digital information that a computer can understand. They are used by researchers to monitor experiments, by scientists to keep track of phenomena in nature as they occur, and by businesses to control production operations as they happen.

Touch screens are interesting input devices because they allow the user to simply touch areas of the monitor to enter data. Several techniques are used in touch screens (Figure 4.8). One of the most common is the use of beams of infrared light that the finger interrupts when the screen is touched. The location where the beam was broken is then translated by software into

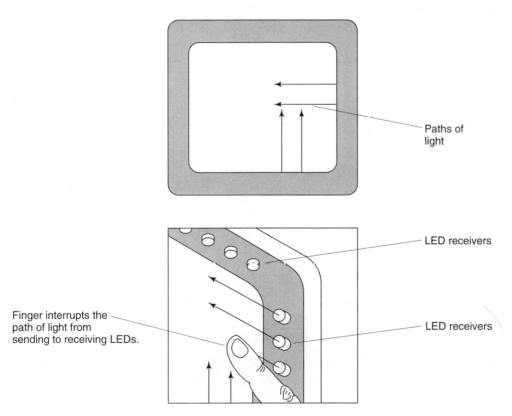

FIGURE 4.8
How a touch screen works: A finger breaks the beam of light from the sending light-emitting diode (LED) to the receiving LED. The X-Y coordinates of this spot are sent to the computer, which calculates the finger's location.

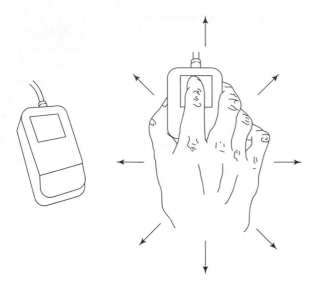

FIGURE 4.9
The mouse is another popular input device. The mouse is held in one hand and pushed around a desktop, which moves a pointer on the screen. The button on the mouse can be pushed (clicked) once, or a series of times, or pushed and held.

data the computer can use. Touch screens are not normally used to enter large amounts of data. They are effective in some situations, however, such as when a student responds to questions in the computer-based lesson when it is natural to point and touch to respond to a prompt. Touch screens are popular to many because the interface between person and machine is considered more natural.

Most computers now use an input device called a *mouse*. The Apple Macintosh computer popularized the mouse, but Xerox computers first used them. A mouse is a small, lightweight device that fits easily in the hand while it is pushed around a flat surface like a desktop (Figure 4.9). As the mouse moves, a cursor on the video screen also moves. The mouse is used to position the cursor at any point on the screen to select options, make drawings, or perform other functions. Selections are made by pressing a button, or buttons, on the top of the mouse.

Those who prefer the mouse as a pointing device think it is easier to use than a touch screen; in addition, it does not require special hardware modifications to the monitor. Disadvantages of using a mouse include the need for clear desk space to move the mouse on and the need to remove one hand from the keyboard to use the mouse.

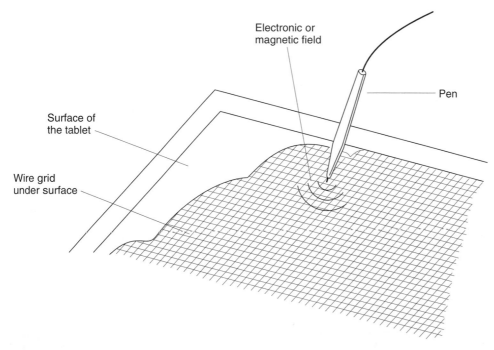

FIGURE 4.10
How tablets work: The pen transmits a magnetic or electromagnetic signal to a receiving grid under the tablet's surface. The X–Y coordinates of the grid determine the pen's location.

Numerous other input-only devices exist, such as game paddles and touch pads (Figures 4.10 and 4.11), and new devices are being invented continually. When categorizing peripheral equipment, input-only devices are those that are used exclusively to enter data into the computer for computation.

Compact disks, also called CD–ROMs, are also used as input devices. One CD can store about 650 megabytes of information. They are excellent storage devices for large data bases or lessons with a number of graphics or other visuals. CD–ROMs are basically the same as the CDs used to play music or that Kodak stores photographs on. As a matter of fact, most new CD players permit the playback of music and the display of photos on the computer screen, in addition to the storage of computer data.

Output-Only Devices.

Just as input-only devices can send information only in one direction, output-only devices only receive data from the computer. The two most important output-only devices are the printer and the cathode-ray tube (CRT).

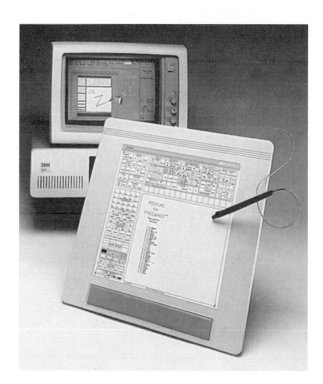

FIGURE 4.11
Digitizing pads, such as this system, permit the teacher or student to touch a "pen" to the palette to create drawings that are immediately entered into the computer's memory and shown on the computer's screen. Photograph courtesy of PENCEPT Corp.

Printers. Five categories of printers generally are used with microcomputers. All print out on some kind of paper. The differences among each category are based on how the printers produce characters on the page. The five categories:

1. Thermal printers
2. Dot-matrix printers
3. Daisy wheel printers
4. Ink-jet printers
5. Laser printers

Chain and band printers are two additional types used exclusively with mainframe computers.

Thermal printers convert output into copy on a temperature-sensitive paper that is similar to the paper used in old-fashioned thermofax machines. While these printers are not widely used, they are relatively inexpensive and work well with small, portable computer systems.

Probably the most widely used printer over the years has been the dot-matrix. These printers derive their name from the way characters are produced (Figure 4.12). A series of small pins press against a printer ribbon and produce symbols on paper (Figure 4.13). The characters produced this way consist of small dots. Dot-matrix printers are fast and can produce complicated

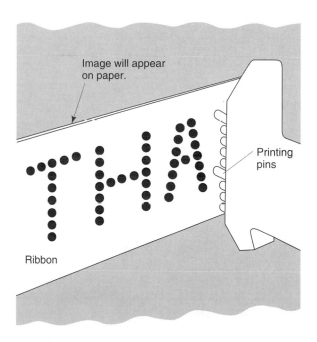

FIGURE 4.12
How a dot-matrix printer works: Printing pins press against a printer ribbon in various combinations to create characters on the paper. The printing head consists of a collection of these pins, such as five wide by seven deep.

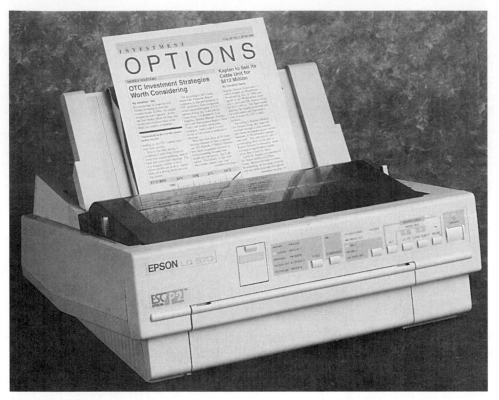

FIGURE 4.13
The dot-matrix printer uses a series of very small pins that press against a printer ribbon to produce characters consisting of small dots. Current dot-matrix printers provide relatively high-quality printing at low cost.
Photograph courtesy of Epson America, Inc.

graphic output very easily. They are also relatively inexpensive when compared with laser printers, but some consider the print quality inferior.

Daisy wheel printers get their name from the fact that they use a wheel with appendages that have characters on them. The appendages look a little like the petals of a daisy. As the wheel spins, a hammer-like device strikes the appropriate letter, which in turn strikes the printer ribbon, which then makes an impression on paper. Daisy wheel printers produce letters and symbols that appear identical to those made by standard electric typewriters, and because of this are often called "letter-quality" printers. Daisy wheel printers work slower than dot-matrix printers, are more expensive, and cannot produce complex graphics. Because of these limitations, daisy wheel printers are not widely used today.

Ink-jet printers use a nozzle to spray liquid ink drops onto the page. They produce relatively high-quality characters and are very quiet. Inexpensive color printing is possible when ink-jet printers are used (Figure

4.14). Ink-jet printers are fast, relatively inexpensive, and produce a fairly high-quality image. They are often used instead of dot-matrix printers by those who cannot afford a laser printer. Ink-jet printers are very popular for color printing.

Laser printers are the most recent addition to the collection of printing devices. Laser printers, as their name implies, produce very high-quality characters on paper using a combination of several printing steps, including one involving a laser. This laser encodes an organic photoconductor, which then attracts particles of toner. When the toner is brought into contact with the paper, an image is produced. Heat and pressure fuse the image. This is basically the same process as is used by photo copiers.

Laser printers have become an important component of desktop publishing (Figure 4.15). This term refers to the use of a microcomputer and laser printer to produce documents such as newsletters, newspapers, resumes, and brochures that are of comparable quality

FIGURE 4.14
Color ink-jet printers, such as this model by Hewlett Packard, allow printing in color.

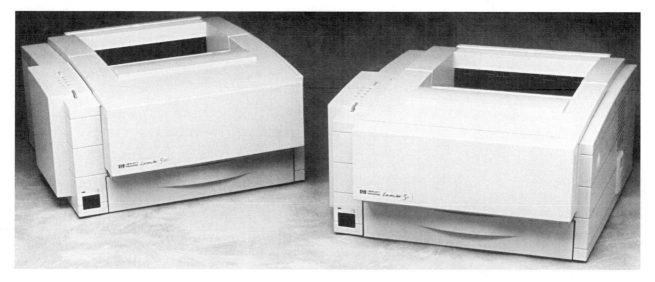

FIGURE 4.15
Laser printers combine high-speed and high-quality printing.
Photographs courtesy of Hewlett Packard Co.

FIGURE 4.16
How a chain printer works

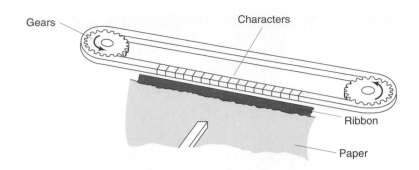

to those produced by commercial printers using printing presses. The high quality of printing is the most notable characteristic of the laser printer.

Printers are also characterized by their speed and by whether they produce letters by impact. Printer speed is an important concern when selecting a printer. Low-speed printers can print from 15 to 600 characters per second. Most low-speed printers are serial printers, meaning they produce characters one at a time. Printers for microcomputers are almost always low-speed printers.

The rate of printing for high-speed and very high-speed printers is stated in terms of the number of lines

printed per minute. Printers that produce 300 to 3,000 lines per minute are called *high-speed printers*. These printers are also called *line printers*.

Very high-speed printers can print in excess of 3,000 lines per minute. Some will even print 20,000 lines per minute. These printers are called *page printers*. Chain and band printers are examples of high- and very high-speed printers (Figure 4.16). They are almost always used with mainframe computers.

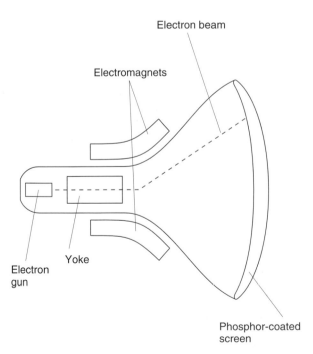

FIGURE 4.17
How a cathode-ray tube (CRT) works: An electron gun sends a beam that is bent by electromagnets so it sweeps up and down and back and forth along the back of the tube's face. Phosphors in the screen are excited, and an image appears.

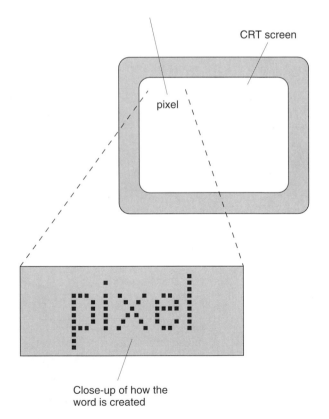

FIGURE 4.18
How pixels create images on a screen: Images appear because dots of light, or picture elements (pixels), are combined to form an image.

Impact printers produce characters when an image is formed when some type of printing mechanism strikes a printer ribbon. Both front and hammer striking (the hammer is behind the paper) impact printers are available.

Nonimpact printers produce a character without striking the paper. Ink-jet and laser printers are nonimpact printers.

Video Output.   Cathode-ray tubes are considered basic components of all computer systems and can be categorized into one of three types: monitors, receivers, or monitor/receivers. For all categories, the CRT, or picture tube (Figure 4.17), is used to generate an image. Most of the CRTs used with personal computers are raster scan monitors. This kind of video device produces an image in the following sequence:

1. The image is sent electronically from the computer to the CRT.
2. An electron gun generates an electron beam.

3. A series of electromagnets directs the beam to the phosphor-coated screen.
4. The electron beam causes the phosphors it strikes to emit a light. This is the image seen on the screen.
5. The beam scans the entire back of the screen 60 times each second.

When CRTs are used with computers, the screen is divided into addressable locations. How this is done varies, depending on the CRT, but each location is a small dot called a *pixel*. The term *pixel* is derived from the term *picture element* (Figure 4.18). Pixels are small dots of light that are formed on the picture tube. These dots are the building blocks for all characters formed on the screen in a method similar to how the huge scoreboards at major league baseball parks produce the score or the number of outs using light bulbs. When pixels are grouped, they form characters, or graphics.

The number of rows and the number of pixels in each row determine the resolution, or quality, of the

TABLE 4.4
Characteristics of computer video displays

Name	Meaning	Computer	Horizontal Scan Rates (KHz)	Vertical Scan Rates (Hz)	Analog (A) or Digital (D)
		FOR PCs			
MDA	Monochrome display adapter	PC, XT, AT	18.02	50.0	D
CGA	Color graphics adapter	PC, XT, AT	15.75	60.0	D
HGA	Hercules graphics adapter	PC, XT, AT	18.02	50.0	D
EGA	Enhanced graphics adapter	PC, XT, AT	21.85	60.0	D
			18.02	50.0	D
			15.75	60.0	D
PGA	Professional graphics adapter	XT, AT	31.50	60.0	A
VGA	Video graphics array	PS/2	31.50	60.0	A
			31.50	70.0	A
			35.50	43.5	A
MCGA	Multicolor graphics adapter	PS/2 #30	31.50	60.0	A
		PC, XT, AT	31.50	70.0	A
DA	Display adapter	XT, AT	Same as VGA		A
		FOR APPLES			
II, IIE, IIGS: Common names for Apple II			15.75	60.0	D
Macintosh, Mac Plus, Mac SE			22.23	60.0	D
Macintosh II			35.00	66.0	A
SuperMac			48.19	59.3	A
(high-resolution cards for Mac II)			55.37	60.1	A

Reprinted with permission from Csuszar, I. A. (1988, March). Television and computer video. *Video Systems*.

FIGURE 4.19
Liquid crystal displays are built in to portable, lap-top computers, such as this Zenith Z-Star EX.
Photograph courtesy of Zenith Dat Systems.

image that is produced. Higher resolution requires more computer memory, so that early inexpensive microcomputers did not have the capability of producing very realistic graphics on their CRT.

Computer displays/monitors have evolved considerably in recent years and will continue to change. Early microcomputer displays were regular television receivers. They were inexpensive but produced a low-quality image. Now, most microcomputers use special monitors that vary according to the following:

1. The number of pixels they produce on the screen.
2. How often images are refreshed by the cathode ray.
3. The number of colors they produce.

Generally, the more pixels, the faster the refresh rate, and the more colors, the better. Macintosh computers either have built-in monochrome screens, or use interchangeable color monitors. DOS/Windows and OS/2 computers use a variety of displays depending on the kind of display adapter that is installed in the computer. The types of displays are summarized in Table 4.4.

Video projectors are similar to other video-output devices in most ways; however, they eliminate the need for the phosphor-coated picture tube. Instead, video "guns" project images onto screens.

Plasma Displays.   A plasma screen consists of a grid of wires sealed between two flat plates of glass. The space between these pieces of glass is filled with neon/argon gas. When an electrical current is sent into the grid of wires, it excites the gas, and this produces a bright, high-quality image with no video flicker. The original PLATO terminals used in the 1970s were plasma screens.

Liquid Crystal Displays.   Liquid crystal displays (LCDs) are used in watches, calculators, portable or small computers, and panels for use with overhead projectors. A liquid crystal material is deposited between two sheets of a polarizing material (Figure 4.19). When an electrical current is passed between crossing wires, the liquid crystals are aligned so that light cannot shine through. Liquid crystal displays are also called *flat-panel displays*. Recently, several manufacturers have offered transparent, LCD output devices for use with overhead projectors. Use of these devices permits large groups to see a computer's output when it is projected on a screen (Figure 4.20).

Other Output-Only Devices.   Plotters are devices that create drawings, charts, and diagrams. There are two types of plotters: pen plotters and electrostatic plotters.

FIGURE 4.20
Liquid crystal display output devices are available for use with overhead projectors so the computer's output can be seen by large numbers of students.

Pen plotters are either flatbed plotters or drum plotters. Both create images on a sheet of paper by the movement of one or more pens over the surface of the paper or by the movement of paper under a pen. Flatbed plotters have a flat surface where the drawing occurs. Drum plotters use a rotating drum over which drawing pens are mounted. The pens move to the left or right while the drum rotates to create a drawing. Drum plotters can produce plots of any length because roll paper can be used.

Electrostatic plotters draw by using a row of styli across the width of the paper. As the paper rotates on a drum, an electrostatic charge is created on the paper. When the paper passes through a developer, an image emerges. Electrostatic plotters are considerably faster than pen plotters.

Voice-output devices produce audible words. There are two voice-output systems. The first uses digitized words stored on a disk or in memory. When a word is selected for output, it is converted back into sound waves by a speaker. Voice synthesizers, the second kind of voice-output device, produce audible output by examining the letters and letter combinations in words (called *phonemes*) (Figure 4.21). The voice-synthesizer software then generates sounds by applying rules of intonation and stress to artificially produce human-like voice output. Telephone companies use voice synthesis as part of their directory assistance systems.

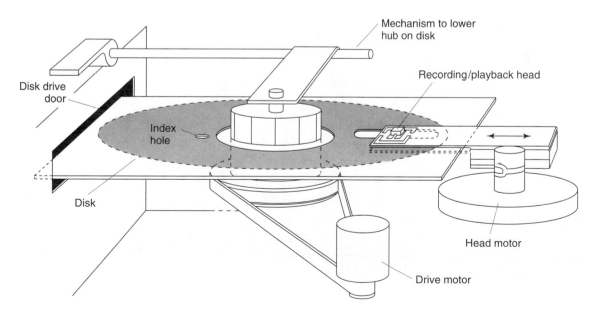

FIGURE 4.21
Inside a disk drive: The disk rotates, and the recording/playback head moves back and forth over it.

Input and Output Devices.   These devices can serve both to enter information into the computer's memory or to receive information from the computer's memory. Floppy-disk drives, hard-disk drives, tape drives, and modems are some of the most important input–output devices. Floppy-disk drives are the most widely used microcomputer storage devices. Like hard-disk drives and tape drives, floppy-disk drives contain transducers. Transducers convert information from one type to another. In the case of the disk drive, electrical information sent from the computer is converted into a magnetic field by the drive's recording head. This magnetic information is then stored on a disk coated with a surface that can be magnetized. When data are loaded in or retrieved from a disk, the magnetic information is converted back into electrical information that is sent to the computer.

More specifically, the heads in the disk drive are electromagnets that magnetize the chromium dioxide or iron oxide surface of a disk. The heads produce circles of magnetic information called *tracks* on the surface of the disk. These tracks are divided into sectors. Sectors and tracks are places where data and programs are stored. In other words, tracks are like file drawers in a file cabinet, and sectors are like file folders in the drawers. At first they are empty, but eventually, information is placed into them (Figure 4.22).

The disk drives work in a manner similar to the recording heads in video and audio recorders. All three (computer disk drives, video recorders, and audio recorders) store information on a magnetizable surface—the tape or disk. Most microcomputer disk drives use 3½ inch or 5¼ inch disks as storage media.

Hard-disk drives, on the other hand, store magnetic information on a rigid disk instead of a flexible one. Hard-disk drives were once called Winchester drives. This name was derived from a code name used by IBM in the 1970s for a disk drive they were developing. Some say the name evolved because the disk drive had two surfaces, each capable of storing 30 megabytes of information. Hence, the drive was called a 30–30 drive. It followed that fans of cowboy movies began to call the drive after the famous .30-caliber Winchester rifle.

Hard disks have a spindle on which a disk platter is mounted. The disks rotate at a high rate of speed, commonly 3,600 revolutions per minute. Access arms, also called *actuators,* contain read–write heads (electromagnets) that store information on the disk or read infor-

FIGURE 4.22
Floppy disks contain flexible plastic disks covered with a metallic oxide that can be magnetized by a disk drive recording head. The most common sizes are 5¼ inches and 3½ inches.

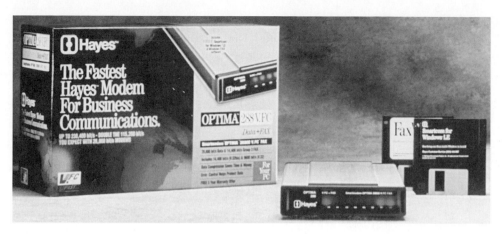

FIGURE 4.23
Modems convert computer output into an audible signal that can be sent over telephone lines or that can convert audible signals received from a telephone line into a signal the computer can process. This is a Hayes external modem.

FIGURE 4.24
The "motherboard" is the primary internal component of the computer. The central processing chip, random-access memory (RAM) chips, read-only memory (ROM) chips, and
peripheral cards are all inserted into the motherboard. Open design is characteristic of
Apple computers, such as this Macintosh SI.

FIGURE 4.25
Increasing sophistication and decreased size have characterized advances in computer technology. A single card from the Apple Macintosh LCII contains the motherboard of the older Apple IIe.

mation from the disk. The heads do not touch the disks but float on a cushion of air about one millionth of an inch above the disk's surface.

There are a number of varieties of hard-disk drives. Some use removable disks that can be taken out of the disk drive and replaced with different ones. Mainframe disk drive systems often use removable disk packs. Some microcomputer disk drive systems use removable disk cartridges. Half-height disk drives are also available. These disk drives are half size but

function the same. Hard-disk drives are normally built into the computer's case, but external hard drives are also available.

Magnetic tape drives were the first magnetic storage system used with computers. Tape drives store computer output, or retrieve information for input, from tape rather than from a disk. Mylar-backed tape, with iron oxide as the storage medium, became the primary storage system for computers during the 1960s. Now high-speed tape drives are used to back up large amounts of data, or to archive information not routinely used by the microcomputer.

Modems are input–output devices that convert a computer's electronic digital information into audible information that can be sent over communication channels, usually telephone lines. At the receiving end, a second modem converts the audible data back into digital data. The term *modem* is derived from the words *modulator* and *demodulator*. There are three categories of modems:

1. External, direct-connect modems
2. Internal modems
3. Acoustic couplers

External, direct-connect modems are stand-alone devices attached to the computer by a cable. The telephone wire connects to the modem to allow for communication over telephone lines (Figure 4.23). Internal modems consist of printer circuit boards installed inside the computer's case. The telephone connector attaches to a jack in the computer's housing that is connected to the modem board.

Acoustic coupler modems permit the telephone headset to be placed in molded rubber cups. The modem is then connected to the computer by a cable. Acoustic coupler modems were once very popular because they could be used anywhere with almost any telephone. Newer telephone systems have made external modems easier to use, and they are more popular than acoustic modems.

Modems transmit and receive data in bits per second. Three hundred, 1,200, 2,400, 9,600, and 14,400 bits per second, called *baud rates*, are the most common speeds for microcomputer modems. This corresponds to about 30, 120, 240, 960, or 1440 characters per second.

"Smart" modems contain a microprocessor that controls functions that make the modem easier to use. Automatic dialing, automatic acceptance of incoming data, and delayed dialing are examples of smart modem functions.

The Central Processing Unit Component

While computer users are most often concerned with ways to input and output information, the central processing unit (CPU) is the most important component of the computer system. The CPU is inside the box we connect input and output devices to. The CPU consists of two major components: the arithmetic/logic unit and the control unit (Figure 4.24 on p. 79).

The arithmetic/logic unit contains the circuitry necessary to perform arithmetic functions such as addition, subtraction, multiplication, and division. It also contains the circuitry required to perform logical operations such as comparing and sorting. Actually, adding, subtracting, dividing, multiplying, comparing, and sorting are the processing functions performed by the central processor. The control unit of the CPU directs and coordinates the activities of the entire computer. This unit controls input and output devices, controls the arithmetic section of the CPU, and transfers data to and from memory (Figure 4.25 on p. 80).

When an instruction is executed, the CPU's control unit receives the instruction from the main computer memory and places it in an instruction register. An instruction register is an area of memory within the CPU that can store a single instruction at a time. Data needed are also called from memory and are also placed in special registers. Control is then turned over to the arithmetic/logic unit, where all necessary computations are performed. The answer, the result of the processing, is then stored in another register. Later, the control unit places this result back in main memory.

While this process may seem cumbersome, computers can perform millions of these operations per second. The basic sequence of finding instructions, finding data, executing the instruction, and computing results is common to all computers, whether they are mainframes, minis, or micros.

8-Bit, 16-Bit, and 32-Bit Computers

Computers are sometimes referred to as 8-bit, 16-bit, or 32-bit computers. This designation refers to the design of the computer's central processor. In general, an 8-bit CPU can process 8 bits (equal to 1 byte) at a time, a 16-bit computer can process 16 bits at a time, and a 32-bit computer can process 32 bits at a time. Eight-bit computers also use 8 bits to make up 1 byte.

Information is moved inside a computer in circuits called *busses*. An 8-bit computer uses an 8-bit bus to send information from one location to another. Sixteen-bit computers move information along 16-bit busses, and 32-bit computers use 32-bit busses. Generally, the more bits that can be handled at one time, the faster the computer. Also, 8-bit CPUs can directly access only 64,000 memory locations, while 16-bit CPUs are directly connected to 512,000 memory locations. Thirty-two-bit CPUs can address more than 16 million storage positions. This makes the larger CPUs more powerful, in the language of computer users. Some personal computers, many minicomputers, and mainframe computers are 32-bit machines.

The Memory Component

Internal Computer Memory.
Since the 1940s, several generations of computers have evolved, and this evolution has been based primarily on the way information was stored in internal memory. The first practical computers used vacuum tubes to store data. Magnetic core memory replaced vacuum tubes. Magnetic core memory consisted of small, ring-shaped pieces of metal that could be polarized or magnetized. Transistors replaced magnetic core memory.

Transistors printed on small chips of silicon are now used for computer memory (Figures 4.26 and 4.27). This kind of memory is called *semiconductor memory*. Transistors are printed on a semiconductor material, such as silicon. These transistors either inhibit the flow of an electrical current or allow the current to pass. Thus, they are either off or on. This permits the binary coding of information on the silicon chip.

Core memory functioned in microseconds (millionths of seconds) and cost hundreds of dollars for each thousand characters stored. Semiconductor memory operates in nanoseconds (billionths of seconds) and costs less than 25 cents per thousand characters stored.

There are several different categories of memory: RAM, ROM, PROM, and EPROM. RAM stands for random-access memory and is the memory used when programs and data are temporarily stored in the computer. RAM is often called user-accessible memory and is the kind of memory referred to when computers are said to be 640K or 4-meg computers. Since K is the metric abbreviation for 1,000, a 640K computer can store approximately 640,000 bytes or characters of information in its main RAM memory. RAM is "volatile," meaning that it is not permanent. When the computer's power is turned off, RAM is erased.

ROM stands for read-only memory. The information stored in this memory is permanent and cannot

FIGURE 4.26
Inside a chip

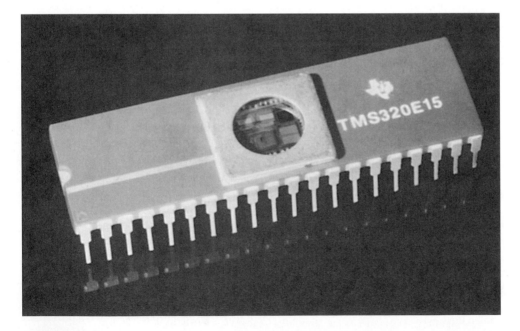

FIGURE 4.27
Close-up of a chip

be erased. Rather, it is activated when the computer is turned on. ROM is recorded when it is manufactured and is used to store data and programs that are not to be altered, such as language interpreters or display controllers.

PROM is short for programmable read-only memory. PROM acts the same as ROM when it is part of a computer. Specifically, it can be read, but it cannot be altered. PROM chips, however, are not recorded when they are manufactured but are recorded by the manufacturer of the computer when it is assembled. A special kind of PROM is EPROM. EPROM is erasable programmable read-only memory. EPROM permits the user to erase the data stored in the memory by using special ultraviolet devices that destroy the EPROM's settings.

External Magnetic Memory.   As was mentioned previously, information can be output from or input to computers. When this information is stored, it is usually stored on some magnetic medium, often a disk. The organization of this information is usually in tracks. Tracks can be linear, as with computer tape, or circular, as in floppy or hard disks.

Tracks are divided into units called *sectors*. Sectors are systematic subdivisions of tracks where bytes of information are stored. For example, Apple's early disk

operating system (DOS) 3.3 uses 35 tracks, each with 16 sectors, when storing information on a 5¼-inch floppy disk (Figure 4.28).

Disks are rated by their capacity to store information and by whether they can store on one side or both sides. Single-density (SD) disks store about 360K of information, double-density (DD) disks store either 720K or 800K, and high-density (HD) disks store about 1.4 meg (1.4 million characters, numbers, or symbols).

Nonmagnetic External Memory.   One of the original memory systems for computers used cards with holes in them, called *keypunch cards*. Although not used often today, keypunch cards once served basically the same purpose as floppy disks. They stored data according to the way holes were punched in them. Each card was 80 columns long, and each column could store one character.

Recently, optical disks have been introduced as storage devices. These disks store digital information in the form of small bumps on the surface of the disk. A laser is used to reflect light off the coding of these bumps and a light sensor is used to translate this information into electrical signals (Figure 4.29). These signals are input to the computer. First called OD-ROM (optical disk–read-only memory) and now called CD-ROM (compact disk–read-only memory), this kind of mem-

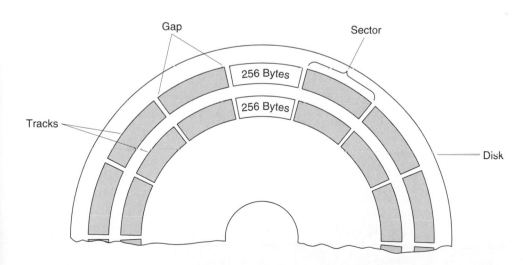

FIGURE 4.28
Information is stored on magnetic disks in circular tracks divided into sectors that are separated by gaps. Each sector holds a certain number of bytes of information. Apple's 3.3 disk operating system places 256 bytes of information in each sector. There are 16 sectors per track and 35 tracks per disk.

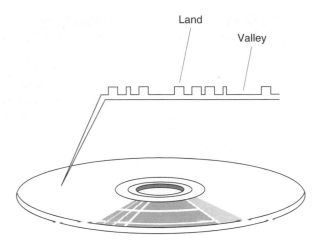

FIGURE 4.29
An optical disk

ory is very inexpensive. It is possible to mass produce optical disks that contain large data bases, such as encyclopedias, dictionaries, and other references.

INFORMATION TRANSMISSION BETWEEN COMPUTERS

There are two basic concerns related to how information is sent from one computer or computer device to another. The first deals with the method of transmission, and the second relates to the device used to carry the information.

Transmission Methods

Serial and parallel data transmission are two important methods used to send information between compo-

nents, such as computers and printers. Serial transmission systems send one bit of data at a time through the transmission medium, usually a wire. Parallel systems send information 1 byte at a time through a multiwire cable (Figure 4.30).

Inside computers, busses move data as bytes in parallel. This means that information is sent 8, 16, or 32 bits at a time. This causes problems when information must be sent out of the computer such as when it is sent serially to a printer, for example. It must be adapted so that only 1 bit at a time is sent. Often, a special circuit board is installed in the computer to allow for serial communication. Parallel transmission is electronically faster than serial, but this is often not a critical factor when information is sent between devices. For example, the mechanical print-head in a dot-matrix printer moves hundreds of times slower than the information that is sent to the printer from the computer, so either parallel or serial transmission is satisfactory when communicating with a printer.

Transmission Media: Wires, Cables, and Fibers

Twisted pair wire, like common telephone line, is one inexpensive way that computer components can be connected. Unfortunately, this kind of transmission medium is susceptible to electrical interference that can cause transmission errors. Twisted pair wire is normally used for low-cost, short-distance, local area networks, such as Appletalk networks.

Coaxial cable is a more commonly used transmission medium. Cable television cable is an example of coaxial cable. There are two kinds of coaxial cable: baseband, which carries one signal at a time, and broadband, which carries multiple signals using different frequencies. Baseband signals in local area networks are

FIGURE 4.30
Common computer cables include the mini DIN 8, the DB 9, the DB 25, the Centronics 50, and the Centronics 50 SCSI Terminator.

digital. Broadband signals are usually analog or continuous ones. Ethernet networks often use coaxial cable.

One commonly used computer cable is the RS-232C, a serial cable. The RS stands for recommended standard, the 232 is a number reference to this standard, and the C indicates that this is the third revision of this standard. Often, RS-232C cables are used to send serial data to and from modems.

One major concern of computer users is the lack of standardization of computer cables. Almost every manufacturer uses slightly different cables that often are not compatible with those of other manufacturers. When equipment is purchased, it is important to specify what kinds of devices will need to be connected so that the correct connecting cables are obtained.

Recently, fiber optics systems that transmit information by light through thin glass strands have become popular. Fiber optics cables have the potential to transmit many times more information, more reliably, than other transmission media.

COMPUTER HARDWARE AND SOFTWARE ORGANIZED IN SYSTEMS

Computers are systematically organized collections of machinery. Programs tell computers how to operate or function to perform a task or tasks. The machinery and the programs interact in specific, logical ways. For example, between the computer and some kind of application software, such as a word processing program, are special programs called *operating systems*. These operating systems permit the application software to direct the computer hardware. Understanding the operating system program is important to understanding how computers work. Four special computer systems will be discussed in this section: (1) operating systems, including DOS; (2) language interpreters; (3) networks; and (4) special function systems.

Operating Systems

Operating systems usually perform three functions. These include start-up functions, interfacing with user functions, and resource management functions.

When a computer is turned on, a set of commands is loaded into the computer's memory from ROM or from a disk. This process is called *booting*. The term's origin lies in some unknown computer scientist's reaction to what happens when the computer is turned on: It begins

to program itself, and this reminded our mystery person of the phrase "Pull yourself up by your own bootstraps."

When the computer is turned on, it actually teaches itself how to operate while it loads the operating system commands into RAM. When a microcomputer is turned on, information stored in ROM issues commands to load the operating system into RAM from either a floppy disk, a hard disk, or a different ROM chip. Operating system information remains in RAM as long as the computer is turned on, or until a replacement operating system is loaded.

Operating system commands permit the computer to correctly process information entered at the keyboard or loaded from a disk. Three types of commands make up the operating system: (1) control commands, (2) resident commands, and (3) transient commands. Control commands, also called supervisor commands, communicate with the user. They cause input–output and give the computer directions.

Resident commands are loaded into RAM when booting occurs and are special utilities that enhance the computer's capabilities. Transient commands are less frequently used functions and are not loaded into the computer's memory. They are loaded from a disk only when they are needed.

Disk Operating Systems.   The DOS is a common operating system used in microcomputers. DOS commands are intended to allow users to use diskstorage systems. As with other computer systems, the DOS consists of hardware and software components.

The disk drive and cable are the most obvious hardware components of the DOS. Usually, there is also a circuit board attached to the computer's main circuit board. The DOS hardware is not really part of the operating system, however. The disk drive merely inputs to the computer's memory the operating system stored on a disk.

Disk hardware is not functional without software to direct it. The DOS software is contained on a special disk that comes with the computer or with the disk drives when they are purchased. This disk is called the *system disk* or the *system master disk*.

The system disk is critical because it contains the operating system commands that are loaded into the computer's memory when a disk is booted. These commands give direction to the disk hardware. When a new, blank disk is formatted or initialized using the system disk, DOS commands are often stored on it so that it will also be capable of booting or starting the system. Additionally, the system disk will usually contain other useful programs, such as a "copy" program (one that

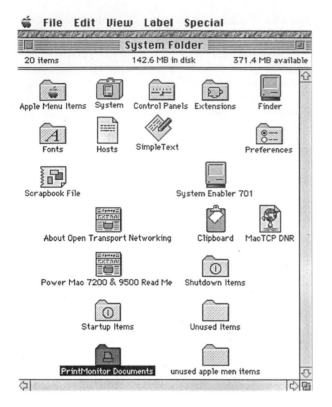

FIGURE 4.31
The Macintosh operating system is displayed using icons, or little pictures, when the System Folder is opened. The Finder is the system that keeps track of where information is stored.

permits the duplication of the contents of a disk) and the "initialization" program (the directions needed to prepare a new disk so lessons can be saved on it). Often, operating systems are stored on the computer's hard drive, so when it is turned on the system is "booted" from the system file on the hard drive.

Several different DOSs are in widespread use. One of the first operating systems for microcomputers was CP/M (control program for microprocessors). Apple II computers use Apple DOS (the last version is 3.3) or Apple ProDOS.

Macintosh computers come with a disk with a set of files called the System Folder that contains its operating system. The Finder is the most visible component of the Macintosh operating system. The Finder supervises the Macintosh operating system and allows the user to control the computer and application software (Figures 4.31 and 4.32). System 7.1 was introduced by Apple in 1991 and significantly improved the Macintosh's operating system capabilities over previous operating systems (Figure 4.33). System 7.5 was introduced in 1994.

MS-DOS—for Microsoft Disk Operating System—is an operating system for IBM and IBM-compatible PCs (Figures 4.34 and 4.35). The newest, proprietary IBM operating system is called OS/2. UNIX is an operating system for minicomputers developed by Bell Laboratories that recently has been modified for microcomputers. The UNIX system is one of the most powerful of the microprocessor-based operating systems, partially because of the large library of utility programs that it supports.

FIGURE 4.32
In the Macintosh system, folders contain files or even other folders. Two folders are shown open: one called *Word,* the other called *Works.*

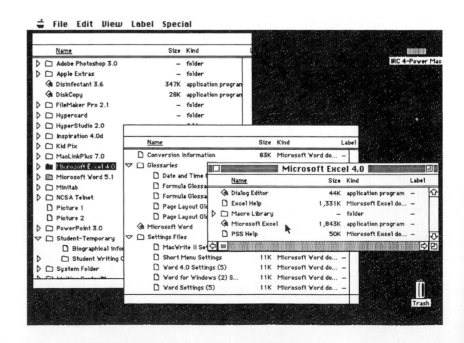

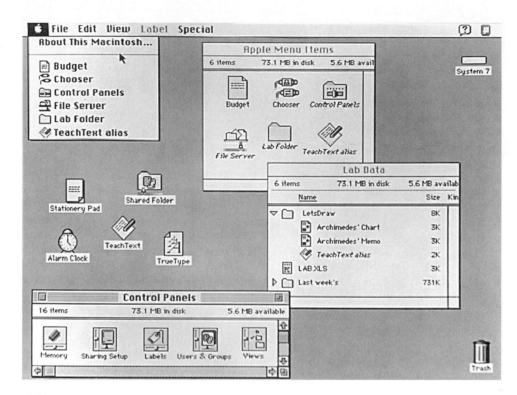

FIGURE 4.33
Apple significantly improved the Macintosh's operating system with the introduction of System 7 in 1991

Photograph courtesy of Apple Computer, Inc.

FIGURE 4.34
Cards are crowded onto the motherboard of an MS-DOS type microcomputer. This design increases flexibility, allowing the custom tailoring of the computer to the needs of individual users.

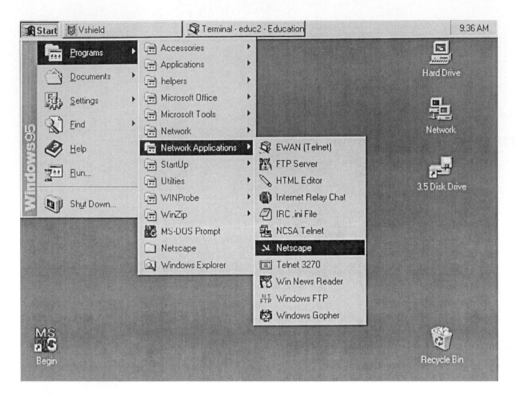

FIGURE 4.35
One popular graphical user interface (GUI) for IBM computers is Windows 95 by Microsoft.

FIGURE 4.36
Example of the directory of files in
drive C

```
Volume in drive C is MS-DOS_5
Volume Serial Number is 175C-5DA3
Directory of C:\

COMMAND     COM              47845      06-03-91     5:00a
AUTOEXEC    BAT                166      09-15-92    11:16a
CONFIG      SYS                149      10-05-92     1:35p
DOS             <DIR>                   10-24-91     4:04p
WINDOWS         <DIR>                   11-02-90     8:06a
LASERPLX        <DIR>                   07-08-92    10:00a
WINA20      386               9349      06-03-91     5:00a
WORKS           <DIR>                   10-28-91     1:04p
WP51            <DIR>                   09-01-92     4:30p
F-PROT          <DIR>                   11-08-91     2:26p
LINKWAY         <DIR>                   11-11-91     6:18a
LWTUTOR         <DIR>                   11-11-91     6:18a
LWWORK          <DIR>                   11-11-91     6:18a
ROLLTEMP                       249      02-10-92     3:24p
SCRAP       PG                  64      02-10-92     3:17p
WORD            <DIR>                   07-13-92    11:34a
         16 file(s)                57822 bytes
                               4511744 bytes free
```

Several other operating systems exist, such as TRS-DOS and "Pick." Unless the correct operating system has been loaded into the computer's RAM, data that were stored using that system cannot be used.

Windows is now the most popular operating system for IBM compatible computers. Windows comes in several versions that operate within the MS-DOS operating system. Version 3.1 and Windows for Workgroups are popular versions. Windows 95 is the latest version, introduced in 1995.

Language Interpreters.   Personal computers use BASIC more than any other high-level language. It is interpreted by the microcomputer similarly to other more sophisticated computer languages. The Apple II series of micros have a system called a *BASIC interpreter* built into their ROM. Because the CPU can understand only machine language, or binary code, the high-level language used by the programmer must be deciphered before it can be processed. Personal computers with BASIC have this deciphering done by the BASIC interpreter.

When a program is written in BASIC, or FORTRAN, Pascal, or any other language, and loaded into RAM, each command must be converted by the interpreter to machine language (binary code) before it can be executed by the CPU. The interpreter is called *system software* and is loaded into the computer's main memory from a disk if it is not a permanent part of the computer's ROM.

Networks.   Networks are special systems composed of two or more computers, connected in some way. There are two basic network configurations: star networks and ring networks.

Star networks use a central computer with multiple terminals or other computers connected outward from it to form a star (Figure 4.37). Often, star networks are used when the central computer has all the information in its memory that the other computers need for processing. In other words, in this type of network, software is shared. In a school media center, there might be a star network that accesses a computerized card catalog. Terminals might be located throughout the school with the main computer containing the data base.

Ring networks, on the other hand, do not use a central, host computer. For example, computers in the school media center, in the principal's office, and in the business department might be connected in a ring network (Figure 4.38). Each department's computer would perform functions needed by that department, but the computers could also share data and information through the network. In this kind of network, each computer would have its own software.

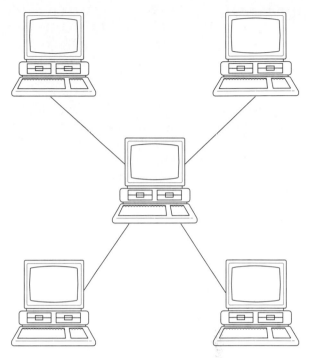

FIGURE 4.37
A star network

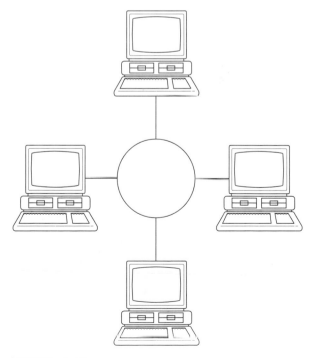

FIGURE 4.38
A ring network

SUMMARY

This chapter has presented some of the terminology used to describe computer systems. Understanding these terms is an important step in becoming computer literate. Computers and terms associated with them can be divided into two categories—hardware and software. Computers have four components—input devices and software, output devices and software, memory devices and software, and the CPU. Computers and computer software are organized into systems. A study of computer systems occurs once the study of computer components is completed. Ultimately, in-depth understanding of computer operation and use will be based on the study of computer systems.

REFERENCES FOR ADDITIONAL STUDY

Bitter, G. (1989). *Microcomputers in education today*. Watsonville, CA: Mitchell Publishing.

Bitter, G. (1992). *Macmillan encyclopedia of computers*. Upper Saddle River, NJ: Prentice Hall.

Bullough, R., & Beatty, L. (1991). *Classroom applications of microcomputers* (2nd ed.). Upper Saddle River, NJ: Prentice Hall.

"The bits and pieces of a computer system." (1983, September). *Consumer Reports*, 462–470.

Csaszar, I. (1988, March). Television and computer video. *Video Systems*, 7–14.

Ditela, S. (1982, April–May). Anatomy of a personal computer. *Technology Illustrated*, 59–62.

Dorf, R. (1981). *Introduction to computers and computer science*. San Francisco: Boyd and Fraser.

Geisert, P., & Futrell, M. (1995). *Teachers, computers, and curriculum* (2nd ed.). Boston: Allyn and Bacon.

Giarratano, J. (1982). *Foundations of computer technology*. Indianapolis: Sams.

Hock, S. (1989). *Computers and computing*. Boston: Houghton-Mifflin.

Kidder, T. (1981). *Soul of a new machine*. New York: Avon.

Lockard, J., Abrams, P., & Many, W. (1994). *Microcomputers for twenty-first century educators* (3rd ed.). New York: Harper Collins.

Lea, C. (1984). *The Apple Macintosh book*. Believe, WA: Microsoft Publishing.

Mansfield, R. (1982, March). How computers remember. *Computer*, 20–22.

Shelly, G., & Cashmere, T. (1984). *Computer fundamentals for an information age*. Brae, CA: Anaheim Publishing.

Tong, H., & Guppy, A. (1984, July). Personal computers. *National Geographic*, 87–107.

Truly, J. (1993). *PCs made easy* (2nd ed.). New York: Observe, McGraw-Hill.

Vockell, E., & Schwartz, E. (1992). *The computer in the classroom* (2nd ed.). New York: Mitchell, McGraw-Hill.

SELF-TEST QUESTIONS

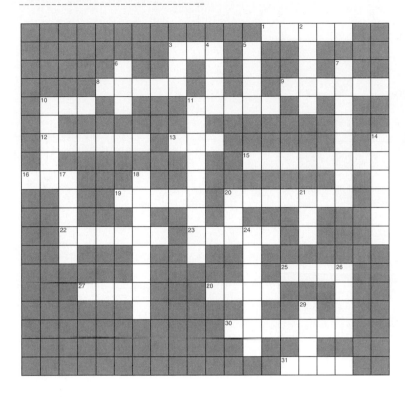

Word List

ASCII	micro
baud	mini
BASIC	modem
binary	mouse
bit	network
bus	OCR
byte	parallel
cathode	RAM
code	ring
CPU	ROM
daisy	scanner
disk	serial
DOS	sector
hardware	software
head	star
laser	switch
LCD	track
mainframe	

Across Clues

1. Where information is stored on a disk.
3. Erasable memory.
8. Used to send information over telephone lines.
9. On or Off.
10. Byte sized transmission within the computer.
11. Smallest computer.
12. How information is stored.
13. Binary digit.
15. Opposite of hardware.
16. Display device.
19. High quality printer.
20. Output device.
22. Transmission type.
23. Pointing device.
25. Speed of transmission.
27. Collection of bits.
28. Type of network.
30. Computers connected to each other.
31. Place where recording on disk occurs.

Down Clues

2. Code for bytes.
3. Permanent memory.
4. Middle sized computer.
5. Type of network with a serving computer.
6. Microcomputer operating system.
7. Opposite of software.
10. Type of high-level language.
11. Large computer.
14. Portion of a track.
17. Type of printer.
18. Byte-sized communication.
20. Brains of the computer.
21. Reading of characters.
24. Device that digitizes graphics.
26. External memory.
29. How computers store information in bytes.

FIGURE 4.39
Computer terms crossword puzzle

ANSWERS TO SELF-TEST QUESTIONS

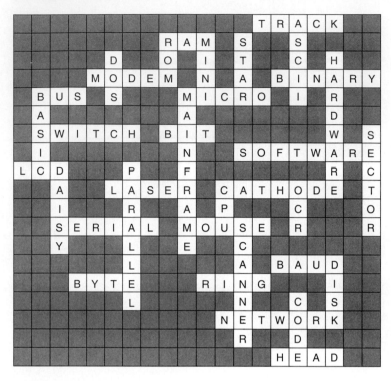

FIGURE 4.40
Crossword puzzle answers

CHAPTER FIVE

TEACHING WITH COMPUTERS:

An Overview of Computer-Based Learning

GOAL

The purpose of this chapter is to provide the reader with an overview of uses of the computer in education.

OBJECTIVES

The reader will be able to do the following:

1. Trace the history of the use of computers in the schools. Describe the views of Papert, Sheingold, Taylor, Maddux, and Dede.
2. Differentiate among the terms *CAI*, *CBI*, and *CBL*, as used in the text.
3. Cite and give examples of the six types of CBL. Cite advantages of using each of the six types.
4. State the categories in the Thomas-Boysen taxonomy of instructional uses of the computer. Describe the advantages of this classification system.
5. Differentiate between type I and type II uses of the computer in education.
6. Describe why teacher training presents a problem with respect to using computers in the school.

The first use of a new technology is quite naturally to do in a slightly different way what had been done without it. . . . Most of what has been done up to now under the name of "educational technology" or "computers in education" is still at the stage of the linear mix of old instructional methods with new technologies.

Papert, 1980, p. 36

CATEGORIES FOR COMPUTER SOFTWARE USED IN EDUCATION

As Papert (1980) suggests, discovering the appropriate uses for the computer in education has been a problem. Few deny the enormous educational potential of this machine, which can handle data with amazing speed and accuracy and is beginning to simulate human thought and behavior, but most seem to agree that we have yet to tap all the possibilities of the technology. In this section, general categories for computer software used in the schools will be presented. The reader is encouraged to consider each category carefully and evaluate the appropriateness of using the computer for that particular purpose.

Drill and Practice

One of the first uses of the computer in education was for drill and practice in arithmetic and reading. As early as 1968, Patrick Suppes and Richard Atkinson of Stanford University were producing computer programs that elicited a student response, provided immediate feedback, and then proceeded to another problem. In the Suppes–Atkinson model, the computer presents students with randomly generated problems of a specific type, and students stay with that type of problem until they achieve a certain level of proficiency. Students then move to problems of a more difficult or different nature (Atkinson & Suppes, 1968).

Drill-and-practice computer software has remained popular and has been widely produced for most subject areas. Although the Stanford work of the 1960s was done on time-sharing mainframe computers, the drill-and-practice model was widely adopted when the microcomputer became available in the late 1970s. In fact, before 1984, about 75% of all educational software produced was of the drill-and-practice variety (Figure 5.1).

In the mid-1980s, numerous computer educators began to criticize the overuse of drill-and-practice programs in education. They suggested that drill and practice was not a good use of the power of the computer and that much of what was being sold as drill-and-practice software could be done just as easily in a workbook or on a "ditto." These critics also said that by emphasizing the use of drill-and-practice activities, educators were using the computer to encourage the teaching of lower-order objectives at the expense of higher-order problem solving skills. One presenter at a Minnesota Educational Computing Corporation Annual Conference reacted to the vehement criticism by titling her talk "Drill and Practice Is Not a Dirty Word."

The battle over drill-and-practice software has cooled, however, and most educators have adopted a middle-of-the-road approach to the topic. Most agree that the computer offers some useful capabilities for drill and practice; most also agree that the computer can do far more than that. Although some drill-and-practice software is still being published, emphasis has switched to more complex programs that emphasize higher-order objectives.

The Initial Popularity of Drill and Practice.
Papert's 1980 statement about first using a new technology to do what had already been done without it is certainly appropriate when looking at the early overuse of the computer for drill and practice. The activity had traditionally been part of the curriculum and could be easily adapted to the microcomputer. Using drill-and-practice programs did not involve changing curriculum or approach. In a sense, it was a safe way for educators to get started with the new technology.

Another factor in the early popularity of these programs was the ease with which they could be written. In the early 1980s, many educators were using microcomputers for the first time and learning BASIC language. Simple drill-and-practice programs in arithmetic and spelling were some of the first programming attempted by many of these educators. Many of these early programs might be considered crude today, but they were honest first attempts at using a new technology and learning a new programming language.

Today's drill-and-practice programs are much more sophisticated. Milliken Publishing Company has produced a mathematics series that has been widely accepted in the schools. In the program, children are tested before beginning the program and placed at the appropriate level. They then proceed through the program, mastering each level before they are allowed to

FIGURE 5.1
Simple drill-and-practice programs like this one just present problems for students to
solve. This kind of computer-based drill is similar to traditional flash cards.

go on. The program keeps track of the students' progress, so they can return to where they left off the day before. The teacher can also print out a record of each child's progress at any time.

Advantages of Computerized Drill and Practice.
While drill and practice is not the only use for the computer in education, it has several advantages over traditional methods.

Immediate Feedback. Probably the most obvious advantage of computer drill and practice is that students receive immediate feedback on their responses. There is no waiting for the teacher to grade the paper. Students do not "practice their mistakes" because they are alerted the first time they make an error. This contrasts with a student doing worksheet-type drill and practice who might make the same mistake 25 times until feedback from the teacher is received.

When using a quality drill-and-practice program, students can progress at their own speed. The program determines when a student has mastered a concept and

then places the student in the next higher level. Students doing paper-and-pencil drill and practice frequently do more (or fewer) items than necessary for mastery of a concept. In computer-assisted drill and practice, the program determines the optimum number of items for each student.

A quality drill-and-practice program need not respond just that a response is right or wrong, it can also give individual feedback about the type of mistake made by the student. Thus, if a student responds that 62–19 is 47, the program can point out that the student has subtracted the bottom number from the top number and explain why this cannot be done.

More sophisticated error-analysis techniques have become available that have been adapted from work in the area of artificial intelligence and involve the ability of the computer to "understand" student errors. *ICAI (intelligent computer-aided instruction)* is a term used to describe software programs that incorporate artificial intelligence. The type of immediate individualized error analysis available in sophisticated drill-and-practice programs is almost impossible for the typical teacher to provide.

Efficient Record Keeping.   Most newer drill-and-practice programs contain fairly sophisticated record-keeping functions. With these functions, information is kept on the progress of each student in a class. At any time, the teacher can access these records and determine at which level the student is operating, the amount of time the student has spent on the program, or specific concepts that have been difficult or easy for the student.

Motivation.   Many computer drill-and-practice programs appear more motivating for students than typical workbooks or teacher-made worksheets. The use of graphics and sound, the motivation of immediate feedback, and the novelty of working on the computer are all factors that may increase time on task for students performing drill-and-practice activities. Research results on this topic are mixed, however, and some studies have indicated that after the novelty effect wears off, much of the motivating power of the computer is lost. Others suggest, however, that quality drill-and-practice software can hold students' attention much longer than traditional methods.

Several computer drill-and-practice programs include factors intended to be highly motivational to students. Math Blasters, for example, uses a video game format to teach math facts (Figure 5.2). Word Munchers is another drill-and-practice program that uses a game format for added motivation (Figure 5.3).

Given the advantages of using the computer for drill and practice and the fact that the use of such software may free up time the teacher would otherwise spend preparing and grading these activities, it does appear that there is a place for quality drill-and-practice software in education.

Tutorial

Computer tutorials, as the name implies, are designed to act as tutors or teachers for students. Concepts are presented and students are given an opportunity to interact with these concepts, much as they would with a teacher.

Like drill-and-practice programs, computer tutorials vary tremendously in quality. Many early tutorials available on the computer were simple and unimaginative in design. Some simply presented information on the computer screen and occasionally questioned the student about the information. This type of tutorial was termed an "electronic page turner" because the computer was used to present information in a sequen-

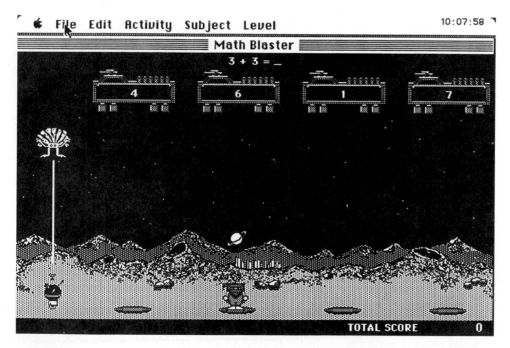

FIGURE 5.2
Math Blasters uses a motivational video game format for practicing math facts.

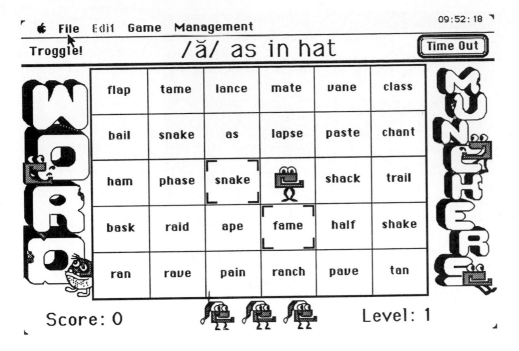

FIGURE 5.3
Word Munchers uses a game format for reviewing sounds.

tial, linear fashion, much as the material would be presented in a book. Most students who have used this type of computer tutorial will testify that such an approach can quickly become boring and tedious. Using the computer to "turn the page" as students read through volumes of material is clearly not a good use of the technology. There are, however, techniques that make good use of the power of the technology in producing effective computer tutorials.

Alphabetic Keyboarding, a program published by South-Western Publishing Company, is an example of a good tutorial program. This program presents information to the student and then gives the student an opportunity to practice using that information. The practice is guided, and the feedback is immediate. Some elementary and middle schools are using this program or similar keyboarding programs as a major portion of the keyboarding curriculum.

Advantages of Computerized Tutorial Programs.   Properly designed tutorial programs can offer some real advantages to both teachers and students. Currently computer tutorial systems cannot reproduce the flexibility and personal knowledge of an individual teacher interacting with a student. On the other hand, they do offer advantages over a single teacher attempting to present material to 30 students at once or over a traditional textbook or programmed text approach. In evaluating tutorials, users should always ask, "What does the tutorial offer that I couldn't obtain through a more traditional method of presenting information?"

Interaction.   A well-designed computer tutorial should offer opportunities for the student to interact with the material being presented. Throughout the tutorial, the student should have the opportunity to actively participate in the learning experience. This participation must involve more than having the learner answer a series of multiple-choice or fill-in questions at the end of sections in the tutorial. Students must have a chance to practice new ideas, ask questions, test hypotheses, and check their learning. One of the distinct advantages of using the computer as tutor is that the student can become a more active participant in the learning process (Figure 5.4).

Individualization.   A good tutorial program can adjust the pace of presentation to the needs of each student, a difficult if not impossible task for a single teacher. Using branching and interactive techniques,

FIGURE 5.4
One popular type of tutorial teaches students how to type using a computer keyboard.

the tutorial can provide additional instruction for students who need it and also let faster students move through material rapidly. One important issue for educators interested in the use of tutorials and the incorporation of individualized techniques in these tutorials is the issue of student control versus computer control. In some tutorials, students control the pace and difficulty of the lesson, while in others, the computer uses complex rules to determine what the student will do next. Research in this area has indicated that computer control techniques tend to work better for student learning than student control techniques. However, students apparently can be taught to monitor and control their own learning before the use of student-controlled tutorials, and these techniques increase the effectiveness of student-controlled programs.

Recent attempts to individualize computer tutorials have included intelligent tutoring systems, that is, tutoring systems based on the principles of artificial intelligence. These ICAI programs contain knowledge of the expert, knowledge about the student, and rules that either explain or reduce the difference between the expert and student models. Thus, an intelligent system contains some type of "production rules" so it can produce strategies on its own. In such a system, the student model usually contains knowledge of student

errors. Once the student model has been created and all errors identified, the teaching module can either diagnose student errors, coach the student, or provide a type of "guided discovery" experience for the student. In a review of research on ICAI programs, Dede (1986) states the following:

> Educational devices incorporating artificial intelligence (AI) would "understand" what, whom and how they were teaching and could therefore tailor content and method to the needs of an individual learner without being limited to a repertoire of prespecified responses (as are conventional computer assisted instruction systems). (p. 329)

Although production of ICAI-type tutoring systems is currently difficult, time-consuming, and expensive, these systems are leading educators into some fundamental areas of educational investigation. Identifying student errors and misconceptions and discovering rules and strategies to respond to these misconceptions should add to knowledge about the teaching and learning process and should help with education both on and off the computer.

Efficiency.   Almost every classroom teacher has been faced with students who need or want individual instruction. One common reason for this need is student absence. The question, "Did I miss anything?" is universally joked about among teachers, but at the same time, most teachers feel a real need to "reteach" students who have missed a lesson. Teachers also find the need to "reteach" slower students. For most teachers, however, time constraints make reteaching a lesson almost impossible. Computer tutorials are an excellent resource in these situations. For some students, the tutorial might provide a second approach for material they have been taught once, while for others, it can make up for the missed classroom presentation. In both cases, the tutorial can save the teacher valuable time.

Although both drill-and-practice and tutorial computer programs provide some unique capabilities for educators, both types are often classified as applications that use the computer to do what has already been done without it. Maddux (1984) defines *type I* (using the computer to teach in traditional ways) and *type II* (using the computer to expand both method and content) uses of the computer. Maddux suggests that much of the early work with computers in schools can be characterized as type I uses of the technology, that is,

using the technology to do in a slightly different way what we are already doing in classrooms. Whereas the majority of drill-and-practice and tutorial programs are examples of type I uses of the computer, the following categories of computer can often be classified as type II uses of the machine:

Computer Simulations

A simulation is a representation or model of an event, an object, or a phenomenon. A simulation is generally a simplified model that contains the essential elements of the thing simulated. Although simulations existed as educational tools long before computers were available in classrooms, the computer has greatly increased the practicality of using simulations in education.

Simulations can be powerful tools for educators. The main advantage of using simulations is that they give the student the power to manipulate various aspects of the model. Students become an active part of the educational environment and can usually see the immediate results of the decisions they make in this environment.

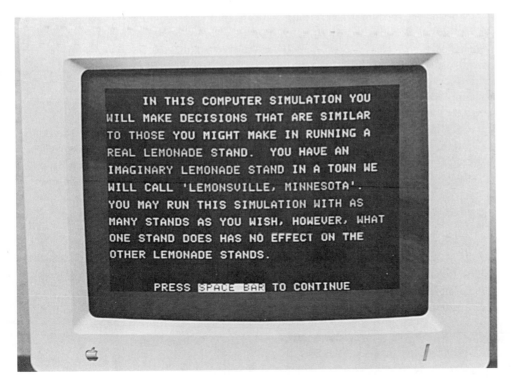

FIGURE 5.5
Lemonade Stand is a classic simulation first offered on the system master disk that came with Apple II+ microcomputers.

FIGURE 5.6
Decision making is an important characteristic of simulation programs. In Decisions, Decisions, students must decide a number of things, as this screen shows.

In a sense, students are given the power to "play" with a model of the subject being studied and to experience the effects of changing different variables in the model.

Because simulations give students an opportunity to apply their learning to a "real-life" situation, these programs tend to address higher-order educational objectives. Usually, a simulation will require the students to perform application-, analysis-, and synthesis-level activities.

Lemonade Stand, a simple simulation produced by Apple Computer in 1979, provides a good historical example of some of the characteristics and value of this approach (Figure 5.5). Lemonade Stand simulates a small-business situation in which students make decisions about several variables in the business and then receive feedback on the results of these decisions. When using the program, students are told how much money they have and are also given a weather report. Students then decide how many glasses of lemonade to make, how much to charge, and how many advertising signs (which cost money) to make. Students may work through the simulation by themselves or in competition with another student. Students make decisions for particular days and receive feedback on how much profit or loss they achieved that day.

A similar decision-making approach is used in the newer simulation titled Decisions, Decisions. Here again, students are asked to make decisions and then deal with the results of these decisions (Figure 5.6).

Using the feedback in the program, students can form generalizations about optimum prices and numbers of glasses to make given certain weather conditions. Through a hypothesis-testing procedure, they can test out these generalizations as they work through successive days. In addition to providing students with experience with simple principles of economics, Lemonade Stand also gives users a chance to use applied mental mathematics. Users must keep track of how much money they have and how much they are spending each day. Like any simulation, Lemonade Stand is most valuable used in conjunction with a classroom unit on applied mathematics or economics and is not designed for use as a stand-alone activity.

Since Lemonade Stand, an increasing number of computer simulations have become available for classroom use. Most of these simulations offer students a chance to test ideas out in a "real-life" situation and thus use the computer to provide problem-solving experiences across different areas of the curriculum. Programs include a simulation of the operation of the human heart, the dissection of a frog, and simulations of stock market and space exploration situations.

Where in the World is Carmen Sandiego? and Where in the USA is Carmen Sandiego? (Figures 5.7 and 5.8) and Where in Time is Carmen Sandiego? are three social studies-oriented simulations that are very popular in schools. These programs allow students to use clues to search for the location of a wanted person.

FIGURE 5.7
Where in the USA Is Carmen Sandiego? is a popular simulation program that gives students direct experiences with U.S. geography.

In the program, students must use knowledge of geography to make use of the clues provided. Students can use information sources that accompany the program and additional almanacs and maps to secure the information they need to locate the missing person. The Carmen Sandiego programs demonstrate that the data-handling, graphics and sound capabilities of the computer make it an effective means for creating realistic educational environments in which students can actively participate.

Sim City is another computer simulation designed to help students learn to apply and synthesize information. In this program, students make decisions about crucial issues involved in managing and developing an urban environment. Issues like waste removal, transportation, type of industry, and energy resources are all part of the decision-making environment. Like the early Lemonade Stand program, the Sim City simulation uses real feedback for students; that is, their city may be plagued by serious problems or may be a financial and social success depending on the decisions that they make (Figure 5.9).

Many educators think that well-designed simulations like the Carmen Sandiego and Sim City series may offer opportunities for students to apply classroom knowledge in more complex, realistic situations and thus expand and enhance the types of learning experiences provided for students. Used properly, computer simulations might provide one example of the type II computer-learning experiences described by Maddux (1984).

Research on the effectiveness of computer simulations on student learning has produced mixed results. Some researchers indicate that it is difficult to show that simulation increases student learning. Others will argue that traditional learning-outcome measures (student achievement tests) focus on low-level, knowledge-type outcomes and do not adequately measure the higher-level skills students may acquire through simulation experiences. In any case, if simulations are to be used effectively in classroom situations, objectives for the use of these programs must be clearly defined and instruments must be created to measure student success in attaining these objectives.

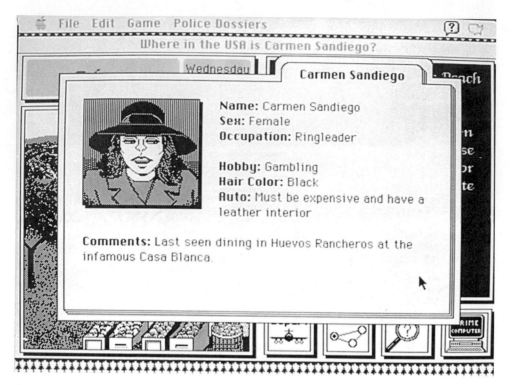

FIGURE 5.8
In Where in the USA Is Carmen Sandiego? students learn information-handling skills.

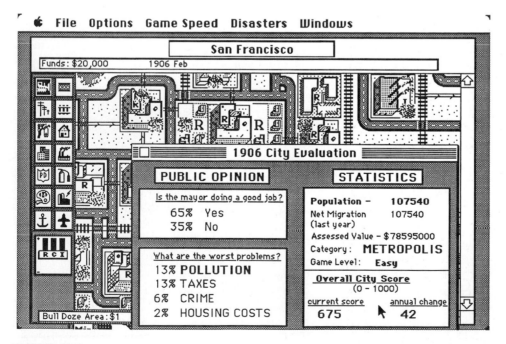

FIGURE 5.9
In SIM City students receive feedback on the effects of their decisions.

Problem-Solving Software

Problem-solving software, like simulation software, uses computer capabilities to enhance the teaching and learning of higher-order problem solving strategies. Most problem solving software is similar to simulation software in that students are placed in situations where they can manipulate variables and then receive feedback on the results of these manipulations. Simulations, however, are attempts to model real-life situations and objects, whereas problem-solving software is a more general category that includes all software designed for teaching problem-solving strategies.

The Factory by Wings for Learning provides a good example of a problem solving software package (Figure 5.10). In The Factory, students are asked to construct a series of processes that will produce a specified product. The program provides students with a variety of problem solving experiences and also includes experiences with visual discrimination and spatial relationships. Specifically, the authors of the program suggest that the program can be used to help develop the following problem solving skills:

- Working backwards
- Breaking a problem into parts
- Identifying necessary and unnecessary information
- Looking for a sequence
- Visual reasoning

One of the strengths of The Factory program is that students are encouraged to test hypotheses about how to make the product and then are provided immediate feedback about the success or failure of their approach. Thus, students see that making a mistake can lead to valuable information on how to improve their approach and thus acquire important experience in the hypothesis testing and revising process.

In one sense, The Factory can be regarded as a "classic" problem solving program. The earliest copies of the Factory ran on Apple II computers; today the program is available for both Macintosh and IBM computers and contains many more options and features than the original program. Throughout its history, however, The Factory has provided many students and teachers opportunities to use the computer to experiment and problem solve.

A second example of problem-solving software is The Incredible Laboratory by Sunburst. In this program, users are asked to discover the ingredients necessary for creating colorful and unusual monsters. This program helps students learn to use trial and error in problem solving and to learn effective note-taking strategies. Like The King's Rule, The Incredible Laboratory has several levels of difficulty.

Adventure games are another category of computer problem-solving software available for classroom use. These games usually place students in a mythical situation and ask them to pursue a well-defined goal. Stu-

FIGURE 5.10
The Factory, a problem-solving software program, contains several levels of difficulty.

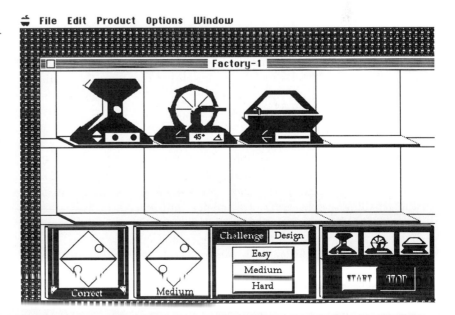

dents make decisions in pursuit of the goal and receive feedback based on these decisions. Most of these games provide students with valuable experiences in reading, memory, following directions, and testing hypotheses.

Some adventure games have roots in academic disciplines. One involves traveling to different planets in the universe where students have to make the correct decisions to keep their spaceship in operation. Other adventure games put students in a particular place in history and allow them to manipulate major features of that historic environment. Generally, adventure game programs are very motivating to students. More work needs to be done, however, to create games that relate directly to academic areas.

Educators are demonstrating an increased interest in using the capabilities of the computer to allow students to test hypotheses in problem-solving situations. Many teachers use these packages with students working in pairs or small groups. Almost all problem-solving software allows the student more freedom to explore than do drill-and-practice and tutorial programs. Increased popularity of this approach can be documented by scanning software publishing house catalogs that now generally contain an entire section on problem solving in addition to problem-solving packages in sections for specific subject areas.

Tool Software

Tool software is the category of educational computer software currently receiving the most attention from educators and is an area of emphasis in this text. Tool software is computer software used as a tool to enhance the teaching and learning of almost all subjects taught in schools. Word processors, data base managers, spreadsheets, hypermedia, graphics programs, and statistical analysis packages are all examples of tool software programs currently used in schools. These types of packages are referred to as tools, because like pencils, paper, rulers, typewriters, and calculators, they help students and teachers accomplish tasks but do not specify the content of these tasks. For example, an elementary school teacher might turn to a data base management system as a tool for the teaching and learning of a science unit on whales. The teacher could have students determine what types of information they would like to collect about whales and then assign each student a type of whale to study. Students could enter the information they collected into a record, and the class would then have a data base with information on 25 or 30 types of whales. Students would determine the template, or format, for the records. A record might include some of the following categories:

> Name of whale
> Typical adult weight
> Color
> Physical description
> Location
> Food
> Enemies
> Endangered?
> Migration habits

The students could then test hypotheses about whales by asking questions and then searching and sorting the "homemade" data base in different ways. Questions like "Do larger whales tend to live in the Pacific Ocean?" could be easily studied by searching for all the records on the largest whales. In this type of exercise, students do not merely memorize information about whales. Instead, they organize, manipulate, and use this information.

The role of the computer in this type of exercise is clearly that of a content-independent tool to expand intellectual capabilities. The concept of a tool is certainly not new to teachers and learners. Throughout the industrial revolution, increasingly sophisticated tools were used to extend human powers. As Bork (1985) indicates, "Just as we can speak of mechanical tools as extenders of human physical powers, we can also speak of intellectual tools as extenders of the human intellect. These tools expand the power of our minds" (p. 43).

Tool software can take a variety of forms, and it appears to be appropriate for all ages. Kid Pix is a popular computer tool designed for young children. Kid Pix enables children to combine prepared graphics and their own original graphics and text in creating their own projects (Figure 5.11). The package contains motivating tools and prepared graphics that open numerous possibilities for creative young minds. Adults also have reported being intrigued by the possibilities contained in the Kid Pix package, which is available on both Macintosh and IBM computers.

Advantages of Tool Software.
As educators strive to discover the most appropriate uses of the computer in the schools, they are discovering many advantages to emphasizing tool software. These advantages include the following:

FIGURE 5.11
This project, created using Kid Pix, was created by first-grader Kate Schmidt of Delmar, Iowa.

- Tool software teaches students to manage information.
- Students learn how to use tool software.
- Tool software is cost-effective.
- Tool software emphasizes active student involvement.
- Tool software gives freedom to the individual teacher.

Tool Software Teaches Students to Manage Information.   As society has moved into the Information Age, the skills necessary for professional success have changed. Working with tool software gives students an opportunity to access, organize, and manipulate information. Such experiences, properly managed, should help students develop the type of problem-solving and information-handling skills necessary for life in the Information Age.

Several of the national studies of education published in the mid-1980s pointed out the need for teaching problem-solving strategies in schools (National Commission on Excellence in Education, 1983; National Research Council, 1989). The authors of these reports suggest that knowledge-level skills are overemphasized in schools and that students are not acquiring the problem-solving strategies necessary for life in today's world. Using the computer to write, organize, and search for information and to display and calculate mathematical relationships should help students develop information-management strategies.

Students Learn How to Use Tool Software.   On a practical level, most students will use tool software programs throughout their academic and professional lives. Students who begin to use word processors and data base managers in elementary school will be able to expand their capabilities with these systems as they progress through the school system. Although the specific software they will use may change as students seek more complex applications of the tool, the basic approaches to using the software will remain constant. Thus, students are given an opportunity to experience "adult uses" of the computer early on and to develop appropriate strategies for effectively using these tools.

Tool Software Is Cost-Effective.   Tool software programs are clearly one of the best bargains for schools. General purpose tool software programs can be used across the curriculum and across grade levels. Rather than purchasing a CAI-type program, which helps in the math curriculum in the second week of the second grade, schools can purchase programs that can be used in K–12 in all areas of the curriculum.

Even if educators decide to purchase special-use tool software such as a data base program appropriate for young children, this program is still equally useful in social studies, science, and language arts and still can be considered a general-purpose program.

Tool Software Emphasizes Active Student Involvement.

Throughout the history of the use of the computer in education, critics have suggested that computers may be intellectually limiting to children. These critics usually suggest that the computer will be teaching the child and that the child, in these circumstances, will become a passive receiver of information. Papert (1980) criticizes this "computer-teach-the-child mode" when he says, "In most contemporary educational situations where children come into contact with computers, the computer is used to put children through their paces, to provide exercises of an appropriate level of difficulty, to provide feedback, and to dispense information. The computer is programming the child" (p. 19). Papert then argues that in a LOGO environment the relationship is reversed and that the child programs the computer. "And in teaching the computer how to think children embark on an exploration about how they themselves think" (1980, p. 19). In a similar way, children using tool software to manipulate information are controlling the computer and are not just being put through their paces.

Tool Software Gives Freedom to the Individual Teacher.

Just as a pencil or calculator can be used in many different ways in the classroom, tool software can be applied to almost any subject and almost any grade level. The teacher can use the tools to help students manipulate and access information in many different ways. Whereas a typical software program comes with specific objectives and approaches, teachers can devise their own objectives and approaches to using tool software in the classroom.

Because educators are making increased use of tool software, companies are developing banks of prepared activities for teacher use. Some of these banks are described in the tool software chapters in this text. But even these prepared activities are usually templates, or outlines, that teachers can manipulate for their own objectives and purposes.

In general, tool software gives each teacher a chance to relate computer capabilities to his own subject and approach and thus encourages teacher creativity. This flexibility makes the integration of the computer into the curriculum a much more natural process. As the classroom teacher develops or adapts tool software activities to accompany existing units of study, the computer is not an add-on or isolated activity, it is an integral tool in the classroom. The computer becomes a natural tool that students turn to just as they turn to other intellectual tools like the calculator or pencil.

Programming

The exact function and place of the teaching of computer programming has been a subject of great debate among computer educators. There are convincing arguments both for and against the teaching of programming at the elementary and secondary school level. There also are convincing arguments for choosing each of several programming languages for this purpose.

Advocates of the teaching of computer programming in schools believe that it is by programming or controlling the computer that children acquire an understanding of the capabilities and limitations of the computer. Luehrmann (1984) is one well-known supporter of the teaching of computer programming in the schools:

> To tell a computer what you want it to do, you must be able to communicate with it. To do that, you will need to learn a language for writing your ideas down so that you can review them, show them to others and improve them. . . . If you can tell the computer how to do the things you want it to, you are computer literate. If you cannot, you will have to depend on others to communicate your needs to the machine. (p. 37)

According to Luehrmann's point of view, the learning of programming gives students the control and power over the machine necessary to successfully function in a technological society. Advocates of programming suggest that a student who knows how to program can control the computer, whereas the student who does not know programming language is controlled by the machine.

A second strong argument for the teaching of computer programming is that the exercise of programming a computer provides a powerful experience in problem solving for learners. Children programming the computer enter step-by-step instructions designed to "teach" the computer a particular skill. In a sense, young programmers may be viewed as teaching the computer how to think, and in carrying out this task, programmers gain interesting insight into their own thinking and problem-solving approaches. However, research results on the effectiveness of programming activities on children's problem-solving capabilities have not yet given strong support to this point of view (Pea & Kurland, 1984).

Some supporters of the teaching and learning of programming contend that, like word processors or spreadsheets, programming can be used as a tool in the teaching of other subjects (Luehrmann, 1984; Papert, 1980). According to this point of view, programming should not be taught just for the sake of learning programming. Thus, in mathematics, children may use BASIC to create a program that will compute the square root of a number. Through the writing of this program, children gain insights into the process of determining square roots and have a high-level encounter with the concept as they attempt to teach the computer. Similarly, learners might use the LOGO language to teach the computer how to write a simple sentence or a Haiku poem.

Those who argue against the widespread teaching of programming in schools contend that few students will become professional programmers and that most adults are not interested in writing their own programs. According to this point of view, user-friendly software designed for particular applications is a much better use of most students' time than are long hours spent producing programs.

In any case, the early years of educational computing in the schools were characterized by frequent teaching of programming at both the elementary and secondary school levels. Becker (1986a) found that 76% of the high schools and 47% of the elementary schools where computers were used offered regular or extensive instruction in programming. At the time of the earlier Johns Hopkins studies (early 1980s), 98% of these schools teaching programming were using the BASIC programming language. LOGO, Pascal, and FORTRAN were each used by 5% of the schools. (Note that some of the schools use more than one language, so the percentages total more than 100.) By the end of the decade, more schools were using PASCAL (the Advanced Placement Test language) and LOGO.

The teaching of programming has steadily declined in U.S. schools. In his 1989 study, Becker found that programming was the single classroom application to decline in use in schools (Becker,

1991a). The tendency to de-emphasize programming as a computer application was further observed in Becker's 1994 study.

Like the teaching of programming itself, the use of the BASIC language in the schools has been extremely controversial. Some authors have suggested that BASIC was originally used because it is built into most microcomputers and requires no additional software. Given the paucity of software in the early years of school computing, BASIC was a natural starting place for schools wishing to offer a computer curriculum. Critics of BASIC programming argue that with higher quality software and more appropriate educational programming languages now available, it is a "scandal" that schools are still clinging to the teaching of BASIC as a major portion of the computer curriculum.

Specific rationales and approaches to working with LOGO are presented in Chapter 12. Whether the individual teacher decides to accept or reject the teaching of programming as part of the curriculum, she must be knowledgeable of the various possibilities for this approach.

Integrated Learning Systems

Integrated learning systems (ILSs) have been available to schools since the late 1960s. Although earlier systems were available on mainframe computers, current systems are microcomputer-based and include multimedia features (Sherry, 1992). A typical ILS includes instructional software and a management system and operates on a local area network. Most ILSs are relatively comprehensive in nature and are designed to teach large "chunks" of the mathematics, science, language arts, reading, and other core curriculum areas.

Typically, an ILS includes a pretest, diagnosis of the learner's level, assignment of an appropriate activity, a post-test, and, if needed, a reinforcement activity. Students work at their own pace, and feedback is consistent and nonjudgmental. Systems also provide a management system that reports results both individually and for the class as a whole (Hopkins, 1991).

In recent years, the overuse of ILS systems by schools has been noted and criticized. Critics suggest that many ILS systems involve merely putting traditional school curriculum on the computer. Although this approach might be easy and popular, many educators suggest it is not an appropriate use of new technologies.

Computer-Managed Instruction

This final category does not directly involve the learner, but its use by the teacher is significant to the learner. Computer-managed instruction (CMI) refers to the teacher's use of the computer to manage instruction in the classroom. Here the computer is used to record and calculate grades, record attendance, keep track of student progress in different subject areas, diagnose and prescribe, write letters home to parents, and, in general, make the operation of the classroom smoother and more efficient. CMI saves teachers time and increases efficiency. It also lets the teacher create a positive role model for students. Watching the teacher use the computer, the student can see the computer as a powerful tool to increase efficiency and productivity.

Numerous teacher utility programs are available that help teachers computerize some of their record-keeping and material-generation procedures. Gradebook programs have been the most popular of these utilities (Figure 5.12). One of these programs, called Gradebook, was written by Texas teacher Mike Mitchell, and received the Texas Computer Association's Best Program of the Year award. The program is available for free through the Texas Computer Association. There are also programs that help teachers gener-

ate tests, produce instructional materials such as crossword puzzles and word finds, write Individualized Educational Plans (IEPs), and keep records of individual student progress. The Minnesota Educational Computing Corporation (MECC) produces numerous low-cost teacher utility programs.

It has been suggested that schools need to emphasize CMI in their work with teachers (Pearlman, 1989). Using computers to improve their own productivity seems to be a natural way for teachers to develop both confidence and competence in computer use. Several authors have suggested that the best way to improve computer use in schools is to provide individual teachers with computers at school or at home so they can use the computer as a productivity tool. Although some school districts have provided teachers with computers for individual use, most districts still place the majority of their computer purchases in computer labs. Those who have emphasized placing computers with individual teachers have reported positive results.

Trends in Computer Software Use

Looking at the categories of computer education software available (not including CMI), it is interesting to

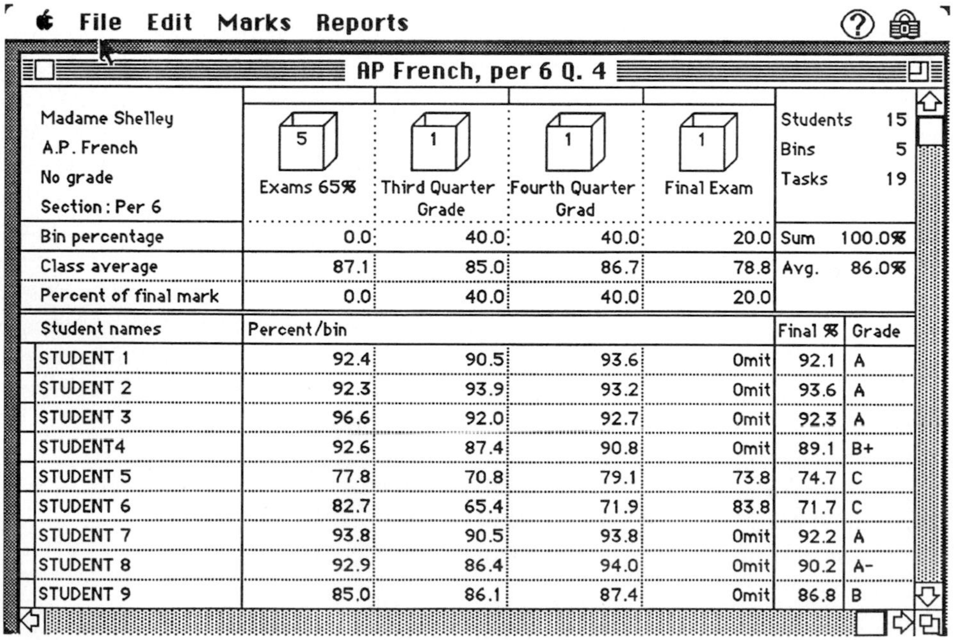

AP French, per 6 Q. 4	Exams 65%	Third Quarter Grade	Fourth Quarter Grad	Final Exam		
Madame Shelley A.P. French No grade Section : Per 6	5	1	1	1	Students 15 Bins 5 Tasks 19	
Bin percentage	0.0	40.0	40.0	20.0	Sum	100.0%
Class average	87.1	85.0	86.7	78.8	Avg.	86.0%
Percent of final mark	0.0	40.0	40.0	20.0		
Student names	Percent/bin				Final %	Grade
STUDENT 1	92.4	90.5	93.6	Omit	92.1	A
STUDENT 2	92.3	93.9	93.2	Omit	93.6	A
STUDENT 3	96.6	92.0	92.7	Omit	92.3	A
STUDENT4	92.6	87.4	90.8	Omit	89.1	B+
STUDENT 5	77.8	70.8	79.1	73.8	74.7	C
STUDENT 6	82.7	65.4	71.9	83.8	71.7	C
STUDENT 7	93.8	90.5	93.8	Omit	92.2	A
STUDENT 8	92.9	86.4	94.0	Omit	90.2	A-
STUDENT 9	85.0	86.1	87.4	Omit	86.8	B

FIGURE 5.12
Gradebook Screen from MacSchool

note that the involvement of the user becomes increasingly more active and controlling in each successive category. With drill-and-practice software, the user simply responds to the questions delivered by the computer, whereas the child who is programming the computer is "telling" the computer what to do. It does appear that the child-in-control type of educational applications, beginning with simulations and including problem solving, tool applications, and programming, are gaining more favor as the most appropriate uses of the technology.

As suggested in Chapter 1, it appears that computers and computer-related technology can support restructuring and transforming schools to more learner-centered environments. Thus, the use of learner-centered tools that expand and enhance students' and teachers' experiences in school seems to be an appropriate focal point for future computer applications.

Dede (1987) suggests that the next generation of educational software will feature cognition enhancers that enable human beings to extend their cognitive powers through computer applications. Dede suggests that three types of cognition enhancers are emerging: (1) empowering environments, (2) hypermedia, and (3) microworlds. Empowering environments are computer tools designed to efficiently handle the routine aspects of a task so the human user can focus on higher-level activities. Dede suggests the possibility of such tool kits for work in writing, art, and even anthropology.

Dede defines *hypermedia* as a framework for nonlinear representation of symbols (graphics, text, images, code) in the computer. In a hypermedia system, data are accessible through associations, and such systems can be viewed as realistic extensions of human memory. Apple's Hypercard system is one example of software taking this approach.

Finally, a microworld allows the user to explore and manipulate artificial realities. In such an environment, students might explore the principles of gravity by manipulating and exploring a microworld where baseball is played in Earth's gravity and then in the gravity of various planets. (The concept of microworld is further explored in Chapter 12, which discusses LOGO.)

All three of Dede's cognition enhancers are clear examples of computer environments that emphasize student involvement and control and learning while doing. These all will be strong themes in computer applications of the future.

Adding to the literature on trends in computer use, Becker (1992) stated three major conclusions in his 1991 study. First, he suggested that, despite the

tremendous increases in hardware and software available in schools, "only a small minority of teachers and students can be said to yet be major computer users—that is, where a large portion of instruction, learning, or productive work in their classes is being accomplished through the use of computers" (p. 10). He cited teacher attitude and lack of teacher education on computer use as two major impediments blocking more effective and appropriate computer use.

Second, Becker suggested that the hardware available in most schools was inadequate to support the more complex computer learning environments available and advocated by futurists like Dede. He said software publishers were severely limited by the constraints of older machines.

Becker's final conclusion was that word processing was the major computer learning activity in U.S. schools. He said, however, that word processing was not yet integrated into the teaching of writing and was taught for its own sake. He saw this as a natural progression, however, in the use of this tool in writing instruction.

In 1994, Becker completed a similar study that reinforced the themes he found in 1991. Although schools in the 1994 study were making progress toward more integration, the 1991 themes were still predominant.

A second large-scale descriptive report of computer use in education was produced by the Office of Technology Assessment (Porro, 1988). The report described the state of technology use in schools at the time and provided recommendations for research and development efforts in this area. The report concluded:

> OTA finds that, although new interactive technologies cannot alone solve the problems of American education, they have already contributed to important improvements in learning. These tools can play an even greater role in advancing the substance and process of education, both by helping children acquire basic skills and by endowing them with more sophisticated skills so they can acquire and apply knowledge over their lifetimes. (p. 4)

Authors of the OTA report reviewed research about computers in education and suggested that the total research in the area created an incomplete and somewhat impressionistic picture. The report suggested, however, the following areas as the most promising current uses of computers in education:

- Drill and practice to master basic skills
- Development of writing skills
- Problem solving

- Understanding abstract mathematics and science concepts
- Simulation in science, math, and social studies
- Manipulation of data
- Acquisition of computer skills for general purposes and for business and vocational training
- Access and communication for traditionally unserved populations of students
- Access and communication for teachers and students in remote locations
- Individualized learning
- Cooperative learning
- Management of classroom activities and record keeping

There now seems to be consensus that the computer can best be used in classrooms to help students develop information handling and problem-solving skills. Tool software, problem-solving software, simulations, and hypermedia environments are all types of computer use that emphasize these goals. These uses of computers in classrooms will not eliminate other effective uses of the tool, however.

CATEGORIES FOR COMPUTER USE IN EDUCATION

The categories cited thus far in this chapter focus on defining types of software available for educational use, but it is also useful to categorize in terms of how the computer is used in education. One of the best known of these categorization systems was proposed by Taylor (1980). Taylor pointed out that the computer can be used as a tutor, as a tool, and also as a tutee. Although the concepts of computer as tutor and tool have already been presented in this chapter, the concept of computer as tutee requires more explanation.

Computer as Tutee

With the computer as tutee, the traditional role of the computer in education is reversed. Instead of the computer presenting information to the student, the student is teaching the computer. To teach the computer, the student must learn a language the computer understands and thus must work with a programming language. Taylor argues that "the computer makes a good Tutee because of its dumbness, its patience, its rigidity and its capacity for being initialized and started over

Notes From the Literature
- -

Becker (1992) studied teachers in 31 schools in 16 states who provided substantial computer-based learning activities to one of their classes. Each class had a computer for every two students, used the computer for at least 1 hour per week in mathematics, and had a comparison class of similarly achieving students, usually taught by the same teacher, using only "traditional" media. After an academic year of instruction, students experiencing traditional media were compared with those having computer-based instruction. The outcomes on five mathematics achievement tests indicated little difference between students. The results suggest that "teachers and schools that provide students with substantial computer experiences will implement a fairly traditional program of instruction that will not be greatly different from the curriculum that the students would have followed without the computer" (p. 8).

Becker continues to argue that "the way that teachers teach is a product of their own schooling, training, and experiences as teachers" (p. 8). Putting computers into the schools will not increase the chances that changes in education will occur.

Becker, H. J. (1991). When powerful tools meet conventional beliefs and institutional constraints. The Computing Teacher, 18(8), 6–9.

from scratch" (1980, p. 4). He suggests that students can teach the computer to be a tutor or a tool, and:

> Learners gain new insights into their own thinking through learning to program, and teachers have their understanding of education enriched and broadened as they see how their students can benefit from treating the computer as Tutee. As a result, extended use of the computer as Tutee can shift focus of education in the classroom from end product to process, from acquiring facts to manipulating and understanding them. (Taylor, 1980, p. 4)

Taxonomy of Educational Uses of the Computer

Another useful classification system for educational uses of the computer has been created by Thomas and Boysen (1984). They contend that the traditional method of classifying by type of software is of no use to the teacher attempting to integrate the computer into the classroom. Knowing that a program is a simulation or a tutorial does not help the teacher who wants to know where and how to use the program in instruction. To address this problem, Thomas and Boysen suggest a taxonomy of computer's use where the classifying variable is the state of the learner with respect to the material. The major value of this is that it gives the teacher direction about where and how to use the computer in instruction. One interesting sidelight of this system is that the same program might be classified in different areas, depending on how the teacher uses the program in instruction.

Experiencing.   At this "lowest" level of the Thomas-Boysen taxonomy, the learner has not yet received formal instruction, and computer programs are used to set the stage for later learning. Used before instruction, programs may provide experiences or models for later instruction. For example, the Lemonade Stand program mentioned earlier in this chapter might be used as an experiencing program before a formal unit on simple economics. Some of the basic concepts presented intuitively in the simulation would be used as common experiences and used as points of reference in formal instruction.

Informing.   At this level, the student is ready for formal instruction, and the computer is used to deliver the information. Programs used at this level will frequently be chosen from the tutorial software mentioned earlier.

Reinforcing.   Reinforcing programs are used after formal instruction to strengthen specific learning outcomes. Drill-and-practice programs will frequently be used at this point in instruction, but sometimes a tutorial will present information in an interesting alternative fashion, providing a useful mode of reinforcing.

Integrating.   Integrating programs let the student apply previous learning to new situations as well as associate previously unconnected ideas. Here students are frequently asked to manipulate and apply information beyond the classroom presentation. Simulations might be especially appropriate for learners at this level.

Utilizing.   Here the computer is used as a tool in the manipulation of the subject matter. At this stage, the student might use a data base or a word processing about whales or a statistical program to analyze research data.

In terms of unique contributions that the computer can make to education, experiencing, integrating, and utilizing programs appear to show the most promise. Before the availability of the computer, providing students quality experiences in these three areas was a problem for teachers. Simulations, problem-solving software, and tool software all provide exciting possibilities for enriching students' experiences before formal instruction and for integrating and using information after instruction.

TERMINOLOGY: CAI, CBI, OR CBL?

The terms *computer-assisted instruction (CAI)*, *computer-based instruction (CBI)*, and *computer-based learning (CBL)* are all used frequently to describe computer applications in education. Although the term *CAI* sometimes refers broadly to all educational software, it usually means a programmed learning approach in which specific educational objectives are achieved through step-by-step instruction. The term *instruction in CAI* is usually interpreted as a view of the computer as delivering information to the student. Thus, for many, the term *CAI* refers to drill-and-practice and tutorial-type computer programs.

The term *CBL* is gaining popularity to describe all student learning related to the computer. This term is considered more general by some because the term *learning* more naturally encompasses situations where the computer is used as an educational tool but is not delivering information or instructing the student. Because tool software computer applications are emphasized in this text, the term *CBL* will be used here as the umbrella term for all educational uses of the computer.

A third term, *CBI*, is also used frequently, but again, the term *instruction* might imply only educational uses of the computer where the computer is delivering information to the student and probably does not include the tool usages of the machine. When this term is used in the text, it refers to use of the computer to deliver information to the student.

COMPUTERS AND OTHER TECHNOLOGIES

As the position of the computer in education continues to mature, the computer is increasingly being coupled with other technologies to create quality learning experiences for students. Used with a telephone through a modem, the computer can be used as a tool to enable communication between classrooms around the country. Coupled with a video disk player, the computer can be used to create tutorial or simulation programs with video input. Coupled with a speech synthesizer, the computer can read students' writing back to them. Thus, CBL is not limited to students, computers, and software but can also include and encompass various combinations of the computer with other advanced technologies to create learning experiences for students. The term *computer-related technologies* is gaining popularity as a way of describing the hardware used in conjunction with computers.

PROBLEMS WITH USING COMPUTERS EFFECTIVELY IN THE CLASSROOM

The capabilities of the computer offer exciting possibilities for educators to expand and enhance the curriculum. With the new technology come some problems and challenges that may keep educators from using the full potential of the computer.

Inadequate Teacher Training

Using the computer for drill-and-practice or tutorial applications requires little additional training for the classroom teacher. Making use, however, of computer software that requires more student involvement (simulations, tools, programming) requires more teacher involvement. These higher-level applications of the technology define and expand the types of computer experiences necessary for teachers to evaluate and use the most powerful classroom computer applications.

Teachers cannot use computer tools in their teaching until they have had an opportunity to use these tools themselves. Unfortunately, most teachers have not had such an opportunity. Certainly, teachers who have never used a data base system cannot be expected to devise classroom applications of such a system, and teachers who have never used a word processor cannot be expected to create writing activities appropriate for word processing.

Unfortunately, learning to use tool applications of the computer is a time- and energy-consuming project. It is clear that teachers are not going to learn these skills in a few two-hour workshops taught after school

on a Monday afternoon. School administrators and school districts must be more willing to furnish funds for extended workshops to help their teachers learn and experience the power of the technology.

Some teachers have worked extensively with computer tools (usually self-taught), and many of them are creating interesting applications for the classroom. Most teachers, however, still have not had the opportunity to attend in-depth workshops on computer applications and thus have problems understanding and devising type II computer applications (using the computer to expand both method and content) for their students.

Lack of Integration into the Curriculum

Many teachers and schools are currently "getting students on the computers," yet the students are having isolated, disconnected encounters with the technology. Some districts have even mandated that students will be on the machines for "30 minutes a week" with little direction as to what students will do during that time. In one school, students spend their 30 minutes a week choosing a disk, running the program, and then choosing another disk and repeating the process. There is no plan, no student accountability, and no connection with any other learning activities going on in the regular classroom.

Lack of teacher training can be cited as one explanation for the lack of integration of the computer into the curriculum. A second reason may be the tendency to place all the computers in a school in a laboratory and hire a computer teacher to run the laboratory. Sometimes, the computer laboratory model encourages teachers to view the computer as something to be taught rather than as a tool to enhance teaching. With this model, the classroom teacher may send the students off to the specialist to "learn computers" just as she might send the students to the music teacher to learn to play the trumpet.

One computer teacher has devised an interesting solution to this dilemma. Although he teaches his computer classes in a middle school as a separate subject, he uses the class to help other faculty in the school become more involved with computers. For the final project for the class, each student is asked to find a teacher in the school and interview the teacher about what type of computer application the teacher would like for her teaching. The student then works with the teacher in designing or locating and implementing the application.

Dynamic Nature of Computing

Given the basic conservative nature of the schools and the perpetual problems with obtaining adequate funds, the fast-paced, dynamic nature of the computer industry presents some real problems. Just as schools are outfitted with computers, the machines become obsolete, and newer, faster, more powerful models are available that will run "the newest software." Needless to say, most school systems are not financially equipped to replace computer equipment every two or three years, as the rate of development of the industry would dictate.

In addition to the problems of paying for the new equipment, the new equipment and new software compound the needs for teacher training mentioned earlier. Obviously, the new equipment requires new training for a staff who may feel that they have just begun to master the older equipment.

Although there is no easy solution for this problem, there are bright spots. Concerning both time and money, it does not seem that schools should be switching software and hardware every year or two, as is the practice in business and industry. First, students and teachers may not need the most up-to-date version of a piece of software to use the basic approach it presents. The basic concept of using a spreadsheet has remained the same for the past 10 years, yet spreadsheets have become more and more powerful and sophisticated during that time. A student could, however, become familiar with and adept at presenting and analyzing quantitative information using one of the versions of VisiCalc available since the late 1970s. When instruction focuses on the concepts and power behind the approach in general, older specific implementations may be quite adequate.

Although perhaps appropriate for using some types of tool software, the argument that schools do not need the newest versions of software does not cover all potential computer use in schools. New developments in computer education emphasize the creation of powerful simulated environments where students can make decisions and apply information. Most of these environments require software beyond what is available for most students in most schools. Becker (1991a) cited lack of up-to-date hardware as one of the three major difficulties in school computer use. Clearly, the problem cannot be ignored.

SUMMARY

Although early uses of the computer in the classroom emphasized the use of the technology as a

delivery device for traditional classroom practices, more recent applications have emphasized the computer as a tool to expand the intellect. More traditional uses have been described as type I (using the computer to teach in traditional ways) and type II (using the computer to expand both method and content). Generally, type II uses require more student control, whereas type I uses emphasize the computer controlling the student. Type II uses of the computer are beginning to facilitate classrooms that are centered on actively engaged students and teachers acting as facilitators.

Type II uses of the computer offer promise for expanding and enhancing the curriculum. Serious problems, however, impede these possibilities. These problems include inadequate teacher training, lack of integration of the computer into the curriculum, the dynamic nature of the computer industry, and equity issues. Educators must be aware of these issues and work to ensure the best use of the computer for all children in school.

SELF-TEST QUESTIONS

1. Define type I and type II computer uses as described by Maddux. Given an example of each.
2. Which is not one of the six major categories of computer software as presented in the text?
   a. Simulation
   b. Drill and practice
   c. Keyboarding
   d. Programming
3. Arthur Luehrmann is an advocate for teaching programming in the schools.
   a. True
   b. False
4. Cite the five categories in the Thomas–Boysen taxonomy. What is the classifying variable for this taxonomy? Why might this approach be useful for teachers?
5. The computer can be a tutor, tool, or tutee. Describe what is meant by the computer as tutee.
6. Suppes and Atkinson worked primarily in the area of developing simulation software.
   a. True
   b. False
7. Seymour Papert is usually associated with which type of classroom computer application?
   a. Drill and practice
   b. Tutorial

c. CMI

d. Programming

8. The term *CAI* is usually considered the most general, all-inclusive term to describe computer uses in education.

a. True

b. False

ANSWERS TO SELF-TEST QUESTIONS

1. Maddux defines type I uses as using the computer to teach in traditional ways. Type II uses involve using the computer to expand both method and content. A drill-and-practice program might be an example of a type I use, whereas the data base exercise on whales might be a type II use.

2. c

3. a. True.

4. The five categories in the Thomas–Boysen taxonomy are experiencing, informing, reinforcing, integrating, and utilizing. The classifying variable is the state of the learner with respect to the material. The strength of this approach is that it helps the teacher determine where to place computer activities within instruction and thus helps integrate computer uses into the curriculum.

5. When the computer is viewed as tutee, the student is teaching the computer how to do something. Usually, this involves the student programming the computer. Through teaching the computer, the student gains a better understanding of the concept that she is trying to teach to the "dumb" computer.

6. b. False.

7. d

8. b. False.

REFERENCES

Atkinson, R. C., & Suppes, P. (1968). *Program in computer-assisted instruction: Final report.* Washington, DC: Office of Education (DHEW).

Becker, H. J. (1986a, August). Instructional uses of school computers. *Reports of the 1985 National Survey, 2.*

Becker, H. J. (1991a). How computers are used in United States schools: Basic data from the 1989 I.E.A. computers in education survey. *Journal of Educational Computing Research, 7*(4), 385–406.

Becker, H. J. (1992). Computer-based integrated learning systems in the elementary and middle grades: A critical review and synthesis of evaluation reports. *Journal of Educational Computing, 8*(1), 1–41.

Bork, A. (1985). *Personal computers for education.* New York: Harper & Row.

Dede, C. (1986). A review and synthesis of recent research in intelligent computer-assisted instruction. *International Journal of Man-Machine Studies, 24*(4), 329–353.

Dede, C. (1987). Empowering environments, hypermedia and microworlds. *The Computing Teacher, 14*(3), 20–24.

Hopkins, M. (1991). Technologies as tools for transforming learning environments. *Computing Teacher, 18*(7) 27–30.

Luehrmann, A. (1984, April). The best way to teach computer literacy. *Electronic Learning, 3*(3), 37–42, 44.

Maddux, C. D. (1984). Educational microcomputing: The need for research. *Computers in the Schools, 1*(1), 35–51.

National Commission on Excellence in Education. (1983). *A nation at risk.* Washington, DC: U.S. Government Printing Office.

National Research Council. (1989). *Everybody counts.* Washington, DC: National Academy Press.

Papert, S. (1980). *Mindstorms.* New York: Basic Books.

Pea, R., & Kurland, D. M. (1984). On the cognitive effects of learning computer programming. *New Ideas in Psychology, 2,* 137–168.

Pearlman, R. (1989). Technology's role in restructuring schools. *Electronic Learning, 8*(8), 8–15, 56.

Porro, J. (Ed.). (1988). *Power On! New tools for teaching and learning.* Washington, DC: U.S. Government Printing Office.

Sherry, M. (1992). The new ILSs: Branching out. *Technology and Learning, 13*(2), 16–29.

Taylor, R. (Ed.). (1980). *The computer in the school: Tutor, tool, tutee.* New York: Teachers College Press.

Thomas, R. A., & Boysen, J. P. (1984). A taxonomy for the instructional use of computers. *AEDS Monitor, 22*(11, 12), 15–26.

REFERENCES FOR ADDITIONAL STUDY

Armour-Thomas, E., White, M. A., & Boehm, A. (1987, April). *The motivational effects of types of computer feedback on children's learning and retention of relational concepts.* Paper presented at the annual meeting of the American Educational Research Association, Washington, DC. (ERIC Document Reproduction Service No. ED 287 446)

Beaver, J. F. (1994). Problem solving across the curriculum—Improving students' problem-solving skills using off-computer & on-computer activities. Eugene, OR: *International Society for Technology in Education.*

Becker, H. J. (1991b). When powerful tools meet conventional beliefs and institutional constraints. *The Computing Teacher, 18*(8), 6–9.

Becker, H. J. (1991). How computers are used in United States schools: Basic data from the 1989 I.E.A. computers in education survey. *Journal of Educational Computing Research, 7*(4), 385–406.

Becker, H. J. (1986b, January). Our national report card: Preliminary results from the new Johns Hopkins Survey. *Classroom Computer Learning,* 30–33.

Bok, D. (1985). Looking into education's high tech future. *Harvard Magazine,* 29–38.

Bruder, I. (1989). Future teachers: Are they prepared? *Electronic Learning, 8*(4), 32–39.

Chanond, K. (1988). The effects of feedback, correctness of response and response confidence on learner's retention in CAI. In M. Simonson (Ed.), *Proceedings of selected research paper presentations* (pp. 134–146). New Orleans: Association for Educational Communications and Technology Individualization.

Clark, R. E. (1983). Reconsidering research on learning from media. *Review of Educational Research, 53*(4), 445–459.

Clark, R. E. (1985). Evidence for confounding in computer-based instruction studies: Analyzing the meta-analyses. *ECTJ, 33*(4), 249–262.

Coyle, K., & Thompson, A. (1988). Computers in education: A call for exemplary software. *Journal of Research on Computing in Education, 20*(3), 245–257.

Edward, C. (1989). Project MICRO. *The Computing Teacher, 16*(5), 11–13.

Gray, B. (1988). Enhancing learning through debriefing. *The Computing Teacher, 15*(9), 19–21.

Hawkins, J. (1985). Computers and girls: Rethinking the issues. *Sex Roles, 13*(3–4), 165–180.

Kulik, C., et al. (1984). *Effects of computer-based education on elementary school pupils.* Paper presented at the annual meeting of the American Educational Research Association, New Orleans.

Kulik, J., Bangert, R., & Williams, G. (1983). Effects of computer-based teaching on secondary school students. *Journal of Educational Psychology, 75,* 19–26.

Kulik, J. A., & Kulik, C. C. (1987). Computer-based instruction: What 200 evaluations say. In M. R. Simonson & S. M. Zvacek (Eds.), *Proceedings of selected research presentations.* Atlanta: Association for Educational Communications and Technology.

MacArthur, C. A., et al. (1987). *Computer assisted instruction with learning disabled students: Achievement, engagement, and other factors related to achievement.* Paper presented at the annual meeting of the American Educational Research Association, Washington, DC.

Moore, J. (1990). Finding the right educational software for your child. *Exceptional Parent, 20*(7), 58–62.

Moursund, David. (1993). Problem solving models for computer literacy—Getting smarter at solving problems. *Journal of Educational Computing Research,* 248 pages.

Reiser, R., & Dick, W. (1990). Evaluating instructional software. *Educational Technology, Research, and Development, 38*(3), 43–50.

Rosengren, K. S., Gross, D., Abrams, A. F., & Perlmutter, M. (1985, September). *An observational study of preschool children's computing activity.* Paper presented at Perspectives on the Young Child and the Computer, Austin, TX. (ERIC Document Reproduction Service No. ED 264 953)

Sheingold, K., Hawkins, J., & Kurland, D. M. (1984). *Classroom software for the information age* (Report No. 22). New York: Center for Children and Technology.

Swigger, K. M. (1985). Intelligent tutoring systems: A tutorial. *AEDS Monitor, 23*(9, 10), 6–9.

Thompson, A. D. (1989a; 1985, May–June). Helping pre-service teachers learning about computers. *Journal of Teacher Education, 36*(3), 52–54.

Thompson, A. D. (1989b). Liveware: The next challenge in computer education. *Computers and Human Behavior, 5*(1), 37–45.

Voogt, J. (1990). Courseware evaluation by teachers: An implementation perspective. *Computers and Education, 14,* 299–307.

CHAPTER SIX

TEACHING ABOUT COMPUTERS

Computer Instruction in the Curriculum

GOAL

The purpose of this chapter is to present the process of teaching about computers, what is often referred to as *computer literacy*.

OBJECTIVES

The reader will be able to do the following:

1. Define *computer literacy*.
2. Define the four components of the definition of computer literacy.
3. Explain the kindergarten through 12th-grade scope and sequence for teaching computer literacy.
4. Explain the content of a junior high school computer literacy course.
5. Explain the content of a high school computer science course.
6. Explain the content of a high school computer programming course.
7. Explain the minimal equipment needs for support of a computer literacy program in an average school system.
8. Discuss the process of programming and the general technique for problem solving with a computer.
9. Define and write an algorithm.
10. Identify the primary symbols used in flowcharting.
11. List the five categories of commands in BASIC and give examples of commands in each category.
12. Explain when and where BASIC programming is used in the curriculum.

117

COMPUTER LITERACY

The need for students to learn about computers has been a concern of educators for almost two decades. After what was perhaps the most complete analysis of national opinions about the importance of computer literacy, Molnar (1978) wrote:

> There is a national need to foster computer literacy. Further, if we are to meet this need, we must ensure that high school graduates have an understanding of the uses and applications of the computer in society and its effect upon their everyday lives. . . . A nation concerned with social needs and economic growth cannot be indifferent to the problems of literacy. If we are to reap the benefits of science-driven industries, we must develop a computer-literate society. (p. 14)

Since Molnar's statement, the term *computer literacy* has become common in the vocabulary of both professional educators and the lay public. Generally, the term indicates that a person knows "about" computers and can "use" them successfully.

Theorists have taken two somewhat opposite views of what *computer literate* means. At one extreme are those who take a literal interpretation of computer literacy. To them the word *literacy* is the key. Writing and reading computer programs is the basic skill of the computer-literate person. In other words, the ability to control a computer effectively and correctly with a well-written program is critical, and educators should concentrate on developing this skill in students.

On the other side of the argument are those who believe that a computer-literate person merely needs to know how to use a computer correctly and that little programming experience or expertise is necessary. One comparison often used by advocates of this position is to the driver of an automobile. Knowing how to drive, knowing the rules of the road, and understanding simple preventive maintenance requirements, such as when to change the oil, are all that a new driver needs to understand about automobiles. Understanding the operation of the internal combustion engine and the mechanics of the automatic transmission are not competencies needed by the driver. The same can be said for the operator of the computer. According to this line of thinking, computer literacy courses would be comparable to driver training.

An increasingly popular third position, however, offers a compromise between the two extremes and, like most compromises, has benefits and consequences. Advocates of this position believe that computer-literate students should possess competencies in four areas:

1. The basic principles of programming.
2. The current and potential applications for computers.
3. The general concepts of computers as systems.
4. A positive, anxiety-free attitude about computers and computer technology.

Computer Literacy Defined

Montag-Torardi (1985) conducted a nationwide survey of instructional computing experts to define *computer literacy,* determine what competencies were the most important for a computer-literate person to possess, and to develop a standardized test of computer literacy so that a uniform method of determining a person's level of competence would be available. This survey, and a follow-up and revision by Oviatt (1990), documented the validity of the following definition of *computer literacy:*

> Computer literacy is an understanding of computer characteristics, capabilities, and applications, as well as an ability to implement this knowledge in a skillful, productive use of computer applications suitable to individual roles in society. (Montag-Torardi, 1985, p. 863)

The knowledge, skills, and attitudes of a computer-literate person were divided further into four categories, each with its own definition.

Computer Applications. This subset of competence refers to an individual's ability to responsibly evaluate, select, and implement a variety of practical computer applications to do meaningful and efficient work based on an understanding of general types of applications, capabilities, and limitations of those applications and societal effect of specific applications.

Computer Systems. This category of computer literacy refers to the appropriate knowledgeable use of equipment (hardware) and programs (software) necessary for computer applications.

Computer Programming. This category refers to the ability to direct the operation of the computer through the skillful use of programming languages. This requires an understanding of problem-solving strategies, algorithms, flowcharts, languages, and programming.

Computer Attitude. Montag-Torardi (1985) determined that there was an affective component of computer literacy. This component consists of an individual's feelings about the personal and societal use of computers in appropriate ways. Positive attitudes include an anxiety-free willingness or desire to use the computer, confidence in one's ability to use the computer, and a sense of responsibility when using computers.

Competencles of the Computer-Literate Person

Montag-Torardi (1985) also identified the specific skills, or competencies, that a person who desires to be computer literate should possess. Oviatt (1990) refined and updated the list of competencies. Eighty-three were identified and organized into categories corresponding to the four subsection definitions of computer literacy. There were 29 computer applications competencies, 25 computer systems competencies, 20 computer programming competencies, and 9 attitudinal competencies. These competencies are listed in Appendixes A through D.

COMPUTER ANXIETY

One area of special interest to educators is computer anxiety. A number of researchers (Maurer & Simonson, 1993–94; Rosen, Sears, & Weil, 1987) and teachers have identified computer anxiety as a negative force that prevents many from becoming computer literate.

Computer anxiety is defined as the fear or apprehension felt by individuals when they use computers or when they plan to use computers. Several observable behaviors are exhibited by computer-anxious individuals:

They avoid computers and the areas where they are located.
They use excessive caution when using computers.
They make negative remarks about computers and computing.
They attempt to shorten the time when they have to use computers.

In a series of studies that dealt with computer anxiety, Maurer and Simonson (1993–94) found it to be a widely held feeling of many people, including groups that normally would not be thought of as having computer-anxious members. Even frequent computer users and people with broad computer backgrounds are not exempt from having colleagues who are computer anxious. Maurer and Simonson demonstrated that computer anxiety is an attitude that affects some members of just about any group.

Notes From the Literature

There is a strong relationship between amount of computer experience and computer anxiety. Hands-on experience in a computer literacy course has been shown to reduce levels of computer anxiety.

Jones, P. E., & Wall, R. E. (1985). Computer experience and computer anxiety: Two pilot studies. Unpublished manuscript, Towson State University, College of Education and Instructional Technology, Towson, MD. (ERIC Document Reproduction Service No. 275 315)

The effect of computer anxiety on computer literacy is an important issue to the educator. It has been found that people who are highly anxious will have more difficulty learning a new skill, and this anxiety influences subsequent use of the skill (Rosen, Sears, & Weil, 1987). Computer-anxious students tend to have a more difficult time learning computer concepts and tend to use the computer less than their friends who are not as anxious.

Researchers and other educators have attempted to deal with the problem of computer-anxious students, and the most promising efforts are based on attempts to identify computer anxious individuals before course work begins so special assistance can be provided. Several kinds of remediation have been proposed.

First, a computer-anxious student must be diagnosed. The paper-and-pencil Computer Anxiety Index

Notes From the Literature

Andrew Yeaman identified seven myths of computerism that refute some commonly held positions about computer literacy, including some discussed in this chapter: (1) Computer anxiety is the biggest obstacle encountered when people learn about computers. (2) People have computer anxiety because effectively using computers demands high math skills. (3) Computers are viewed as a single entity with a human capacity to create fear. (4) People are afraid of breaking computers. (5) Computer stress is caused by the keyboarding skills prerequisite to computer use. (6) Fear of computers is greater among women than among men. (7) People can be educated out of being computer anxious.

Yeaman, A. (1992). Seven myths of computerism. Tech Trends, 37(2), 22–25.

(Simonson, Montag-Torardi, & Maurer, 1987) is an easy and accurate way to identify students who might have anxiety-related problems. Next, these students need to be placed in situations where successful use of the computer is guaranteed and where they can receive human assistance when they need it. This can be accomplished in several ways. One-on-one teacher–student tutoring has been successful in helping students overcome their anxieties. Peer tutoring can also be effective if the tutor is knowledgeable, patient, and personable.

The key to successful remediation of anxious students is for them to experience success with the computer. This is often accomplished by having them participate in a period of systematic, well-organized, supervised contact with computers. These experiences are designed to desensitize them. Computer anxiety is overcome in much the same way small children are taught not to be afraid of the water or the dark. The person should be confronted with the fearful situation in small, controlled increments. These situations should produce positive, successful experiences, and the anxious person should always have a positive role model to emulate.

Research has demonstrated that computer anxiety is a real phenomenon that needs to be dealt with in a positive, active manner (Maurer & Simonson, 1993–94). The teacher who uses computers should understand that students may not be successful at computer-based tasks, not because they are unmotivated or dull, but because they are overly anxious. Of special concern are the preliminary data that indicate that girls and women seem to exhibit anxiety toward computers to a greater extent than do boys and men. Anxiety should be reduced before formal course work begins.

TEACHING ABOUT COMPUTERS

Many educators believe teaching about computers is a necessary prerequisite for teaching and learning with computers, the ultimate use of the computer in education. Teaching about computers begins with simple information about keyboards and culminates in advanced programming.

A comprehensive scope and sequence of computer topics should be developed for each school where computers are being used (Figure 6.1). This sequential plan is designed in the same manner that the scope and sequence for math skills or language com-

petencies are identified. Normally, awareness activities that familiarize students with computers and their operation occur first, then more in-depth understanding is introduced, and last, high-level competence is offered.

Teaching About Computers in the Elementary School

In elementary school, students should have their first formal experiences with computers. One assumption is at the foundation of elementary school computer activities: Students should realize they can easily control the computer. First, this means that they need to know how to turn it on, how to make a program run, and how to operate the keyboard, mouse, and other input devices to control the computer. These activities come under the broad heading of keyboarding skills.

Next, students should have a slightly more formal "controlling" experience with computers. Often, programming in LOGO is the activity chosen to allow students to control the computer, or a problem-solving lesson is assigned that will give students a sense of being in charge of their own learning.

Keyboarding. A modest controversy has occurred in elementary education about when keyboarding should be presented and who should do the presenting. Before examining these concerns, however, it is important to discuss what is meant by keyboarding. *Keyboarding* refers to more than learning how to touch-type. While typing skills are important, the computer is controlled by keyboard manipulations

FIGURE 6.1
K–12 Scope and Sequence for Teaching About Computers

Elementary School
1. Keyboard use
2. LOGO programming

Junior High/Middle School
1. Computer literacy course for all students
2. Enrichment activities for "special students"

Senior High School
1. Computer science course
2. Programming course(s)

that go beyond traditional typewriter use. The special function keys, the mouse, and the multiple keying requirements of computer keyboards make them different from typewriters.

Keyboarding also involves more than just using keys. It implies that the student should know how to turn the computer on and off, how to use output devices such as printers and video monitors, and how to use special input devices, such as a mouse or a touch screen. In other words, the elementary student needs to know how to input and output information to and from the computer.

Typing skill, however, is probably one of the most important new competencies expected of elementary school students because of the computer. Most educators agree that touch-typing, or using the "home row," is the correct strategy to present. Students should be able to type 20 to 40 words per minute, depending on their age, without looking at the keyboard.

Determining the appropriate time to teach typing concerns many elementary educators. The physical development of a child's hand and hand–eye coordination obviously relates to ability to touch-type. Some advocate teaching typing as soon as children begin to use computers, as early as kindergarten, or even preschool. Others say this is too early and that more maturity is required before children can learn to type without extreme anxiety being produced in them. Some even advocate waiting until junior high school before typing is formally taught.

The major disadvantage of delaying the teaching of typing is that if students are to use computers in regular course work before they are taught typing, they will probably revert to the hunt-and-peck mode of typing, and this has been demonstrated to inhibit the learning of efficient typing later. Considerable research on the question of when to teach typing to students expected to use computers needs to be conducted to either support the trend to teach keyboarding in the second, third, or fourth grade or to offer other options.

Most schools that offer keyboarding in the elementary school seem to be introducing it in the third grade. Although little research-based data support this trend, many contend that the third grade is a good compromise. Certainly, additional exploration is necessary.

Another concern of the elementary educator involves who should teach keyboarding. Three alternatives are available: (1) the regular classroom teacher, (2) software tutorial, or (3) a special instructor from the outside.

The main advantages of having the regular classroom teacher teach keyboarding are the low cost and ease of implementation. Because the teacher is already employed by the school, there is no need to hire additional support staff, and because this teacher is also the one who will make regular class assignments that involve using the computer, many consider it a good idea to have this teacher also present keyboarding information.

There are, however, several disadvantages to this option. The regular classroom teacher is probably not trained in typing and may not even be a typist. The teaching of typing is an important skill that business education teachers spend considerable time learning. If an untrained person teaches keyboarding, then there is a possibility that skills may be taught inefficiently.

A second option is to purchase computer software that teaches typing. These programs are usually tutorials that present typing routines and then provide the student with opportunities to practice skills until they are learned. The main advantages of this option are also cost and availability.

Keyboarding tutorials are relatively inexpensive and take advantage of the computer as a patient and individual tutor. Disadvantages relate to effectiveness. If students do not, or cannot, learn from the computer tutorial, then their subsequent experiences with computers may be influenced negatively.

Notes From the Literature

Effectiveness of keyboarding instruction has been found to be increased when it is combined with reading, writing, and spelling activities in the elementary school.

Balajthy, E. (1988). Keyboarding, language arts, and the elementary school child. The Computing Teacher, 16, 40–43.

Notes From the Literature

A study of second graders was performed to determine if teaching keyboarding could be effective in the primary grades. After 6 weeks of touch-typing instruction, both boys and girls made significant gains in keyboarding speed without sacrificing accuracy.

Britten, R. M. (1988, April). The effects of instruction on keyboarding skills in grade 2. Educational Technology, 28(4), 34–37.

The third option is to hire a special keyboarding instructor trained in elementary education, instructional computing, and typing. Obviously, this option is the most expensive, although it may be the most desirable. Just as obviously, more educators are needed who possess the skills to be an elementary computing expert.

Combinations of these three options are also possible. Some schools hire specialists to introduce students to the computer, and to keyboarding. Students then engage in laboratory work using tutorials supervised by the regular classroom teacher. Elementary school media specialists often coordinate this kind of program.

Eventually, many think all preservice elementary education programs will require teachers-in-training to become proficient not only in using computers but also in teaching how to use computers. In addition to the many other skills that elementary teachers must possess, they will also be expected to teach keyboarding. The teaching of keyboarding should be part of the elementary school curriculum.

LOGO Programming.   The language LOGO probably did as much to popularize computing in the school during the 1980s as did any other innovation. Seymour Papert, working with colleagues at MIT's Artificial Intelligence Laboratory, is considered the father of LOGO. His book *Mindstorms: Children, Computers and Powerful Ideas* (1980) describes the philosophical foundation of LOGO and has become a best-seller in the educational computing community.

LOGO, described in more detail later, is a language based on several important ideas. First, it is based on Piaget's ideas of concrete learning. Next, it is designed so students can control the learning environment

themselves and so that, left to themselves, children will learn things. LOGO also allows students to learn by first mastering seemingly simple ideas, then moving to more complex, powerful concepts.

LOGO programming is often presented several times in the elementary grades. It is sometimes introduced to students by having them create simple graphics by using the turtle, a small mechanical device with wheels that moves on the floor, or more often by a graphic of a turtle the computer creates on the computer monitor. Children as young as 5 have successfully created LOGO graphics. Slightly older students develop more complex drawings by combining simple graphics. Recursion and other advanced topics are presented later, usually as class assignments.

It is important to remember that the school's computer literacy curriculum committee should develop a systematic sequence of LOGO-programming activities. One reason LOGO is presented in the elementary school is to give students a successful, enjoyable experience using a computer. There are other positive consequences derived from using LOGO, also. They will be discussed in a later chapter.

Electronic Mail and Messages.   A number of elementary teachers use the Internet and the World Wide Web to familiarize children with the power of computers. Often educators use an electronic version of the old stand-by, the pen pal. Corresponding with kids from schools in other states or countries is a powerful method of familiarizing students with the computer and its capabilities as a telecommunications tool.

Junior High School Computer Literacy

When the President's Commission issued its report *A Nation at Risk* (National Commission on Excellence in Education, 1983), one of its recommendations was that all students should be required to take a one-semester computer science course. While specific recommendations for the content of this course were not made, many school systems around the country have interpreted this recommendation to mean that students should have a course similar to the one outlined in this chapter. This course is often taken by students between fifth and ninth grade.

The primary purpose of this course is to teach students to understand the applications of computers, to understand how computers work as systems, to understand programming principles, and to understand that a positive, anxiety-free attitude is necessary for computer-literate individuals. School systems usually develop their own objectives for their computer literacy course. Courses are generally divided into the six areas shown in Figure 6.2.

At the completion of the computer literacy course, junior high school students should have a working knowledge of computers, but more important, they should be able to use a word processor to write a term paper, use a record-keeping system to maintain data files, use an on-line data base to access information sources and to correspond with experts, and prepare a budget using a spreadsheet. These computer-related skills can then be applied to assignments in other courses. For example, English papers can be written using a word processor after data sources, such as the Magazine Index, are used to obtain information about the topic of the paper.

The goal of a computer literacy course is to make the junior high student a frequent and comfortable user of the computer. After completing a computer literacy course, the middle school student should be able to

FIGURE 6.2
Major Topics of Computer Literacy Courses

Unit 1: History of Computers

A. Precomputer developments
B. Mark I computer
C. Atanasoff-Berry computer
D. Development of the four generations of computers

Unit 2: Languages

A. Levels of languages
   1. Machine language
   2. High-level languages
B. Different languages and their applications

Unit 3: Computer Applications

A. Uses of computers in society
B. Computer occupations
C. Future of computers
D. The "Big Four" applications of computers
   1. Word processing
   2. Record keeping
   3. Spreadsheets
   4. Telecommunications
E. Computer-based instruction and computer-managed instruction
F. Robotics

Unit 4: Terms, Words, and Acronyms

A. Terminology
B. Abbreviations
C. Names and dates

Unit 5: Computer Systems

A. Basic components of computers
B. Types/categories of computers
C. Time sharing and networking
D. Input and output devices
E. Computer processing sequences

Unit 6: Flowcharting and Algorithms

A. Programming procedures and techniques
B. Problem solving by programming
C. BASIC, LOGO, and PASCAL

routinely use computers in other courses. Normally, this would be the only course related to computers that all students would take. Although no additional coursework that teaches about the computer would be required of all students, many high schools would probably find that many students would want to take one of several second-level courses in computer science or computer programming.

Computer Science Course.   *Computer science* is the study of computers and the consequences of their use. It is the art and science of representing, storing, processing, and presenting information. Computer science involves several activities:

The development and design of computers
Study of the improvement of the operation of computers
Study of how computers solve problems in society
Study of the choice of practical ways to use computers

A high school computer science course would probably be an elective taken by juniors or seniors who had previously taken the junior high computer literacy course and who had taken advanced mathematics. However, it might be a second-semester course taken by students as a continuation of the semester-long computer literacy course (Figure 6.3).

FIGURE 6.3
Major Topics of a High School Computer Science Course

Unit 1: Literacy

A.   Vocabulary and terminology
B.   Applications of computers
C.   Architecture of computer systems

Unit 2: Using a Computer

A.   Data base management
   1.   Inventories
   2.   Mailing lists
   3.   Sorting routines
   4.   File maintenance
   5.   File transfers
   6.   Report generation
B.   Standard package utilization
   1.   Business operations: payroll and general ledgers
   2.   Spreadsheets
   3.   Word processors
C.   Communications systems
   1.   Hardware: modems and multiplexers
   2.   Software protocols
   3.   Data Bases

Unit 3: System Operation

A.   Protocols
B.   Security systems: passwords
C.   Processing: batch and on-line
D.   Priority assignments
E.   System utilities
F.   Programming principles
   1.   Generalized algorithms
   2.   Inputs and outputs
   3.   Strings
   4.   Sorts
   5.   Loops
   6.   Files
G.   Compilers

Until recently, computer science was a discipline reserved for the college classroom, and because many high school students will be taking college-level computer science, the information presented in high school computer science courses should be in accord with what is presented in postsecondary courses. It is also important to remember that many secondary students want and need a second-level course before they graduate from high school.

Computer science course content should be developed locally by the school system's computer literacy curriculum committee. The purpose of this computer science course is to provide the student with the *why* and *how* of computer operation. For example, the student would learn how a word processor works, not just how to use one. In this way computer science differs from both the computer literacy course, where use of word processing is presented, and the programming course, where a student might write a program that converts a general purpose computer into a word processor.

Computer Programming Course.

Computer programming involves defining a problem, developing a series of steps to solve that problem, and writing a series of instructions so the computer will carry out the solution. A program is a detailed and explicit collection of instructions that direct a computer to perform input, arithmetic, logical, and output operations. Programs are written in languages (e.g., BASIC, PASCAL, LOGO, FORTRAN, and C) that are compatible with the computer system, or hardware, being used.

A language is a set of words and rules for constructing sentences that can be used for communicating. Languages have a syntax or grammar that is made up of rules for formation of words and their relationships. The semantics of a language define what the words and statements of the language mean.

Many high schools offer programming courses (Figure 6.4). Sometimes these courses are for a specific language, such as programming in PASCAL or BASIC. In other situations, they are generic programming courses where the similarities and differences between languages are taught. High-level languages, ones that use English-like instructions, are taught as examples of these rules.

Although it is important that a local computer literacy curriculum committee develop the specific content for programming courses, the nine topic areas shown in Figure 6.4 are usually included in these kinds of courses.

Notes From the Literature

Research shows that although programming may foster cognitive skill development, conventional programming instruction is not designed for this purpose and the investment of time studying programming required for transfer to occur would be unreasonable in most educational settings.

Salomon, G., & Perkins, D. N. (1987). Transfer of cognitive skills from programming: When and how? Journal of Educational Computing Research, 3(2), 149–169.

Of all the courses taught in the high school in the computer literacy curriculum, it is most critical that programming courses be taught by specialists. If students learn incorrect programming techniques, they will find it extremely detrimental to them in subsequent programming courses they might take. Just as it is harmful to English students to learn this language poorly, computer language students must be presented the syntax and organization of languages properly, or they may be forced to "unlearn" before acquiring advanced programming skills.

Equipment Requirements for the Computer Curriculum

It is difficult to project the equipment needs of schools very far into the future. New inventions and advancements of existing hardware produce overnight changes in the availability of computer equipment. In the 1970s, futurists were saying that by the 1980s every school would have a computer, and many were shaking their heads in disbelief. Well, today, most schools do have computers, and usually quite a few. The futurists of this decade are now saying that in the next few years all schoolchildren will either own or have access to a computer for their personal use.

The projections listed in Table 6.1 are considered to be what is needed to support the coursework previously described. Specific brands of computers may vary among schools, but two considerations should be taken into account when hardware is purchased. First, sufficient software must be available for the equipment purchased to support the needs of the local curriculum. Second, students should be given the opportunity to use more than one brand of computer hardware as they are learning about computers.

FIGURE 6.4
Major Topics of a High School Programming Course

Unit 1: Terminology and Background

Unit 2: Algorithmic Thought

A.   Basic concepts
B.   Task analysis
C.   Flowcharting

Unit 3: Computer Languages

A.   Machine code
B.   Assemblers
C.   High-level languages
D.   Compilers and interpreters
E.   System languages

Unit 4: Programming Principles

A.   Instruction sets: syntax
B.   Character types
C.   Counters
D.   Input–output commands
E.   Branching
F.   Loops
G.   Sorts
H.   Subroutines

Unit 5: File Structures

A.   Sequential files
B.   Relative files

Unit 6: Advanced Topics

A.   Subscripts
B.   Standard techniques
C.   Library routines
D.   Graphics

Unit 7: Interface Techniques

A.   Input routines
B.   Output routines

Unit 8: On-Line Techniques

A.   Menus
B.   Program modules
     1.   Linking
     2.   Branching
C.   System calls
D.   Relocatable subroutines
E.   Customization

Unit 9: Gaming and Simulation

A.   Learning programs
B.   Artificial intelligence
C.   Interactive video
D.   Inferential-predictive programs

Notes From the Literature

An analysis of the errors committed by students while doing BASIC programming showed that many students did not understand the computer's capabilities and had only a fuzzy idea of the general language features. Assignments often emphasized getting a program to run, leading to trial-and-error programming without regard for higher level thinking skills such as planning and debugging.

Putnam, R. T., Sleeman, D., Baxter, J. A., & Kuspa, L. K. (1986). A summary of misconceptions of high school BASIC programmers. Journal of Educational Computing Research, 2(4), 459–472.

For example, the school computer literacy curriculum committee may decide that the Power Macintosh 6100/60 will be used in the computer curriculum. The business education department may also decide that Zenith Pentium computers will be used in business education classes. Similarly, the drafting program may decide to use Macintosh computers. These business education and drafting program hardware decisions are supplemental to the primary hardware decision to select the Power Macintosh 6100/60 as the machine used to teach students computer literacy.

These lists of equipment represent recommendations for average-size schools. Peripheral devices such as disk drives and printers are not included in Table 6.1, but are necessary. The assumption is that adequate peripherals will be purchased along with computers.

It is increasingly apparent that computers should be connected to local area networks within schools and these local area networks should be connected to external networks that link buildings. Ultimately,

Notes From the Literature

When teaching BASIC, emphasize problem-solving skills and let students learn programming commands as they need them to solve problems. Get kids onto computers as soon as possible in the course and assign "real" problems whenever possible to build motivation and demonstrate the relevance of the skills being learned.

Kwajeski, K. (1986). Teach BASIC through programming, not lecture. The Computing Teacher, 14(2), 7–11.

TABLE 6.1
Microcomputer Hardware Needs for Average-Size Schools

Level	Today's Needs	Reasonable Goal	Optimum

Elementary	5 in IMC
	1 per classroom
		10 in IMC
		2 per classroom
		15 in computer
		  classroom (networked)
		1 per teacher
			15 in IMC
			5 per classroom
			30 in computer
			  classroom (networked)
			1 per teacher
			Building network

Junior high/
middle school
	5 in IMC
	1 per classroom
	15 in computer
	  classroom
		10 in IMC (networked)
		2 per classroom (networked)
		30 in computer classroom
		  (networked)
		1 per teacher (networked)
			10 in IMC
			5 per classroom (networked)
			60 in two computer classrooms
			  (networked)
			1 per teacher (networked)
			Building network

Senior high	5 in IMC
	1 per classroom
	30 in computer
	  classroom
		10 in IMC (networked)
		2 per classroom (networked)
		30 in computer classroom
		  (networked)
		1 per teacher (networked)
			10 in IMC (networked)
			5 per classroom (networked)
			60 in two computer classroom
			  (networked)
			1 per teacher (networked)
			Building network

school networks should be part of the Internet. At the very least, school networks should have modems that permit logging on the Internet through a commercial provider of this service, such as America Online, CompuServe, or Prodigy.

FUNDAMENTALS OF PROGRAMMING

But to tear down a factory or to revolt against a government or to avoid repair of a motorcycle because it is a system is to attack effects rather than causes; and as long as the attack is upon effects only, no change is possible. The true system, the real system, is our present construction of systematic thought itself, rationality itself, and if a factory is torn down but the rationality which produced it is left standing, then that rationality will simply produce another factory. If a revolution destroys a systematic government, but the systematic patterns of thought that produced that government are left intact, then those patterns will repeat themselves in the succeeding government. There is so much talk about the system. And so little understanding. (Pirsig, 1974, p. 94)

Computers are systems, and computer programs are also systems. As stated in Chapter 2, programming of computers involves the use of systems theory and the systems approach. The systems approach is a form of logical problem solving, like the scientific method. It is a self-correcting and logical methodology for decision making that applies a rational procedure to designing a set of directions for attaining specific objectives. Computer programming is an example of the systems approach put to practice. It involves an exact way of thinking and requires a thorough understanding of the problem to be solved.

Computer programmers usually follow a three-step process when they write a program. First, they develop a verbal plan that gives the solution to the problem the computer program is supposed to solve. This verbal plan is called an *algorithm*. Next, they translate this verbal solution into a flowchart, which includes both verbal and visual elements. Last, the flowchart is used as the basis for writing a program in some "high-level language," such as PASCAL or BASIC (Figure 6.5). In other words, when the program is written, the strategy visually described by the flowchart is translated into a code that uses "human-like" words and phrases. This series of statements is called the *computer program*.

This three-step process could be compared to how directions might be given to a stranger in town who wants to find a motel. A friendly native of the town

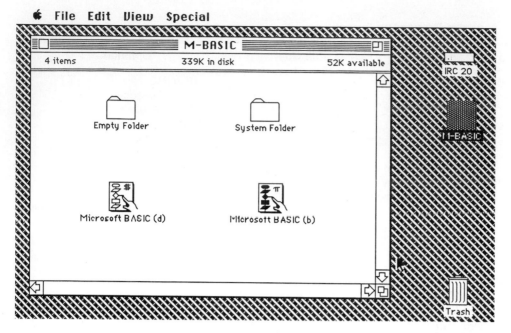

FIGURE 6.5
Macintosh Screen Showing Microsoft BASIC

might give directions such as, "Go down this street until the third stop light, then turn left. Go three more blocks, then turn right. . . ." These directions would be similar to an algorithm. If finding the motel is difficult, the person giving directions might draw a map showing the route to the motel. The map would probably include a sketch with some written directions. The map would be similar to a computer flowchart. The most elaborate way to direct this person to the motel would be to take them there. This method would be most like a final computer program written in precise computer code. The stranger would be assured of reaching the destination, unless of course the native really didn't know where the motel was, either.

Certainly, there is more to computer programming than giving directions. Computer languages have rules and procedures for their correct use, and understanding the syntax of a computer language is no trivial task. This section will present the basic process of computer programming.

Algorithms

An algorithm is a procedure for organizing a logical series of steps with words to solve a problem. Logic in this case refers to the problem-solving pattern for doing things in a specific order. Because computers work logically and sequentially, the instructions used to guide them also must be organized that way.

When an algorithm is written, five general steps usually are followed:

1. The programmer determines the specific problem. If there is more than one problem to solve, or if the problem can be easily divided into parts, the programmer divides the solution into sections and organizes them sequentially.
2. The programmer lists each step needed to solve the problem, or subproblem.
3. Each step in the problem's solution is organized sequentially.
4. The programmer tries the process out to see if the problem can be solved every time by following the sequence.
5. The programmer combines all subcategory solutions to solve the complex problem and tries out the complete solution.

Useful algorithms have the following characteristics:

- Unambiguous
- Precise
- Finite
- Effective

Notes From the Literature

After programming instruction, both ability to use mathematical variables and mathematic problem-solving ability scores were significantly improved.

McCoy, L., & Burton, J. (1987–88). The relationship of computer programming and mathematics in secondary students. Computers in the Schools, 4(3/4), 159–166.

For example, consider these two algorithms for hard-boiling an egg. A poor algorithm would be "Put an egg in a pan of water, and boil it for three minutes."

A better algorithm would be:

Take a quart-size copper-bottom pan.
Put four inches of water in the pan.
Put an egg in the pan.
Put the pan on the burner, and turn on the heat.
When the water begins to boil, start the timer.
Boil the water for three minutes.
Remove the egg.
Turn off the burner, and dump out the water.
Crack the egg, remove the shell, and serve.

This procedure is finite, and each step is clearly defined and limited. It would be improved by adding steps such as "salt the egg before eating," and even this addition could be made more effective by indicating the exact amount of salt.

An old parlor trick can be used as another example of an algorithm. This algorithm gives an exact procedure for determining a person's age:

1. Write down someone's age.
2. Subtract any one-digit number from this age.
3. Multiply the result of step 2 by the number 9.
4. Add the age written in step 1 to the product obtained in step 3.
5. Add together the last two digits of the result of step 4 to get the one's place for the age. (If the number is larger than 9, one should be added to the number found in step 6.)
6. Use the next digit of step 4 in the ten's place, and you have the person's age.

Obviously, this algorithm could be clarified by defining all the terms used, but it does provide an unambiguous, precise, finite—and as you will show your friends at your next party—an effective method of determining a person's age. That is the purpose of the algorithm, and when developed correctly, the algorithm makes subsequent flowcharting and programming easier.

Flowcharts

A flowchart is a diagram drawn in symbols with words used to describe the steps for a solution to a specific problem. Flowcharts are based on algorithms and use graphic symbols. Each symbol in a flowchart has a different meaning. Words are used to clarify the symbols (Figure 6.6).

There are four main reasons that flowcharting is such a helpful process:

1. The flowchart shows in pictorial form the logical process followed to solve a problem. This allows for easier checking for the correctness of the solution.
2. The flowchart is a means of communicating to others. It is a compact method of showing an algorithmic solution.
3. Flowcharts can be divided into parts so the problem solver can develop solutions to large problems, one section at a time. These parts can then be connected to make a master flowchart.
4. The flowchart is a record that can be easily consulted later.

Many symbols are used in flowcharting, but programmers use five most often. They are the oval, the parallelogram, the rectangle, the diamond, and the circle.

The oval is used to represent terminal operations. Words like START, STOP, BEGIN, and END are written in the oval.

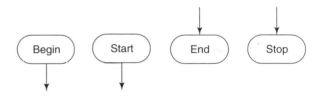

Notes From the Literature

Middle-school students successful in programming were not necessarily high-ability students in other areas, and access to a computer at home was not a reliable predictor of success. Most had gained their programming skills primarily from classroom instruction, although few obtained generalizable problem-solving skills as a result.

Mandinach, E. B., & Linn, M. C. (1987). Cognitive consequences of programming and achievements of experienced and talented programmers. Journal of Educational Computing Research, 3(1), 53–72.

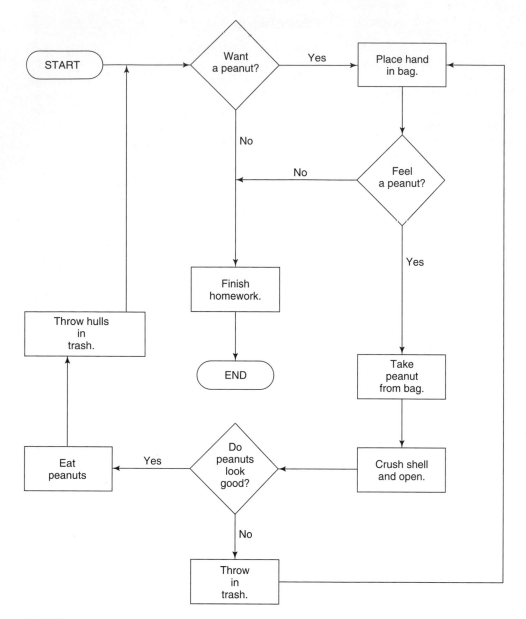

FIGURE 6.6
Flowchart For Eating a Peanut

Note: Reprinted with permission from Simonson, M. R. (1984). *Media planning and production* (p. 81). Upper Saddle River, NJ: Prentice Hall.

The parallelogram is used to symbolize input or output from an outside source. Statements are written inside the symbol to explain what is being input or output.

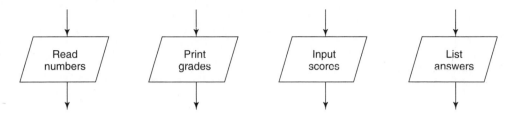

Rectangles are used to represent processes or define variables. Often, one step of an algorithm corresponds to what is placed in the rectangle.

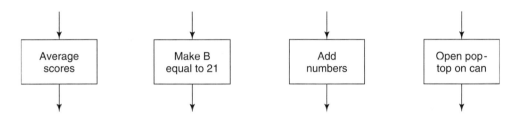

Diamonds indicate decisions. Questions that are to be answered are written within the diamond. Two possible answers, yes or no, are written outside two of the points of the diamond, indicating the direction of flow determined by the decision made.

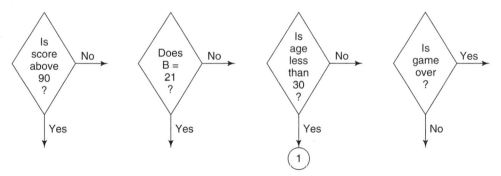

Circles are used to connect one portion of a flow-chart diagram to another. Numbers or letters are placed in the circle. Circles are always used in pairs.

The symbols of a flowchart are connected by lines with arrows that indicate the direction of flow. Normally, flowcharts are written so that the direction of the solution moves down the page and from left to right.

Programming

Traditionally, one of the most widely used programming languages for microcomputers has been BASIC (Beginners All-Purpose Symbolic Instruction Code). It was developed in the early 1960s at Dartmouth University by Professors John Kemeny and Thomas Kurtz. Originally, BASIC was designed for use by nonprogrammers as an alternative to the FORTRAN (FORmula TRANslation) language, which was considered too difficult for students who had not had a formal course in programming.

BASIC proved to be so easy to use and so powerful that it became very popular. In the late 1970s and early 1980s, almost all microcomputer manufacturers built BASIC into their machines' read-only memory (ROM). Because BASIC was built in, it was free, and because it was easy to learn, it was widely used. Many schools began to offer courses in BASIC programming as an initial attempt to make students computer literate.

Unfortunately, some educators believe BASIC is not a good language to teach students who will have little additional computer training. Many think it should be taught as a component of a computer literacy course or as one of several programming languages taught in a computer programming course taken after a computer applications course, rather than as a first course for students who are not computer literate and who may not take another instructional computing course.

One problem encountered by computer programmers generally, and BASIC programmers specifically, is the interesting phenomenon called *language dialects.* Dialects are different versions of the same language. These dialects are all slightly different from each other and therefore may not be compatible with one another. In other words, a program written in Applesoft BASIC, the version used on Apple II computers, may not work in an IBM PS/2, a Power Macintosh, or a Zenith. Each of these microcomputers uses a slightly different dialect of BASIC.

The Structure of the Languages— An Example

Traditional programs have two parts, a line number and the program code. The line number indicates the sequence in which the computer executes the program code. The program code is the BASIC command that tells the computer what to do.

Any number can be used as a BASIC line number. It would be possible to begin with number 1 for the first command in a program and to give the second com-

mand the number 2, and so on. There is one problem with this approach for assigning line numbers, however. If a command is omitted, or if the programmer wants to change a program by adding additional information to the lesson, the entire program must be retyped. To expedite the editing and revision of BASIC programs, most lesson designers use increments of 10 or 100 for line numbers. This allows for considerable flexibility during the editing or debugging phase of program development.

There are five categories of commands in languages such as BASIC: (1) program commands, (2) operational or functional symbols, (3) variables, (4) branching/decision commands, and (5) system commands.

Program Commands.   Program commands tell the central processing unit (CPU) to complete some function. Program commands are the most-often used category of command.

Operational or Functional Symbols.   The next category of commands includes symbols that indicate something is to occur. They are characters such as slashes and parentheses, and punctuation marks such as colons and commas, rather than terms or words.

Variables.   Variables are the next category of commands in the BASIC language. Variables are quantities that may change while a program is being run. When data are processed, variables are assigned names and values that are stored and recalled when needed.

Branching and Decision-Making Commands.   The category of commands considered the most powerful are the branching and decision-making commands. These commands are used to produce the sophisticated kinds of programs that make computers the useful tools they are. These commands permit choosing options and performing different portions of the program. Branching commands are usually based on yes/no decision, or on the answer to whether some input is equal to or not equal to some value or statement.

System Commands.   System commands direct the computer's CPU how to run or what to do with a program. They are not instructions used to solve a problem. Rather, they are directions for handling programming instructions. Often, system commands are typed directly into the computer at the keyboard, without line numbers. Sometimes, however, they are part of a program. A subcategory of system commands comprises disk-operating system (DOS) commands. These are commands that direct the DOS, rather than the CPU, to do something with a computer program (Table 6.2).

TABLE 6.2
Summary Sheet—BASIC Facts

1. Program commands	2. Operational or Functional Symbols	3. Variables	4. Branching and Decision Commands	5. System Commands
REM — Remarks about the program	The semicolon (;) separates variables to be output	Numeric variables Assigned number values (A, A1)	If–then — Permits matching and decision making	NEW — Clears working memory
PRINT — To output information to the screen or printer	The comma (,) indicates that spaces are to be skipped	String variables Assigned to words and/or numbers in phrases (A$, A1$)	For–next — Permits looping a preset number of times	LIST — Lists program code in memory
INPUT — To enter data to the program	The colon (:) indicates that more than one programming command is to be performed for one line number		GOSUB — Permits branching to a subroutine, then to return	DEL — Permits deletion of lines of program code
LET — To assign values to variables	Parenthesis ( ) indicate that functions within them occur first			RUN — Directs CPU to execute program
DATA, READ — To assign values to several variables	The asterisk (*) indicates that two variables are to be multiplied times each other			TRACE — Shows line number of program code on screen as it executes (NOTRACE)
END — Indicates the completion of the program	The slash (/) indicates division			DOS Commands
GR — Places computers in the graphics mode	The plus (+) indicates addition			INIT — Initialize a disk
TEXT — Sets the screen to the full-text mode	The minus (–) indicates subtraction			SAVE — Saves a program from memory to a disk
COLOR — Sets the color for graphics	The pyramid or up-arrow (^) indicates exponentiation			LOAD — Loads a program on disk
PLOT — Used with GR to indicate where "dots" are placed				CATALOG — Shows a disk's catalog on screen
HLIN, VLIN — Used with GR to draw horizontal or vertical lines				

Programming in the School's Curriculum

Most often, programming is taught as a language in one of four areas of the school curriculum: (1) junior high school computer literacy courses, (2) high school computer programming courses, (3) as part of students' math-applications assignments, or (4) as graphics techniques taught in design, drafting, or art courses.

Junior High School Computer Literacy.
Programming fundamentals are often presented twice in computer literacy courses. First, teachers often introduce students to computers by having them complete some kind of a simple programming tutorial during the first few class sessions.

Later in many computer literacy courses, students have a more in-depth unit on programming. In this unit, the five categories of commands are presented, and students learn the syntax of the language. The goal of this unit is normally not to make programmers out of students but rather to familiarize them with the concept of high-level computer languages and how they work to control the computer. An introductory programming assignment might be like the one shown in Figure 6.7.

Obviously, the program in Figure 6.7 is simple, but it gives students the opportunity to write a program based on an algorithm. Perhaps each student could write an algorithm and a flowchart for a different problem and then write the code that corresponds to the algorithm. The graphic programming assignment that follows is another often-used introductory activity; many teachers use it to introduce junior high students to programming. The primary reason to teach programming at this level is not to attempt to solve some grand problem but to give students a fun activity that will show them how to solve a problem using the computer.

High School Computer Programming.
The purpose of this semester-long experience is to make students fairly expert programmers of some high-level language. The entire process of programming is presented, including the concepts of algorithms, flowcharts, and high-level languages. The most notable difference between this course and the programming unit in the computer literacy course taken in junior high is the depth of coverage.

FIGURE 6.7
Simple, Introductory Programming Assignment

```
Write a Program That Determines a Person's Age

100 PRINT "This program will determine your age, just answer the following
questions."

110 Print "Subtract any single digit (we'll call this number the SECRET NUMBER)
from your age."

130 Print "Now multiply by 9 the number you got from subtracting the SECRET
NUMBER from your age."

140 Print "Now, in your head, add your age to the number you just obtained.
We'll call this new, large number the MAGIC NUMBER."

150 Print "Using the keyboard number keys, type the last two digits (two rightmost
numbers) of the MAGIC NUMBER, separated by a comma."

160 Input A, B

170 C=A+B

180 Print "Now type MAGIC NUMBER'S third digit from the right of the MAGIC
NUMBER, followed by a 0 (zero). For example, if the MAGIC NUMBER's third digit
from the right is 2, then type 20. If the MAGIC NUMBER doesn't have a third digit,
just type 0, followed by a RETURN."

190 Input D

200 Print "Your age is" C+D

210 End
```

Programming the computer to play a game is an interesting final activity that is often assigned to high school programming students. It is fairly difficult to write a program that would play checkers or blackjack, but several example programs are available that can be used as models for students to follow. Sometimes teams of students are assigned to prepare a game program. In this case, the project is partitioned so individual programmers complete sections of the overall assignment.

Applications in Mathematics Classes.
Because BASIC was derived from FORTRAN, it has many easily used and powerful math functions. Algebra teachers like to have students enter algebraic formulas in BASIC programs because the computer will give the student immediate feedback concerning correctness and accuracy. Programs that solve a mathematical problem make excellent projects and assignments for students, as an alternative to writing a paper or taking a test (Figure 6.8).

Graphics Applications in Design, Drafting, and Art Classes.
An example of a homework assignment involving the computer that an art teacher might give would be as follows:

```
90   REM TO DRAW A SAILBOAT
100  HOME
110  DIM X1(100),X2(100),Y(100)
120  GR
130  COLOR = 6
140  FOR I = 1 TO 100
150  READ X1(I),X2(I),Y(I)
160  IF X1(I) = 40 THEN 190
```

FIGURE 6.8
A Simple BASIC Program

```
Write a program that inputs any three numbers and outputs their sum, product,
and product squared.
100 Print "This program permits you to input any three numbers and output their
sum, product, and product squared."
110 Print "Type any three positive numbers, other than zero, at the keyboard
separated by commas. Type the numbers, not the words for the numbers."
120 Input A,B,C
130 D=A+B+C
140 E=(A*B*C)
150 F=(E*E)
160 Print "The numbers you input were A;B;C"
165 Print
170 Print "The sum of these numbers is D"
180 Print
190 Print "The product of these numbers is E"
200 Print
210 Print "The product squared of these two numbers is F"
220 Print
230 Print "Would you like to try this program again? If you would, type YES."
240 Input Y$
250 If Y$="YES" Then 100
260 If Y$="Yes" Then 100
270 Print "See you next time."
```

```
170   HLIN X1(I),X2(I) AT Y(I)
180   NEXT
190   END
210   DATA 20,20,5,19,20,6,18,18,7,20,20,7
220   DATA 17,17,8,20,20,8,16,16,9,20,20,9
230   DATA 15,15,10,20,20,10,14,14,11,20,20,11
240   DATA 13,13,12,20,20,12,12,12,13,20,20,13
250   DATA 11,20,14,20,20,15
260   DATA
      10,27,16,11,26,17,12,25,18,13,24,19,40,40,40
```

Another possible art project follows:

```
450   REM ANIMATION—CAR
460   HOME
470   Y = 25
480   GR
490   FOR X = 0 TO 30
500   COLOR = 6
510   GOSUB 560
520   COLOR = 0
530   GOSUB 560
540   NEXT X
542   COLOR 6
544   GOSUB 560
548   END550 REM DRAW THE FIGURE
560   HLIN X + 3,X + 5 AT Y
570   HLIN X + 2,X + 5 AT Y + 1
580   HLIN X + 1,X + 7 AT Y + 2
590   PLOT X + 2,Y+ 3
600   PLOT X + 6,Y + 3
610   RETURN
```

Programming can be presented in other topic areas, but the four mentioned here represent those applications used most. Because BASIC is easy, it is popular, and if used correctly, it can have a valuable place in the curriculum (Figure 6.9).

SUMMARY

Teaching about computers is to a certain extent a necessary prerequisite to teaching with them. Computer literacy, the primary thrust of a program that teaches about

computers, has become an important topic for schools. Generally, curriculum plans that teach about computers have a scope and sequence that begin in the elementary school, continuing until high school graduation.

The curriculum plan that teaches students about computers has four major components. In the elementary school, students become familiar with computer operation. Primary objectives of these experiences are to provide students with successful encounters with computers and to show them how to control computers. Keyboarding, telecommunications activities such as sending electronic mail, and LOGO programming are examples of activities that allow these objectives to be met.

In junior high school, students take a computer literacy course. This course is designed to teach students how computers work, how they can be programmed, and how to use applications of computers. The primary goal of this course is to give students the skills they need to use the computer successfully as a tool in subsequent courses that they take and outside, and after, schooling.

The high school curriculum contains the final two courses that teach about computers. First, computer science could be offered. Next a programming course, or a series of programming courses, could be made available. These courses would be elective.

The specific sequence of activities that teach students about computers should be developed locally by a computer literacy curriculum committee. The school system's needs would be determined by this committee. Equipment should support the needs of the computer curriculum.

Most educators agree that teaching and learning with computers is ultimately more important to education than teaching about them. Once computer literacy competencies are learned, however, it is easier to use the computer, especially when new computer hardware and software become available.

Computers are systems. The programs that control computers are also complex systems. Users who understand the systematic processes that are used in the development of computers and programs are more likely to use them effectively.

A systematic process is followed when computer programs are written. First, it is important to understand that computers are problem-solving machines. When a program is planned, it is written to "do" something.

When programming, a highly logical and relatively simple procedure is followed to organize the components of a computer to solve a problem. This set of steps, normally called a *program*, begins with the development of an algorithm, which is a logical sequential

FIGURE 6.9
Current Major Programming Languages—A Timeline

	1950			1960	
BUSINESS APPLICATIONS	**FORTRAN (1954)** FORmula TRANslator. Developed by an IBM team headed by John Backus. FORTRAN was the first high-level language. Known as a scientific language because of its facility for number crunching, FORTRAN also has good array-handling features.	**COBOL (1959)** COmmon Business-Oriented Language. Developed by the Department of Defense. COBOL was fine-tuned by Capt. Grace Hopper of the U.S. Navy. COBOL is one of the most widely implemented computer languages; it is primarily known for business applications. Highly structured but wordy. COBOL's syntax is English-like and intrinsically self-documenting.	**RPG (1962)** Report Program Generator. Created by IBM, RPG is generally classified as a nonprocedural language for producing business reports.	**BASIC (1964)** Beginner's All-purpose Symbolic Instruction Code. Developed at Dartmouth College by T. E. Kurtz and J. G. Kemeny, BASIC was created to teach students programming. Features of BASIC include array and string manipulation. It is widely used on microcomputers and minicomputers for educational and business applications. BASIC is easy to understand and learn and is appropriate for solving small problems.	
SCIENTIFIC APPLICATIONS		**ALGOL 58 (1958)** ALGOrithmic Language. ALGOL 58 was designed by a committee of members of the Association for Computing Machinery and European computer industry representatives. ALGOL 60 and ALGOL 68 were later versions. Useful for mathematical problem-solving, ALGOL was the first block-oriented language.	**APL (1962)** A Programming Language. Developed by Kenneth Iverson and used mainly in scientific applications. APL is known for its scope, compactness, and facility with arrays. APL has a highly specialized character set, which may be mapped to the keyboard.		

FIGURE 6.9
(continued)

	1950						1960					

SYSTEMS APPLICATIONS

SPECIAL APPLICATIONS

LISP (1960)
LISt Processing. Created by John McCarthy, LISP uses the data type list as its basic element. Many artificial-intelligence applications are written in LISP.

SNOBOL 4 (1963)
StriNg-Oriented symBOlic Language. Developed by David Farber, Ralph Griswold, and Ivan Polonsky of Bell Labs, the current version of SNOBOL is still in use for text applications, including databases and editors.

FIGURE 6.9
(continued)

	1970			1980
BUSINESS APPLICATIONS	**PL/1 (1964)** The name is not an acronym, although many think of it as Programming Language 1. IBM created PL/1 to replace COBOL and FORTRAN, but this expectation has not been fulfilled.			
SCIENTIFIC APPLICATIONS		**Pascal (1971)** Named after the 17th-century mathematician Blaise Pascal. Niklaus Wirth invented Pascal to teach his students the art of programming. Pascal procuces structured programs, simple to follow and maintain, and is extensively used on microcomputers.	**Ada (1979)** Named after Ada Augusta, the Countess of Lovelace, assistant to Charles Babbage. Ada, based on Pascal, was created by a group of programmers headed by Jean Ichbiah under contract for the U.S. Department of Defense. It is used throughout the federal government for applications beyond its original purpose—weapons system tracking.	**MODULA-2 (1979)** MODUlar LAnguage 2. MODULA-2 was written by Pascal designer Niklaus Wirth in response to the need for an enhanced Pascal. It is a multiprocessing language with coroutines that may be executed simultaneously.

FIGURE 6.9
(continued)

	1970		1980
SYSTEMS APPLICATIONS	**PROLOG (1970)** PROgramming LOGic. Written by Alain Colmerauer at the University of Marseilles, France, PROLOG is used largely for artificial-intelligence applications. It is a logic-oriented language, arriving at a problem's solution by "reasoning" its way to the answer. It is declarative rather than procedural, solving problems based on rules that the programmer has input.	**C (1975)** The successor of a language named B. Dennis Ritchie created C for the Unix operating system. C is used for systems and general applications and is known for compactness, memory conservation, and power.	**C++ (1983)** Designed and implemented by Bjarn Stroustrup at Bell Labs, this is an object-oriented superset and extension of C. Rumor has it that Bell Labs calls C++ "C" and C "Old C."
SPECIAL APPLICATIONS	**FORTH (1974)** Should have been called "Fourth" (as in *fourth generation*), but the computer used by its developer, astronomer Charles Moore, accepted only five-character names. An object-oriented language originally created to control telescopes, FORTH's key ingredient is the word. Words (like atoms) may be strung together and may have pointers to the locations of other words. The extensibility of FORTH is a key to its ever-growing popularity.		**Smalltalk 80 (1980)** Developed at Xerox's Palo Alto Research Center and implemented with the help of Alan Kay, Smalltalk is an object-oriented language used for Xerox's original graphical windows system. Actor, the language for *Microsoft Windows*, is derived from Smalltalk.

series of steps written in English that lead to the solution of the problem of interest. The algorithm is translated into a flowchart. Flowcharts are graphic representations of solutions to problems. They use visual symbols, words, and directional lines to show how a program will execute.

After a flowchart is written, it can be translated into one of several collections of codes called *programming languages*. These "high-level" languages allow human beings to communicate easily with computers. BASIC is a high-level language for many microcomputers. It also is a simple language to learn and is relatively powerful. Other popular languages are PASCAL and C. Languages have five categories of commands (program commands, operational/functional symbols, variables, branching and looping commands, and system commands).

SELF-TEST QUESTIONS

1. What are the four components of the definition of *computer literacy*?
2. Define *computer anxiety.*
3. What are two observable behaviors of a computer-anxious person?
4. At about what grade level should a required computer literacy course be taught?
5. *Keyboarding* is computer terminology for typing.
   a. True
   b. False
6. At what grade level do most schools teach keyboarding?
7. Programming in LOGO should not normally be taught until after a student has taken a computer literacy course, usually in the high school.
   a. True
   b. False
8. According to most professional educators, which is ultimately going to have the greatest effect on education, teaching about computers, or teaching with them?
9. Programming the computer is the most important skill a student can learn about computers.
   a. True
   b. False
10. What group or person in a school system makes decisions about the scope and sequence of the computer literacy curriculum?
11. Define an *algorithm.*
12. What are the five most commonly used flowchart symbols?

13. Write a flowchart for sharpening a pencil.
14. Organize these five statements into the most logical sequence:
    a. Translate into binary code.
    b. Identify the problem.
    c. Develop a flowchart.
    d. Write an algorithm.
    e. Translate into a high-level language.
15. What are the five categories of commands in BASIC?
16. Describe the results that are displayed when this program is executed:
    ```
    100   LET A = 5
    110   LET B = 25
    120   LET C = -11
    130   LET T = A * C
    140   LET X = (T * T)/B
    150   PRINT "THE RESULT OF SOLVING
          THIS EXAMPLE PROBLEM IS "; X
    ```

ANSWERS TO SELF-TEST QUESTIONS

1. The four components of the definition of *computer literacy* are computer systems, computer applications, computer programming, and computer attitudes.
2. *Computer anxiety* is defined as the fear or apprehension felt by an individual when using computers or considering using computers.
3. Behaviors of computer-anxious individuals include the following:
   a. Avoidance of computers and the area where they are located
   b. Excessive caution when using computers
   c. Negative remarks about computers and computing
   d. Attempts to shorten the time when computers must be used
4. Computer literacy, as a course, is usually taught sometime between fifth and ninth grade, during junior high or middle school years.
5. b. False. Typing and keyboarding are not the same. Keyboarding implies much more than typing, although typing is a major component of the teaching of keyboarding.
6. Most schools now teach keyboarding during the third grade.

7. b. False. Although comprehensive LOGO programming may be taught in high school, many schools are using LOGO in the elementary school as a positive way to present computers to young children.

8. Teaching with computers is considered the most important effect of using computers in schools. Teaching about computers is to facilitate using them.

9. b. False. Although programming in the traditional sense may be the ultimate goal of some students and some curriculum plans, many now believe that using the computer as a tool is the most important goal of K–12 computer literacy courses of study.

10. In the school, a committee of teachers, administrators, students, and parents, often designated as the Computer Literacy Curriculum Committee, is the group that determines the specific scope and sequence of computer topics for that school system.

11. An algorithm is a procedure for organizing a logical series of steps to solve a problem. Algorithms are written in English and are the first step used when writing a computer program.

12. The five most commonly used flowcharting symbols are the oval (entry/exit points), the rectangle (definitions or processes), the parallelogram (inputs/outputs), the diamond (decisions), and the circle (connectors).

13. Flowchart for sharpening a pencil (see Figure 6.10).

14. b, d, c, e, a

15. The five categories of programming commands presented in this chapter are the following:
    a. Program commands
    b. Functional symbols
    c. Variables
    d. Decision and looping commands
    e. System commands

16. This program would print this statement on the screen.

    THE ANSWER PRODUCED AFTER SOLVING THIS EXAMPLE PROBLEM IS 121.

REFERENCES

Maurer, M., & Simonson, M. (1984). Development and validation of a measure of computer anxiety. In M. R. Simonson (Ed.), *Proceedings of selected research paper presentations at the annual convention of the Association for Educational Communications and Technology* (pp. 318–330). Ames, IA: Iowa State University.

Maurer, M., & Simonson, M. (1993–94). The reduction of computer anxiety. *Journal of Research on Computing in Education, 26*(2), 205–219.

Molnar, A. R. (1978). *The next great crisis in American education: Computer literacy.* Paper presented at the annual convention of the Society for Applied Learning Technology. (ERIC Document Reproduction Service No. ED 191 733)

Montag-Torardi, M. (1985). The development of a computer literacy assessment instrument. In M. R. Simonson (Ed.), *Proceedings of selected research paper presentations at the annual convention of the Association for Educational Communications and Technology* (pp. 860–888). Ames, IA: Iowa State University.

National Commission on Excellence in Education. (1983). *A nation at risk: The imperative for educational reform.* Washington, DC: U.S. Government Printing Office.

Oviatt, L. (1990). *Development of a standardized test of computer literacy.* Unpublished master's thesis, Iowa State University, Ames, IA.

Papert, S. (1980). *Mindstorms: Children, computers and powerful ideas.* New York: Basic Books.

Pirsig, R. M. (1974). *Zen and the art of motorcycle maintenance.* New York: Bantam Books.

Rosen, L. D., Sears, D. C., & Weil, M. W. (1987). Computerphobia. *Behavior Research Methods, Instruments, and Computers, 19*(2), 167–179.

Simonson, M., Montag-Torardi, M., & Maurer, M. (1987). Development of a standardized test of computer literacy and a computer anxiety index. *Journal of Educational Computing Research, 3*(2), 231–247.

REFERENCES FOR ADDITIONAL STUDY

Apple Computer, Inc. (1981). *The DOS manual.* Cupertino, CA: Apple Computer, Inc.

Apple Computer, Inc. (1983). *PRODOS user's manual.* Cupertino, CA: Apple Computer, Inc.

Arch, J. (1986). Computer literacy: Time for a new direction. *The Computing Teacher, 13*(8), 4–5.

Bullough, R., & Beatty, L. (1991). *Classroom applications of microcomputers* (2nd ed.). Upper Saddle River, NJ: Prentice Hall.

Castek, J. E. (1988). *Structured BASIC programming on IBM personal computers.* New York: John Wiley & Sons.

Charles, P. (1988). The C mystique. *PC Magazine, 7*(15), 92–108.

DeVoney, C. (1988). *MS-DOS user's guide* (3rd ed.). Carmel, IN: Que Corp.

Duffy, T. (1992). *Computing concepts* (2nd ed.). Belmont, CA: Wadsworth Publishing.

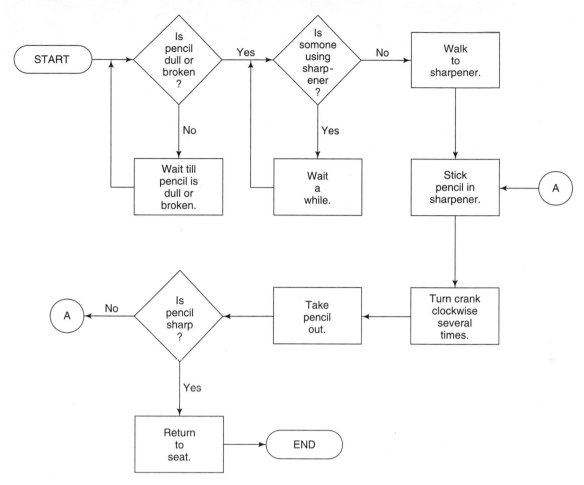

FIGURE 6.10
Flowchart for Sharpening a Pencil

Gallini, J. K., & Gredler, M. E. (1989). *Instructional design for computers: Cognitive applications in BASIC and LOGO.* Glenview, IL: Scott, Foresman.

Geisert, P., & Futrell, Y. (1990). *Teachers, computers, and curriculum.* Needham Heights, MA: Allyn & Bacon.

Harper, D. (1989). *LOGO: Theory and practice.* Belmont, CA: Brooks/Cole.

Heimler, C., Cunningham, J., & Nevard, M. (1987). *BASIC for teachers.* Santa Cruz, CA: Mitchel.

Hock, S. (1989). *Computers and computing.* Boston: Houghton Mifflin.

Kronsjo, L. (1979). *Algorithms: Their complexity and efficiency.* New York: Wiley.

Lewis, H., & Papadimitriou, C. (1978). The efficiency of algorithms. *Scientific American, 238*(14), 50–62.

Quasney, J., & Maniotes, J. (1984). *BASIC fundamentals and style.* Boston: Boyd & Fraser.

Ross, S. M. (1986). *BASIC programming for educators.* Englewood Cliffs, NJ: Prentice Hall.

Stern, N. (1975). *Flowcharting: A tool for understanding computer logic.* New York: Wiley.

Vockell, E., & Schwartz, E. (1992). *The computer in the classroom* (2nd ed.). Watsonville, CA: Mitchell McGraw-Hill.

CHAPTER SEVEN

COMPUTER ETHICS AND EQUITY

GOAL

In this chapter, the reader will be introduced to issues of computer ethics and equity and given practical suggestions for dealing with these issues.

OBJECTIVES

The reader will be able to do the following:

1. Cite specific suggestions for teaching computer ethics issues to children.
2. List and describe typical computer ethics problems that occur in schools.
3. Cite examples of inequitable school experiences of males and females with respect to computers.
4. Cite examples of inequitable home experiences of males and females with respect to computers.
5. Cite examples of methods of addressing gender equity problems with respect to computer use.
6. Differentiate between the ways that computers are used in lower socioeconomic group schools and in more wealthy schools.
7. Differentiate between the ways that computers are used with lower achieving children and higher achieving children.
8. Describe inequities in computer access for minority students.
9. Distinguish between computer access and computer use.

A PERSONAL REFLECTION

I asked ten friends of mine, all girls and women of color, to paint a picture for me of the person who came to mind when I said the words "computer scientist." Nine out of ten said he was white and wore a tie. Unfortunately, this is both the image and the reality of computer science professionals—mostly male, mostly white, mostly from middle class or aspiring middle class backgrounds.

Where are women of color in computer science? In image, nowhere. Well, not completely . . . there is one Asian woman among the professionals . . . a few African-American and Hispanic women word processing in the back. One in the front, and a few in the back—that image, although not quite accurate, does reflect the implications of computer culture as they exist today for women of color. Yet, as Sam Cooke sang so beautifully, " . . . but I know a change is gonna come."

Edwards, 1992, p. 57

G iven the potential power of the computer to influence and improve the learning process, it is imperative that schools handle computer use in a manner that is both ethical and equitable. Students need to be ensured equal and fair access to computers and computer-related technology, and they need to experience ethical use of this technology modeled and directly taught. During the early years of computing in schools, many teachers, schools, and districts did not pay adequate attention to issues of ethics and equity. As computer work in schools expands, teachers must develop a sophisticated understanding of computer ethics and equity issues. In addition, teachers need to be aware of specific strategies for dealing with these issues with students.

MORE ATTENTION TO COMPUTER ETHICS

Why Are Computer Ethics Important?

As use of computers has expanded, issues of computer ethics have become increasingly important to educators. Like government, business, and industry, schools have become infected with computer viruses, their information destroyed or changed, and files have been illegally accessed. In many cases, copyright laws and policies have been ignored and disks have been illegally copied. These occurrences, both in the larger society and in the schools, have made it clear that schools must adopt policies on computer ethics and that students must be educated in this area.

Many educators have been astounded that students do not automatically carry values from other parts of their lives to their work with the computer. For many students, computer crimes seem not to be as serious as other crimes. A student who would never think of breaking into an office to change a grade might find it acceptable to change the same grade electronically. Similarly, there are students who would never think of stealing property or money from their classmates, but would steal files of information from them.

The speed of our movement into the Information Age has made it difficult for many educators to deal adequately with the topics of computer ethics. Many schools, some schools districts, and some states, however, have begun to set up explicit standards for ethical behavior with respect to computers and information and have incorporated the teaching and discussion of these standards into the curriculum. As information accessible through computers rapidly becomes the most valuable commodity in our society, it is clear that all students must be educated on the ethical use of this information.

Many teachers have had similar problems with respect to computer ethics. Given the rapidity of the infusion of computers into schools and the pressures to use the computer with students, some early computer users failed to understand or obey copyright laws. Needs for classroom sets of software were sometimes met through illegal copying. These types of behavior created inappropriate models for many students.

As computer use in schools matures, it is extremely important that both teachers and students become knowledgeable about computer ethics and that they practice appropriate ethical behavior in this area. Schools must deliberately teach and live the topic of computer ethics.

Teaching Computer Ethics

Determining appropriate methods for teaching computer ethics to students has been difficult. Simply listing major points in a code of ethics or preaching about computer ethics does not make the issue real for students. Structured discussions on the topic are more likely to encourage students to become involved in the issues and begin to practice some ethical decision making with respect to computers (Hannah & Matus, 1984).

Weller, Repman, Rooze, and Parker (1992) have created a hypermedia program to enable students to actively participate in computer ethics decision making. The program includes the following elements: (1) examining each ethically difficult situation from the points of view of the persons involved, (2) determining the best action to be taken by each person in the situation, and (3) experiencing the consequences of the decision. The software currently has some limited audiovisual effects. Field tests of the program on junior high school students have indicated that the program is effective in helping students develop ethical values toward computers.

According to Weller et al. (1992), the four major ethical areas of concern for computer users are the following:

1. *Software piracy*—making illegal copies of software.
2. *Privacy*—accessing private information about people, businesses, and other organizations, without their permission.
3. *Theft of goods and services*—using a computer to steal money, valuable items, or services.
4. *Theft of information*—using a computer to gain access to individual or company secrets that cost them money and time to get.

Given these categories of concern, Weller et al. (1992) built scenes in the hypermedia program that illustrate examples of each. Students choose an area of concern to explore and then are asked to make decisions in that area. Results of the student decisions are reported in the program. Certainly, this type of program helps make computer ethics a more realistic and personal concern for students.

In addition to directly teaching about computer ethics, schools must model appropriate ethical behavior related to computers. Students attending schools that take computer ethics seriously and pay attention to making students aware of proper behavior in this area are much more likely to develop appropriate behavior. Clearly, a student who observes a teacher pirating software is getting a message that this behavior is acceptable. In response to this challenge, many schools have developed or are developing computer codes of ethics. Typical codes of computer ethics usually make explicit the following points:

• Use of another person's computer account or files is illegal and unethical.

• The use of invasive software, such as worms and viruses destructive to hardware and software and files, is illegal and unethical.
• Sending rude, obscene, or harassing material via any electronic mail or bulletin board facility is strictly forbidden.
• Copyrighted software must only be used in accordance with its license or purchase agreement.

Clearly, students who are learning to use computers also need to learn ethics of this use. Teachers cannot assume that students' morals and ethics will automatically transfer to the electronic world. Students need both the knowledge to protect themselves from computer crimes and the values to avoid illegal and immoral computer activities themselves.

Computer Viruses

A computer virus is simply a bit of programming code designed to replicate itself and perhaps perform another simple task like erasing a screen. Unfortunately, the other simple task that a virus performs may be very damaging to a computer program.

A virus spreads by burying itself deep within a computer's operating system, which is the system that tells the computer how to operate. The virus then gives commands to make room for a copy of itself on every data diskette or every program stored on the hard disk in the infected computer. Every time a new diskette is used, the virus goes along with it. When that diskette is introduced into a clean computer, it spreads the virus to its operating system.

Typically, a computer virus program includes the following features:

1. It can execute or carry out instructions held in the program code.
2. It can replicate or make copies of itself.
3. It can alter other executable software programs to include copies of itself (Maxwell & Lamon, 1992).

Because viruses operate without visible instructions from the user, they can exist and operate without the user's knowledge. Most users have no idea that a virus exists until the virus has done some harm.

Often, a virus is written so that it acts much like a time bomb; thus, it can enter a computer and not do anything for several days and then erupt and destroy the system. Although simple, a virus can shut down a mainframe computer or wipe out the contents of a hard drive. It is almost impossible to keep viruses out of machines, because some viruses have entered from sealed, newly purchased commercial software as well as from pirated software or unauthorized users.

Current trends toward connecting computers and sharing information over electronic bulletin boards make the computer virus problem even more severe. One business executive tells how he brought work home and "caught" a virus through some software that his second-grader had brought home from school.

In today's world, most users find that they need some type of virus detection and removal software. Many of these programs are called *disinfectant programs;* many are very effective for detecting and removing viruses (Figures 7.1 and 7.2). Many of these programs are transparent and operate in the background to guard against virus invasion and thus do not affect the everyday visible operation of the machine. It should be noted, however, that virus detection and removal programs must be continually updated because new viruses that are resistant to existing disinfectant programs are continually developed.

In addition to using disinfectant programs, many users are becoming more cautious about the software they bring into their machine. Because sharing software is how viruses are spread, care is called for in deciding what software is entered into a machine.

EQUITY ISSUES

As with issues of ethics, issues of computer equity were seldom noticed or addressed in the early years of computers in schools. In the excitement of getting the machines up and running, the relatively subtle issue of computer equity was pushed into the background.

In recent years, educators have begun to recognize the seriousness of computer inequity issues. Sutton (1991) notes, "The evidence indicates that computer use during the 1980s did not bring education closer to equal educational opportunity. Rather, it maintained and exaggerated existing inequities in education. Children who were minority, poor, female, or low-achieving were likely to be further behind after the introduction of computers into schools."

As computers are used more and more in the schools, however, four major equity issues are emerging. One of these issues involves equal access to computer technology by both boys and girls. The other issues involve equal access for children of lower socioeconomic status, minority children, and average to low-ability children. All four issues have important implications for computer education.

Any discussion of equity issues needs to include a distinction between use of computers and access to computers. Today, most children in schools have equal access to computers in that there are computers available for them to use. However, the actual use of this access, both in time on the computer and the type of work done on the computer, can be much different for different groups of students. Thus, those who dismiss equity issues by citing statistics on the availability of computers are missing the point. The following sections will include discussions of key issues of computer use for different groups of students.

Sex Equity

Differences Between Male and Female Students. Because females in our society still have fewer environmental experiences in mathematics and science because of the nature of their free time and play activities, appropriate computer problem-solving environments may be particularly beneficial in improving meaningful science and mathematics learning for female students. Evidence suggests, however, that computers in schools tend to be used more by male students than by female students (Becker, 1986b). It also appears that many teachers are not sensitive to computer equity issues and do not recognize the differential use between males and females. In addition, more males than females appear to be taking leadership roles in computer education, and thus students may be get-

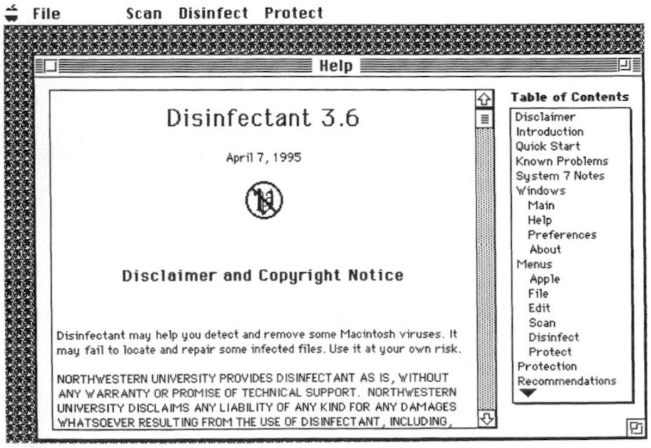

FIGURE 7.1
Disinfectant 3.6 is a software program designed to detect and eliminate computer viruses.

FIGURE 7.2

The Disinfectant 3.6 program can be used on any disk, either a hard disk or a floppy disk. The program will disinfect the entire disk.

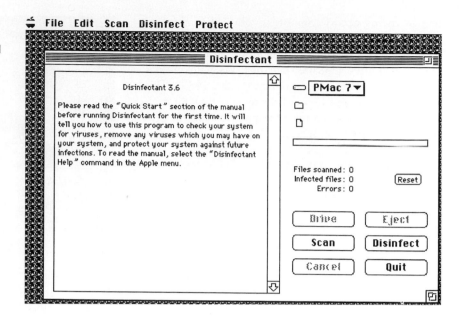

ting the message that "computers are for boys" because of the lack of adequate female role models. Computer specialists and teachers in the schools tend to be male. Without intervention, current uses of the computer in schools could actually help widen the existing gap in mathematics and science achievement between young males and females. In addition, the inequity could cause females to have fewer options when they are ready to enter the work world.

Young females tend to differ from young males both in terms of experiences with computers and attitudes toward their ability to use computers. Both areas should be of concern to educators.

Although no gender differences are found for computer use in preschool, by the third and fourth grade, there are gender differences in both attitude and performance on computer-based education tests. These differences become even more pronounced at the high school level (Nelson & Watson, 1991). Some researchers have found differences as early as first grade (e.g., Collis & Lloyd, 1990).

Becker's studies of computer use in school suggest that girls are taking almost as many computer courses as boys, but that males dominate computer use before and after school. At the typical middle school in Becker's study, only 15% of the before- or after-school users were girls (Becker, 1986b).

Boys also seem to pursue more recreational use of computers. In one study, researchers found boys outnumber girls 3 to 1 at the video arcade. In addition, the researchers found that many of the girls who were in the video arcade were there to watch the boys, not to participate (Kessler, 1985). Although playing video games may be viewed as quite different from classroom computer use, confidence in dealing with the technology and ability in following directions may be gained from video game experience.

In terms of attitude toward ability to use computers, several researchers have noted that females tend to express an attitude toward computers that can be summarized as "We can, but I can't." That is, many females believe that, in the abstract, women are as capable as

---

Notes From the Literature

In a study of first grade students using computers for the study of language arts, the children's attitude toward the computers was measured. Although reading and writing were not perceived by the first graders as being associated with either girls or boys, computers were seen as masculine by both sexes. Even though the children in the study participated in more than 6 months of relatively intense computer work, this attitude persisted.

Collis, B., & Lloyd, O. (1990, Fall). The effect of computer use on grade 1 children's gender stereotypes about reading, writing and computer use. Journal of Research and Development in Education, 14–20.

men with respect to computers. Thus, these women will answer true to a statement such as "Women are as good as men at working on computers." Yet, these same women will often indicate that they personally are not capable at working on computers (Collis, 1985). This attitude can be very harmful for females making decisions about whether to take computer courses or pursue computer topics at school.

Possible Reasons for the Differences. Families apparently provide more encouragement for boys to pursue an interest in computers than for girls. Parents are more likely to purchase a computer for a son than for a daughter and more likely to send a son to a computer camp than send a daughter (Miura & Hess, 1984).

Other, more subtle differences in family treatment of male and female children with respect to computers also seem to affect computer use. In general, parents tend not to motivate their female children to be involved with computer-based technology as much as they motivate their male children. Parents also tend to purchase more computer games for boys than for girls, and frequently, the father and sons are the main computer users in the home (Nelson & Watson, 1991).

The media are also contributing to the equity problem with respect to computer use. In a recent study by the Women's Action Alliance, it was determined that only 24% of the people shown in two popular computer magazines were women. Of this 24%, the majority were not shown working at the computer, but as providing support for men who were doing the computer work. Certainly, this type of media coverage must influence self-perceptions of young women reading the magazines.

In addition to the lack of appropriate female role models depicted in the media, there also exists a lack of real role models for young girls in schools. Frequently, the computer specialist in a school or district is male. Girls need to see their female teachers working with computers, leading computer clubs, teaching computer classes, and enjoying computer work. Role models from everyday life in school will be very important to female students (Figure 7.3).

Obviously, teachers must be sensitive to these problems and make every effort to ensure equal access and opportunities with the computer for both boys and girls in their classrooms. All teachers need to develop specific approaches for helping females develop their full capabilities with respect to computer use.

FIGURE 7.3
Students need female role models who are expert computer users.
Photograph courtesy of International Business Machines Corporation.

Specific Strategies

Teachers must be sensitive about the type of software they select for classroom use. Although newer software tends to be less male dominated, much of the current educational software contains elements that tend to be much more appealing to males than to females. For example, much software uses only males as the action figures in the program. In addition, a large number of educational programs emphasize violent and competitive activities as motivators for learning. It is suggested that teachers keep these issues in mind as they make decisions about classroom computer software.

Notes From the Literature

Informal experience working with computers was found to help girls develop positive attitudes toward computers. Formal computer course work did not have the same positive effect on computer attitudes. Thus, the authors conclude that informal activities that encourage girls to gain computer experience must be developed and made available.

Aman, J. (1992). Gender and attitudes toward computers. In C. Martin & E. Murchie-Beyman (Eds.), In search of gender free paradigms for computer science education. Eugene, OR: International Society for Technology in Education.

Similar to results from research in gender differences in mathematics and science education, studies have suggested that girls working on computers with other girls perform better than girls working with boys (Martin, 1991) (Figure 7.4). Thus, teachers are encouraged to construct situations where girls are allowed to work together on the technology. Some have even created computer clubs for girls only, although there are some other equity problems inherent in excluding males from these types of opportunities.

Equal access to computers has also been a problem for young women. Studies indicate that boys tend to use computer laboratories during free time during the day and before and after school far more than do girls (Nelson & Watson, 1991). Teachers observing this type of behavior need to structure situations to ensure that girls learn to take advantage of the computer resources in the school.

Many schools and school districts have formed computer equity teams to help increase teacher awareness of equity issues and to suggest strategies for addressing these issues. These teams present programs on computer equity for faculty members, publicize newsletters on the topic, evaluate software recommended for use in the school, and create specific activities for students under-represented in computer use. In general, the existence of computer equity teams has been a positive force in schools. In one study, the authors found that sexism was least likely in schools with strong equity teams (Lee, 1992).

In addition to equity teams at the local level, there is now emerging a national concern about computer equity issues. *Computer Equity News* is a newsletter for educators promoting gender equality in computers, math, and science. Published by the Women's Action Alliance in New York, the newsletter contains information and ideas about equity projects around the country. The newsletter is a product of the Computer Equity Expert Project and is funded by the National Science Foundation, IBM Corporation, American Express, Chevron, Hewlett Packard, Intel Foundation, Xerox Foundation, and The Westinghouse Foundation. The newsletter contains specific ideas and strategies for dealing with computer equity problems.

It seems obvious that teachers must devise additional methods to combat sex equity problems with respect to computer use and attitudes. The severity of the current problem is summarized in a review by Nelson and Watson (1991):

> The computer initially was described as a revolutionary, technological advancement which would benefit all members of our society equally. After two decades of computer enhancement, however, research findings show that extreme gender-based differences still exist. Males are encouraged from preschool years to engage in computer-based activities. Females typically are generally more ignored both at home and at school. Most of the software that is marketed and then purchased by families and schools is based on male-oriented themes. (p. 351)

Low Socioeconomic Group Children

Evidence seems to indicate that children from lower socioeconomic groups are being deprived both in terms of the amount of time they spend on computers and the type of computer activities selected for them. Both issues are significant.

FIGURE 7.4
Girls working with other girls tend to achieve more while working on computers.
Photograph courtesy of International Business Machines Corporation.

Although federal grants are increasing funds to provide computers for children from low socioeconomic groups, there are still far more computers in schools that draw students from wealthy neighborhoods. In more affluent areas, parent organizations are becoming increasingly active in raising money to buy more computers for the schools. In schools that may already have larger budgets because of the tax base, concerned parents are adding to the funds to ensure computer education for their children. Although the motives of these parents are good, the results may widen the gap of opportunity between the rich and poor in this country.

In addition to having less access to computers, once they are on the computer, children from lower socioeconomic groups may not be getting the same quality activities as other schoolchildren. Research has suggested that teachers in low socioeconomic schools are much more likely to use drill-and-practice and tutorial-type software with their students, whereas schools in wealthier areas tend to use more problem-solving, student-controlled activities. These results suggest that many children from low socioeconomic groups are using computers in schools to do what they were already doing without the computer in a slightly different way. Although the real educational power of the computer lies in its ability to help students learn the problem-solving and information-handling skills so important for life in the Information Age, many poor children are not having the opportunity to use the computer in this way. Thus, the wealthier children may be benefiting more from the power of the technology than the poorer children. Again, inadvertently, teachers may be using the computer to widen already existing gaps in achievement.

Minority Students

Research indicates that minority students, like females, have less access to computers and may be the victims of stereotyping with respect to computer use. As shown in Figure 7.5, black and Hispanic children have less access to computers at home and in school than white children. Given that computer access and informal computer experience are strong predictors of computer use and computer proficiency, this type of inequity must be recognized and addressed.

Like females, minority populations also tend to be under-represented in computer journals and in computer products. In one study of computer clip art, it was shown that blacks appeared in only 1.7% of the available pictures (Brownell & McConnaughy, 1991). Because blacks make up 12.4% of the population, this is a clear discrepancy. Given that clip art is used by students for pictures in papers and projects, this type of inequity forces students to produce computer projects that do not adequately portray a diverse population. This lack of available art depicting blacks was found in clip art packages for both Apple and IBM computers.

Middle- and Low-Achieving Children

High-achieving children and children identified for talented and gifted programs get more access to computers than average- and below-average achieving students. In some schools, computer time is used as a reward for students who finish their work, and thus a student who works slowly may get little or no computer time during the year. In other schools, computers are reserved for talented and gifted programs. Other students not

FIGURE 7.5
Statistics make it clear that minority students have less use of computers and computer-related technology.

Race Gaps in Computing			
Children who use school computers in grades K–8, 1989:		Homes that have computers, 1989:	
Black children	38%	Black homes	15%
Hispanic children	43%	Hispanic homes	14%
White children	61%	White homes	36%

Data from *USA Today,* July 19, 1992.

selected for these programs receive limited or no access to the machines. Becker (1986a) states, "As much as boys dominate computer use, higher-ability students use computers at least as disproportionately" (p. 4).

No research evidence suggests that high-achieving students benefit more from computer time than other students. The practice of giving less computer time to average and below-average students, however, might widen achievement gaps between students. This allocation of computer time needs to be carefully considered in schools. The assumption that "smart kids need computers more" is an unsubstantiated prejudice and may prove harmful for society as a whole.

SUMMARY

As computer use in schools matures, teachers need to pay increasing attention to issues of computer ethics and equity. Teachers and schools must model ethical behavior with respect to hardware and software and also overtly teach principles of this behavior. It seems apparent that students do not automatically generalize ethical principles into the computer area and that schools must take specific actions to help students develop ethical behavior and attitudes in this area.

In general, computer equity issues focus on four groups of children in schools who have had other equity problems in the educational system: females, children from low socioeconomic groups, minority children, and average and low achievers. The computer has potential for enhancing the education of each of these groups. Unless, however, current practices are monitored and improved, the computer could widen existing gaps in achievement between these groups and the "more privileged" groups.

SELF-TEST QUESTIONS

1. Schools have traditionally emphasized issues of ethics and equity with respect to computer use.
   a. True
   b. False
2. Describe the characteristics of a computer virus.
3. If your computer has a virus, what should you do about it?
4. Computer viruses are relatively uncommon.
   a. True
   b. False

5. List three points that should be included in a school's computer code of ethics.
6. Describe two methods for helping to make computer ethics a meaningful and relevant topic for students.
7. Girls tend to spend more time on computers than boys.
   a. True
   b. False
8. Girls work best with other girls with respect to computer work.
   a. True
   b. False
9. Teachers are generally aware of gender differences in computer use.
   a. True
   b. False
10. Describe the "We can, but I can't" phenomenon.
11. Which of the following computer uses are most common for children from low socioeconomic groups?
    a. Problem solving
    b. Tool software
    c. Drill and practice
12. In general, low-achieving children spend more time on computers than high-achieving children.
    a. True
    b. False
13. Distinguish between computer use and computer access. Why is the distinction important?

ANSWERS TO SELF-TEST QUESTIONS

1. b. False. In the early years of educational computing, many teachers were not made aware of the importance of issues of computer ethics and equity. It is important that these issues now be carefully addressed.
2. Viruses can alter other executable software programs to include copies of themselves and can alter and harm other software programs. Viruses tend to be invisible in a software program and are frequently not noticed until they do their harm.
3. Software programs called *disinfectants* are available to identify and eliminate viruses. You may use such a program to rid your software of viruses.
4. b. False. Computer viruses are becoming increasingly common.

5. The four points listed in the chapter that might be included in a code of ethics:
   a. Use of another person's computer account or files is illegal and unethical.
   b. The use of invasive software, such as worms and viruses destructive to hardware and software and files, is illegal and unethical.
   c. Sending rude, obscene, or harassing material via any electronic mail or bulletin board facility is strictly forbidden.
   d. Copyrighted software must only be used in accordance with its license or purchase agreement.
6. One method for making computer ethics more meaningful to students is to use a hypermedia program, like the one mentioned in this chapter, to involve students in decision making in this area. Such programs allow students to make decisions in the area of ethics and then view the results of these decisions. Such approaches tend to be much more meaningful to students than having them study principles of computer ethics.

   A second idea of making computer ethics more meaningful to students is to have students collect current events items in this area. Students locating and hearing about real cases of computer ethics violations should begin to see the significance of the issue.
7. b. False. Girls tend to spend less informal time on computers than boys.
8. a. True. Similar to results in math and science education, studies have indicated that girls working with other girls are more successful with computer work than girls working with boys.
9. b. False. Studies have indicated that most teachers are unaware of the gender inequities in computer use. This fact itself, unless addressed, will serve to encourage the continuing of these inequities.
10. "We can, but I can't" is an attitude common to many females today. Females with this attitude subscribe to the general idea that females are as good as males at computer work but believe that they themselves are not capable in this area. Computer educators need to be aware of this attitude and work to help young females develop more confidence in their abilities.
11. c. In many low socioeconomic class schools, children are encouraged to use computers for remedial drill-and-practice activities. Although this is not a computer use that expands and enhances intellectual opportunities for chil-

dren, it still tends to be emphasized in poorer schools. With children in higher socioeconomic schools using computers for problem solving, simulations and intellectual tool purposes, there is a serious potential inequity in this emphasis on drill-and-practice use.
12. b. False. Currently, high-achieving children are given more access to computers than low-achieving children. Many teachers tend to believe that high-achieving students are better suited to computer experiences. This assumption indicates a basic misunderstanding of the technology on the part of these teachers.
13. Computer access refers to the availability of computers in schools and is usually described in terms of the ratio of the number of computers to the number of children in a school. Computer use, however, refers to both the amount and type of computer use actually engaged in by children. Often, groups of children do not receive equitable use of computers in schools, even though the access statistics look similar for these groups.

REFERENCES

Becker, H. J. (1986a, August). Instructional uses of school computers. *Reports of the 1985 National Survey, 2.*

Becker, H. J. (1986b, January). Our national report card: Preliminary results from the new Johns Hopkins Survey. *Classroom Computer Learning,* 30–33.

Brownell, G., & McConnaughy, K. (1991). What's wrong with this picture? *The Computing Teacher, 18*(8), 54–55.

Collis, B. (1985). Sex differences in secondary school students' attitudes toward computers. *The Computing Teacher, 12*(7), 33–36.

Collis, B., & Lloyd, O. (1990, Fall). The effect of computer use on grade 1 children's gender stereotypes about reading, writing and computer use. *Journal of Research and Development in Education,* 14–20.

Edwards, C. (1992). Implications of the computer culture for women of color. In C. Martin & E. Murchie-Beyman (Eds.), *In Search of Gender Free Paradigms for Computer Science Education* (p. 57). Eugene, OR: International Society for Technology in Education.

Hannah, L., & Matus, C. (1984). A question of ethics. *The Computing Teacher, 12*(1), 11–14.

Kessler, S. (1985). Gender relations in secondary schooling. *Sociology of Education, 58*(1), 34–38.

Lee, V. (1992). *Sexism in single-sex and co-ed schools.* Unpublished manuscript. University of Michigan, Ann Arbor, MI.

Maxwell, J., & Lamon, W. (1992). Computer viruses: Pathology and detection. *The Computing Teacher, 20*(1), 12–15.

Martin, R. (1991). School children's attitudes towards computers as a function of gender, course subjects and availability of home computers. *Journal of Computer Assisted Learning, 7,* 187–194.

Miura, I. T., & Hess, R. D. (1984). Gender difference in enrollment in computer camps and classes. *Sex Roles, 13,* 193–203.

Nelson, C., & Watson, J. (1991). The computer gender gap: Children's attitudes, performance and socialization. *The Journal of Educational Technology Systems, 19*(4), 345–353.

Sutton, R. (1991). Equity issues in educational computer uses. *Review of Educational Research, 61*(1), 1–24.

Weller, H., Repman, J., Rooze, G., & Parker, R. (1992). Students and computer ethics: An alternative to preaching. *The Computing Teacher, 20*(1), 20–22.

REFERENCES FOR ADDITIONAL STUDY

Aman, J. (1992). Gender and attitudes toward computers. In C. Martin & E. Murchie-Beyman (Eds.). *In search of gender free paradigms for computer science education.* Eugene, OR: International Society for Technology in Education.

Cole, M., Griffin, P., & the Laboratory of Comparative Human Cognition. (1987). *Contextual factors in education: Improving science and mathematics education for minorities and women.* Paper prepared for Committee on Research in Mathematics, Science, and Technology Education, Commission on Behavioral and Social Science and Education, National Research Council. Madison, WI: Wisconsin Center for Education Research.

Hawkins, J. (1985). Computers and girls: Rethinking the issues. *Sex Roles, 13*(3/4), 165–180.

Kramer, P., & Lehman, S. (1990) Mismeasuring women: A critique of research on computer ability and avoidance. *Journal of Women in Culture and Society, 16*(1), 158–172.

Martin, C., & Murchie-Beyman, E. (1992). *In search of gender free paradigms for computer science education.* Eugene, OR: International Society for Technology in Education.

Mayo, J. L. *Computer viruses: What they are, how they work, and how to avoid them.* Blue Ridge Summit, PA: Wintercrest Books.

McAdoo, M. (1994) Equity: Has technology bridged the gap? *Electronic Learning, 13*(7), 24–34.

Sanders, J., & Stone, A. (1987). *The neuter computer: Why and how to encourage computer equity for girls.* New York: Women's Action Alliance.

PART TWO

APPLICATIONS OF EDUCATIONAL COMPUTING

CHAPTER EIGHT

MANAGING TEXT

Word Processing and Desktop Publishing

GOAL

This chapter will introduce the reader to the basic capabilities of the word processor and applications of these capabilities in education.

OBJECTIVES

The reader will be able to do the following:

1. Describe the basic characteristics of all word processing programs.
2. Describe types of word processing programs frequently used in education.
3. Define *desktop publishing*. Describe desktop publishing programs frequently used in education.
4. Describe the advantages of using a word processing or desktop publishing system.
5. Indicate types of uses teachers can make of word processing systems.
6. Define the four major stages of the writing process and describe specific word processing activities that can help with each of these stages.
7. Describe at least two applications of word processing technology in each of the following areas: reading, science, social studies.

If freewriting silences that inner censor who is so instrumental in preventing people from committing their words to paper, then typing on the computer terminal is better than freewriting . . . it is easier to suspend your judgment about what you are writing. My writing has more of a voice, my sentences are more textured, simply because I enjoy the ease with which I can type at the terminal without the encumbrances of keys that get jammed or the fear of making mistakes.

Aversa, quoted in Daiute & Taylor, 1981

WHAT IS WORD PROCESSING?

Although hundreds of word processing programs are available to educators, all share certain characteristics. A word processing program is computer software designed to facilitate the efficient collecting, revising, storing, and printing of text.

Common Characteristics of Word Processing Programs

Almost all word processing programs provide the following features:

  Collecting text
  Editing and revising text
  Saving text
  Printing text

Collecting Text.   A word processing program allows the user to enter text with the computer keyboard. The text is displayed on the computer monitor and stored temporarily in the computer. With most systems, text is entered much as it would be typed with a typewriter. Unlike most typewriters, however, the majority of word processing systems have something called a "wrap-around" feature. This feature allows the word processing program to determine the end of each line of text and automatically move the cursor to the next line. Users never use the return key unless they wish to force a return, such as at the end of a paragraph. Although this wrap-around capability is convenient for later formatting of the text, experienced typists initially have trouble remembering not to press the return key at the end of a line of text.

With any word processing system, erasing mistakes at the time of text entry is very simple. Usually, the user

simply presses the delete or backspace key to erase the character immediately to the left of the cursor and then types the correct entry. In addition, most systems allow the user to move the cursor anywhere in the text and add or delete information. Thus, corrections can be made as the text is entered, or later in the process.

Editing and Revising Text.   Obviously, there must be more to word processing systems than enabling simple entry and correction of text. Most modern typewriters now provide easy correction at the time of entry. In addition to these features, the word processor enables the typist to revise and edit text after it is initially entered. Almost all word processing systems provide the following revising and editing features: replacing, moving, inserting, and deleting.

Replacing.   If the writer realizes that she has misspelled *commitment* several times in a document, all misspellings can be corrected with one command. The writer merely calls the replace function, types in the misspelled word, and then enters the correct spelling of the word. Typically, the prompt will appear on the screen and resemble the prompts below:

  Replace what? comitment
  With? commitment
  One at a time?

The program then locates each misspelling of the word and corrects it. The question "One at a time?" is asking the writer if she wants all the occurrences replaced at once or whether she would like to make a decision about each occurrence individually.

Moving.   Before word processors, writers usually moved paragraphs around their document by cutting out pieces of the text, and taping them into the new spot. With the word processor, the writer just highlights the text she wishes to move, then moves the cursor to the new location and clicks. The text flows in at the new location. Some systems even have an automatic "move-back" capability that allows the writer to move the text back to the original location if desired. In any case, the writer can always use the move commands again to locate and move the text if she does not like the move.

Inserting and Deleting.   With most systems, the user can move the cursor to any position in the text to add or delete information. After the insertion or deletion, the text is automatically reformatted or reorganized.

Saving Text. As text is entered with a word processing system, it is temporarily stored in the computer. All systems also allow the permanent storage of text in a secondary storage location, usually on a disk. With one or two strokes on the keyboard, the writer can save work to a file on a disk. A typical microcomputer disk will store numerous files and hold more than 100 pages of text. Any of these files can be accessed easily, revised, and printed in minutes.

Printing Text. Obviously, none of the capabilities mentioned would be of much use without the ability to obtain a printed copy of the text. All word processing programs provide some means for interfacing with a printer for printing out the completed copy. Most programs offer extra printing features such as underlining, italics, boldface, page numbering, and optional print sizes and fonts.

Hardware Configurations

To use a word processor, you usually need both hardware and software. Most schools own general-purpose microcomputers that can be turned into word processors with the appropriate word processing software package. Printers are needed to obtain "hard copy" of student and teacher work.

Systems Frequently Used in Education

As more word processing systems come on the market, selecting the best system for a school or classroom has become more difficult. Systems that have gained popularity in education are usually easy to use and reasonably priced. These systems can be categorized as follows:

Learner-oriented systems
Single-function (word processing), "adult systems"
Multifunction, integrated systems
Desktop publishing systems

Elementary teachers usually select their software from the learner-oriented systems, whereas secondary teachers usually desire the more advanced features available in the word processors in the second and third categories. There are, however, multifunction systems appropriate for use in the elementary school.

Learner-Oriented Systems

In the early 1980s, Bank Street College produced the first version of the Bank Street Writer, a word processing system designed for learners. At a time when word processing programs tended to be both complicated and cumbersome, the Bank Street Writer was advertised as an easy to use, intuitive system, appropriate for home and classroom use. Instructions were printed on the screen, language was simple and nontechnical, and teachers and students were attracted to the system and used it extensively. Some have suggested that the popularity of the Bank Street Writer was that teachers could learn the system easily. Most students had few problems with the early, more cumbersome programs, but some of these were difficult for teachers. In any case, others have followed with "learner-oriented word processors," but the Bank Street College must be given credit for the first such system and for doing much to make word processing readily available in the schools.

Because of advancing technology, most word-processing systems are now user-friendly and fairly easy to learn. Many of the advantages of the Bank Street Writer are now standard features on all systems.

The Bank Street Writer itself has been continually updated and is now much easier to use and more powerful than initial versions and is still used extensively in the schools. New versions of the system include advanced features such as an on-line speller and thesaurus. There is also a 20-column version of the Bank Street Writer, which allows entry and printing of primary-size type included in the package and has a built-in calculator.

Two other learner-oriented systems frequently used in the early years of elementary and middle school computer use are the Magic Slate by Sunburst and FrEdwriter. Magic Slate is a versatile system that has gained popularity because it allows young students to collect text in primary-size type. Although many word processing systems now offer the choice of 20, 40, or 80 columns, Magic Slate was the first to offer this option. Magic Slate also makes extensive use of icons in its menus so young writers can select options by using pictures. Other options include split screen, definable function keys, and choices of type styles. Thus, in addition to providing a good first experience for young word processors, Magic Slate offers more sophisticated features for middle and high school students. The newer version of Magic Slate, called Magic Slate II, offers a built-in speller, a variety of fonts, and prompted writing (discussed later in this chapter), among other features.

One of the most appealing early educational word processing programs was the system called FrEdwriter (stands for Free Education Writer), published by Steele Publishing, through The San Diego County Office of Education (Figure 8.1). FrEdwriter, produced by the authors of the original top-selling Applewriter program, is a freeware processing program produced by and for educators. The authors of FrEdwriter state, "This program is freeware. You are free to distribute copies, but you may not sell them." FrEdwriter contains all the basic word processing functions, operates on the entire Apple II family of computers, and is available in Spanish and English. Because it is freeware, and thus students and teachers can have their own copies of the system, FrEdwriter is widely used in the schools. In an article on FrEdwriter, computer coordinator Gwen Solomon (1987) states the following:

> Since it's hard to beat free, I decided to compare the other word processors [with] FrEdwriter to see if there is good reason to spend money on a word processor for our English classes. I found that, although it doesn't have all of the frills and features of the more expensive programs, FrEdwriter stands out if you need something basic. (p. 30)

FrEdwriter also has a feature that allows teachers and students to easily produce prompted writing activities for students. Given this capability, teachers can write instructions, called *prompts*, to aid student writing. Students write their responses below the prompts and can print out their documents with or without the prompts.

Prompted writing has been compared to the use of training wheels on a bicycle; students first write correctly with the prompts and soon no longer need them.

FrEdwriter comes with a set of 10 disks. The first disk is the word processor itself, and the other disks contain information about using FrEdwriter and model lesson plans for teaching the writing process to students in grades 3 to 12. These model lessons were produced by classroom teachers.

The producers of FrEdwriter have also set up a system so that teachers can share the writing exercises they produce on the system. Teachers can submit their student activities and receive copies of activities produced by other teachers.

Storybook Weaver (Figure 8.2) enables young writers to create their own stories with a simple word processor and to illustrate these stories. Students can use prepared graphics in the program to build their own illustrations. Based on themes popular to children, the package has been used successfully by elementary teachers to motivate student interest in writing and producing creative products.

Another learner-oriented word processing program gaining popularity in elementary schools is Kid Works 2. By combining word processing and painting capabilities, pictures, and sound, Kid Works 2 provides a holistic writing environment for young children. The program's special features enable emergent writers to make the connections between symbols and printed words, while it supports more advanced learners to write, illustrate and listen to their own stories.

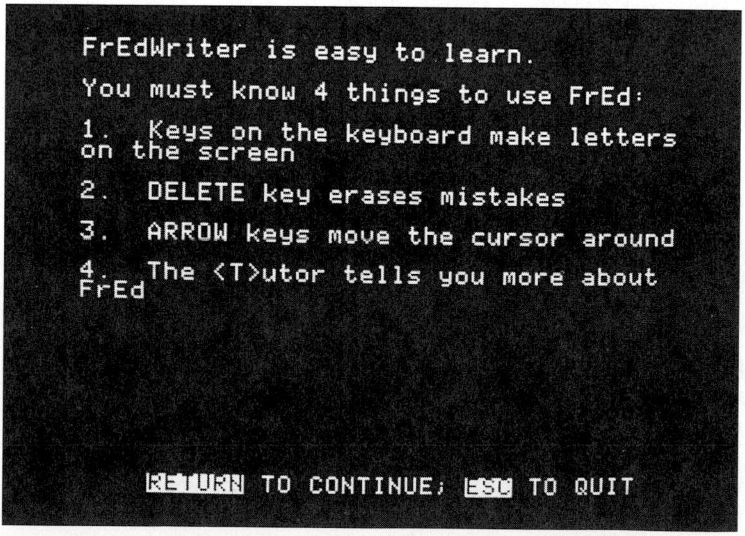

FIGURE 8.1
FrEdwriter is a full-function word processing package that can be duplicated by teachers and distributed to students at no charge.

```
FrEdWriter is easy to learn.
You must know 4 things to use FrEd:
1.   Keys on the keyboard make letters
on the screen
2.   DELETE key erases mistakes
3.   ARROW keys move the cursor around
4.   The <T>utor tells you more about
FrEd

         RETURN TO CONTINUE; ESC TO QUIT
```

FIGURE 8.2
Storybook Weaver is an excellent writing tool for young children.

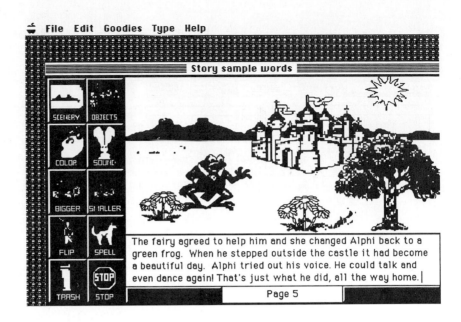

Single-Function, "Adult" Systems

Many schools use single-function, general-purpose word processing systems in instruction. This is especially true at the middle and high school level. Microsoft Word, available for both Macintosh and IBM computers, is a popular single-purpose system used in schools (Figure 8.3).

Newer versions of Microsoft Word have several sophisticated features useful for school writing activities. For example, Microsoft Word 6.0 contains a grammar checker that gives students information about the quality of their writing. The grammar checker indicates the reading grade level of the writing, so students know that their writing is readable at the 5th- or 7th- or perhaps 12th-grade level. The grammar checker also looks for common student writing mistakes such as clichés or passive voice. The checker, of course, does not change any of these usages; it merely points them out to the student.

Multifunction, Integrated Word Processors

There are also software packages available that combine word processing capabilities with additional tool uses of the computer. These integrated packages usually combine word processing, spreadsheets, and data bases. Some also include graphics capabilities. Integrated packages allow the user to combine tables and text quite easily. These packages also facilitate learning different tool applications because the basic computer commands and procedures remain constant across the different applications. Thus, whether the user is word processing or creating a budget on a spreadsheet or organizing information on a data base, the basic commands for operating the system remain the same. A third advantage of these systems is that they are usually less expensive than the software for each of the tools purchased individually.

AppleWorks was one of the first such integrated packages frequently used in classrooms (Figure 8.4). AppleWorks contains word processing, spreadsheet, and data base management capabilities. Companion packages may be purchased to add graphics capabilities. Using the AppleWorks system, tables from the data base or the spreadsheet can be easily pasted into the word processor and become part of the written document. To do this, users first create the appropriate files in the data base or spreadsheet. These files are then printed to something called the clipboard. During this process, the files are not printed out in hard-copy form; instead, they are printed into a format that is readable by the word processor part of AppleWorks. Once the file is printed onto the clipboard, the user can open a word processing document and select the desired location for the table. The user then instructs the program to move the contents of the clipboard to the location of the cursor. From elementary school through high school, AppleWorks has gained tremendous popularity in the schools. Although Apple II and GS computers

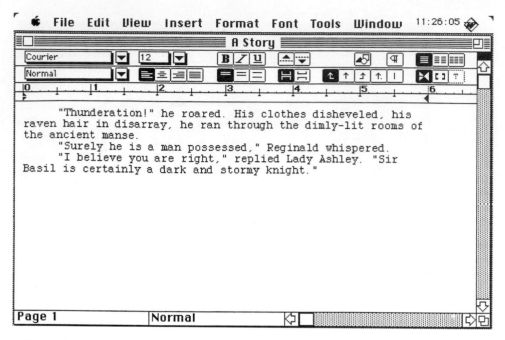

FIGURE 8.3
Microsoft Word is a word processing program with multiple capabilities.

are being phased out of schools, use of improved integrated programs similar to AppleWorks that run on Macintosh or IBM computers is increasing in schools.

Microsoft Works, available for the Macintosh and IBM microcomputers, is another integrated package that is gaining widespread use in schools. Similar to AppleWorks, Microsoft Works contains word processing, data base, and spreadsheet capabilities (Figure 8.4). In addition, telecommunications, desktop publishing, and graphing capabilities are included in the package. Simple manuals on using Microsoft Works in classrooms are now available for teachers.

ClarisWorks is a Macintosh or IBM software package that allows access to tools and features from word processing, graphics, spreadsheets, charting, data base management, and communications. The graphics capabilities of this package are flexible and feature graphics tools so that students can easily create their own graphics as well as select prepared graphics. ClarisWorks is currently a very popular integrated program for school use.

LOGOwriter is a multifunction word processing system of a different type. LOGOwriter combines word processing capabilities with LOGO programming. With LOGOwriter, students can write text to accompany

their programming and graphics projects. This is in addition to using the system only as a word processor or only as a programming language.

WHAT IS DESKTOP PUBLISHING?

Desktop publishing software is being used increasingly in schools, and usually features the ability to produce and combine text and graphics, arrange text in

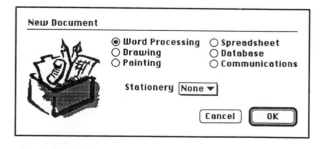

FIGURE 8.4
Microsoft Works is an integrated word processing package that is used extensively in schools.

columns, and vary fonts and styles. These special-purpose systems enable students and teachers to produce high-quality, professional-looking bulletins, newsletters, and newspapers right in the classroom. More advanced desktop publishing systems allow users to produce professional-looking magazines and journals.

Desktop Publishing Used in Schools

The Print Shop from Broderbound was one of the first such systems and has been very popular in classrooms. The Print Shop combines graphics and text capabilities and allows users to produce signs, banners, greeting cards, and letterheads. The program is extremely user-friendly. The user need only follow the instructions on the screen to produce very professional-looking products.

Because it is so easy to use, The Print Shop can be a good program to involve reluctant or anxious teachers in using the computer. Generally, teachers are very impressed with the products they obtain quickly and efficiently using The Print Shop. As the advertisements for the program suggest, anyone who can read instructions on the screen can successfully use The Print Shop. Many schools report that The Print Shop disk gets worn out because so many teachers use it so often. This very simple desktop publishing capability may be just the "hook" necessary to get these teachers interested in additional classroom uses of the computer.

The Print Shop, however, does not allow the use of large amounts of text. It can be used for communicating short messages, but the educator interested in producing newspapers and longer bulletins must look to other desktop publishing software.

The Children's Writing and Publishing Center also combines graphics and text and allows users to produce illustrated newspapers and newsletters (Figure 8.5). With The Children's Writing and Publishing Center, students and teachers can produce fairly professional-looking newspapers in the classroom. This system, available for both Apple II and Macintosh computers, is simple to learn and use.

PageMaker is a powerful desktop publishing system available for the Macintosh computer. With PageMaker, teachers and students can produce professional-looking printed products ranging from bulletins to entire journals (Figure 8.6). Increasingly, schools and districts are deciding to buy a powerful system like PageMaker instead of spending money on professional printing.

Notes From the Literature

When desktop publishing, use one type style per publication, avoid the liberal use of italics, bold, underline, or outline text. Use a complementary typeface for headlines and subheads such as sans serif headlines for serif text. Serif typefaces for text are usually best. Use all-capitals sparingly.

The optical center of a page is ⅖ of the way down from the top, so optimize this space. The lower right-hand corner is the least read portion of the page. This is a good place for the table of contents or an unimportant article. Place photos above corresponding text not below.

Rose, S. Y. (1988). A desktop publishing primer. The Computer Teacher, 15(9), 13–15.

FIGURE 8.5
The Children's Writing and Publishing Center can be used to create newsletters and newspapers, as well as illustrated stories.

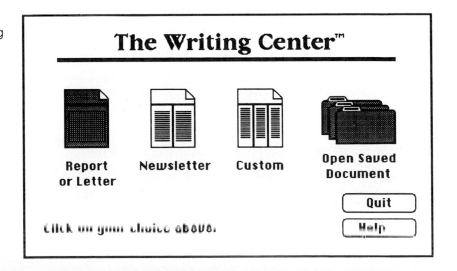

Journal of
Computing
in
Teacher Education

Volume 7 Number 4 • Summer 1991

A refereed publication of the ISTE Special Interest Group for Teacher Educators

FIGURE 8.6
PageMaker can be used to publish journals like this one "at home."

Newer programs are beginning to combine word processing and desktop publishing capabilities into one system. The Writing Center is a combination word processing–desktop publishing program designed primarily for elementary and middle school writers. The program contains many of the capabilities of both a word processor and a desktop publisher and can import files from other systems. Combining text and graphics with the system is very simple. In addition, The Writing Center also includes a spell checker and thesaurus.

WHY WORD PROCESSING AND DESKTOP PUBLISHING?

The capabilities provided by word processing and desktop publishing systems offer tremendous possibilities for educators. Specifically, it appears that word processing and desktop publishing, properly used by the teacher, can help improve the quality of student writing and also students' attitudes toward writing.

In 1990, the most common use of the computer in schools was for word processing (Becker, 1991). These results were replicated in Becker's 1994 study. Becker noted in both his studies that most schools were teaching the skill of word processing itself, however, and not emphasizing word processing as a tool for improving writing. Thus, it is imperative that teachers begin to understand how to use the word processor in the teaching of writing and that they understand that word processors themselves do not improve writing. It is only the combination of the capabilities of the word processor and the facilitation of a knowledgeable teacher of writing that will enable the potential of the word processor to be realized in the classroom.

Given the characteristics of word processors outlined in the previous section, it seems obvious that word processing has the potential to improve the teaching and learning of writing. Research on the effects of word processing on the writing process is still in its early stages, but studies have begun to suggest that word processing can improve student attitudes toward writing, increase the amount of time students spend writing, and also increase students' willingness to revise their writing. Properly managed and encouraged, all of these factors can be used to improve student writing.

Students writing using word processing systems can easily and quickly revise and edit their work. Before word processing, elementary students typically wrote one draft of a writing assignment and only rewrote the draft if it was judged unsatisfactory by the teacher. With the advent of the word processor came the opportunity for the teacher to ask students to incorporate suggestions in drafts of their writing. The first draft might be critiqued by peers and then revised for submission to the teacher. The second draft might then be critiqued by the teacher and then revised into "final" form. Given this type of model, young writers can learn to write, expecting to revise and improve their work.

Built-in capabilities also can help encourage students to revise their work. Spelling and grammar checkers give students an opportunity to obtain suggestions for changes in their work and provide motivation for changing the work.

Combined with other communication capabilities, the word processor or desktop publishing system can also be used to enhance the young writer's sense of audience. With the addition of a telephone modem and communication software, the classroom computer can become a vehicle for written communication among students at different schools, in different states, and even in different countries. In these situations, the students are writing to "real" audiences and have an opportunity to experience a heightened sense of writing as communication with a real person. Students are no longer writing just as an exercise for the teacher; they are writing with a specific communication goal in mind.

Students in one Midwestern school were recently connected with students of the same age in a school in a southern state. For this project, students had the opportunity to do some direct, on-line communication, in addition to sending information previously collected to and saved on disks. In initial exercises, students were asked to exchange information about their schools and communities. The students in the Midwestern school immediately began to comment on the poor spelling and grammar they were reading in the work of their southern partners. When the Midwestern teacher asked her students if they thought the partner students might be making the same observation about their writing, the Midwestern students became much more conscious of their own writing. The teacher immedi-

Notes From the Literature

School access to word processing, which is certainly a type of cognitive enrichment software, is probably inequitably available to school children simply by virtue of the fact that poor children have fewer computers in their schools than do middle- and upper-class children. But, beyond this general condition, it may well be that students have unequal opportunities to write with word processing based on class, race, or gender differences within school and classroom settings (p. 146).

Cole, M., Griffin, P., & the Laboratory of Comparative Human Cognition. (1987). Contextual factors in education: Improving science and mathematics education for minorities and women. Paper prepared for Committee on Research in Mathematics, Science, and Technology Education, Commission on Behavioral and Social Science and Education, National Research Council. Madison: Wisconsin Center for Education Research.

ately observed more self-checking and also more requests to have other students proofread work. It became clear that the awareness of writing to a "real" audience improved student interest in correct grammar, spelling, and punctuation.

Others have also confirmed the value of having students use word processors and telecommunications to enable writing to real audiences. "When writing became a way to share their ideas across time and distance, teachers reported a surprising enthusiasm among students for writing and revision. Students worried about the accuracy of their information as well as the form of their writing" (Riel, 1990, p. 35).

In a similar way, desktop publishing software allows students to produce professional-looking bulletins, newsletters, and newspapers for their peers or parents. Again, the act of writing takes on new meaning as students write with a specific message and audience in mind. Before word processing and desktop publishing capabilities, students all too often viewed writing as an exercise carried out with only the teacher as audience.

In addition to potentially improving the quality of writing, word processing allows the writer to operate much more efficiently. The initial collecting of text is faster and more easily corrected. The writer can store a large number of files on disk and access these files very easily. Any can be called up, revised, and printed in a matter of seconds.

It should be noted, however, that not all writers enjoy working with a word processor. Some think text is collected too quickly on the processor and that the slow speed of the pencil is more conducive to thoughtful writing. Others suggest that obtaining a nice-looking printout early in the writing process can be deceiving—the product may look better than it really is. In any case, most agree that the capabilities of the word processor have possible applications in the teaching of writing.

make good instructional decisions about the appropriate use of the word processor with their students. Word processing is clearly a powerful capability, but teachers must experience this power themselves before attempting to use it in the teaching of writing.

Teachers beginning to work with a word processing system should use the same software they plan to use with their students. In their initial work with the system, teachers will encounter many of the questions and problems students will have with the system.

Letter writing is usually a good way to begin to learn a word processing system. Formatting is simple, the product is usually short, and the revision capabilities of the system can be used to modify the letter for different audiences. Usually, it is easiest to begin with personal letters. Learners can experience the power of some of the revision capabilities by writing to a relative, saving and printing the letter, and then revising it so it can be sent to a second friend or relative. In the revision, the salutation can be changed, information pertinent to the new audience can be added, and irrelevant information for the new audience can be deleted. After these initial experiences, teachers can create form letters for field trips, clubs, progress reports, and then modify these for individual parents or occasions. Time saved, even with this very basic use of the word processor, can be considerable.

As teachers advance in their abilities to use the word processor, class files can be created, printed, and saved on the system. Course outlines, quizzes, tests, spelling lists, and assignments can all be created and saved on a word processor. Desktop publishing programs can be used to produce newsletters for students, organizations, or parents. Teachers can then easily and efficiently update and revise all of these materials. Materials can also be easily individualized for students as teachers make changes in the basic document appropriate for each student or group of students.

WORD PROCESSING FOR THE TEACHER

Before classroom teachers can best use word processing capabilities with their students, teachers must use word processors for their own writing tasks. As indicated previously, word processing changes the writing process. Through using the word processor, teachers will experience the flexibility and efficiency afforded by the word processor. These experiences should equip teachers to

WORD PROCESSING IN THE TEACHING OF WRITING

It seems clear that the ease and flexibility of writing with a word processing system offer intriguing possibilities for teachers of writing. Since most teachers from kindergarten through graduate school are in one way or another teachers of writing, these possibilities should be of almost universal interest among both preservice and in-service teachers.

The word processor itself, of course, is not a teacher of writing. It is only when the capabilities of the word processor are combined with the expertise of the individual teacher that activities making good use of the available technology can be developed. Reviews of the research on word processing in the teaching of writing suggest that the effect of word processing on student writing quality is directly affected by the type of use an individual teacher makes of a word processor (Cochran-Smith, 1991). Thus, as was stated in the previous section, teachers are strongly urged to become familiar with the technology themselves before they attempt to develop teaching applications. Throughout this text, teachers will be encouraged to become familiar with the different types of software for their own use before using the tools with their students.

Many schools use word processors, but in many cases, the system's true capabilities are not used in the teaching of writing. In one school, students are permitted to enter a document on the word processor only after they have it in perfect form. All the editing and revising is finished before the document ever enters the system. Obviously, such a use of the word processor ignores some of the unique reasons for using the technology in the first place.

As classroom teachers become more familiar with word processing capabilities, they develop a growing list of activities and ideas for appropriately using this technology in the classroom. The Bank Street Activity Files were among the first sets of published materials designed to provide teachers with a range of prepared activities to use with the word processor. The Bank Street Activity Files are a two-volume set of prepared activities for use with The Bank Street Writer.

Since the publication of The Bank Street Activity Files, other companies have followed with prepared word processing activities for the classroom. Several publishers have produced similar files for use with Magic Slate, AppleWorks and Microsoft Works. As mentioned earlier, the publishers of FrEdwriter are also committed to the creation and sharing of activity files for teachers.

Keyboarding

To obtain the full benefit from a word processing system, students need to be able to enter text easily and efficiently. The term *keyboarding* refers to entering information on electronic equipment through the use of a typewriter-like keyboard. Keyboarding is the skill that enables an individual to use a computer keyboard efficiently. Keyboarding differs from typing because it does not include the formatting and business communication skills usually included in a typing class.

Because most elementary and middle school children have not had a formal class in keyboarding and/or typing, most of them do not possess this capability. One need only look around in a class of 3rd- or 4th-grade students using computers to see that most of these students have developed all types of "creative" and inefficient methods for finding and hitting keys on the computer keyboard. One educator has suggested that unless schools address the keyboarding issue soon, an entire generation of typists with bad habits will be created.

As indicated in Chapter 6, on computer literacy, there is much discussion and concern among computer educators about the need to teach keyboarding in elementary school so that students can make full use of word processors. Many elementary schools have instituted programs to teach keyboarding in grades 3 and 4 and have reported positive results from these programs (Figure 8.7). Many of the programs use computer software (Paws and Keyboarding are two examples) as the basis of their instruction. None have reported any psychomotor problems with children learning keyboarding skills at this age.

Notes From the Literature

Cochran-Smith (1991) considered the benefits of word processing for children in elementary classrooms. After analyzing the extensive body of research she concluded, "The literature clearly indicates that the ways word processing is used for writing result from the interaction of teachers' goals, the social organizations of classrooms, and the features of word processing. But we need to know more about what those ways are, what they look like at various grade levels, and how they are played out over relatively long periods of time in individual classrooms. Instructional intervention is important and the effectiveness of word processing for writing depends on the nature of instruction that accompanies its implementation. We need to know more about the kinds of instruction teachers provide when they teach writing with word processing to beginning writers, and we need to know how this instruction changes over time" (p. 147).

Cochran-Smith, M. (1991). Word processing and writing in elementary classrooms. A critical review of related literature. Review of Educational Research, 61(1), 107–155.

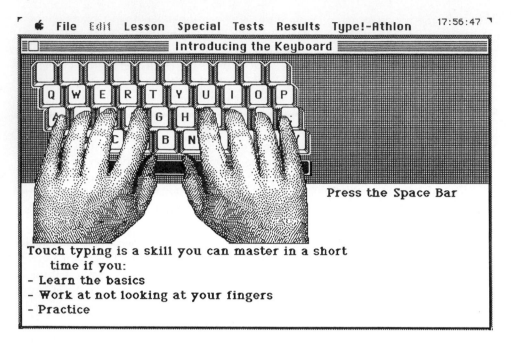

FIGURE 8.7
Several programs have been quite successful in helping children develop keyboarding skills.

There is debate, however, about the appropriateness of teaching keys in the elementary school. Some business educators argue that elementary teachers are neither trained nor equipped to teach correct skills. Many insist that only business educators are qualified to teach keyboarding in the elementary schools. Others suggest that perhaps the business educators could design the keyboarding curriculum and instruct the elementary teachers, who would then work with the students. Some argue that a course meeting one hour a day for at least one semester is necessary to teach these skills. Still others suggest that there is no time in the elementary school curriculum for the teaching of keyboarding.

It seems clear to most educators, however, that by the late 1990s, elementary schoolchildren will be making extensive use of computer tools in the learning process. Although some educational computing programs require little keyboarding skill, it is clear that high-level keyboarding skills are required for entering computer programming code and for word processing.

For many years, ninth grade was considered the most appropriate time to teach typing skills. Most students did not have access to typewriters before their high school years, so earlier instruction would not have been practiced much outside the class. Needs have

changed, however, and 9th or 10th grade is no longer the most appropriate time to teach keyboarding. Educators must resolve the problem and devise a method of meeting the needs of children.

The amount of time necessary to teach keyboarding skills appropriate for word processing is currently under study and discussion. Wetzel (1985) suggests that, based on his review of the research, most students in grades 3 through 5 will average 10 words per minute after receiving teacher instruction and practice on a microcomputer 35 minutes a day for 4 weeks. If this schedule is extended to 9 weeks, the average student will type 15 to 20 words per minute. Wetzel suggests that word processing can begin when students achieve 10 words per minute.

Assuming that learners have basic keyboarding skills, word processing can be used effectively to enhance each stage of the writing process. The writing process is frequently divided into four major stages: prewriting, composing, revising, and editing. Word processing provides unique capabilities for the teaching of each of these stages. In the following sections, each of these phases of the writing process will be briefly described, and word processing activities for that phase will be suggested. Readers are encouraged to devise their own word processing activities for these stages.

Prewriting

The prewriting phase of the writing process is the time for exploration of ideas before the more formal composition. During prewriting, the writer can collect ideas, make notes, brainstorm, play with ideas and approaches, and sketch out a structure or outline for later work. Generally, the prewriting time should be free and open and encourage the production of ideas for later specific development.

The ease of adding, deleting, and revising text with a word processor encourages teachers and students to focus more attention on the prewriting phase of the writing process. With a word processor, students can freely collect ideas, then later go back and add structure and detail, finally forming it into the finished product.

Several techniques have been developed to use word processing in the prewriting process. One idea is to have students brainstorm a list of possible essay topics and then save these topics in a file. Each time the student thinks of another topic, it is added to the list. When the student is ready to write an essay, he goes to the file to search for a topic.

The concept of free-writing can be used effectively as a prewriting exercise with the word processor. In a free-writing exercise, writers are encouraged to sit down at the computer and write as they think. Writers are encouraged to let ideas flow freely and easily and not to worry about form, structure, or details of grammar and punctuation. A free-writing exercise can serve to collect ideas and themes for later work, much like a brainstorming session. Instructions for a typical free-writing exercise might be, "You now have a few minutes to let your mind go and write down everything you are thinking about. Relax and do not worry about structure or organization; just write as the words come to you." Ideas collected and recorded in such a session can later be more formally and carefully developed.

Daiute (1985) suggests that free-writing techniques are valuable in writing instructions for several reasons.

> After freewriting, students see that they have ideas and information to express. . . . Freewriting techniques are most useful for limbering, practicing, and recording. Exploration with the techniques gives teachers and students insights into their own unique writing processes. Writers who use this technique begin by discovering what they have to say and finding their voice. Polishing comes later.

Invisible writing is another possible prewriting word processing activity (Marcus & Blau, 1983). Students are given a topic or a "started sentence" and then asked to turn off the monitor of their computer. Students are then asked to relax and write freely and quickly about the topic. They are instructed not to worry about errors in their writing. Because they cannot see their work, students quickly forget about editing and focus on developing and expressing ideas. Several researchers have collected student reactions to the invisible writing experience, and the following student reaction is somewhat typical:

> At first I felt really frustrated because I knew I was making mistakes and couldn't see or fix them. After a while, though, I just thought "what the heck" and concentrated on what I was writing. Once I did that, I was able to write freely and easily and really enjoyed the experience. All I thought about was the ideas and not the editing. (Thompson & Jarchow, 1985, p. 4)

Teachers can also produce questions and activities that aid students in the prewriting phase. These activities can help students both generate and focus ideas for later writing. One example of this type of activity is the "My Most Unusual Relative" activity (Figure 8.8). Obviously, the idea development and focus procedure exemplified in this activity can be adapted to many topics and subjects.

Commercial programs that help in the prewriting phase are also available. Some of these programs are templates for particular word processors, while others are self-contained programs focused on one aspect of the prewriting process.

Although traditionally, teachers and students of writing have tended to skip over the prewriting phase of writing and emphasize more formal composing, word processing provides a tool for emphasizing the idea-generating and exploration part of the writing process. As educators continue to develop activities and ideas for encouraging prewriting, young writers will share more and more in the joy of exploration, until recently only enjoyed by the professional writer.

Composing

Up to this time, many writing teachers have focused on the composing stage of writing. During this phase, writers produce the first formal draft of their work. Attention is focused on organization, incorporation of details, grammar, and usage. Certainly, word processors facilitate this part of the writing process. Writers can easily enter text, revise as they write, and save their work when they take a break from writing. They can then return to their work and take up entering text

FIGURE 8.8
Exercise to Aid Students in the Prewriting Phase

My Most Unusual Relative

Make a list of the names of all your close relatives. Begin the list with your closest relatives (mother, father, brothers, sisters) and then expand to grandparents, aunts, uncles and cousins.

List of My Relatives

Looking over your list, choose the person who is your most unusual relative. Name that person below. Use a complete sentence.

My Most Unusual Relative

Now, describe the physical characteristics of that relative. What does his/her face look like? Color of hair? Height? Unusual physical features? How does he or she usually dress?

Now describe the personality of this relative. Is he or she friendly? talkative? intelligent? funny?

Explain what you find unusual about this relative. Include as much detail as possible.

right where they stopped. At any time during the process, the writer can obtain a nicely formatted printout of the document in progress.

When using a word processor, writers are freed from the straight sequential writing pattern dictated by a typewriter or paper and pencil. The writer can write sequentially but also go back and insert an idea at any point in the text. The writer can also write about a particular idea and later decide where to insert it into the text.

Given the flexibility of the word processor, authors can easily incorporate their prewriting work into the composing phase of the process. Outlines constructed in prewriting activities can be expanded into the actual document. Free-writing activities can be revised and edited and also serve as the base document for later work.

Using a technique called *prompted writing,* teachers can also aid students with the structure and organization during the composing process. As mentioned earlier, these prompted writing activities can

FIGURE 8.8
(continued)

Go back to the original list of relatives, and find the relative who dislikes this unusual relative the most. Describe why this relative dislikes him or her.

_____

_____

Now find a relative who likes this unusual relative. Describe what this relative likes about him or her.

_____

_____

Finally, describe how you feel about your most unusual relatives. Be sure to give your reasons.

_____

_____

Now you are ready to remove the original list of relatives and all the writing prompts. Only your writing should remain. When you have done this, go back and revise and edit your essay entitled "My Most Unusual Relative." Be sure you add good transition sentences between main titles.

_____

_____

---

be much like the use of training wheels for young bicycle users. After a few prompted writing exercises, students no longer need the prompts as the responses to the questions become an automatic part of the writing process.

Figure 8.9 is an example of a prompted writing exercise that is structured to help young writers include more explicit detail in their writing. Note that students write below the prompts. Many programs then allow the students to print out their writing without the teacher prompts. If this capability is not built in, of course, students can just delete the prompts before printing.

Prompted writing offers numerous possibilities for teachers attempting to help students structure their writing during the composing phase of the writing process. Simple prompts can be used to encourage students to write topic sentences, include supporting details, and write summary statements in paragraphs. More complex prompts can be used to encourage specific structure or style in specific writing situations.

FIGURE 8.9
Prompted Writing Exercise

CHARACTER DESCRIPTION
ANNE TYLER
IN
THE ACCIDENTAL TOURIST

Macon wore a formal summer suit, his traveling suit—much more logical for traveling than jeans, he always said. Jeans had those still, hard seams and those rivets. Sarah wore a strapless terry beach dress. They might have been returning from two entirely different trips. Sarah had a tan, but Macon didn't. He was a tall, pale, gray-eyed man, with straight fair hair cut close to his head, and his skin was that thin kind that easily burns. He'd kept away from the sun during the middle part of the day.

For this exercise, you will collect text after each item below. Collect text for item 1 and then move the cursor below item 2 to collect the appropriate text for that item. Follow this procedure until you are finished.

_____

1. Notice that the author begins by telling us what Macon is wearing. Start your description the same way.

_____

2. The author then describes why the character has chosen to wear this outfit and contrasts it with another possibility. Do the same for your character.

_____

3. The author then describes the dress of the character's spouse. Do the same for the companion of your character.

_____

Because of the word processor's flexibility, it also is an ideal environment for encouraging collaborative writing by young authors (Figure 8.10). Collaborative writing encourages students to make writing a group, rather than an individual, project. Collaborative writing activities might involve setting up structures for children to comment on the writing of others in the class, or children might actually create a document together. Research has indicated that making the writing process more interactive is beneficial to young writers. Specifically, these activities seem to benefit both planning and revising strategies. When children work together on computers, they encourage each other's imagination, point out problems, and suggest improvements in work they create together.

Dual-mode writing (Marcus & Blau, 1983; Thompson & Jarchow, 1985) is another technique to encourage collaborative writing. Like the students doing invisible writing, dual-mode writers cannot see the writing they do on the computer. In this case, however, the student's com-

FIGURE 8.9
(continued)

---

4. She contrasts the dress of the two. Do that for your characters.

---

5. She then adds details about the major character. Do that in your paragraph.

Now go back and delete the numbered suggestions and asterisks, so that only your text remains.

Read your text carefully and revise it. Then check your text for spelling and punctuation errors, and change these. Print your final copy.

Excerpt from *The Accidental Tourist* (p. 1) by Anne Tyler, 1985, New York: Knopf. Copyright ® 1985 by Anne Tyler Modarressi, et al.

puter is connected to a neighbor's monitor, so the neighbor can view the other writer's work. Using various codes, the neighbor is encouraged to respond to the work on request from the writer. Thus, the writer can get suggestions for improving the document during composing.

Many students in a dual-mode writing experience have remarked on the added dimension partnership writing offers. The writers enjoy being able to get ideas from their partners: "She helped stimulate my creative thought with only a few words or a statement. It's good to get outside help while you are actually writing" (Thompson & Jarchow, 1985). Readers also seemed to find the process of being involved in a partner's writing process an interesting experience. One reader com-

Notes From the Literature

Simple collaborative writing projects include strategies for getting writers to read and comment on the writing of others. For example, students are asked to load a document written by another student and make comments in capital letters within the document. The document is then returned to the writer, who can revise her work, based on the comments within the text.

Students using word processors tended to enjoy, and have a more favorable attitude toward, writing than students writing traditionally.

Schromm, R. M. (1989). The effects of using word processing equipment in writing instruction: A meta analysis. Unpublished doctoral dissertation, Northern Illinois University.

rience and the heightened sense of writing to an audience. "Pretty soon I found that I was writing right to my partner." Another writer remarked, "I felt like I was talking to the other person and I wanted feedback, just like in a conversation."

In general, a word processor makes the composing phase of the writing process easier and more efficient for the writer. Using a word processor also creates flexibility in the composing process. Writers can collect, save, and print their work at any time. Writers are no longer limited to a linear sequence in the writing process. They can collaborate with others during the composing process. Understandably, many writers who are accustomed to a word processor become "addicted" to the convenience and say they have difficulties composing without the word processor. Increasingly, both teachers and students may acquire this same addiction.

mented, "It was fun sitting here, watching her story develop and thinking of ideas in my brain and waiting for her to need them" (Thompson & Jarchow, 1985).

Many participants also commented on the phenomenon of turning writing into an immediate social expe-

Revising

In the revising phase of the writing process, the writer changes and rearranges the content of the writing. In this phase, writers are concerned with identifying and

FIGURE 8.10
Collaborative writing is an excellent word processing activity.
Photograph courtesy of Apple Computer, Inc.

Notes From the Literature

- -

Junior high students using word processors had more positive attitudes about their writing ability and about their writing instruction than students receiving traditional writing instruction.

Kurth, R. J. (1987). Using word processing to enhance revision strategies during student writing activities. Educational Technology, 27(1), 13–19.

Notes From the Literature

- -

When using a word processor, second and third graders wrote longer pieces and made more revisions than when they wrote papers by hand.

Kahn, J. (1987). Learning to write with a new tool: Young children and word processing. The Computing Teacher, 14(9), 11–12, 56.

solving problems of organization and coherence. Professional authors generally spend long hours in revision, while young writers in school frequently do no revising at all.

Before the word processor, the revision process was extremely tedious. Revising implied recopying or retyping a paper and thus long hours of tedium. With the word processor, however, revising has become a much simpler and even enjoyable task. Given the capabilities of the word processor outlined in this chapter, writers can add text, move paragraphs, delete text easily, and almost instantly obtain a nicely formatted printed copy incorporating the revisions. No longer must writers think in terms of two or three drafts for a document. Now they can continue to revise until the document is the best it can be.

Current research suggests, however, that the capabilities of the word processing program alone will not ensure that students will do more revising. It appears that, at first, students need feedback from the teacher or other students to encourage revision (Balajthy, McKeveny, & Lacitignola, 1986–87). Students must be taught the importance of revision and techniques for revision. It is up to individual teachers to create approaches and activities that encourage students to take advantage of revision possibilities.

Editing

The final step in the writing process involves checking for spelling, grammar, and usage errors. Too often, students attempt to combine the revision and editing processes. Because looking for spelling errors generally is easier than looking for logic errors, students who combine the two may be tempted to ignore the revision stage.

However, after the revision process it is time to make a technical check of the document. Many word processing programs come with software that usually accompany the word processor that can help with editing. The

most widely used of these programs are the spelling programs (Figure 8.11). These programs will identify any words in the text that are not contained in the dictionary for the spelling program. Students are usually given a list of these words and several options for changing each of the words. It is important to note that spelling programs do not supply the correct spelling of a word. They simply identify words not in the speller's dictionary. Some programs may offer suggestions as to how the word could be spelled, but the student, not the computer, makes the final decision on the spelling of each word. A program that offers suggestions will usually take a commonly misspelled word such as *receive* and suggest the correct spelling to the user.

Most spelling programs will check the entire text against the dictionary that accompanies the spell-checker. After the check is completed, the writer is informed that a certain number of suspect words were located.

Because the program identified a word as suspect does not always mean the word was actually misspelled. The checker simply flags words in the text that are not in the dictionary. Most proper nouns in a document will be flagged as suspect words. The speller used for this book flagged *microcomputer* as a suspect word. Obviously, that word was not in the dictionary supplied with the speller. Fortunately, most spellers allow the user to add words to the dictionary. In this case, the author added the word *microcomputer* to the dictionary, and the word was no longer flagged during spell check.

Usually, the spell-check program offers the writer several options for the flagged words. These options usually include changing just that occurrence of the word, changing every occurrence of the word in the text, ignoring the suspect word, and adding the suspect word to the dictionary. Each suspect word is handled individually, and the writer makes an individual choice for each word.

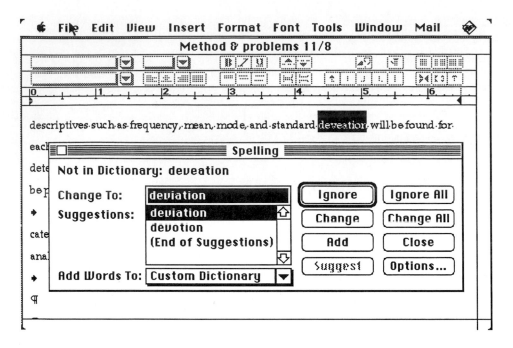

FIGURE 8.11
Spell-check programs are built into many word processors, or can be added on later.

Spelling checkers have met with mixed reactions among classroom teachers. Some teachers do not allow their use, saying these programs inhibit the learning of good spelling habits. Many of these teachers seem to believe the spelling checker spells for the student, which of course is not true.

The majority of teachers who have worked with spelling checkers are enthusiastic about the possibilities. Spelling checkers seem to encourage students to edit their writing. Spelling errors generally are not careless mistakes; they indicate that the student really does not know how to spell the word. Therefore, it usually is difficult for students to independently identify their own spelling errors. Using the spelling program to flag possible errors, students are given a specific list of words on which to focus attention. Students may need to look up some of these words in a dictionary. Using a spelling checker usually means that students will do more spelling work when writing a paper than they would without it.

There clearly are limitations to working with spelling checkers. Some of the early programs have such small dictionaries (less than 50,000 words) that they are not useful to most students. Generally, a dictionary should have the capacity of at least 80,000 words, or an inordinate number of words will be flagged

as suspect. The flagging of proper nouns also irritates some users, but commonly used proper nouns can always be added to the dictionary.

Checkers also do not catch words that are correctly spelled but misused. Thus, if a student uses *there* instead of *their*, this error will not be flagged. Even with these limitations, however, most educators agree that spelling checkers offer significant advantages to writers in the editing phase.

In addition to spellers, there are other programs that will evaluate writing on several different criteria. AT&T developed one of the first of these programs, called Writer's Workbench, to help its technical writers check the quality of their work. The initial development of this program was on a mainframe computer, but AT&T has since made versions of the program available for microcomputers and schools. Writer's Workbench analyzes writing in many ways. A few of the analyses follow:

- *Organization*—The first and last sentence of each paragraph are printed out. The writer can then check the logic of the text and look for smooth transitions between paragraphs.
- *Development*—The length of each paragraph is computed. Short paragraphs are marked.

- *To-be verbs*—To identify possible passive construction, the entire text is printed out, with all the inflectional forms of the verb *to be* marked.
- *Suggest*—More concise alternatives are suggested for wordy expressions.
- *Style*—This program computes readability levels (four of them), number of sentences, number of words, average sentence length, average word length, number of question sentences, number of imperative sentences, number of short sentences, number of simple and compound sentences, and more.

Writer's Workbench also contains programs that analyze vagueness, commonly misused words, punctuation, grammar, and other style characteristics.

Other style-analysis programs have followed Writer's Workbench and include many of the same features. Writer's Helper by Conduit is one such program. Writer's Helper is available for the Apple IIc and IIe and contains a series of miniprograms that help student writers plan what to write and begin to revise what they have written. Eleven of these miniprograms help with the editing and revision stages of writing. These programs count the number of words in each paragraph, compute readability, calculate sentence length, search for homonym and usage errors, check for sexist language, and print out a word-frequency table.

As mentioned earlier, there is a grammar checker in Microsoft Word that provides useful feedback to students on both the quality and quantity of their work. Using the grammar checker, students can receive information on the level of their writing, common grammar and usage errors, and suggestions for improvement.

Like the spelling checkers, computer style checkers have some problems. Computer programs do not understand language, and thus style is checked through a series of quantitative measures, which obviously have limitations. Like the spelling checkers, however, the style checkers do increase student awareness of the editing process and focus attention on possible areas for improvement. In one sense, both the spelling checkers and the style checkers can make students a bit more analytical and critical of their writing. Just as with the spelling checkers, the final decisions about style are, and clearly should be, left to the individual student.

Writing Assessment

If computers can in fact provide useful feedback about the quality of writing, it seems apparent that teachers

of writing might be able to use computer programs to help with assessing student writing. All teachers who have been faced with the challenge of evaluating student writing recognize the extremely time-consuming nature of this task, and most would welcome help in this area. If computer programs could help teachers assess student writing more efficiently, teachers would not have to limit the number of student writing assignments because of the time available to evaluate these assignments.

One example of a student writing assessment project uses an instrument called the Computerized Instrument for Writing Evaluation (CIWE) (McCurry & McCurry, 1992). College student essays are analyzed using the CIWE in the following areas: fluency, sentence development, word use or vocabulary, and paragraph development. When compared with teacher evaluations in these same areas, the results from the CIWE correlated at the .95 level, providing "solid evidence that the CIWE was measuring the same qualities that teachers look for in student writing" (McCurry & McCurry, 1992, p. 36). Although the correlations were somewhat smaller for evaluation of younger students' writing, they were all statistically significant and above .6. Results suggest that using computers to help assess student writing will soon be a major tool for teachers of writing.

USING THE WORD PROCESSOR ACROSS THE CURRICULUM

In addition to using the word processor to facilitate the teaching of writing, recent attention has focused on using this technology in the teaching of reading. The basic idea here is that the learning of reading and writing are interrelated and that students will perform better in both subject areas if the teaching of the two subjects is integrated. IBM has produced a program titled Writing to Read, which is directed at encouraging young readers (kindergarten and first-grade level) to write and then read their own stories. New meaning and relevance are given to the reading process when students read and share their own stories. With the program, students as young as 5 collect and print out their own stories. Both student and teacher reactions to the program have been positive. Research results on the effectiveness of the approach are pending, but early indications are that the program has positively influenced student achievement in both reading and writing skills.

Writing is certainly a part of almost every subject taught in the elementary and secondary schools, and many of the ideas and approaches suggested in the previous section can be adapted to particular subject areas. For example, the prompted writing activities suggested for the composing stage of writing can be used to help students develop habits using the writing style and structure of a particular task for a particular discipline. The science teacher can use prompted writing techniques to train students to efficiently and professionally organize the writing of lab reports. The social studies teacher can use collaborative writing techniques for group research projects. The math teacher can have students write word problems, share them with other students, and then revise these problems, based on the suggestions of peers.

SUMMARY

Word processing programs are increasingly available for use in educational settings. All these programs share certain common features, including capabilities for collecting, revising, storing, and printing text.

Notes From the Literature

In a study of fourth-grade to ninth-grade classes, attitudes toward language arts improved with the use of word processing. Basic skills were also significantly improved, even though time had been taken away from these subjects to learn the word processing system.

The educational effects of word processors. County of Lacombe, No. 14. Alberta Department of Education, Edmonton. (ERIC Document Reproduction Service No. ED 287 457)

Numerous word processing software packages are available for use in the schools, varying from simple programs appropriate for first graders, to sophisticated integrated packages that combine word processing with other tool software capabilities.

Although the potential of the new technology is great, word processors by themselves will not improve the teaching of writing. Teachers must become familiar with the technology and work to apply and develop approaches to taking advantage of the unique capabilities of word processing in the teaching of writing. Given this commitment on the part of teachers and educators, word processing capabilities have the potential to vastly improve written communication.

SELF-TEST QUESTIONS

1. List the basic characteristics common to almost all word processing systems.
2. Which of the following is the most unique characteristic of FrEdwriter?
   a. It is freeware.
   b. It is used in education.
   c. It is a single-use, "adult" word processor.
   d. It has several different fonts.
3. Dedicated word processors are frequently used in classroom settings.
   a. True
   b. False
4. Which of the following is not one of the four stages of the writing process discussed in this chapter?
   a. Prewriting
   b. Postwriting
   c. Revising
   d. Editing
5. Describe two types of software programs that can be useful in the editing phase of the writing process.
6. AppleWorks is an example of a single-function, "adult" word processing system.
   a. True
   b. False
7. Identify and describe one software package available for desktop publishing activities.
8. Describe what is meant by collaborative writing. Why does the word processor help with this process?

9. Prompted writing activities can be used most frequently in the prewriting phase of the writing process.
   a. True
   b. False
10. Third graders do not seem to have achieved the psychomotor skills necessary to learn to keyboard.
    a. True
    b. False

ANSWERS TO SELF-TEST QUESTIONS

1. Almost all word processors contain capabilities for collecting, editing and revising, saving, and printing text.
2. a.
3. b. False.
4. b.
5. Spelling checkers, programs that read through a document and flag suspect words, can be useful in editing. Style-analysis programs, like Writer's Workbench, can also be helpful in locating problems with grammar and usage.
6. b. False.
7. The Print Shop allows the classroom teacher to make cards, signs, and banners easily.
8. Collaborative writing is writing in groups of two or more. The ease of entering text and the ease of revising with a word processor make this process much easier. Students can write, discuss, and revise very quickly.
9. b. False.
10. b. False.

REFERENCES

Balajthy, E., McKeveny, R., & Lacitignola, L. (1986–87). Microcomputers and the improvement of revision skills. *The Computing Teacher, 14*(4), 28–31.

Becker, H. J. (1994). *Analysis and trends of school use of new information technologies.* Prepared for the Office of Technology Assessment, U.S. Congress (Contract: No. K3-0666.0). Irvine, CA: University of California, Department of Education.

Becker, H. (1991). How computers are used in United States schools: Basic data from the 1989 I.E.A. computers in education survey. *Journal of Educational Computing Research, 7*(4), 385–406.

Cochran-Smith, M. (1991). Word processing and writing in elementary classrooms: A critical review of related literature. *Review of Educational Research, 61*(1), 107–155.

Daiute, C. (1985). *Writing and computers.* Reading, MA: Addison-Wesley.

Daiute, C., & Taylor, R.P. (1981). Computers and the improvement of writing. In *Proceedings of the Association of Computing Machinery, 1981.* ACM08979. Washington, DC: Association of Computing Machinery.

The educational effects of word processors. County of Lacombe, No. 14. Alberta Department of Education, Edmonton. (ERIC Document Reproduction Service No. ED 287 4571)

Marcus, S., & Blau, S. (1983). Now seeing is believing: Invisible writing with computers. *Educational Technology, 23*(4), 12–15.

McCurry, N., & McCurry, A. (1992). Writing assessment for the 21st century. *The Computing Teacher, 19*(7), 35–37.

Riel, M. (1990). Building a new foundation for global communities. *The Writing Notebook: Creative Word Processing in the Classroom, 7*(3), 35–37.

Solomon, G. (1987). A free word processor that stands up in the crowd. *Electronic Learning, 6*(1), 30–31.

Thompson, A., & Jarchow, E. (1985). *An experiment in dual mode writing.* Unpublished manuscript, Iowa State University, College of Education.

Wetzel, K. (1985). Keyboarding skills: Elementary, my dear teacher? *The Computing Teacher, 12*(9), 15–19.

Word processing in the classroom: Its effects on freshman writers. Unpublished manuscript, Poughkeepsie, NY: Marist College and IBM Corporation. (ERIC Document Reproduction Service No. ED 276 062)

REFERENCES FOR ADDITIONAL STUDY

Boone, R. (1991). *Teaching process writing with computers.* Eugene, OR: International Society for Technology in Education.

Bracey, G. (1989). Word processing: Helps adults revise, and young students simply like it. *Electronic Learning, 8*(6), 24–28.

DeGroff, L. (1990). Is there a place for computers in whole language classrooms? *The Reading Teacher, 43*(8), 568–572.

Hall, J., & Yoder, S. (1992). *Beyond word processing in Microsoft Word 5.0.* Eugene, OR: International Society for Technology in Education.

Kahn, J. (1987). Learning to write with a new tool: Young children and word processing. *The Computing Teacher, 14*(9), 11–12, 56.

Kurth, R. J. (1987). Using word processing to enhance revision strategies during student writing activities. *Educational Technology, 27*(1), 13–19.

McCarthy, R. (1988, June). Stop the presses! An update on desktop publishing. *Electronic Learning, 7*(6), 24–30.

Penso, R. (1989). No more scribbles and hieroglyphics: Computer composition with beginners and slow learners. *The Computing Teacher, 16*(5), 19–22.

Pons, K. (1988). Process writing in the one-computer classroom. *The Computing Teacher, 15*(6), 33–37.

Rathje, L. (1990). *AppleWorks for educators—A beginning and intermediate workbook.* Eugene, OR: International Society for Technology in Education.

Rose, S. Y. (1988). A desktop publishing primer. *The Computer Teacher, 15*(9), 13–15.

Schromm, R. M. (1989). *The effects of using word processing equipment in writing instruction: A meta analysis.* Unpublished doctoral dissertation, Northern Illinois University.

Wetzel, K. (1992). *Microsoft Works for the Macintosh—A workbook for educators.* Eugene, OR: International Society for Technology in Education.

MANAGING INFORMATION
Data Managers

GOAL

This chapter will introduce the basic capabilities of a data base manager and possible applications of these capabilities in education.

OBJECTIVES

The reader will be able to do the following:

1. Define the following terms: *data, information, knowledge,* and *Information Age*.
2. Describe the characteristics of a data base management system.
3. Define the following terms: *record, field,* and *template*.
4. Differentiate the capabilities of a computer data base manager from those of more traditional data management systems.
5. Describe the characteristics of at least three types of data base management systems frequently used in education.
6. Cite three major goals for teaching with data base management in the classroom.
7. Cite three ways teachers can use data base management programs for administrative purposes.
8. Describe the three stages in learning to use data base management systems.
9. Describe activities appropriate for each of the stages in the preceding objective.
10. Cite examples of classroom data base activities in the following subject areas: science, social studies, and English.
11. Cite original examples of how data base management can be used in your own teaching.

Sometime, during the second half of the 20th century, Western Society evolved from an industrial to a post-industrial, or to be precise, an Information Society.

Education for an industrial society centered on teaching the Three Rs: "Reading, 'Riting, and 'Rithmetic." Its aim was to produce a disciplined work force—punctual, conformist, specialized—to operate the brute machinery of the nation-state. Education for an Information Society will center on the Three Cs: "Children, Computers, and Communication." Its aim will be to produce a creative work force—adaptable, entrepreneurial, interdisciplinary—to help solve the problems of this planet.

Stonier & Conlin, 1985

Throughout education, talk of skills for life in the Information Age has become commonplace. For many, however, exactly what is meant by the *Information Age* and what skills will be necessary for this age remain a little fuzzy. Terms like *data, information, knowledge, knowledge explosion,* and *Information Age* are often thrown around with little precise definition.

To clarify the discussion of data base managers in education, definitions of key terms involving information and information management will first be discussed and defined.

WHAT IS THE INFORMATION AGE?

Before considering what is meant by the *Information Age,* it is important to define the terminology associated with this period, starting with the terms *data* and *information.* Data provide the raw material, the building blocks for information. Data on their own provide no meaning. Information, however, is data interpreted in a meaningful and useful form. For example, the raw numbers obtained from a yearly census are data; when those numbers are arranged meaningfully in a table or through a data base manager, the numbers become information.

Knowledge is the next step on the hierarchy, and it is here that the interaction of the human being and the information becomes important. Information becomes knowledge when it is acquired (and transformed) by a person and used. Knowledge involves human beings using information to form insights and judgments.

The *information explosion* refers to the tremendous rate of increase in the amount of available information about particular topics. Depending on whom you ask, you may hear that information doubles every year or every five years or more or less. This statistic is fairly meaningless to most of us. Statistics in specific content areas, however, show that the amount of available information is increasing rapidly. In the field of mathematics, for example, the number of articles published in periodicals doubled between 1960 and 1970 and then more than doubled again between 1970 and 1980.

The growing significance of quality, up-to-date information in a modern economy has led to the assertion that information is the fourth major resource in any society—with the other three being land, labor, and capital. Information is quickly becoming the most important of the four commodities in our society. Stonier (1983) describes the place of information in current society:

> Information has upstaged land, labour, and capital as the most important input into modern productive systems. Information reduces the requirement for land, labour and capital. It reduces the requirements for raw materials and energy. It spawns entire new industries. It is sold in its own right, and it is the raw material for the fastest growing sector of the economy—the knowledge industry. (p. 8)

Thus, effectively handling information has become a major role for business and industry and is crucial for economic growth in today's world. Many believe society has now passed into the Information Age.

Clearly, the information explosion and the events of the Information Age will continue to affect our educational system. As information and knowledge expand, skills in accessing and using this information will be important. The ability to locate and use quality information will be more important than the ability to memorize facts. Teachers will be seen less as the dispensers of information and more as facilitators in helping students learn the process of using information.

It is equally clear, however, that one cannot totally separate acquisition of facts from acquisition of problem-solving and information-handling skills. Obviously, these sets of skills are interrelated. Students ignorant of the basic facts and events of the American Revolution, for example, are in no position to search for relevant information on that period. Information, as well as information-handling skills, will continue to be an important part of the curriculum. In this chapter, the emphasis is on information-handling skills as these provide the "new" part of the curriculum necessitated by the demands of the Information Age.

The computer data base manager is one of the most powerful tools to help children learn some of the skills necessary for life in the Information Age. Through use of the data base manager, students will have experiences in organizing, collecting, and using information. The emphasis in all work with a data base manager is on effectively manipulating information, not on memorizing the information. The data base manager enables teachers to provide quality student activities in the area of analysis and synthesis of information and to surpass the emphasis on memorizing information in today's schools.

WHAT IS A DATA BASE MANAGER?

To understand exactly what a data base manager is, one first must understand the term *data base*. A data base is simply a collection of data, and all of us encounter hundreds of these data bases every day. Collections of recipes, magazines, stamps, student records, and household bills are all data bases. Data bases existed long before the advent of the computer.

Although most of us are surrounded with our personal data bases, many of these data bases lack any well-defined organization system. Magazine collections provide an excellent example of this phenomenon. Many people save and collect back copies of their favorite magazines, but few have effective methods for organizing these collections. A growing stack of *National Geographic* magazines, for example, is actually of very little use. Generally, the major reason for saving the magazines is so that articles on a particular subject may be later located and used. The problem is that when the need does arise, finding the appropriate article(s) can be a monumental task. The larger the collection, the more difficult it is to locate a particular article or set of articles. Thus, most collectors rapidly realize that they need more than a data base; they also need some way to organize that data base so they can use the information "buried" in it.

Certainly, people organized data bases long before the advent of the computer. These systems vary from the very crude (throwing all the baseball cards in a shoe box) to the very useful (recipe card file systems). Card files, address and record books, and file cabinets are all quite useful and common noncomputer methods for organizing data bases.

With the computer, however, came a type and level of data base organization never before possible. Computer management systems enable the user to enter, store, update, access, and manipulate data bases with great flexibility. Given a computer data base management system and an appropriate data storage format, the collector of the *National Geographic* magazines could immediately access all the articles on penguins, or all the articles on penguins who live at the South Pole, or all the articles about penguins who live in zoos.

Basic Features of a Data Base Management Program

The flexibility provided through a data base management system can best be understood by first examining the basic parts of any management program. Generally, most systems can be described in terms of three levels: file, record, and field (Figure 9–1).

File. A file is a collection of information about a particular topic. All the information collected on the topic is in the file. Thus, the information on the *National Geographic* described earlier would all be contained in the file. Similarly, a class studying whales could place all the information they collect in a data base management file called "Whales."

Record. A record contains all the information about one entry in a file. Thus, a record in the *National Geographic* example might be one article out of one magazine. A record in the whales file could contain the information about one of the whales under study. A record in an address file might contain all the information about a particular person (Figure 9–2).

Field. Within each record are fields that organize the information in the record. Within the *National Geographic* record, fields might include title of article, date of magazine, page number, major subject, minor subjects, and locale of the subject of the article. Thus, a sample selection of fields for a record for this file might look like this:

MAJOR SUBJECT(S):
ARTICLE NAME:
MAGAZINE DATE:
PAGE NUMBERS:
MINOR SUBJECTS:
LOCALE:

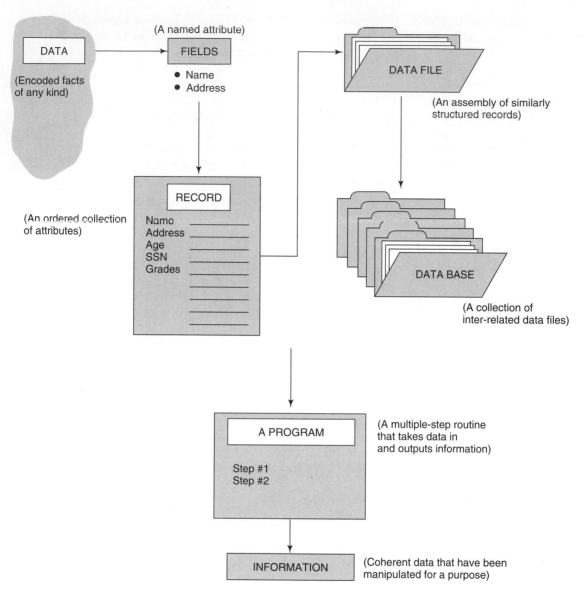

FIGURE 9–1
Data base terminology.

The fields for the whales file record might include the name of the whale, average length, scientific name, habitat, migration habits, and whether the whale is toothed or not toothed. A sample record for this file might look like this:

COMMON NAME: GRAY WHALE

SCIENTIFIC NAME: ESCHICHTIUS

AVERAGE LENGTH: 50 FEET

HABITAT: NORTHERN PACIFIC; COASTAL
    WATERS

LIFE EXPECTANCY: 25 YEARS

MAJOR FOODS: SMALL CRUSTACEANS

GROUP: TOOTHED

Once the fields for a file are determined, all records in the file are stored using the same field. A field, however, can be left blank if it does not apply to a particular entry or if that information is not available. Using the vocabulary just defined, a third example of a data base file would be one used for administrative purposes within a school. The individual record in this file would

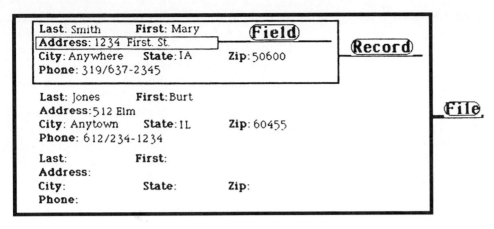

FIGURE 9–2
Sample fields, records, and file.

obtain information about one student in the school. Possible fields might include name, age, grade, sex, teacher, parents' name, composite test scores by year, and special needs. Thus, a sample record from this file could look like this:

LAST NAME: STANLEY

FIRST NAME: JOSEPH

AGE: 11

GRADE: 5

SEX: M

TEACHER: JONES

PARENTS' NAME: JOHN AND ANITA

ADDRESS: 3212 FRIAR STREET

PHONE: 292-0113

1992 COMPOSITE ACH: 67

1993 COMPOSITE ACH: 75

1994 COMPOSITE ACH: 68

1995 COMPOSITE ACH: 76

1996 COMPOSITE ACH: 78

SPECIAL NEEDS: HEARING IMPAIRED

Differences From Noncomputer Data Organization Systems. The major advantage of a computer data base manager over other data organizational systems is the flexibility provided by the fields in the system. In a typical noncomputer data organization system, rapid searches can be conducted by one "field" only. In the whales example, a student might organize a card file by type of whale. The student could easily access all the information collected about gray whales, but would have no easy way to locate all the information collected about toothed whales longer than 50 feet. That task would require reading through each card in the file. Similarly, the student would find locating all the whales that live in coastal waters a difficult, time-consuming task.

Recipe files provide a second example of a noncomputer data organization system. Typically, a recipe file is organized by type of food and has categories such as meat, fish, salad, vegetable, and so on. Searching the field for meat recipes is a fairly easy task. But searching the file for all recipes that contain tuna and take less than one hour to prepare is a much more complicated task.

Using a computer data base management system, however, a student can bring up information on whales or the recipe file through any of the fields chosen for the records. Using the record format in Figure 9–2, the student could search for all whales that eat herrings, or all whales longer than 50 feet, or all whales that are toothless and eat crustaceans.

Similarly, a recipe file on a data base management system can be searched using several criteria at one time. One possible search might be for all recipes that use cheddar cheese and take less than 30 minutes to prepare. Another search could be for all main dishes without meat that take less than 45 minutes to prepare. Obviously, these searches would be difficult and time-consuming to carry out with a traditional record-keeping system. With a data base system, however, each search should take less than five seconds.

Data Base Management Software for Education

Hundreds of data base management programs for microcomputers are available today. Like word processing programs, data base management programs come in varying prices and capabilities.

Single-Purpose, "Adult" Systems.   These systems are software programs that perform data base management functions exclusively. They tend to be used most in business situations where data base management is one of the major computer uses. In general, these systems tend to be more powerful and capable than integrated systems and can hold more records. Filemaker Pro is a single-purpose data base management program popular for office use.

Multipurpose, Integrated "Adult" Systems. These systems offer data base management capabilities in addition to other tool capabilities. Here, data base management is one of a group of compatible computer tools. The AppleWorks integrated system discussed in Chapter 8 offers data base management capabilities in addition to word processing and spreadsheet capabilities. The data base management functions of AppleWorks use the same basic commands as the word processing functions. Thus, students who have learned to use the word processor portion of the AppleWorks system can easily generalize many of their skills to the data base management portion of the program. Microsoft Works offers a similar integrated system (Figure 9–3).

As indicated in Chapter 8, one advantage of the integrated systems is that students can "paste" their data base files into a word processing document. (*Paste* is a term used in many computer programs that means inserting an item—a table, graphic, or text block—into a designated spot in a given file. For instance, the sample records cited earlier in this chapter were simply inserted into the word processing part of the docu-

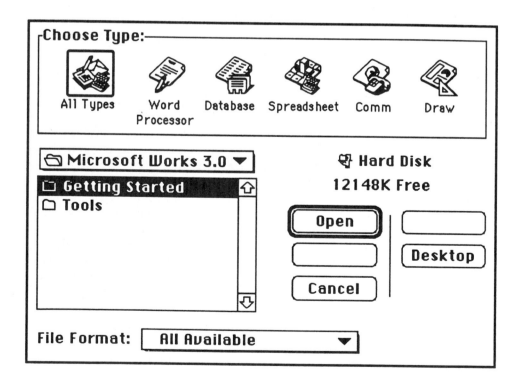

FIGURE 9–3
Microsoft Works has a data base manager as one of its integrated systems. Microsoft Works, like most Apple Computer Inc. software, uses visuals—or icons—to represent ideas. In Works, the file folder outline is used to represent different files.

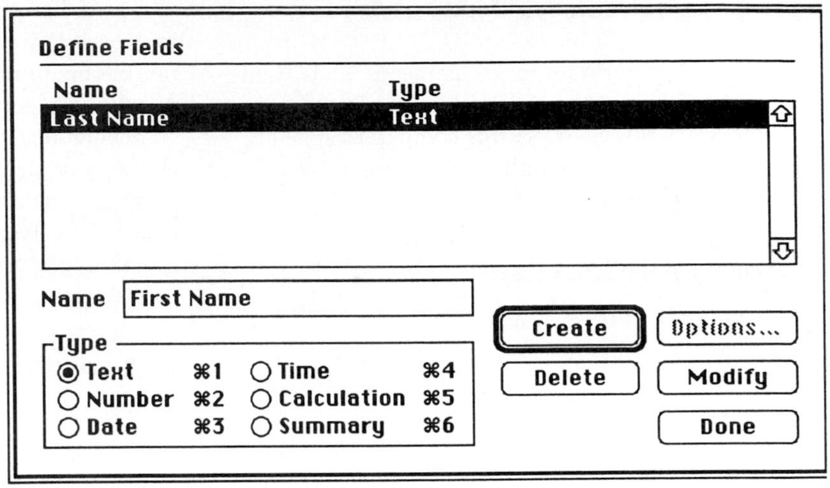

FIGURE 9–4
Microsoft Works includes a data base management system. Defining a field in Works is accomplished by following simple directions.

Define Fields

Name	Type
Last Name	Text

Name [First Name]

Type
- ⦿ Text ⌘1   ○ Time ⌘4
- ○ Number ⌘2   ○ Calculation ⌘5
- ○ Date ⌘3   ○ Summary ⌘6

[Create] [Options...]
[Delete] [Modify]
[Done]

ment.) The students writing a report on whales can insert a table into their essay detailing the characteristics of whales longer than 50 feet.

In many ways, the AppleWorks and Microsoft Works data base programs are similar to the FileMaker Pro system. The terms *file*, *record*, and *field* apply in the same way. Although the details of setting up the data base are somewhat different, the AppleWorks and Microsoft Works systems also provide for a "tables" format printout. In the tables format, records are printed out horizontally with the field labels at the top of each column. A tables printout from the whales file might look like the one shown below.

Notice that to make the table fit within the margins of the word processing document, only four of the fields were selected for the table.

Because AppleWorks and Microsoft Works are used extensively in schools, there exist a growing number of commercial and teacher-made data bases for use with these systems. Both the design and collection of data for a useful data base take a tremendous amount of time, so sharing existing data bases is certainly a useful trend for educators. Obviously, educators who wish to share data base management systems should select data base software that is frequently used by other educators.

Learner-Oriented Data Base Management Systems. Several software publishers have produced data base management programs appropriate for use in the elementary school. Although the concept behind these systems is identical to that of the adult systems, these systems are written with the needs of the young learner in mind.

Bank Street Filer is an example of a learner-oriented data base management system. Produced by the authors of the Bank Street Writer, the Bank Street Filer is a simplified version of a powerful, adult computer tool. Like most of the learner-oriented systems, this system has prepared data bases that accompany it.

Bank Street Filer is a menu-driven program, which means users can always see the available options. The on-screen menus remind learners about the various capabilities of the program and provide a learning tool for beginners.

To ensure ease of use, most learner-oriented systems are quite simple in terms of number of records used, and number and types of fields allowed. These systems allow students to learn data base management techniques and concepts in a friendly environment and should be increasingly useful in the elementary school.

Common Name	Scientific Name	Length	Food
Gray Whale	Eschrichtius	60 feet	small crustaceans
Fin Whale	Balaenoptera physalus	75 feet	crustaceans

WHY DATA BASE MANAGEMENT?

Although computer data base management is used extensively in business and industry, educators have been somewhat slower to use this computer capability. There are, however, three rather compelling reasons to include data base management in the curriculum.

Learning the Tool Itself

We are surrounded by data bases and data base management systems every day. The travel agent searching for an appropriate flight, the stockbroker accessing information on IBM stock, the bank teller searching for a client's balance are all using data base management systems. Almost all students today will make extensive use of data base management systems in their personal and professional lives. At the very least, then, students need to understand how to create and operate data base management systems.

Initial work with data base management systems should focus on the basics of using the tool. Students should understand the concepts of file, record, and field. They should know how to perform different types of searches on the data base. They also need to know how to select appropriate fields in terms of capabilities for later searches.

At this level, students will work with a specific data base system. But while they must become familiar with the particular syntax of that system, they also need to learn general data management skills. Thus, while learning to search the whales file for all records of whales shorter than 30 feet, students should learn the basic features of performing a numeric search in any data base system. Once the concepts are taught, skills learned in one software system should be easily generalizable to another system.

Teaching Higher Level Problem-Solving Skills

Given the rapidly expanding information and knowledge bases in the Information Age, students must have the abilities needed to use these bases. Initial work with data bases will help them acquire the skills to create and manipulate such systems. But while the "how-to" part of using data base management systems is an important initial step, it is only the first step in learning to work with data files. More advanced work should help students acquire valuable skills for using information and knowledge in problem solving situations.

Critics have suggested that the educational system has been slow to develop a curriculum appropriate for the Information Age. Although most educators recognize that students need more work with problem solving, curriculum development in this area has been problematic. A good data base management system can create a computer environment where students can manipulate information. Working in this environment, students are acquiring problem-solving skills in organizing information, accessing information, and hypothesis testing.

Organizing Information

Most students have experienced the need for an effective system for organizing data. They collect large

Notes From the Literature

Ehman, Glenn, Johnson, and White (1990) used a case study approach to investigate what happens in the classrooms of experienced computer-using social studies teachers and to describe the issues, problems, and opportunities encountered while using computer data bases as part of a problem-solving instructional unit. After receiving a 10-day problem-solving unit using a computer data base as an integrated element, student teams produced an oral report. Based on that report, the researchers concluded that the most successful students had teachers that "acted as 'metacognitive guides' who provided students a clear road map of the unit at the beginning, and then gave continuous reinforcement and guidance to show individuals, groups, and their whole classes where they had been, where they were at the time, and where they were going" (p. 27). In addition, the researchers identified the importance of avoiding time pressure by integrating the activity into the current curriculum rather then tacking it onto the traditional curriculum. Successful teachers also dealt with students' lack of sufficient entry level knowledge on the content and specific data base categories before leaving them to the task of problem solving with data base tools. Finally, the study identified small, noncompetitive groups of students as the most conducive to successful problem solving.

Ehman, L., Glenn, A., Johnson, V., & White, C. (1990, November). Using computer data bases in student problem solving: A study of eight social studies teachers' classes. Paper presented at the Annual Meeting of the National Council for the Social Studies, College and University Faculty Assembly, Anaheim, CA.

Notes From the Literature

The use of a computerized file management program helps high school social studies students learn how to locate, gather, organize, and evaluate information for solving specific problems.

White, C. S. (1986). The impact of structured activities with a computer-based file management program on selected information processing skills (Doctoral dissertation, Indiana University, 1985). Dissertation Abstracts International, 47, 513A.

amounts of information for a paper or project and then have difficulty using this information. Sometimes they merely write the information on a pad of paper and then find that they must read through all the information time after time, searching for particular topics, authors, or facts. The sheer tedium of this search process often keeps students from effectively using the information they have collected.

As the size of an information base grows, so grows the need to organize that information. The student who writes the most effective report may not be the student who has collected the most data. The successful report writer usually has been taught effective organizational skills in addition to writing and research skills.

Work with data base management systems provides students with valuable opportunities to develop organizational skills. The data base management program itself provides only the opportunity to effectively organize the data. How the user develops the organization system determines how accessible and usable the information actually is.

For example, suppose a group of students has set up the record format for a student file. Hearing about the project, the principal would like to use the data base to determine how many students come from single-parent families. He asks the students to provide these numbers, but the design of the record in the file does not provide this information. The existing record has a field for parents' name but does not differentiate how many names are in that field. The information the principal desires may be contained in the file, but it is effectively "buried" and not available for easy access. The students will need to redesign their record to provide the necessary information. In discussing possibilities for the new record format, students will probably consider many organizational options. Each option will provide slightly different information.

One direct solution is to add a field that asks "Are you living with both parents?" If this is the solution the students decide on, a search for all the "no" answers for this field will locate the records for students who are not living with both parents and appropriate pieces of these records could then be printed out for the principal's study.

Students (or the principal) might also decide that they want to obtain more specific information about the adults with whom the child is living. Fields involving questions about step-parents or nonrelated adults living with students in the school might be added. In any case, through considering their options, students learn valuable lessons about organizing information for later use.

One useful test for a data base management system is to have someone else use it. After a group of students has designed a data base and collected information for it, another class could use the data base for research purposes. Problems encountered by the students in the other class can be communicated to the designers of the data base management system, and the system can be further refined.

Students who have worked with the creation and use of data bases will rapidly understand the importance of carefully determining appropriate fields. The initial organization system determines the later usefulness of the file. Although students cannot be expected to predict all possible uses of a file, they can gain skill in creating flexible, usable initial organization systems.

Accessing Information

To solve a problem requiring information, students need to know how to access the appropriate information. As the amount of this information multiplies, the need for sophisticated abilities in this area grows. Learning to communicate with a data base involves defining an area of search, evaluating the results of initial searches, and continually narrowing or expanding a topic.

One of the great advantages of computer data bases is the capability of communicating with large central systems. The number and type of accessible data bases have increased tremendously in the last few years. In Chapter 10, some of the national and international data bases are discussed. Tapping these rich sources for the appropriate information can be an extremely challenging task for the beginner.

Students can develop strategies for searching data bases using small, local "homemade" data bases. For initial activities, teachers can have students search student-made, teacher-made, or purchased data bases.

Most of the skills necessary for accessing information in a large data base are the same as those used in a small data base. These same skills can then be generalized to the larger, more sophisticated data bases.

The whales data base mentioned previously would be a good starting point for students learning to access information. Students could be asked to define a topic for study and then develop strategies for searching the data base for all the information on this topic. Students with similar topics could compare their search strategies and results and thus expand their strategies.

On-line searches can provide valuable learning experiences for students developing their search skills. In an on-line search, students enter descriptors and immediately see the result of the search. Students can search national bases containing information about resources on a particular topic. If the number of articles is too large, or some of the articles are slightly off base, students can narrow the field by adding additional or alternative descriptors. The on-line experience helps students refine the search as they see results.

The DIALOG data base system discussed in Chapter 10 provides a useful means for learners to develop skill in searching data bases. The DIALOG system uses the basic logic of set theory to help students search the data. With DIALOG, symbols are used for the intersection and union of sets, and users are taught to use these symbols in searches. For example, students can search for all articles about computers *or* math education, or they can search for articles about computers *and* math education. Clearly, the first search will yield many more articles than the second. A typical search might begin with the user just asking for all the articles on computers. When the system supplies an enormous number of possible articles, the user begins to use the idea of the intersection of sets to narrow the field. For the next search, the descriptors "computers" and "schools" are used. When the system again reports a very large number of articles, to narrow the search, the user may search for "computers," "schools," and "secondary."

Alternatively, if a search yields too little information, users may want to broaden the area of search. For work on this chapter, for example, an initial search using the descriptor "data base management" was performed. The number of articles identified was small, so a second search using two descriptors was performed. The descriptors for the second search were "data base management" or "tool software." The thinking was that articles on the use of tool software might provide information or background on the use of data base managers in the classroom.

Given experiences with local, "homemade" data bases and large, central data bases, students learn to define problems and access information appropriate for the solution of those problems. The focus of all these activities is on giving students valuable experience in the manipulation and use of information as applied to specific problems.

Hypothesis Formulating and Testing

With an existing data base, students can be given activities that encourage them to formulate and test hypotheses about the information they collect. After having collected the whales file mentioned earlier, for instance, students could be asked to formulate and test hypotheses such as "The largest whales live in the Pacific Ocean" or "Toothed whales are larger than nontoothed whales."

To test the first hypothesis, students might search separately for the largest whales and for whales that live in the Pacific Ocean. Students can then perform a third search for whales that meet both criteria. Then they can compare the results from all the searches to see how many of the largest whales actually live in the Pacific Ocean. Most likely, the initial hypothesis will not be totally confirmed, and the students will need to reformulate the hypothesis.

This process of refining or reformulating the hypothesis is an extremely important part of the hypothesis-testing process. From the searches for the initial hypothesis, students will gain valuable information about their first ideas. By carefully examining the results of these searches, students may discover that the largest whales have features other than habitat in common. Students can then use a similar process to test second- and third-level hypotheses.

Students can test the second initial hypothesis by searching first for all whales over a certain length and then for all the large whales that are toothed. By comparing the results from these searches, the students can either confirm or refine the original hypothesis.

In most cases, students will find that their initial hypotheses are not proven. The information gathered from these first searches, however, will enable them to make better guesses on their subsequent searches. Students will learn to interrogate the data base to formulate and test possible relationships among the data. As they test their initial hypotheses, they will find the errors in their ideas. Given experience with this "debugging" phase of hypothesis testing, students learn to learn from their errors. Students are having valuable curricular experiences in the analysis and use of information.

Papert (1980) argues that far too much emphasis has been placed on students getting the right answer to a problem the first time. He contends that students begin to believe that making an error is bad and thus do not gain the valuable ability to learn from errors and build meaningful knowledge gained from mistakes. He suggests that computer activities can help students accept errors as learning opportunities.

As they organize data for future use, access data for a particular problem, and test hypotheses, students learn skills for managing information. The focus in all these activities is teaching students to *use* information, not merely memorize it.

DATA BASE MANAGEMENT APPLICATIONS FOR TEACHERS

As emphasized in Chapter 7, teachers must be able to use computer tools themselves before they can design and implement tool activities for their students. Teachers learning to use a data base management system will find numerous useful applications for professional and personal purposes. They will gain expertise in the operation of the system and ideas on how the system can best be used with students.

Organizing Information About Students

One of the first uses of data base management that occurs to most teachers is organizing the mounds of information they have collected about their students. As mentioned earlier, the organization of this information then implies more efficient use of the information.

An instrumental music teacher in a small Midwestern town provides a good example of data base system use. This teacher enrolled in a computer applications course primarily to gain credits on the salary schedule. At the beginning of the course, he did not believe computer applications would really affect his teaching of music.

When the concept of data base management was introduced in the course, however, the teacher quickly saw its advantages. Because he taught instrumental music to students at both the middle schools and high schools in town, he worked with a large number of students. His traditional organization system consisted of pink cards for his female students and blue cards for his male students. On the cards, the teacher had recorded information including the instrument the student played, the level of the book in which the student was working, and times that the student was available for lessons. The teacher would sort through the cards to schedule (and reschedule!) lessons and events. He guessed he spent the equivalent of 10 working days a year sorting through his cards for one reason or another.

For his class project on data base management, this teacher put the information from his cards into a PFS file. (PFS is an inexpensive data base management program.) The design of his record was quite simple and included fields for name, grade, school, sex, instrument, level, schedule, and free periods.

BAND STUDENT INFORMATION

LAST NAME:

FIRST NAME:

AGE:

GRADE:

SCHOOL:

INSTRUMENT:

LEVEL:

FREE PERIODS:

PERIOD 1:

PERIOD 2:

PERIOD 3:

PERIOD 4:

PERIOD 5:

PERIOD 6:

After the information was entered, class lists could be collected and printed in a matter of seconds. The teacher could search for all Level II flute players in the middle school who were free during Period 2 and then immediately print out his class list. In a similar manner, he could search for students who played appropriate instruments at appropriate levels for performances and print out lists of performers. Needless to say, the teacher was pleased with the efficiency of the system. He ended up persuading his principal to purchase a computer for him.

In a Canadian school district, a data base management program is used by administrators to track student discipline problems (Hauserman, 1992). The data, taken primarily from student information sheets that are filled out when students are referred to the office, include the following fields:

NAME:

GRADE:

DATE OF INFRACTION:

DESCRIPTION OF THE PROBLEM:

SOLUTION TO THE PROBLEM:

ACTION TAKEN (FILLED OUT BY
     ADMINISTRATOR):

To simplify searches, common descriptors for several of the fields are used. For example, infractions are classified into one of the following categories: fighting, rude behavior, swearing, leaving campus, lunchroom disturbances, throwing things, vandalism, stealing, truancy, and lack of homework. Similarly, actions taken are classified as counseling, detention, apology, cleanup, suspension, homework contracts, and payments.

Thus, information on discipline problems can be sorted and analyzed by any of the fields included. When a student enters the office, a list of that student's previous infractions can be quickly printed out. In addition, discipline problems for the school as a whole can be analyzed; in the example cited, sorting of the data base revealed that 40% of the infractions were for fighting.

Obviously, this same type of information management system could be used by teachers and administrators for scheduling reading groups, club meetings, interest groups, and group projects. Because almost all teachers are involved with managing and scheduling large groups of students, data base management is an efficient tool for teachers to have at their disposal.

One idea that might motivate teachers to use data base management involves collecting information about students on the first few days of school. Traditionally, the information that teachers collect remains "buried" in the card file and difficult to access. But on the computer, teachers can set up a record that includes fields for name, age, sex, hobbies, instruments played, clubs, and brothers and sisters. Teachers can set up a station at the computer for students to fill in their own records. When all the student records have been entered, the teacher and the students together can search the file for all students who are interested in collecting baseball cards or all students who play the violin.

This start-of-school activity serves several purposes. First, the students see immediately that the computer will be an important tool in the classroom. Second, students realize the power of a data base system. The information collected on the computer can be immediately used to access information about students who share interests, live in the same part of town, or belong to the same clubs. In a sense, the information collected "comes alive" as students see how it can be manipulated and accessed. The teacher might want to suggest the first searches, but soon students will suggest searches also. Very early in the school year, students see the power of an effective information management system. Throughout the year, the information can be continually updated and used.

Accessing Teaching Materials

Data base management techniques can also help teachers locate and acquire resource materials for teachers. Increasingly, teachers have the capability of accessing large central data bases for information and ideas on teaching particular topics.

In the mid-1980s, Minnesota Educational Computing Corporation (MECC) introduced an interesting pilot project that exemplifies some of the advantages of central data bases for teachers. The MECC project was designed primarily for social studies teachers interested in teaching current events. The basic idea of the project was to have a group of skilled social studies teachers locate appropriate current events articles each evening and design student activities to accompany the articles. Each evening, about 10 articles and activities would be placed in the central data base, and the next morning, teachers from around the country would have the opportunity of accessing and using the materials. Teachers could thus obtain current materials prepared by outstanding educators. Similar sharing-type networks are currently being established through central data base facilities such as DIALOG, CompuServe, and McGraw-Hill's MIX.

On a smaller level, teachers within districts or local areas are establishing data bases for sharing ideas in particular disciplines. Thus, a chemistry teacher might access a chemistry teachers' network to locate ideas stored on teaching a particular topic. Isolation and the inability to share teaching techniques and ideas have been longstanding problems in education; with the advent of data base management and communication technology, new solutions are emerging.

In addition to accessing teaching ideas and activities, teachers can also use some of the techniques mentioned for students to organize and access content material. Thus, an English teacher might start a file of 19th century British novels read by students in an advanced literature class. Students in the class could access the file to choose a book to read. A science teacher might create a file recording the main features of student science fair projects. Students looking for a project idea could search the file for all projects in the area in which they wish to work and build on ideas of other students. Basically, the creation of such files will make student and teacher work much more accessible to students.

Some teachers also use data base management programs to keep student grades. Although spreadsheet programs have been the most popular for numerical record-keeping purposes (see Chapter 8), there are advantages to using data base management programs. Obviously, the data base management program chosen for such a purpose must possess calculation capabilities. The major advantage of putting student grade records on a data base is that teachers can immediately search for all students who scored below (or above) a certain grade on a particular test or activity or combination of activities. In general, the data base program gives the teacher a greater capability for manipulating the data entered than does a spreadsheet.

In the role of manager of students and information, the classroom teacher will find the capabilities of data base management systems very useful. As individual teachers define and implement these applications, they will also be preparing to effectively design data base learning activities for students.

TEACHING ABOUT DATA BASE MANAGEMENT SYSTEMS

Initial teaching about data base management systems will probably require some instruction on the use and design of the systems themselves. As computer use in education advances, however, most students will begin to acquire the basic data base management skills early in elementary school. Eventually, upper elementary and secondary teachers will be able to focus more on teaching with data base systems and less on teaching about these systems. Until then, however, many teachers will need to focus some instruction on teaching about data base management systems. Hunter (1985) suggests that these skills can be developed in three consecutive stages.

Stage 1: Using

In this first stage of work with data base management systems, students use files that have been developed by someone else, either the teacher or students in other classes. Alternatively, these files may be purchased from software companies selling data base files for educational use, or the files may be obtained from other teachers or other schools.

Students who are doing their first work with a data base management system should probably begin by working with some noncomputer data bases. Creating, working with, and sorting simple card files will help students acquire a concrete idea of what a data base is and some of the problems with working with a noncomputer system.

Once students have had experiences with noncomputer data bases, they can begin to learn the mechanics of working with a computer data base system. Having the concrete model available, students should easily learn the concepts of file, record, and field. They will soon be ready to begin to search, sort, and print out results from existing data bases. Teachers can prepare activities designed to help students practice these skills.

Once students have mastered the mechanics of the system, they are ready to use the data in the system. Again, students need to start with teacher-prepared questions and activities designed to give students practice in accessing information and testing hypotheses. As students work with the data, activities can progressively become more open-ended and student directed, so that students are encouraged to formulate and test their own hypotheses about the data.

Stage 2: Building

At the second level, students are encouraged to develop research and organizational skills as they gather and enter information into record formats created by the teacher. These ready-made record formats are usually called *templates*. During this phase of the process, students locate and gather data for the file and learn to categorize these data.

Initial activities for this phase might involve simply adding records to the prepared files the students were working with during Stage 1. Having seen how the creator of the file recorded data should give students a good start for adding their own data to the file.

After they are comfortable with adding information to an existing file, students can be given just a template so they can build an entire file of records on their own. This task might best be approached as a class project, with each student or pair of students responsible for collecting a certain category of records. At the end of the project, the class should have a large file for their own use or to share with another group of students.

Stage 3: Designing Files

Having used and built data base files, students should be prepared to design their own templates for files. Here students are involved in all stages of the research process from defining the problem to analyzing the results.

Notes From the Literature

Sumitra Unia (1991) explored Beverly Hunter's (1985) widely accepted three-step sequence of data base instruction; using, building, and designing. Rather than progress through the steps in the traditional order, she introduced data bases to her fifth-grade students by initially designing, followed by building and then using a data base to test predictions. Given the direction of interviewing people through a neighborhood survey, students designed 17 questions and conducted the interviews. After the data were collected, students were introduced to building a data base to analyze their data. They then used the completed file to refute or confirm various student-generated predictions. Following this step, they discussed questions asked in the last national census and explored how other people and organizations used data bases. Based on her experience, Unia concludes, "it is not imperative to begin by using ready-made data bases. . . . Children can learn about data bases in meaningful contexts, reversing the often-cited instructional sequence described at the outset" (p. 34).

Unia, S. (1991). Exploring information. *The Computing Teacher, 19*(1), 33–34.

As indicated earlier, designing files involves careful planning and organization. Students must anticipate the uses they will wish to make of the data to define appropriate fields. Activities for this stage might include "pilot designs" where students design a template, enter about five records, and then have other students attempt to use the data file. Discussion of improvements in design could follow.

TEACHING WITH DATA BASE MANAGEMENT

Although it is useful for organizational purposes to separate teaching *about* data base management from teaching *with* data base management, there is clearly overlap between the two. Teachers using data base management activities with their students will be constantly suggesting new search and organization techniques appropriate to the task at hand. Just as all teachers teach reading and writing skills appropriate to their subject area, all teachers will teach data base management skills appropriate to their subject area.

Following are several specific data base management classroom activities. Although these activities are organized by subject area, the basic idea of most of the activities can be generalized across subject areas.

Social Studies

Data base management activities can help introduce students to the problem-solving methods of social studies. In a sense, students using a data base in a history or geography class are in an environment where they have the opportunity to define and discover historical or geographical relationships.

Using either simulated or real data, a history teacher could provide students with interesting raw material for problem solving in history. Students are encouraged to consider historical methods, trends, and events through the examination of source materials and evidence. The study of local census returns, parish registers, wills, and other records gives students an opportunity to experience history on a real, personal level.

Some teachers are beginning to search out these sources for their students. One West London school used the parish register for the village Adel for the years 1693 to 1702. Youngsters were given activities to help them enter the data from the register into a useful data base system and then were asked to interrogate the data base. Questions such as "How many children died before they were 5 years old?" and "How many people died of fever?" help the study of history come alive for children. These particular records are now available in a number of London schools.

Although there are obvious difficulties in making primary source information available for classroom use, this appears to be an exciting possibility for social studies teachers. The sharing of such records, once they are located, will make this method more universally available.

In addition to some of the exciting possibilities offered by use of primary source data, a growing number of commercially prepared data bases are available for uses in the social sciences. Scholastic has published data bases for U.S. history and U.S. government, which can be used with the PFS system. Data base files are also commercially available for AppleWorks and The Bank Street Filer. As suggested earlier, using and interrogating these data bases can help students develop skills for creating and using their own data bases.

Science

The use of data base management programs in science can bring the student a little closer to some of the actual processes of science. Through organizing and using material in data bases, students can form and test hypotheses.

One method of keeping students close to "real" data is to use a data base system to organize and record results of student observations and experiments. In a high school chemistry class, each student or lab group can insert their results from a particular experiment into a record. By the end of a school day, the file contains all the individual results from the day. Students can then compare their results with those of others in the class or formulate and test hypotheses about the composite results of the experiment. Using the data base, students can use the results from an experiment. Such a system will also increase student concentration on performing the experiment accurately; knowing that their results will be one record in a file will undoubtedly make students more accountable for their work. Few students will want their data identified as "outlying" or faulty.

One teacher reports using a homemade data base to encourage student questioning and hypothesis testing (Goldberg, 1992). Using a collection of shells belonging to the teacher, students classified the shells by color, size, shape, texture, and group name. Common descriptors were defined for each field; thus, for the shape field,

the descriptors *oval, rectangle,* and *circle* were used. For the size field, students agreed on definitions of sizes 1 through 4, with 1 being the smallest and 4 largest.

Once the data base was constructed, students began to ask questions and test hypotheses. For example, several students noticed that the smaller shells seemed lighter in color than the darker shells. The SORT command was used to arrange the shells by size from smallest to largest, and students discovered that the hypothesis was correct. That is, the smaller shells tended to be gray and white in color, while the larger shells tended to be blue and orange.

At the end of the activity, the teacher concluded that the data base manager added several dimensions to the shell activity. Students were able to swiftly sort and search the data base and were encouraged to ask more and varied questions. In previous work with the shells, the teacher had constructed all the questions. With the addition of the data base manager, he could let the students construct questions and explore. He also found that students discovered that there were many questions that could not be answered though searching and sorting the data base and that these questions required further reading and investigation. In general, the computer data base manager made the shell work more dynamic and open-ended.

Students can also use data base managers to form files of records of natural phenomena observed. An elementary class studying birds might create a file of birds observed by students in the class during the unit. Again, students can use this file to form generalizations about the types of birds observed in a particular locale. These types of data bases are especially useful since the students feel an ownership of the information in the system.

An increasing number of commercial and teacher-made data bases are available for use in science. One teacher-made file contains all the common elements studied in a science class and various properties of these elements. Students can use this file to form generalizations about properties of certain elements.

English

One obvious use of data base files for students of all ages is to record the books students have read. Instead of book reports, students can save a record on a particular book. The record can include items such as topic of the book, number of pages, and student ratings of different aspects of the book. This type of book report is much more usable than the traditional book report, because other students can easily access and use the recorded information.

For more advanced students, data base systems can provide a method for studying characteristics of writers and books. For example, students wishing to study characterizations of a particular author can create a template to record characteristics of each character in a novel or group of novels. Once the file is complete, students can interrogate the file to search for similarities and differences in the characters in the novel(s). For example, hypotheses about differences in female and male characterizations by a particular author can be tested and refined.

SUMMARY

Many of the activities suggested here add a slightly different dimension to the classroom. Students storing information in a data base can actually see that this information will be used by others. Rather than just turning in a science lab report or a book report to the teacher, students in essence make their information public for "the world to see." Rendering student information useful to others both expands and enhances the learning process. Just as the word processor can enhance students' sense of audience for writing, so can the data base system expand students' sense of audience for information. Assignments are no longer merely tasks to complete for the teachers; they are contributions to an expanding base of information and knowledge.

Effective and efficient use of data base management systems is and will continue to be an important skill for life in the Information Age. As the technology advances, teachers and students will be able to collect and use larger and more varied data bases. In the meantime, existing data base management systems provide exciting potential for teaching problem-solving skills across the curriculum. Each individual teacher can contribute to the realization of this potential through implementing and refining data base activities in the classroom.

SELF-TEST QUESTIONS

1. List the three basic units of organization common to all data base management systems.
2. Give an example of a data base that belongs to you. Could you make this data base more usable by putting it on a data base management system?

Describe what a record for this data base might look like.

3. Which of the following is a characteristic of the program called Bank Street Filer?
   a. It is freeware.
   b. You can store only one data file per disk with it.
   c. It is designed for young learners.
   d. It holds at least 5,000 records.
4. Describe at least three rationales for including data base management activities in the curriculum.
5. Which of the following is not one of the major commodities in modern society?
   a. Information
   b. Land
   c. Industry
   d. Capital
   e. Labor
6. Designing a data base management system is a good initial activity for students learning about data base management.
   a. True
   b. False
7. List the three phases involved in learning to use a data base management system.
8. Suggest a sample activity for each of the phases from Question 7.
9. Describe the major advantage of a computer data base management system over a noncomputer data organization system.
10. Describe how use of a data base management system can increase student accountability for schoolwork. Give an original example.
11. Devise two activities that use a data base management system in the subject(s) area and grade level you will be teaching. Define the objectives for each of these activities.

ANSWERS TO SELF-TEST QUESTIONS

1. The basic units of organization are the file, record, and field. In some systems, the record is called a *form,* but the concept is the same.
2. Personal data bases might include recipe collections, record collections, address books, and magazine collections. Almost any data base will be more efficiently accessed if it is organized into a computer management system. Possible fields should include all those criteria by which you might later

want to search your data base. For example, if you plan to search for all the jazz records in your collection, type of music should be included as a field.

3. c.

4. a. Teaching data base management gives students experience with the basics of using a data base management system.

   b. Data base management systems enable students to perform hypothesis testing.

   c. Creating data base management helps students develop organizational skills.

   d. Students develop skill in techniques of accessing information.

   e. Students are better able to communicate their data to other students.

5. All are major commodities.

6. a. True.

7. a. Using a data base system created by someone else.

   b. Building by adding information to a template created by someone else.

   c. Designing original templates and collecting data.

8. **Using:** Students could search an existing data base on U.S. presidents for data on all the presidents who served before 1800. They could then print out their results in table form and include the table in a report. **Building:** Given a teacher-created template for information about types of microcomputers, students could each research a type of microcomputer and enter a record about that machine. The class could then form and test hypotheses about commonalities and differences among microcomputers. **Designing:** Having completed an experiment in a physics laboratory, students could design a template to organize and store the data from each of the different lab groups. Each lab group's results would make up a record. After the template is designed, each group could enter its results. Analysis and comparison of results could follow.

9. The major advantage provided by a computer data base management system is the flexibility provided by the fields in the system. Although the noncomputer system can be organized by one criterion only, the computer system can be organized by several criteria simultaneously. Thus, the computer system can be searched in many ways.

10. The easy accessibility of data on a data base management system can make student data collection a more meaningful experience. If student data are entered in a data base management system, the data can be compared and analyzed. In a sense, each student's data becomes "public" and thus is not just collected for the teacher to grade.

REFERENCES

Ehman, L., Glenn, A., Johnson, V., & White, C. (1990, November). *Using computer data bases in student problem solving: A study of eight social studies teachers' classes.* Paper presented at the Annual Meeting of the National Council for the Social Studies, College and University Faculty Assembly, Anaheim, CA.

Goldberg, K. (1992). Data base programs and the study of seashells. *The Computing Teacher, 19*(7), 32–34.

Hauserman, C. (1992). Discipline tracking with data bases. *The Computing Teacher, 20*(3), 20.

Hunter, B. (1985). Problem solving with data bases. *The Computing Teacher, 12*(8), 20–27.

Papert, S. (1980). *Mindstorms: Children, computers and powerful ideas.* New York: Basic Books.

Stonier, T. (1983). *The wealth of information: A profile of the post-industrial economy.* London: Methuen.

Stonier, T., & Conlin, C. (1985). *The three C's: Children, computers and communication.* Chichester, England: John Wiley & Sons.

Unia, S. (1991). Exploring information. *The Computing Teacher, 19*(1), 33–34.

White, C. S. (1986). The impact of structured activities with a computer-based file management program on selected information processing skills (Doctoral dissertation, Indiana University, 1985). *Dissertation Abstracts International, 47,* 513A.

REFERENCES FOR ADDITIONAL STUDY

Dunn, S., & Morgan, V. (1987). *The impact of the computer on education: A course for teachers.* London: Prentice Hall.

Elder, C., & White, C. (1989). A world geography database project: Meeting thinking skills head-on. *The Computing Teacher, 17*(3), 29–32.

International Society for Technology in Education. (1992). *The Process Writing Kit.* Eugene, OR: Author.

Kleiman, G. M. (1984). *Brave new schools: How computers can change education.* Reston, VA: Reston.

Lodish, E., & Caputo, A. (1987). ReSEARCHING on line: Schools and electronic data bases. *The Computing Teacher, 14*(7), 10–12.

Parker, J. (1986). Tools for thought. *The Computing Teacher, 14*(2), 21–23.

Salant, A. (1990). A fully integrated instructional database: Promoting student research skills. *Educational Technology, 30*(4), 55–58.

Schiffman, S. (1986). Productivity tools for the classroom. *The Computing Teacher, 13*(8), 27–31.

Sheingold, K., Hawkins, J., & Kurland, D. M. (1984). *Classroom software for the information age (Report No 22).* New York: Center for Children and Technology.

Strickland, A., & Hoffer, T. (1989). Databases, problem solving and laboratory experiences. *Journal of Computers in Mathematics and Science Teaching, 9*(1), 19–28.

Watson, J., & Strudler, N. (1988–1989). Teaching higher order thinking skills with data bases. *The Computing Teacher, 16*(4), 47–50.

Wellington, J. J. (1985). *Children, computers and the curriculum: An introduction to information technology and education.* London: Harper & Row.

CHAPTER TEN

MANAGING NUMBERS

Spreadsheets and Statistical Analysis

GOAL

In this chapter, the reader will be introduced to computer spreadsheets and possible applications of this tool in the classroom.

OBJECTIVES

The reader will be able to do the following:

1. Define the terms *cell, label,* and *value.*
2. Cite at least two major advantages of using a computer spreadsheet program over traditional paper-and-pencil numerical records.
3. Describe what is meant by a *formula* or *function* with respect to spreadsheets.
4. Describe at least three spreadsheet software programs, giving the distinguishing characteristics of each.
5. List at least three reasons that spreadsheets should be included in the curriculum.
6. Describe two ways teachers can use spreadsheets for administrative purposes; cite the advantages to using spreadsheets for these applications.
7. Describe the steps in learning to use a spreadsheet program.
8. Describe the spreadsheet applications in the following subject areas: mathematics, science, social studies, and English.
9. Describe an original spreadsheet activity, applicable to the subject and level in which you are teaching or plan to teach.
10. Explain the characteristics and purposes of statistical software.
11. Explain the difference between spreadsheet programs such as EXCEL and statistical spreadsheet programs.

There is the model of rote learning where material is treated as meaningless; it is a dissociated model. Some of our difficulties in teaching a more culturally integrable mathematics have been due to an objective problem: Before we had computers there were very few good points of contact between what is most fundamental and engaging in mathematics and anything firmly planted in everyday life. But the computer—a mathematics-speaking being in the midst of the everyday home, school and workplace—is able to provide such links. The challenge to education is to find ways to exploit them.

Papert, 1980, p. 47

With the advance of technology in society has come an increased concern about the teaching and learning of sophisticated quantitative skills in schools. Quantitative approaches and analyses are becoming more and more common in almost every field. Every well-educated adult needs skills in mathematical estimation, modeling, and problem solving. Many have suggested, however, that traditional approaches to mathematics teaching in schools are not giving students experiences with the quantitative problem solving skills they need for life in the Information Age.

As Papert (1980) points out, teaching quantitative skills in a meaningful environment has been traditionally problematic in education. He reemphasizes this point when he states, "our education culture gives scarce resources for making sense of what they are learning" (p. 47). In his remarks, Papert is primarily building a case for the teaching of LOGO; however, computer spreadsheets provide another possible computer environment for the teaching of meaningful, "culturally integrable" mathematics.

The spreadsheet gives the classroom teacher the power to create environments where the student is an active participant in numerical problem-solving situations. With a spreadsheet program, teachers can create quantitative environments for children that closely model the real-life mathematics of business and industry and the home.

WHAT IS A SPREADSHEET?

Initially, the basic concept and use of a spreadsheet program are deceptively simple. The idea of a computer spreadsheet arose from the observation that much of the numerical work done by adults in our society was done with a pencil, eraser, and paper. Typically, these tools were used to arrange numerical data into an organized set of rows and columns. Of course, the contents of these rows and columns would vary according to the task at hand. For teachers, the rows might contain student names, and the columns, student grades on different assignments. At home, the rows might be items in a family budget, and the columns, expenditures for different days, weeks, or months. For a small business, the rows might contain income and expenditure items, and the columns, different days of the month. Looking at the samples in Tables 10–1 and 10–2, one can see a similarity in format.

Although the contents of the two examples are quite different, the basic arrangements of the numerical data are similar. You probably have many similar arrangements of numerical data pertaining to budgets, grades, club records, income taxes, gas mileage, and schoolwork.

Such systems of arranging data into rows and columns have worked well for centuries. From the professional accountant to the student struggling to make ends meet, people have made good use of this simple and logical method of organizing numerical data.

The major difficulty with systems using pencil and paper is their inflexibility. One change in one of the sample tables, for instance, requires much erasing and changing of related data. For example, if the car expenses for February are changed to

TABLE 10–1
Sample grades spreadsheet.

Mrs. Jones' Grades					
Student Name	Quiz 1	Quiz 2	Project	Total	%
Sue Smith	10	10	50	70	100
John Jones	8	7	40	55	56
Stan Robbins	9	8	48	65	93

TABLE 10–2
Sample budget spreadsheet.

The Thompson Family Budget				
Expenses	January	February	March	Total
Rent	345	345	345	1,035
Utilities	125	100	75	300
Food	250	225	275	750
Clothes	75	75	75	225
Car	225	250	300	775
Misc.	100	75	100	275
Total	1,120	1,070	1,170	3,360

$275 in Table 10–2, the totals for both February and for car expenses must be recalculated and changed. If John Jones improves his project grade by 5 points (Table 10–1), the total and the percentage must be recalculated. Obviously, this process is tedious and time-consuming.

A computer spreadsheet program uses the same basic organization pattern of arranging figures into rows and columns. Generally, the rows and columns in a system are labeled with numbers and letters, and a typical system offers more than 100 rows and columns. A typical "empty" spreadsheet program is shown in Figure 10–1.

Notice that each location on the spreadsheet can be identified by using the row and column identification. Thus, C4 identifies a position three units over and four units down. Each of the locations on a spreadsheet is called a *cell*. The location of a cell is specified by its row and column location. In Figure 10–1, cell G16 is down in the lower left corner of the screen. Depending on the size of the spreadsheet created, there may be hundreds of available cells.

In a spreadsheet program, two types of data can be entered into a cell: labels and values. A label is a collection of characters and usually is used to identify categories on the spreadsheet. In our gradebook example, the student names are labels. In the budget example, the categories for expenditures are labels. The title of a spreadsheet is also entered as a label.

Notice that in Table 10–3, the following items are treated as labels: the title of the spreadsheet (Mr. Smith's Algebra Grades), the student names, the column headings (student name, Quiz 1, Quiz 2, Test, Homework, Total, Percentage), and the heading "Possible."

The second data type used in a spreadsheet, values, are numerical data. In Mr. Smith's gradebook example, the grades, totals, and percentages are all numerical data. In the Thompson family budget example, the actual expenditures and totals are numerical data and thus are treated as values.

Obviously, there must be more to a spreadsheet program than merely the entry of labels and values into cells that are arranged in rows and columns. The only advantage that such a program would provide over the paper-and-pencil method would be neatness and storage. The real value of a spreadsheet program lies in its ability to accept formulas as values. A formula in a spreadsheet program is generally a function that describes the relationship between various values in the spreadsheet. In the gradebook example, the contents of a "Total" cell may be specified as a formula that adds up the contents of the cells containing specific grades. Thus, if the grades were contained in cells C6, D6, E6, and F6, the entry in the total cell might be (C6 + D6 + E6 + F6). This entry would be treated as a value.

The use of formulas or functions in a spreadsheet program provides at least two major advantages over alternate methods of data representation. The first advantage is that the computer performs the calculation indicated by the formula. In the example indicated, the total is calculated instantly by the computer.

The major advantage of using formulas or functions in a spreadsheet program is the ease with which data can be changed. When a number in a cell is altered, all the related data are automatically changed. Thus, if Carl receives 10 more points on his homework assignments, his total and percentage are immediately recalculated and changed. Then, the spreadsheet would look like that shown in Table 10–4.

Similarly, a family budget could be entered into a spreadsheet program. The Moss family budget for the first quarter of a year has been entered into a spreadsheet program, and the budget is shown in Table 10–5. Now if the family wishes to change any item in their

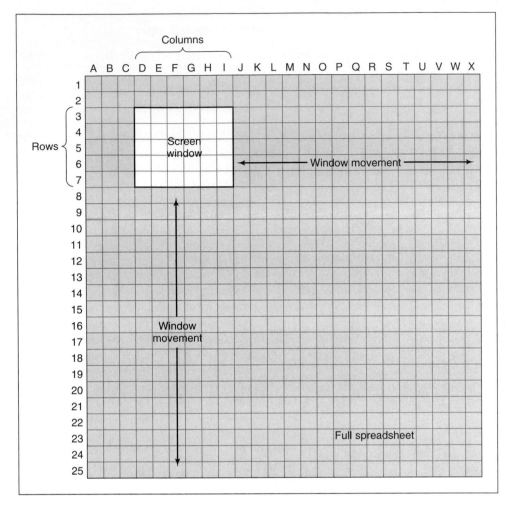

FIGURE 10–1

Electronic spreadsheets have columns designated by letters and rows designated by numbers. It is possible to move the video screen "window" to see any portion of the spreadsheet.

TABLE 10–3

Sample grades spreadsheet.

Mr. Smith's Algebra Grades						
	Quiz 1	Quiz 2	Test	Homework	Total	Percentage
Possible	10	10	100	60	180	
Name						
Smith, Sam	8	9	93	56	166	92.22%
Jones, Joe	9	10	86	57	162	90.00%
Coe, Carl	6	4	67	48	125	69.44%
Betts, Sue	9	10	97	60	176	97.78%
Moe, Ann	3	7	78	57	145	80.56%

TABLE 10–4
Revised sample grades spreadsheet.

Mr. Smith's Algebra Grades					
	Quiz 1	Quiz 2	Test	Homework	Total	Percentage
Possible	10	10	100	60	180	
Name						
Smith, Sam	8	9	93	56	166	92.22%
Jones, Joe	9	10	86	57	162	90.00%
Coe, Carl	6	4	67	58	135	75.00%
Betts, Sue	9	10	97	60	176	97.78%
Moe, Ann	3	7	78	57	145	80.56%

budget, they can make the changes easily. If they decide to trade in their car and purchase a cheaper, used car with payments of $250 per month, they could make those changes in their budget instantaneously. The new budget would look like that shown in Table 10–6.

In Table 10–6, every item related to the change in the car payments (total for car expenses of the quarter, total expenses for each month, total expenses for the quarter, savings for each month, and savings total for the quarter) has been automatically changed to reflect the new amounts in car payments.

The sample formulas in both the gradebook and budget example are simple. Spreadsheets, however, offer much more sophisticated numerical and financial modeling. Notice that in the budget example (Tables 10–5 and 10–6), Joe's salary is variable. Possibly, the couple might want to reflect that variability in the amount they budget for "optional" items. They could, for example, budget 10% of Joe's salary for entertainment, 10% for clothes, and 10% for miscellaneous. Thus, the amount allotted for these items would vary with the amount Joe earned (Table 10–7).

TABLE 10–5
Sample family budget spreadsheet.

Moss Family Budget 1993				
	January	February	March	Quarter
Income				
Ann's Salary	1,550	1,550	1,550	4,650
Joe's Salary	1,235	1,645	765	3,645
Investments	78	98	76	252
Totals	2,863	3,293	2,391	8,547
Expenses				
Rent	900	900	900	2,700
Utilities	176	158	143	477
Food	348	347	345	1,040
Credit Card	140	150	120	410
Car	456	456	456	1,368
Insurance	234	234	123	591
Gas	47	98	65	210
Clothes	144	234	32	410
Entertainment	125	134	97	356
Misc	145	167	100	412
Total Monthly	2,715	2,878	2,381	7,974
Monthly Savings	148	415	10	573

TABLE 10–6
Revised sample family budget spreadsheet.

Moss Family Budget 1993				
	January	February	March	Quarter
Income				
Ann's Salary	1,550	1,550	1,550	4,650
Joe's Salary	1,235	1,645	765	3,645
Investments	78	98	76	252
Totals	2,863	3,293	2,391	8,547
Expenses				
Rent	900	900	900	2,700
Utilities	176	158	143	477
Food	348	347	345	1,040
Credit Card	140	150	120	410
Car	250	250	250	750
Insurance	234	234	123	591
Gas	47	98	65	210
Clothes	144	234	32	410
Entertainment	125	134	97	356
Misc.	145	167	100	412
Total Monthly	2,509	2,672	2,175	7,356
Monthly Savings	354	621	216	1,191

Although the formula does not show on the printed copy in Table 10–7, the entry in the cell for clothes for January reads .1*B8. B8 is the location for Joe's January salary. Similarly, the entry for Miscellaneous for March reads .1*D8, where D8 is the cell containing Joe's March salary.

The design for a particular spreadsheet is called the *template*. The template usually contains all the labels and formulas that make up the spreadsheet. The template can be thought of as the data-free design of the spreadsheet. Although most people design their own templates, numerous special-purpose, commercially prepared templates are available. Many of these templates are available on disk, although some are suggested in books and are entered by the user. Commercially prepared templates include templates for small business accounting, for teachers, and for home use.

A simple template for recording inventory in a small company is shown here. The template contains no data but is in a format that might be applicable to several different small businesses.

Beginners working with spreadsheets will quickly discover they can easily modify existing templates or design new templates to meet their individual needs.

Spreadsheet Software

Like the other tools, spreadsheet software is available in three major forms: single-purpose software, integrated software, and learner-oriented software. Currently, the most popular spreadsheet programs for use in the schools are parts of the integrated system Apple-Works and the integrated system Microsoft Works. The examples in this chapter use the AppleWorks and Microsoft Works spreadsheet programs.

Single-Purpose Software.   Because spreadsheet programs are so popular for business and home financial management, hundreds of single-purpose programs are available. VisiCalc, originally available for

INVENTORY

	Item	Color	Size	Price	Cost	Value	Total Cost	Total Value
Totals								

TABLE 10–7
Sample family budget spreadsheet showing variability in budgeting.

Moss Family Budget 1993				
	January	February	March	Quarter
Income				
Ann's Salary	1,550	1,550	1,550	4,650
Joe's Salary	1,235	1,645	765	3,645
Investments	78	98	76	252
Totals	2,863	3,293	2,391	8,547
Expenses				
Rent	900	900	900	2,700
Utilities	176	158	143	477
Food	348	347	345	1,040
Credit Card	140	150	120	410
Car	250	250	250	750
Insurance	234	234	123	591
Gas	47	98	65	210
Clothes	123.5	164.5	76.5	364.5
Entertainment	123.5	164.5	76.5	364.5
Misc.	61.75	82.25	38.25	182.25
Total Monthly	2,403.75	2,548.25	2,137.25	7,089.25
Monthly Savings	459.25	744.75	253.75	1,457.75

Apple computers in the late 1970s, was the first widely used single-purpose spreadsheet program available for microcomputers. The popularity of VisiCalc was responsible for the early popularity of the microcomputer. Although VisiCalc is no longer produced, it still must be regarded as the "grandparent" of current spreadsheet programs. Old versions of VisiCalc are still used in many schools, and the spreadsheet portion of AppleWorks is quite similar to VisiCalc in format and operation.

Many single-purpose spreadsheet programs, such as EXCEL, are used primarily by small businesses for financial and accounting purposes. Schools, however, tend to use integrated spreadsheet programs because of the financial advantages of obtaining several tool packages in one.

Integrated Software. LOTUS 1-2-3 is one of the most widely used of the integrated programs. With LOTUS 1-2-3, users can integrate their spreadsheet work with compatible graphics and data base programs. Information from the spreadsheet can be immediately graphed or entered into a data base format for sorting and searching. LOTUS is available for IBM and IBM-clone machines as well as for Macintosh computers.

Although less powerful than LOTUS 1-2-3, the integrated AppleWorks program is less expensive and runs on the Apple computers used extensively in schools. With AppleWorks, students can integrate their spreadsheets with the word processor and use the spreadsheet tables to illustrate points made in the text. Data from the spreadsheet can also be transferred to the data base program for searching and sorting. There are no graphing capabilities within AppleWorks, but a related program called Graphworks can be used to graph data from spreadsheets. Because so many schools use AppleWorks, an increasing number of curriculum materials based on this system are becoming available.

Similarly, Microsoft Works has a spreadsheet program that can be easily integrated with Microsoft Works word processing, data base, and graphic capabilities. As more and more schools obtain Macintosh or IBM computers, Microsoft Works is becoming an increasingly popular spreadsheet choice for schools.

Learner Programs. Interestingly, few learner-oriented spreadsheet programs are available on the market. This lack of software seems to be related to a lack of use of the spreadsheet tool in the classroom. Although one can argue that spreadsheet programs are appropriate only after students have studied algebra, there are in fact some simple record-keeping functions of the tool that could be useful for younger children. In fact these simple functions might be useful initial algebra experiences for students. For example, fifth-grade students could construct budgets for themselves or for school events.

It should be noted that including a chapter on spreadsheets is somewhat unusual for beginning educational computing textbooks. When the first edition was published, this text was the only text with such a chapter. Given the power of the spreadsheet to introduce students to useful mathematical ideas, it seems ironic that the spreadsheet has been the computer tool slowest to catch on in the classroom.

WHY SPREADSHEETS?

Learning the Tool Itself

Like the word processor and data base manager, the spreadsheet is an important tool for organizing and manipulating numerical data. At the lowest level, students need to learn the basics of spreadsheet operation. They need to understand the tool and its practical applications.

The basic concept of the spreadsheet has certainly become popular in the business world. In fact, it was the VisiCalc spreadsheet software that made the initial Apple computers so popular for small businesses in the late 1970s and early 1980s. Many specialized programs are now available that adapt basic spreadsheet capabilities to a particular field.

Several years ago, an introductory computer class for preservice teachers invited an agricultural software producer to demonstrate her products. Following her demonstration of rather expensive software, students were encouraged to ask questions. One student asked, "Does that software do anything you couldn't do yourself with a basic spreadsheet program?" The presenter admitted that, in fact, a basic spreadsheet program could be used to obtain the same results as her programs. This, of course, assumed that the user had experience and knowledge about working with spreadsheets. The student asking the question demonstrated a good basic knowledge of the spreadsheet tool itself; she was able to critically evaluate the software manufacturer's claims. Both

the ability to evaluate spreadsheet-type software and the ability to create spreadsheets for particular situations are important skills for students.

This familiarity with the tool can be characterized as a form of computer literacy. Through work with spreadsheets in school, students can acquire the ability to know when and how to use spreadsheet software.

Organizing Numerical Data

As anyone who has attempted to teach mathematics can verify, many students have difficulty learning to organize their work with numbers. From the second grader attempting to arrange a set of figures into a column to the algebra student attempting to arrange the data from a word problem, students can benefit from the "built-in" organizational patterns of the spreadsheet. Students who have worked with spreadsheets can be expected to develop habits of arranging data into labeled, ordered rows and columns.

Work with spreadsheets also gives students practice categorizing numerical data. When setting up a spreadsheet system, students must decide how to divide the data into meaningful categories. In Table 10–7, the creator of the spreadsheet template chose the categories of income and expense and months of the year. Had those categories not served her purpose, she could have gone back to change them. In any case, the creator divided up numerical data into meaningful pieces.

Encouraging Projections, "What-If" Thinking

Critics of current teaching practices in mathematics suggest that students need more experience in numerical problem solving. Just as data base management systems provide students with experiences in hypothesis testing with respect to verbal information, the spreadsheet provides opportunities for hypothesis testing with respect to numerical information.

"What-if" thinking involves testing different hypothetical situations. "What if my rent goes up $50 per month?" is a simple example of this exercise. "What if we doubled our inventory?" is a question that might be useful to small business operators. If the template for the spreadsheet is correctly designed, every item that depends on the changed value will be automatically changed.

Many mathematics students lack an effective intuitive feel for numbers. This problem often becomes evident when a student is working out a word problem.

Students get so involved in the details of how to organize and work the problem that they lose sight of the big picture. Often, students will come up with answers that are unreasonable in terms of the data given, yet they are unable to check themselves. The mathematics teacher who asks, "Does your answer make any sense?" is typically responding to this situation.

The failure of the current mathematics curriculum to help students develop this feel for numbers is well documented in the literature. The National Council of Teachers of Mathematics reports:

> Unfortunately, the applied mathematics experiences that our students get in schools or college courses are only limited and shallow imitations of the real-world process. Secondary school "applications" are almost exclusively limited to well-defined word problems selected to represent familiar types. Problem statements provide all the needed information, rarely more. The solution requires writing an appropriate equation, usually following a textbook example with similar structure and solving for that externally unknown x. Students are seldom invited to challenge the assumptions of the proposed model, make intuitive "guesstimates" of the answers, or to test the reasonableness of computed results. They get precious little experience grappling with the ambiguity and fuzziness of realistic problems. (Fey, 1984)

"What-if" thinking gives students this chance to play with numbers and build important estimation and intuitive mathematics skills. The spreadsheet can create a mathematical environment where students are free to play, guess, and experiment. It can help develop the intuitive sense for numbers and numerical relationships that many students lack. Building this intuitive sense for numbers can also help students develop mathematical and numerical self-confidence, an important asset in almost any field in today's world.

A simple spreadsheet set up to allow students to investigate the effects of putting various values into the equations $y = 2x$ and $y = x^2$ is a good example of using spreadsheets to encourage intuitive mathematics. Using the teacher-made spreadsheet, students are encouraged to enter specific values for x, guess the result, and then let the spreadsheet calculate the answer. The activity can be done with an entire class or by small groups of students. At the conclusion of the activity, students should verbally describe the difference between doubling and squaring a number. A sample of some possible study or experiments with this environment might include the following values:

Linear and Quadratic Equations

$y = 2x$	x	y
	5	10
	10	20
	100	200
	1,000	2,000
	4	8
	40	80
	400	800
	4,000	8,000

$y = x \wedge 2$	x	y
	5	25
	10	100
	100	10,000
	1,000	1,000,000
	4	16
	40	1,600
	400	160,000
	4,000	16,000,000

A second example of a spreadsheet for "what-if" thinking uses a student-constructed spreadsheet designed to record income and expenses for the production of a student play. Students might set up the spreadsheet like the one in Table 10–8.

Using this template, students could "play" with their options to maximize their profits. They could try out various options for the sale of food and drinks. They might contrast buying more drinks and candy and selling them for a lower price, with buying fewer and selling them for a higher price. They can ask "What if we don't sell all the candy or drinks?" Similarly, students can experiment with different ticket prices for adults and students and immediately observe the effect on profits.

Students could aim for a particular profit and adjust ticket prices and food sales to meet that profit. For example, if the students wished to project a profit of $250, the values shown in Table 10–9 might be used in the spreadsheet.

Used properly, spreadsheets can provide students with valuable experience in developing estimation and numerical problem-solving skills. A good spreadsheet template eliminates the need for much tedious calculation, allowing students to focus on the formation of mathematical generalizations and concepts. Traditional paper-and-pencil mathematics still has an important place in the curriculum, however. Students must

TABLE 10–8
Sample student-constructed spreadsheet.

Play Profits			
	Number	**Price**	**Total**
Income			
Tickets			
Adults	45	$1.50	$ 67.50
Students	50	$ .50	$ 25.00
Drinks	100	$ .15	$ 15.00
Candy	100	$ .25	$ 25.00
Total			$132.50
Expenses			
Drinks	100	$0.10	$ 10.00
Candy	100	$0.07	$ 7.00
Total			$ 17.00
Total Profit			$115.50
Food Profit			$ 23.00
Ticket Profit			$ 92.50

TABLE 10–9
Revised sample student-constructed spreadsheet.

Play Profits			
	Number	**Price**	**Total**
Income			
Tickets			
Adults	45	$3.00	$135.00
Students	50	$1.00	$ 50.00
Drinks	97	$ .35	$ 33.95
Candy	96	$ .50	$ 48.00
Total			$266.95
Expenses			
Drinks	100	$0.10	$ 10.00
Candy	100	$0.07	$ 7.00
Total			$ 17.00
Total Profit			$249.95
Food Profit			$ 64.95
Ticket Profit			$185.00

develop such basic skills to benefit from the estimation and "what-if" experiences provided through work with spreadsheets.

Practical Work With Formulas, Functions

Spreadsheets provide an ideal environment for students to apply concepts about functions and formulas. In creating a template for a spreadsheet, students must work out formulas that express the relationships between the values in the spreadsheet. Thus, students have an opportunity to apply their knowledge of functions.

Often, learners are taught about functions without any context in which to use their knowledge. For too many math students, functions exist only in the mathematics textbook. In a spreadsheet environment students can apply their mathematics to real-world situations. Spreadsheets can be used both as a tool for the teaching of functions and as an application exercise for students who have already been introduced to functions.

The spreadsheet provides the type of mathematical application exercise so necessary in the development of strong quantitative skills. When creating templates, students are analyzing and expressing the relationships among various variables in a situation. They are active participants and creators of a mathematical environment. Setting up a template for a small business can be

regarded as a very complex algebra word problem. Students have to define the variables and then express the relationships between them.

TEACHERS' ADMINISTRATIVE USE OF THE SPREADSHEET

To become familiar and comfortable with the capabilities of the spreadsheet, teachers should first use them for their own purposes. They will quickly find that this initial use of the spreadsheet is far more than a "practice" exercise; the spreadsheet can be an extremely useful tool for many of the management and administrative functions of the typical classroom teacher.

Grade Records

Numerous gradebook software programs are available, but many teachers prefer using a spreadsheet program for recording grades. The major advantage of a spreadsheet over a prepared gradebook program is that teachers can create their own templates that reflect their personal needs and styles. They can weight grades, figure percentages, and calculate group statistics on assignments, for example. Category labels can describe or number specific assignments.

Why Use a Spreadsheet for Grades?

Ease and efficiency of calculation are other advantages of using a spreadsheet for grade records. Once the template is set up, totals and percentages are automatically updated each time a new score is added. Average scores for individual tests and other statistics can be calculated as soon as the data for a test are entered. Teacher and students can always access up-to-date information about student performance. At the end of the semester, as soon as the last grades are entered, final calculations are automatically performed, making late nights with a gradebook and a calculator a thing of the past (Figure 10–2).

Spreadsheets also make revising student data much more efficient. If a grade on an exam is changed, the new value is entered, and the total for that student is automatically changed. If a new student enters the class, that student's name can be immediately inserted in the correct place alphabetically.

Finally, spreadsheets provide a convenient method of saving student data. Generally, an entire year's worth of student data can be saved on one disk. Teachers can easily keep several years of student data in a small disk storage box, making student data from previous years readily accessible.

Getting Started.

The first step in setting up student grades on a spreadsheet is locating the appropriate software package. Because a typical grade file is simple and comparatively small, almost any spreadsheet program would be adequate for the task. Generally, the software that teachers plan to use with their students is a good choice because in setting up and using the grading system, teachers gain valuable experience with the software. Students are also introduced to the package as teachers explain the grading system to them and provide a printed copy of their records.

The next step is designing a template. The template will contain a place for student names and might include other student demographic information. Some type of student personal identification number is usually a valuable part of a template; teachers can then print out grades by student number rather than name and ensure confidentiality.

After entering student demographics, teachers will want to label all graded assignments for the grading period. (This initial template can be changed, and additional graded assignments can easily be entered later.) Formulas for student totals, weighted totals, percentage scores, test averages, and standard deviations can then be entered. Once the template is set up, all

---

FIGURE 10–2
Electronic gradebooks are easy to create using a spreadsheet program.

Last name	2. GFX, WP (10)	3. D.E. (5)	4. I'NET (10)	5. IMAGING (5)	6. AUD, VID (5)	7. PRJ. FAIR (10)	8. H'STUDIO (20)	9. DTP (15)	10. DB (10)	11. SS (10)	12. PROJ-I (10)	13. PROJ-II (10)	TOT LAB	PROJ GRADE	Q1	Q2	Q3	TOT QUIZ	FINAL EXAM	TOTAL POINTS	PERCENT
DS	10	5	10	5	5	10	18	15	9	10	10	10	117		19	16	20	55	54	226	94%
CG	10	5	10	5	5	10	18	15	9	9	10	10	116		17	16	19	52	47	215	90%
NJ	10	5	10	5	5	10	19	15	10	10	10	10	119		16	16	16	48	49	216	90%
TR	10	5	10	5	5	10	19	15	10	10	10	10	119		15	16	17	48	44	211	88%
YS	10	5	9	5	5	10	18	15	9	8	7	10	111		20	17	17	54	48	213	89%
BK	9	5	8	5	5	9	17	14	9	8	10	10	109		20	18	18	56	47	212	88%
PT	9	5	7	5	5	9	18	14	10	10	10	10	112		16	16	19	51	48	211	88%
JW	10	5	10	5	5	10	18	13	10	10	8	10	114		19	13	13	45	39	198	83%
ND	10	5	10	5	5	10	19	14	9	8	10	10	115		15	15	14	44	45	204	85%
CS	9	5	10	5	5	10	18	13	10	10	10	10	115		16	10	18	44	44	203	85%
RL	10	5	8	5	5	10	19	14	10	10	10	10	116		16	11	15	42	43	201	84%
MA	10	5	10	5	5	0	19	14	10	9	10	10	107		18	17	14	49	41	197	82%
ZT	10	5	10	5	5	10	18	12	9	9	10	10	113		14	12	15	41	43	197	82%
LP	9	2	10	5	5	10	12	13	9	9	10	7	101		14	12	14	40	41	182	76%
HR	10		9	5	5	10	16	13	10	6	10	10	104		15		18	33	41	178	74%
MS	10	5	9	5	5	9	12	10	9	8			82		12	9	12	33	36	151	63%

these calculations will be performed every time new data are entered in the spreadsheet. The template shown in Table 10–10 is a simple example of types of information teachers might want to include in their work. Note that one change in a student grade in the spreadsheet will automatically be reflected in the class average, student total, student weighted total, and student percentage.

Class or Club Financial Records

Spreadsheets can be used to keep the financial records for classes and clubs and also allow for some financial projecting. For example, having entered club financial data on a spreadsheet, students can ask, "What if we raised the dues by $2?" They could change the entries for amount of dues and also number of members, if they think the increase will reduce membership. They could then observe the corresponding changes in other areas. If they are not happy with the results, they might try several possible raises until they have found the best combination of dues and membership.

The financial records of the student play presented earlier in the chapter illustrate a different type of financial modeling made possible by spreadsheets. Students and teachers can decide how much money they need to raise from an event and then manipulate the variables to model a situation in which they will be likely to meet their goal. They can try raising admission prices, lowering food prices, getting people to donate the raw materials, and numerous other financial strategies. Basically,

the spreadsheet gives students and teachers an opportunity to do some fairly sophisticated financial modeling as they attempt to optimize income for their clubs and class projects. In addition to increasing the financial efficiency of these organizations, students receive valuable experiences in real-life mathematics.

Athletic Records

Spreadsheets are an ideal means for providing young athletes with immediate statistics on their performance. As soon as the data are entered, an updated information sheet can be printed out for each athlete. The baseball coach can compute new statistics for each player as soon as the data from each game are entered. The swimming coach can summarize each swimmer's statistics for a meet and compare these statistics to the swimmer's best times and those of others. Table 10–11 shows a spreadsheet created by a swimming coach to provide data to her swimmers immediately after their performance in a meet.

An increasing number of coaches and managers are recognizing the value of computers for recording student statistics, and computers are becoming an integral part of school athletic events. Many coaches appoint students to enter data into a spreadsheet right at the sports event. The spreadsheet also can supply students with immediate feedback on their performances. Coaches routinely provide students with printouts summarizing their performance at a particular athletic event and comparing these data with previous performances.

TABLE 10–10
Template for teacher's record-keeping spreadsheet.

	Ess.1	Qz.1	Poem	Qz.2	Total	W.T.	%
Honors English Grades Period 2 Fall 1993							
Possible	30	18	42	20	110	148	
Student Name							
Abe, Joe	25	12	32	15	84	111	75.00%
Brown, Betty	27	15	40	17	99	131	88.51%
Downs, Ralph	29	18	40	17	104	139	93.92%
Miller, Sue	26	14	36	15	91	120	81.08%
Taylor, Todd	22	12	30	14	78	104	70.27%
Class Average	25.8	14.2	35.6	15.6	91.2	121	81.76%

W.T. = weighted total

TABLE 10–11
Swim meet spreadsheet.

File:	AMES1993		
Report:	Meet summary		
Name	Class	Event	Performance
Ann Miller		100 Freestyle	R 1:27.34
Ann Miller		100 Freestyle	D.Q.
Ann Miller		100 Freestyle	1:29.58
Beth Dinsmore		100 Backstroke	1:24.33
Beth Dinsmore		100 Freestyle	R No Split
Beth Dinsmore		100 Backstroke	1:25.41
Beth Dinsmore		100 Freestyle	1:12.07
Beth Dinsmore		50 Freestyle	38.84
Beth Dinsmore		100 Freestyle	1:10.80
Beth Dinsmore		500 Freestyle	6:49.60
Beth Dinsmore		100 Backstroke	1:22.58
Beth Dinsmore		50 Backstroke	38.55
Beth Dinsmore		500 Freestyle	6:36.79
Beth Dinsmore		50 Backstroke	39.50
Beth Dinsmore		500 Freestyle	6:34.63
Beth Dinsmore		50 Backstroke	38.45
Beth Dinsmore		500 Freestyle	6:34.00
Beth Dinsmore		100 Freestyle	R 1:09.74
Beth Dinsmore		50 Backstroke	39.07
Beth Dinsmore		500 Freestyle	6:30.26

TEACHING ABOUT SPREADSHEETS

Spreadsheet programs are among the simplest computer tools to learn. The entering of labels, values, and formulas is an uncomplicated process. As students wish to model complex relationships among variables, however, the mathematics involved in constructing spreadsheets can become quite complicated. The tool itself can be as simple or as complex as the needs of the students dictate.

Students who have never used a spreadsheet program should begin with paper-and-pencil exercises that simulate the spreadsheet operation. These initial exercises might involve setting up personal budgets, compiling record sheets for class science experiments, or projecting population changes over a period of years. With these exercises, the students have a concrete model to which they can relate their later activities on the computer. Also, students who have had the experience of hand-calculating totals, percentages, and averages will be in a position to appreciate the value of the formulas or functions in the spreadsheet. After the initial paper-and-pencil work, the data can be transferred to the spreadsheet. Here, students will immediately see the value of formulas for saving entry and calculation time.

Using Spreadsheets

Students normally begin by using spreadsheet environments created by someone else, usually the classroom teacher. Spreadsheets are not yet used as extensively in education as data base management programs, so there are not as many commercially available templates for spreadsheets.

Initial spreadsheet environments can be simple opportunities for students to enter data and observe results. One simple program is based on a model of estimating and testing. Here, the teacher sets up a program with a simple mathematical relationship such as squaring a number. Students are given a worksheet on which to enter their data. Each time a number is supplied, students are asked to estimate the square of the number, enter the number, and then record the actual result. The teacher, the student, or other students can all supply "interesting" numbers to test. At first, students will probably start with whole number values; rapidly, however, they will move to exploring the difference in the squares of numbers such as .01 and .001. In addition to obtaining experience entering data and observing the effect of a formula entered by someone else, students build valuable estimation skills.

Teachers can also set up templates to help students organize, record, and calculate results from classroom or school surveys. Students could enter the individual information, and the spreadsheet could calculate statistics on the information. Some programs will also produce graphs summarizing the information entered. A sample of such a survey is shown in Table 10–12.

Creating Spreadsheets

Students will probably begin creating their own spreadsheets by modifying templates created by others. In the school survey example in Table 10–12, students could easily add columns for the number of music activities and the number of sports activities. They would then need to enter a formula for computing the averages for these columns, and thus they would begin the process of creating their own spreadsheets.

To create meaningful complex spreadsheet programs, students need to be able to work with formulas and functions. As suggested earlier, the spreadsheet provides a natural arena in which to apply information learned about functional relationships. Teachers must,

however, proceed with caution and remember that younger students probably do not possess the skills and mathematical maturity necessary to create their own spreadsheets.

USING SPREADSHEETS ACROSS THE CURRICULUM

Although students need to learn the mechanics of working with spreadsheets, the real value of the tool is its application to quantitative problems across the curriculum. Students will not build estimation, modeling, and problem solving skills just from learning how to operate spreadsheets; it is important that teachers devise activities with spreadsheets that will help students benefit from the real problem-solving value of the tool.

Understandably, much of the emphasis in the initial work with spreadsheets in education has been in the area of mathematics. Quantitative approaches, analyses, and modeling techniques are becoming increasingly significant, however, in many subject areas. The spreadsheet is a valuable tool for enabling students to experience some of these approaches. Using the spreadsheet across the curriculum will help students perceive the importance and usefulness of quantitative methods outside the mathematics classroom and help them learn to apply mathematical techniques in real-world situations. Papert (1980) says using spreadsheets across the curriculum may help make mathematics more "culturally integrable" for students. Given that the Professional Standards for Teaching Mathematics produced by the National Council of Teachers of Mathematics (1991) emphasize integrating mathematics with other subjects and teaching mathematics across the curriculum, the spreadsheet provides an especially valuable tool to enable this type of integration.

TABLE 10–12
Spreadsheet for student survey data.

	Elm Street School					
Student Name	Age	Ht.	Brothers	Sisters	Pets	Schools
Smith, Sue	11	43	2	1	5	2
Tiber, Tim	7	36	1	0	1	1
Williams, Joe	9	40	1	1	7	1
Average	9.0	39.7	1.3	.7	4.3	1.3

Mathematics

The majority of educational applications of spreadsheets has been developed for use in mathematics classes. Generally, these applications are structured to give students experience in estimation and scientific problem solving with numbers.

A simple program designed by a British mathematics teacher illustrates the power of spreadsheet applications in mathematics. This program enables students to experiment with the effects of changing a dimension of a cube on the volume of a cube. Students start with a spreadsheet that calculates the volume of a cube, given the dimensions. The initial spreadsheet program looks like this:

Volume of a Cube

Dimension	Length	Height	Breadth	Volume
1	1	1	1
2	2	2	8
3	3	3	27
4	4	4	64
8	8	8	512
12	12	12	1,728

Students can experiment with changing the dimensions of a cube and can see the effect on the volume. The spreadsheet can be used by the entire class at one time, with the teacher asking students to predict changes before the computer calculates them. Questions such as, "What happens when you multiply the side of the cube by 2?" will provide interesting student speculations. These speculations can then be tested using the template.

After work with this template, the teacher can introduce a second template that enables a different type of projection. Here the students can choose to increase a side by a certain amount and then observe the effects of this increase.

Volume of a Cube
Increase by .5

Dimension	Length	Height	Breadth	Volume
1	1	1	1
1.5	1.5	1.5	3.375
2	2	2	8
2.5	2.5	2.5	15.625
3	3	3	27
3.5	3.5	3.5	42.875
4	4	4	64
4.5	4.5	4.5	91.125
5	5	5	125

If the problem is to find the side of a cube whose volume is 15, the students can use this template to help

Notes From the Literature

By using a spreadsheet to solve "story problems" in math, students are able to concentrate on the process of developing a solution. Students feel free to experiment, using the skills of estimation and approximation, while the computer does the calculations.

Arad, O. S. (1986–1987). The spreadsheet: Solving word problems. The Computing Teacher, 14(4), 13–15.

solve the problem. From the first experiment, it is evident that the solution is close to 2.5, but slightly less than 2.5. Students can now use 2.4 as a starting point and use the increase program again; this time the increase will be .01.

Volume of a Cube
Increase by .01

Dimension	Length	Height	Breadth	Volume
2.45	2.45	2.45	14.706
2.46	2.46	2.46	14.886
2.47	2.47	2.47	15.069
2.48	2.48	2.48	15.252
2.49	2.49	2.49	15.438
2.50	2.50	2.50	15.625

Students can now see that the side is slightly more than 2.46. If they desire a more precise answer, they can go back to the increase template and change the initial value to 2.46 and the increase to .005 or .001. Obviously, the process can go on for a long time. The students, through use of the template, gain skills in approximation and problem solving and also probably enjoy the fun of the search.

From upper elementary school through college, the spreadsheet can be used to create dynamic mathematical environments for learners. The type of experimentation modeled in the simple cubing example can be replicated in situations throughout the mathematics curriculum.

Social Studies

Quantitative analysis and modeling are increasingly important techniques across the social sciences. Both statistics and "what-if" projecting techniques are useful in helping social scientists understand the past and predict the future. Spreadsheets can make some of these techniques accessible to students.

Notes From the Literature

Much of the software distributed for use in algebra classes treat students as spectators rather than involving them as participants. To address this problem, some instructors ask students to write computer-based programs to perform algorithms; however, without sufficient programming experience, too much time is spent learning and debugging programs that have nothing to do with the understanding of the algorithm. Other instructors ask students to rely on pencil, paper, and calculator to solve problems involving algorithms. The amount of work seems to exceed that which is necessary to understand a particular problem-solving technique. Pinter-Lucke (1992) views application of a computer spreadsheet as the optimal vehicle at the pre-calculus level for working through numerical algorithms: "A spreadsheet displays more values at one time than a calculator can display, and it involves the user in a more interactive way than a computer program can. A spreadsheet best replicates the process of working out the problem by hand without a lot of tedious calculations. With all three devices, several examples can be computed in a short amount of time. Only with a spreadsheet, however, are intermediate values likely to be displayed. It is by making general observations about these values, in addition to the final values, that students get a better understanding of the methods" (p. 93).

Pinter-Lucke, C. (1992). Rootfinding with a spreadsheet in pre-calculus. *Journal of Computers in Mathematics and Science Teaching, 11,* 85–93.

In social studies, students can use spreadsheets to organize and interpret quantitative data. Data from a school survey, tables in geography books, town records, or records kept by students can be arranged and manipulated using a spreadsheet. Students can compute statistics, test relationships, and model changes in these data. Through such work, social studies can become a more vital, dynamic area for learning. Social studies becomes something more than material written in a book; it becomes a lively, changing discipline where relationships can be discovered and tested.

Hannah (1986) describes one spreadsheet exercise for social studies classes. In this activity students were first asked to rank a number of cities from the "best place to live" to the "least desirable place to live." Using a spreadsheet, weightings were assigned, and each city received an average class rating. Hannah writes:

The students next were introduced to the inspiration for this activity, *Rand McNally's Places Rated Almanac: Your Guide to Finding the Best Places to Live in America.* In the Rand McNally ranking of 329 metropolitan areas in the United States, the students' favorites didn't do quite as well. Honolulu was 61st rather than 1st. (1986, p. 14)

Students then studied the various criteria that different "raters" used to come up with data on ranking cities for "quality of life." They saw how selecting and weighting criteria can determine which cities come out on top and how changing the criteria and weightings can make dramatic differences in the ratings.

The final assignment for the students was a competition. Groups of students drew from a hat the name of the city they would represent. The students were then asked to devise a spreadsheet that showed that their city was the No. 1 place to live. The students who drew Philadelphia included number of sports teams, major museums, city parks, crime rates, major zoos, population, and number of hospitals in their criteria for rating. The students participating in Hannah's (1986) activity received valuable experience in learning how statistics and models can be used and manipulated in social science. Rather than just studying about procedures and techniques involved in ranking quality of life in major cities, the students became active mathematical modelers.

English

Although a few may protest that numbers have no place in the study of English, this field also is adopting some quantitative techniques. At the college and graduate level, the computer is used increasingly to perform numerical style analyses of different authors. In one such study, comparisons are made between women and men characters on the number of questions asked by each. Data are collected from all the novels of a particular author, and then statistics are calculated on these data to determine one aspect of the different characterizations of males and females by a particular author.

On a simpler level, students can perform similar analyses of works they are reading in an English class. Data could be collected on many aspects of a written work from grammar through style, entered on a spreadsheet and analyzed or compared with other works. Such quantitative exercises may help students focus on individual aspects of style and how these affect the overall written work.

Record-keeping applications of spreadsheets might also be especially useful in the English class. Students could keep records of their own writing, using templates that calculate statistics such as average number of misspellings per 100 words or average number of sentence fragments per 100 words. Through keeping a record of successive assignments, students can chart their progress and also determine areas where their writing skills need special attention.

A second record-keeping application useful for teachers of speech is suggested by a speech teacher (Dribin, 1985). Dribin suggests a method of using spreadsheets for helping students learn to evaluate other students' speeches more effectively. Dribin describes how student evaluation of other student speeches is often imprecise and not very useful to the student being evaluated. She mentions that frequently the popularity of the student speaker is the major criteria for evaluation. She suggests using a spreadsheet to help students to learn to evaluate in more objective and useful ways.

This particular spreadsheet is set up to compare each student evaluator's ratings with the teacher's ratings on particular criteria. If a student rates a speaker's eye contact as 9 and the teacher rates it as 2, the evaluator receives a -7 for her evaluation on that criteria. Thus, in addition to the speaker receiving feedback on the student evaluations, each evaluator receives a score on her evaluation. The results for both the speaker and the evaluators can be obtained immediately when the data are entered into the prepared template.

Obviously, this technique can be applied to many situations in which students are asked to evaluate other students, such as in judging each other's writing.

Science

A spreadsheet can be used for hypothesis testing and revision, making it a natural tool in the science curriculum. With a spreadsheet, students can organize and record data and then hypothesize mathematical relationships among the data. Students can then immediately see how well their projections fit the data. The use of the spreadsheet to enhance a standard first-year high school physics experiment illustrates this approach.

Typically, high school physics students perform some type of laboratory experiment to explore the relationships between mass, acceleration, and time. Usually, students work with a mechanism that allows them to roll a ball down an inclined plane and measure the distance the ball has traveled at different time intervals.

The teacher could start out this laboratory session by suggesting that students will be asked to determine the general equation for the distance the ball travels in a given amount of time. The teacher can suggest the following equation as an initial guess when the incline is 30 degrees and ask the students to determine the value of k through recording data from several observations.

$$x = k(t = 2)/1$$

The first experimental situation will involve simply rolling the ball down the inclined plane. Students will be asked to perform the experiment 10 times under these circumstances and record their data on a prepared spreadsheet. On the spreadsheet, students will record time and distance traveled. Students can enter their prediction equation for the distance traveled, and this value will be automatically calculated for each entry. Another column in the spreadsheet might show the difference in the predicted distance (from the equation) from the actual distance. By observing the results and adjusting the value for k, students should be able to come up with a reasonable approximation of k.

Notes From the Literature

Spreadsheet programs can be used by students studying economics to generate "manageable models" on the computer that will help them to understand complex theoretical principles.

Balestri, D., Cochrane, H., & Thursh, D. (1984, December). High tech, low tech, no tech: Three case studies of computers in the classroom. AAHE Bulletin, 11–14.

Notes From the Literature

The use of spreadsheets in science labs frees students from performing complex mathematical calculations and allows them to concentrate on analysis of the data. Emphasis is on using the microcomputer as a tool for learning science concepts, and students are encouraged to observe how the spreadsheet manipulates the data entered.

Pogge, A. F., & Lunetta, V. N. (1987). Spreadsheets answer "what if . . ." The Science Teacher, 54(8), 46–49.

Inclined Plane Experiment
Experiment 1

Trial	Time (ti)	Distance (xi)	k Prediction	Difference
1				
2				
3				
4				
5				
6				
7				
8				
9				
10				

Experiment 2

Trial	Time (ti)	Distance (xi)	k Prediction	Difference
1				
2				
3				
4				
5				
6				
7				
8				
9				
10				

After the initial experiment, students use an apparatus that releases the ball with a specified initial velocity. Students can use the same spreadsheet template for this second experiment. They will immediately notice that as the actual time increases, the error in their prediction equation increases. Students then revise their predictions for the relationship, given this new situation. They then enter their "guesses" for the function describing the relationship and immediately observe the error terms for their guesses. Through revising their functions, they should be able to minimize the error and see that in the second case they need to add the initial velocity as a constant to their equations. They can test and see that this more general equation will also work in the first case, where the initial velocity is, of course, zero.

Given the power of the spreadsheet, students can focus their attention on the "big picture" of the experiment and not on individual calculations. They are free to model ideas about physical relationships and immediately observe the accuracy of their models. This type of experimental exercise is readily adaptable across the science curriculum.

STATISTICS AND SPREADSHEETS

Increasingly, sophisticated statistical computer applications that once required mainframe computers are becoming available for microcomputers. Complex statistical analyses used by educational researchers can be rapidly and easily computed with software such as StatView II or Statistica. Even the most powerful and widely used statistical applications such as the Statistical Package for the Social Sciences (SPSS) are now available in microcomputer versions.

Statistical programs are tools that permit the user to input large amounts of numerical data into spreadsheets so they can be analyzed. Statistical spreadsheets have powerful mathematical formulae built into them. For analysis, data need only be correctly entered into a spreadsheet format. A generic spreadsheet such as LOTUS 1-2-3 or EXCEL could be used, but researchers would have to understand the mathematics well enough to be able to enter formulae themselves. Statistical software makes complex mathematical computations available at the click of a mouse button, or the stroke of a key.

Statistics

The study of statistics gives educators methods for describing and summarizing data. Statistics are used to explain a collection of numbers or to compare two or more sets of numbers. Educational researchers use statistics to test hypotheses and answer research questions. Teachers use statistics to help students understand concepts, or to show relationships among variables. As Blommers and Lindquist said more than 35 years ago, "Statistical methods are techniques used to facilitate the interpretation of collections of quantitative or numerical data" (1960, p. 3).

Statistical tests are often divided into two types: descriptive or inferential. Descriptive statistics are used to reduce large quantities of data to a manageable size and describe them precisely. Average, standard deviation, and range of scores are examples of descriptive statistics (Table 10–13).

Inferential statistics permit the comparison and identification of relationships between collections of numbers. Correlations, t-tests, and analysis of variance are examples of inferential statistical tests.

Statistics is the analysis of numbers, and the numbers used are obtained by measurement. For example, teachers give grades. Grades are often expressed as numbers, such as a score on a vocabulary test, 35 out of a possible 40. The number 35 is one score and is only meaningful when it is compared with other students' scores. If a vocabulary test is given to 30 students in a language arts class, there will be 30 scores. One way to describe the class performance on this test would be to average all 30 scores. If the average is 29, then a student with a score of 35 would be "above average." If the scores range from 21 to 37, and if the standard deviation is $3\frac{1}{2}$, then the teacher and students would have a better understanding of the relationship of any one score, such as the 35, to the entire collection of scores. The average (often expressed as the mean), standard deviation, and range are examples of descriptive statistics.

Inferential statistics permit more sophisticated analyses. The language arts teacher might want to see if the boys in her class perform differently from the girls. The appropriate test for this analysis would be a t-test that would compare the average, or mean, score for the girls with that of the boys. Or the teacher might compare the scores from the 40-question vocabulary test with scores from a writing assignment. The appropriate analysis would be a correlation. Both the t-test and correlation are examples of inferential statistical tests (Table 10–14).

Statistical analyses use numbers to represent events or characteristics. Numbers are obtained by measuring. There are four levels of measurement: nominal, ordinal, interval, and ratio. *Nominal* measures classify objects, people, or observations into categories where no ordering is implied. Examples of nominal measures are the color of automobiles, the political affiliations of college students, or the day of a week when a test was

TABLE 10–13
Course grading: Distant versus local students' scores.

		Local Student Scores	Distant Student Scores	Combined Scores	t	p<
Quiz	$\bar{X}=$	68.0	66.8	67.7	.54	.60
Scores	SD=	5.8	3.8	5.3		
Minor Project	$\bar{X}=$	71.8	70.2	71.3	1.6	.12
Scores	SD=	2.3	2.7	2.5		
Final Project	$\bar{X}=$	77.8	76.9	77.6	1.0	.32
Scores	SD=	2.3	2.2	2.6		
Final Exam	$\bar{X}=$	31.9	33.6	32.4	−1.2	.25
Scores	SD=	3.4	3.4	3.4		

TABLE 10–14
Course grading: Correlations.

	Final Project	Final Exam	Minor Projects	Quizzes
Final Project		$r = .41$ $p = 03$	$r = .65$ $p \leq .01$	$r = .48$ $p = .01$
Final Exam			.42 .03	.49 .01
Projects				.64 $< .01$
Quizzes				

given. *Ordinal* measures are used when it is possible to detect degrees of differences among observations and ordering and when ranking is possible. The sizes of cars, the heights of students, and the sequences of classes are examples of ordinal data.

Interval measurement is used when the intervals between numbers used to represent observations represent equal quantities. IQ scores and the Fahrenheit temperature scale are examples of interval measurement. *Ratio* measurement assumes that there is an absolute zero point where the number scale originates.

The zero point indicates the total absence of the phenomena being measured. Very few variables in education lend themselves to the ratio scale. The Kelvin scale for measuring temperature has an absolute zero point and is an example of interval measurement.

Generally, teachers categorize students into groups, such as boys and girls, or first period and third period, and compare test scores between these groups. The groupings are examples of nominal measures, and the test scores are examples of interval measures.

Statistics in the Curriculum

Virtually all microcomputer-based statistical systems use a spreadsheet for data storage. Rows in spreadsheets are used to store information about one person or object, and each column in a row is where observations about each individual or object are entered. For example, a language arts teacher could prepare a spreadsheet that has a row for each of the 30 students in her class, and columns in the spreadsheet could be used to store information about each student (Figure 10–3).

When a statistical package is used to store student records, it is easy for the teacher not only to calculate grades but also to analyze the trends of scores and the relationship among scores (see Table 10–13). For exam-

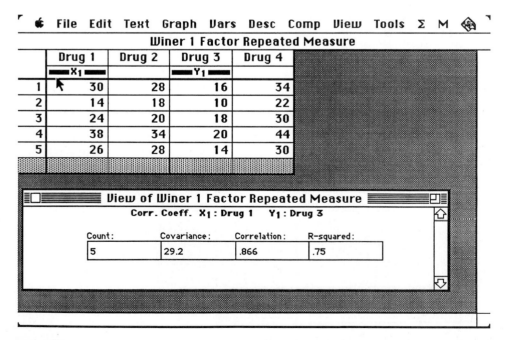

FIGURE 10–3
Statview II is a statistical package designed for use with microcomputers.

ple, students often worry about the first few quizzes given in a class. They wonder if they score poorly will their final course grade be affected. A simple correlation between quiz score and final grade for students in the course in a previous term would let students know how much their score on the first quiz is related to their final course grade. Statistical analyses also let teachers determine trends in their grading.

Hypothesis testing is where statistics have their greatest effect. Hypotheses are used to predict relationships between variables being studied. For example, a hypothesis about student attitudes toward distance education might be stated as follows:

> There is no difference in attitude toward the effectiveness of a course between students who are located in the same site as the teacher and students who are located at a remote site connected to the teaching site by two-way interactive television.

To test this hypothesis, the attitudes of students would be measured. Probably, a reliable and valid test measuring the construct "attitude toward course effectiveness" would be given to students at both the local and remote sites. Researchers consider the attitude test score to be a dependent variable because a student's score on the attitude test depends on the student's experience in the course. The location where students learn is called an *independent variable*, because it is independent of any manipulation and does not change during the study. A t-test would be used to determine the difference between the attitudes of the two groups of students. When a t-test is computed, the mean or average scores from the attitude test from the two groups of students are compared to identify the statistical significance of the difference between them.

Obviously, the interpretation of statistical test results is not the intent of this book. However, the use of simple yet powerful microcomputer-based statistical applications makes it possible for educators not only to keep records and compute grades but also to answer sophisticated research questions and to test experimental hypotheses. Action research, which is research conducted by practitioners to answer real-world questions, has become considerably easier because of the availability of powerful microcomputer statistical packages.

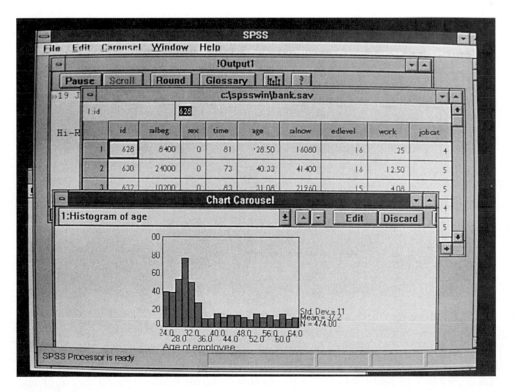

FIGURE 10–4

Statistical Package for the Social Sciences (SPSS) is a powerful statistical package. Formerly available only to users with access to a mainframe or minicomputer, it also is now packaged for use with microcomputers.

Elementary Curriculum.

Elementary applications fall into two categories. First, teachers use statistical software to keep records of grades and to analyze the relationships between groups of students. Increasingly, the results of portions of nationally standardized tests such as the Iowa Tests of Basic Skills are being used by teachers, school counselors, and administrators to diagnose students' aptitudes and characteristics and to prescribe correct instructional activities for them.

Second, teachers use statistical software to analyze data collected by students in classes. For example, in a second-grade class, the weights of two baby gerbils can be measured as they grow and compared with how much they eat. Also, students in a fifth-grade class can record outdoor temperatures for several months and compare these data with the time between sunrise and sunset. These data can be correlated and plotted. Some classes use a computer and modem to collect weather data from computer pals located in schools in other states or other countries. Data collection and sharing among classes give students something to correspond about with their distant friends.

At the elementary level, use of statistical packages prepares students for more sophisticated uses in secondary school. It may not even be necessary to purchase software. Some elementary science texts now come packaged with simple statistics software.

Secondary Curriculum.

At the secondary level, statistical software can be especially useful for administrative purposes. Many school counselors use sophisticated analyses of student records including test scores to help them make curriculum decisions. In science classes, students use statistical software to help them analyze data collected during experiments and laboratory activities. In social studies classes, vast amounts of data are available from sources such as the census bureau, the stock market, and the various sports leagues. Much of these data are available on-line from information utilities and can be downloaded into local computers for analysis. (*Download* means to transfer a file from a central computer to a personal computer.) For example, it is possible for students to use statistical tests to compare stock market trends to demographic data. One interesting application in a physical education class involved the use of data from the Professional Golf Association (PGA). Information about the players on the PGA tour was compared with local golf team data, and conclusions were drawn about how to improve. Sta-

tistics are used to make learning of abstract concepts more realistic and to provide a constructivist foundation for classroom activities.

Postsecondary Curriculum.

In college, statistics are often used by students to analyze data they have collected. For many majors, students are required to take at least one course in statistics. Increasingly, these courses use microcomputer-based software. Undergraduate and graduate students analyze data collected from surveys, interviews, and experiments. Most often, data are used to test hypotheses and respond to research questions. At the advanced graduate student level, statistics are a basic tool. Most graduate students take several courses in statistics, and many use statistical tests to analyze data for their theses and dissertations. As a matter of fact, in many social sciences, statistics have replaced foreign language study as a basic requirement.

In all cases, statistics are tools used to solve problems. Just as word processors assist writers, and data base packages help record keepers, statistical systems assist students and teachers who wish to answer questions about the characteristics of people, events, or objects. Statistics software uses spreadsheets to store numerical data and contain powerful built-in mathematical formulae that permit the easy analysis of data. Statistical systems are a sophisticated subset of the spreadsheet category of computer software.

SUMMARY

The spreadsheet provides exciting potential for improving the teaching of quantitative skills to students. Specifically, the spreadsheet can be used to create environments where students can develop mathematical estimation and problem-solving skills. The spreadsheet makes numerical modeling and "what-if" projection techniques readily available for teachers and students. Similarly, spreadsheet-based statistical packages enable students to learn and apply statistical concepts easily and efficiently and make the work of statistics much more accessible to students at an earlier age.

Educators are just beginning to discover the potential of the spreadsheet for use in the classroom. The spreadsheet is not only for the mathematics teacher; it is also a tool that can help students experiment with the power and application of mathematics in almost every subject area. Individual educators need to become familiar with the power of the tool and develop appropriate applications for their subject and grade level.

SELF-TEST QUESTIONS

1. Arithmetic operations can be performed on labels in a spreadsheet.
   a. True
   b. False
2. Within a spreadsheet, a change to one cell automatically implies changes to all cells that are related to that cell through formulas.
   a. True
   b. False
3. List at least three reasons for including work with spreadsheets in the curriculum.
4. Describe the steps in learning a spreadsheet program.
5. Describe what is meant by "what-if" thinking.
6. Explain why "what-if" thinking is an important tool for students.
7. Describe two ways teachers can use spreadsheets for administrative purposes.
8. Cite an example of a spreadsheet application in social studies. Your example should include opportunities for "what-if" thinking in social studies.
9. Cite an example of a spreadsheet application in English.
10. Cite one way you could use a spreadsheet program in your own subject area.
11. What is the primary difference between a statistical package and a generic spreadsheet package?
12. What is the difference between descriptive and inferential statistics?

ANSWERS TO SELF-TEST QUESTIONS

1. b. False.
2. a. True.
3. a. Students need to learn how to use spreadsheets because they are tools used in almost every area of professional life.
   b. Spreadsheet work helps students develop skills in organizing numerical data.

c. Work with spreadsheets encourages "what-if" thinking.
   d. Spreadsheets provide practical applications for work with formulas and functions.
4. The steps in learning to use a spreadsheet program include (1) using spreadsheets created by others and (2) creating student-authored templates for spreadsheets.
5. "What-if" thinking involves testing out different hypothetical numerical situations. Students are encouraged to project the implications of making certain numerical changes.
6. "What-if" thinking is an important skill because it encourages students to estimate and build intuitive mathematical skills. It can help develop the intuitive sense for numbers that many students lack.
7. a. Teachers can use spreadsheets for recording and calculating grades.
   b. Teachers can use spreadsheets for keeping class and club financial records.
   c. Teachers can use spreadsheets for keeping athletic statistics for students.
8. Spreadsheets can be used in social studies to enable students to test hypotheses about historical, social, or economic trends.
9. In an English class, students could use a spreadsheet to analyze their writing by keeping track of the number of words in sentences, sentences in paragraphs, and paragraphs in stories. The lengths of words used in writing assignments also could be entered into a spreadsheet.
10. Share your answer to question 10 with a classmate and compare. Collaborate with one another.
11. Statistical packages have sophisticated formulae built into their spreadsheets that permit the computation of statistical tests such as t-tests and analysis of variance tests. Generic spreadsheet packages usually have no formulae built in. Formulae must be entered by the user.
12. Descriptive statistics give the characteristics of a group of related numbers, such as the test scores for a class of language arts students. For example, they give information about the collection of numbers' distribution (range, variance, standard deviation) and the numbers' central tendencies (average, median, mode). Inferential statistics are used to compare or draw inferences from two or more collections of related numbers, such as a comparison of the test scores of girls versus boys. Examples of inferential statistics include correlations, t-tests, and analysis of variance tests.

REFERENCES

Arad, O. (1986–1987). The spreadsheet: Solving word problems. *The Computing Teacher, 14*(4), 13–15.

Balestri, D., Cochrane, H., & Thursh, D. (1984, December). High tech, low tech, no tech: Three case studies of computers in the classroom. *AAHE Bulletin,* 11–14.

Blommers, P., & Lindquist, E. (1960). *Elementary statistical methods.* Boston: Houghton Mifflin.

Brown, J. M. (1986–1987). Spreadsheets in the classroom I. *The Computing Teacher, 14*(3), 9–12.

Brown, J. M. (1987). Spreadsheets in the classroom II. *The Computing Teacher, 14*(5), 9–12.

Dribin, C. (1985). Spreadsheets and performance: A guide for student-graded presentations. *The Computing Teacher, 12*(9), 22–25.

Hannah, L. (1986). Social studies, spreadsheets and the quality of life. *The Computing Teacher, 13*(4), 13–17.

National Council of Teachers of Mathematics. (1991). *Professional Standards for Teaching Mathematics.* Reston, VA: Author.

Papert, S. (1980). *Mindstorms: Children, computers and powerful ideas.* New York: Basic Books.

Pinter-Lucke, C. (1992). Rootfinding with a spreadsheet in pre-calculus. *Journal of Computers in Mathematics and Science Teaching, 11,* 85–93.

Pogge, A., & Lunetta, V. (1987). Spreadsheets answer "What if . . ." *The Science Teacher, 54*(8), 46–49.

REFERENCES FOR ADDITIONAL STUDY

Abacus Concepts. (1991). StatView II. Berkeley CA: Abacus Concepts.

Arganbright, D. (1985). *Mathematical applications of electronic spreadsheets.* New York: McGraw-Hill.

Baras, E. M. (Ed.). (1986). *Guide to using Lotus 1-2-3.* Berkeley, CA: McGraw-Hill.

Beaver, J. (1992). Using computer power to improve your teaching, Part II: Spreadsheets and charting. *The Computing Teacher, 19*(6), 22–24.

Blank, D. (1985). Stepping through fast-food land: A spreadsheet tutorial. *The Computing Teacher, 12*(9), 26–28.

Borg, W., & Gall, M. (1990). *Educational research* (5th ed.). New York: Longman.

Choate, J. (1986). Using VisiCalc and DYNAmo to make models and solve problems in high school math classes. *Computers in the Schools, 3*(1), 75–81.

Dyril, E. (1986). Electronic spreadsheets in the curriculum. *Computers in the Schools, 3*(1), 47–54.

Elzey, F. (1987). *Introductory statistics: A microcomputer approach.* Belmont, CA: Wadsworth.

Fey, J. T. (Ed.). (1984). *Computing and mathematics: The impact on secondary school curricula. Report of a conference sponsored by the National Science Foundation.* Reston, VA: National Council of Teachers of Mathematics.

Henderson, T., Coll, D., & Coll, G. (1983). *Spreadsheet software from VisiCalc to 1-2-3.* Indianapolis: Que Corporation.

Leedy, P. (1993). *Practical research planning and design* (5th ed.). Upper Saddle River, NJ: Merrill/Prentice Hall.

Luehrmann, A. (1986). Spreadsheets: More than just finance. *The Computing Teacher, 13*(7), 24–28.

Miller, M. (1988). Using NFL statistics to teach the spreadsheet. *Computing Teacher, 15*(6), 45–47.

Parker, J. (1986). Tools for thought. *The Computing Teacher, 14*(2), 21–23.

Verderber, N. (1991). Fibonacci numbers and the spreadsheet. *Mathematics and Computer Education, 25*(2), 192–196.

Vest, F., & Griffith, R. (1991). The mathematics of the return from home ownership. *School Science and Mathematics, 91*(7), 300–305.

Wolfram, S. (1991). *Mathematica* (2nd ed.). Redwood, CA: Addison-Wesley.

CHAPTER ELEVEN

MANAGING INFORMATION

Telecommunications and the Internet

GOAL

The purpose of this chapter is to present the techniques that permit computers to send and receive information from each other, and from information utilities, and to explain the Internet.

OBJECTIVES

The reader will be able to do the following:

1. Explain what computer communication systems are and how they work.
2. Explain the differences among local area, wide-area, and telephone communication systems.
3. Define the basic components of a computer communication system.
4. Explain some services available when computers communicate with each other.
5. Explain how computer communication systems can be used in the school.
6. Explain the services offered by national data base services called information utilities, such as DIA-LOG and America Online.
7. Define and explain the Internet and the World Wide Web and give examples of their uses in teaching.

Knowledge is Power.

(Francis Bacon, 1597)

In a time of turbulence and change, it is more true than ever that knowledge is power.

(John F. Kennedy, 1962)

One fundamental characteristic of a democratic society is free access to information. The computer may be the most powerful tool since the printing press to permit large numbers of citizens to easily, rapidly, and accurately obtain access to all kinds of information.

In an earlier chapter, the uses of data bases in education were discussed. The emphasis was on local, single-computer data bases. This chapter will extend that discussion to include communication between computers and the accessing of information stored in one computer by another computer in a remote location. The emphasis will be on communication and access to information.

In the last few years access to the Internet has increased and is widely accessible to teachers and students. This chapter will discuss the Internet, the World Wide Web, and how this aspect of telecommunication relates to distance education.

INTRODUCTION TO COMPUTER COMMUNICATION SYSTEMS

Computer communication systems are also called *data communication systems* or *telecommunications systems*. All refer to the transfer of data from one computer to another via a communications medium such as a telephone line. Computer communications systems allow nearly instantaneous transmission of information and for the storage of that information in the receiving computer until it is ready to be used.

Communication means the exchange of information. *Telecommunication* refers to the exchange of information over long distances. In 1876, Alexander Graham Bell began the modern electronic era of communication when he said, "Mr. Watson, come here. I want you," into his first telephone. Calculating devices were attached to telegraph lines in 1940 by George Stibitz. He connected a calculator at Dartmouth College to one in New York City.

The next development in telecommunications technology occurred in 1954 when International Business Machines Corporation (IBM) introduced a device that transmitted punched card data to computers at remote locations. Other similar developments that allowed data to be sent through wires to remote locations were tried in the 1950s, and most were successful. However, although these developments permitted data to be sent over relatively long distances, they were not really computer communication systems because transmission was one way, only one computer was used, and the systems were not practical.

The first truly useful computer communication system was the Sabre airline reservation system developed by IBM and American Airlines. It used 2,000 terminals scattered throughout the United States that were connected to a central computer. When it became operational in 1962, any ticket agent at any terminal could check airline schedules and instantly book seats for a passenger. The Sabre system has evolved into an industry-wide computer-based airline ticketing system that is still in use. One way microcomputer users can access part of this system is by using a data base known as the Official Airline Guide.

Types of Computer Communication Systems

Today, nearly all kinds of computers can communicate with one another and with remote terminals. There are basically three combinations of computers in these communication systems.

- Small computer or terminal with large host computer
- Large computers with large computers
- Small computers with other small computers

Computers can be connected to one another in networks. There are three kinds of communication networks: local area networks (LANs), wide-area networks, and telephone networks.

A local area network provides for communications within a limited area, such as a building or an office. A wide-area network provides communications in a larger area, such as a city, a state, or a country. Telephone networks, also called *dial-up networks*, connect computers in different locations using telephone lines and telephone equipment. Telephone computer networks use regular telephone lines and telephone numbers; in high-volume systems, they may use leased lines. Leased lines are telephone lines that are reserved for a computer communications network.

The main difference between a wide-area network and a telephone network is that communication in a telephone network is usually intermittent rather than continuous. When a user at a remote site wants to communicate with the central computer, a connection is made, in much the same way that a telephone call is accomplished. Wide-area networks, on the other hand, normally have computers connected with each other at all times. Educators are most likely to use local area networks, or telephone networks, although large school districts are beginning to establish wide-area networks that connect all schools in the system. Increasingly, schools are connecting their school district networks to networks in other schools and businesses and these connected networks are being linked to the Internet, the network of networks.

Local Area Networks. Local area networks cover limited geographical areas (Figure 11–1). They are usually found in offices or buildings. In a school, the media center card catalog might be stored on a computer's hard disk accessible by other computers placed throughout the school. For example, a social studies teacher could search the catalog to determine what materials were available in the media center on the *Reconstruction* period following the U.S. Civil War, or a student could search the file for the return date of a videotape that had been checked out. The microcomputer and hard disk in the media center, the micro-

computer in the teacher's lounge, and the microcomputer in the study hall would all be part of the media center's local area network.

Information sharing is one reason local area networks are established. Hardware sharing and electronic mail–text transfer are the other primary reasons for establishing local area networks. For example, if a school has only one laser printer, a local area network could be established so this relatively expensive printing device could be used by many in the school. Also,

FIGURE 11–1
A local area network.

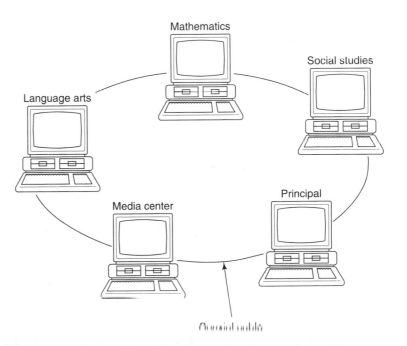

the school may need or want to share information through an electronic bulletin board. Electronic bulletin boards are similar to the bulletin boards found in the lobbies of college dormitories where students leave messages such as "Chemistry 101 text wanted" for others to see. Bulletin board messages can be entered from any computer in the network. Electronic messages also can be sent to any or all of the computers connected to the network.

Local area networks have three characteristics: (1) They have an organization plan, called *network topology*, (2) they use a specific kind of communication *channel*, and (3) they have a *network access* procedure that permits communication.

Network topology refers to the pathways used by devices in the network to communicate with one another. The three most common configurations are bus, ring, and star. When bus topology is used, all devices in the network are connected to, and share, a single cable. Information is transmitted in any direction between any computers in the network. Ring networks also have computers connected to a single communication cable that forms a circle. Messages are sent from one computer to another through the ring. Special codes in the message permit the receiving computer to recognize the signals intended

for it. Star configurations, on the other hand, use a central, controlling computer that handles and routes messages.

Communication channels permit the transmission of messages in a local area network. *Channels* refer to the wires used to send data. Usually, either twisted pair wire or coaxial cable is used.

Network access, the last component of a local area network, refers to the procedures used to allow personal computers to send and receive data. Two methods of network access are used: (1) carrier-sensed multiple access (CSMA) and (2) token passing. CSMA is used in bus networks. When a microcomputer tries to send data, it electronically listens to the network to see if any other computer is sending data. If one is, it waits a short time and listens again, and again, until the channel is clear; then it transmits its message. Token passing is used with both bus and ring networks. A token is a string of bits that constantly travel through the network. A token is a little like a baton passed between racers in a relay race. When a microcomputer on the network wants to send a message, it listens for the token, and when it receives the token, it is permitted to send its message. Possession of the token is permission to transmit.

When schools expand their use and application of computers beyond the simplest stand-alone systems, local area networks are one of the first improvements made. Schools use local area networks to share hardware and information, and to send electronic mail.

Telephone Networks.   Telephone networks are so called because computers use telephone numbers, lines, and switching systems to communicate (Figure 11–2). Besides two computers, two devices called *modems* and two programs (one for each computer) called *communications software* are needed. Several con-

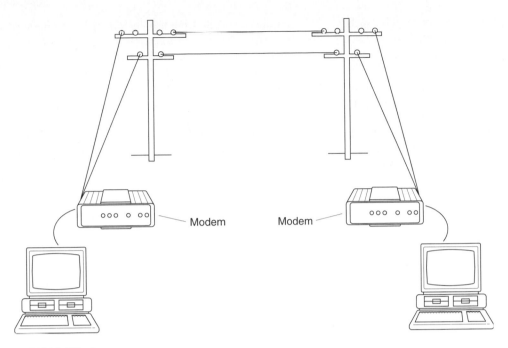

FIGURE 11–2
A telephone network.

cepts critical to telephone communication networks are used by this kind of a system. They determine how information is sent, received, and processed.

The output of a computer is digital information, but telephone lines are designed to carry audible information such as voices, which are analog data (also called continuous data). A modem converts the digital output of a computer into an analog signal that can be transmitted over regular telephone lines. Actually, the modem creates a tone that represents the computer's output and carries the digital computer signal. (Details about modems are presented in Chapter 3.)

Information is sent serially by modems. This means that one bit of information is sent at a time. A bit is one binary digit. Usually 8 or 16 bits are used to represent one character—a letter, number, or symbol. These groupings or bits are called *bytes.* Computers internally process information in bytes rather than bits. Parallel communication is when 8 or 16 bits are transmitted simultaneously in a special communication system called a *bus.*

Before data can be sent from one computer to another by a modem, they must be converted from parallel transmission (how computers internally transmit data) to serial transmission (how modems send data). Usually, this is accomplished by a special series of cir-

cuits in the computer. Old Apple IIe computers required that a special circuit board be placed in a peripheral slot. The Super Serial Card was an example of such a board. It converted parallel data into serial data. Most computers now have one or more built-in serial outputs so data can be transmitted serially to modems and printers.

The speed of transmission over telephone lines is measured in something called *baud rate,* which refers to

---

Notes From the Literature

McDaniel, McInerney, and Armstrong describe how educationally oriented networks can range from in-school LANs to global computer networks. In Indiana, schools and homes are connected through at-home computers in the Buddy Project, and students and educators are linked to the State Department of Education through IDEAnet, which provides on-line data bases, conferencing, e-mail, and file transfer over toll-free lines.

McDaniel, E., McInerney, W., & Armstrong, P. (1993). Computers and school reform. Educational Research Technology and Development, 41(1), 73–78.

bits per second (binary digits per second). The speeds most commonly used are 300; 1,200; 2,400; 9,600; 14,400; and 28,800 bits per second. What this means is that about 300; 1,200; 2,400; 9,600; 14,400; or 28,800 binary digits are sent each second from the sending modem to the receiving modem. If 10 bits are used to send each character, then 30; 120; 240; 960; 1,440; or 2,880 characters are sent each second. At 300 baud it would take about 1 minute to fill a standard computer screen with text; at 1,200 baud, it would take 15 seconds to fill the screen; and at 9,600 baud a screen would be filled in about two seconds.

Information is sent through modems using either asynchronous or synchronous communication procedures. *Asynchronous* means that one character at a time is sent or received. Each time a character is sent, a start bit is sent first, and after each series of bits that refer to a character, a stop bit is sent. Because each character must be preceded by a start bit and followed by a stop

bit and because idle time usually occurs between characters, asynchronous transmission is relatively slow. On the other hand, synchronous transmission allows for characters to be sent in groups rather than individually. The modem keeps track of characters by timing them.

There are three basic ways that communication channels are used for transmitting data: (1) simplex, (2) half duplex, and (3) duplex. A simplex channel allows data to be transmitted in one direction only. For example, a computer that transmits using a simplex channel can send but not receive. Data sent from a computer to a printer is an example of a simplex system.

Half-duplex channels permit data to be sent in both directions but in only one direction at a time. Normally, half-duplex transmission is used between a microcomputer and a mainframe computer. The information from the microcomputer is sent to the mainframe, and when transmission is complete, the mainframe responds. Duplex—or full-duplex—trans-

FIGURE 11–3
Modems allow computers to send and receive information from each other and from information utilities via telephone lines. This is a Hayes external modem.

mission permits the sending of data in both directions at the same time. Speed is the main advantage of duplex transmission.

A Typical Telephone Network. The hardware and software for a typical Macintosh telephone network would be configured as follows:

First, a modem is needed. Inexpensive modems that transmit 9,600 or 14,400 baud work nicely. The modem is connected to the serial output on the back of the computer and to an active telephone line using a standard telephone wire (Figures 11–3 and 11–4).

Once this hardware is assembled and connected, software is needed to direct the computer to use this system correctly. Many kinds of *communications software* are available, including free programs. One often used with the Macintosh microcomputer is the communications portion of the Microsoft Works integrated software system. This program permits the user to store telephone numbers and other codes that the program can be directed to use. For example, if a teacher wanted to access the information utility Dialog, the communications module of Microsoft Works would be loaded, the teacher could select the correct service from the menu, and wait for the computer to dial and

log onto the service. Microsoft Works, like most communications software, completes the call for the teacher and enters the utility so it can be easily used.

Any telephone number can be called by a telephone network system, so if two computer users want to send information to one another, they merely need to set up systems like the one described. It is even possible to send messages between computers without the need for a person to receive the information. The communication software directs the computer to receive the message and to store it for later use.

Wide-Area Networks. Wide-area networks hold considerable promise for education, especially when used for sending electronic mail, posting bulletin board notices, and accessing information utilities. As educators gain more experience with communications software, they are bound to discover many more than these three major applications. The Internet, for example, is a wide-area network of many smaller networks.

Electronic Mail. Electronic mail is the transmission of correspondence via computer communications channels. It combines techniques used in traditional telephone calls with conventional mail. Electronic mail

FIGURE 11–4
Some computers have built-in modems. This Hayes modem is on a card from a laptop computer.

is instantaneous, like the telephone, but one can send longer, more detailed messages. Also, messages do not interrupt the person they are sent to because they can be stored in the receiver's computer, or in a host computer, until they are ready to be read.

Electronic mail software is needed to send and receive messages. Once a message has been entered at the keyboard, the electronic mail software looks up the telephone number of the recipient's computer and transmits the message. The receiving computer answers, accepts the message, and stores it until it is read.

Bulletin Boards.   It is estimated that there are thousands of bulletin board services (BBSs) available free for personal or school use. Almost all BBSs run on microcomputers. They have been set up by individuals, computer clubs, and companies. Bulletin boards are places where messages can be posted for others to read. Most messages are available for anyone to look at, although some systems permit protecting messages with passwords to limit viewing of the message.

Generally, BBSs are established to deal with single topics, such as those for Zenith computer owners, social studies teachers, or school media specialists. This fosters the development of a "clubiness" for BBS users. BBSs bring a human element to computers because they promote the sharing of ideas and the interaction of computer users. Teachers like to use BBSs because they are inexpensive and bring the outside world into the classroom. Ideas generated during classroom discussions can be shared with others, and questions can be asked of experts outside the classroom. Students who use BBSs also quickly see the power of computer communication.

Information Utilities.   The microcomputer revolution has brought about many new terms, such as *information utility,* to explain new ideas. The idea of the information utility is new and potentially very important, especially to educators.

Utility is not a new word. The gas company, the electric company, water and sewage service, and the telephone company are considered utilities. They provide basic services to anyone who needs them. Utility services are usually fundamental ones that are provided by the government if there is no private enterprise to deliver them. Information utilities provide fundamental access to information. They provide communication and access, and although most are commercial enterprises, many institutions such as public libraries and schools are also beginning to provide access to information through utilities.

Information utilities usually sell their services. A person subscribes to the service in much the same way a person subscribes to a newspaper, signs up for cable television, or has a telephone installed. After paying a fee, users are given a password that permits use of the utility with a computer and modem. Bills usually include a monthly fee and a fee for services provided. The services commonly provided by information utilities are discussed next. Several well-known information utilities are Dialog, America Online, CompuServe, and Prodigy.

Access to Data Bases.   Probably the most important function of information utilities is to provide on-line access to national data bases. Such data bases include the following:

- The Magazine Index, a listing of popular magazine articles similar to *The Reader's Guide to Periodical Literature*
- The Associated Press News Service, a report on current news events
- The Movie Index, an annotated report that reviews and describes motion pictures currently being shown in theaters.

Access to data bases is such an important function of information utilities that the following section of this chapter will discuss the use of national data bases.

Access to News.   Electronic versions of newspapers such as *The Washington Post* are available from information utilities. Specialized news, such as sports scores and stock quotations, are also available.

Conferencing.   Information utilities are often used for ongoing discussions devoted to a particular topic. Computer conferences are similar to electronic bulletin boards, except they deal with a specific topic, rather than a variety of ideas, and participants often communicate on-line with one another, rather than at different times. Many conferences are now interactive. For example, America Online and other services offer forums where subscribers can send messages and receive answers from governmental leaders, movie stars, sports celebrities, or famous artists.

Electronic Catalogs. Electronic catalogs provide information about a company's products and allow users to place orders electronically. Normally, a person charges with a credit card number, and goods are shipped by mail.

Securities Trading. Stocks, bonds, and other securities can be traded electronically by clients of brokerage firms. Users can buy and sell or merely check the status of their accounts.

Program Sharing. Several utilities distribute computer programs to their subscribers, free of charge or for a fee. For example, math teachers looking for a program to help teach the quadratic formula might find one in a catalog list they could request electronically. The program would then be downloaded from the information utility's computer to the subscriber's microcomputer. At the end of the month, the cost of the downloaded math lesson would appear on the bill sent from the information utility.

Internet Access. The Internet is a large collection of regional wide-area networks that use the TCP/IP protocol. The TCP/IP protocol stands for "Transmission Control Protocol/Internet Protocol" and is a family of data transmission rules that define how data are passed over the network. Many information utilities offer access to the Internet. Several important services are available using the Internet: (1) Electronic mail. There are millions of Internet users worldwide, and sending mail to them is a relatively simple task. (2) File transfer. It is possible to transfer files and programs using the Internet File Transfer Protocol (FTP). (3) File access. Finally, it is possible to access another computer's files and use them. ERIC is available from several host computers using the Internet.

ON-LINE DATA BASES: THEIR USE AND EFFECT

Access to information is one of the most important uses of computers. Knowledge obtained through computer networks can be used to improve work, school, and recreation. For example, a standard fixture of many businesses in the past was a wire service ticker tape. Business leaders would use this up-to-date information

to stay abreast of current events that might influence their businesses. In school, students have for decades had to write term papers that required them to review the *Reader's Guide* to find current magazine articles on their topic, and many movie fans read the newspaper to find reviews of films currently showing in town.

In each of these examples, the user is looking for information, and the information is in a data base. They are the kind of data bases that have been used for decades, and they are valuable. However, what happens if a business cannot afford to subscribe to the wire service, if the library's collection of magazines is inadequate (or if pertinent articles have been torn out), or if the newspaper's reviewer did not see the movie you are interested in? Obviously, access to these traditional data bases is limited, and because of this, decisions are often made in the absence of adequate knowledge.

Information utilities were established to make it easier to access information. Instead of duplicating wire service printouts in several businesses in town, duplicating the subscriptions to periodicals in all school media centers, and expecting the newspaper's reviewer to see every movie, those services can be centrally located so they can be accessed by anyone using a microcomputer and modem, or by a direct connection

Notes From the Literature

One of the most exciting applications of telecommunications involves the use of the Internet, which is a worldwide network of more than 3,000 computer networks. Estimates indicate that between 2 million and 5 million people worldwide have access to the Internet, most of them associated with colleges or universities. Increasingly, K-12-grade teachers and students are obtaining access to the Internet and its services, usually through a local college or university, and many states are developing plans to provide easy access to all schools.

The Internet provides four basic types of information exchange: (1) person to person, (2) person to group, (3) person to computer program, and (4) person to information archive.

Four kinds of activities occur: (1) electronic mail to send messages, (2) computer conferencing to participate in group discussions, (3) interactive sessions to search for information, and (4) file transfer to obtain copies of documents that have been found.

Harris, J. (1992). Electronic journeys by electronic mail. *The Computer Teacher, 20(1),* 36–38.

through the Internet. Information utilities are still new, especially to educators, but many believe that in the future using utilities will be a basic skill needed by students and teachers.

Several information utilities are available in the marketplace (Table 11–1). They all differ slightly, but as with word processing programs, a person who knows how to use one will find it relatively easy to learn how to use the others. Three information utilities and their various advantages will be described next—America Online, CompuServe, and Dialog.

America Online

America Online (AOL) is a subscription service that offers a huge variety of information on its own data base as well as through a direct Internet connection or with a modem. Following is a list of the commonly used departments of AOL:

Today's News
Personal Finance
Clubs & Interests
Computing
Travel
Marketplace

TABLE 11–1
Selected On-Line Services

America Online
8619 Westwood Center Drive
Vienna, VA 22182-2285

CompuServe
5000 Arlington Centre Blvd.
Columbus, OH 43220
(800) 848-8990

Dialog Information Services, Inc.
3460 Hillview Ave.
Palo Alto, CA
(800) 3-DIALOG

Dow Jones News/Retrieval
Box 300
Princeton, NJ
(800) 345-8500

MCI Mail
1133 19th St., NW
Washington, DC
(202) 872-1600

People Connection
News Stand
Entertainment
Education
Reference Desk
Internet Connection
Sports
Kids Only

AOL greets subscribers with a graphical interface that makes it simple to navigate through the services provided (Figure 11–5). The user need only point to a service and click a mouse button to access it. Pull-down menus provide a broader range of navigation tools.

AOL software is free, but subscribers are charged a monthly rate that permits a certain amount of free connection time. Charges for extra time on AOL are billed monthly to a credit card. Software is available for Macintosh, Apple, and DOS/Windows computers.

AOL is connected to the Internet and recently purchased part of the Internet backbone, so it is possible to access many Internet services, most notably the Internet's worldwide e-mail system. AOL is an example of a commercial information utility that targets both professional and personal users of computers.

CompuServe

CompuServe originally supplied time-sharing services to businesses. Through this system, a company, a school district, or a university could connect to Com-

Notes From the Literature

According to the April 30, 1995, *Des Moines Register,* the current prices for on-line services are the following:

- America Online—$9.95/month with 5 free hours. $2.95 per extra hour.
- CompuServe—$8.95/month for unlimited access to basic services. $4.80/hour for extended services.
- Prodigy—$9.95/month for 5 hours. $2.95 per extra hour.
- e-World—$8.95/month for 4 hours. $2.95 per extra hour.
- GEnie—$8.95/month for 4 hours. $3.00 per extra hour.
- DELPHI—$10.00/month for 4 hours. $4.00 per extra hour.

FIGURE 11–5A
When subscribers connect to America Online, they are greeted by this welcome page.

FIGURE 11–5B
The main menu is a graphical interface that enables subscribers to easily navigate through the services provided by America Online, including a connection to the Internet.
Copyright 1995, America Online, used with permission.

puServe's mainframe computers using regular telephone lines and use CompuServe's powerful computers to complete accounting, payroll, or inventory tasks. To cut down on the costs of maintaining its huge mainframe computers, CompuServe began to offer access to its mainframes to microcomputer users. More recently, CompuServe has started to offer its subscribers access to other data bases and other computers (Figure 11–6).

CompuServe uses a menu-driven system. A typical menu offers a list of numbered choices. Users can jump ahead to a new menu that is more specific. Even if a user does not know the name of the data base she wants, she can select options from menus that will quickly narrow choices until the correct information is found. Once the user knows the name of the data base, she can bypass the menus and go directly to the data base. CompuServe's easy use is one of its main selling points. Some examples of services provided by CompuServe follow:

Communications.
Electronic mail services and a variety of special interest group forums (bulletin boards).

FIGURE 11–6
CompuServe is an information utility that allows users of microcomputers access to a variety of data bases and powerful mainframe computers.

```
    CompuServe Information Service
     14:45 CST Thursday 07-Jan-93 P
           (Executive Option)
      Last access: 06:11 22-Dec-92

          Copyright (c) 1993
         CompuServe Incorporated
           All Rights Reserved

    GO RATES for current information

 Y&   1 Access Basic Services
  2   Member Assistance (FREE)
  3   Communications/Bulletin Bds.
  4   News/Weather/Sports
  5   Travel
  6   The Electronic MALL/Shopping
  7   Money Matters/Markets
  8   Entertainment/Games
  9   Hobbies/Lifestyles/Education
 10   Reference
 11   Computers/Technology
 12   Business/Other Interests
 Y7   JEnter choice number !2
 HjAssistance (FREE)Y k HELP
```

News.
CompuServe offers news, weather, and sports information from Associated Press, Business Wire, McGraw-Hill News Snapshot, and other news services.

Entertainment and Games.
Multiplayer and single-player games are available as well as entertainment news and movie reviews.

Hobbies, Lifestyles, and Education.
Members can access a variety of services of personal interest including personal financial information, health and fitness, art, music, and literature.

Computers and Technology.
CompuServe offers a forum for virtually every brand of computer hardware and software on the market.

Business.
Aviation, business management data bases, data processing, and professional forums (health, legal, engineering, and media) are available.

Dialog

Probably the information utility of greatest interest to educators is Dialog. It focuses more on access to technical and scientific information than on personal uses (Figure 11–7). Dialog also is accessible through the Internet (address: Telnet Dialog.com)

In the 1960s, Dialog was established to keep track of the millions of documents produced as part of the space program. As it grew, it provided access to other kinds of data. Over the years, many corporations, governmental agencies, and universities have produced research reports and scientific information that had been kept in archive data files. Recently, these organizations have started to put this information in computer-based record-keeping systems. Dialog has purchased copies of, or has access to, the computer files of these corporations and governmental agencies and makes them available to subscribers. Additionally, Dialog has added several specialty data bases to its list of services. Today, Dialog offers access to more than 250 data bases that contain the most up-to-date information on specialty and technical topics. It has quickly become the most important information utility for educators.

The first service listed in the Dialog system is the most important one for educators. Educational Resources Information Clearinghouse (ERIC) is the basic indexing and abstracting source for information about education. ERIC has two parts. The first,

FIGURE 11–7
With its emphasis on access to technical and scientific information, Dialog is an information utility especially useful to educators.

```
                *** DIALOG HOMEBASE Main Menu ***
      Enter an option number and press ENTER to view information
      on any item listed below; enter a BEGIN command to search
      in a different database.

            1 Announcements (new databases, price
              changes, etc.)
            2 DIALOG HOMEBASE Features
            3 DIALOG Free File of the Month
            4 DIALOG Database Information and Rates
            5 Database Selection (DIALINDEX/OneSearch
              Categories)
            6 DIALOG Command Descriptions
            7 DIALOG Training Schedules and Seminar
              Descriptions
            8 DIALOG Services

            9 Begin DIALOG Menus (sm)
           10 Begin DIALOG Business Connection (r)
      Enter an option or a BEGIN command and press ENTER.
           /H = Help    /L = Logoff    /NOMENU = Command Mode
```

Resources in Education (RIE), indexes nonperiodical publications such as grant reports and conference proceedings. RIE also gives a detailed abstract of the report. All the information is available on-line through Dialog.

The second part of ERIC is the *Current Index to Journals in Education (CIJE)*, which indexes the hundreds of periodicals about education. *CIJE* is the equivalent to *The Reader's Guide to Periodical Literature* for educators interested in information about education.

Another valuable data base for teachers is *The Magazine Index,* which indexes most of the popular magazines that students might want to use to write a term paper for social studies or English. Both *CIJE* and *The Magazine Index* necessitate going to the actual journal or magazine to read the relevant article, but soon that information may also be available on-line.

The Dialog system is relatively complex, and serious users are encouraged to enroll in training seminars offered in most major cities. However, once the basics of on-line searching using the Dialog system are mastered, the largest collection of technical, scientific, and reference information from any information utility is available. Also, almost all Dialog data bases are searched the same way, so skills learned from searching one data base are easily transferred to others. Costs for using Dialog vary, but many schools subscribe to a special education service that provides teachers and students access to most of Dialog's education-oriented data bases at significantly reduced rates.

Searching Dialog Data Bases—An Example of On-Line Searching. Once a person has logged on the Dialog system, decisions must be made as to what procedure to use to move around in the Dialog utility. Those procedures will be presented next. While they may vary depending on the specific data base searched, they are general ones used for all routine searches, not just those using Dialog.

First, define the information that is needed. For example, if a teacher wants information about "using microcomputers in the teaching of high school language arts," the ERIC data base would probably be the best one to search. If, on the other hand, the topic is "the influence of the space program on the development of technology in society," the correct data base might not be so obvious. In this case, *The Magazine Index* might work. For topics that are less easy to define, Dialog offers a service called DIALINDEX that lets the user scan several data bases to see which one offers the most information. In any case, key words related to the topic should be identified. For our first example, the key words would probably be *microcomputers, teaching,* and *language arts.* For the second example, the key words would be *space, technology,* and possibly *development* and *society.*

Dialog uses several commands for searching. Because Dialog is an on-line system, searches are the result of interaction between the computer and the user. Whenever the computer is ready for input from the user, a "?" (question mark) prompt is given. The user then replies with a command (followed by pressing the return key) that directs the computer to do something. The most important commands in Dialog follow:

Begin.   This command lets the user select the data base to be searched. "Begin" can be used any time there is a ? prompt. (Example: "Begin 47" would tell the computer to access data base No. 47, which is *The Magazine Index*.) "B" can be used as an abbreviation for Begin.

Select.   The select (S) command is always followed by the term to be searched for or by the number of a previously retrieved collection of articles to be searched. The results of the search will be placed in a special set or storage location. (Example: "Select Microcomputer" would retrieve all records that contain the word microcomputer anywhere in the basic document in the ERIC data base. For standard data bases, the basic document would include the title, abstract, and subject descriptors.)

Normally, several searches of key words are made, with the results of each search placed in a separate set (storage location). When all key word searches are completed, the sets are searched and compared, and matches are placed in new sets. For example, if the search for the term *microcomputer* found 500 articles and they were placed in set 1, and if the search for the term *teaching* found 3,000 records, and they were placed in set 2, then a third search would be conducted that compares sets 1 and 2 to find records that contain both terms. This new search might produce 200 matches, and they would be placed in set 3. This searching process would continue until all key words had been searched for and all matches had been made.

Type.   The type (T) command allows the results of selecting to be seen immediately on the screen. Type is always followed by three kinds of information separated by slashes (/). The first number is the number of the set of articles to be displayed on the screen. The next number, immediately following the slash, is a format number indicating how much of the record is to be displayed. The last number, after the second slash, gives the number(s) of the records to be displayed. For example, "Type 3/5/1-2" would show the complete (indicated by the 5 in the middle) versions of the first and second records (indicated by the 1-2 after the last slash) of set number 3 (indicated by the 3 before the first slash).

Following are other commonly used format numbers and their output:

2 = COMPLETE RECORD EXCEPT ABSTRACT
3 = BIBLIOGRAPHIC CITATION
5 = COMPLETE RECORD
6 = RECORD ACCESSION NUMBER AND TITLE
7 = BIBLIOGRAPHIC CITATION AND ABSTRACT
8 = RECORD ACCESSION NUMBER, TITLE, AND INDEXING INFORMATION

Print.   The print (P) command causes the results to be printed on paper, off-line. This printout is then mailed to the address of the Dialog subscriber. Sets, formats, and records desired are indicated after the print command just as they are for the type command. (Example: "Print 3/5/1-2.")

Logoff.   The logoff command ends the search session. The user is disconnected from Dialog, and the cost of the search session since the last begin command is displayed. A number of other commands are available, but these five are the ones used most often.

Logical Connectors.   Almost all computer searching systems use terms called *logical connectors. And, or,* and *not* are the most commonly used.

And identifies records that include both search terms, or both search sets, on either side of the *and*. In other words, the command "microcomputer *and* teaching" would cause a search for records that include both key words *microcomputer* and *teaching.* Similarly, "S1 *and* S2" would identify records that are found in both set 1 and set 2.

Or identifies records that are not duplicates or are not found when both key words or sets on either side of it are searched. In other words, "microcomputer *or* teaching" would identify records that were found when either key word was searched for. Specifically, all nonduplicate records would be stored in a new set.

Not eliminates one search term from another search term. For example, if all microcomputer-based language arts teaching applications were identified and placed in set 8, the *not* term could be used to eliminate some records, such as those aimed at remedial studies, or with gifted students. Example: "Select S8 *not* remedia?" The ? is used in this case to truncate the word so that all terms that begin with the letters *remedia* are identified, and their records eliminated. This would identify words such as *remedial, remediate,* and *remediation.* The results of this search would be placed in a new set (probably 9). "Select S9 *not* gift?" could be run to further limit the searching process by identifying all records with words beginning with *gift*. These records would be eliminated from set 9 and placed in a new storage location, set 10.

There are more efficient methods of searching Dialog data bases, which users can learn as they gain experience with the system. Nonbibliographic data bases, such as those with statistical records or directories, are searched differently. Each data base available through Dialog is described in a "bluesheet" that gives the user specific instructions about searching. Once the basic searching procedures are mastered, other techniques come easily.

THE INTERNET

A commonly asked question is "What is the Internet?" The reason such a question is asked so often is that there's no agreed upon answer. The Internet can be thought about in relation to its common protocols, as a physical collection of routers and circuits, as a set of shared resources, or even as an attitude about interconnecting and intercommunication. Some definitions include the following:

- A network of networks based on the TCP/IP protocols.
- A community of people who use and develop those networks.
- A global collection of resources that can be reached from those networks by millions of users.

Today's Internet began as an experiment more than 20 years ago by the U.S. Department of Defense to connect an experimental network called the ARPAnet with various radio and satellite networks. The ARPAnet was designed to support military research in particular, research about building networks that could withstand partial outages and still function.

In the ARPAnet model, communication always occurs between a source and a destination computer. To send a message on the network, a computer put data in an envelope, called an Internet Protocol (IP) packet, and "addressed" the packets correctly. The communicating computers—not the network itself—were also responsible for ensuring that the communication was accomplished. The philosophy was that every computer on the network could talk with any other computer.

Responding to market pressures, Internet developers in the United States, the United Kingdom, and Scandinavia began to put their IP software on every conceivable type of computer. It became the only practical method for computers from different manufacturers to communicate. This was attractive to the government and to universities, which did not necessarily buy their computers from the same vendors.

At about the same time the Internet was coming into being, local area networks (LANs) were developed. This technology matured quietly, until desktop work stations became available around 1983. Some of these work stations came with UNIX, which included IP networking software. This created a new demand: Rather than connecting to a single, large timesharing computer per site, organizations wanted to connect the ARPAnet to their entire local network. This would allow all the computers on that LAN to access ARPAnet facilities.

Also at the same time, other organizations started building their own networks using the same communications protocols as the ARPAnet—namely, IP and its relatives. It became obvious that if these networks could talk together, users on one network could communicate with those on another.

One of the most important networks was the NSFnet, commissioned by the National Science Foundation (NSF). In the late 1980s, the NSF created five supercomputer centers. Up to this point, the world's fastest computers had been available only to weapons developers and a few researchers from very large corporations. By creating supercomputer centers, the NSF made these resources available for any scholarly research. Only five centers were created because they were so expensive—so they had to be shared. This created a communications problem: The NSF needed a way to connect the centers and to allow the clients of these centers to access them. At first, the NSF tried to use the ARPAnet for communications.

Later, NSF built its own network, based on the ARPAnet's IP technology. It connected the centers with 56,000 bits-per-second (56k bps) telephone lines. (This is roughly the ability to transfer two typewritten pages per second. That's slow by modern standards, but was reasonably fast in the mid-1980s.) Because access to telephone lines is billed by the mile, it was obvious that if they tried to connect every university directly to a supercomputing center, the NSF would go broke. One line per campus with a supercomputing center at the hub, like spokes on a wheel, add up to lots of miles of phone lines.

In response, the NSF created regional networks. In each area of the country, schools were connected to their nearest neighbor. Each chain was connected to a supercomputer center at one point and the centers were connected together. With this configuration, any computer could eventually communicate with any other by forwarding the conversation through its neighbors.

The most important aspect of the NSF's effort is that it allowed everyone to access the network. Up to that point, Internet access had been available only to computer science researchers, government employees, and government contractors.

The NSF promoted universal educational access by funding campus connections only if the campus had a plan to spread the access around. So everyone attending a four-year college could become an Internet user.

The demand keeps growing. Now that most four-year colleges are connected, people are trying to get secondary and primary schools connected. College graduates know what the Internet can be used for, and talk their employers into connecting corporations. All this activity points to continued growth, networking problems to solve, evolving technologies, and job security for networkers.

The answer to the question "What is the Internet?" changes over time. A few years ago the answer would have been easy: "All the networks, using the IP protocol, that cooperate to form a seamless network for their collective users." This would include various federal networks, a set of regional networks, campus networks, and some foreign networks.

But more recently, some non-IP-based networks wanted to provide their services to the Internet clientele. So they developed methods of connecting their networks (e.g., BITNET, DECnets, etc.) to the Internet. At first these connections, called "gateways," merely transferred electronic mail between two networks. Some, however, have grown to translate other services between the networks as well.

Governance

The Internet has no president or chief operating officer. The constituent networks may have presidents and CEOs, but that's a different issue; there's no single authority figure for the Internet as a whole.

The ultimate authority for the Internet rests with the Internet Society, or ISOC. This is a voluntary membership organization whose purpose is to promote global information exchange through Internet technology. It appoints a council, which has responsibility for the technical management and direction of the Internet.

The council is a group of invited volunteers called the Internet Architecture Board (IAB). The IAB meets regularly to set standards and allocate resources such as Internet addresses. The Internet works because there are standard ways for computers and software applications to talk to each other. This allows computers from different vendors to communicate without problems. It's not an IBM-only or Sun-only or Macintosh-only network. The IAB decides when a standard is necessary, and what the standard should be. When a standard is required, it considers the problem, adopts a standard, and announces it via the network.

The IAB also keeps track of various numbers (and other things) that must remain unique. For example, each computer on the Internet has a unique 32-bit address; no other computer has the same address. How does this address get assigned? The IAB considers these questions. While it doesn't actually assign the addresses, it makes the rules about how to assign addresses.

Internet users express their opinions through meetings of the Internet Engineering Task Force (IETF). The IETF is another volunteer organization; it meets regularly to discuss operational and near-term technical problems of the Internet. When it considers a problem important enough to merit concern, the IETF sets up a "working group" for further investigation. Anyone can attend IETF meetings and be on working groups; the important thing is that they work. Working groups have many functions, ranging from producing documentation, to deciding how networks should cooperate when problems occur, to changing the meaning of the bits in a packet. A working group usually produces a report. Depending on the recommendation, it could be documentation made available to anyone wanting it, it could be accepted voluntarily as a good idea for people to follow, or it could be sent to the IAB to be declared a standard.

Costs

There currently is no Internet, Inc., that collects fees from all Internet networks or users, even though the backbone infrastructure is being privatized. Instead, everyone pays for their part. The NSF pays for NSFNet. NASA pays for the NASA Science Internet. Networks get together and decide how to connect and fund these interconnections. A college or corporation pays for its connection to some regional network, which in turn pays a national provider for its access.

Effect on the User

The concept that the Internet is a collection of networks means little to the user. Users want to do something useful—run a program, or access data—they should not have to worry about how everything works. Consider the telephone system—it's an Internet, too. Pacific Bell, AT&T, MCI, British Telephone, and so on, are all separate corporations that run pieces of the telephone system. They worry about how to make it work together; all callers have to do is dial.

International Connections

The Internet has been an international network for a long time, but it only extended to the United States' allies and overseas military bases. Today it is found in more than 50 countries, and the number is rapidly increasing. Eastern European countries longing for Western scientific ties have wanted to participate for a long time, but were excluded by government regulation. This ban has been relaxed. Third world countries that formerly did not have the means to participate now view the Internet as a way to raise their education and technology levels.

In Europe, the development of the Internet used to be hampered by national policies mandating different protocols. These policies prevented development of large scale Internet infrastructures except in the Scandinavian countries, which embraced the Internet protocols long ago and are well-connected today. In 1989, RIPE (Reseaux IP Europeens) began coordinating the operation of the Internet in Europe and currently about 25% of all hosts connected to the Internet are in Europe.

Currently, the Internet's international expansion is hampered by the lack of a good infrastructure, namely a decent telephone system. In both Eastern Europe and the Third World telephone connections are limited to the speeds available to the average home anywhere in the United States: 9,600 bits/second. Typically, even if one of these countries is "on the Internet," only a few sites are accessible. Usually, it is the major technical university for that country.

Commercialization

Many big corporations have been on the Internet for years. For the most part, their participation has been limited to the research and engineering departments. The same corporations used some other network (usually a private network) for their business communications.

But running multiple networks is expensive, and some businesses are looking to the Internet for "one-stop" network shopping. They had been scared away in the past by policies that excluded or restricted commercial use. Many of these policies are under review and will change. As these restrictions drop, commercial use of the Internet will become more common.

Privatization

Right behind commercialization comes privatization. For years, the networking community has wanted the telephone companies and other for-profit ventures to provide "off the shelf" IP connections.

Although most people in the networking community think privatization is a good idea, there are some obstacles. Most revolve around the funding for the connections that are already in place. Many schools are connected only because the government pays part of the bill. If they had to pay their own way, major research institutions would probably stay on the Internet; but some smaller colleges might not. The costs also probably would be prohibitive for most secondary schools, not to mention grade schools.

In 1995, NSFNet decided the Internet experiment was over and the concept had proven itself, so users were advised to find commercial providers for their Internet connections. Today, the infrastructure of the Internet is commercial, and NSFNet has been turned off.

INTERNET SERVICES

The Internet supports research and education through sharing of computer resources and data. These services correspond to the basic functions of the Internet: electronic mail, remote logon, and file transfer.

Electronic Mail

Electronic mail, or e-mail, allows computer users to exchange messages. To use e-mail, the sender composes a message and addresses it to the intended recipient using a program designed to support e-mail operations (Figure 11–8).

Messages can contain anything from a few words to long documents, such as the text of reports, articles, and even books. Most e-mail systems make it easy to insert and send longer documents created with word-processing programs and other computer applications.

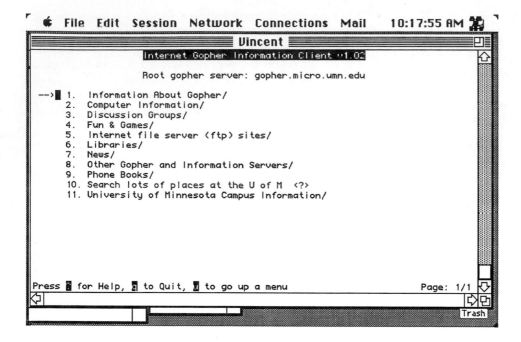

FIGURE 11–8
The Internet allows communication among millions of users worldwide via a collection of regional networks.

Some can even include graphics and programs. E-mail can be forwarded simply by re-addressing an outgoing message. (See Figure 11–9.)

E-mail is a quick, reliable, and efficient way of transmitting information one-to-one. There are also ways to use mail to communicate with larger numbers of people. One of the most important of these are listservers, sometimes called listservs, computer programs that manage large mailing lists and are the heart of hundreds of on-line discussion forums. The forums are collections of e-mail users sharing common interests. Users join a forum by sending a command via e-mail to

Notes From the Literature

"To use a metaphor, the U.S.A. already has a network of information superhighways, but customers are connected to these highways by a local network of unpaved (that is, predominantly analog) single lane roads."

Galbreath, J., & Andreotta, R. J. (1994). Developing and using the national information infrastructure. Educational Technology, 34(4), 15–20.

Notes From the Literature

A study investigating the effect of direct and unrestricted access to the Internet for a group of Florida high school teachers suggested that the teachers required the following:

- Ongoing Internet training
- Technical support
- Home Internet access
- Time to learn and incorporate the Internet into their classes.

Additionally, the study found that the use of the Internet increased teachers' self esteem, improved their attitudes towards computers and education, and encouraged them to restructure their classes and schedules to accommodate Internet resources in their classrooms.

Gallo, M. A., & Horton, P. B. (1994). Assessing the effect on high school teachers of direct and unrestricted access to the Internet: A case study of an east central Florida high school. Educational Technology Research and Development, 42(4), 17.

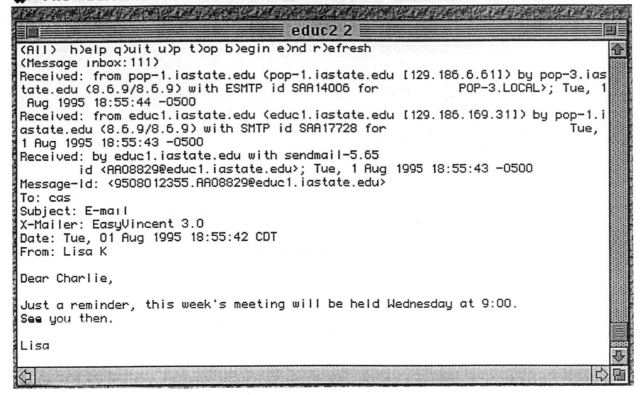

 File   Edit   Session   Network   Connections

```
                              educ2 2
(All) h)elp q)uit u)p t)op b)egin e)nd r)efresh
(Message inbox:111)
Received: from pop-1.iastate.edu (pop-1.iastate.edu [129.186.6.61]) by pop-3.ias
tate.edu (8.6.9/8.6.9) with ESMTP id SAA14006 for          POP-3.LOCAL>; Tue, 1
 Aug 1995 18:55:44 -0500
Received: from educ1.iastate.edu (educ1.iastate.edu [129.186.169.31]) by pop-1.i
astate.edu (8.6.9/8.6.9) with SMTP id SAA17728 for                         Tue,
1 Aug 1995 18:55:43 -0500
Received: by educ1.iastate.edu with sendmail-5.65
        id <AA08829@educ1.iastate.edu>; Tue, 1 Aug 1995 18:55:43 -0500
Message-Id: <9508012355.AA08829@educ1.iastate.edu>
To: cas
Subject: E-mail
X-Mailer: EasyVincent 3.0
Date: Tue, 01 Aug 1995 18:55:42 CDT
From: Lisa K

Dear Charlie,

Just a reminder, this week's meeting will be held Wednesday at 9:00.
See you then.

Lisa
```

FIGURE 11-9
Electronic mail allows computer users to communicate with each other. It is instantaneous, like a telephone call, but can be delivered even when the recipient is away from
the computer. This message was delivered via the Internet.

the listserver program that supports that forum, asking to subscribe. Once added to the list, a subscriber receives all messages posted to the list and can send messages to all the other members.

Some listserver forums have thousands of subscribers in dozens of countries. Giving users the ability to correspond with so many colleagues at electronic speeds has created profound changes in scholarly communication. Forums provide an informal place to test new ideas, to validate findings, and to communicate with colleagues outside of the cumbersome formal research channels.

There are hundreds of these on-line forums, covering every topic imaginable. In addition to discussions on academic research, listserver forums are used for an endless variety of communication, for example, to debate presidential elections, provide support services to companies' customers, and announce job vacancies and important meetings.

Besides on-line forums, listservers are also used to support publication of electronic periodicals, ranging from newsletters to current awareness services to formal, refereed journals.

Remote Logon

Remote logon, also called Telnet, allows users to connect to other computers and the services they run. One of the original ideas behind the Internet was to allow researchers to use programs and resources mounted on computers at other facilities. The current Internet features thousands of computer services accessible via remote logon.

To use most computer systems, a person needs to be registered and have a password. There are some exceptions. Hundreds of on-line library catalogs, growing numbers of community bulletin boards, campus information services, and other public information systems are open to anyone on the network.

Using Telnet requires giving a command to the local system to connect to the remote system, specified by its network address. Once Telnet makes the connection the remote system's rules and its structure take over. A certain amount of awareness, intuition, and ability to work with ambiguity is required to explore an unknown system. There are also a growing number of gateways—systems that provide simple access to other systems—often with useful tips and instructions about procedures.

Telnet makes distance unimportant. It is possible to sit in an office and use a computer on the other side of the world as if it were next door. Government agencies are using Telnet to provide information services to their constituencies. Corporations, relatively new to the Internet, are also starting to provide services and products on-line. Already, many data base providers, such as Dialog, can be reached over the Internet using Telnet at higher speeds, with better reliability, and at lower costs than dial-up access. New services are announced every day.

At the host system's command line, users type **Telnet site.name** and hit enter to connect to a Telnet site. Every Telnet site has two addresses—one composed of words that are easier for people to remember; the other a numerical address better suited for computers. The "escape character" is good to remember.

SOME INTERESTING TELNET SITES

Agriculture

Telnet: psupen.psu.edu
User name: PNOTPA

PENPages, run by Pennsylvania State University's College of Agricultural Sciences, provides weekly world weather and crop reports from the U.S. Department of Agriculture. These reports detail everything from the effect of the weather on palm trees in Malaysia to the state of the Ukrainian wheat crop.

Telnet: caticsuf.cati.csufresno.edu
Login: public

California State University's Advanced Technology Information Network provides similar information as PENPages, but focuses only on California crops. It also maintains lists of upcoming California trade shows and carries updates on biotechnology.

Art

Telnet: ursus.maine.edu
Login: ursus

The National Gallery of Art in Washington maintains a data base of its holdings, which can be searched by artist (Van Gogh, for example) or medium (e.g., watercolor). You can see when specific paintings were completed, what medium they are in, how large they are, and who donated them to the gallery.

Congress

Telnet: locis.loc.gov
Password: none needed

The Library of Congress Information Service can be searched for current and past legislation (dating to 1982). Users get a main menu of several data bases, including the Library of Congress card catalog (with book entries dating to 1978) and a data base of information on copyright laws.

Current Events

Telnet: info.umd.edu

Every year, the CIA publishes a Fact Book that is essentially an almanac of the world's countries and international organizations, including such information as major products, type of government and names of its leaders. It's available for searching through the University of Maryland Info Database.

Users choose a terminal type and hit enter (or just hit enter if the terminal type is VT100). At the main menu, choose the number next to "Educational Resources." Then select the number next to "International," followed by "Factbook." Elements can be searched by country or agency.

This site also maintains copies of the U.S. budget, and documents related to the North American Free Trade Agreement (NAFTA) and other government initiatives. At the "Educational Resources" menu, select the number next to "United States" and then the one next to "Government."

Environment

Telnet: envirolink.org
Login: gopher

Envirolink is a large data base and conference system about the environment, based in Pittsburgh.

Telnet: epaibm.rtpnc.epa.gov

No password or user name is needed. At the main menu, type **public.**

The U.S. Environmental Protection Agency maintains on-line data bases of materials related to hazardous waste, the clean lakes program and cleanup efforts in New England. The agency plans to eventually include cleanup work in other regions, as well. The data base is actually a computerized card catalog of EPA documents—you can look the documents up, but you'll still have to visit your regional EPA office to see them.

Telnet: hermes.merit.edu
Host: mirlyn
Login: meem

The University of Michigan maintains a data base of newspaper and magazine articles related to the environment, with the emphasis on Michigan, dating back to 1980.

Geography

Telnet: martini.eecs.umich.edu 3000

The University of Michigan Geographic Name Server can provide basic information, such as population, latitude and longitude of U.S. cities and many mountains, rivers, and other geographic features.

No password or user name is needed. Type in the name of a city, a zip code, or a geographic feature and hit enter. The system doesn't like names with abbreviations (for example, Mt. McKinley), so spell them out (Mount McKinley).

By typing in a town's name or zip code, users can find out a community's county, longitude, and latitude, among other things. Not all geographic features are yet included in the data base.

Health

Telnet: fdabbs.fda.gov
Login: bbs

Type **topics** after logging in.

The U.S. Food and Drug Administration runs a data base of health-related information.

Hiring and College Program Information

Telnet: fedix.fie.com
User name: fedix (for the federal hiring data base)
or   molis (for the minority-college system)

The Federal Information Exchange in Gaithersburg, MD, runs two systems at the same address: FEDIX and MOLIS. FEDIX offers research, scholarship and service information for several federal agencies, including NASA, the Department of Energy and the Federal Aviation Administration. Several more federal agencies provide minority hiring and scholarship information. MOLIS provides information about minority colleges, their programs and professors.

History

Telnet: forsythetn.stanford.edu
Account: socrates

At the main menu, type **select mlk** and hit enter.

Stanford University maintains a data base of documents related to Martin Luther King Jr.

Scholarships

Telnet: fedix.fie.com
or
Telnet: 192.111.228.33

Offers information on scholarships, minority assistance, and so on.

Space

Telnet: spacelink.msfc.nasa.gov

Users are given an overview of the system and asked to register and choose a password.

NASA Spacelink in Huntsville, Ala., provides all sorts of reports and data about NASA, its history and its missions. You'll find detailed reports on every probe, satellite, and mission NASA has ever launched along with daily updates and lesson plans for teachers.

The system maintains a large file library of GIF-format space graphics, but they cannot be downloaded through telnet. If you want them, you have to dial the system directly, at (205) 895-0028.

Telnet: ipac.caltech.edu
Login: ned

The NED-NASA/IPAC Extragalactic Database lists data on more than 100,000 galaxies, quasars and other objects outside the Milky Way.

Telnet: cfa204.harvard.edu
Login: einline

Users can learn all about quasars, novae, and related objects on a system run by the Smithsonian Astrophysical Observatory in Cambridge, Massachusetts.

Telnet: spacemet.phast.umass.edu
Login: user's name and a password

The physics department at the University of Massachusetts at Amherst runs a bulletin-board system that provides extensive conferences and document libraries related to space.

Supreme Court Decisions

Telnet: info.umd.edu

Users choose a terminal type and hit enter (or just hit enter if the terminal type is VT100). At the main menu, choose the number next to "Educational Resources" and hit enter. Select the number next to "United States" and, at the next menu, choose the one next to "Supreme Court." The University of Maryland Info Database maintains U.S. Supreme Court decisions from 1991 on.

Time

To find out the exact time:

Telnet: india.colorado.edu 13

The screen will look something like this:

Escape character is ' ^]'.
Sun Nov 17 **14:11:41** 1996
Connection closed by foreign host.

The middle line gives the date and exact Mountain Standard Time, as determined by a federal atomic clock.

Transportation

Telnet: metro.jussieu.fr 10000

The Subway Navigator in Paris can help you learn how long it will take to get from point A to point B on subway systems around the world.

Users choose a language in which to search (English or French) and then a city to search. They are then asked for the station of departure and the station of arrival.

Weather

Telnet: madlab.sprl.umich.edu 3000
                 (note the 3000)

The University of Michigan's Department of Atmospheric, Oceanographic and Space Sciences supplies weather forecasts for U.S. and international cities, along with skiing and hurricane reports.

File Transfer Protocol (FTP)

File Transfer Protocol (FTP) allows users to move data files from computer to computer. The vast quantity and range of resources available through FTP makes it one of the most popular features of the Internet. Hundreds of systems connected to Internet have file libraries, or software archives, accessible to the public. Much of this information consists of free or low-cost shareware programs for virtually every make of computer. But there are also libraries of documents, such as U.S. Supreme Court decisions, and copies of historical documents, from the Magna Carta to the Declaration of Independence. Users can also find song lyrics, poems, and even summaries of every "Star Trek" episode.

A typical session involves connecting to a remote FTP host, specified by its network address, moving around in the directories on the host, and requesting the system to retrieve the desired files. As with Telnet, access via FTP is usually limited to registered users. Many resources, however, can be used by unregistered or anonymous users—where users identify themselves literally as "anonymous." This "anonymous FTP" is a rich cache of free public information.

At the host system's command line, users type **ftp site.name** (for example, ftp spacelink.msfc.nasa.gov) and hit enter, where "site.name" is the address of the desired FTP site. Then they log in as "anonymous" and the system provides information on what to type for a login and a password. The following list of commands will help with file transfers:

ls—lists all the files in the current directory
cd directory.name—changes the current directory
get file.name—copies the specified file from the host computer to the individual's account (download)
put file.name—copies the specified file from the individual's account to the host computer (upload)

SOME INTERESTING FTP SITES

Internet—Network Service Center

nnsc.nsf.net

or

128.89.1.178

A gold mine of documents and training materials on Internet use.

Libraries

ftp.unt.edu

The library directory contains numerous lists of libraries with computerized card catalogs accessible through the Net.

Macintosh Software

sumex-aim.stanford.edu

This is the premier site for Macintosh software. After logging in, users switch to the info-mac directory, which will bring up a long series of subdirectories of free- and shareware Mac programs.

ftp.uu.net

Lots of Macintosh programs can be found in the systems/mac/simtel20 directory.

Music

cs.uwp.edu

The pub/music directory has everything from lyrics of contemporary songs to recommended CDs of baroque music. It's a little different—and easier to navigate—than other FTP sites.

potemkin.cs.pdx.edu

This is a Bob Dylan archive. Interviews, notes, year-by-year accounts of his life and more can be found in the pub/dylan directory.

ftp.nevada.edu

Guitar chords for contemporary songs can be found in the pub/guitar directory, in subdirectories organized by group or artist.

Native Americans

pines.hsu.edu

Home of IndianNet, this site contains a variety of directories and files related to Indians and Eskimos, including federal census data, research reports and a tribal profiles data base. Look in the pub and indian directories.

Pictures

wuarchiv.wustl.edu

The graphics/gif directory contains hundreds of GIF photographic and drawing images, from cartoons to cars, space images to pop stars. These are arranged in a long series of subdirectories.

Photography

ftp.nevada.edu

Photolog is an on-line digest of photography news, in the pub/photo directory.

Shakespeare

atari.archive.umich.edu

The Shakespeare directory contains most of the bard's works. A number of other sites have his works as well, but generally as one huge file. This site breaks them down into various categories (comedy, poetry, history, etc.) so that individual plays or sonnets can be downloaded.

Space

ames.arc.nasa.gov

Stores text files about space and the history of the NASA space program in the pub/SPACE subdirectory. In the pub/GIF and pub/SPACE/GIF directories, users can find astronomy and NASA-related GIF files, including pictures of planets, satellites, and other celestial objects.

Weather

wuarchive.wustl.edu

The /multimedia/images/wx directory contains GIF weather images of North America. Files are updated hourly and take this general form: CV100222. The first two letters tell the type of file: CV means it is a visible-light photo taken by a weather satellite. CI images are similar, but use infrared light. Both these are in black and white. Files that begin with SA are color radar maps of the United States that show severe weather patterns as well as fronts and temperatures in major cities. The numbers indicate the date and time (in GMT—five hours ahead of EST) of the image: the first two numbers represent the month, the next two the date, the last two the hour. The file WXKEY.GIF explains the various symbols in SA files.

Extended Services

Internet utilities and services that present network resources in a new way have begun to emerge. While most of the original Internet applications are difficult to master, these new services are intended to make resources accessible to non-experts and users with less computing experience. Using friendlier interfaces, such as menus, they avoid the clumsy commands and the lack of clues typical of earlier applications. These new services also provide pointers to resources once known only to those with more network experience.

One of the most popular of these extended services is Gopher, a program developed at the University of Minnesota. First, its hierarchical menus allow users to cruise the Internet and read, print, and download the information found there without having to know addresses or commands. Second, it works with other network services, such as e-mail, Telnet, and FTP, making it an all-in-one Internet tool. Finally, it takes advantage of the interactive nature to pull together widely distributed information and present it through a single, seamless interface. Gopher is used for many public information services, such as community bulletin boards, because it is easy to use but still powerful.

An index, called Veronica (for Very Easy Rodent-Oriented Net-wide Index to Computerized Archives), offers a keyword search of most Gopher-server menus in the entire Gopher web. Veronica connects directly to the data source. Because Veronica is accessed through a gopher client, it is easy to use, and gives access to all types of data supported by the Gopher protocol.

The result of a Veronica search is a Gopher menu, customized according to the user's keyword specification. Items on this menu may be drawn from many Gopher servers. These are functional Gopher items, immediately accessible via the Gopher client—users just double-click to open directories, read files, or perform other searches—across hundreds of Gopher servers. There is no need to know which server is actually involved in filling requests for information. Items that appear particularly interesting can be saved in the user's bookmark list.

Notice that these are *not* full-text searches of data at Gopher-server sites. Veronica indexes the *titles* on all levels of the menus, for most Gopher sites in the Internet.

SOME INTERESTING GOPHER SITES

Agriculture

cyfer.esusda.gov

This site offers an extensive list of agricultural statistics and regulations.

usda.mannlib.cornell.edu

More than 140 types of agricultural data can be found here, most in Lotus 1-2-3 spreadsheet format.

Animals

saimiri.primate.wisc.edu

Information on primates and animal-welfare laws.

Architecture

libra.arch.umich.edu

Maintains on-line exhibits of a variety of architectural images.

Art

seq1.loc.gov

The Library of Congress runs several on-line galleries of images from exhibits at the library. Many of these pictures, in GIF or JPEG format, are huge, so users should carefully consider what to download. Exhibits include items such as art from the Vatican, copies of once-secret Soviet documents, and pictures of artifacts related to Columbus' 1492 voyage.

galaxy.ucr.edu

The California Museum of Photography maintains its own on-line gallery here. At the main menu, select "Campus Events," then "California Museum of Photography," then "Network Exhibitions."

Astronomy

cast0.ast.cam.ac.uk

A Gopher devoted to astronomy, run by the Institute of Astronomy and the Royal Greenwich Observatory, Cambridge, England.

Census

bigcat.missouri.edu

Detailed federal census data for communities of more than 10,000, as well as for states and counties, can be found at this site. At the main menu, select "Reference and Information Center," then "United States and Missouri Census Information," then "United States Census."

Computers

wuarchive.wustl.edu

Dozens of directories list software for all sorts of computers. Most programs are compressed and have to be expanded before they can be used.

sumex-aim.stanford.edu

This system is similar to wuarchive.wustl.edu, with an emphasis on Macintosh programs and files.

Environment

ecosys.drdr.virginia.edu

Copies of Environmental Protection Agency fact sheets on hundreds of chemicals, searchable by keyword. Select "Education," then "Environmental fact sheets."

envirolink.org

Dozens of documents and files related to environmental activism around the world.

gopher.econet.apc.org
nceet.snre.umich.edu
or
telnet 141.211.152.61

Education

schoolnet.carleton.ca

Canada's SchoolNet

gopher.ed.gov

U.S. Department of Education

chronicle.merit.edu

Chronicle of Higher Education

gaia.sci-ed.fit.edu

Florida Tech Education Gopher

informns.k12.mn.u Internet for Minnesota Schools
goldmine.cde.ca.gov

California Department of Education

gopher.ed.uiuc.edu

UIUC: College of Education

shiva.educ.kent.edu

Deaf Education Resources

info.asu.edu

The following sites are of special interest to K–12:

Entomology

spider.ento.csiro.au

All about creepy-crawly things, both the good and the bad.

Geology

gopher.stolaf.edu

Select "Internet Resources," then "Weather and Geography" for information on recent earthquakes.

Government

marvel.loc.gov

Run by the Library of Congress, this site provides numerous resources, including access to the library's card catalog and information about the U.S. Congress.

gopher.lib.umich.edu

Variety of government information, from Congressional committee assignments to economic statistics and information about NAFTA.

ecix.doc.gov

Information on conversion of military installations to private use.

sunsite.unc.edu

Copies of current and past federal budgets can be found by selecting "Sunsite archives," then "Politics," then "Sunsite political science archives."

wiretap.spies.com

Documents related to Canadian government can be found in the "Government docs" menu.

stis.nih.gov

Select the "Other U.S. government gopher servers" for access to numerous other federal gophers.

Health

odie.niaid.nih.gov

National Institutes of Health data bases on AIDS, in the "AIDS-Related Information" menu.

helix.nih.gov

For National Cancer Institute fact sheets on different cancers, select "Health and Clinical Information" and then "Cancernet Information."

nysernet.org

Look for information on breast cancer in the "Special Collections: Breast Cancer" menu.

welchlink.welch.jhu.edu

This is Johns Hopkins University's medical gopher.

Internet

gopher.lib.umich.edu

Home to several guides to Internet resources in specific fields, for example, social sciences. Select "What's New & Featured Resources," then "Clearinghouse."

Israel

jerusalem1.datasrv.co.il

This Israeli system offers numerous documents on Israel and Jewish life.

Japan

gopher.ncc.go.jp

Look in the "Japan Information" menu for documents related to Japanese life and culture.

Music

mtv.com

Run by Adam Curry, an MTV video jock, this site has music news and Curry's daily "Cybersleaze" celebrity report.

Nature

ucmp1.berkeley.edu

The University of California at Berkeley's Museum of Paleontology runs several on-line exhibits on this site. Users can obtain GIF images of plants and animals from the "Remote Nature" menu. The "Origin of the Species" menu provides access to Darwin's work or it can be searched by keyword.

Sports

culine.colorado.edu

Look up schedules for teams in various professional sports leagues here, under "Professional Sports Schedules."

Weather

wx.atmos.uiuc.edu

This site offers weather facts and forecasts for North America.

Other new Internet applications are Archie, Wide-Area Information Server (WAIS), and the World Wide Web (The Web, WWW, or W3). The Archie service is a collection of resource discovery tools created to keep track of the contents of anonymous FTP archive sites. It is being expanded to include a variety of other on-line directories and resource listings. Currently, Archie tracks the contents of more than 800 anonymous FTP archive sites containing some 1 million files throughout the Internet. Collectively, these files represent more than 50 gigabytes (50,000,000,000 bytes) of information, with additional information being added daily.

WAIS is a more radical approach, making a real-time connection to other WAIS servers and searching their indexes. WAIS then lets the user go directly to the selected site to retrieve the item.

The World Wide Web (WWW) merges the techniques of information retrieval and hypertext to make an easy but powerful global information system. The WWW consists of documents and links to other items that may be located elsewhere on the network. Indexes are special documents which, rather than being read, may be searched. The result of such a search is another document containing links to the documents found.

The Web contains documents in many formats. Documents that are *hypertext* contain links to other documents, or places within documents. All documents, whether real, virtual or indexes, look similar and are contained within the same addressing scheme. To follow a link, users click with a mouse (or type in a number). To search an index, users give keywords (or other search criteria). These are the only operations necessary to access any of the data on the Web.

SOME INTERESTING WEB SITES

Education

K–12 Resources
http://edu-52.sfsu.edu/dit_home.html
http://www.tc.cornell.edu/Kids.on.Campus/KOC94/
http://web66.coled.umn.edu/ [Web 66]
http://www.teleport.com/~vincer/starter.html
http://edweb.cnidr.org:90/
(EdWeb K12 Resource Guide)
http://www.manymedia.com/show-n-tell/
(Show-n-Tell)
gopher://is.internic.net/11/infoguide/resources/k-12/

K-12 Schools
http://hillside.coled.umn.edu/others.html [Map]
http://toons.cc.ndsu.nodak.edu/~sackmann/k12.html
http://forum.swarthmore.edu/mathmagic/what.html

MathMagic! Offers a problem-solving project with teams of students "talking" about math.

Science Education

http://cea-ftp.cea.berkeley.edu/Education/
Science education: This site offers CEA Education Outreach tools

http://www.umi.com
A listing of dissertations.

http://ftp.clearlake.ibm.com/ERC/HomePage.html
http://ecosys.drdr.virginia.edu/Environment.html
These sites offer a virtual library of environmental information.

http://www.nnu.edu/aftaera/home.html
The homepage for the American Educational Research Association.

http://galaxy.einet.net/GJ/education.html
A catalog of education facilities on the Internet.

gopher://gopher.ed.gov/
The Department of Education's Gopher server.

http://www.mit.edu/people/cdemello/univ.html#U6
Listing of all college and university home pages.

http://forum.swarthmore.edu/
This site offers a geometry forum.

http://tecfa.unige.ch/info-edu-comp.html
Educational technology web server

http://www.amherst.edu/~drsharp/thedoc.html
The doctor's office.

http://george.lbl.fov/ITG.hm/pq.docs/dissect
A frog dissection.

http://www.xmission.com/~jayhall/
Information about genealogy.

http://pubweb.parc.xerox.com/map
A listing of maps.

http://www.cs.indiana.edu/metastuff/bookfaq.html
A list of books on line.

Computers

Multimedia
http://mistral.enst.fr/~picoh/louvre/
Virtual tour of the Louvre.

http://rever.nmsu.edu/~elharo/faq/Macintosh.html

The Well Connected Mac

http://www.iastate.edu/
Iowa State University web server (Figures 11–10, 11–11).

Searching

http://nearnet.gnn.com/wic/
The Whole Internet Catalog.

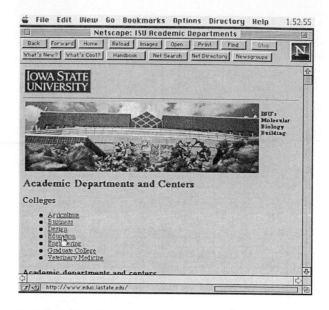

FIGURE 11–10

Iowa State University's homepage, accessed via the World Wide Web, offers links to documents containing information about the school.

FIGURE 11–11

The address of the Iowa State University College of Education homepage is displayed in the lower left corner of the ISU Academic Departments page.

http://www.cs.colorado.edu/home/mcbryan/
    WWWW.html
The World Wide Web Worm

http://web.nexor.co.uk/archie.html
Archie servers—WWW

http://cui_www.uniqe.ch/meta-index.html
W3 Search Engines

http://akebono.stanford.edu/yahoo/
Yahoo—A Guide to WWW

http://www.awa.com/yellow/yellow.html
Interactive Yellow Pages

http://cs.indiana.edu/internet/internet.html
Listservers for the World Wide Web.

gopher://gopher.uoregon.edu
List of telephone area codes.

Miscellaneous

http://medoc.gdb.org/best/fund.html
Funding opportunities.

http://www.internet.net/stores/infoworld/index.html
InfoWorld home page

http://www.i-link.com/lcsb/Welcom.html
Iowa legislative

http://www.nara.gov/
National archives

http://lcweb.loc.fov/homepage/lchp.html
Library of Congress home page

http://the-tech.it.edu/KPT/KPT.html
Kai's Tips on using Adobe Photoshop.

http://www.cs.yale.edu/HTML/YALE/CS/HyPlans/
    loosemore-sandra/clipart.html
Sandra's Clip Art

Music

http://www.cs.cmu.edu:8001/afs/cs.cmu.edu/user/
    jdg/www/music_artists.html
Music artists.

http://128.194.15^{32}/~ahb2188/elvishom.html

Elvis Presley home page.

http://www.stones.com/
The Rolling Stones web site

Weather—Space

http://adswww.harvard.edu/MITSA/weather.html
Weather Page-MITSA

http://www.atmos.uiuc.edu/wxworld/html/top.html
Worldwide weather

http://www.lanl.gov/~cjhamil/SolarSystem/homepage.
   html
Solar system home page

COMPUTER COMMUNICATION AND NATIONAL DATA BASES IN THE CURRICULUM

As with other computer topics, computer communication and the use of national data bases can be presented two ways in the school curriculum: teaching *about* them and teaching *with* them. As with other computer tools, teaching *with* is more significant than teaching *about*.

Teaching About Computer Communication and National Data Bases

Three topics are normally included in the curriculum plan that deal with teaching about computer communication and national data bases.

1.   General topics related to the use of references and searching for information using references are presented in the elementary school. Usually, this kind of instruction is not computer based but uses the school's media center as a local resource. Students are taught the importance of, and techniques for, finding references about an idea that they have. Obviously, these skills have been a part of the elementary school curriculum for a long time and are part of the widely accepted goal of education to produce independent learners who understand how to find information about a topic. Computer communication and searching of national data bases are usually used in demonstrations to show students that

additional information is available about their topics or to show them how to find information on difficult or unusual topics. Usually, the regular classroom teacher presents this information.

2.   Data base searching strategies are taught as separate skills, important in themselves. Often, they are presented in a special unit titled Media Center Use or Library Skills. Normally, the school's media specialist, or librarian, teaches these skills. These topics also have been a component of the curriculum for years. The difference is that now on-line searching is presented, and access to a wider variety of data bases is stressed. Data base concepts are also taught as well as how they are organized. Additionally, the use of the logical connectors *and, not,* and *or* is presented, as are more traditional topics such as the correct procedures for writing footnotes, references, and citations.

Basically, this second category of topics about computer communications and use of national data bases complements what traditionally has been presented in the library-use course. In this course students are taught topics such as use of *The Abridged Reader's Guide to Periodical Literature* and the card catalog, and note taking. Usually, each level of organization within the school system, such as the elementary school, the junior high, and the high school, will have their own course of this type so students can learn to use the resources available to them.

3.   Computer communications and use of national data bases are taught in the junior high school's computer literacy course. The topics presented deal with how computers communicate with one another, how modems work, and how data bases are searched. The purpose of this component of computer literacy education is to develop an understanding of how telecommunications work and the technical details of computer communication. The use of the Internet and its various searching tools is an increasingly important topic for any basic computer literacy course.

Teaching With Computer Communications Systems, National Data Bases, and the Internet

The most important effect of computers on education occurs when they are used to facilitate learning. Computer communications systems permit the classroom teacher to access information worldwide and to bring information into the classroom that otherwise would not be available. A three-phase approach to teaching with computer communications systems is used most often:

1. *Phase I: Awareness Activities in the Elementary School.* Elementary school applications are designed to introduce the concept of communicating using computers. Often, teachers introduce students to computer communications by having them post messages on BBSs. These messages are used as a kind of "pen-pal" approach to computer communications. Teachers have also had success identifying other schools with communications systems so the schools can become "sister" or "brother" schools. Students can input daily schedules and diaries of events in their school for their "sisters and brothers" to read. The purpose of these activities is to acquaint elementary school children with computer communications.

Next, teachers often present basic concepts of information sources to elementary school students. Initially, teachers present traditional techniques for organizing and accessing information. Then they demonstrate to students how to access information on-line. Local school media center catalogs and data bases are used first; then distant data bases are searched. The purpose of these activities is to make children aware of how information is organized and accessed.

2. *Phase II: Individual Uses of Computer Communications.* Usually in the middle school, or junior high school, teachers begin to make assignments that require students to do research. Traditionally, this research is done in the school media center, the city library, or elsewhere in the community. Increasingly, teachers and students are using computer communications to supplement resources available locally.

First, students must be instructed in the techniques of on-line searching. Generally, because of the cost, local computer data bases are searched first. Junior high school students can probably learn the procedures for searching data bases just as effectively using the computerized card catalog of the school media center as they can when accessing an information utility such as Dialog, or data sources available via the Internet. The purpose of these activities is to develop searching skills in students. Usually, the junior high computer-literacy course has a unit that covers these topics.

Next, students are given assignments that can be accomplished using computer communications. Current events projects and book reports that might require searching the *New York Times* or the *Washington Post* indexes, or that would use the *Magazine Index,* are often assigned. Projects such as these have traditionally been given to junior high students.

3. *Phase III: Sophisticated Uses of Computer Communications.* By the time students reach high school, they should have a good working knowledge of computer communications techniques and capabilities. At this level more advanced uses of communications systems can be explored. On-line conferencing, information requests from experts, and searching of technical data bases are examples of advanced uses of computer communications for high school students. Technical information utilities such as Dialog are often used for sophisticated searches, because Dialog makes available hundreds of data bases such as the following:

- Medline, a data base of biomedical information.
- D&B—Dun's Financial Records, a compilation of financial information about 700,000 U.S. businesses.
- CA search, a condensed version of Chemical Abstracts.

Information available through the Internet is almost limitless and accessing these data should be a basic skill of all students.

The primary reason computer communication is growing in importance in school is that it provides easy, inexpensive, and comprehensive access to information. Information searching has traditionally been an important skill for students to possess. This skill has merely been broadened by the addition of computer searching. As has been stated many times in this textbook, the computer's primary contribution to education is related to its effect on doing what schools have always done. Learning with the assistance of computers, and using computers to improve the learning process, must be the criteria by which the importance of computer technology is judged.

SUMMARY

Computer communications are the combination of computer technology and communication technology. What computer communications systems are, common system features, and the services available when using computer communications systems were presented. Uses of computer communications in the curriculum were also identified.

The use of the computer to communicate and to access information remotely are less commonly understood techniques than those presented in the other chapters in this section. The next chapter will discuss important issues such as copyright and software and hardware selection.

SELF-TEST QUESTIONS

1. When a microcomputer in a social studies classroom is used to access the school media center's on-line card catalog, this is an example of:
   a. A telephone network
   b. A local area network (LAN)
   c. A wide-area network
   d. A simplex system
2. When data are sent over telephone lines, how are they configured?
3. Define *half duplex*.
4. Which of these components are not needed for a telephone computer communications network?
   a. A telephone
   b. A modem
   c. Communications software
   d. Serial data
5. Define *information utility*.
6. When using Dialog, what command is needed to start a search of a new data base?
7. If a science teacher wanted to identify documents in an on-line data base that discussed magnetism and superconductivity, what logical connector would be used between these key words?
8. Teaching with computer communications systems is more important than teaching about them.
   a. True
   b. False

ANSWERS TO SELF-TEST QUESTIONS

1. b. LAN. Accessing information within a school building is an example of a local area network.
2. When sent over telephone lines, data must be sent serially, one bit at a time.

3. *Half duplex* refers to the sending of data between two terminal devices, in one direction at a time. In other words, when one computer is sending, the other computer cannot send but must wait until the first has finished. Normal telephone conversations are full-duplex transmissions, because both people on the line can talk and listen (if that is possible) at the same time.
4. a. A telephone is often not needed for a telephone network, just the live telephone line.
5. An information utility provides access to information in data bases it owns or subscribes to.
6. Begin (or B) is the command used to start a search of a data base. For example, "Begin 1" would be the first command entered to start a search of ERIC.
7. The logical connector *and* is used between two key words when documents that contain both words are sought.
8. a. True. Teaching with computers and with computer communications systems is of primary importance to most educators.

REFERENCES FOR ADDITIONAL STUDY

Arms, V. (1988). Computer conferencing. *Educational Technology, 28*(3), 43–45.

Azarmsa, R. (1987). Computer conferencing: Models and proposals. *Educational Technology, 27*(12), 28–32.

Badgett, T. (1987a, May 12). On-line databases: Dialing for data. *PC Magazine,* 238–258.

Badgett, T. (1987b, May 12). Search software: Directory assistance. *PC Magazine,* 263–267.

Caputo, A., & Lodish, E. (1987). Researching on-line: Schools and electronic data bases. *The Computing Teacher, 14*(7), 50–51, 60.

Desey, D. (1995). All aboard the Internet. *Tech Trends, 40*(1), 11–12.

Dodge, B., & Dodge, J. (1987). Readiness activities for telecommunications. *The Computing Teacher, 14*(7), 7–8, 22.

Elmer-Dewitt, P. (1993, December 6). First nation in cyberspace. *Time,* 62–64.

Friedlander, B. (1985). Get your class in-line and on-line with a modem. *Electronic Education, 5*(3), 14–15, 23.

Goldberg, F. (1988, May). Telecommunications in the classroom. *The Computing Teacher, 15*(5), 26–35.

Guthrie, J., & Crane, B. (1992). Online retrieval adds realism to science projects. *The Computing Teacher, 19*(5), 32–33.

Hannah, L. (1987). Teaching data base search strategies. *The Computing Teacher, 14*(9), 16–17.

Harris, J. (1995). Educational telecomputing projects: Information collections. *The Computing Teacher, 22*(4), 44–48.

Harris, J. (1995). Educational telecomputing projects: Interpersonal exchanges. *The Computing Teacher, 22*(3), 60–64.

Harris, J. (1995). Organizing and facilitating telecollaborative projects. *The Computing Teacher, 22*(2), 66–69.

Harris, J. (1992). Telnet sessions on the Internet. *The Computer Teacher, 19*(10), 40–43.

Harris, S., & Kidder, K. (1995). *Netscape: Quick tour for the Macintosh.* Research Triangle Park, NC: Ventana Press.

James, D. (1983, July). Networking: A powerful tool for personal communication. *Personal Computing,* 45–54.

Manning, R. (1987, May). Guide to communications software. *Family Computing,* 18, 20.

Neuman, D. (1987). Local and long distance computer networking for science classrooms. *Educational Technology, 27*(6), 20–23.

Shelly, G. B., & Cashman, T. J. (1984). *Computer fundamentals for an information age.* Brea, CA: Anaheim Publishing.

Snider, M. (1995, March 22). Growth spurt causes traffic tie-ups on Internet. *USA Today,* p. 6D.

Snyder, J. (1994, December). Taming the Internet. *Macworld,* 114–117.

Streeter, A. (1992, October 12). How to get your company on Internet. *MacWEEK,* 22–25.

Wedemeyer, D. (1986). The new age of telecommunications: Setting the context for education. *Educational Technology, 26*(10), 7–13.

CHAPTER TWELVE

MANAGING COMPUTERS

Selecting Software and Hardware

GOAL

This chapter will present the procedures for the selection and purchase of computer software and hardware.

OBJECTIVES

The reader will be able to do the following:

1. Identify sources of information about computer software.
2. Explain important criteria for software evaluation.
3. Explain copyright regulations as they relate to computer software.
4. Describe a system for school software circulation.
5. Identify sources for information about hardware.
6. Explain the process of selecting and purchasing computer hardware.
7. Describe simple repair and maintenance procedures for computer hardware.

The cartoon in Figure 12–1 was used by a computer software company, Microrim, to advertise a data base manager it was selling. The caption, "It's not how hard you work. It's how much you get done," was designed to attract the attention of computer users who were interested in results rather than reputation.

The cartoon is one of the better examples of the advertising used to promote computer software. It is

FIGURE 12–1

"It's not how hard you work. It's how much you get done." Software advertisement.

Illustration compliments of Microrim, Inc. Reprinted with permission from Gill, B., Dick, W., Reiser, R., & Sahner, J. (1992). A new model for evaluating instructional software. *Educational Technology, 32*(3), 39–44.

creative, thought provoking, and relevant. Although it is likely Microrim's data base manager is a good one, the potential customer has little way of knowing if the software will actually do what is needed. Ads normally do not give unbiased evaluations of the software being promoted. As a matter of fact, identifying reliable information about computer products is difficult.

This chapter is divided into two sections. First, the process of identifying, evaluating, taking inventory, and circulating software will be presented. Software copyright regulations will also be discussed. Next, the process of identifying, evaluating, ordering, and distributing hardware will be examined. General information about computer maintenance will also be presented.

SOFTWARE DECISIONS

The primary problem for those who want to purchase the best computer software is that no single source gives all the information needed. As a matter of fact, information about computer software is located in hundreds of places, and theoretically, a potential buyer should examine most of this information before making a decision. To simplify matters, this discussion will be limited to an explanation of the primary sources of information about computer software and major procedures for software acquisition.

Step 1: Locating Software

Finding out what programs are available may be the most difficult step in the process of software acquisition. Traditionally, educators have had a hard time locating all competing and comparable instructional materials to evaluate them. Often schools have had to purchase materials based only on input from salespeople or on product exhibits at conventions.

There are five primary sources of information about microcomputer software:

1. Vendor catalogs, advertisements, and software brokers
2. Professional journals
3. Indexes
4. On-line services
5. Educational organizations

As many of these sources as possible should be consulted before purchasing decisions are made.

Vendor Catalogs, Advertisements, and Software Brokers.   Most software distributors issue catalogs with information about the products they sell. These catalogs usually list titles, descriptions, target audiences, and prices. Vendor catalogs are distributed monthly, quarterly, or yearly. Many companies also send special announcements whenever a new product is introduced and advertise extensively in computer magazines such as *Macworld, MacWEEK, PC Magazine, PC Computing,* and *BYTE.*

Catalogs are often sent unsolicited to teachers as third-class mail. While some consider this kind of "junk mail" a nuisance, the announcements and information contained in vendor catalogs can be helpful when purchasing decisions are made.

It is relatively easy to be placed on mailing lists. The school's computer coordinator or school media specialist should send postcards to vendors who advertise in computer magazines, asking for copies of company catalogs. In a short time, most company sales departments will routinely send current catalogs and will place the coordinator on lists for future mailings.

In many schools, these catalogs are placed in some kind of vertical file, usually in alphabetical order by vendor. Efficient schools also have a subject listing of software offered by vendors. It is important to remember that catalogs are not an unbiased source of information because they present only positive information about products.

Many software brokers publish catalogs of software from a number of different companies. *PC & Mac Connection, MicroWarehouse, The Mac Zone,* and *MacMail* are four software brokers who publish comprehensive catalogs.

Professional Journals.   Many computer software companies advertise in educational computing magazines. Often, lists of advertisers are included in each issue, and sometimes a yearly directory of advertisers is published. Although it takes a great deal of time to scan different issues of several magazines, this is a good way to get up-to-date information about computer software. Many journals publish lists of new software that include descriptions and even ratings.

Indexes.   For education software, there are "union lists," or comprehensive listings, of what is commercially available. For example, the National Information Center for Educational Media (NICEM) indexes list most commercially available instructional materials, such as motion pictures, videotapes, and filmstrips. *Books in*

Print and *El-Hi Books in Print* are the primary indexes for books and textbooks. Unfortunately, no single comprehensive index for microcomputer software exists.

There have been several one-time attempts at indexing software. These sources have become outdated, but still contain valuable background information about tried-and-true software. The *Educational Software Directory*, published by Electronic Communications Inc., of Tallahassee, Florida, and *The Software Guide*, published by Micro Information Publishing Inc., of Prior Lake, Minnesota, are two such comprehensive indexes. Both were published in the mid-1980s. Often, school media specialists collect these indexes and others and keep them in the school's curriculum laboratory. Regional media centers, serving multiple school districts, and college of education curriculum laboratories also collect indexes such as these.

On-Line Services.   On-line services, such as information utilities like America Online and CompuServe, have lists of software that can be downloaded. A number of freeware and shareware software packages are available, also.

Education Organizations.   Often, schools order instructional materials that other schools are using and consider effective. Also, state and regional educational organizations, such as state departments of education, publish lists of recommended software. These lists can become the core collection for a school.

One additional source for microcomputer software is the Minnesota Educational Computer Consortium (MECC). MECC began as a consortium of teachers in Minnesota who shared software they had created. Over the years, a large collection of uniformly high-quality, teacher-produced software was developed. In

FIGURE 12–2
Software packages typically include the software itself, on one or more floppy disks and/or compact discs, as well as a user's manual, instructions for loading the software into the computer, and information about customer support services.

the early 1980s, the collection of MECC software was offered to schools, regional educational service organizations, and even statewide groups. Schools obtained hundreds of computer-based lessons for as little as $2 or $3 each. MECC now offers its software collection in a catalog. Prices are still low, and many schools use the MECC software as the core of their microcomputer software collection.

Other states and regions have established similar teacher collections of software. Most of these lessons are drills and tutorials, and few are aimed at high-level concepts. However, because they are low-cost and developed by teachers, many schools find them attractive.

Locating software is the key step in the acquisition process. Once programs have been identified, they need to be compared to the needs of the school and to each other, so the best instructional package is selected.

Step 2: Evaluating Software

Evaluation is the task of every user. Only the person with a need for a software package can make the final decision about whether her needs were met, or if learning has occurred. It is also important, however, for teachers to purchase software that is most likely to meet curricular objectives. A considerable body of literature has been published about the process of evaluating computer software (Zahner, Reiser, Dick, & Gill, 1992). Models for software evaluation based on learning have been tested and found to be useful (Reiser & Dick, 1990). These models have several steps to follow when evaluating software.

First, teachers should review software, identify the objectives the software is designed to teach, and develop tests and attitude questionnaires related to the objective and software. During a one-on-one evaluation phase, students should be observed as they individually work through the program. Next students should be tested on the skills they learned and asked about their attitudes toward the lesson. In a small-group evaluation phase, 10 to 20 students should use the lesson in a realistic setting, and then they should be tested. Data from the students should then be analyzed to determine if the computer lesson is effective (Figure 12–3).

Most often, evaluation occurs in two phases. First, published reviews or testimonials are located and used to screen software. Next, local reviews based on locally established criteria are conducted. Many computer software companies permit potential buyers to preview their programs. This gives educators an excellent opportunity to select only the most appropriate lessons.

> ### Notes From the Literature
>
> Variability among raters of educational software appears to be related to computer/software experience, awareness of similar products (for comparison), and the actual time spent on the evaluation process.
>
> *Callison, D. (1987–1988). Experience and time investment factors in public school evaluation of educational microcomputer software. Journal of Educational Technology Systems, 16(2), 129–149.*

Published Reviews and Testimonials. Computer educators love to talk about their favorite software. Teachers who are "tapped in" to computer-use networks will often hear about new software packages, or they can ask colleagues about their favorite software. One of the best sources of information are on-line discussion groups and bulletin boards. Conventions and conferences often feature presenters who talk about packages and how they fit in their school's curriculum. Although these sources are hit and miss, they can be helpful because people's opinions about computer software usually are based on actual experiences using the lesson.

Numerous journal publishers have begun to offer critical reviews of new computer software (Figure 12–4). Often these reviews are written by teachers who give the kind of information other educators need. However, finding reviews of specific lessons can be a problem. Back issues of journals need to be scanned, and this can be time-consuming. It is sometimes possible to contact journal editors to find out if a certain package has been reviewed. Software manufacturers themselves might have lists of the publications that have reviewed their software.

Two review aids are available, also. The Microcomputer Index, accessed through information utilities such as Dialog, gives on-line information about computer software. Additionally, the Educational Products Information Exchange (EPIE) publishes reviews of both computer software and hardware. EPIE, a subscription service, has been used by educators for decades and is a valuable source of information about all kinds of educational products. School and regional centers often subscribe to EPIE and have back issues of reviews.

Local Software Reviews. Ultimately, all lessons should be evaluated by those who will use

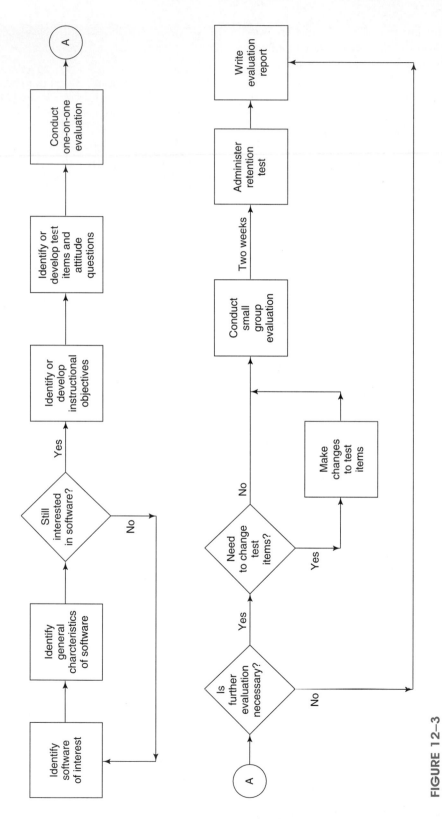

FIGURE 12–3
A new model for evaluating instructional software.

FEBRUARY 1995

Microsoft Word 6.0

Word Processor

PROS: Dazzling array of new features; many interface improvements; works identically to Windows version. **CONS:** Slow; can't use ruler to adjust tabs and margins with their dialog boxes open; dual-platform manual makes finding Mac-specific information difficult. **COMPANY:** Microsoft Corporation (206/882-8080). **COMPANY'S ESTIMATED PRICE:** $329.

MW ★★★

THE LATEST VERSION OF THE Macintosh world's most popular word processor has been out for several months now. It's been lynched online and at user groups, it's been tossed in the Trash and returned to dealers, and it's lost market share to Novell's WordPerfect, which had for years been a relatively minor player among high-end Mac word processors.

What happened? Three things: First, Microsoft made Word's interface identical to that of Word 6.0 for Windows, and the differences annoyed many 5.1 loyalists. Second, Microsoft included such a huge array of add-on utilities, document templates, and gimmicky autoformatting Wizards that a full installation of Word 6 swallows 25MB of hard disk space. Third and most significant, Microsoft shipped a program that is often dramatically slower than its predecessor—so much so that it doesn't run acceptably on 68010-based Macs, or even on slower 68040 Macs such as the Quadra 610.

Some of Word's reported performance problems are genuine, but much of the criticism leveled against the program has been a bit overblown. There are flashes of brilliance in Word 6; and the new cross-platform compatibility is a boon to businesses that mix Macs and Windows machines. But before you

vations against its greed for hard disk space and horsepower.

A Fancy Face-lift

Word 6 sports an entirely new look and feel, featuring a multitude of tool bars and attractive 3-D dialog boxes, many of which display previews as you select formatting options (see "The Latest Word"). I'm not a big tool-bar fan—when I'm writing, my hands spend far more time on the keyboard than on the mouse. Fortunately, you can hide all the tool bars or show only those that you use. You can create your own tool bars, which you can also turn into floating palettes.

Word 6 joins WordPerfect and Claris's MacWrite Pro in providing zoom features that let you magnify or shrink a document while still being able to edit

adjust ruler settings in Word 6's greatly enhanced Print Preview window—something WordPerfect doesn't allow.

Word 6's ruler is a good example of the good news/bad news changes that Microsoft has made. Adjusting column widths is much easier than in Word 5.1. Also, a new vertical ruler appears when you're in page-layout view and lets you adjust top and bottom margins. And best of all, if you press the option key while dragging any ruler or tab marker, Word displays precise numeric measurements in the ruler itself. That's useful because the bad news is that Word 6, unlike its predecessor, doesn't let you adjust the ruler's tab or margin markers while the Paragraph or Tabs dialog box is open.

Word has always been a shortcut-lover's paradise, and Word 6 continues

FIGURE 12–4
Many computer magazines publish reviews of software. Often, a year's reviews are indexed in the December issue.

them. Normally, reviews should be based on predetermined, teacher-identified criteria. Specifics may change, but the general characteristics of good computer software are well known and should be identified before purchasing decisions are made. For computer-based instruction (CBI) materials, three areas are normally evaluated during the software review process: content, use, and administration. (Figure 12–5).

Content Questions.   Content evaluation can be organized into three sections: objectives, content accuracy, and methodology of instruction. The lesson's objectives should be clearly stated. Specifically, objectives should indicate what students should be able to do after completing the lesson and should indicate the minimum acceptable level of performance expected of students. For example, an objective for a mathematics drill-and-practice lesson might be as follows:

Given previous instruction on long division, a student will use this computer-based drill-and-practice lesson until 9 of the last 10 problems attempted are completed correctly.

An objective for a tutorial on how to use a micrometer might be as follows:

Given a computer-based lesson on how to use a micrometer, an industrial education student will use the program to learn how micrometers measure and will work problems until five in a row are solved correctly.

Both of these examples have the three basic components of a correctly stated performance objective. They state the conditions under which learning should occur, the observable action expected of the student, and a minimum acceptable level of performance.

Accuracy is mandatory in teaching, and CBI is no exception. Errors of fact cannot be tolerated. When instructional materials are considered for purchase, they must be closely examined by a knowledgeable teacher. Errors of fact in computer materials not only cause problems in learning, they also erode the credibility of the medium.

Methodology is the last category of concern when CBI is evaluated. It is also the most overlooked area. *Methodology* refers to the techniques used to present the information contained in the lesson. The methodology used should take advantage of the characteristics of computers, should be based on theories of instruction and learning, and should incorporate what is known about the target audience.

Because the computer is the most interactive of media-delivery systems, CBI should be interactive, both physically and intellectually. Computers are primarily individual tools, so CBI should be designed with the individual learner in mind. Computers are also graphic, so effective instruction should use more than words to present concepts. One question evaluators should always ask when examining CBI is, "Could the information be presented just as effectively at a lower cost, using an alternative medium?"

Because CBI draws heavily from several theory bases, those theories should be used to form much of the foundation for evaluation of CBI. Behaviorism indicates the following to educators:

- The correct results should be given to students as they work through lessons.
- Reinforcement helps students retain what they have learned.
- Small instructional steps are effective.

FIGURE 12–5
Computer-based instruction evaluation form.

Material Title: ―――――――――――――――――――――――――――――――――
Producer/Distributor: _____
Address: _____
Computer System Needs: _____
Other Hardware Needed: _____Cost_____
Backups Provided: _____ yes _____ no
Copy Protected: _____ yes _____ no

  I. Content
      A. School Subject_____
      B. Grade Level: _____
      C. Objective(s): _____

        _____

      D. Content Description: _____

        _____
        _____
        _____

      E. Accuracy of Content:_____
      F. Reading Level: _____

      G. Is the package unbiased? _____ yes _____ no
      H. Level of Cognitive Domain
          Knowledge
          Comprehension
          Application
          Analysis
          Synthesis
          Evaluation

     I. Level of Affective Domain
          Receiving
          Responding
          Valuing
          Organization
          Characterization

Cognitive theory, as described in Chapter 2, implies that individualization of the rate of presentation and variation of the route students take through an instructional sequence are teaching methods that should be used in CBI. How fast a student works, the rate of learning, the skipping or repeating of information, and the route of instruction should be variable in computer-based lessons.

Branched instruction—lessons that vary the route of teaching—should provide for remediation when students need help and for rapid movement through the program when students are already competent in certain concepts. Cognitive theorists also advocate the preassessment of the target audience so instruction is correctly tailored in terms of prerequisite skills needed and the complexity of the new information that is presented. Hypermedia lessons that do not have predetermined routes that must be followed give considerable control to the learner and permit the application of many of the principles of cognitive theory.

Constructivist-based instruction should permit learners to define their own learning objectives, and to develop a learning strategy based on individual experiences and expectations. Extremely flexible computer-based systems with a wealth of instructional components are needed to provide a constructivist instructional situation.

FIGURE 12–5
(continued)

II. Methodology Used

	Little			Considerable	
A. Level of Interactivity	1	2	3	4	5
B. Branching	1	2	3	4	5
C. Visualization	1	2	3	4	5

	Poor			Good	
D. Feedback/Reinforcement	1	2	3	4	5

III. Utilization

A. Type of Lesson: Drill   Tutorial   Game   Problem Solving

Simulation   Other

B. Approximate time to complete program: _____ minutes

C. Ease of Use:	Poor			Good	
	1	2	3	4	5

D. Help Procedures:	None			Many	
	1	2	3	4	5

E. "Crash Proofness":	Poor			Good	
	1	2	3	4	5

F. Documentation:	Poor			Good	
	1	2	3	4	5

Describe Documentation:_____

_____

_____

- -

Reviewer's Name: _____

Date of Review: _____

Recommendation: Check one box

☐ Excellent—purchase
☐ Good—purchase if funds available
☐ OK—purchase only if substitute not available
☐ Poor—do not purchase

Gagne (1985), a cognitive psychologist, listed nine events of instruction that should be included in CBI:

1. Gain the student's attention.
2. Inform the student of the lesson's objective.
3. Stimulate the recall of information learned previously.
4. Present stimuli distinctively.
5. Guide the student's learning.
6. Elicit performance from the student.
7. Provide informative feedback.
8. Assess performance levels.
9. Enhance retention and transfer of learning.

Systems theorists stress the value of feedback and the effectiveness of the logical organization of instructional sequences. Systems research also indicates that designers should attempt to anticipate contingencies that might occur when a lesson is used.

These theories promote the idea of using organized sequences that let the learner move through instructional events systematically. Often, developers of CBI use

Bloom's (1956) taxonomy as the basis for sequencing information. Knowledge-level information, Bloom's lowest level of cognitive learning, is recommended for presentation first, often using tutorial and drill lessons. Subsequent instructional events should promote comprehension, application, analysis, synthesis, and evaluation.

Simulation lessons are often used to present higher level ideas such as the synthesis of several concepts and the evaluation of generalizations. Usually, CBI is organized so that basic concepts are presented early to provide students with the foundation needed to learn more complex ideas.

Utilization Considerations.

Utilization considerations deal with how easily and effectively students interact with the computer materials. Software evaluators should consider several factors in this area. First, the methodological category of the lesson should be identified. These categories (drills, tutorials, games, problem solving, simulations, and materials generation) give teachers clues to where the lesson might fit in the school's curriculum. Next, the ease or difficulty of use of the software should be determined. Related to this are the availability of help within the lesson, the "crash-proofness" of the lesson, and the type and quality of documentation that accompanies the lesson.

Help routines give the user of the lesson a chance to have questions answered about using the program and come from within the program itself. For example, if a student cannot remember the keystroke sequence that branches to a vocabulary list needed to complete a lesson, there should be a simple command such as "ESCape" that would route the student to the lesson's directions. The student should also be able to branch back to the spot just left. Most Macintosh programs offer "balloon help," a feature in which the user positions the mouse over an item on the screen, prompting a balloon to pop open with help information about that item.

Crash-proofness refers to the ability of the lesson to accept erroneous keystrokes, or commands, without crashing the program. A well-written program not only ignores incorrect commands but also recognizes them as wrong and tells the students they are typing or attempting something inappropriate. Just as a teacher would correct a student who answers a question with a date instead of a name, a computer lesson should recognize and point out if a student types the word *one* when the numeral *1* is required.

Documentation, usually in the form of a printed teacher's manual, should explain the lesson's objectives and should clearly state the target audience. Special commands and directions for using the package should be clearly explained, and a comprehensive index of these commands and directions should be provided. Last, documentation manuals often give references, titles of related computer lessons, and lists of homework and classwork that can be used with the CBI. Documentation for CBI is similar to the teacher guides that accompany 16mm films and instructional videotapes.

Management Considerations.

A number of administrative, or managerial, questions should be considered when CBI is evaluated. First is cost. An inexpensive, or free, lesson that is methodologically unsophisticated but still accurate may be more attractive than a lesson costing several hundred dollars. Next, hardware compatibility must be considered. Many schools still use Apple II computers, and new software may not work correctly with these computers. Special hardware needs, such as dual-disk drives, color monitors, or extra memory must be noted as well.

Evaluators also should look for copy-protection schemes, which are hidden codes in programs that prevent easy copying, and the availability of backup copies of the software. Although many companies are abandoning the copy protection of their software, it is still a problem in many instances. Copyright laws and regulations must be followed, but it is just as important for a school to have replacement or backup copies of all lessons.

If a school district plans to use a specific package in many classrooms with a large number of students, information about site licenses and multiple-copy discounts should be requested from vendors. Some software companies offer site licenses, or special pricing arrangements, giving purchasers the right to make unlimited copies of software for use within the school (the site). While 30 individual copies of a $50 CBI program would cost $1,500, a site license could cut that cost by two-thirds.

Obviously, other issues might be of concern to specific teachers or schools. That is why it makes good sense to locally prepare evaluation procedures. The school's computer curriculum committee should develop a systematic process for software evaluation. See Figure 12–5 for a typical CBI evaluation form.

Step 3: Ordering Software

In many schools, the administration handles purchasing after selection decisions have been made. When requisitions for purchases are prepared, however, teachers usually write them. The following information is normally needed in a purchase requisition:

Name of the software package

Format of the software, such as compact disk, 5¼-inch floppy, or 3½-inch floppy

Computer brand and model the software is to be used with

Manuals needed

Supplier/distributor address

Approximate cost

If possible, it is a good idea to include copies of advertisements that describe the lesson being requested.

Step 4: Inventorying and Distributing Software

As soon as software is delivered, it should be checked against the purchase order to be sure that everything requested has been received. Once the order is verified, the software should be inventoried and prepared for distribution within the school. This is a four-part process.

1. The software should be checked to make sure that it runs correctly. If possible, the entire lesson should be tested to identify any internal errors.

2. A backup, archive copy of the lesson should be made, or if a backup is provided by the software company, it should be tested. This backup should not be used or circulated. Rather, it should be stored in a safe location for use if the circulation copy of the lesson is damaged. Most educators agree that using both the circulation copy and the backup copy of a computer lesson violates copyright regulations. The archive copy is meant to be used only if the original is damaged.

3. The new lesson should be cataloged. Usually, listings by title, curriculum area, descriptors, and company are adequate. A short synopsis of the lesson's content also should be included.

4. The software should be distributed to its storage location. The closer the software is stored to its intended users, the more likely that it will become part of instruction. Software for students should be located in the school media center or computer laboratory. Materials for teachers should be located where teachers can use them easily. For example, science lab problem-solving software should be assigned to the science lab.

Unless a school has a large software budget, teachers and students will need to share programs. Centralized storage of software in the media center or computer laboratory makes sharing easy. Unfortunately, if the media center is not conveniently located, usage may suffer. One solution is to include a citation in the media center's catalog that gives all storage locations. Then lessons can be distributed on "long-term" checkout to a primary user, and others can have access to them if necessary.

Software also can be placed on a server machine so that anyone connected to the local area network can access it. File sharing capabilities of the Macintosh operating system and of Windows systems makes sharing of software relatively simple.

Certainly, a school should develop an easy-to-use system of software circulation that satisfies both short-term and long-term users. The school media specialist is usually responsible for making and implementing these decisions.

COPYRIGHT

In 1976, Congress enacted a copyright law that dramatically restructured the concept of "fair use" of commercially prepared instructional materials. The law contained little guidance for users, so in 1980 Congress passed the Computer Software Copyright Act that clarified appropriate use of computer software. This law did a great deal to explain what copying was legal and what was not. However, much of the information available to educators about media center and classroom use of computer software has not been subjected to judicial scrutiny. The information offered in this section is based on what legal advisors to the education profession are saying about copyright.

First, when a school orders software, it is a good idea to indicate on the purchase order that "Purchase is for media center circulation and student use." This is because a significant percentage of computer software is licensed rather than sold, and many licensing agreements attempt to prevent rental or lending. In other words, distributors are attempting to limit the program's use to only one person. If a notice that the software is to be used in a school media center is included with the purchase order, then the school could argue that these terms apply, rather than those of the licensing agreement.

Schools may make one archive copy of copyrighted material. This copy must be stored for backup purposes and should contain the copyright notice. If the circulation copy is destroyed, it is permissible to make a second circulation copy from the backup. However, only one copy of the program should be used at one time.

Most legal advisors agree that it is permissible to make a copy of a program that uses a copy-protection scheme, even if a special copy-decryption program is needed. Copy-decryption programs override copy-protection schemes.

When lessons are circulated, the copyright notice should be visible on the label. License terms, if any, should be circulated with the software package. Schools, however, generally are not considered to be liable for unknown copyright infringement committed by borrowers.

If a school owns only one copy of a program, it should be used in only one machine at a time. Loading a lesson into several computers at once is normally considered copyright infringement. For example, if a teacher plans to teach 25 students simultaneously, using a copyrighted lesson on 25 machines, then 25 copies of the software are needed. The proliferation of computers with internal hard drives and computers connected to networks has increased problems for schools, too. A liberal interpretation of the copyright laws would indicate that if only one person is using a computer program at any one time, then having it available to users over a network is acceptable. Realistically, however, it is difficult to prevent more than one person from using the lesson. A more conservative approach would be to purchase copies of software for all computers when the computers are ordered or to order network licenses for software.

Computer labs should have signs posted that tell patrons that copying may be illegal. One recommended sign says: "Many computer programs are protected by copyright. Unauthorized copying may be prohibited by law."

Teachers should be aware of copyright regulations. Computer programs are creations, just like books and films. They should not be illegally copied, and teachers are responsible for promoting the proper, legal use of instructional materials.

HARDWARE SELECTION DECISIONS

The procedure for selecting computer hardware closely parallels the four-step process used for choosing software:

Step 1: Selecting Hardware for Purchase

Five categories of hardware are needed for a computer system:

1. The computer
2. Input devices
3. Output devices
4. Firmware
5. Cables and connectors

Catalogs from computer manufacturers and from computer retailers are the best source of information about hardware. Often, advertisements in computer magazines also give up-to-date information, but a school normally needs a collection of catalogs. Several dozen catalogs would be enough to cover the different options and categories of equipment.

Computers.   Because there are only a few manufacturers of microcomputers for schools, and because most have educational representatives, locating computer hardware is relatively easy. Most of these manufacturers, such as Apple and IBM, offer packages of equipment that include a complete configuration of hardware. This is an attractive option for schools because it usually is less expensive to buy computers as complete systems.

The most difficult decision a school has to make is whether to stick to one brand. There are pros and cons to this, although most schools seem to be standardizing. If, for example, a school purchases nothing but Macintosh PowerPC 6100 computers, then software compatibility is not a problem, equipment maintenance is simplified, training in operating procedures is easier, and discounts for large-quantity purchases can be negotiated. Unfortunately, the PowerPC may not be the best computer for all uses. For example, the business education program may be better served if IBM compatible computers are used, and laptop computers may be more suitable for some students.

Many school systems select one computer type as the primary teaching machine and then purchase other computer brands in smaller quantities for specialty needs. The decision to standardize should be made by the school's computer curriculum committee.

Input Hardware.   Disk drives usually are purchased with the computer. Most computers have built-in floppy and hard disk drives. Additional disk drives may be needed so that computers have the added flexibility and power offered by a second storage device. There is a move away from the traditional 5¼-inch floppy disk to the 3½-inch disk, and to compact disks. Many software manufacturers distribute their software in both formats. Probably, 3½-inch disks and CD drives will be the standard for the next several years.

Notes From the Literature

For those just beginning to plan for classroom technology, here are nine suggestions:

1. Begin a comprehensive strategic plan that includes a vision statement and a definition of strategies to get you there.
2. Involve everyone who will implement the plan.
3. Start a technology library by accumulating magazines, handouts, conference notes, technical reference sources, videotaped training sessions, etc.
4. Find a "guru" or create one to manage the technical aspects of your plan. This will usually not be the same person who guides curricular uses of technology or trains others.
5. Planning needs to be for the long term, and it needs to be systemic.
6. Expand your definition of basic skills; information exchange is a driving force in the global marketplace and your curriculum should take advantage of technology to promote those skills.
7. Communicate with and listen to the local business community in helping make decisions.
8. Solve problems, don't buy toys.
9. Do LOTS of research before plunking down your money.

Edwards, J. L. (1994). Get started on technology. Education Digest, 59(5), 46–51.

Other input devices, such as a mouse, modems, external speakers, video cameras, scanners, graphics tablets, and light pens may need to be purchased, also. It is generally best to purchase these when other computer hardware is ordered.

Output Devices.   Once again standardization is important. If all dot-matrix printers are one brand, such as Epson or Apple, then ordering, maintaining, and operating are simplified. However, once a school decides on a certain brand of equipment, it loses flexibility. A new printer may be offered by another manufacturer that is faster and less expensive, and if the school has decided to standardize, it might not be able to take advantage of this new piece of equipment.

Video displays are normally purchased with the computer, but several options are available. Color monitors are effective for large group presentations. Other output devices, such as large-screen TVs, liquid crystal display (LCD) projection equipment, letter-quality printers, and laser printers should be considered by schools to supplement their instructional computing program. Catalogs and magazine advertisements are good sources of information about these devices. Exhibits by vendors at state, regional, or national conventions are also excellent places to find up-to-date information, because the actual hardware can be seen and demonstrated, and comparisons can be made between competitive brands.

Peripheral Firmware Devices.   Firmware devices, the small boards that are added to a computer's peripheral slots, are probably the most difficult to purchase. Because so many options are available, such as accelerators, video cards, audio cards, and networking cards, and because many boards are produced by third-party manufacturers, it is difficult to know how much firmware is really needed. Memory-expansion is one of the most misunderstood peripheral devices. Most of the time, more memory is good. However, if software cannot take advantage of the extra memory, or if only a few of the school's computers have the extra memory, then the cost of the additional memory may not be worthwhile.

Cables and Connectors.   Cables and connectors are an often-overlooked category of "hardware." Although standard cables normally are provided with the computer system, specialty cables are not. Extra-long video cables to connect computers to video projectors, long telephone cables for connecting modems to telephone receptacles, and adapters that convert connectors (8 pin to 15 pin, for example) should be available in the well-equipped school media center. Accessories are usually listed together near the back of equipment brochures and catalogs.

Step 2: Ordering Equipment

After specific items of equipment have been identified, the next step is to issue orders. While schools handle orders differently, there are several considerations that the teacher, administrator, or computer curriculum committee member should take into account when purchase requisitions are prepared.

First, a decision must be made whether to buy a complete computer system or separate components. Usually it is simpler to buy a complete system, but sometimes it is less expensive and more effective to mix and match computer components from several manufacturers.

Most computer manufacturers sell their computers as systems. For example, Apple sells a Macintosh system that includes the computer, one 3½-inch drive, a 500 mg hard drive, a color monitor, mouse, and modem. It is possible to purchase these items separately, although the total price would be higher.

Second, if a school decides to order components instead of a complete system, four pieces of information are needed:

1. The name of the item, including the model number.
2. What is included with the item, such as the component parts of the system or the cables needed.
3. What this piece of equipment must be compatible with, such as a particular printer or scanner.
4. The approximate price of the item.

Third, the vendor must be chosen. This means the school must decide whether to solicit bids. In the bid process, a purchase order is sent to several potential suppliers, who are asked to submit a proposal indicating the cost of the items listed. These bids are kept confidential, and the vendor who submits the lowest is awarded the order. Obviously, this means the school gets the most for its money. Unfortunately, this also means that local vendors may not be the low bidders. Many small, local equipment distributors cannot compete with large mail-order operations, because their volume of sales is too small. If a school decides it wants to support local or regional businesses, or if the school believes that servicing and installation of the equipment will be more convenient if a local company is involved, then the low-bid process may not be desirable.

Fourth, the decision about accessories and peripheral devices must be made. Obviously, this decision is closely related to the other three. It makes good sense to order printers, video projectors, LCD displays, cables, and other accessories when major hardware systems are purchased. This reduces the likelihood of compatibility problems, or that a necessary item will not be available when it is needed.

Step 3: Inventorying and Distributing Equipment

When new equipment arrives, it should be checked against purchase orders, inventoried, set up to be sure it works correctly, and distributed. Usually, one person in the school is responsible for these duties. In very small schools, the superintendent, principal, or a desig-

nated teacher carries out these activities. In larger schools, the computer coordinator or media specialist is responsible for equipment inventorying.

Check Deliveries Against Purchase Orders. As soon as possible after the order is received, all boxes should be opened and the equipment examined. Items should be turned on and checked to be sure they operate. If anything is missing or does not seem to work, the dealer or the manufacturer should be contacted. Often, it is possible to solve problems informally if they are identified early. Several computer manufacturers have representatives visit schools to inventory and set up all equipment. This service reduces the responsibilities of local school officials.

Inventory New Equipment. After purchase orders and equipment have been checked, the new computer hardware should be entered into the school's inventory system. Most organizations have inventory procedures to keep track of equipment they own. While computer equipment should be entered in this schoolwide inventory system, it also makes sense to develop an inventory system just for computer hardware. This computer inventory can be either a subset of the master inventory or a separate, stand-alone system.

Generally, seven kinds of information are recorded in an inventory:

1. Model numbers and names of items.
2. Serial numbers.
3. Purchase date.
4. Lists of components, such as network cards, installed in the piece of equipment.
5. Warranty information.
6. Locally developed inventory control numbers.
7. Storage location for the equipment.

After each item of equipment has been inventoried, it should be marked as the property of the school. Large, easy-to-see labels should be permanently attached to each piece of equipment.

Distribution of equipment to laboratories, classrooms, and media centers comes next. The school's computer curriculum committee should establish a priority plan for the distribution of new hardware. This plan should be publicized so teachers know when equipment will be made available to them and so they can participate in establishing priorities. A distribution plan might look like this:

Priority 1: Computer classroom—30 additional computers
Priority 1: Media center—5 additional computers
Priority 1: Teacher's work room—5 computers
Priority 2: Computer classroom—30 computers
Priority 2: Media center—5 computers
Priority 2: Science, math, language arts classrooms—5 computers each
Priority 3: Remaining classrooms—5 computers each
Priority 4: Business classroom—15 computers
Priority 5: All classrooms—2 additional computers each

Peripheral hardware would need to be distributed using a similar priority system. When equipment is assigned to a specific location, it makes sense to assign items to a specific person, too. This teacher or administrator would be responsible for security and routine maintenance.

Step 4: Maintaining Computer Equipment

One often overlooked area of computer use is computer maintenance. Computers are relatively durable, reliable pieces of equipment, but because they are used by many different people, they need to be maintained systematically. Usually, one person is assigned responsibility for equipment maintenance, and normally that person is either the school media specialist or the school computer coordinator. This person carries out four kinds of maintenance:

1. Conducting preventive maintenance
2. Making simple repairs
3. Replacing inoperable equipment from a backup pool
4. Coordinating repair with outside agencies

Once a year, each piece of computer equipment should be inventoried and cleaned. Preventive maintenance (PM) for computers is relatively simple, because they have so few moving parts. Generally, cleaning and dusting are all that is needed. Dust should be vacuumed out of the inside of computers; disk drive heads should be timed, demagnetized, and cleaned; monitor screens should be dusted; and printer heads cleaned. Special diagnostics disks are available to help teachers with this kind of PM. A checklist of PM procedures can be prepared; then the teacher responsible for each computer can carry out PM by following this list. Very efficient schools keep track of PM using a computerized inventory system.

If malfunctions are located during PM, or if equipment fails to operate at any time during the semester, one of three second-level maintenance procedures should be followed. The equipment should be fixed, replaced, or sent to a repair facility.

Simple Repairs. Often, teachers can repair malfunctioning computers. Often, diagnostic, self-test procedures are built into read-only memory (ROM) chips in the computer or printer. These diagnostics tell the user if the computer is operating correctly and even give advice about what repairs are needed. Special floppy disks are also available that help identify malfunctions. One common disk drive problem is the calibration of its speed. A diagnostic disk can identify this problem and will give directions for correcting it. Norton Utilities is a software package that diagnoses problems with floppy and hard drives.

The substitution method is the simplest way to identify causes of malfunctioning computer systems. For example, when a floppy disk fails to boot, one of several problems is probably responsible. One piece of equipment at a time should be substituted until the component that contains the malfunction is located. Usually, software is substituted first because most problems are with software rather than hardware and disks are easier to substitute than pieces of equipment. Once it has been determined that the software works correctly (by running the lesson successfully on another, identical computer), one component of the computer system should be substituted at a time.

Establish a Backup Pool. Approximately 5% to 10% of a school's computer hardware should be kept in reserve to replace malfunctioning equipment. Replacement equipment should be readily available so broken equipment can be substituted quickly. In many schools, the temptation will be to use all hardware all the time, and this may be necessary early in the equipment acquisition process. However, once a substantial collection of hardware is purchased, a backup pool should become a priority.

Establish Repair Agreements. Schools usually enter into repair contracts with outside agencies or pay for maintenance by the piece. Repair agreements and contracts are similar to the extended warranty packages some new car owners purchase for new automobiles. They are most cost-efficient when schools have relatively large equipment inventories. Piece-by-piece repairs are best for specialty, low-quantity items that do not malfunction often, such as monitors and laser printers. In either case, repair agencies should be identified before they are needed, and contacts should be made with them so they know they will be called on for repair work. Repair agencies most often used by schools are university audiovisual departments, large corporation electronic sections, local TV repair shops, and repair services established by computer dealers.

Maintenance records should be kept on all major pieces of equipment. Sometimes an item will have several related malfunctions. Often, machines have undiagnosed problems that contribute to secondary breakdowns. A track-record of maintenance and repair work for a computer is nearly as important as a health record for a person. The latter helps the doctor determine the physical well-being of a patient; the former helps the repair technician determine the mechanical and electronic status of a machine.

SUMMARY

This chapter summarizes the major procedures followed when software and hardware are evaluated, selected, and purchased. These procedures parallel each other.

Locating good software comes first. Catalogs, advertisements, indexes, broker catalogs, and information from educational organizations are sources of information about computer software. After lessons have been identified, they should be evaluated. Reviews in computer magazines and recommendations from other educators who are familiar with the software are two sources of evaluation information. All software also should be locally reviewed.

When software is ordered, backups and manuals should also be purchased. If multiple copies are needed, duplication licenses or quantity discounts should be negotiated with the vendor. When software arrives at the school, it should be matched against purchase orders, checked for malfunctions, inventoried, backed up, and then distributed to the computer site where it is to be used. Generally, the school's computer curriculum committee coordinates software selection, evaluation, and distribution. The school, through its teachers and computer committee, is also responsible for ensuring strict adherence to copyright regulations.

Procedures for the purchase of hardware generally are the same as those for software. First, appropriate hardware must be located. Catalogs, advertisements,

and information from other educators can be used. When equipment is ordered, a decision must be made about whether to order complete systems or individual components. Complete systems are easier to order and may be less expensive. Components, on the other hand, may provide more computer power and increase purchasing flexibility.

When equipment items arrive, they should be inventoried and distributed according to a priority system. Equipment maintenance should be a continuous and systematic process so that the hardware remains reliable. In short, an equipment-acquisition plan should be systematically planned and designed to support the school's curriculum.

SELF-TEST QUESTIONS

1. What are the primary sources of information about computer software?
2. What categories of questions should be asked when software is reviewed before purchase?
3. Define *crash-proofness.*
4. What kind of information should be contained in computer documentation, such as manuals?
5. Is it legal to make a backup copy of a copyrighted, copy-protected computer lesson?
6. Is it best to store computer software in a central location or to distribute it permanently to users?
7. Is it legal to load a copyrighted computer lesson into more than one computer at a time?
8. What are the best sources for information about computer hardware?
9. Define PM.
10. What group should normally determine the priority for distribution of computer equipment in the school?

ANSWERS TO SELF-TEST QUESTIONS

1. Catalogs from vendors, advertisements in journals, indexes, broker catalogs, and other educators or educational organizations are the main sources of information about computer software.
2. Content questions, use questions, and management questions should be asked when software is evaluated.

3. *Crash-proofness* refers to the capability of the computer lesson to accept erroneous keystrokes without malfunctioning. Well-written programs will even recognize wrong entries and diagnose them for the student.

4. Computer manuals should normally give the lesson's objectives, state the target audience for the lesson, explain all commands, and provide references for additional study.

5. Most educators believe that copyright law says it is legal to make one backup copy of any computer software for the archives.

6. The question of where to store software is a difficult one that must be answered by each school, depending on local needs and the availability of local resources. Computer software will be used more if it is easy to obtain. On the other hand, if teachers need to share a program, it should be easy for anyone to access. Most schools use a centralized storage and inventory system with long-term checkout for certain one-user packages.

7. It is not legal to load a software package into more than one computer at a time, unless the school owns multiple copies of the lesson or has negotiated a site license for duplication of the package.

8. The best sources of information about computer hardware are vendor catalogs, computer magazine advertisements, other educators, and exhibits at conventions.

9. PM stands for preventive maintenance.

10. Many schools have established a computer curriculum committee to coordinate all aspects of the instructional computing program in the school, including the priority system for hardware distribution. In small schools, the principal and superintendent often make these decisions.

REFERENCES

Bloom, B. (1956). (Ed.). *Taxonomy of educational objectives: Handbook I: Cognitive domain.* New York: David McKay.

Gagne, R. M. (1985). *The conditions of learning and the theory of instruction* (4th ed.). New York: Holt, Rinehart & Winston.

Reiser, R., & Dick, W. (1990). Evaluating instructional software. *Educational Technology Research and Development, 38*(3), 43–50.

Zahner, J., Reiser, R., Dick, W., & Gill, B. (1992). Evaluating instructional software: A simplified model. *Educational Technology Research and Development, 40*(3), 55–62.

REFERENCES FOR ADDITIONAL STUDY

Becker, G. (1984). Software copyright looks fuzzy, but is it? *Electronic Education, 4*(2), 18–19.

Bitter, G., & Camuse, R. (1988). *Using a microcomputer in the classroom* (2nd ed.). Boston: Allyn & Bacon.

Borton, W., & Rossett, A. (1989). Educational software and published reviews: Congruence of teacher, developer and evaluator perceptions. *Education, 109*(4), 434–444.

Brownell, G. (1987). *Computers and teaching.* St. Paul, MN: West.

Bullough, R., & Beatty, L. (1991). *Classroom applications of microcomputers* (2nd ed.). Upper Saddle River, NJ: Merrill/Prentice Hall.

Dukelow. R. (1992). *The library copyright guide.* Washington, DC: Association for Educational Communications and Technology.

EPIE Institute. (Monthly). Write to Box 839, Water Mill, NY 11976.

Gader, B., & Hodar, M. (1985). *Apple software for pennies.* New York: Warner Books.

Gill, B., Dick, W., Reiser, R., & Sahner, J. (1992). A new model for evaluating instructional software. *Educational Technology, 32*(3), 39–44.

Glossbrenner, A. (1984). *How to get free software.* New York: St. Martin's Press.

Hannafin, M. J., & Peck, K. L. (1988). *The design, development, and evaluation of instructional software.* Upper Saddle River, NJ: Merrill/Prentice Hall.

Heller, D., & Heller, D. (1984). *Free software for your Apple.* San Jose, CA: Enrich/Ohaus.

International Communications Industries Association. (1993). *Equipment directory of audio-visual, computer, and video products.* Washington, DC: Author.

Johnson, S. (1993). *Appraising audiovisual media: A guide for attorneys, trust officers, insurance professionals, and archivists in appraising films, video, photographs, recordings, and other audiovisual assets.* Washington, DC: Association for Educational Communications and Technology.

Krathwohl, D., Bloom, B., & Masia, B. (1964). *Taxonomy of educational objectives: Handbook II: Affective domain.* New York: David McKay Co.

Lee, H. (1984). *Where to find free programs for your TRS-80, Apple, or IBM microcomputer.* Pasadena, CA: Pasadena Technology Press.

Lockard, J., et al. (1991). *Microcomputers for educators* (2nd ed.). Boston: Little, Brown.

Merrill, P., et al. (1986). *Computers in education.* Englewood Cliffs, NJ: Prentice-Hall.

Miller, J. (1989). *Official fair-use guidelines.* Washington, DC: Association for Educational Communications and Technology.

Philips, G. (1984). *IBM PC public domain software.* Culver City, CA: Ashton-Tate Publications

Pollard, G. (1987). The price is right. *The Computing Teacher, 14*(5), 30.

Reed, M., & Stanek, D. (1986). Library and classroom use of copyrighted videotapes and computer software. *American Libraries, 17*(2), 120A–120D.

Sinofsky, E. (1994). *A copyright primer for educational and industrial media producers* (2nd ed.). Washington, DC: Association for Educational Communications and Technology.

Stephenson, J., & Cahill, B. (1988). *Microcomputer troubleshooting and repair.* Indianapolis: Howard Sams & Co.

Talub, R. (1989). *Copyright and instructional technologies: A guide to fair use and permissions procedures.* Washington, DC: Association for Educational Communications and Technology.

Wright, E., & Forcier, R. (1985). *The computer: A tool for the teacher.* Belmont, CA: Wadsworth.

CHAPTER THIRTEEN

LOGO

A Visualization Language for Learners

GOAL

The purpose of this chapter is to introduce the reader to the LOGO programming language as an active tool for student visualization and construction of knowledge.

OBJECTIVES

The reader will be able to do the following:

1. Describe the major characteristics of the LOGO programming language.
2. Describe how Piaget influenced the work of Papert.
3. Describe the difference between Piaget's perspective and Papert's perspective.
4. Describe Papert's conception of a computer microworld.
5. Cite and describe two reasons for LOGO's inclusion in the curriculum.
6. Describe the four powerful ideas from the LOGO programming language presented in this chapter.
7. Create a LOGO example of the use of the four powerful ideas described in the previous objective.
8. Describe the concept of "top-down" programming and how the structure of LOGO encourages this approach.
9. Describe the three data types supported by LOGO.
10. Cite specific applications of LOGO in the teaching of at least two different subject areas.
11. Describe the term *debugging* and how this term relates to the LOGO experience.
12. Describe the LEGOLOGO TC environment.
13. Explain the statement, "LOGO has no threshold and no ceiling."
14. Make a case for including LOGO as the major programming language in an elementary school curriculum.
15. Explain why the LOGO language is extendable and can grow with the user.

This child is curious. He wants to make sense out of things, find out how things work, gain competence and control over himself and his environment, and do what he can see other people doing. He is open, perceptive, and receptive. He does not shut himself off from the strange, confused, complicated world around him, but takes it, touches it, hefts it, bends it, breaks it. To find out how reality works, he works on it. He is bold. He is not afraid of making mistakes. And he is patient. He can tolerate an extraordinary amount of uncertainty, confusion, ignorance and suspense. He does not have to have instant meaning in any new situation. He is willing and able for meaning to come to him—even if it does come very slowly, which it usually does. . . . School is not a place that gives much time, or opportunity, or reward, for this kind of thinking and learning.

Holt, 1970, p. 14

LOGO, a programming language and learning environment created by Seymour Papert and his colleagues at MIT in the late 1960s, has had a profound effect on both theory and practice in the field of educational computing. The use of LOGO in schools and in teacher education has steadily increased since the early 1980s and continues to grow. Versions of LOGO are now available for almost every major microcomputer, and educational computing publications are filled with articles about using LOGO in classrooms. Regional, national, and international conferences are conducted annually to enable educators to share their ideas about LOGO. Even critics of LOGO and the LOGO approach have to admit that the language has had a substantial effect on both the theoretical and practical uses of computers in education.

LOGO, based on constructivist theories of knowledge and learning, allows learners to construct and test visual models of complex mathematical relationships. While similar visualization tools are available to assist in teaching and learning, LOGO remains a simple initial experience for educators interested in this type of computer application.

WHAT IS LOGO?

LOGO is a computer programming language as well as a philosophy of education. Both aspects of the language must be experienced and understood to adequately answer the question "What is LOGO?"

LOGO Is a Programming Language

LOGO is a modern, procedural programming language based on the artificial intelligence language LISP. It is a language designed for learners. As an initial programming language, it has replaced BASIC as the major language taught in schools. As a programming language, LOGO has several distinguishing characteristics. Each of these characteristics is discussed in the following paragraphs.

LOGO Is a Language With Easy Entry. LOGO is a programming language that has easy entry points for beginners. With five minutes of instruction, even early elementary-age children can engage in interesting explorations and problem-solving activities with the language (Figure 13–1). Because of this, some people have the idea that LOGO is a "baby language" or a trivial learning language for later, more sophisticated languages. This is not true. Although it has easy entry points, LOGO is a highly sophisticated language with capabilities that should interest even the expert programmer. The LOGO language is extendable and can grow with the needs of the user. LOGO, like the artificial language LISP, is based on the idea of composition of functions. Because of this, users can define their own procedures and thus build all the complexity they need into the language. LOGO has been used successfully in first-grade classes and in introductory college programming courses. The combination of simplicity and complexity is one of the unique features of LOGO.

LOGO Is a Procedural Language.   Programming in LOGO is based on structuring commands into blocks called *procedures*. Once a procedure is written, it can be used in other procedures. A procedure in LOGO might contain the directions for drawing a square or for finding the standard deviation of a group of numbers. The procedural structure of LOGO is similar to that of other modern languages such as PASCAL and PL/1.

FIGURE 13–1
Originally, a floor turtle was controlled by a microcomputer. It moved over paper on the floor and created LOGO graphics.
Photograph courtesy of Terrain, Inc.

LOGO Is an Interactive Programming Language.   Both commands built into the LOGO language and commands defined by the user can be executed by simply typing the command at the keyboard. Thus, the programmer receives immediate feedback on how the procedure works and exactly where the bugs are.

LOGO Has Turtle Graphics.   An important feature of the LOGO language is the incorporation of turtle graphics. Although other languages have since incorporated the idea, LOGO was the first language with these capabilities (Figure 13–2).

The LOGO turtle is usually a small triangle that responds to commands from the user by moving around the display screen. When told "FD 50," the turtle will travel 50 units in the direction that it is heading and leave a path 50 units long. The direction of the turtle can be changed with a right turn (RT) or left turn (LT) command. Like the forward command, the turning commands require that the user tell the turtle how far to turn. For example, the command LT 90 causes the turtle to turn 90 degrees to the left. LOGO also supports floor turtles that are robotlike objects that respond to the same commands as the triangle on the screen.

LOGO Uses Lists as Data Objects.   Although many people believe turtle graphics are the major feature of the LOGO language, LOGO's capabilities far surpass the turtle. Students can manipulate numbers, characters, and words in the LOGO language. In addition to characters, words, and numbers, LOGO contains compound data structures called lists. These lists are groups of words and make LOGO a powerful language for symbol manipulation. Thus, LOGO is useful for writing programs that manipulate language.

LOGO Is a Philosophy for Computer Use in the Classroom.   Papert (1980) presents a documented theory of how and why computers should be used in the classroom. Papert is perhaps the only writer and thinker to have developed a complete theory about the role of the computer in education, a theory that involves a well-developed and supported argument about such fundamental issues as epistemology, learning, and thinking (Dunn & Morgan, 1987).

The theoretical background for Papert's work can be found in the area of artificial intelligence and in the work of Jean Piaget, with whom Papert studied in Switzerland. Piaget (1954) asserts that children build

FIGURE 13–2
Many versions of LOGO use an on-screen turtle that looks like a triangle. LOGOWriter, however, uses a turtlelike shape.

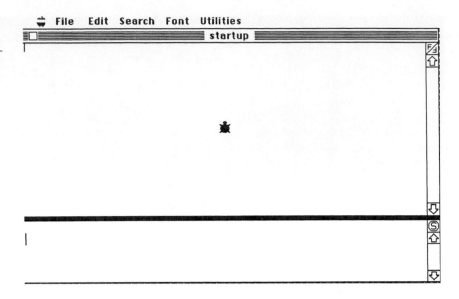

their own intellectual structures as a result of their interaction with the environment. Through experiences, children form theories about the world and constantly modify, revise, and develop these theories as a result of experience.

Papert believes the computer is best used in education as an "object to think with" and not as a dispenser of information. In a frequently quoted statement, Papert (1980) summarizes his views:

> In many schools today, the phrase "computer-aided instruction" means making the computer teach the child. One might say that the computer is being used to program the child. In my vision, the child programs the computer and, in doing so, both acquires a sense of mastery over a piece of the most modern and powerful technology and establishes an intimate contact with some of the deepest ideas from science, from mathematics, and from the art of intellectual model building. (p. 5)

To Papert, LOGO is an environment where the student can explore and discover powerful ideas. Students working with LOGO can speak mathematics to the computer and learn math in "mathland," much as students living in France naturally learn French. Through LOGO, Papert has created an environment where learners can experience mathematics. They can build, test, and revise theories within the LOGO environment, expanding their mathematical experiences.

Papert's emphasis on having children interact with this mathematical environment relies heavily on the assumptions of Piaget. Papert differs from Piaget, however, in his view on intervention into the world of the

learner. Piaget contends that children will develop cognitively in a set sequence and is opposed to "hurrying up" this sequence. But Papert (1980) says:

> My perspective is more interventionist. My goals are education, not just understanding. So, in my own thinking I have placed a greater emphasis on two dimensions implicit but not elaborated in Piaget's own work: an interest in intellectual structures that could develop as opposed to those that actually at present do develop in the child, and the design of learning environments that are resonant with them. (p. 61)

According to Papert, the rich LOGO environment provides experiences that will alter and improve children's mathematical intellectual development. Piaget views this development as relatively fixed, whereas Papert sees enriching the child's environment and experiences as a means for altering intellectual development.

Papert argues that our culture does not provide a rich mathematical environment for children. He contends that much of school mathematics is disassociated from the real world and taught in a rote, meaningless manner. He says this is the major reason so many adults in our society hate and fear mathematics. He believes that experiencing the meaningful mathematical environment created by LOGO may help combat this cultural problem that he terms "mathophobia."

In addition to mathematics applications, Papert sees other possibilities for using LOGO and LOGO-type environments to enhance school learning across the curriculum. He tells the story of Jenny, a young student who had a history of difficulties learning English grammar. Jenny had viewed the study of grammar as pointless and a waste of time. She could see no reason to learn the information. When using LOGO to generate poetry, however, she found that she needed to know the difference between a noun and a verb to teach the computer how to write a poem. After her experience, Jenny reported to her teachers, "Now I know why we need nouns and verbs." For Jenny, the LOGO experience gave a meaning to an otherwise meaningless subject. She needed to teach the computer to write poetry, and in teaching the computer, she began to understand and see meaning in the material herself.

The concept of "microworld" is one that Papert has used to describe LOGO and LOGO-like environments. A microworld is an environment for learning in which children are free to experiment, test, and revise theories, and invent their own activities. A microworld focuses on a particular problem area and creates an environment in which students can explore this problem area. LOGO is a microworld for geometry learning; LOGO has been extended to create microworlds for work in Newtonian physics, Cartesian coordinates, and English grammar.

A microworld, according to Papert, must provide the student with some opportunity to use the ideas in the environment to produce a product. The product must be something that the child wishes to create. He contends that the creation of a product that is meaningful to the child is an important part of the learning process. In turtle graphics, the product is the graphic programmed by the learner.

Versions of LOGO

The initial work with LOGO used mainframe computers. With the advance of technology, however, microcomputers became powerful enough to support LOGO, and thus began its widespread use in schools. The original microcomputer versions of LOGO were available first in 1979 for the TI 99/4 home computer and the Apple II computer. Since that time, versions of LOGO have been written for almost every major brand of microcomputer.

LOGO has an initial disadvantage when compared with BASIC because the BASIC language is built into most microcomputers. Thus, if BASIC is the language taught, no additional software is needed. With LOGO, the software containing the language is used. Legally, a separate software package is needed for each machine in use.

Probably the most widely used microcomputer software versions of the language have been developed by LOGO Computer Systems, Inc. (LCSI). Versions of LCSI

Notes From the Literature

Clements (1991) studied the enhancement of creativity for students learning in a LOGO environment compared with those receiving non-LOGO creativity treatment and those in a nontreatment control group. After 25 weeks he concluded that "the LOGO programming group had significantly higher scores than either of the other groups on the total assessment of figural creativity, and both the LOGO and comparison group had significantly higher scores than the control group on verbal creativity. Certain aspects of both figural and verbal creativity (e.g., originality) were more strongly affected than other aspects (e.g., fluency). This extends previous research by indicating that certain LOGO environments can enhance creativity in verbal, as well as figural, domains. These results militate against the sole acceptance of a domain-specific hypothesis of LOGO's influence on creative performance (i.e., enhancement of figural associative networks); instead, both this domain-specific hypothesis and a process-based hypothesis (i.e., metacomponential enhancement) received some support. An implication is that certain computer environments may offer unique opportunities for the enhancement of both figural and verbal creativity" (p. 150).

Clements, D. (1991). Enhancement of creativity in computer environments. *American Educational Research Journal, 28*(1), 173–187.

LOGO are now available for both Apple and IBM computers. Another popular version of the language is called Terrapin LOGO. It is available for the Apple II family of computers and is similar to LCSI LOGO.

In 1986, LCSI released a version of LOGO called LOGOWriter, which combines LOGO programming capabilities with word processing capabilities. Samples of student work done with LOGOWriter are included in the word processing chapter (Chapter 6). The LOGO programming portion of LOGOWriter is similar in syntax to Apple II LOGO. LOGOWriter is the version of the language used in the examples in this text.

Site licenses can be purchased for LOGOWriter, allowing schools to make enough copies of the software for each of the machines at the school (Figure 13–3).

The versions of the language are generally similar enough that users can move from one version to another with relative ease. The examples for this chapter use LCSI LOGOWriter but can be easily implemented on other systems with only minor changes.

FIGURE 13–3
LOGOWriter here is pictured on an Apple IIGS machine. LOGO is available for most micro-computers.

In addition to the "full-blown" versions of LOGO, several simplified LOGO packages are available. Most of these packages are relatively inexpensive and contain just the turtle graphics portion of the language. EZ-LOGO and Quick-LOGO are two such packages.

Some educators argue that these simplified versions emphasize the trivial portions of the language and do not provide a true LOGO experience. Rather than using simplified versions of LOGO, many early elementary teachers develop or use microworlds that allow students to explore with LOGO in the immediate mode (Yelland, 1992–1993). These microworlds involve thematic units or games.

Object LOGO is a version of LOGO that emphasizes object-oriented programming. Object LOGO is a more advanced version of the LOGO language and can provide a tool for object-oriented programming experiences for middle and high school students.

WHY LOGO?

During the early years of computer use in the schools, there were some heated debates about which program-

ming language should be taught. Generally, the debates centered on whether BASIC or LOGO should be the major language of the schools, and both sides were vehement in their arguments. One LOGO enthusiast indicated that BASIC is the junk food of computer programming. Another suggested that students who have learned to program through BASIC are mentally mutilated beyond repair.

There are some sound educational reasons to choose LOGO as a first educational programming language, and there are also some sound reasons to choose BASIC. Each of the characteristics of LOGO mentioned in the previous section could be used as an argument to use it in schools. The advantages of LOGO as an initial programming language can, however, be summarized into two major categories: (1) LOGO is an intellectually honest beginning for programming, and (2) LOGO is expandable across the curriculum.

LOGO Is an Intellectually Honest Introduction to Programming

Because of the sophisticated structure of the language, LOGO provides a sound introduction to the field of modern computer programming. "Someone who learns LOGO is likely to have a very clear idea of the nature of variables, procedures, and most other programming constructs" (Harvey, 1982, p. 263). The procedural nature of the language is a sound introduction to other procedural languages like PASCAL, LISP, and PL/1. The programming approaches and habits encouraged by the LOGO language generalize easily to more advanced languages.

LOGO Is an Expandable Learning Experience, Applicable Across the Curriculum

The real goal for the LOGO experience as conceived by its developers, however, was not to create just an introductory language.

> LOGO . . . isn't supposed to be an easy introduction to something else. It's not specifically for computer science majors, and it isn't a tool for teaching the same math curriculum people are already teaching. Instead, it's a door into the territory of the computer as an object for intellectual exploration. . . . LOGO is for learning learning. (Harvey, 1982)

Thus, it is a mistake to view LOGO as another programming language vying for a spot in the curriculum. LOGO is a computer learning environment.

Students working with LOGO learn thinking and problem-solving skills applicable across the curriculum. Two of the major problem-solving skills students can learn in the LOGO environment are how to debug a program and how to learn from one's own errors. The friendly, interactive nature of the language creates an ideal environment for experimenting and learning hypothesis-testing skills.

The developers of LOGO contend that in traditional school situations, children are taught that making an error is a negative experience that should be avoided at almost all costs. In the LOGO environment,

however, children learn to learn from, even to enjoy, their own thinking errors. An error in LOGO provides natural feedback for users: The program does not do what users think it should. Learners then revise their "false theory" and try again. The interaction is nonjudgmental and children learn to view mistakes as a positive part of the learning process.

Research on LOGO

A growing number of researchers are interested in examining both the cognitive and affective effects of LOGO experiences. Although much of this research is just beginning and many of the results are conflicting, a few generalizations are emerging.

In the area of mathematical achievement, it appears that the LOGO experience may facilitate achievement gains. Positive effects have been found in the areas of angle estimation, concepts of variable, and concepts of coordinates. To maximize these gains, teachers should emphasize the mathematical content of LOGO activities and the connection between the LOGO activities and the rest of the curriculum (Clements, 1985).

Although results are conflicting, research evidence shows that LOGO experiences may facilitate some problem-solving behaviors. Specifically, students who have worked with LOGO performed better than students who worked with computer-assisted instruction (CAI) on certain metacognitive tasks: deciding on a problem, obtaining a mental representation of a problem, and monitoring comprehension (Clements, 1985).

In the affective area, evidence indicates that LOGO can serve as a powerful tool in encouraging prosocial interaction, positive self-image, positive attitudes toward learning, and independent work habits

Notes From the Literature

Nastasi, Clements, and Battista (1990) investigated the effect of LOGO environments and computer-assisted instruction (CAI) problem-solving software on students' cognition. After 42 treatment sessions, students working in pairs were videotaped. The results indicate that children with the LOGO experience revealed more cognitively oriented conflict, attempts at and successful resolution of conflicts, rule making, and pleasure at discovery than students experiencing CAI-based problem solving. The findings suggest that LOGO may foster cognitive growth through opportunities for resolving cognitive conflict and may enhance effectance motivation.

Nastasi, B., Clements, D., & Battista, M. (1990). Social-cognitive interactions, motivation, and cognitive growth in LOGO programming and CAI problem-solving environments. Journal of Educational Psychology, 82(1), 150–158.

(Clements, 1985). In general, evidence suggests that working in pairs is the most advantageous arrangement for LOGO programming.

It should be noted that the LOGO research effort is just beginning and the results cited are tentative. In a review of research on LOGO, Clements (1985) concludes that research results on LOGO are sufficiently suggestive to justify further study of the means to maximize these benefits. Clements writes, "LOGO does appear to hold potential to combine the abstract and mathematical with the concrete and aesthetic; the analytical with the intuitive; and culturally transmitted knowledge with personal introspection and self-discovery" (Clements, 1985, p. 69).

GETTING STARTED WITH LOGO

Some educators contend that LOGO is an ideal starting point for teacher work on the computer. Through work with LOGO, teachers are introduced to a philosophy of using the computer as well as to a beginning programming language. If LOGO is a first experience with the computer, the learner immediately controls the computer rather than being controlled by it. In addition, teachers are introduced to a language that can be used as a tool for learning across the curriculum.

LOGO is assuming an expanding role in the curriculum for both preservice and in-service teachers.

Generally, initial experiences focus on introducing teachers to the LOGO learning environment, as well as the LOGO programming language.

Although not all teachers will be teaching mathematics, the LOGO approach to learning is generalizable across the curriculum and is an important model for computer learning for all educators. As mentioned earlier, more and more LOGO-like environments are becoming available in different subject areas. Through experience with LOGO, all teachers can begin thinking about developing and using similar learning environments in their own subject areas.

The introductory LOGO concepts presented here are by no means a complete introduction to the language. The intent is to provide some introductory experiences so the reader can better understand the power and potential of the language.

You should embark on your journey into LOGO as discoverers and testers of new ideas and use the computer as a vehicle to test out your ideas. You should also remember that LOGO is not a series of computer commands to be memorized but an environment for learning. As the details of the language are presented, the environment will slowly expand. Each new idea presents new possibilities for exploration and learning. After you have had some experiences with LOGO, go back and read the "What Is LOGO?" and "Why LOGO?" sections again, this time bringing your own experience with the language to your reading.

The LOGO programming material begins with a section of turtle graphics. After these initial experiences, some of the LOGO words and lists capabilities will be introduced.

The LOGO language material will be presented in terms of powerful ideas from the language. Experiment and feel comfortable with each powerful idea and its educational potential before you advance to the next one. The examples use the LOGOWriter version of

Notes From the Literature

Instruction in LOGO programming appeared to facilitate problem-solving in third graders 2 years after the LOGO training occurred.

Clements, D. H. (1987). Longitudinal study of the effects of LOGO programming on cognitive abilities and achievement. Journal of Educational Computing Research, 3(1), 73–94.

the language, so you will need a copy of LOGOWriter to get started in your exploration. If you boot up the disk and choose NEW PAGE, you will be ready to begin experimenting.

Powerful Idea 1: The Primitives

Some powerful capabilities are built in the LOGO languages. These capabilities are in the form of commands that LOGO "knows" how to execute and are called the LOGO primitives. There are more than 100 LOGO primitives relating to many different aspects of the language, but beginning users can get started by using just a few of these commands.

LOGO primitives provide easy access to the language for beginners and are also building blocks (see Powerful Idea 2) for more advanced use of the language. With just a few of the beginning primitives, students and teachers can enter the LOGO graphics world and create interesting mathematical experiences.

To start working with LOGO, the language must be loaded into the machine. With LOGOWriter, choose NEW PAGE from the table of contents, and the LOGO turtle appears on the graphics screen. Remember that the turtle's perspective becomes your perspective; to drive the turtle around, you must pretend you are sitting on the turtle's back (Figure 13–4).

The screen is divided into the graphics screen (upper part where the turtle is located) and the command center (lower part). You will type your instructions into the command center.

Some beginning primitive commands are listed in Figure 13–5. Start off by just using FD (forward), followed by a space, and the number of units you wish the turtle to travel. Then press the return and see what happens. Your command might look like this:

FD 50

If you received an error message, make sure you entered FD in capital letters and that there is a space between the FD and the 50. Notice that the FD command needs an input; that is, you must enter a number to tell the turtle how many forward units to travel (Figure 13–6). Thus, FD with no input results in no action by the turtle.

After you have used the forward command several times with different inputs, you're ready for more commands—driving the turtle in a straight line is not a very interesting activity. The turning commands, RT (right turn) and LT (left turn), allow you to change the direction of the turtle. Try RT 30 and notice what happens to the direction of the turtle. The turtle doesn't go anywhere, it just changes direction. Enter FD followed by an input and notice that the turtle moves in a different direction. Notice that RT, LT, FD, and BK (backward) all need input function.

With the ability to move the turtle forward, backward, right, and left, you can create interesting graphics on the screen. After you have experimented a little with these primitives, create a graphic design on the screen. You might want to have the turtle trace your initials, or draw a house, or make a cube or a spaceship, or . . .

As you work on your graphic, the PU (Pen Up) command may be useful. PU allows you to take the pen

FIGURE 13–4
Remember that your perspective when drawing is just as though you are sitting on the turtle's back.

```
BK
FD
LT
RT
PU
PD
HOME
CG
```

FIGURE 13–5
These LOGO primitives are enough to get started with the language.

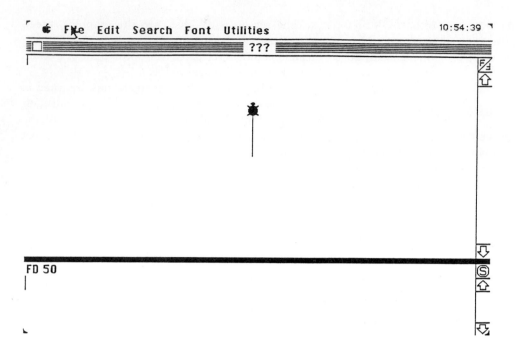

FIGURE 13–6
The FD 50 command produced this image.

up and move the turtle around without making a mark on the screen. Be sure, however, to type PD (Pen Down) when you are ready to begin marking again. Notice that PU and PD take no inputs. You simply use the command PU, and for all commands after that, the turtle leaves no marks until you give the command PD. Thus, after you have entered the command PU, you still must indicate what you want the turtle to do now that the pen is up.

There are also LOGO primitives that will help you "clean up" your screen and start over again. The primitive

HOME

takes the turtle back to its starting position. The primitive

CG OR CLEARGRAPHICS

clears all your graphics off the screen. Thus, if you type

HOME CG

the turtle will return to the starting position, and all your graphics will be removed from the screen.

After you have worked on a few projects with LOGO primitives, you may notice that you are repeating the same commands. A time-saving primitive command called REPEAT tells the turtle to repeat the directions following the command a certain number of times:

REPEAT 4[FD 50 RT 90]

This tells the turtle to repeat the direction FD 50 RT 90 four times. Thus, the turtle will go forward 50, turn right 90, go forward 50, turn right 90, go forward 50, turn right 90, go forward 50, turn right 90. What figure will these commands construct?

With the REPEAT command, you can construct interesting geometric shapes quickly and efficiently. If you are looking for a challenge, you might try to construct a triangle (you may be surprised here) or a circle (this is not trivial). In any case, practice using the REPEAT command, remembering that after you type the REPEAT command, you must enter the number of times you wish the commands within the brackets repeated. The command

REPEAT [FD 30 RT 60]

is not executable because the user failed to include the number of times FD 30 RT 60 is supposed to be repeated.

Almost invariably, young students introduced to the REPEAT command will soon try things like REPEAT 12,345[FD 5 RT 12 FD 3]. They watch with great glee as the turtle dutifully carries out the instruction the required number of times. Fortunately, all versions of LOGO contain some capability for stopping a procedure that is being executed. Thus, in LOGOWriter, if a student decides she does not really want to watch the turtle perform the commands 12,345 times, she can press the Open-Apple key and the ESC key to stop the turtle.

LOGO primitives open the door to the LOGO learning environment for both teachers and students. Generally, learners can take the tool and devise numerous interesting projects on which to work. A good example of this phenomenon occurred in a Midwestern fourth-grade class. The children had about five minutes of group instruction on the LOGO primitives and then were set loose to explore the power of the commands. One group in particular became intensely involved in their LOGO creation. They received permission to work through recess and finally, after about an hour, they raised their hands for help. The project was a detailed diagram of the planet Saturn, complete with rings, and included an artificial satellite circling the planet. The question that the group had for the instructor was, "Should we program a picture of a camera on the satellite? Then the camera could be taking a picture of Saturn."

Powerful Idea 2: Procedures, or Teaching the Turtle New Tricks

The LOGO primitives provide easy access to the language and interesting possibilities for student projects and learning. The primitives, however, are also the basic building blocks for expanding the language. Recall that LOGO is an expandable language with no ceiling. As you begin to use the primitives as building blocks to expand the language, this concept of no ceiling will become more meaningful to you.

Writing procedures in LOGO is the means used to add capabilities to the language. At first you will be working in turtle graphics, and through your procedures, you will be teaching the turtle "new tricks."

As you know, the turtle already knows how to go forward, backward, and turn right and left. The turtle does not know, however, how to draw a square. In fact, if you type SQUARE, LOGO will respond, "I don't know how to SQUARE." You can, however, teach the turtle how to SQUARE by collecting a set of primitive commands. To do this, you must be in the LOGOWriter editor.

Once you have entered the editor, type

    TO SQUARE

This instruction indicates that you wish to write a procedure, that is, to build a new capability into the language. You are naming the procedure SQUARE, but you can name it anything you want. If you wanted to name the procedure HARVEY, you would type TO HARVEY. In general, it is a good idea to get in the habit of giving procedures names that describe what they do.

When you press the return after entering "TO SQUARE," you will find that you have entered the LOGO editor. In the upper right corner of your screen, you should see the words Flip Side. The editor is the means by which you can collect commands to write procedures. Notice that as you enter your commands, the commands are merely recorded on the screen, but no graphics appear. In the editor, you merely collect commands for future use. When you exit the editor, you can run your new procedure and see how the commands work. From your previous work, you probably recognize that the easiest way to enter the commands for the turtle to draw a square is:

    REPEAT 4[FD 50 RT 90]

After you have entered these commands, you can type END to indicate that you are finished writing your first procedure. Your screen should now look like this:

    TO SQUARE
    REPEAT 4[FD 50 RT 90]
    END

To test your procedure, you must first exit the editor. Once you are out of the editor, if you type

    SQUARE

you will see that the turtle does indeed know how to SQUARE (Figure 13–7). After you have typed SQUARE the first time, move the turtle around a bit, and then type SQUARE again. Notice that this command works just like the primitives. It is like a new primitive that has been added to the turtle's vocabulary. Thus, in addition to the primitive commands, your turtle now knows how to SQUARE.

Perhaps, however, your SQUARE procedure did not work like you planned. You may even have received an error message when you typed the command. To fix bugs in the procedure, you return to the editor and delete, insert, and change your instructions. When you

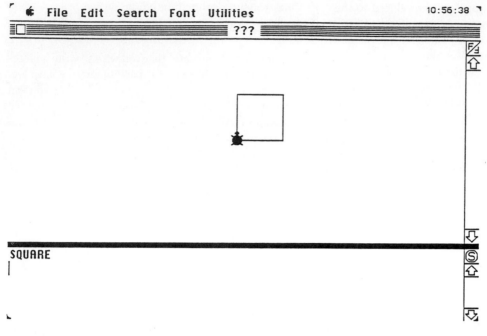

FIGURE 13–7
Square.

have finished your changes, you can then exit the editor and run the procedure again. Remember that to run the procedure, you just type the name of the procedure. To summarize, to create a procedure, you enter the editor and type

TO NAME-OF-THE-PROCEDURE

To run the procedure, you must exit the editor and type the name of the procedure.

Now that you know how to teach the turtle new tricks, practice writing some more procedures. You might want to write a procedure that will draw a triangle or a pentagon. You could write a procedure that will draw your first initial on the screen, or draw a tree, or a house, or . . . Try some simple procedures and keep working until you are comfortable with moving in and out of the LOGO editor and running your procedures.

The following procedure is a sample procedure that writes the letter "A" on the screen. The next procedure writes the letter "T."

TO A
RT 30
FD 50
RT 120

FD 50
BK 25
RT 120
FD 22.5
END
TO T
FD 45
LT 90
FD 15
BK 30
FD 15
LT 90
FD 45
RT 180
END

These procedures can be used now to form a third procedure that will write AT on the screen. This new procedure will be called AT. In the editor, enter:

TO AT

and then "call" the two procedures that have already been written. You call a procedure within a procedure by typing the name for the procedure. Thus, in the following procedure (AT), the A in line 2 tells LOGO to run the procedure named A, and the T in line 3 tells LOGO to run the procedure called T.

```
TO AT
A
T
END
```

After exiting the editor, you can call this new procedure by typing AT. Notice that there is a little bug in this new procedure! The problem, as you see, is that the "T" is drawn from the position of the turtle when it finished the A. The turtle's position must be changed for it to be in proper position to draw the T. This can be done by returning to AT and inserting some commands between the A call and the T call.

```
TO AT
A
PU BK 50
LT 90
FD 25
RT 180
PD
T
END
```

Although this approach works, a slightly more elegant way to attack the problem is suggested:

```
TO AT
A
MOVE
T
END
TO MOVE
PU
BK 50
LT 90
FD 25
RT 180
PD
END
```

Notice that in the second solution, MOVE is written as a separate procedure and then called within the procedure AT. Here MOVE is called a subprocedure because it is called by another procedure. Notice that within AT, both A and T are also used as subprocedures. As you begin using your procedures as building blocks, you will find that the second AT program is a much better model to follow. Usually, the final procedure is a call to several subprocedures. These subprocedures may themselves call other subprocedures. The final procedure should be short and clear and should not contain long strings of primitives. If you name them meaningfully, someone should be able to look at your final procedure and make a good guess at what it does.

A second example of using procedures as building blocks involves the use of the SQUARE procedure you wrote earlier. You can now use SQUARE in more complex procedures. By moving the turtle around a little between the calls to SQUARE, you can create a design of SQUARES all over the screen. One possibility is to move the turtle forward a little between each square. A procedure for doing this might look like this:

```
TO DESIGN
REPEAT 6[SQUARE PU FD 10 PD]
END
```

After you try DESIGN, you might write a similar procedure, but this time turn the turtle a little between the calls to SQUARE. Keep revising this procedure to get the design you want. You also may wish to use some of the other polygon procedures you have written as pieces of designs. Remember that the turtle "knows" all the procedures you have taught it now, and you can use these procedures as tools.

The procedure and subprocedure capabilities of LOGO lead to a problem-solving style that Papert calls breaking the problem down into "mind-sized" bites and that computer scientists call top-down programming style. Using this style, the learner first considers the total goal for the project and then begins to divide the problem into "do-able" chunks. Thus, the final procedure for a project calls numerous subprocedures. The subprocedures themselves might also call subprocedures. The program called AT provides a simple first example of this approach. The goal for the program was to put the initials AT on the screen. The problem was immediately divided up into chunks; the first chunk involved creating a procedure for the A, the second chunk was the MOVE, and the third chunk involved creating a procedure for the T. The chunks were then combined into the final program. Using this programming style, the final procedure is extremely simple and easy to read. The final procedure is just a call to a number of subprocedures. A second example of this approach follows.

The goal for this next program is to create a forest of trees (Figure 13–8). For the beginning programmer, this task might appear impossible. Remember, however, that you will divide this problem into "mind-sized" chunks, similar to the A, T, and MOVE in AT. A breakdown of the problem might look like this:

```
TO GROVE
REPEAT 5[TREE MOVE]
END
```

TREE is the next procedure that needs to be broken down into smaller pieces, and that breakdown might look like this:

```
TO TREE
TRUNK
BUSH
END
```

TRUNK will be easy to program, because it is just a straight line. BUSH, however, still needs to be simplified.

```
TO BUSH
REPEAT 5[BRANCH]
END
```

And then BRANCH can be broken down:

```
TO BRANCH
REPEAT 5[LEAF MOVE]
END
```

At this point, you have written only general procedures that outline our approach to solving the problem. If you tried to run one of these procedures, LOGO would respond, "I DON'T KNOW HOW TO GROVE" or "I DON'T KNOW HOW TO TREE" because you have not yet written the contents of that procedure.

You begin writing procedures with the simplest "mind-sized bite." In this case, that is the LEAF. A first attempt at LEAF might look like this:

FIGURE 13–8
Grove.

```
TO LEAF
LT 45 FD 10 BK 10
RT 90 FD 10
END
```

You can now write the next procedure:

```
TO BRANCH
REPEAT 5[FD 10 LEAF]
END
```

If you try out this second procedure, you will find the first bug—obviously, something went wrong. Looking at the resulting graphic, it becomes evident that the problem is in the procedure LEAF. At the end of LEAF, the turtle is left out on the end of the LEAF, and the following command, that is, FD 10, is executed from that location. You can, however, change LEAF so that the turtle ends up where it started. The new procedure might look like this:

```
TO LEAF
LT 45 FD 10 BK 10
RT 90 FD 10 BK 10 LT 45
END
```

Now the turtle ends up in the middle of the LEAF, pointing straight up. Run BRANCH again. Notice that BRANCH uses the newest definition of LEAF, and the bug has been fixed.

The next step is to write the procedure for BUSH. In this procedure a number of branches will be drawn on the screen. A first try for BUSH might be:

```
TO BUSH
REPEAT 5[BRANCH RT 30]
END
```

After entering and running this procedure, you will notice a couple of bugs. First, BRANCH, like LEAF, needs to end with the turtle in the starting position. That problem is easy to fix by altering BRANCH to look like this:

```
TO BRANCH
REPEAT 5[FD 10 LEAF]
BK 50
END
```

Notice that the BK 50 moves the turtle back to the starting point for the turtle and makes it easier to use BRANCH as a piece of another procedure.

The second bug in the procedure BUSH involves the number and arrangement of the branches. There are many ways this could be solved. To begin BUSH, the turtle should be pointing left. The command LT 90 should turn the turtle 90 degrees to the left. By the end of BUSH, the turtle should have turned 180 degrees to the right, and the turn between branches must be related to the number of branches. If you choose to draw eight branches, a good guess for each turn is 180/7. (LOGO will even perform this calculation for you. If you are using Apple LOGO II, be sure to leave a space on either side of the slash mark. Otherwise, you will get an error.) Trying that approach, BUSH can be modified to look like this:

```
TO BUSH
LT 90
REPEAT 8[BRANCH RT 180/7]
END
```

When you run this procedure, you will notice that the turtle makes a turn at the end of the last branch and is thus facing 180/7 degrees right of the horizontal starting line. A good modification is to turn the turtle back up to the horizontal line. This can be done by adding a command to the procedure:

```
TO BUSH
LT 90
REPEAT 8[BRANCH RT 180/7]
LT 180/7
END
```

The procedure for TRUNK in TREE is easy to construct:

```
TO TRUNK
FD 50
BK 50
END
```

To combine the two procedures, a procedure called TREE can be written. The only tricky part of TREE is ensuring that the turtle is in the correct position to run each of the subprocedures. Noting that at the end of BUSH, the turtle is pointing left, a turn of 90 degrees right will turn the turtle so that it is pointing straight down. Thus, TREE could look like this:

```
TO TREE
BUSH
```

RT 90
TRUNK
END

Now you are ready to write the final procedure, GROVE. Note that the procedure was written at the beginning of the problem-solving exercise and looks like this:

TO GROVE
REPEAT 5[TREE MOVE]
END

The only problem involves writing the MOVE procedure. Notice that the MOVE procedure will take the turtle from the end of one TREE to the beginning of the next one. Looking at TREE, you can see that the turtle ends up at the end of the trunk facing down. To start the next TREE in the correct position, the turtle needs to be a certain number of units to the right of the first tree and at the center of the BUSH, facing up. A possible MOVE follows:

TO MOVE
LT 90
PU
FD 50
LT 90
PD
END

Further adjustments to GROVE can move the turtle to get the GROVE to start on the left corner of the screen. See if you can add commands to GROVE to accomplish this.

In solving the GROVE problem, you used procedures as building blocks for other procedures. You also became involved with the LOGO debugging process. You tried an approach, saw the results, and when the procedure did not run as you expected, you returned to edit the procedure to remove the bugs. This constant testing and revising of ideas is a significant part of the LOGO procedure-writing process and the LOGO learning environment.

Many students initially have difficulties debugging their procedures. Instead of editing, some will want to totally rewrite a procedure that does not work the way they expected. The idea of testing and editing procedures is an important part of the LOGO experience, and teachers must initially help students to see that

they do not need to throw out a procedure that does not work. All they need to do is fix it.

The clown project shown in Figure 13–9 is another example of a LOGO project built with procedures. The code for the clown project demonstrates the procedural nature of the project.

You should now be ready to create a simple LOGO project of your own. Remember to break your project up into "mind-sized" pieces. Your final procedure should be a simple collection of calls to subprocedures. The procedure for the house project looks like this:

TO HOUSE
FRAME
ROOF
MOVE1
WINDOWS
MOVE2
DOOR
END

You may wish to actually write the subprocedures for HOUSE or create a LOGO project of your own.

Powerful Idea 3: Using LOGO Variables

As you experimented with LOGO procedures, you may have had to write separate procedures to get different-size squares, triangles, or circles. For example, you might have written one procedure that made a square of side 50 and called that procedure SQUARE. When you needed a smaller square, you had to write a second procedure with a different name. Some of those steps can be eliminated, because LOGO allows you to write one general procedure for a figure and then enter the size of the figure when you call the procedure.

You can do this by naming a variable location in your procedure definition. This indicates that you will provide a value for the variable location each time you run the procedure. For example:

TO SQUARE :SIDE
REPEAT 4[FD :SIDE RT 90]
END

Notice that this new procedure looks like the SQUARE procedure you wrote earlier, except for the addition of :SIDE. :SIDE is the name of the variable location for this procedure. Each time you call

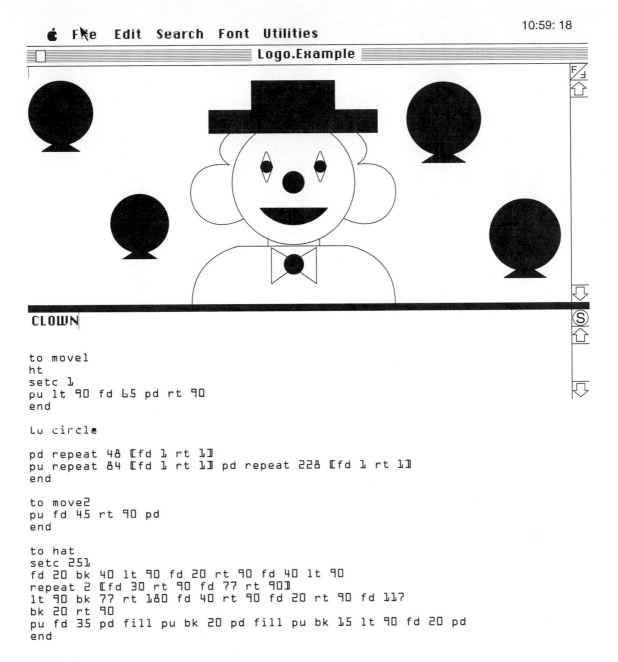

FIGURE 13–9
The clown project is another example of procedural programming with LOGO.

SQUARE, you must supply a value for the variable :SIDE. You do this by typing the procedure name and a value for the variable. Thus, the procedure name must be followed by an input. For example, the command

SQUARE 50

will draw a square with side 50. While

SQUARE 10

will draw a square of side 10. If you call SQUARE without a value for :SIDE, LOGO will respond,

FIGURE 13–9
(continued)

```
to clown
move1
circle
move2
hat
hairL
MOVE3
HAIRR
MOVE4
FACE
MOUTH
BODY
TIE
move5
ball 16 .6 4
end

TO MOVE3
pu rt 41 fd 85 lt 90 fd 77 rt 90 fd 17 pd
end

to hairL
fd 15
setc 14
repeat 150 [fd .25 lt 1]
rt 160
repeat 231 [fd .5 lt 1]
end

TO HAIRR
setc 14
PD
REPEAT 150 [FD .25 RT 1]
LT 160
REPEAT 231 [FD .5 RT 1]
END

TO MOVE4
PU
LT 40 FD 60 RT 90 FD 30 PD
END

TO FACE
setc 5
REPEAT 360 [FD .17 RT 1]
pu
rt 90 fd 5 pd fill pu bk 5 lt 90
setc 184
PU RT 90 FD 10 LT 90 FD 15 LT 90 FD 30 RT 90 PD
REPEAT 400 [FD .1 RT 1]
pu rt 90 fd 2 pd fill pu bk 2 lt 90
  pd setc 1 LT 20 FD 10 RT 130 FD 10
BK 10 LT 130 BK 10 RT 20
    setc 184 REPEAT 170 [FD .1 RT 1]
    setc 1 LT 9 FD 11 RT 125 FD 10
PU RT 120 FD 50 RT 90
FD 3 LT 210
PD BK 10 LT 125 BK 11 RT 9
    setc 184 REPEAT 360 [FD .1 RT 1]
rt 90 pu fd 2 pd fill pu bk 2 lt 90
RT 180
pd sect 184 REPEAT 72 [FD .1 LT 1]
sect 1 RT 9 FD 10 LT 125 FD 10
END
```

```
TO MOUTH
  setc 5 PU LT 22 FD 30 LT 90  FD 10 RT 90 REPEAT 20 [FD .5 RT 1]
PD REPEAT 140 [FD .5 RT 1]
PU REPEAT 20 [FD .5 RT 1] RT 180 FD 10 LT 91 PD FD 55
pu rt 180 fd 10 lt 90 fd 10 pd fill pu bk 10 lt 90 fd 10
END

TO BODY
setc 1
PU RT 90 FD 30 PD FD 5 LT 90
setc 6 FD 15 REPEAT 85 [FD 1 RT 1]
RT 95 PD FD 195
RT 95  REPEAT 85 [FD 1 RT 1] FD 15 LT 90
setc 1 FD 5 bk 5 rt 90
setc 6 fd 50 bk 50 lt 90 fd 5
END

TO TIE
setc 233
PU RT 180 FD 32 LT 90 FD 26
PD REPEAT 405 [FD .15 LT 1]
RT 75 FD 20 LT 120 FD 32 LT 120 FD 20
RT 75 REPEAT 90 [FD .15 LT 1]
RT 75 FD 20 LT 120 FD 32 LT 120 FD 20
pu fd 7 pd fill
end

to move5
pu fd 160 lt 130 fd 40 rt 71 fd 40 pd
end

to ball :y :z :x
if :x<1 [stop]

setc :y repeat 360 [fd :z rt 1] rt 70 pu fd 10 pd fill pu  bk 10 rt 90
repeat 80 [fd :z lt 1] pd rt 140 fd 10 lt 150 fd 32 lt 140 fd 10 lt 40 fd 15 rt
270 pu fd 3 pd fill pu fd 70 lt 90 fd 50 pd lt 90
ball :y*2 :z-.05 :x-1
end
```

FIGURE 13–9
(continued)

SQUARE NEEDS MORE INPUTS.

Because SQUARE is now followed by a name for a variable location in the definition line, SQUARE cannot run without an input for the indicated variable. Just like the primitive command FD cannot operate without an input, a procedure with a variable name in the definition line cannot run without an input for that variable.

You can name the variable in the procedure anything you want, as long as it begins with a character. For example, :SIDE could be called :X or :Y or :HARVEY. The colon indicates that you are naming a variable location, and every time you refer to the variable location in the procedure, you must place a colon (:) before the name of the location. When you call the procedure, however, you must supply the value for the variable location, and you do not include the colon.

You can now revise some of our procedures to include variables. For example, if you have a procedure for a triangle that looks like this:

TO TRIANGLE
REPEAT 3[FD 50 RT 120]
END

instead of a procedure that just makes a triangle with side length 50, you can revise your procedure to construct a triangle with a variable side length. To do this, you first must indicate in the definition line (TO TRIANGLE) that the procedure will contain a variable. You do this by adding a variable location name. Thus, the first line of your procedure needs to look like this:

TO TRIANGLE :S

You also need to change the FD input within the procedure. The turtle no longer goes FD 50; instead it should go FD :S, where the value for :S is given each time you call the procedure. Thus, your triangle procedure now looks like this:

```
TO TRIANGLE :S
REPEAT 3[FD :S RT 120]
END
```

Here, the name chosen for the variable location is :S. Typical calls to the triangle procedure now look like this:

```
TRIANGLE 50
TRIANGLE 10
TRIANGLE 100
```

You could now write a procedure that draws different-size triangles from the same point (Figure 13–10). The procedure could look like this:

```
TO MANYTRIES
TRIANGLE 10
TRIANGLE 15
TRIANGLE 20
```

```
TRIANGLE 25
TRIANGLE 30
END
```

Procedures can have more than one variable. For example, if you wish to write a general procedure for a rectangle, you will need an input for length and an input for width. Your procedure might look like this:

```
TO REC :LEN :WID
REPEAT 2[FD :LEN RT 90 FD :WID RT 90]
END
```

To call REC, you must supply two variables, one value for :LEN and one for :WID. Thus,

```
REC 50 10
```

will create a rectangle with length 50 and width 10. Try calling REC with some different values for the variables. Make a short, fat rectangle and then a long, skinny one.

Now try inserting some variables into some of the procedures you have already written. Remember that each time you call a procedure with a variable, you must supply a value for that variable location.

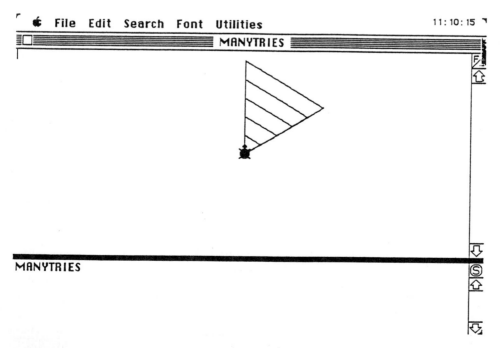

FIGURE 13–10
MANYTRIES command produces the image shown.

Powerful Idea 4: Using Recursion

LOGO beginners are often confused about whether they are in the LOGO editor. The following program is a fairly typical beginner's LOGO error:

```
TO SQUARE
REPEAT 4[FD 50 RT 90]
SQUARE
END
```

Typically, the novice programmer will try to call the program SQUARE from within the editor. If the programmer then exits the editor and types a call to SQUARE, he may be quite surprised. The turtle draws a square as instructed, but the turtle never stops drawing; it just keeps tracing over and over the square.

Careful examination of the program reveals that the turtle is merely following directions. It performs the REPEAT command and then gets to the command SQUARE. This command is called to do SQUARE, so the turtle performs the SQUARE commands again, which contains the REPEAT sequence and returns to the call to SQUARE, and it performs the commands for SQUARE again, and continues, never reaching the END statement.

This beginning programmer has inadvertently stumbled onto a powerful idea. He has written a procedure that calls itself, and is therefore using recursion. While this example is a mild use of recursion, the idea can be used to create some interesting and useful programs. Consider the following example:

This problem involves writing a program that will produce a series of squares arranged in a spiral. Each square in the program should be slightly larger than the preceding square. The REPEAT command will not work for this task because the size of the square needs to change each time the procedure is executed. Recursion offers the perfect tool for this situation.

```
TO SPIRAL :SIDE
SQUARE :SIDE
RT 10
SPIRAL :SIDE+5
END
```

Tracing this program when five is used as input, a square with side 5 is drawn and then the turtle turns right 10 degrees. SPIRAL then calls itself, but this time the value for :SIDE is increased by 5. The value for :SIDE on the second time through the procedure is

thus 10. Now the turtle draws a square with side 10, turns right 10 degrees, and SPIRAL is called again, this time with a value for :SIDE of 15. The program has no stopping point, so it will continue to run until stopped by the user or until the computer runs out of space.

The recursive program SPIRAL can be stopped in the program if a conditional statement is used (Figure 13–11). A conditional statement in LOGO follows the primitive IF and instructs the program to do a particular command under a specified condition. In this case,

```
IF :SIDE > 100 STOP
```

tells the program to stop when the value of :SIDE gets bigger than 100. The program SPIRAL now looks like this:

```
TO SPIRAL :SIDE
IF :SIDE > 100 STOP
SQUARE :SIDE
RT 10
SPIRAL :SIDE+5
END
```

Each time the procedure executes, the current value of :SIDE is checked in line 2 of the procedure. When :SIDE reaches 105, the IF statement is true, and the procedure stops. Thus, the last square that is drawn has side 100.

Using turtle graphics, you have rapidly experienced four major powerful ideas from the LOGO language. These ideas are also applicable in different parts of the language. Whether you are working in turtle graphics, music, or words and lists, the ideas of primitives, procedures, variables, and recursion are all powerful and useful LOGO tools. Turtle graphics is a convenient way to introduce the ideas, but LOGO has numerous capabilities in addition to turtle graphics.

LOGO Numbers, Words, and Lists

LOGO programs can work with three different types of data: numbers, words, and lists. A list in LOGO is a structure that allows the programmer to combine words or numbers. The three LOGO data types and simple commands to manipulate are presented next.

Numbers.   You used some of LOGO's numerical capabilities in the work with turtle graphics. With numerical data, LOGO "knows" how to add, subtract, multiply, and divide, using the symbols +, -, *, and /

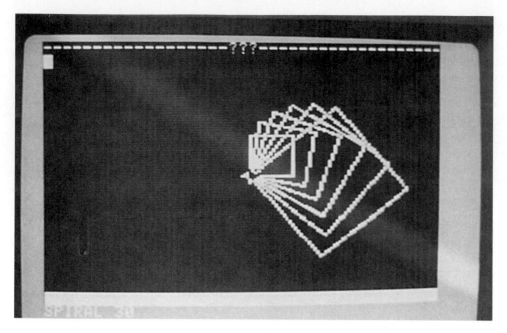

FIGURE 13–11
Spiral.

The command PRINT (3 15)/2*8 in LOGO will output 32.

Using some of these LOGO numerical capabilities, you can write procedures to manipulate numbers. For example, the procedure CUBE:

```
TO CUBE :X
PRINT :X*:X *:X
END
```

This procedure will print the cube of any number that is entered as a variable. Thus, if you call

```
CUBE 5
```

LOGO will print 125.

Notice that you can write numerical procedures and then use them as tools in other procedures. With the simple CUBE procedure, you have expanded the LOGO language to include the capability to cube a number. Basically, you can "teach" LOGO almost any numerical capability, making it a potentially powerful language for mathematics use.

Words.   In LOGO, any string of characters not separated by a space is considered a word. To indicate the data-type word in LOGO, you type a quotation mark in front of the string. For example, the command

PRINT "MISSISSIPPI will cause LOGO to print out the word MISSISSIPPI. Numbers are treated as words in LOGO, but they do not require the preceding quotation mark. Thus, PRINT 64 will cause LOGO to print out the number 64. PRINT "64 gives the same result. PRINT MISSISSIPPI will, however, result in an error message. LOGO assumes that the string of characters MISSISSIPPI is a procedure name unless it is preceded by a quotation mark.

In LOGO, there are several primitives used for manipulating words. The four most commonly used primitives for manipulating words are the following:

```
FIRST
```

Outputs the first character of the word.

```
LAST
```

Outputs the last character of the word.

```
BUTFIRST
```

Outputs the word without its first character.

```
BUTLAST
```

Outputs the word without its last character. For example:

```
PRINT FIRST "SHOW
```

will print S and

    PRINT BUTLAST "DOWN

will print DOW.

LOGO Lists.   LOGO's list-processing capability allows you to manipulate long and complex sets of information quite easily. In LOGO, a list is a group of words and is indicated with brackets. Thus, PRINT [TODAY IS TUESDAY] will print TODAY IS TUESDAY. The primitive commands FIRST, LAST, BUTFIRST, and BUTLAST also work for manipulating lists, but with lists, they operate on words instead of characters. Thus, PRINT BUTLAST [TODAY IS WEDNESDAY] will print TODAY IS.

One interesting educational application of LOGO's list-processing capability involves getting learners to teach the computer "how to talk." Using LOGO words and lists, learners can teach the computer how to create sentences or how to write poetry. In teaching the computer how to talk, the learner may for the first time begin to understand the significance of the parts of speech. The following LOGO program will generate random sentences from the parts of speech given. Although you have not yet experienced all the commands used in the program, you should be able to follow the general idea.

To supply the data for the program, students can define variables that are lists containing the various parts of speech. Thus, the LOGO variable :ADJECTIVES contains four adjectives:

    MAKE "ADJECTIVES SLEEPY WEEPING
        SMASHING BRILLIANT
    MAKE "VERBS EAT SLEEP JUMP FLY
    MAKE "NOUNS PEACOCKS LIONS
        ANTEATERS FISH

After the variables have been defined, students need a procedure that will randomly pick from each list. This procedure can be written by advanced students or supplied to students as a tool. The procedure that will pick randomly from a list could look like this:

    TO RANPICK :OBJECT
    OUTPUT ITEM (1 RANDOM COUNT
        :OBJECT) :OBJECT
    END

With this tool, students can write a procedure called TALK.

    TO TALK
    DEFINE
    PR (SENTENCE RANPICK :ADJECTIVES RANPICK :NOUNS RANPICK :VERBS)
    END

If students would like to generate many sentences at once, they can use the REPEAT command.

    REPEAT 4 TALK.

A sample output from using this command follows:

    BRILLIANT LIONS FLY
    SLEEPY ANTEATERS JUMP
    SMASHING PEACOCKS EAT
    BRILLIANT FISH FLY

The program can also be easily modified so that the user can insert new words into the sentence generator. Of course, the learner will need to supply words that are the correct part of speech for each category to keep the computer talking coherently and correctly. Notice that the program can easily be expanded to include other parts of speech and generate more complicated sentences. Similar programs can also be written to "teach the computer" to write poetry.

LOGO Music

In addition to graphics, numbers, words, and lists capabilities, most versions of LOGO also have music capabilities. Using a few simple primitives and the powerful ideas presented earlier in the chapter, students can write simple music on the computer. The procedural nature of LOGO simplifies the music-writing process. Once a procedure for a particular portion of the music is written and debugged, the procedure can be called whenever it is needed.

Most versions of LOGO music have a command for music followed by two inputs. One input is for the frequency of the note to be played and the other is for the duration. The frequency is the number of times a second a sound wave vibrates. A high frequency number produces a high-pitched sound and a low number produces a low-pitched sound. Duration is the length of the sound. In LOGOWriter, TONE 262 56 produces a middle C with duration 56, whereas TONE 524 56 produces a C an octave higher than middle C.

Several music commands can be combined and then played all at once. To play the music, exit the editor and type the name of the procedure. Of course, a song can be created that is a series of calls to subprocedures:

```
TO FIRST
TONE 252 56/8
TONE 349 56/4
TONE 262 56/8
TONE 262 56/8
TONE 294 56/4
TONE 262 56/2
TONE 330 56/4
TONE 349 56/2
END
```

This example could then be part of a larger procedure,

```
TO MUSIC
REPEAT 5 FIRST
SECOND
THIRD
END
```

This procedure will play the music in FIRST five times and then play the musical procedures SECOND and THIRD. You may wish to write pieces of music for the SECOND and THIRD procedures now. You will probably be surprised to see how easy it is to create recognizable songs.

Notice that 56 is the duration of the whole note in the example FIRST. A smaller value will give you a faster tempo, and a larger value will produce a slower tempo. Once the tempo is chosen, you divide the value for the whole note to obtain half or quarter or other notes.

Some students might use the music capabilities of LOGO to write sound effects to accompany their graphics procedures. Others may just use the music capabilities. Either way, once they have worked with the four basic powerful ideas from LOGO, generalizing to music programming is simple.

LOGO CLASSROOM APPLICATIONS ACROSS THE CURRICULUM

Although the majority of LOGO programs in schools have focused on using LOGO as a tool for teaching and learning mathematics, LOGO applications have been successfully implemented in many different sub-

ject areas. Some of the problem-solving experiences inherent in working with the language involve learning and using techniques that are applicable in almost every subject area. The debugging experiences and the experience of breaking down a problem into smaller pieces are two of the general problem-solving skills experienced in LOGO. In many schools, the study of problem solving is becoming a subject in itself, and LOGO is used as one of the experiences for teaching and learning. In addition, the specific tool uses of LOGO in different subject areas are increasing.

LOGO in Mathematics

Mathematics educators have used the LOGO language in many phases of the mathematics learning process. Some use the language as an open-ended discovery experience for learners, whereas others have imposed a more specific structure on LOGO learning experiences.

LOGO supplies an environment where students can explore and experience concepts in numerous specific subject areas in mathematics. These areas include simple geometry concepts, estimation skills, concepts of variables, polar coordinate systems, vector methods, and topology. At one end of the curriculum, LOGO is used to help students experience the concept of "angle." At the other extreme, Abelson and DiSessa (1980) have written an entire textbook on LOGO applications in undergraduate mathematics.

LOGO in Language Arts

The list-processing capabilities of the LOGO language make it a useful tool for exploring concepts of language. Although students may not possess the expertise necessary to write complex list-processing programs, these programs can be supplied to learners as tools for exploration and learning. Recall that with LOGO, the teacher or programmer can build in as many capabilities as necessary to create a particular learning environment.

As discussed earlier, computer-based environments where children can teach the computer to write sentences or poetry have been used in numerous language classes. In these environments, children have to teach the computer parts of speech, tense, gender, and subject–verb agreement. Generally, the learners supply the words for the generation of language and thus can make the computer produce all types of communication.

LOGOWriter also has interesting capabilities for language and arts teachers. Using LOGOWriter, children can combine word processing and programming

Notes From the Literature

The LOGO language can be used to help geometry students more completely understand terms used in geometry such as angle, complimentary angle, supplementary angles, bisection, parallel line segments, intersecting line segments, and perpendicular.

Niess, M. (1988). LOGO learning tools build informal geometry ideas: Part III. The Computing Teacher, 15(8), 12–15.

projects. Thus, learners can be encouraged to create text to describe and enhance their graphics work. They can also easily produce illustrated stories, newspapers, and announcements.

Some authors have also suggested that children working on LOGO problems in pairs may be developing their abilities to verbally describe their problem-solving and thinking processes (Clements & Nastasi, 1988). Although research in this area has just begun, the development of abilities to communicate problem-solving strategies may be a valuable portion of the LOGO experience.

LOGO in Science

Obviously, the hypothesis-testing nature of the LOGO experience can provide valuable scientific problem-solving experiences for students. In addition, a number of LOGO microworlds are available in which students are free to experiment and test theories about basic concepts of science.

The dynaturtle, developed by DiSessa, provides one example of a scientific LOGO microworld; the dynaturtle environment models the world of Newtonian motion. Using the dynaturtle, students can test theories about Newtonian physics. The dynaturtle remains at rest or travels with uniform velocity in a straight line except when acted on by forces. The forces are supplied by the student, who can cause the dynaturtle to speed up, slow down, or change direction. By learning through experimentation how to "control" the dynaturtle, students experience and explore basic principles of Newtonian motion.

LEGOLOGO TC is a relatively new extension of the LOGO environment that is being used in elementary and middle school science classes. As the name suggests, LEGOLOGO combines the use of LEGOs with the LOGO programming language. Children build objects

with LEGOs and then write programs to control the movements of the objects they build. Children can build cars, ferris wheels, or Morse code generators and then use LOGO to create the action and motion. Teachers have observed that children are highly motivated to work in the LEGOLOGO environment and learn a great deal of physics and problem-solving in the process.

LOGO in Social Studies

LOGOWriter has opened some interesting possibilities for social studies teachers. The combined graphics and text capabilities of LOGOWriter make it an interesting tool for creating maps and map-reading environments for learners. Many teachers have their students create maps for other students and then debug their environments using feedback from their peers.

Students studying data base management techniques in social studies can have an in-depth experience with the structure of these systems by using LOGO. The list-processing capabilities in the LOGO environment allow students and teachers to create their own data base managers. With LOGO, data base managers for particular purposes can be easily programmed by novice programmers. Students who create their own data base management programs develop a deeper understanding of this valuable social science tool.

When using LOGO to create data base managers and LOGOWriter to create map-reading environments, social studies students become active participants in the study of social studies. In both cases, students are creating tools for the learning and understanding of social studies concepts, and in doing so increase their own understanding of these concepts.

SUMMARY

For many computer educators, the LOGO experience has had a profound effect on their conceptions of computer use in the classroom. Although few would argue that LOGO by itself is the answer for computer education, LOGO sheds much light on the concept of how children can best learn with computers. Characteristics of the LOGO environment are appearing in other computer environments made available for children. The idea of creating dynamic, visual computer environments where the computer is used as an interactive object "to think with" expands and enhances the educational experiences that can be created in schools.

Through LOGO and LOGO-like environments, many principles of scientific visualization and modeling are made available to learners. Many argue that these environments provide high-level learning experiences for children and exhibit the potential of the computer as a tool to improve student learning. LOGO's most significant contribution to the use of computers in school may be its use as a model that encourages educators to create other dynamic, visual, learner-controlled environments for students.

SELF-TEST QUESTIONS

1. List and describe at least three characteristics of the LOGO programming language.
2. Which of the following is not a LOGO data type?
   a. Word
   b. Number
   c. Sentence
   d. List
3. The following program uses recursion:

   TO MYSTERY

   REPEAT 4[FD 3 RT 75]

   SQUARE

   REPEAT 4[FD 3 RT 75]

   SQUARE

   a. True
   b. False
4. Write a LOGO program that will draw a rectangle.
5. Compare and contrast the works of Papert and Piaget.
6. List and describe the four powerful ideas from LOGO programming presented in this chapter.
7. Describe the LOGO dynaturtle. Explain its significance.
8. Predict the output from the following LOGO program:

   TO MYSTERY

   REPEAT 3[FD 50 RT 120]

   END

   a. The program draws a square.
   b. The program draws a triangle.
   c. The program draws three connected lines.
   d. The program draws three squares.
9. Describe what is meant by the statement "LOGO is an extendable language."
10. Describe the major characteristics of a microworld.

11. LOGO is available only for Apple and IBM computers.
    a. True
    b. False
12. The LOGO primitive BUTFIRST works for both words and lists.
    a. True
    b. False

ANSWERS TO SELF-TEST QUESTIONS

1. a. LOGO is a language with no threshold and no ceiling. Thus it can be used as a simple beginning computer experience for students and is also applicable for uses in advanced computer science.
   b. LOGO is a procedural language. Like other modern languages, LOGO is structured to encourage breaking a program down into blocks or procedures.
   c. LOGO has turtle graphics. Using turtle graphics involves giving the LOGO turtle commands to direct its actions on the screen.
   d. LOGO uses lists as data objects. In addition to turtle graphics, LOGO contains powerful capabilities to allow manipulation of words, numbers, and lists.

2. c.
3. b. False. To use recursion, the program must call itself. There is no call to MYSTERY within the program.
4. The following LOGO program will draw a rectangle:

   TO RECT

   REPEAT 2[FD 50 RT 90 FD 100 RT 90]

   END

   A solution using variables might look like this:

   TO RECT :LEN :WID

   REPEAT 2[FD :LEN RT 90 FD :WID RT 90]

   END

5. Papert and Piaget both believe that children learn best through experience. They both contend that children build their own intellectual structures as a result of their interaction with the environment in which they live. Papert, however, tends to be more interventionist in his theories than Piaget.

That is, Papert believes enriching the child's environment and experiences can enhance intellectual development.

6. a. *Primitives.* These are the commands built into the language. These are procedures that have already been programmed into the language.

   b. *Procedures.* LOGO can "learn new tricks" when primitive commands are combined to form instructions for more complex actions. Using the LOGO editor, procedures can be written by the user and can be called by other procedures.

   c. *Variables.* LOGO procedures will accept variables; thus, a general procedure can be written to perform a particular task, and variables can be entered for specific implementations of the task. In a procedure, SQUARE :S is written to draw a square with variable length sides; SQUARE 50 draws a medium-sized square, whereas SQUARE 10 draws a small square.

   d. *Recursion.* In LOGO, a procedure can call itself.

7. The LOGO dynaturtle is an example of a LOGO microworld. The dynaturtle remains at rest or travels with uniform velocity in a straight line except when acted on by forces. The student supplies these forces and observes the consequences of applying them.

8. b.

9. The LOGO language is limited only by the abilities of the programmer. Through writing procedures, the programmer can extend the language almost any way desired.

10. A microworld is an environment for learning where a learner is encouraged to experiment, test, and revise theories. A microworld focuses on a particular topic. In the microworld, the student must be able to produce a meaningful product.

11. b. False. LOGO is available for almost all brands of microcomputer.

12. a. True.

REFERENCES

Abelson, H., & DiSessa, A. (1980). *Turtle geometry.* Cambridge: MIT Press.

Clements, D. H. (1991). Enhancement of creativity in computer environments. *American Educational Research Journal, 28*(1), 173–187.

Clements, D. H. (1987). Longitudinal study of the effects of LOGO programming on cognitive abilities and achievement. *Journal of Educational Computing Research, 3*(1), 73–94.

Clements, D. H. (1985). Research on LOGO in education: Is the turtle slow but steady, or not even in the race? *Computers in the Schools, 2*(2/3), 55–71.

Clements, D. H., & Nastasi, B. K. (1988). Social and cognitive interactions in educational computer environments. *American Educational Research Journal, 25*(1), 87–106.

Dunn, S., & Morgan, V. (1987). *The impact of the computer on education: A course for teachers.* Englewood Cliffs, NJ: Prentice-Hall.

Goodyear, P. (1984). *LOGO: A guide to learning through programming.* New York: John Wiley & Sons.

Harvey, B. (1982). Why LOGO? *Byte, 7*(8), 263–293.

Holt, J. (1970). *How children learn.* New York: Penguin.

Killian, J., Nelson, J., & Byrd, D. (1986). Child's play: Computers in early childhood programs. *The Computer Teacher, 12,* 13–16.

Nastasi, B., Clements, D., & Battista, M. (1990). Social-cognitive interactions, motivation, and cognitive growth in LOGO programming and CAI problem-solving environments. *Journal of Educational Psychology, 82*(1), 150–158.

Niess, M. (1988). LOGO learning tools build informal geometry ideas: Part III. *The Computing Teacher, 15*(8), 12–15.

Papert, S. (1980). *Mindstorms.* New York: Basic Books.

Piaget, J. (1954). *The construction of reality in the child.* New York: Basic Books.

Rieber, L. (1986). The effect of LOGO on young children. In M. R. Simonson, E. Coble, & J. Hayward (Eds.), *Proceedings of selected research paper presentations* (pp. 562–597). Las Vegas, NV: Association for Educational Communications and Technology.

Yelland, N. (1992–1993). Introducing young children to LOGO. *The Computing Teacher, 20*(4), 12–14.

REFERENCES FOR ADDITIONAL STUDY

Abelson, H. (1982). LOGO for the Apple II. In *Byte.* New York: McGraw-Hill.

Dalton, D. W. (1986). A comparison of the effects of LOGO use and teacher-directed problem-solving instruction on the problem-solving skills, achievement, and attitudes of low, average, and high achieving junior high school learners. In M. R. Simonson, E. Coble, & J. Hayward (Eds.), *Proceedings of selected research paper presentations* (pp. 119–152). Las Vegas, NV: Association for Educational Communications and Technology.

DiSessa, A., & White, B. (1982). Learning physics from a Dynaturtle. *Byte, 7*(8), 324.

Kinzer, C. K., Littlefield, J., Delclos, V. R., & Bransford, J. D. (1984). *Different LOGO learning environments and mastery: Relationship between engagement and learning* (NIMH-MH-30235). Bethesda, MD: National Institute of Mental

Health. (ERIC Document Reproduction Service No. ED 262 751)

Pea, R. D., & Kurland, D. M. (1984). *LOGO programming and the development of planning skills* (Technical Report No. 16). New York: Bank Street College of Education, Center for Children and Technology. (ERIC Document Reproduction Service No. ED 249 930)

Shimabukuro, G. (1989). A class act: Junior high students, LEGO and LOGO. *The Computing Teacher, 16*(5), 37–39.

Watt, D. (1983). *Learning with LOGO.* New York: McGraw-Hill.

Watt, M. (1982, October). What is LOGO? *Creative Computing,* 112–126.

Yoder, S. (1988). *Introduction to programming in LOGO using LOGOWriter.* Eugene, OR: International Council for Computers in Education.

Yoder, S., & Moursund, D. (1990). LOGOWriter for educators: A problem-solving approach. Eugene, OR: International Society for Technology in Education.

CHAPTER FOURTEEN

HYPERMEDIA AND MULTIMEDIA WITH HYPERCARD AND LINKWAY

GOAL

This chapter will introduce the reader to the basic capabilities of a hypermedia system and applications of these capabilities in classrooms.

OBJECTIVES

The reader will be able to do the following:

1. Describe the basic features of a hypermedia system.
2. Describe the advantages for teachers using a hypermedia system.
3. Describe the advantages for students using a hypermedia system.
4. Cite examples of specific hypermedia use for teachers.
5. Cite examples of specific hypermedia use for students.
6. Cite three possible problems with hypermedia use in education.
7. Describe the specific capabilities of the HyperCard system.
8. Identify the following HyperCard terms: stack, card, button, field, and background.
9. List the components of LinkWay Live!
10. Develop a lesson with pages containing buttons, text, and drawings using LinkWay Live!
11. Compare and contrast the features of HyperCard and LinkWay.
12. Explain the structure and function of HyperStudio.

Research at Harvard has shown that each of us has components of seven distinct intelligences, any of which can be our dominant intelligence. An educational system that teaches to all of these intelligences honors the thinking styles of each individual and can help retain the natural joy of learning.

Thornberg, 1992, p. 40

WHAT IS HYPERMEDIA?

A single definition of *hypermedia* has yet to be agreed on by educators. Many educators confuse hypermedia with multimedia and ignore the differences between the two. Whereas *multimedia* refers to the use of a variety of media, *hypermedia* can be defined from the two words that make up the term. *Hyper* refers to over, above, or more than the average, and *media* is information represented in many formats. Thus, hypermedia suggests having different types of information presented in a variety of formats. Educational technology futurist Dede (1987) defined *hypermedia* as a framework for nonlinear representation of symbols. He considered hypermedia an external associational memory in which the technology helps users organize and access information.

Hypermedia is an extension of hypertext, the electronic representation of text that takes advantage of the random access capabilities of computers. This random access capability permits the user to overcome the strictly sequential medium of print on paper (Marchionini, 1988). Hypermedia, according to Marchionini, extends the means of information representation to include access to graphics, sound, animation, and other forms of information transfer.

Notes From the Literature

"At times the world of hypertext seems almost anti-narrative. You click on Martin Luther King, you hear the beginning of a speech that can make you cry because it's so beautiful. Then the speech ends and you're back at the menu. And you say, 'Wait a minute—don't stop me in the middle of nowhere. What about Selma? Fit this in for me. I'm only a kid (or only an adult). I need context.' "

Snyder, T. (1994). Computers: Ready or not, here they come! The Executive Educator, 16(3), 36–40.

Hypermedia, then, combines methods of representation, such as video, graphics, animation, and text, and connects the information represented in these formats in a multitude of paths to create an environment that affords immediate, yet random, access to large amounts of information (Figure 14–1). Such accessibility has been made possible by advances in information storage technology; in particular, the computer has allowed the information storage and control necessary for hypermedia environments.

The nature of a hypermedia environment is interactive and exploratory. That is, such an environment requires the input or action of users, and users direct their own paths through the environment. Computer technology affords the highest level of interaction between the user and the information stored in a hyperdocument. A hyperdocument is the actual lesson or product of a hypermedia system. Hypermedia systems are hardware and software systems used to create and display hyperdocuments (Marchionini, 1988). The computer is the most common component of hypermedia systems. The user interacts with the computer to access information. A typical hypermedia environment may include a videodisc and a computer interacting with the learner to allow access to graphics, video, sound, animation, and text.

IBM has produced several prototype hypermedia programs that illustrate some of the power and the flexibility of the approach. In one program, students explore numerous facets of Tennyson's poem *Ulysses*. Students can do the following to interact with the program:

- Select different actors' voices to read the poem or portions of the poem.
- View critics discussing aspects of the poem.
- Watch scenes of Ulysses' adventures on which the poem is based.
- Watch modern characters quoting from the poem in speeches.
- Access more information about the poet.
- Ask for more information on specific words and references in the poem.

Students are free to take their own approach in exploring the information, locating information about the poem that interests them. In total, the hypermedia document for the poem *Ulysses* makes the experience of the poem a meaningful reality for students.

A second example of a hypermedia environment fitting the definition offered previously is an environment that allows students to explore information about bird anatomy. In this environment, students can select in-

FIGURE 14–1
Example of a Hypermedia Work Station.

depth information about the anatomy of a bird and access line drawings, slides, video, text, and audio information about different parts of the bird. Students can investigate a particular section of the bird, such as the head, and then examine more deeply a particular part of the head, such as the eye. In one sense, the environment offers a multimedia encyclopedia of information on bird anatomy for the student. Students can explore this environment in the way they choose.

A third example of a hypermedia environment is a program called Phillipe that is designed for use with advanced high school French students. The program includes text, graphics, and audio and video capabilities. In the program, students help Phillipe (who has been kicked out by his girlfriend) find an apartment in Paris. Using both video and audio capabilities, students hear authentic French, experience Paris from the point of view of someone looking for an apartment, listen to Phillipe's phone messages, read newspaper ads, and have other experiences connected with the task. The student users make decisions aimed at the goal of finding an apartment. Through the program, the students

Notes From the Literature

One quality of virtual environments is verity (derived from *veritas* meaning "true to life"). Verity is used to denote a continuum of simulation experiences that range from recreations of the physical world as we know it to depictions of abstract ideas which have no physical counterparts. On one end of the verity dimension, VRs simulate real-world counterparts which respond to natural laws; on the other end of the scale, some VRs represent abstract ideas that are so novel that they may not resemble any aspect of the world as we know it.

Thurman, R. A., & Mattoon, J. S. (1994). Virtual reality: Toward fundamental improvements in simulation-based training. Educational Technology, 34(8), 56–64.

Poohkay, B., & Szabo, M. (1995). Effects of animation and visuals on learning high school mathematics. In M. Simonson & M. Anderson, (Eds.). Proceedings of Selected Research and Development Presentations at the Annual Convention of the Association for Educational Communications and Technology, Anaheim, CA.

gain experience in French and also experience in Paris. Throughout the program, the students control what they do next.

It is important to distinguish hypermedia from both multimedia and interactive multimedia. Multimedia is the combination of many forms of media or the combination and display of multiple visual and/or audio elements. Interactive multimedia allows the user to interact with the multimedia; however, this interaction does not necessarily alter the linear direction of the presentation. The term *interactive multimedia* has been used somewhat interchangeably with *hypermedia,* however. Given the definition of hypermedia suggested here, it seems clear that a multimedia environment that allows high-level interaction with the user and allows random access to the information is quite similar to a hypermedia environment. However, the term *interactive multimedia* does not inherently imply the nonlinear access feature of a hypermedia system.

WHY USE HYPERMEDIA?

Exploratory Learning

Hypermedia enables educators to simulate the way human beings naturally learn new things. Most learners do not proceed in a linear manner through a body of knowledge. Rather, they become interested in a topic, pursue various aspects of the topic that interest them, make connections among concepts, and gradually become knowledgeable in a particular area. For example, the student who has gained expertise in art history probably began with an interest in a particular artist. This

interest may have been stimulated by a visit to an art museum or by reading an art history book or through a magazine article or television show. When the student sought more information about this artist, the student discovered additional artists with similar styles and then perhaps other artists with different styles. Information was probably gathered from a large variety of sources possibly including books, conversations, art museums, television specials, and magazines. Through a process of self-initiated investigation and discovery, the student gradually accumulated a large body of interrelated knowledge in the area of art history. Note, however, that this knowledge is usually not acquired by reading a textbook from cover to cover, but by gathering and interpreting related pieces of information.

A similar description of the learning process could be created for a young learner who has become an expert in a particular sport. An interest in baseball may be started through watching a game on television, listening to an adult conversation, talking with peers, or watching a movie. The young learner acquires information through television, newspapers, magazines, conversations, and other data sources. The path the information collection follows will be different for different learners. One learner may begin with a focus on an individual player; a second learner may begin by collecting data about a particular team; and a third learner may begin with an interest in understanding baseball statistics. In each case, the learner collects and assimilates information and develops a steadily expanding area of expertise. In both the art history and baseball examples, the learner is free to explore a variety of sources to collect information and can choose the aspect of the topic and the source of information she wishes to explore.

Simulating the type of informal learning described in these examples has been a difficult challenge for educators. Typically, students in classrooms have not enjoyed the opportunity to pursue a topic in their own ways. Although structured opportunities to do this type of learning might help students develop vital skills for lifelong learning, schools and teachers have not had the resources to provide students frequent experiences with independent learning.

Hypermedia applications may enable the type of individualized, student-initiated learning described here. With an appropriate hypermedia program or tool, students might be able to use different intelligences (see Thornberg's, 1992, quote at the beginning of the chapter) to pursue and integrate knowledge. A hypermedia program on birds, for example, might let stu-

---

Notes From the Literature

Major publishing houses are forging ahead with multimedia CD-ROMs that will accompany textbooks. Materials to be provided include animations, demonstrations, simulations, and video footage, as well as material that can be converted into overhead transparencies. Publishers are trying to tap the full visualization power of the technology rather than turn out CD-ROM "page turners"—conventional textbooks simply written on a CD-ROM.

Illman, D. L. (1994, May). Multimedia tools gain favor for chemistry presentations. Chemical & Engineering News, 34–40.

dents access video, graphics, text, and audio information on various aspects of this topic. If the students' investigations into flight caused an interest in a different topic about birds, the students could then pursue this topic. Some students could pursue one topic in depth, while others may prefer to study several related topics on birds.

Student Projects

In addition to participating in exploratory learning environments designed by others, students can use hypermedia capabilities as a communication tool. Similar to the word processor or the data base manager, a hypermedia system enables students to organize and communicate information in innovative and efficient ways.

Through constructing their own hypermedia projects, students can learn to choose appropriate information, choose the media that best communicates the information, organize the information so that learners can explore it in their own ways, and learn to locate various forms of information stored through various types of media. Thus, student work with hypermedia can help students gain valuable Information Age skills.

Cautions

Although the advent of hypermedia applications offers exciting potential for learners and teachers, numerous educators have suggested that the most appropriate and productive uses of hypermedia in classrooms have yet to be defined. A former executive for Apple Computer has called hypermedia "a solution waiting for a problem."

One fear is that hypermedia capabilities may be used as simply another way to deliver material using traditional teaching methods. A hypermedia system is not inherently interactive and could be constructed to deliver information to students in much the same way it is currently delivered through textbooks, films, and lectures. Students would not be encouraged to construct their own knowledge or explore information in their own ways, and would enjoy only limited interactivity with the program.

A second caution is related to early use of BASIC programming in the early 1980s. Many have suggested that hypermedia capabilities will enable teachers to construct their own lessons and applications. Usually, this type of curriculum development is extremely time-consuming and might take teachers away from activities more immediately useful to their students. Previous attempts at making teachers software authors (BASIC, Apple Super-Pilot) have not been successful, because teachers discovered that creating quality software was an extremely challenging and time-consuming activity. In general, most of the high-quality software currently used in classrooms was created by professional publishers, not by classroom teachers. It is very possible that teachers will find hypermedia authoring takes too much time and that professional publishers should again assume the responsibility for authoring software. It also seems possible that hypermedia tool kits for teachers will be increasingly available and that these tool kits will markedly simplify the authoring process.

A third caution for possible educational hypermedia applications involves the relatively costly and somewhat complex hardware necessary to run such systems. Video-disk and CD-ROM (compact disk read-only memory) players are not yet routine pieces of equipment in classrooms. In addition, setting up and connecting a hypermedia system can be a relatively challenging task; many teachers have neither the interest nor the knowledge to set up and maintain these systems as they currently exist.

Assessment of student learning will also create a challenge for teachers using hypermedia applications with students. Instead of all students learning the same thing, students using hypermedia environments will be learning different things. Thus, the old model of assessing student progress with one common test will no longer work. One

---

Notes From the Literature

In an experiment dealing with animation and accompanying narration, one group of students watched an animation of the operation of a bicycle pump or automobile braking system then listened to a narration of that operation. Another group of students listened to the narration as they watched the animation. A third group of students only watched the animation, and still another group only heard the narration. On a test of problem solving, the concurrent animation-narration group outperformed all other groups, which did not differ from one another. "An instructional implication is that pictures and words are most effective when they occur contiguously in time or space."

Mayer, R. E., & Anderson, R. B. (1992). The instructive animation: Helping students build connections between words and pictures in multimedia learning. Journal of Educational Psychology, 84(4), 444–452.

Notes From the Literature

The authors summarize research concerning the use of animation and other visuals in multimedia instruction. They offer 10 recommendations based on this review and their own research:

1. Analyze relevance of graphics/animation to learning and use only appropriate ones.
2. Opt for simpler graphics in animations.
3. Examine graphics/animations for:
   a. perspective
   b. ability to convey the information in a single viewing or allow for multiple viewings
   c. clarity of representation
   d. desirability of showing from multiple perspectives
   e. ability of the learner to interact with the graphic/animation
4. Use input from graphics specialists.
5. Test prototypes of the lesson with target audience.
6. Test prototypes on different machines.
7. Complex animations may not be the best for beginning learners.
8. Interactive graphics may be the best use of visuals.
9. Engage learners by having them create and use mental imagery during instruction.
10. Use the same graphics/animations in testing situations as were used in lessons.

Poohkay, B., & Szabo, M. (1995). Effects of animation and visuals on learning high school mathematics. In M. Simonson & M. Anderson (Eds.). Proceedings of Selected Research and Development Presentations at the Annual Convention of the Association for Educational Communications and Technology, Anaheim, CA.

possible solution is to have students create hypermedia projects that demonstrate and communicate what they have learned about a particular topic.

It has also been suggested that students will need to learn some basic skills and approaches to effectively use hypermedia systems. That is, teachers may need to teach a type of hypermedia literacy to students. Students who are accustomed to studying material in a linear manner will probably need some structured help to begin to handle the open-ended nature of a hypermedia environment. In fact, studies have demonstrated that initial student use of a hypermedia system may be rather chaotic and unfocused. One unknown computer user described it as "students lost in hyperspace."

These cautions are not meant to suggest that use of hypermedia is inappropriate in schools, but rather that educators need to ensure that hypermedia is put to its most appropriate use in classrooms. The following sections suggest some uses.

HYPERMEDIA APPLICATIONS FOR TEACHERS

Hypermedia tools offer teachers an opportunity to create learning environments for students. Because the software used with hypermedia makes writing programs relatively simple, the technology allows teachers to create their own hypermedia documents. Using hypermedia, teachers will be able to adapt instructional materials to individual students' learning styles (Marchionini, 1988). Hypermedia offers teachers the opportunity to quickly and efficiently create their own hyperdocuments and thus may be the first practical authoring tool for teachers. Measuring the effectiveness of these teacher-made hyperdocuments will offer interesting information to researchers.

Hypermedia offers the potential of altering the roles of teachers and learners and the interactions between them. The nature of hypermedia environments, based on the principles of cognitive theory, grants more control to the learner and encourages the teacher to become a facilitator rather than a deliverer of information. As students work through hyperdocuments, the teacher's role becomes that of guide. The teacher may provide strategies for interacting with the environment and direction in terms of goals for the experience, but the student is given primary responsibility for learning and discovering the material.

Hypermedia programs such as HyperCard and LinkWay are valuable, flexible computer tools for teachers. Computer education journals present dozens of descriptions of teacher-initiated hypermedia projects. Teachers are creating hypermedia environments for presentations, assessments, simulations, record keeping, accessing data bases, problem solving, hard disk management, and numerous other purposes.

The ease of authoring of hypermedia documents makes hypermedia a valuable tool for students as well as teachers. Given the tools for work with hypermedia, students can create their own hyperdocuments. Student term projects might involve creating a hyperdocument on a period in history or on a poem or novel they have read. Observing and measuring outcomes from such student work offer yet another promising research direction.

Finally, hypermedia environments provide researchers a valuable window through which to observe student learning and learning styles. If hyperdocuments are constructed so that students "leave a track," researchers can gather information on how individual students explored an environment. Given the interest of cognitive psychologists in examining learning processes, the window into these processes provided by the tracks left by a student exploring a hyperdocument will be a valuable tool. This information will be useful to hyperdocument designers and to researchers interested in understanding and defining different learning styles.

Educators and researchers seem to agree that hypermedia provides new and interesting possibilities for the teaching–learning process. The extent of the ability of hypermedia to influence student learning has yet to be determined, however. Levels of learner control, need for organizers and cognitive maps, information on how students use these environments, and the use of hypermedia environments in altering roles of teachers and students are all areas in need of research.

TEACHING ABOUT HYPERMEDIA

Two widely used hypermedia programs that illustrate features of hypermedia are Apple's HyperCard and IBM's LinkWay. A brief introduction into specific features of each of these systems follows. These are certainly not the only hypermedia tools available to teachers and students, but they provide good examples of the structure of such programs. A third program, HyperStudio, is gaining popularity in schools because of its simplicity. Students or teachers who have worked with HyperCard should be able to switch to using HyperStudio with little instruction.

HyperCard on the Macintosh

To better understand the capabilities and limitations of authoring programs, educators need to do some initial work and experimentation with these programs and see some sample programs written in an authoring language. HyperCard is currently only available for use on Macintosh computers, but it appears that the approach of the language may be available soon for other types of computers. Because many readers may not have the

hardware necessary to run the HyperCard program, this section provides a general view of authoring with HyperCard, without requiring hands-on experience.

WHAT IS HYPERCARD?

HyperCard creator Bill Atkinson says the system is an authoring tool and an information organizer. He states, "You can use it to create stacks of information to share with other people or to read stacks of information made by other people. So it's both an authoring tool and sort of a cassette player for information" (Goodman, 1987, p. xxi). Others suggest that HyperCard is a hypermedia tool kit, designed to allow users to create environments where video, audio, and computer information can be organized and used easily.

HyperTalk is the programming language that is a part of the HyperCard system. HyperTalk allows users to create their own HyperCard stacks; however, the system is designed so that users can create their own stacks with little or no knowledge of the language. The HyperTalk language is modular in structure and encourages users to modify already written programs (or scripts) to meet their needs. Thus, users who wish to use HyperCard to control interaction with a video disk can use programs already written and merely replace the addresses of various locations on the video disk with the ones that users wish to use.

A typical HyperCard stack allows users to explore the information in the stack in their own ways. For example, a HyperCard stack exists for use with a video disk containing pictures from the National Gallery of Art. Using the HyperCard stack, students can explore the pictures on the disk in a variety of ways. They can search for and rapidly locate all the paintings by a particular artist or search for and rapidly locate all the paintings that have a horse in them, or indicate that

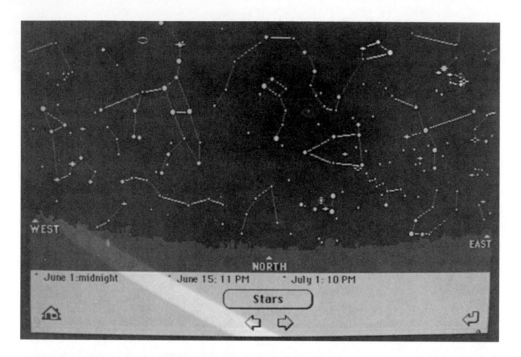

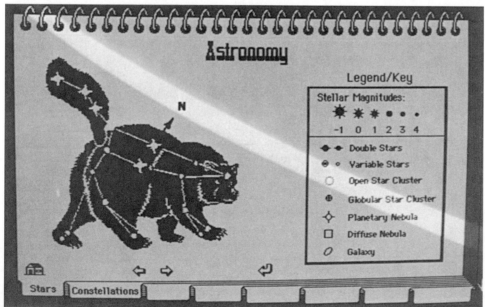

FIGURE 14-2
Cards From Constellations Stack.

they want more information about a particular aspect of a painting. Students using a HyperCard driver program with the National Gallery video disk can explore the gallery as if they were browsing the gallery in person. They can look at all the paintings by a particular artist, or all the paintings in a particular period, or all the paintings with flowers in them. The HyperCard stack makes all the information on the video disk easily accessible to the student using the stack.

A second example of a HyperCard stack was developed by graduate students at Iowa State University to allow students to freely explore and obtain information about the constellations (Figure 14–2). Given a picture of a particular part of the sky at a particular time of year, students can indicate which constellation they wish to examine and obtain more graphics and information about that constellation. Students can also choose to examine a different part of the sky or a different time of year. In one sense, the constellation stack is a large data base that contains both graphic and text information about the constellations. Unlike a traditional data base manager, however, the HyperCard system allows students to explore the information in almost any way they desire.

Another HyperCard stack allows students to locate commonly used Chinese words (Figure 14–3). Students can find the Chinese characters for the word and also press a button to hear the word pronounced.

Typically, the information to be explored using HyperCard includes some combination of text, graphics, audio, and video information. In many cases, this information is a large and varied data base that students can explore and use in a variety of ways.

HyperCard and HyperTalk address some of the problems of authoring languages mentioned earlier in this chapter. The system is designed so that learners with little previous programming experience can create sophisticated educational stacks quite easily. Because authors are free to "borrow" pieces of existing programs or scripts, much of the time for programming a new application is reduced. In fact, many of the current books and articles written about HyperCard contain scripts that users are encouraged to use.

Because HyperCard facilitates the free connection of idea applications, the system also encourages the creation of exploratory, learner-centered educational programs, rather than the drill-and-practice programs encouraged by the structure of many authoring languages.

There also have been strong efforts to coordinate and share the teacher-created products produced with HyperCard. Apple Computer makes available disks of sample programs created by educators. The first of

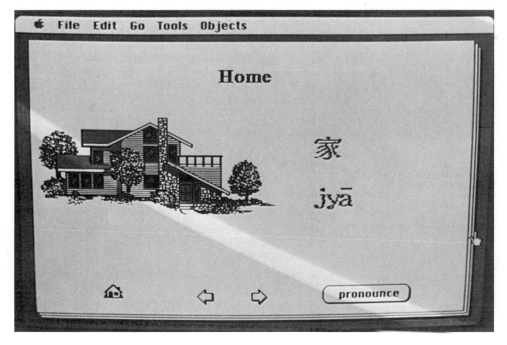

FIGURE 14–3
Card from Chinese Stack.

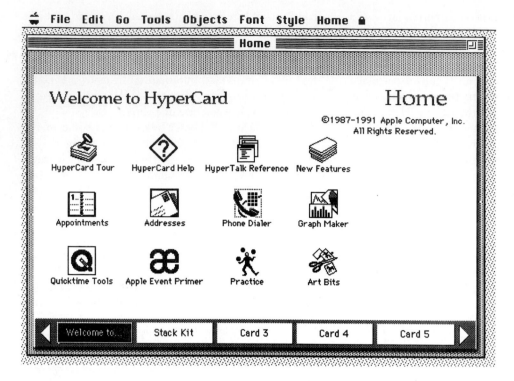

FIGURE 14–4
HyperCard's Home Card is an entry point for using HyperCard.

these disks is titled, "HyperCard: The First Year," and contains programs such as writing and photography. Currently, teacher-created HyperCard stacks are also shared through large central systems such as CompuServe, and teachers can easily access the stacks created by others. There are also publishing houses (Kinko's is one example) that sell educator-created HyperCard stacks at reasonable rates.

GETTING STARTED WITH HYPERCARD

There are five major elements in the HyperCard environment:

1. Stacks
2. Backgrounds
3. Cards
4. Fields
5. Buttons

The stack is much like a recipe box; the background is a constant background found on each card

in the box; fields are sections for particular information on a card. Buttons, as will soon be obvious, have no logical partner in the recipe box analogy, and buttons are the feature that give the HyperCard system its unique power.

Stacks

A stack in HyperCard is like a file in other computer systems; a stack is usually opened by clicking the mouse on a picture (or icon) that symbolizes a stack. The stack is a collection of cards, and usually the cards contain information about a particular subject. A stack might be a collection of information about birds, a driver program to control interaction with a video disk, or an address book. Generally, learner-oriented stacks are a collection of information that students can access and manipulate in a variety of ways.

HyperCard supports two basic types of stacks. Homogeneous stacks have one stack background that appears on every card in the stack. The Chinese dictionary mentioned previously is a homogeneous stack because each card in the stack has the same background.

Heterogeneous stacks combine multiple backgrounds in one stack. The constellations stack mentioned earlier is a heterogeneous stack, because several different backgrounds are used in the stack. These backgrounds vary, some emphasizing textual entries and some emphasizing graphics. Even a heterogeneous stack, however, usually has an underlying theme or reason for grouping the information in the stack. A stack can have as many backgrounds as the author wishes, depending on the purpose of the stack.

The HyperCard system is set up so that users can browse stacks in the system or create their own stacks. A typical user begins work with HyperCard by browsing around existing stacks and learning HyperCard navigation techniques during this process. The HyperCard system includes a Home Card (Figure 14–4) that is a collection of stacks for beginners to browse through and use. These stacks include an introduction stack, an address stack, a slide show stack, and a "To Do" list stack.

The Home Card also contains a stack called Stack Ideas, which contains cards to help users start their own stacks. After new users have browsed several sample stacks, it is time for them to begin to customize these stacks or create their own stacks starting from Stack Ideas. After modifying and adapting existing stacks, most users begin to create entirely new stacks.

It is simple for new users to create a stack of their own using HyperCard (Figures 14–5a and 14–5b). Typically, beginners start by choosing an existing template that is similar to the stack they want to create. Thus, they open the HyperCard stack titled Stack Ideas and choose the card that will be the basis of a new stack (Figure 14–6).

As an example, new users can choose the stack titled To Do List and then choose New Stack from the pull-down file menu. Users can then choose to copy the background on the stack and type in a name for the new stack. At this point, users make any desired modifications in the stack background. They can add text or graphics to the background, and HyperCard automatically saves any changes made in the new stack. After the To Do list background has been designed, new cards can be obtained by simply choosing New Card from the menu.

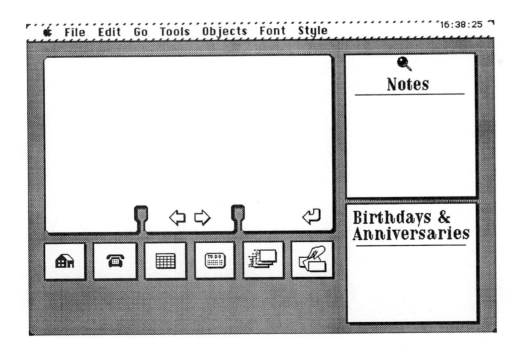

FIGURE 14–5A
Background in a HyperCard address stack. Note that the background will remain the same, but different cards will have different specific information (as shown in Figure 14–5b).

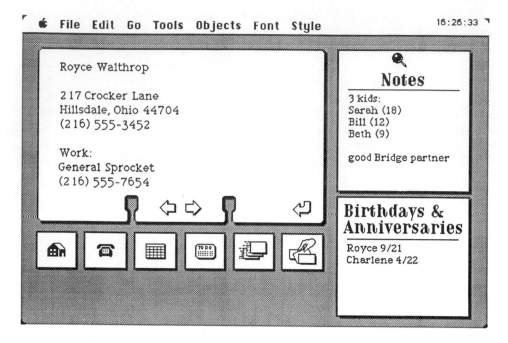

FIGURE 14–5B
HyperCard Address Card with Information Entered.

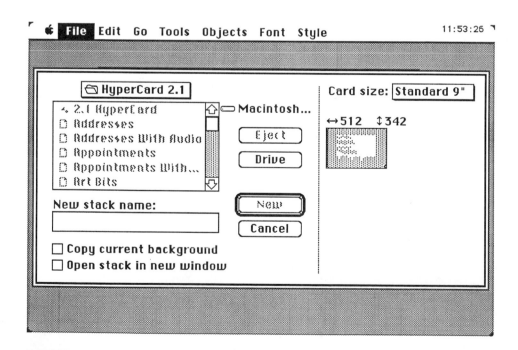

FIGURE 14–6
When users indicate they want to make a new stack, a card appears asking for the stack name.

Backgrounds

Stacks can have one or more backgrounds; these backgrounds usually appear on multiple cards and give a constancy to the way information is handled and displayed on the cards. The background is the part of a card that remains constant from card to card. Thus in the To Do example, the background has a graphic on it, a title, and a place for the user to enter a list of things to do. An address stack might have just one background that contains labels for inserting names, phone numbers, street addresses, and other information (see Figure 14–5b). The background might also include a graphic, if desired. A stack may contain just one background, or it may contain multiple backgrounds. The HyperCard program has a stack that is a collection of possible backgrounds for user-created stacks. As in the To Do example, most users will use at least part of these backgrounds in their first attempt to create stacks of their own.

Cards

In one sense, the card is the basic unit of the HyperCard system. Generally, all information is entered on a particular card, and a collection of cards composes a stack. If the stack is a collection of information about birds, an individual card might contain the information about one of the birds described. If the stack is a collection of addresses, an individual card might contain the information about one person on the address file. In the To Do example, each card might be a To Do list for a particular day. In an address stack, an individual card might contain information about one person or family.

The cards or a group of cards in a single stack usually have a common look. This look might include a common graphic and common areas where information is entered. Each card in the stack may have its own graphics and information as well as the information shared with other cards. As mentioned earlier, the information shared with other cards is called the background for the card.

To modify and create cards, users will use a tools menu (Figure 14–7). This menu allows the user to select tools that are useful in working on cards.

Fields

Fields are the areas on cards where the information is recorded. In the stack on birds, a field on a card might contain information about where the bird is found or how large the bird is. Usually, a card will contain several fields. Text fields in HyperCard are primarily of the fill-in-the-blank variety. Text that remains constant in all cards in a stack is included in the background for the stack; text that varies in different cards usually appears in fields. Thus, the label on a field might appear in the card background, whereas the specific entry for the field appears on only one card. In the address stack, the label address is in a background and individual addresses are entered on each card (Figure 14–8).

Buttons

Up to this point, readers might think the description of the HyperCard system sounds much like a traditional data base system, with capabilities for video and audio interaction thrown in. But it is the HyperCard button

---

 File Edit Go Tools Objects Font Style   12:11:17

FIGURE 14–7
HyperCard Tools Menu.

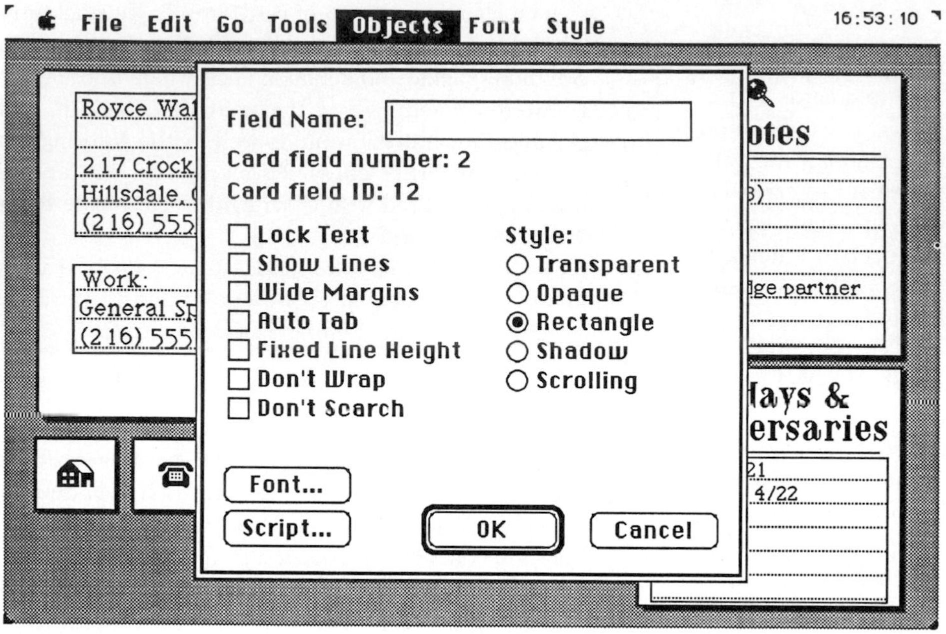

FIGURE 14–8
The HyperCard field tool enables the creation of new fields.

that distinguishes the system from existing data base systems (Figure 14–9).

Buttons on the cards allow the user to immediately access another card in the stack or a card in a different stack or perform other actions. In Figure 14–10, buttons for obtaining information on area codes, help, and access to the home card are pictured. For example, in the bird stack mentioned earlier, the user can select a button to hear the call of the bird. When this button is selected, HyperCard goes to the card that contains the directions for playing the call of the bird and executes these directions. From the users' point of view, however, all that happens is that they hear the call of the bird. In the Chinese dictionary example, the user can select a button on the card that plays the Chinese pronunciation of the word. In the National Gallery of Art example, the user can select a button to find out more about the artist of a particular painting. In the "To Do" list example, the user might want to include a button that would immediately go to the "To Do" list for the next day or the previous day. When the button is selected, the system goes to a card that contains this information. The information might be textual or audio, depending on the stack.

The button in HyperCard gives users immediate access to numerous avenues of exploration about a particular subject. Carefully constructed buttons give the

HyperCard stack its power as a user-controlled environment in which users have maximum opportunity to explore the stack freely.

Creating and programming buttons in HyperCard is a simple procedure. The stack author simply selects the button tool and the option to create a new button. The new button appears on the card, and the author can move it, select a different appearance for it, and enter the directions that accompany the button. The easiest directions to enter are to simply link the button to another card; this can be accomplished with one command in the system. Thus, if I create a button to hear the bird's call in my bird stack, I can link it to the call card with one command.

The script for a HyperCard button is easy to write and interpret. It is written in HyperTalk, which is the programming language for HyperCard, and is usually quite direct. If users want to write directions for a button that will take them to the next card in the stack, the script will read:

ON MOUSEUP
　_GO TO NEXT CARD
END MOUSEUP

Similarly, the following script will take users to the first card in a stack:

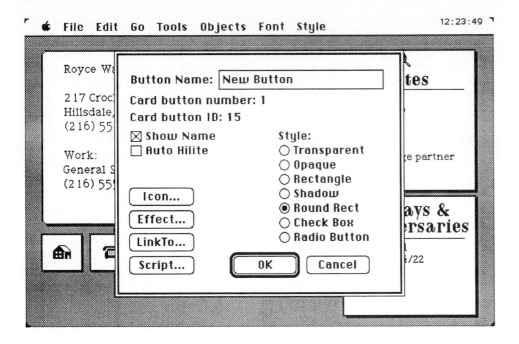

FIGURE 14–9
The HyperCard button tool enables the creation of new fields.

ON MOUSEUP
GO TO FIRST CARD
END MOUSEUP

Authors can refer to specific cards by the name of the card, an identification number for the card, or the order of the card in the stack.

HyperTalk

The HyperCard system uses a friendly, direct language: HyperTalk. For HyperCard users in English-speaking countries, the HyperTalk vocabulary is all English, with full English words. Commands are complete English sentences. If you'd tell a friend, "Go next door," then

FIGURE 14–10
View of HyperCard Buttons.

you can tell HyperCard, "Go to the next card" (Goodman, 1987, p. 345).

In the following example, the user wants the data entered in each new card created in the To Do list stack. Assuming that the user had created a field for date, the script to accomplish this task looks like this:

ON NEWCARD
__PUT THE DATE INTO FIELD "DATE"
END NEWCARD

Because "the date" is a value built into the system, HyperCard always knows what the date is and simply inserts it into the correct field on command.

HyperCard and Educator Authoring

HyperCard is used by numerous educators to design and produce stacks for their students. HyperCard offers the potential for educators to create quality, discovery-oriented learning environments relatively easily. Because HyperCard enables the easy interface of audio and video equipment with the computer, the educator/author can also easily create multimedia learning environments for learners.

One of the major impediments to the widespread use of HyperCard is that the system currently is available only for the Macintosh computer, and many classroom teachers do not have this hardware readily available to them. As the hardware becomes more widely available or if HyperCard-like systems are written for types of computers currently available to teachers, it seems likely that it will be the most practical authoring language for educators.

HyperStudio for Classrooms

Similar to HyperCard in format and structure, Hyper-Studio is extremely easy to use and has been adopted in many classrooms for student project work. Available for both Macintosh and IBM Windows environments, HyperStudio is designed to encourage student project use of hypermedia. Using HyperStudio, students are able to produce hypermedia projects that incorporate sound, graphics, video, scanned pictures and several additional features. Easy enough for second graders to use, HyperStudio has become a valuable tool for teachers wanting to make interactive multimedia projects a possibility for their students.

One fourth-grade teacher uses HyperStudio as a tool for student reports on themselves and their families. Using the capabilities of HyperStudio, students are able to put together reports that include pictures of themselves, narrations in their own voices, and videos of themselves and their families. Students organize the projects in individual ways, creating buttons to let the viewer find more information on everything from their pets to the books they like to read.

Hypermedia With LinkWay

The software system for MS-DOS and OS/2 computers comparable to Apple's HyperCard is IBM's LinkWay. Version 1.0 of LinkWay was introduced in 1989, and the most recent version, LinkWay Live!, was made available in 1992 and replaced version 2.01 (Figure 14–11). LinkWay is a true hypermedia system, although IBM prefers to call it a multimedia package. What is possible with HyperCard is also possible with LinkWay, but LinkWay has characteristics that Hyper-Card does not make as accessible to the user.

LinkWay permits the creation of complex lessons that are nonlinear, nonsequential, user controlled, and highly visual. A variety of external devices can be controlled by LinkWay lessons, including laser disk, compact disks, digital–video interactive (DVI) systems, and videotape players. The real strength of LinkWay is its ease of use. It is intuitive and straightforward. The most difficult aspect of LinkWay is its interface with DOS (disk operating system).

Notes From the Literature

A hyper-reference is an on-line electronic aid that provides immediate access to adjunct information with a direct return path to the target information. Eighty foreign language learners participated in a comparison of hyper-reference and conventional paper dictionary use. Hyper-reference users consulted over two times as many definitions as conventional dictionary users. Analyses of efficiency (consults per minute) found a higher consultation rate for hyper-reference users than for conventional dictionary users.

Bilingual (Spanish/English) dictionary users consulted 25% more definitions than did monolingual dictionary users. Bilingual dictionary users completed reading in 20% less time than monolingual dictionary users. Differences in comprehension were, however, not significant.

Aust, R., Kelley, M. J., & Roby, W. (1993) The use of hyper-reference and conventional dictionaries. Educational Research Technology and Development, 41(4), 63–73.

USING LINKWAY

LinkWay Live! comes bundled with excellent documentation, including a Reference Guide, Installation and Learning Guide, and even a comic booklike manual titled *Getting a Quick Start with IBM LinkWay Live!* Possibly the easiest way to learn about LinkWay is to use the tutorial that is loaded when the program is installed. The tutorial gives step-by-step instructions about how to use LinkWay.

System Requirements

LinkWay uses 300 KB (kilobytes) to 640 KB of conventional memory and about 800 KB of additional memory (extended memory, expanded memory, or virtual RAM). A mouse is required, and the software supports any of the current display monitors used with IBM-compatible computers (CGA, EGA, MCGA, VGA, and XGA). LinkWay Live! works in a DOS rather than Windows environment and requires at least DOS 4.0. One major advantage of LinkWay is its ability to control almost any peripheral device that can be attached to a computer. LinkWay also can be enhanced by adding firmware cards to the computer and software commands to the lesson.

Lesson Components

LinkWay lessons are built on *pages* that are collected into *folders* (Figure 14–12). This is similar to HyperCard's use of cards collected into stacks. There are two kinds of pages: the base page and all other pages. Every folder has one base page and zero or more other pages. Pages have five categories of objects used to create lessons:

1. *Fields* are used for textual information.
2. *Pictures* are objects that display graphics such as drawings.
3. *Buttons* cause actions to occur when they are clicked on by the mouse. Common button actions include moving to a new page, showing pop-up text, or moving to a different folder.
4. *Lists* present a body of text from which a selection is made.
5. *Media* control audio, video, or animation.

It is also possible to write background script commands to control actions in a LinkWay lesson. Advanced authors can write directions that automatically exit LinkWay and use other components of DOS and then return without the user noticing.

When a new lesson is created, the author first selects the graphics mode (such as EGA or VGA) that

FIGURE 14–11
LinkWay Live! is the most recent version of IBM's sophisticated hypermedia authoring system. Included with the software is a comic-book-like instruction manual.

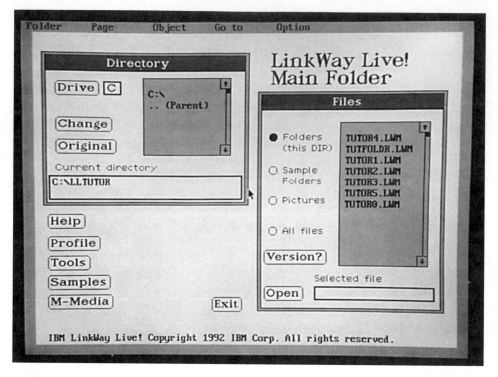

FIGURE 14–12
The main folder from IBM's hypermedia authoring system, LinkWay Live!

will be used. VGA is becoming a standard for IBM-compatible computers. The advantage of creating lessons in the VGA mode is high resolution. The disadvantage is that VGA lessons cannot be used on systems that do not have VGA capability. Many educators create lessons in MCGA (the LinkWay default mode), which is fairly high quality but compatible with almost all hardware systems in widespread use.

The second step in lesson development is to open a new folder. When a new folder is started, a base page is created immediately. The base page is one of the powerful characteristics of LinkWay. It is a background page that shows up behind the information on all other pages in a folder. It is also the first page accessed when a folder is opened, unless a command on the base page or within a linking button from another folder accesses a different page within the folder. The base page permits the author of the lesson to provide access to fields, pictures, or buttons that are needed on all of the pages in the folder. Often, page-turning buttons, menu buttons, and background graphics are placed on the base page.

Next, additional folder pages are created. These pages contain the various components of the lesson, including text, pictures, and buttons. Obviously, the most critical aspects of any lesson are its content and

organization. Effective hypermedia lessons must be organized well. Usually, lessons are built around a metaphor, such as a book, or a tour, or a story, or an event. The lesson's metaphor gives students something familiar and concrete to relate to as they explore the new information in the lesson.

Next, high-quality hypermedia lessons have a straightforward navigation system, or way to move through the lesson. Buttons permit the easy use of the lesson and give the student control over the process of learning. The navigation system standardizes the process of movement within the lesson (Figure 14–13). HyperCard uses a Home Card as a central point where users access different sections of lessons. LinkWay uses a *Main* Folder with a main page to accomplish the same thing.

Finally, hypermedia lessons need a *cognitive map* that visualizes the structure of the lesson. For example, this textbook's cognitive map is based on its table of contents, chapters, appendixes, and index, all of which reference the book's page numbers. Because the pages of computer lessons, except for the page on the screen, are invisible to the user, it is important that students have a clear indication of where they are within the lesson. If not, the student may become confused and disoriented. Cognitive maps can be as simple as page museum that shows its floor plan with an arrow pointing to a spot that says "You are here."

LinkWay permits the simple development of these components of hypermedia lessons. As a matter of fact, the LinkWay tutorial is a model of the effective design of a hypermedia lesson.

Other Capabilities of LinkWay

Many tools are available to the user of LinkWay Live! Most notable are the built-in paint program, the text editing program, the font editor, and the image capture capabilities.

LwPaint. LinkWay Live! includes a simple yet powerful paint program called LwPaint that can be used to create new visual designs or modify existing pictures. It is also possible to produce drawings in other graphics packages and convert them to LinkWay files.

numbers (e.g., p. 33 of 120), or supplemented in small graphics that show the structure of the lesson with a blinking light indicating where the student is in the lesson. This kind of cognitive map is similar to a map in a

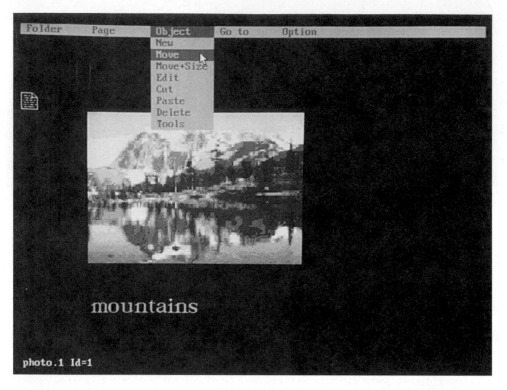

FIGURE 14–13
A page from a LinkWay Live! project, combining a button, type, and a photograph.
Words and numbers in the lower left corner of the page provide information about the
location of the page in the project.

LwEdit.   LwEdit is a word processing program that permits the creation, editing, and printing of standard ASCII text files. LwEdit can also create "hot text," which are words that function as navigational buttons when they are clicked on with the mouse.

LwFonted.   LwFonted is a font editor that permits the creation of custom icons, little pictures, and character fonts for use within a folder. Icons provided with LinkWay can be changed, or new icons can be added using LwFonted.

LwCaptur.   LwCaptur is a terminate-and-stay-resident (TSR) utility. It is used to import and convert graphic images from other programs into the appropriate LinkWay Live! display format. Almost any graphic image available for DOS computers can be incorporated into LinkWay, including scanned pictures, portions of screens from other programs, and images created by sophisticated drawing, painting and graphics packages. PC Paintbrush, a widely used DOS graphics package, stores pictures with a .PCX extension. For these files to be used in LinkWay, they must have the correct file extension for the graphics mode they were created in or be converted using LinkWay's PCX2LW utility.

Like LwPaint, LwFont, and LwEdit, LwCaptur resides in memory until it is used. To capture a graphic from another application, the user exits LinkWay and launches LwCaptur. The graphic to be captured is displayed on the screen, and the user presses the Shift+PrtSc keys. LwCaptur saves the image in the proper format for use within LinkWay.

LinkWay can be used in classrooms that are networked and is an excellent companion to HyperCard. Both multimedia–hypermedia platforms are inexpensive and permit the development by students and teachers of powerful computer-based instruction. Many school computer committees have replaced programming in BASIC with lesson development using LinkWay or HyperCard in computer courses.

TEACHING WITH LINKWAY

Because LinkWay is not only powerful but also easy to learn, many educators begin using it in the upper elementary grades. At this level students prepare visualized reports that include text, drawings, and buttons. For example, fifth-grade geography students could prepare a lesson on the countries of South America. The Main Page for the lesson might be a drawing of South America with the countries labeled. Students could be organized into work groups that develop a section of the lesson about one South American country. Each country's lesson would be a separate folder that is linked to and accessed from the lesson's Main Page.

In high school, more sophisticated lessons can be created using LinkWay. For example, in a science class students might prepare lessons about the periodic chart of the elements. When the name or symbol of an element—molybdenum, for example—is clicked on with the mouse, the learner branches to a folder dealing exclusively with this metal. In addition to giving facts, the molybdenum lesson might include scanned color pictures and access a video disk that shows science experiments using molybdenum. The development of this lesson about the periodic chart could be a project for several sections of a chemistry class.

LinkWay is also sophisticated enough to be used outside of school to solve real-world instructional problems. Recently, the U.S. Navy developed a LinkWay hypermedia lesson to help officers learn the facts about something they call the Threat Matrix. The Threat Matrix is a scheme for organizing thousands of facts about navies. Naval officers have to memorize the capabilities of ships, aircraft, submarines, weapons, and sensors for the navies of all countries of the world. Specifically, they learn how ships and weapons might be military threats (Figures 14–14 and 14–15).

LinkWay was chosen as the system for developing this lesson for the following reasons:

1. It is DOS based, and the U.S. Navy uses DOS computers almost exclusively.
2. It is inexpensive.
3. It is easy to use.
4. Lessons are easy to modify.
5. Multimedia is included in lessons.
6. Copies of lessons could be made and used without the need to purchase or install LinkWay.
7. LinkWay has a "run-time" utility that permits the use of LinkWay lessons on computers that do not have the full version of LinkWay installed.
8. It is powerful enough to meet all needs.

The Threat Matrix lesson is organized around the metaphor of a book. The book is divided into sections: one for the United States; one for the former Soviet Union, now called the Commonwealth of Independent States (CIS); and one for the countries of the rest of the world. Each section of the lesson is divided into chapters with pages that include information about the components of naval forces, and finally, like a real book, the lesson includes a table of contents, an index, and self-test questions. A standard cognitive map is placed in the upper left corner of each page, and a standard navigation system of buttons is located in the upper right corner of each page. Like most hypermedia lessons, the Threat Matrix requires active involvement by the learner and uses many visual stimuli.

LinkWay specifically, and hypermedia generally, are tools for students as much as they are for teachers. Students can design reports, projects, and presentations that are content rich and instructionally stimulating. Many believe use of hypermedia by students may be one of the most valuable ways to have students learn *with* computers instead of learning *about* them.

SUMMARY

Hypermedia is the newest technology receiving attention in the field of education. Through hypermedia environments, students can explore vast quantities of information delivered through varied media, students can explore this information in a nonlinear format using their own style.

Initial research efforts in the field have suggested that the interactivity afforded by hypermedia environments may positively influence student learning. Early research also has indicated that the various mediated approaches afforded by hyperdocuments may help to create meaningful contexts in which students can effectively learn.

SELF-TEST QUESTIONS

1. Define *hypermedia*.
2. What is a hyperdocument?
3. Cite two reasons for students to use hypermedia systems.
4. Cite two reasons for teachers to use hypermedia systems.
5. In the HyperCard system, a stack is similar to a file in other systems.
   a. True
   b. False
6. What does *nonlinear* mean with respect to hypermedia?

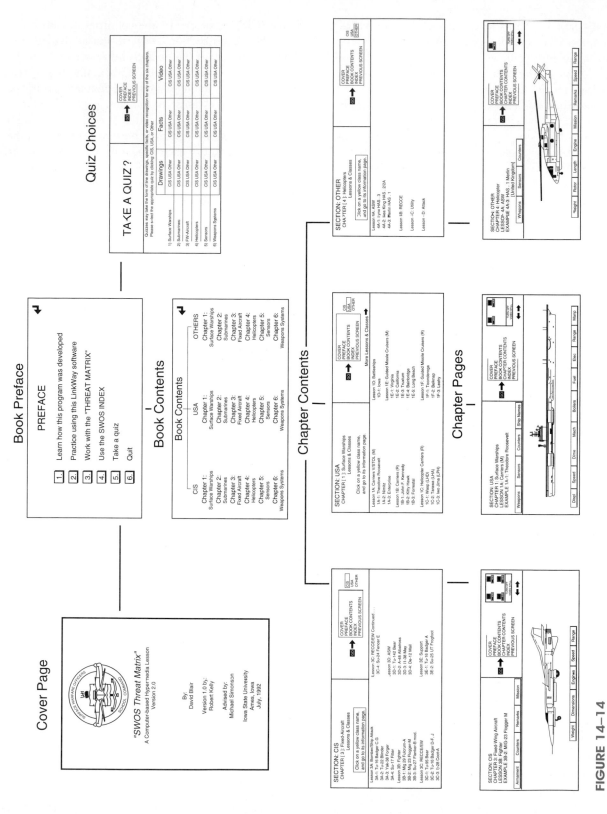

FIGURE 14–14
Sample LinkWay Live! Pages from the U.S. Navy "Threat Matrix" Lesson.

Sample Linkway Page
from the
US Navy "Threat Matrix" Lesson

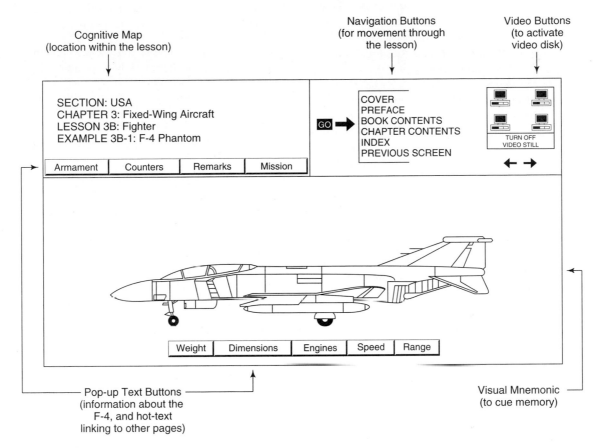

Cognitive Map
(location within the lesson)

Navigation Buttons
(for movement through
the lesson)

Video Buttons
(to activate
video disk)

SECTION: USA
CHAPTER 3: Fixed-Wing Aircraft
LESSON 3B: Fighter
EXAMPLE 3B-1: F-4 Phantom

| Armament | Counters | Remarks | Mission |

GO →

COVER
PREFACE
BOOK CONTENTS
CHAPTER CONTENTS
INDEX
PREVIOUS SCREEN

TURN OFF
VIDEO STILL

← →

| Weight | Dimensions | Engines | Speed | Range |

Pop-up Text Buttons
(information about the
F-4, and hot-text
linking to other pages)

Visual Mnemonic
(to cue memory)

FIGURE 14–15
Close-up of a Sample LinkWay Live! Page from the U.S. Navy "Threat Matrix" Lesson.

7. HyperCard has been characterized as a combination of an authoring system and a:
   a. Programming language
   b. Data base management system
   c. Spreadsheet system
   d. Video disk system
8. HyperCard facilitates the creation of which type of environments?
   a. Teacher controlled
   b. Student controlled
   c. Multimedia
   d. b and c
   e. a and c
9. Describe the function of the button in the Hyper-Card system.
10. Cards are to Stacks or _____ are to Folders.

11. Give three characteristics of LinkWay Live! that differ from HyperCard.
12. When a lesson designer prepares a standardized way for users to move through a LinkWay Live! lesson, the designer is developing the _____.

ANSWERS TO SELF-TEST QUESTIONS

1. Hypermedia combines methods of representation, such as video, graphics, animation, and text, and connects the information represented in these formats in a multitude of paths to create an environment that affords immediate, yet random, access to large amounts of information.

2. A hyperdocument is the project that is completed using a hypermedia system.

3. Hypermedia can provide a tool to help students engage in exploratory learning experiences. That is, students can use a hypermedia environment to explore a topic in their own way. Hypermedia also provides students with a useful tool for building multimedia projects and reports.

4. Teachers can use hypermedia as an authoring tool to put together learning environments for their students. Hypermedia environments also encourage teachers to move into the role of facilitator in the classroom. Teachers can also use hypermedia environments to track students' learning styles and approaches to problems.

5. a. True.

6. Students can move randomly through the lesson.

7. a.

8. b.

9. The button is the portion of the HyperCard system that provides the action for the system. Buttons appear on cards, and when buttons are selected, some action takes place. Frequently, selecting a button will move the learner to a different card.

10. Cards are to Stacks as Pages are to Folders.

11. Characteristics of LinkWay Live! not available with HyperCard are:
   a. LinkWay offers color.
   b. LinkWay comes with a built-in graphics package, icon maker, and image capture system.
   c. LinkWay lessons can be used on computers that do not have LinkWay in a Runtime version.
   d. LinkWay runs on DOS and OS/2 computers.

12. Cognitive map.

REFERENCES

Dede, C. (1987). Empowering environments, hypermedia and microworlds. *The Computing Teacher, 14*(3), 20–24.

Goodman, D. (1987). *The complete HyperCard handbook.* New York: Bantam Books.

Marchionini, G. (1988). Hypermedia and learning: Freedom and chaos. *Educational Technology, 28*(11), 8–12.

Thornberg, D. (1992). *Education, technology and paradigms of change for the 21st century.* Eugene, OR: International Society for Technology in Education.

REFERENCES FOR ADDITIONAL STUDY

Becker, H. J. (1991). When powerful tools meet conventional beliefs and institutional constraints. *The Computing Teacher, 18*(8), 6–9.

Best, A., & Mathis, J. (1994). *The 1994–95 educational software preview guide.* Eugene, OR: International Society for Technology in Education,

Butler, M. (1994). *How to use the Internet.* Eugene, OR: International Society for Technology in Education.

Flewelling, G. (1994). *Math activities using Logo Writer: High school math.* Eugene, OR: International Society for Technology in Education,

Heller, R. S. (1990). The role of hypermedia in education: A look at the research issues. *Journal of Research on Computing in Education, 22*(4), 431–439.

International Business Machines. (1992). *IBM LinkWay Live!* Atlanta: Author.

Kaehler, C. (1988). *HyperCard power: Techniques and scripts.* Reading, MA: Addison-Wesley.

Kheriaty, L., & Mei Wang, L. (1992). *Getting a quick start with IBM LinkWay Live!* Atlanta: International Business Machines.

Levin, S. P. (1991). The effects of interactive video enhanced earthquake lessons on achievement of 7th grade Earth science students. *Journal of Computer-Based Instruction, 18*(4), 125–129.

Megarry, J. (1988). Hypertext and compact discs: The challenge of multi-media learning. *British Journal of Education Technology, 19*(3), 172–183.

Morariu, J. (1988). Hypermedia in instruction and training: The power and the promise. *Educational Technology,* 17–20.

Muhlhaauser, M. (1992). Hypermedia and navigation as a basis for authoring/learning environments. *Journal of Educational Multimedia and Hypermedia, 1*(1), 51–64.

Muir, M. (1991). Building houses and learning HyperCard: An introductory lesson. *The Computing Teacher, 19*(3), 8–13.

Salem, J. (1992). HyperCard: The two-dimensional manipulative. *The Computing Teacher, 19*(6), 47–49.

Schafer, D. (1988). *HyperTalk programming: Revised edition.* Indianapolis: Hayden Press.

Smith, J. (1992–1993). Goin' wild with HyperCard. *The Computing Teacher, 20*(4), 24–27.

Sydow, D. P. (1994). *QuickTime Macintosh multimedia.* Eugene, OR: International Society for Technology in Education.

Yoder, S., & Moursund, D. (1994). *Introduction to microworlds: A Logo-based hypermedia environment.* Eugene, OR: International Society for Technology in Education.

Yoder, S. (1994). Introduction to programming in Logo using LogoWriter (3rd ed.). Eugene, OR: International Society for Technology in Education.

CHAPTER FIFTEEN

COMPUTERS IN EDUCATION

Past, Present, and Future

GOAL

The purpose of this chapter is to provide an overview of the history of the use of computers in education and projections for future uses of the technology.

OBJECTIVES

The reader will be able to do the following:

1. Cite reasons for the study of the history of computers in an education class.
2. Describe the first "real" computer, its inventor, and uses.
3. Describe the contributions of each of the following people to the development of modern-day computing: Pascal, Babbage, Leibnitz, Jacquard, Hollerith, Turing, and Atanasoff.
4. Characterize the first three generations of modern computing.
5. Describe the following "early" educational computing projects: Computer Curriculum Corporation, PLATO, SCHOLAR, MYCIN, and LOGO.
6. Describe the major contributions of each of the early projects in the preceding objective.
7. Describe current limitations of artificial intelligence applications in schools.
8. Describe major projected directions for future development of computer applications in education.
9. Define *virtual reality*.
10. Explain how computers can work as a tool in the movement to restructure schools.

If the teacher, if anyone, is to be an example of a whole person to others, he must first strive to be a whole person. Without the courage to confront one's inner as well as one's outer worlds, such wholeness is impossible to achieve. Instrumental reason alone cannot lead to it. And there precisely is a crucial difference between man and machine: Man, in order to become whole, must be forever an explorer of both his inner and his outer realities. His life is full of risks, but risks he has the courage to accept, because, like the explorer, he learns to trust his own capacities to endure, to overcome. What could it mean to speak of risk, courage, trust, endurance, and overcoming when one speaks of machines?

Weizenbaum, 1976, p. 280

The history of computers has held a rather tenuous place in a typical introductory course in educational computing. When such courses were first taught, in the early 1980s, typically more than one third of the course was devoted to a detailed study of the development of the computer. In retrospect, it seems that much of this emphasis was created by default rather than by design. With little hardware and software available, the instructor for such a course may have emphasized computer history because that was a topic that could be handled easily through lecture and textbook work.

As the availability of hardware and software increased, however, educational computing courses began to take on a new look. Emphasis was placed on using the computer as a tool; educators were taught how to teach *with* the computer, not *about* the computer. With the changing emphasis, the pendulum then swung abruptly in this opposite direction; little, if any, mention of the history of the computer was found in a typical introductory computers in education course in the mid-1980s. In fact, some educators became critical of any teaching of the history of computers, insisting that a student did not need to know about computers to use them.

WHY STUDY COMPUTERS IN EDUCATION?

Although the history of computers in education should clearly not be the main focus of an introductory course on computers in education, this information is an important part of these courses. Educators learning to teach with the computer need to know about the development of the technology and the educational uses of the technology to make informed decisions about how to best use the computer in the classroom. Knowledge of the development of the computer removes much of the mystique that novice users attach to the machine and provides a realistic view of both the capabilities and limitations of the machine.

There has been an unfortunate tendency for computer educators to act as though the computer and computer education first came into being in the late 1970s and early 1980s. The reason for this phenomenon is clear. The late 1970s marked the widespread availability of the microcomputer and thus was the first time educators could realistically begin thinking about computer uses in the classroom. In their enthusiasm for this "new" machine, many educators failed to learn from and build on the decades of work in educational computing already completed by researchers and educators using mainframe computers. This failure has caused many computer educators to "reinvent the wheel" as they made some of the same mistakes made in the 1960s and 1970s by educators using mainframe computers.

To provide a background that will enable educators to make informed decisions about hardware and software, this chapter will briefly trace both the history of the computer and the history of its use in education.

BRIEF HISTORY OF THE DEVELOPMENT OF THE COMPUTER

The history of the development of the computer can be characterized by a single underlying theme: the human desire to simplify the process of data and information manipulation and storage. The history of the development can be viewed as the progression of attempts to create devices to collect and handle increasingly complicated information. From the abacus to the supercomputers of the 1990s, continually more complex and capable devices have been created to expedite the information-handling process. Tracing the development of these devices enhances the understanding of both the structure and function of modern computers.

Early Systems

The exact beginning of the history of computers is difficult to determine. Almost as soon as human beings began to live in organized societies and cooperate with each other, the need for organized systems of handling information arose. The need for records of information such as hunting achievements, agricultural products, and population statistics necessitated systems beyond the use of the 10 digits on the hands. These early systems included markings on caves, where numbers were grouped (usually in 10s), and piles of stones, where the size of the stone might determine the place value. The groupings in these early systems marked the beginnings of later more complicated systems of place value. The systems themselves marked the beginning of information-handling techniques.

These earliest systems allowed only for storage and not for manipulation of data, however. One of the earliest devices to simplify the manipulation of data was the abacus. The abacus, still in common use in many Eastern cultures, was developed at least 5,000 years ago by the Babylonians. The abacus began as a board with grooves in it. Pebbles within the grooves were manipulated to perform simple calculations. Soon, the abacus changed form to the more portable and manipulatable bead-and-frame design still common today. Although the exact system is different on different types of abacuses, place value is denoted by the position of the beads on the frame, and skilled operators can perform rapid and accurate calculations with the abacus.

Mechanical Calculators.   The abacus is, of course, operated by the user and offers no possibility for automatic arithmetic operations. The first mechanical calculators appeared in the 17th century. The two most famous of these devices were designed by Blaise Pascal and Wilhelm von Leibnitz. Pascal's machine, called the Pascaline, was a simple, gear-driven device, which was operated by turning dials to enter the numbers for calculation. The Pascaline could perform only addition and subtraction operations, but a similar machine developed a few years later by Leibnitz could also perform multiplication and division operations. It is interesting to note that neither Pascal's nor Leibnitz's machines were reliable because of the state of the mechanical parts available at the time. This theme of creative inventors identifying concepts far beyond the practical capabilities of their times is a common

one in the history of computing. Again and again, inventors have created machines that represented conceptual advances but that were practically useless in their own time.

More practical and reliable mechanical calculators were of course developed later and were in common use until the 1970s. At that time, the first electronic calculators became available, and quickly replaced the mechanical devices.

Jacquard's Loom.   It may seem strange that the invention of a loom designed to expedite the process of weaving cloth would be included in a brief history of development of the modern computer. The work of the French inventor Joseph-Marie Jacquard in the development of the automated loom, however, marked a significant chapter in the progress toward the modern computer. Jacquard's contribution was the idea of using punched cards to record the patterns to be produced on the loom. The patterns on Jacquard's cards determined which threads were raised and lowered in the weaving process. In one sense, Jacquard produced the first machine that could be "programmed"; that is, the behavior of the machine could be controlled through the use of punched cards, just as the behavior of later computers would be controlled by punched cards.

The First "Real" Computer

Charles Babbage, a rather eccentric 19th-century mathematician, is usually credited as the "father of the computer." Babbage actually created two computerlike devices. The first was called the Difference Engine and the second, the Analytical Engine. Babbage set out to create a machine that would tabulate and print out accurate mathematical tables. During Babbage's time, the creation of these tables was a long and tedious job, and the tables often contained errors. The Difference Engine was Babbage's first attempt at a "table-creating device," but Babbage ran into practical problems in implementing his ideas. Babbage remained undaunted, however, and went on to work on a similar device, called the Analytical Engine. Babbage's Analytical Engine was steam driven and contained all the parts of a modern computer: input, central processing unit (CPU), memory, and output. Although Babbage's basic concepts for the Analytical Engine must be regarded as brilliant, the actual machine was never completed because of the state of the technology at the time. Like Pascal, Babbage had ideas that far surpassed the practical capabilities of his own era.

The 1890 Census: The Beginning of Computer Data Processing

Facing another slow and difficult compilation of census information in 1890, the Census Bureau announced a contest to identify better ways of processing data. The challenge was to create the fastest, most efficient method. Herman Hollerith won the contest with his method of using punched cards. Hollerith created electric machines that sensed patterns of punched holes in cards and carried out the proper action of each card. His work marked the beginning of large-scale computer electronic data processing. Hollerith went on to market his machines, and eventually this firm became IBM Corporation.

In 1936, mathematician A. M. Turing made a conceptual advance for computing when he thoroughly described the nature and theoretical limitations of modern computers, years before a single programmable electronic computer was built. Turing's paper "On Computable Numbers" provided a symbolic description of a computer. A Turing Machine, as his description came to be called, exists only on paper as a set of specifications, but no computer built since has surpassed these specifications (Turing, 1936). Once again, the theory of computing far surpassed the technological capabilities of the times.

Electronic Machines

Whereas Babbage's Analytical Engine was completely mechanical, the first practical automatic computing devices were electromechanical. Electricity replaced the complex and awkward mechanical arrangements of early machines. The first completely electronic computer was invented during the 1940s. There has been some argument about the person responsible for the development of this first electronic digital computer. It is now agreed, however, that the first machine in which computing, control, and memory were all electrical was developed by John V. Atanasoff of Iowa State University in the early 1940s. Atanasoff, with the help of his graduate student Clifford Berry, designed a machine to solve linear algebraic equations. Their computer, called the ABC (for Atanasoff-Berry Computer), is recognized as the first electronic digital computer (Figure 15–1).

FIGURE 15–1
The ABC computer, invented in the 1940s by John V. Atanasoff and Clifford Berry of Iowa State College, was the prototype of a modern computer.

Soon after the ABC, another electronic digital computer, the ENIAC, was developed. The ENIAC was used by the military for creating firing tables for new weapons. The ENIAC was 500 times faster than the best electromechanical computer of the times, was powered by vacuum tubes, and filled up a room 20 feet by 40 feet wide. Because Atanasoff's machine was smaller and less visible than the ENIAC, for years the ENIAC was identified as the first fully electronic digital computer. Legal action, however, determined that Atanasoff's ABC should be awarded the honor of being the first electronic digital computer.

A succession of electronic digital computers followed the ENIAC, and over the next several decades technological developments enabled the creation of smaller, more powerful, and more efficient machines. Vacuum tubes were replaced with smaller transistors, beginning in 1959. The transistor era did not last long, however. By 1964, integrated circuits began to replace transistors, and computers became smaller, faster, and more reliable.

The more recent developments in modern computing are frequently referred to in terms of generations. The first-generation computers are usually characterized as those that used vacuum tubes for calculation and control. These machines were common in the 1940s and 1950s. The use of bulky, energy-consuming vacuum tubes made the computers of this period large, expensive, and somewhat impractical.

By the late 1950s, the transistor was replacing vacuum tubes, and computers quickly became smaller and more reliable. The use of transistors in computers marked the second generation of modern computing. It was during this "generation" that higher level programming languages first appeared.

The theme of making computers smaller and more reliable was continued into the third generation. This period was marked by the use of integrated circuits in computers. Integrated circuits incorporated hundreds of transistors on a small silicon chip. By the 1970s, large-scale integrated chips became available. These chips contained tens of thousands of circuits on a single chip and made both microcomputers and embedded computers possible.

In 1977, a small computer company called Apple introduced the Apple II microcomputer (Figure 15–2). The Apple II was a compact, self-contained desktop computer and was quickly accepted in businesses, homes, and schools. In 1981, the IBM PC appeared and quickly became the best-selling personal computer. Since then, microcomputers have become steadily smaller, less expensive, and more powerful.

In one sense, the computers that are increasingly present in today's schools are very similar to Babbage's Difference Engine. They all contain capabilities to input data, process it, store it, and output results. The technology has advanced, but the machine is basically just an information-handling device that performs those four functions.

Most computer historians also characterize fourth and fifth generations of modern computing, but there is currently little agreement on the specific features of these generations. Whereas the first three generations are clearly classified by the advancing state of the technology, the later generations are usually characterized by changing functions of the machine. Artificial intelligence, attempts to program the computer to simulate human thought, is almost always included as one aspect of later generations of modern computing.

FIGURE 15–2
The Apple II series of computers popularized microcomputers in education.

A. M. Turing, the inventor of the Turing Machine, also made a significant early contribution to the area of artificial intelligence. In 1936, Turing published a major paper, called "Computing Machinery and Intelligence," asserting that computers would imitate human intelligence perfectly by the year 2000. Turing even included specific criteria for determining the "humanness" of this machine. He stated that a human would be able to question the machine and that in one case out of three the questioner would mistake the machine for a human being (Turing, 1936).

Turing's 1936 claim provided fuel for a growing number of computer scientists and cognitive psychologists interested in investigating the possibilities of artificial intelligence. It also provided fuel for critics who found the idea of a "thinking machine" unrealistic, impractical, and sometimes, repulsive. One of the most well-known critics of the concept of computer intelligence is Joseph Weizenbaum, professor of computer science at Massachusetts Institute of Technology (MIT). Weizenbaum warns of the dangers involved in using the computer as a metaphor for the human mind:

> I have argued that the individual human being, like any other organism, is defined by the problems he confronts. The human is unique by virtue of the fact that he must necessarily confront problems that arise from his unique biological and emotional needs. The human individual is in a constant state of becoming. . . . No other organism, and certainly no computer, can be made to confront genuine human problems in human terms. (Weizenbaum, 1976, p. 223)

Although the question of whether a computer can totally simulate the problem-solving process is indeed arguable, the fact that the computer is increasing in power and capability is not. The increased sophistication of the technology has brought the processes of the computer closer to those of humans. The exact limits of the technology are yet to be determined.

HISTORY OF COMPUTERS IN EDUCATION

It has long been recognized that the computer, with its information-handling capabilities, has obvious possibilities for the educational process. Whether teachers are attempting to transmit information or help students learn to manage and organize information, the computer can provide valuable tools. The major theme of the relatively brief history of the use of the computer in education can best be characterized by educators continuing to search for the most effective applications of the technology to the learning process.

As mentioned earlier, it is important to realize that the history of the use of the computer in education dates far earlier than the advent of the microcomputer. Before its availability, at least 20 years of work on computer applications in education had been conducted. Work in educational computing in the 1960s was performed on large, mainframe computers. By the 1970s, many of the computers in education were smaller minicomputers. By the end of the 1970s, the first microcomputers became available, and fairly quickly, these machines replaced the large time-sharing machines of the previous two decades.

Early Projects

During the 1960s and 1970s, an increasing number of computers became available for educational work. This period in the history of educational computing was marked by several large, usually federally funded projects designed to investigate various educational applications of the technology. All these projects were initially developed and carried out on large, mainframe computers or minicomputers. Because few of the products of these projects are used in microcomputers today, some writers have characterized these early efforts as failures. Actually, the results of these early pilot efforts provide valuable insights for educational computing today. The Computer Curriculum Corporation at Stanford, the PLATO project at the University of Illinois, SCHOLAR, MYCIN, GUIDON, and Papert's work with LOGO at MIT are six projects that illustrate some of the diverse efforts of this period. These projects have influenced present-day educational computing. Software from some of the projects is now available for and used on microcomputers.

Computer Curriculum Corporation.

Patrick Suppes of Stanford began his project in 1963. Suppes was primarily interested in using the computer to aid in the effective teaching of mathematics. The project was based on using the computer for both tutoring and drill and practice. Suppes and his associates attempted to define each step of the process of learning mathematics and to create programs that sequentially advanced students through the carefully defined segments of the curriculum. By 1967, computer-aided instruction (CAI) programs were available for 14 strands in a curriculum developed for grades 1 to 6.

Thousands of students were involved in the testing of the programs, and research results were kept on the achievement of students working with the programs (Solomon, 1986).

The Suppes materials were tested on large numbers of students. Results from these pilot tests were then used to modify the programs. Suppes used the results obtained from students working on his programs to refine his ideas on how students naturally structure and sequence mathematics as they learn. Thus, later versions of the materials reflected what Suppes and his colleagues learned from student results provided earlier. By the 1980s, the material had been revised for use on microcomputers and redefined into 12 strands for grades 1 to 7.

Suppes's associate, Richard Atkinson, developed and studied similar materials for the teaching of reading. Among other topics, Atkinson studied the issue of computer control versus student control of these programs. In a computer-controlled program, the computer determines the sequence and difficulty of student questions, whereas in a student-controlled program, the student takes responsibility for many of these decisions. Atkinson's work indicated that computer-controlled programs were more effective than student-controlled programs.

Although Suppes's materials were developed for a large, mainframe computer, similar materials are available for and widely used with microcomputers. The products of the Suppes project are generally regarded as quality examples of computer software used for drill and practice and tutorials and are frequently used as prototypes for developers interested in publishing this type of software. The programs have been developed and tested over two decades, representing some of the most carefully developed CAI software available.

Drill-and-practice software was widely used when microcomputers first became available in schools. Unfortunately, much of the early drill and practice available for schools ignored many of the findings of Suppes and others who had spent years examining this type of educational computer application. Although there is less emphasis on drill and practice and tutorial software today, the software of this type that is being produced tends to be of much higher quality than earlier microcomputer lessons and tends to incorporate many of the principles developed by Suppes and his colleagues.

PLATO. The PLATO project is one of the best known of the early computer education efforts. PLATO (Programmed Logic for Automatic Teaching Operation) was begun in the 1960s at the University of Illinois. Initially, the goals for PLATO included creating quality educational software that would be available to schools on a widespread basis. All the PLATO materials were developed on a large, mainframe computer. Special terminals that accessed this computer were then used in the schools and at other remote sites.

Although PLATO was committed to the production of quality educational software, early development did not reflect a particular philosophy of the best use of computers in schools. PLATO material was developed by a variety of educators, and all the major categories of educational software were developed. Later emphasis of the project materials, however, tended toward discovery-oriented, simulation programs. The Fruit Fly Program, a program where students learn principles of genetics through breeding fruit flies, is frequently cited as a sample of the type of materials developed through PLATO.

The TUTOR authoring language was developed as part of the PLATO project and was widely used by PLATO authors. The language provided powerful and flexible capabilities for educational software authors. It should be noted, however, that many educators indicated that they had difficulties learning and working with the language.

Although the hundreds of software programs produced through PLATO never reached the number of students first envisioned by project directors, some of the PLATO software has served as prototype software for later developers. When the advent of the microcomputer made the concept of accessing a large, central computer less attractive to educators, PLATO materials began to be marketed for the microcomputer. Like the Suppes materials, much of the PLATO software is high-quality, carefully debugged material that reflects two decades of work in computer education.

SCHOLAR. The SCHOLAR program, developed by Carbonell, was an ambitious initial attempt to make the computer simulate the behavior of a human tutor. In SCHOLAR, the computer conducts a dialogue with the student on the geography of South America. In the dialogue, both the student and the computer are permitted to ask and answer questions.

In SCHOLAR, facts, concepts, and procedures are stored in a data structure in the form of a network. Each element of the network is related systematically to other elements in the network. The meaning of each element is determined by its relationship with other elements. This type of network is called a *semantic net-*

work. When a student asks a question, the network is searched for the topic of the question and the relationship. For example, if a student asks, "What is the climate of Brazil?" Brazil is located in the network, and then the relevant relationship "climate" is found.

Specific answers for specific questions are not stored in SCHOLAR. Instead, SCHOLAR contains an organized knowledge base and rules that allow the system to "generate knowledge" when asked a specific question. This relational system was designed to simulate the way a human tutor responds to questions.

A sample student SCHOLAR dialogue is listed in Figure 15–3. Notice that the program does contain some capability to interact with varied student responses, but clearly the program does not closely reflect the flexible dialogue possible between a human tutor and a student. Also notice that the program is a mixed initiative dialogue. That is, both participants can take the initiative and ask a question of the other.

Although limited in scope and capability, SCHOLAR was one of the first attempts to program the computer to act like an intelligent human tutor. The semantic network approach for storing and retrieving data gave the program far more flexibility than earlier tutorial programs. The SCHOLAR program marks a first attempt to deal with programming the computer to generate information and understand natural language.

MYCIN.   MYCIN is usually regarded as a pioneer effort in artificial intelligence rather than in educational computing. Increasingly, however, these two fields are merging, and the influence of the approach and techniques incorporated in MYCIN and the related program GUIDON is beginning to be felt in education. Both MYCIN and GUIDON were developed on large, powerful computers, and at this point, no microcomputers are powerful enough to accommodate this type of program. The history of the technology clearly suggests, however, that this limitation will vanish within the next few years, and some of the approaches of this type of artificial intelligence will become more readily available and practical for educators.

The MYCIN program was developed to diagnose bacterial infections in the blood and suggest appropriate treatment. The goal of the project was to produce an expert system that would diagnose as accurately as the best human expert. Knowledge is stored and used in MYCIN in the form of production rules. A production rule is an if–then statement, such as, "If you have

hay fever, then take an antihistamine." To make the diagnosis, the program questions the user to obtain the information it needs.

The GUIDON (Clancey, 1979) program uses the MYCIN expertise for teaching purposes. In GUIDON, the student engages in a tutorial dialogue about her diagnosis of a particular problem. The program compares the student approach to the diagnosis with the MYCIN approach and provides appropriate feedback to the student. In other words, the questions the student chooses to ask to obtain the necessary information are compared with those asked by MYCIN, and the final diagnoses are compared.

Through both MYCIN and GUIDON, the reasoning process of the program is made transparent to the user. That is, the user not only receives the diagnosis but also can receive information about the reasoning process used by the program. In one sense, the programs enable the user to see how the expert thinks as she makes a diagnosis.

LOGO.   The work of Seymour Papert on the development and implementation of the LOGO language is detailed in Chapter 12. His work began in the 1960s on large mainframe computers at MIT. In addition to developing an educational computer programming language, Papert and his colleagues articulated new theories on how the computer can best be used in education. Papert (1980) describes his vision of the future of computer use in education. Papert emphasizes the creation of computer environments (e.g., LOGO) where students can use the computer to think with, to manipulate information, and to test ideas. Papert's views, first published in the early 1970s, were probably a bit ahead of his time. By the 1990s, however, these views had a significant influence on software development efforts.

Clearly, each of these pioneer mainframe computer education projects created a base for later quality microcomputer software development. Suppes's work marked one of the first efforts to produce drill-and-practice software based on knowledge of student learning patterns. Some of the first simulation and discovery-oriented programs came from the PLATO project. Both SCHOLAR and MYCIN provide valuable knowledge for educators interested in developing intelligent computer tutorials and programs teaching problem-solving skills. Finally, Papert's work and theories marked the beginnings of student-controlled computer learning environments.

FIGURE 15–3
Sample Student SCHOLAR dialog.

```
Computer:
    Use one of the following:
        Sucre
        French
        Argentina
        Spanish
        to answer the question:
            What is the language of Chile?
Student:
    Spanich
Computer:
    You should have written "Spanish."
    Very Good.
    The capital in Chile is Santiago.
    Correct or incorrect?
Student:
    Correct
Computer:
    That's right.
    Approximately, what is the area of Brazil?
Student:
    2,500,000 square miles
Computer:
    Wrong.
    Please indicate if the following is correct or incorrect:
    The area of Paraguay is approximately 47,432 square miles.
Student:
    What is the area of Brazil?
Computer:
    The area of Brazil is approximately 3,600,000 square miles.
    Now answer the question you didn't answer before.
Student:
    False
Computer:
    Rephrase your statement. I can't understand it.
```

MICROCOMPUTERS IN SCHOOLS: EARLY YEARS

Although microcomputers became available in the late 1970s, they were still too expensive for schools to purchase in quantity. By the early 1980s, however, prices had dropped to the point where many schools were able to acquire several microcomputers, and some laboratories containing 10 to 20 machines began appearing in both elementary and secondary schools.

Many have characterized the early 1980s as the period of hardware acquisition for the schools. But much of this early purchasing was done without a clear picture of how the computers would be used in the classrooms. The most frequent solutions to the problem "Now we have the computers, what do we do with them?" were to teach BASIC programming and use the computer for drill-and-practice activities. Student game playing on the machines was also fairly common during this exploratory period.

As indicated in Chapter 4, there were some logical explanations for those early decisions about computer use. BASIC was immediately available on the machines and required no additional software purchase. Drill-

FIGURE 15–3
(continued)

Student:
   Incorrect
Computer:
   Very good.
   The area of Paraguay is approximately 157,000 square miles.
   The language of Brazil is French.
   Right or wrong?
Student:
   Wrong
Computer:
   You are correct.
   The language in Brazil is Portuguese.
   Is it true that the capital of Brazil is Brazilia?
Student:
   Yes.
Computer:
   That's fine.
   Approximately, what is the population of Brazil?
Student:
   60,000,000
Computer:
   Approximately true, but a more exact value is 70,000,000.
   What is Brazil?
Student:
   Tell me something about Peru.
Computer:
   Wait a minute. I'm checking my files.
   Let's proceed now.
   Peru is a country.
   It is in South America.
   The population is approximately 7,000,000 people.
   The capital is Lima.
   Now answer the question you didn't answer before.

---

and-practice software provided a means to fit the computer activities easily into the current curriculum. Games were an easy way to get students (and teachers) started on the machines and were something that students could do at the computer at any time with little help from the teacher.

It should be noted that there was tremendous pressure on schools to use the computers once they were purchased, and this pressure may have led to some inefficient uses of the machine. Much of this pressure came from parents who could see the importance of the computer in the larger society and were concerned that their children not be "left behind." Some administrators reacted to this pressure by dictating that every child in a school would be on the computer for a certain amount of time each week. Usually, this dictate did not specify how the computer would be used, just that it would be used. Some schools even dictated that all students in the school would be on the computer for a certain number of minutes each week; this type of plan typically led to herding children in and out of computer labs and having them spend the allotted time running programs that had little connection with their classroom work.

Notes From the Literature

- In 1981 there were, on average, 125 students per computer; in 1991, there were 18.
- In 1985, students used computers in school labs a little more than 3 hours a day; in 1989 it was 4 hours a day.

"These numbers give a sense of expanding technological base in schools. A closer inspection of those figures and others, however, reveals that individual students who use computers (and not all do) spend, on the average, a little more than one hour a week (or 4 percent of all instructional time) with computers."

Cuban, L. (1993). Computers meet classroom: Who wins? Teachers College Record, 95, 185–210.

By the mid-1980s, however, clear trends in computer use in the schools began to emerge. Uses of the computer that emphasized the machine as an alternative delivery device (drill and practice and tutorials) were increasingly criticized. Uses of the computer that demanded active student involvement and emphasized the teaching of thinking and problem-solving skills were emphasized. These uses included simulations and tool software.

In a sense, the field of computer education began to "settle down" by the end of the 1980s. Approaches to using computers in classrooms became less faddish and more thoughtful and theory based. Educators interested in computing began to draw more heavily on cognitive psychology and cognitive science as they sought to develop and research appropriate computer use. Solomon (1986) reflects this trend as she traces the underlying pedagogical theories that drive major uses of the computer in schools today. As one reviewer indicated, "She goes beyond chitchat about 'software packages' and she thinks through the ideas that ought to guide the educational use of computers" (Sheldon White, quoted in Solomon, 1986).

It should be noted, however, that schools and teachers have been quite slow in allowing computers and computer-related technology to change what happens in school. In a study of computer use in U.S. schools, Becker (1990) found that the majority of teachers were not making powerful use of the new technologies. The challenges for computer use for the 1990s include helping teachers integrate powerful computer use into their teaching.

It is interesting to note that in the early history of the computer in education, many teachers were concerned with the question "Will the computer replace the teacher?" As teachers became more familiar with the capabilities and limitations of the technology, however, concerns in this area dissolved. The new question that emerged is "How can the computer as a tool best expand the capabilities of the teacher?"

WHAT WILL THE FUTURE BRING?

It is impossible to predict precisely how the computer will be used in the schools in the next decade, but several directions for development and expansion are clear. These directions emphasize complex learning environments that combine computer technology with other technologies and allow students to access a variety of information from many different sources.

Discovery Learning Environments

Computer learning environments will continue the trend to use the computer to produce student-controlled, discovery environments that allow students to explore and test hypotheses in particular content areas. The environments will focus on developing higher-order thinking and problem-solving skills and will be based primarily on the work of cognitive psychologists. In the past several years, increasing emphasis has been placed on using computers in schools to teach higher-order problem-solving skills. Teachers have been encouraged to use the computer for helping children learn to organize, interpret, and use data. It is argued that these types of computer applications will help learners acquire the problem-solving skills necessary for their lives in the Information Age. Software packages

Notes From the Literature

In assessing the necessary skills students must have for the future, Pettersson claims that information literate students have learned how to learn, and they are sophisticated users of information and of information technology. Pettersson also offers a somber projection, that students who lack the skills for using modern informational resources may become the new underclass.

Pettersson, R. (1994). Learning in the information age. Educational Research Technology and Development, 42(1), 91–99.

aimed at achieving these goals have included tool soft-ware (word processors, data base managers, spread-sheets, and telecommunications packages), simula-tions, LOGO, and LOGO-type learning environments.

Interactive Video and Other Combined Technologies

In the next decade, the computer will no longer stand alone as an instructional device in the class-room. The power of the computer to support student interaction and involvement will be married with other technologies to produce multimedia student-centered learning environments. This marriage of technologies has been termed *hypermedia* and was discussed in Chapters 4 and 13.

The development and increased availability of the video disk is probably the single most important factor influencing the interface of the computer with other technology. The video disk enables the rapid access of thousands of frames of slide and video material. Before

the use of video disk technology, educators used video-tape to store video and slide pictures; with tape, the material could only be accessed sequentially, and thus access was slow. With a video disk, which typically can hold 54,000 frames of video information, material can be accessed anywhere on the disk in less than two seconds.

In the classroom of the future, a science lesson on bees might include student-controlled experiences with video, audio, still picture, graphics, and text files. The entire experience will be interactive with the student's input controlling what media is used at what particular time. If a student's response indicates that he does not understand the structure of the bee hive, he will be shown both still and video pictures of hives. If the stu-dent wishes to examine characteristics of the queen bee, he can select audio, video, slide, and text material to conduct this investigation.

Students in early elementary school will also use these multimedia capabilities to control their own learning. Children learning to read will have the oppor-tunity to work with student-controlled computerized

FIGURE 15–4
Just Grandma and Me provides a computer-controlled, multimedia reading experience for students.

books such as Grandma and Me (Figures 15–4 and 15–5). With Grandma and Me—available on CD-ROM—young readers can have books read to them, have words pronounced, choose to have the book read in different languages, and investigate themes in the book. In addition, the motivating graphics and audio in the program can make reading very enjoyable for a young user.

These multimedia experiences for students will require more sophisticated hardware configurations than are currently available in most schools and classrooms. Classrooms of the future will probably require multimedia work stations for both students and teachers. A typical station might include a computer, hard drive, video disk player, speaker, CD-ROM player, optical scanner, and modem.

Artificial Intelligence Applications

As researchers continue to investigate the capabilities of the computer to learn and adapt to different students, the possibility of using these findings to create

classroom applications is increasing. In the near future, intelligent tutors may be available for classrooms. The tutors will be able to adapt to different student responses and guide students through the learning process much as a human teacher would. In the classroom of the future, each student may have an individual computerized tutor in each subject area.

Expert systems, like the MYCIN program, which emulate the processes of experts in different subject areas may also soon be available for classrooms. Students may be able to access and attempt to emulate the process of experts in subject areas from English to science. It is expected that, like the GUIDON program, these programs will allow students to examine the problem-solving strategies of the experts emulated in the systems. These systems should provide students the chance to compare their own problem-solving strategies with those of experts in a particular field and thus make appropriate modifications in their own strategies.

Some relatively simple expert system shells are now available for use in classrooms. These shells allow students to construct their own expert systems by entering

FIGURE 15–5
With Just Grandma and Me, students can choose a variety of options including having the story read in different languages.

a knowledge base into the shell. The shells eliminate the need for complex programming to create the systems and allow the students to focus on obtaining and organizing the information needed for the knowledge base. Knox-Quinn (1988) describes how three girls in her class wrote a system to advise men and women what kind of shoes to buy. She noted that the girls included rules about foot shape and health as well as style. Another group created a system to advise people about healthful eating. She notes that through using the expert system shells to create their own systems, students must think systematically about the knowledge they are entering into the system. In one sense, the students have to teach the computer everything it needs to know to solve problems in a particular domain.

More Emphasis on Telecommunications and Networking

Networking will continue to gain more acceptance in the schools as the reasons for doing it become more evident. Currently, the emphasis is usually on sharing printers, sharing files (both application and data files), and electronic mail. As new and more powerful software is developed for networking and more educational data bases become available for student and teacher use, computer networks will begin to open up classrooms to the outside world. Students will routinely access and use national data bases on subjects they are studying; for example, students in Idaho will share science information with students in Alaska. And on a more local level, networking will help facilitate the sharing of information between and among students working together in a class or a school.

Classroom teachers will also find that the isolated nature of their profession will change as they can easily access teachers from around the country via computer networks. Teachers wishing to collect new ideas on presenting a particular topic will be able to access the ideas of teachers all around the country. Teachers with similar interests or teaching similar subjects will be able to talk to each other and share ideas. Up to this time, this type of communication has been difficult for teachers who are isolated in classrooms for the majority of the working day. With electronic networking, teachers will be able to communicate with other teachers and outside resources at times convenient for the teachers and thus broaden their sphere of communication.

Distance Education

The two-way audio and video capabilities currently available in many distance education facilities will continue to expand. Teachers and students at remote sites can now easily communicate with each other; education at a distance can emphasize interactivity and project-centered experiences in the same ways that they are emphasized at individual sites. Students in U.S. schools will routinely communicate and interact in meaningful ways with students in other countries, and distance education capabilities will provide yet another way for technology to expand the walls of the classroom.

As distance education opportunities continue to expand and computer networks grow in accessibility, it is possible that traditional expectations about students' learning may change. Students may begin to access information and opportunities from a variety of locations other than school. Some have even suggested that the need for traditional school buildings as we know them may disappear. In any case, opportunities offered by technology will undoubtedly change where students learn and how much time they spend in school buildings.

More Powerful Microcomputers

Classroom applications involving artificial intelligence will require more powerful microcomputers than those currently available in classrooms. With each passing year, microcomputers have become more powerful and relatively less expensive. This increased power enables the creation of some of the powerful learning environments described in this text. Schools will have to continue to budget to upgrade their equipment to use new and more powerful educational applications.

More Attention to Liveware

Newer approaches to using the computer in classrooms require careful attention to educating teachers to adequately use these approaches. One author has termed this problem *liveware* (Mills, 1985). In the first wave of educational use, the emphasis was on purchasing hardware at the expense of software. Schools seem to have recognized that problem and are allocating more money for software. The next challenge is allocating both time and money for proper attention to the liveware, or teachers, who are at the heart of the opportunity for using computers to expand and enhance education.

The models of the learner, learning, and the role of the teacher implicit in many of the newer classroom computer applications are foreign to many teachers. These models reflect the assumptions of cognitive psychology, but most teachers have been trained with models that reflect the assumptions of behavioral psychology. In newer computer applications, emphasis is placed on learning processes, meaningful learning, and active learner involvement with the material. In these newer computer environments, students are constructing knowledge through experience, and thus the learner is viewed as an active participant in the concept-building process. Many of the goals for these experiences focus on acquiring process skills. Neither the educational experience nor the professional preparation of most teachers has prepared them for this

change. Most teachers currently lack both the theoretical and practical tools to successfully implement and integrate these newer computer uses.

Thus, future teacher training in computer applications must include background in the underlying assumptions of these applications, as well as "how-to" experiences with the applications. This need has been reflected in the approach of this textbook, but most in-service teachers will not have had the benefit of this approach. Time and money must be devoted to helping in-service teachers acquire the background necessary to successfully implement student-centered, discovery-oriented learning environments in their classrooms.

Use of Technology for Restructuring Schools

As discussed in Chapter 1, U.S. schools in the 1990s have been increasingly involved in movements termed *restructuring* or *transforming*. The basic assumptions of the movements are centered on the need to change schools to keep pace with the demands of life in the Information Age. Advocates of restructuring suggest that schools need to change in both structure and function to better meet the needs of today's students.

As pointed out at the beginning of the text, most educators agree that students in today's schools need to acquire skills that include the following:

1. Problem solving and critical thinking.
2. Information handling (organizing, accessing, manipulating, and evaluating).

3. Global awareness.
4. Technology skills.
5. Ability to cooperate and collaborate with others.

Along with these goals come new views of teachers and students; the focus is on making students active learners and teachers facilitators of this learning. Emphasis is on helping students engage in authentic tasks and produce authentic projects (Figure 15–6).

As indicated throughout this text, computers and computer-related technology provide natural tools for pursuing new goals and approaches for education.

> Computer software tools, such as word processors and graphing programs, can help organize and structure complex tasks for students. Video and video disk technologies can provide visual examples of real-world phenomena, events, and stories that students can use for problem-finding and problem-solving activities. Computer networking and satellite communications technologies can help promote local and long-distance collaboration and communication among students and teachers and can help them become part of the larger world of scholars and scientists. . . . The production capabilities of computers and video cameras enable students to create attractive, professional-looking products of their own design, which can easily be changed or revised. In addition, the public nature of computer work in classrooms can help foster collaboration, discussion, and reflection. Other software allows

students to simulate complex scientific, economic, or historical events and phenomena, thus exploring the variables and relationships that constitute these phenomena. (Sheingold, 1991, p. 20)

This type of authentic, problem-focused work for students will also demand changing schedules, spaces, and structures in schools. A more project-oriented, technology-rich curriculum demands that students have longer periods of time to work. The traditional 50-minute period provides inadequate time for students engaged in constructing a complex hypermedia project or investigating a science simulation. The project-oriented approach also demands a variety of spaces and work areas in schools and student and teacher connections to the outside world.

Currently, many model projects and schools around the country are experimenting with using technology, combined with new structures, schedules, and spaces to promote active student learning. In Rochester, New York, middle school students are now working in team-taught grade-level clusters in a project called Discover Rochester (Sheingold, 1991).

Discover Rochester is an interdisciplinary effort designed to develop thinking and problem-solving skills. Students, working in groups, collect information about the Rochester environment from a scientific, mathematical, historical, cultural, and literary perspective. Students communicate their work through text, audio, graphics, music, and maps on Macintosh com-

FIGURE 15–6
Technology can provide students with the opportunity to engage in motivating, authentic tasks.

puters. One day each week is devoted to student project work. Student multimedia projects are displayed at the Rochester Museum and Science Center. Preliminary results from the project are encouraging. Students and teachers are enthusiastic about the project, and the quality of student work has improved. Student attendance has also improved.

Use of Portable, Laptop Computers. New possibilities for restructuring schools and using technology are available with the smaller laptop computer. If all students are furnished with their own laptops, needs for special spaces for school computer labs could disappear.

Computers could become a natural part of the school day as students take class notes on their laptops, bring them to the library, work easily at home, and never need to go to a special place to "use computers." The laptop offers the possibility of making computers accessible and transportable for all teachers and students and may mark the most common type of school computer use in the future (Figure 15–7).

Virtual Realities.   The field of virtual realities marks one of the newer trends for computer use in schools. A virtual reality is a computer-generated environment where the user is an active participant. In such a system, the user usually wears a head-mounted display system composed of optical stereo liquid crystal display (LCD) video goggles and headphones. The user participates in a three-dimensional "realistic" situation and uses a data-glove to interact with the environment. The glove may be used to point, grasp, and rearrange objects within the environment, and facilitate movement through the environment.

In newer virtual reality environments, called caves, users enter the environment without all the gear required in more traditional virtual reality environments. In the cave, the user can negotiate in the virtual reality almost unobstructed and unaided.

In a best-selling book on virtual reality, Rheingold (1991) called the first chapter "Grasping Reality Through Illusion," a title that seems to summarize much of what virtual realities are about. Rheingold emphasizes the point that the heart of the virtual reality movement is the opportunity to expand human experience.

Virtual reality environments are still too expensive and complex for typical classroom use, but the possibilities offered by these simulated experiences are intriguing. Students could explore underwater or outer-space environments and hearing sounds and feeling the pressures in these environments as they manipulate virtual tools.

As virtual reality tools improve, students and teachers will be able to both participate in these environments and create environments of their own. These experiences may provide yet another active dimension for the classroom.

FIGURE 15–7
Laptop portable computers may enable each student in school to have continuous access to a computer.
Photograph courtesy of Gateway 2000

SUMMARY

Teachers designing and using computer applications in their classrooms should possess a basic knowledge of the history of the technology and its use in education. Both areas have been marked by striving to create and use technology that will enhance and expand the human intellect. Although the extent to which the computer can perform this function remains debatable, the future of the computer in education clearly will involve continuing efforts to expand and enhance classroom experiences for learners.

This textbook begins and ends with a discussion of the uses of technology in dramatically transforming schools for the 21st century. Throughout the text, emphasis has been placed on computer and computer-related technology applications that will help schools become more learner-centered, motivating environments where students and teachers are engaged in authentic and meaningful work.

SELF-TEST QUESTIONS

1. Who is usually credited with the invention of the first "real" computer?
   a. Pascal
   b. Turing
   c. Babbage
   d. Hollerith
   e. Jacquard

2. What contribution did the invention of the auto-mated loom make to the development of the computer?
3. Characterize the three generations of modern computing.
4. Who is now credited with the invention of the first electronic, digital computer?
   a. Pascal
   b. Atanasoff
   c. Babbage
   d. Turing
   e. Hollerith
5. What were Turing's criteria for determining that a machine could fully simulate human intelligence?
6. Computers were first used for educational purposes in the late 1970s.
   a. True
   b. False
7. Summarize the intent of the work of Suppes and his colleagues at Stanford.
8. Later emphasis in the PLATO project was on dis-covery-oriented simulation programs.
   a. True
   b. False
9. How did the SCHOLAR program differ signifi-cantly from earlier tutorial programs?
10. Differentiate the goals of MYCIN and GUIDON.
11. How are projected computer applications for the classrooms of the future usually characterized?
    a. Drill-and-practice programs
    b. Tutorial programs
    c. Interactive student-controlled environments
    d. Programming experiences.
12. Which of the following is not a projected direction for future computer use in classrooms?
    a. Combining computer capabilities with other technologies
    b. Applications of artificial intelligence work
    c. Use of mainframe computers
    d. Use of telecommunications
13. Describe what is meant by virtual reality.

ANSWERS TO SELF-TEST QUESTIONS

1. c.
2. In his automated loom, Jacquard used punched cards to record the patterns to be produced on the loom. In one sense, Jacquard was using punched cards to program the loom. This concept of enter-ing data through punched cards was a significant advance for computing.
3. First-generation computers are usually character-ized by the use of vacuum tubes for calculation and control and were common in the 1940s and 1950s. Second-generation computers used tran-sistors instead of vacuum tubes; high-level pro-gramming languages first appeared during this generation. The third generation in modern computing was marked by the use of integrated circuits. Large-scale integrated circuits made possible the advent of the microcomputer in the late 1970s.
4. b.
5. Turing stated that a human being would be able to question the machine, and in one case out of three, would mistake the machine for a human being.
6. b. False.
7. Suppes studied the sequential development of stu-dent mathematics knowledge and designed pro-grams that sequentially advanced students through carefully defined segments of the curriculum. Sup-pes's programs are frequently cited as examples of carefully developed and tested drill-and-practice and tutorial programs.
8. a. True.
9. The SCHOLAR program was designed to simulate the way a human tutor works with a student. In the program, students are allowed to question the tutor as well as respond to the tutor's questions. The program was designed to be much more flexi-ble and responsive than a typical tutorial program and contains some capabilities to generate infor-mation and understand natural language.
10. MYCIN is an expert system designed to diagnose bacterial infections in the blood and suggest appropriate treatment. GUIDON adapts the MYCIN program for teaching purposes. Through GUIDON, students can compare their own diag-noses and thought processes with that of an expert system.
11. c.
12. c.
13. A virtual reality is a computer-generated environ-ment where the user can operate as an active par-ticipant. The virtual reality might be a simulated undersea environment or an experience in outer space. User control is an important part of these environments.

REFERENCES

Becker, H. J. (1990). When powerful tools meet conventional beliefs and institutional constraints. In *National survey findings on computer use by American teachers.* Report No. 49. Baltimore: Center for Research on Elementary and Middle Schools.

Clancey, W. J. (1979). Tutoring rules for guiding a case method dialogue. *International Journal of Man–Machine Studies, 11,* 25–49.

Dede, C. J. (1990). The evolution of distance learning: Technology-mediated interactive learning. *Journal of Research on Computing in Education, 22*(3), 247–264.

Knox-Quinn, C. (1988). A simple application and a powerful idea: Using expert system shells in the classroom. *The Computing Teacher, 16*(3), 12–15.

Mills, G. M. (1985). Categories of educational microcomputer programs, theories of learning and implications for future research. In *Aspects of educational technology XVIII.* Kogan.

Papert, S. (1980). *Mindstorms.* New York: Basic Books.

Rheingold, H. (1991). *Virtual reality.* New York: Touchstone.

Sheingold, K. (1991, September). Restructuring learning with technology: The potential for synergy. *Phi Delta Kappan, (73)*1, 17–27.

Solomon, C. (1986). *Computer environments for children: A reflection on theories of learning and education.* Cambridge, MA: MIT Press.

Turing, A. M. (1936). On computable numbers, with an application to the entscheidungsproblem. *Proceedings of the London Mathematics Society, 42*(2nd ser.), 230–265.

Weizenbaum, J. (1976). *Computer power and human reason.* San Francisco: W. H. Freeman.

REFERENCES FOR ADDITIONAL STUDY

Bolter, J. (1982). *Turing's man: Western culture in the computer age.* New York: Penguin Books.

Carbonell, J. R. (1970). AI in CAI: An artificial intelligence approach to computer-assisted instruction. *IEEE Transactions on Man–Machine Systems, 11,* 190–202.

Ferrington, G., & Loge, K. (1992). Virtual reality: A new learning environment. *The Computing Teacher, 19*(7), 16–19.

Goldstine, H. (1972). *The computer from Pascal to von Neumann.* Princeton, NJ: Princeton University Press.

Harris, J. (1994). *Way of the ferret: Finding educational resources on the Internet.* International Society for Technology in Education.

Metropolis, E. (1981). *A history of computers in the twentieth century.* New York: Academic Press.

Moursund, D. (1989). A computer virus. *The Computing Teacher, 16*(6), 4.

O'Shea, T., & Self, J. (1983). *Learning and teaching with computers: Artificial intelligence in education.* Brighton: Harvester Press.

Schrum, L. M., & ISTE. (1994). Special Interest Group for Telecommunications. *Directory of Educational Telecommunications Services.*

Sharp, V. F. (1994) *HyperStudio in one hour* (2nd ed.). International Society for Technology in Education.

Shortliffe, E. H. (1976). *Computer-based medical consultations: MYCIN.* New York: American Elsevier.

Stern, N. (1981). *From ENIAC to UNIVAC.* Bedford, MA: DigitalPress.

Yoder, S. (1993). *LinkWay scripting: An introduction.* International Society for Technology in Education.

COMPUTER SYSTEMS

The content of *Educational Computing Foundations* is partially based on a series of concepts that the competent computer user should possess. These concepts are listed in Appendixes A, B, C, and D in the form of objectives. This list of 64 cognitive objectives and 9 affective objectives was identified by Mary Montag-Torardi in 1985 during a national survey of instructional computing experts. In 1990, Lori Oviatt updated and refined the list of objectives. The objectives were used to develop definitions of computer literacy, and the subcategories of computer applications, computer systems, computer programming, and computer attitudes. The *Standardized Test of Computer Literacy* and the *Computer Anxiety Index* are two measures of the objectives in these four appendixes. Chapter 6 has more information about computer literacy and computer anxiety.

The term *computer system* refers to the appropriate, knowledgeable use of equipment (hardware) and programs (software) necessary for computer applications. This requires understanding and abilities in the following areas: computer functions, computer hardware, computer software, computer systems configuration, computer terminology, historical development, and the operation of computers.

GENERAL COMPUTER FUNCTIONS

1. Define the binary system and demonstrate an understanding of its functional relationship to digital computers.
2. Demonstrate an understanding of the process of data processing in a computer (the transformation of data by means of a set of predefined rules) and how computers process data by searching, sorting, deleting, updating, summarizing, and moving.
3. Demonstrate an understanding of the primary functions of a computer system (the input of information, processing of information, and output of information).
4. Demonstrate an understanding of the idea that a computer is an impersonal, literal machine (hardware) incapable of functioning without a program of instructions (software).
5. Demonstrate an understanding of analog and digital computing operations.
6. Demonstrate an understanding of the process of networking/networks (e.g., LAN, star, ring).

COMPUTER SYSTEM CONFIGURATION

7. Define and be able to use computer system terminology (e.g., *hardware, software, CPU, memory, input, output, network, bit, byte, kilobyte, megabyte, gigabyte, terabyte, K, on-line, off-line, LAN, chip, mainframe, microprocessor, DOS, binary, time share, RAM, ROM, BASIC, integrated circuit, viruses, bug, peripheral, disk, disk drive, printer, keyboard, microprocessor, program, CRT, networking, CD-ROM, hard drive, optical storage, modem, mouse, telecommunications, ASCII, laser printer, dot-matrix printer,* etc.).
8. Identify and distinguish between special purpose and general purpose computers.
9. Identify and demonstrate an understanding of the distinctions between multiuser and multitasking computers versus single-user and single-task computers (mainframe, mini, and micro).
10. Demonstrate an understanding of the concepts of networking and time-sharing computer systems.
11. Demonstrate an understanding of parallel and serial communication.

12. Demonstrate an understanding of the function of an operating system (e.g., DOS, MS-DOS versus OS/2, MAC OS versus Apple ProDOS/3.3).
13. Demonstrate a general problem-solving strategy in response to hardware and software failures (e.g., viruses, cable connections, computer environment, power source).
14. Demonstrate an understanding of the proper care and maintenance of hardware and software devices.

COMPUTER HARDWARE

15. Demonstrate an understanding of the capabilities and limitations of computer hardware.
16. Identify and demonstrate an understanding of the function of the major components of a computer system: input, output, central processing unit (control unit, arithmetic/logic unit), secondary storage, and memory.
17. Define and distinguish among the characteristics of RAM, ROM, floppy disk memory, hard disk drive memory, volatile, nonvolatile, WORM, TAPE memory, CD-ROM, and other types of memory.

COMPUTER SOFTWARE

18. Define and distinguish among different categories of computer software (e.g., system software and application software).
19. Demonstrate an understanding of the general capabilities and limitations of computer software.

HISTORICAL DEVELOPMENT

20. Understand the historical development of computers and be able to discuss the resulting societal effects of the past, present, and future.
21. Identify several early computing systems and understand the significance of each to modern computers.
22. Identify and distinguish between the stages of computer development: vacuum tubes, transistors, integrated circuits, and microprocessors.

THE OPERATION OF COMPUTERS

23. Generalize common characteristics of operating a variety of computer systems.
24. Demonstrate the ability to operate a microcomputer system (e.g., on–off sequences, loading, running, saving, copying, and printing).
25. Demonstrate an understanding for system functions such as load, run, copy, code, unlock, catalog, list, save, and delete.

REFERENCES

Maurer, M., & Simonson, M. (1984). *Computer opinion survey: Version AZ.* Ames, IA: Iowa State University Research Foundation.

Oviatt, L, Montag, M., & Simonson, M. (1992). *Standardized test of computer literacy: Version LO.* Ames, IA: Iowa State University Research Foundation.

COMPUTER APPLICATIONS

The term *computer applications* refers to the ability to responsibly evaluate, select, and implement a variety of practical computer applications to do meaningful and efficient work based on an understanding of the following:

- General types of applications
- Capabilities and limitations of applications
- Societal effect (past, present, and future)
- Evaluation and selection techniques
- Specific applications (word processing, data base management, spreadsheet–financial management, statistical analysis, graphics, and educational applications).

GENERAL APPLICATIONS

1. Identify general types of computer applications and give examples of how the applications can be used in personal or professional disciplines:
   a. Information storage and retrieval-record keeping, data base management
   b. Simulation and modeling
   c. Process–machine control—robotics
   d. Computation (numerical–statistical analysis of data)
   e. Data processing
   f. Word processing
   g. Graphics
   h. Speech synthesis
   i. Artificial intelligence

    j. Computer-assisted instruction
    k. Computer-managed instruction
    l. Problem solving
    m. Networking
    n. Market research
    o. On-line communications
    p. Hypermedia environments
    q. Telecommunications
    r. Multimedia
    s. Desktop publishing
    t. Desktop presentations
    u. Interactive video disk

2. Demonstrate an understanding of the idea that computer applications are most effective for information-processing tasks that require any of the following:

    a. Handling large amounts of information (searching, sorting, deleting, updating, summarizing, communicating, organizing)
    b. Rapid handling of information
    c. Accuracy
    d. Repetition
    e. The storage and retrieval of information in an accessible form

3. Identify some of the factors to consider when making decisions regarding the appropriate use of computers for various problem situations:

    a. Cost
    b. People's attitudes (fears, anxieties)
    c. Availability of suitable hardware and software/applications
    d. Hardware limitations (memory capacity, lack of peripherals)
    e. Complexity of some computer-supported applications
    f. Application appropriateness
    g. Ethical and moral considerations
    h. Compatibility

4. Demonstrate an understanding of the idea that a user communicates with the computer system rather than the system controlling the user (e.g., computers do not make mistakes, people make mistakes).

SOCIETAL IMPACT

5. Demonstrate an understanding of past, present, and future applications and implications of computers in relation to the effect on society.

6. Demonstrate an understanding of legal and ethical computer-related issues (e.g., copyright law, computer crime, privacy, security, viruses) and make responsible decisions based on this understanding.

7. Demonstrate an understanding of the different computer-related occupations that exist.

SPECIFIC APPLICATIONS

8. Define *word processing* and understand the common capabilities and limitations as well as the advantages and disadvantages of using word processing.

9. Demonstrate the use of word processing software programs to create, edit, save, and print documents regularly for academic, professional, or personal uses.

10. Define *data base management* and understand the common capabilities and limitations as well as the advantages and disadvantages of using data base management software.

11. Demonstrate an understanding of the use of a data base management system to create, search, sort, retrieve, edit, and print files.

12. Define spreadsheet–financial management software and understand the common capabilities and limitations as well as the advantages and disadvantages of using spreadsheet–financial management software.

13. Demonstrate an understanding of the use of a spreadsheet software system.

14. Define and demonstrate an understanding of the use of simple statistical programs.

15. Demonstrate an understanding of the uses of computer-generated graphics software (e.g., bit-mapped graphics versus object-oriented graphics).

16. Demonstrate an understanding of the use of the computer in telecommunications and telecomputing.

17. Demonstrate an understanding of the use of the computer in desktop publishing (creating newsletters, brochures, and resumes).

18. Demonstrate an understanding of the use of the computer in multimedia, hypermedia, and interactive video.

EDUCATIONAL APPLICATIONS

19. Identify the major uses of computers in education (computer-assisted instruction, educational games, word processing, data management, administrative

uses, interactive multimedia, desktop publishing, and telecommunications).

20. Identify and demonstrate an understanding of the characteristics of categories of computer-assisted instruction software.
21. Demonstrate an understanding of the functioning of computer-managed instruction systems.
22. Demonstrate an understanding of the uses of simulations as teaching tools.
23. Identify computer languages well suited to educational applications (e.g., authoring languages for writing interactive instructional programs).
24. Demonstrate an understanding of the capabilities of using educationally oriented languages (e.g. LOGO, Hypercard, LinkWay).
25. Demonstrate the ability to identify effective instructional computer programs.

26. Demonstrate the ability to design and/or select and appropriately use computer programs to enrich and extend regular course instruction.
27. Identify different methods of integrating computer uses into the classroom.

EVALUATION AND SELECTION

28. Determine what computer hardware and/or software features are necessary to solve particular problems or suit certain applications.
29. Identify computer hardware and software evaluation criteria, and demonstrate the ability to evaluate and select appropriate computer hardware and software in terms of usefulness to particular applications or problems.

COMPUTER PROGRAMMING

The term *computer programming* refers to the ability to direct the operation of the computer through the skilled use of programming languages. This requires an understanding of problem-solving strategies, algorithms and flowcharts, languages, and programming skills.

PROBLEM-SOLVING STRATEGIES

1. Demonstrate an understanding that traditional programming is a problem-solving process.
2. Demonstrate the ability to analyze problems and select and/or develop appropriate problem-solving strategies for their solution.

ALGORITHMS/FLOWCHARTS

3. Define and demonstrate an understanding of algorithms and flowcharts.
4. Read an algorithm or flowchart, and identify the outcome or results that are produced.
5. Identify and demonstrate an understanding of the function of the symbols used to develop a flowchart.
6. Demonstrate an understanding of why flowcharts are helpful in developing computer programs.
7. Demonstrate the ability to develop algorithms and flowcharts for the solutions to problems.

LANGUAGES

8. Define and distinguish among the different levels of languages (machine, assembly, high-level, authoring) and related terms (*compiler, interpreter*).

9. Identify high-level programming languages and distinguish between their characteristics in relation to their appropriateness for various applications and grade levels (e.g., BASIC, PASCAL, COBOL, FORTRAN, LOGO, HyperCard, LinkWay, Hypertext).

10. Demonstrate an understanding of the use of authoring languages and systems to write interactive instructional programs.

PROGRAMMING

11. Define and be able to use computer programming terminology (e.g., *variable, string variable, linear programming, branched programming, bug, debugging, coding, statement, syntax, looping, unconditional branch, conditional branch, pseudocode, recursion, object-oriented, systems analysis, system design, functional specifications*).

12. Identify the steps in creating a computer program, from problem definition through implementation.

13. Identify and be able to interpret user-oriented documentation for computer programs.

14. Identify the characteristics of structured/modular programming style.

15. Read a simple program, demonstrate an understanding of the statements and logic of the program, and identify the output.

16. Identify characteristics of computer programs that run efficiently.

17. Demonstrate the ability to translate a given algorithm or flowchart into a high-level programming language.

18. Given a program (or flowchart) containing errors (syntax and logic), identify the error and debug the program so it will execute properly.

19. Modify computer programs written by others.

20. Demonstrate the ability to write simple programs in a high-level language (e.g., BASIC, PASCAL, LOGO).

ATTITUDINAL COMPUTER LITERACY COMPETENCIES

1. Demonstrate positive attitudes toward the appropriate use of computers.
2. Demonstrate confidence in the use of computers as tools in the home, school, and work environment.
3. Demonstrate comfort with the use of computers.
4. Demonstrate an attitude of acceptance of the computer as a fast and accurate problem-solving tool (a helper rather than a threat).
5. Demonstrate willingness to use a computer for tasks associated with school, work, or personal life.
6. Demonstrate an appreciation for the potential threats to personal privacy that computers pose.
7. Demonstrate an attitude of responsibility for the ethical use of computers (issues dealing with the misuse of computers, such as stealing computer programs, breaking security codes, and borrowing codes without acknowledgment are considered unethical).
8. Demonstrate an attitude that computers usually are not responsible for "computer error" and that computer users are responsible for instructing the computer.
9. Be free of fear and intimidation when using a computer.

GLOSSARY

ABC   Abbreviation for the Atanasoff-Berry-Computer, the first electronic digital computer that was designed and built by John Atanasoff and Clifford Berry at Iowa State College (now Iowa State University) in Ames, Iowa.

access controls   Protect the computer equipment and facilities.

access time   The time needed to retrieve information from a disk or to send information to a disk.

access point   The method of connection between the computer and the network.

acoustic coupler   A type of modem that permits the use of a standard telephone headset. The headset is inserted into two cuplike devices. This permits the sending and receiving of computer signals using a standard telephone headset.

actuators   Parts of disk drives that contain the read–write heads.

ADA   A high-level programming language developed for the U.S. Department of Defense.

adapter   A device that permits interconnection of two connectors or devices that do not directly match.

ADC (analog to digital converter)   A device that converts an analog signal into its equivalent digital signal.

address   A particular storage location in random-access memory.

ADP   Automatic, or automated, data processing.

algorithm   A set of calculations that produces a logical sequence of steps in a process written in human language to solve a problem or to manipulate the record key to find a record. The first step in computer programming is writing the algorithm.

aliasing   The jagged, stair-stepped effect along the edges of computer graphics; also called "the jaggies."

alphanumeric   All the symbols used by a computer, including numbers, letters, and symbols.

alphanumeric keys   Keys with numbers, letters, and special characters that appear on a keyboard device.

ALU (arithmetic logic unit)   The component of the central processing unit that carries out the four mathematical functions (addition, subtraction, multiplication, and division), and the two logic functions (comparisons and sorts).

American Standard Code for Information Interchange (ASCII)   A standard method of representing a character with a number inside the computer. Knowledge of the code is important only if you write programs.

amplifier   A device that supplies power to and strengthens an incoming signal for output.

analog   The variation of an electrical signal or information to represent the original image or sound that is being processed or reproduced for continuous information, or signals. Examples of devices that provide analog information are slide rules, mercury thermometers, regular electric clocks with sweep hands, and traditional sweep car speedometers.

analog film recorder   A film recorder that registers the image as it comes from the computer screen and at the same resolution as the screen.

analog monitor   A monitor that uses an analog signal and displays an infinite number of shades of the primary colors or gray scale. Voltage varies continuously.

analytical engine   A device for solving mathematical problems invented by Charles Babbage in the mid-1800s.

animation   A process of creating movement of images on-screen.

Anonymous FTP   A system that allows people to log into remote computers and transfer files by logging in as anonymous.

ANSI   Abbreviation for the American National Standards Institute. The organization responsible for most standards used for U.S. audiovisual and computer equipment.

anti-aliasing   An image-processing technique that reduces the appearance of aliasing on a graphics display. It makes the edges appear smoother and less "jagged".

Apple DOS   A disk-operating system for Apple II microcomputers. The most popular version is designated DOS 3.3. This version organizes a 5¼-inch floppy disk into 35 tracks, each with 16 sectors.

Apple ProDOS   A disk-operating system for Apple II computers newer than DOS 3.3. It is often used with hard-disk systems.

Apple II   One of the first microcomputers. Developed by Steve Jobs and Steve Wozniak.

Applesoft   A version of BASIC built in the read-only memory of Apple II computers. An application program with a precoded set of generalized instructions for the computer, written to accomplish a certain goal.

ARCHIE   An Internet search program that locates files available on FTP sites.

arithmetic/logic unit   Performs the arithmetic operations of addition, subtraction, multiplication, and division and any comparisons required by the program.

arrays   A series of related data items and fields usually stored in rows and columns.

arrow keys   Keys (down, up, right, and left) found on the numeric keyboard and typically used to move a pointer or cursor.

artificial intelligence (AI)   The process of using computer technology by constructing computer-based hardware–software systems to simulate the thought process of human experts.

ASCII   Has two meanings: (1) ASCII is a universal computer code for English letters and characters. Computers store all information as binary numbers. In ASCII, the letter "A" is stored as 01000001, whether the computer is made by IBM, Apple or Commodore. (2) ASCII also refers to a method, or protocol, for copying files from one computer to another over a

network, in which neither computer checks for any errors that might have been caused by static or other problems.

aspect ratio   In computer graphics, the ratio of the horizontal to vertical dimensions of a frame or image. The ability to maintain or control this ratio is important in the transfer and reproduction of an image for displays or for printed material.

assembler   A computer language-translation device that changes symbolic code into machine code.

assembly language   A low-level language that uses short, mnemonic words instead of the human language-like words of high-level languages.

asynchronous   The transmission of one character at a time over a communication line using a start and stop bit.

asynchronous protocol   Transmits data one character at a time.

Atanasoff, John   Designed and built the first digital computer. (See **ABC**.)

ATR   Audiotape recorder.

audio signal   A varying voltage that carries information representing sound.

authoring language   A simplified programming language used by teachers to create computer-based instruction. PILOT is a commonly used authoring language for microcomputers.

authorware   Development software programs that provide tools used to create interactive multimedia presentations, specifying elements—such as video and audio—that need to be included.

autoanswer   A feature found in some modems that allows the computer to answer the phone.

autodial   Feature frequently found in modems that lets you place a call to a specified number without having to dial it yourself.

backup and recovery   Backup refers to copies made of the data base used to restore (recover) from any disasters. This ensures that no data (or only a minimal amount) are lost.

band printer   A fast printer that uses a horizontal, rotating band containing characters.

bandwidth   The grade of transmission media, measured in hertz. The wider the bandwidth, the greater the number of bits per second can be transmitted.

banked memory   Usually two sets of 64K memory used to give a computer a total memory of 128K. Only one set of 64K can be active at a time. Used in early computers.

bar chart   Horizontal or vertical bars that are stacked, floating, or clustered side by side.

bar code   A series of vertical lines of different widths that represent information, often used in inventory systems.

bar code reader   An electronic device that reads data represented in the parallel lines of the universal product code (UPC).

base band   A coaxial cable that carries one signal at a time.

BASIC   Beginners All-Purpose Symbolic Instructional Code. A high-level, easy-to-learn computer language that is the standard for most microcomputers. It is built into read-only memory in the Apple II series of micros. The advanced version of BASIC is called BASICA. BASIC was developed by Kemeney and Kurtz at Dartmouth College in 1963 and has proved to be the most popular language for personal computers.

batch processing   A method of processing data in which all data records are grouped together and processed at one time. Traditionally, this meant that all computer cards were entered in the computer's memory from a card reader at one time.

baud   Bits per second. A measurement of the speed at which binary digits are transmitted.

baud rate   Speed at which modems can transmit characters across telephone lines. A 300-baud modem can transmit about 30 characters per second.

Beta   A ½-inch videotape format incompatible with the VHS format.

bilevel mode   A scanning mode that scans only black and white.

binary   The base-2 number system used by computers as machine language. All information is represented by groupings of binary digits, of 0 and 1, with each digit in a binary number representing a power of 2. Most digital computers are binary. A binary signal is easily expressed by the presence or absence of an electrical current or magnetic field.

binary digit   (See **bit**.)

binary notation   The use of 0's and 1's to create characters or numbers on which the computer performs operations.

bit   A single binary digit with a value of 0 or 1. Bits are normally collected into groups called *bytes*. For example, the Apple IIe is called an 8-bit computer because 8 bits, binary digits, are used for each byte, and bytes are used to represent alphanumeric characters in the computer's memory. The smallest amount of information a computer can hold.

bit-map display   A display format in which the intensity or color of each point (pixel) on the screen corresponds to the value of a bit of computer memory.

bit-mapped font   Text characters that are built using a pattern of dots.

bits per inch   (See **bpi**.)

BK   A LOGO language primitive meaning back up. Example, BK 50.

block   Designated portion of text, consisting of one or more lines, that is to be copied, moved, or deleted.

BNC   A connector for coaxial cable (coax) that twists into place. BNC connectors are used for analog video signals in most semiprofessional and professional video equipment.

board   A plastic card, or large circuit board, that holds chips and contains circuitry for a computer or peripheral devices, as in the mother board.

Boolean   Pertains to the processes used in the system of algebra developed by George Bool. Pertains to the operations of informal logic.

boot record   Record that resides on sector 1 of track 0 of a file and contains the program responsible for loading the rest of DOS into the microcomputer.

booting   The process of loading an operating system into the computer's memory, usually the disk-operating system.

border   Set of labels for the rows and columns of a worksheet. The columns are labeled with letters, and the rows are labeled with numbers.

boundary   Defines the limits of a component, the collection of components, or the entire system.

bounce   What your e-mail does when it cannot get to its recipient—it bounces back to you—unless it goes off into the ether, never to be found again.

bpi   Bits per inch. A measure of the recording capabilities of a disk.

bps   Bits per second. (See **baud**.)

bridge   The component of a local area network that lets it communicate with other networks.

broadband   Coaxial cable that carries many signals at one time. Each signal is carried by a different frequency in the cable.

buffer   An area in a computer that temporarily stores data before they are processed.

bug   An error or mistake in a computer program. Derived because the first computers used relay switches, and a real bug was found in one. A hardware bug is a physical or electrical malfunction or design error; a software bug is an error in programming, either in the logic of the program or in typing.

bulletin boards   Computer files that store announcements and messages that may be accessed by computer users at remote locations using modems. Information utilities often have bulletin boards for their subscribers

bulletin board system (BBS)   A system consisting of a computer and one or more modems that is used to store messages, programs, or data for anyone having access to the system.

bus   A connection inside or outside a computer through which information is sent that enables the computer to pass information to a peripheral and to receive information from a peripheral.

bus network   Connects several nodes or computers with a single cable along which computers can send messages in either direction.

byte   A collection of binary digits, bits, used to represent letters, numbers, or symbols in a computer's memory. Eight bits, 16 bits, and 32 bits are the common sizes of bytes for microcomputers. A byte usually has 8 bits, so its value can be from 0 to 255. Each character can be represented by 1 byte in ASCII.

C   A high-level language.

CAD/CAM   (See **computer-aided design/computer-aided manufacturing**.)

CAI   (See **computer-assisted instruction**.)

camera ready   A high-quality printed output that is ready for reproduction.

card   Smaller than a board, or circuit board. Usually an accessory added to a computer in an expansion slot to increase the capabilities of the computer.

card reader   A computer input device that reads data and program code from punched cards, also called Hollerith cards.

cardioid microphone   A microphone that accepts sound in a somewhat heart-shaped sensitivity pattern. These microphones are sensitive to sound coming from the front and relatively insensitive to sound coming from the rear.

cartridge   Removable hard-disk storage unit that typically holds 10 or more megabytes of storage.

CASE   (computer-assisted systems engineering)   Software that facilitates the process of systems analysis and development.

cathode-ray tube (CRT)   The tube that produces the image on a monitor screen.

CBI   (See **computer-based instruction**.)

CD-ROM   (compact disk–read-only memory)   A format standard for placing any kind of digital data on a compact disk. Typically, more than 640 million bytes of data can be stored on a single CD-ROM.

CD-ROM XA (compact disk–read-only memory extended architecture)   A CD-I (compact disk interactive) format with computer data, video, and audio that have been designed for use as a computer peripheral.

cell   Intersection point of a row and a column in a spreadsheet. It is referenced by the cell address COLUMN/ROW.

cell animation   An animation technique in which the animated portions consist of separate images that are shown in sequence.

centering hole   Large hole on a diskette that allows the mylar plastic disk inside the diskette envelope to center on the capstan for proper rotation.

central processing unit (CPU)   Device in a computer system that contains the arithmetic unit, the control unit, and the main memory. Also referred to as "the computer."

centronics   Standard method of passing information through a parallel data port.

chain printer   An impact printer that contains all alphanumeric characters and symbols on a rotating chain. Used with mainframe computers.

channel   A single audio signal path.

character   Any graphic symbol that has a specific meaning to people. Letters (both uppercase and lowercase), numbers, and various symbols (e.g., punctuation marks) are all characters.

character generator   A device that electronically produces text displayed over a video image. Also called "titlers."

characters per second (CPS)   A measurement of printing speed most often applied to dot-matrix and impact printers.

charge-coupled device (CCD)   Storage unit used to store data in electrical charges in locations on a silicon chip.

chasing   The process that occurs when a tape machine or sequencer changes its location to match that of another device.

Chat   An option in some telecommunications systems that makes it possible for users to communicate by typing on their respective computers. The text is immediately displayed on the other computer.

chip   Electronic entity containing one or more semiconductors on a wafer of silicon, within which an integrated circuit is formed. A chip has thousands of electrical circuits that have been photographically imprinted and etched on it. Used for CPU, ROM, and RAM.

chroma (chrominance)   The amount and brightness of a hue as measured in the video signal. Without this signal, the video picture appears in black and white.

circuit A path electricity follows from the source of the current through the wiring.

circuit board An arrangement of electronic circuits on a plastic board that functions as a unit.

click Using a mouse—pushing the button on it is called *clicking*.

Client Software on the user's computer that provides a way to access networked services.

clip art Art that is ready to be placed within a desktop publishing application.

clipboard A random-access memory location that stores information that has been cut or copied so it can be transferred to another application—a feature used mostly with Macintosh computers.

clock A device in the computer that generates periodic signals used to synchronize a computer's operation.

clock speed Measured in millions of cycles per second (megahertz, or Mhz), indicates how fast a computer can process information and is a function of the ease with which electricity passes through the CPU.

closed-bus system Type of computer system that comes with plugs, called *established ports*, that accept device cables from the peripheral.

CMI (See **computer-managed instruction**.)

coaxial cable (coax cable) A high-quality communication medium containing several wires in a cable enclosure. The same type of cable is often used to connect a television set. Capable of carrying up to 10 megabits of data at a time.

COBOL (Common Business-Oriented Language) A high-level language often used for business applications and oriented toward organizational data processing procedures.

code The way the computer is controlled, because commands are coded information. The ASCII code represents characters in terms of binary numbers; the BASIC language represents algorithms in terms of program statements. CODE also may refer to programs, usually in low-level languages. Also, an invisible command to WordPerfect that tells it how to display or print text.

cognitive science The psychological science that deals with how people process and use information.

color bars Standard color chart for adjusting the color balance in video equipment.

color cycling animation Changing the color mapping of pixels to create an animated image.

color graphics adapter (CGA) The first (and poorest) color video interface standard established for the IBM PC and compatibles.

color monitor Monitor sometimes referred to as RGB (red, green, and blue).

command An instruction given to the computer, usually in a high-level language.

command.com Command processor of DOS, containing built-in functions or subroutines that enable users to copy a file or get a directory listing of a disk.

command processor The portion of the operating system that stores DOS commands that will be contained in RAM once DOS is loaded into RAM.

compact disk (CD) A laser technology disk that stores computer data. Basically the same as the compact disk now commonly used for recorded music.

compact disk interactive (CD-I) A specification for an interactive product in which still images, computer graphics, audio, and computer data are stored on one disk. This technology is starting to show up in the consumer entertainment market and has great potential for education.

compiler A program, also called a *translator*, that converts high-level programming language code into machine language. As it performs this translation, it also checks for errors made by the programmer.

composite video A video output format in which the three color signals (red, green, blue) are combined with the timing (sync) signal into one composite signal that can be sent over one cable or broadcast through the airwaves. This is the format used when a VCR or some computers are connected to a video monitor.

Comprehensive Crime Control Act of 1984 Prohibits an unauthorized person from accessing computer records to obtain information protected by the Right to Financial Privacy Act of 1978 or data in the files of a consumer-reporting agency.

compressed files Reduced-size files that are easier to transfer across the Internet or from disk to disk. Programs like PKZIP are used to decompress them after they are transferred.

compression A method by which video or audio signals can be stored or transmitted with much greater efficiency than the raw signal itself. Compression typically requires special equipment or programs.

computer An electronic device, controlled by commands stored in its internal memory, that can accept and store data, perform arithmetic and logic functions, and output information without the need for human intervention. Or any device that can receive and store a set of instructions in a predetermined and predictable fashion. The definition implies that both the instructions and the data on which the instructions act can be changed; a device whose instructions cannot be changed is not a computer.

computer animation   The process of using computer-generated images to produce animation, or cartoons.

computer-assisted design (CAD)   Use of the computer to assist in designing other items.

computer-assisted instruction   (See **computer-based instruction**.)

computer-based instruction (CBI)   Most current term for teaching with computers; using programs that either teach students new information, reinforce concepts they have learned previously, or change their attitudes in some predetermined way. (Formerly called *computer-assisted instruction.*)

computer coordinator   The person in the school who oversees the use of computers.

computer crime   The commission of unlawful acts by using computer technology.

Computer Fraud and Abuse Act of 1986   An attempt by Congress to define computer crime and establish penalties.

computer lab   A centralized collection of computer hardware and software organized to serve students in classes and for homework activities.

computer-managed instruction (CMI)   Computerized system of record keeping that keeps track of a student's progress. Some advanced systems diagnose a student's progress, provide instruction, and analyze progress automatically.

computer output microfilm (COM)   A process of using photographic techniques and reduction to hold large amounts of data in computer storage.

computer system   Computer hardware collection consisting of the four major components of computers: inputs, CPU or processing, memory or storage, and outputs.

concentrator   A multiplexor with built-in circuitry that makes the transmission process more efficient. Also performs rudimentary editing on the data to be transmitted.

conditional jump   A movement to another place in a computer program once some predetermined condition has been met, such as if the user types "yes" at the keyboard.

configuration control   Allows only the DBA to make changes to the schema of a data base.

console log   Devices that record what actions users perform on the machines. These devices even log what tapes were mounted on which drives by the operators, which files the operator altered, and what responses the operator gave to the computer's prompts or instructions.

constant   A specific number that does not change. The opposite is variable, which may change when a program is run.

constant angular velocity (CAV)   In laser video disk recordings, a format in which each frame takes exactly one track, allowing frame-accurate freezing of the image.

constant linear velocity (CLV)   In laser video disk recordings, a format in which the disk rotates at varying speeds so the speed along each track is constant. This allows longer recording times (extended play) but does not allow freeze-frame capabilities on most players.

continuous-form paper   Paper that has all sheets attached to provide a continuous flow of paper to the printer.

contrast ratio   The ratio of brightness between the white and black areas of an image.

control character   Normally nonprinting ASCII code running "behind the scenes"; controls the operation of hardware or performs other functions.

control total   A total generated by a program to help an operator determine whether data have been entered or processed correctly. Typical control totals include the total number of records processed or the grand total of an amount field.

control unit   Part of the CPU that directs and coordinates the activities of the entire computer.

convergence   Proper alignment of the vertical and horizontal lines, as in a video projector, for example.

convert utility   A program that allows the user to change one file format to another for use on different devices. The availability of these programs allows, for example, Macintosh and MS-DOS computer users to exchange text and picture files.

coprocessor   Microprocessor chip that is placed in a microcomputer to take the burden of manipulating numbers off the CPU, allowing it to perform other tasks.

copy protection   Makes it difficult to make a copy of a disk, often by organizing it in a nonstandard way that copy programs do not recognize.

copy stand   A device for holding a video camera for shooting flat art or still items.

counter   A part of the computer memory that is reserved for a total count. Used in programs to keep track of the number of cycles through a program's loop.

CPI (characters per inch)   The compressed CPI mode for dot-matrix printers is 10 pica/12 elite CPI.

CP/M (computer program/microcomputers)   The first operating system for microcomputers.

CPS (characters per second)   Indicates the number of characters printed each second by a printer.

CPU   (See **central processing unit**.)

crash Involuntary shutdown of a computer program, or computer hardware system, as in "the system crashed."

crawl The movement of credits or other graphic material across a video screen.

cross fade An effect in which one sound or picture fades out while the next one fades in over it. Also called a *cross dissolve*.

CRT (cathode ray tube) The picture tube in a television receiver; used as the primary output device for microcomputers.

cue control A device for rapidly advancing or rewinding a tape to sample the content or find a special area. Sometimes called a *shuttle control*.

cursor A symbol on the screen, often a blinking square or line, that indicates where the next character will be typed from the keyboard.

cut An abrupt, instantaneous transition between two scenes in a production. Also slang for a video edit.

cybernetics Study of similarities between humans and machines. The science of communications engineering.

DAC (See **digital analog converter**.)

Daemon A harmless Unix program that normally works out of sight of the user. On the Internet, you'll most likely encounter it only when your e-mail is not delivered to your recipient—you'll get back your original message plus a message from a "mailer daemon."

daisywheel printer A printer with a wheel with printable characters on the ends of petal-like protrusions that produces a solid-font print. Also called *letter-quality printer*.

data (datum) Information of any kind.

data base An integrated set of records with the collection of data related to one specific type of application. Data base is often used synonymously with FILE.

data base administrator (DBA) An individual appointed by management, who works with users to create, maintain, and safeguard the data found in the database.

data base management system (DBMS) Complete set of programs that help users to organize, update, and store records and files in virtually unlimited ways.

data base server In some LANs, a special computer dedicated exclusively to the data base needs of the network users.

data communications The electronic transfer of data from one computer device to another.

data controls Safeguards for data and their input. Batch-control slips with control totals and hash totals are examples.

data-definition language (DDL) Used to design the logical structure of the data base. Used to give information such as field name, data type, and size, as well as to limit access to these data.

data dictionary Contains the meaning of each piece of datum found in the data base; it includes data names, type of data, field size; and describes any interrelationships between this piece of datum with other data items.

data entry Inputting information into a computer's memory.

data-flow diagram Graphical method for documenting systems. A physical data-flow diagram documents the current system, whereas a logical data-flow diagram documents the design of the new system.

data integrity Relates to the problem of errors occurring in data that are stored in files.

data interchange format (DIF) A system that permits grabbing data from one program and bringing it into another.

data-manipulation language (DML) Has all the stored routines that allow a user to store, retrieve, change, delete, or sort data or records within the data base.

data processing The process of systematic, orderly manipulation of data by automatic methods to produce information for use in making decisions.

data redundancy The same data are stored in more than one location.

DBA (See **data base administrator**.)

DBMS (See **data base management system**.)

debugging The process of locating and correcting errors in a program.

decibel (Db) A measure of sound or signal intensity measured against a reference level.

decision-support system (DSS) Provides user-friendly languages or programs that a decision maker can employ to retrieve or store data and perform modeling to solve unstructured problems.

decision table The graphic representation of a decision-making process that contains the following parts: decision stub, decision entry, action stub, and action entry.

deck A collection of punched cards.

decode To translate from computer language to human language.

decoder/encoder A decoder translates a composite video signal into separate RGB signals. An encoder combines separate RGB signals into a composite video signal.

default   A decision made by the user, which the computer will use if the user does not change this decision.

definition   The sharpness or resolution of a picture.

demand report   Used to obtain information that may be needed for a specific problem.

demodulation   The conversion of analog signals to digital signals.

desktop organizer   Primarily RAM-resident software package that includes such capabilities as calculators, notepads, automatic dialers, and appointment calendars.

desktop presentations   The use of computer-based multimedia tools to create presentations. The term can be used for everything from the design and printing of overhead transparencies to the production of interactive multimedia presentations involving a wide range of presentation equipment.

desktop publishing (DTP)   Gives the user typeset quality such as you see in newspapers and textbooks. Also allows combining of text and pictures.

dial-in connection   A type of connection used to access the Internet in which modems are used to dial another computer that serves as the host.

dial-up connection   Connecting to an Internet service provided through a modem and telephone line. After you are connected, your computer acts like a terminal on the service provider's computer.

difference engine   A mechanical device invented in 1822 by Charles Babbage to calculate. Used the method of difference.

digit   A number between 0 and 9.

digital   Computers that perform calculations in digits. Electronic computers are digital. Slide rules are analog computers.

digital analog converter (DAC)   A device that converts digital signals used by the computer into analog signals. These devices are used in music and speech synthesizers, for example.

digital audio   A format for audio recording in which the sound is recorded as a string of numbers used for the noise-free reconstruction of the sound.

digital audiotape (DAT)   An audio-recording format that produces CD-quality sound on special cassette tapes.

digital monitor   A display that uses a digital signal. Voltage varies in discrete steps.

digital signals   Signals that represent the values 0 and 1 by the presence or absence of voltage.

digitize   To capture an analog signal (video or sound) and convert it to digital form for storage and reconstruction in a computer. For example, the audio signals on CDs have been digitized. The CD player reconstructs the original audio using a DAC.

digitizer   A device that translates analog information into digital information. In computers, this term often refers to the capture of video signals.

digitizing tablet   A flat drawing surface used with some graphics applications. The tablet allows users to enter commands with a drawing device rather than a mouse or keyboard.

direct-access method   Uses algorithms or indexes to locate a record.

direct-connect modem   A modem that permits the user to directly connect the telephone into a receptacle in the computer because the modem circuitry is located on a printed circuit board inside the computer.

direct connection   A type of connection used to access the Internet in which a computer or computer network has a cable connecting it directly to the Internet. In any direct connection, your computer is the host having continuous on-line access to the Internet.

discussion groups   Commonly called *news groups*, these discussion groups contain messages called articles from people around the world with interest in a particular topic. There are thousands of topics.

disk   A rotating flexible or rigid medium, on whose surface data can be stored and later retrieved through an electromagnetic or other process.

disk buffer   A location in random-access memory that stores often-used information also stored on a disk. Often the directory is stored here.

disk drive   Rectangular box, connected to or situated inside the computer, that reads and writes into diskettes.

disk-operating system (DOS)   The program responsible for enabling users to interact with the many parts of a computer system. DOS (pronounced "doss") is the interface between users and the hardware. To perform system functions, DOS commands are typed on the keyboard, but DOS is actually a collection of programs designed to make it easy to create and manage files, run programs, and use system devices attached to the computer. DOS controls information input and output using disk drives. DOS 3.3, ProDOS, and MS-DOS 6.0 are examples of disk-operating systems.

diskette   A circular, mylar-coated disk used to store information magnetically. Also called a *floppy disk*.

display size   The screen area of a monitor. It is represented by the diagonal measure of the screen.

distributed data processing (DDP) Distributes and manages resources among several computers or terminals.

dither mode Scanning mode that scans shades.

dithering In computer graphics, a method for blurring the transition from one color to another.

documentation The written text or manual that details how to use a computer device or piece of software.

DOS (See **disk-operating system.**)

DOS prompt Indicates that DOS is ready to receive an instruction. It also tells which drive DOS will try to execute the instruction against, unless told otherwise. Typical DOS prompts are A>, B>, C>, and D>.

DOS shell A piece of software that makes the disk-operating system easier to use by introducing menus or some type of graphic user interface.

DOS.SYS Hidden DOS file that handles any information to be passed to disk.

dot-matrix printer A printer that uses pins to produce tiny dots on paper that are grouped to form alphanumeric characters. Often used with microcomputers because of speed and low cost. The printer generates characters by firing tiny print heads against a ribbon.

dot pitch The distance between dots on the monitor screen. The smaller the dot pitch, the denser the image appears.

double density Diskettes and drives that can record approximately 5,876 bits per inch (720K or 800K).

double-density disks Disks with about twice the storage of a single-density disk. They use a higher quality read–write surface on the disks, so that data can be stored in a denser format.

double-sided disks Disks on which data can be stored on both surfaces. A double-sided disk has been certified (tested) on both sides.

double-sided drives Disk drives that are configured so that they can record data on both sides of the diskette.

download The process of sending information from a large, mainframe computer to a smaller computer, such as a micro. Also slang for making a "personal" copy of something.

downloading Receiving a file from another computer.

downsizing The process of moving applications from a mainframe environment to a microcomputer environment. It also refers to performing a given amount of work with fewer people.

dragging Clicking and holding down the mouse button as the mouse is moved.

drawing tool A set of tools contained in a graphics package for drawing lines, filling areas of the screen with specific colors or patterns, or performing other tasks such as erasing.

DR DOS 5.0 A disk-operating system from Digital Research that contains a graphic user interface and allows users to utilize RAM above 640K.

drill and practice The simplest category of computer-based instruction. The student is presented problems to solve by the computer. The computer checks answers and keeps track of progress. Generally, new information is not presented.

driver A computer program used to control external devices or run other programs. CD-ROM drives, video disk players, and printers all require special driver programs to control them.

dropout During playback, the instantaneous loss of a recorded signal that is due to imperfections in the tape.

drop frame time code SMPTE standard time code that drops frame number :00 and :01 each minute, except for every 10th minute, to compensate for NTSC variance from real clock time.

drum plotter A plotter that uses a rotating drum or cylinder with pens that move right and left and draw while the drum rotates.

dub To copy a tape; also called *dupe.*

dumb terminals An ASCII terminal that contains no built-in processing powers; it simply sends data to a computer located elsewhere or receives data from a remote computer. It processes no information internally.

dump To copy the contents of a storage device; also to display, print or store the content of the computer memory, or the printing of a screen image.

DVI Digital–video interactive. A technology that allows a range of interactive products to deliver moving and still images, audio, dynamic graphics, and computer data. A DVI disk is a CD-ROM with this special information on it. Compressed video footage can be expanded in real time (30 frames per second) on a personal computer.

Dvorak keyboard A keyboard devised by August Dvorak that improves typing efficiency because it places the most used keys under the strongest, easiest to use, fingers. An alternative to the QWERTY keyboard.

dynamic range The highest and lowest signal levels of a specific device.

EBCDIC An 8-bit code used by IBM-based computer systems to present letters, numbers, and symbols.

edit controller A device that controls two or more VCRs to accomplish smooth, accurate video editing.

editing   Verifying that the text of a document has been entered correctly.

editing decision list (EDL)   A time-code list of edit points in a production. When the list is fed into a computerized edit controller, the EDL allows the system to auto-assemble the master tape from time-coded original raw footage.

EDP   Electronic data processing.

EDVAC (electronic discrete variable automatic computer)   The first computer built in the United States that featured a stored program unit.

EGA   (See **enhanced graphics adapter**.)

Electronic Cottage   A society where the home is the central point of education, business, and entertainment.

electronic editing   Inserting or assembling program elements without physically cutting the tape.

electronic funds transfer (EFT)   A banking system that electronically records deposits and withdrawals as they occur.

Electronic Industries Association (EIA)   The association that determines recommended video and audio standards in the United States.

electronic mail   A type of software that provides for the easy sending and receiving of messages from one computer to another.

electronic spreadsheet   Program used to manipulate data that can be expressed in rows and columns.

electronic viewfinder   A small picture tube or LCD built into a video camera to allow the operator to see what is being scanned by the camera.

electrostatic plotter   A plotter that produces drawings with a row of styli across the width of the paper.

element   A single entry in an array.

emulate   To imitate or duplicate the behavior of a product or standard, as when an EGA adapter emulates CGA behavior. One brand of computer can sometimes be made to imitate, or emulate, another brand.

encryption   The coding of information so it cannot be understood without decoding first.

end users   People who directly use computers to help them with their jobs.

enhance   The act of altering a basic image to conform to better design standards and visual understanding.

enhanced graphics adapter (EGA) monitor   Video device capable of presenting clear, vivid graphics. Uses a 640 x 350 (or more) dot resolution to present crisper, more colorful images. A color video interface standard developed after CGA (color graphics adapter).

ENIAC (electronic numerical integrator and calculator)   A completely electronic digital computer. Designed by Mauchly and Eckert in 1946.

environmental interaction   Any system that accepts inputs from the environment, processes those inputs, and generates outputs back into the environment.

EPIE   An independent product evaluation agency.

EPROM (erasable programmable read-only memory)   Memory that is not normally erasable except with a special device.

erase head   A separate head in a disk drive, audio or video recorder that erases a previously taped signal before it is rerecorded.

ergonomics   The science of adapting work and working conditions to suit the individual worker.

ethics   The study of conduct and moral judgment.

exception report   Alerts management that an activity or process needs correction.

expanded memory   RAM above the 640K base memory limit.

expansion board   Printed circuit board that can be inserted into an open-bus expansion slot, expanding the computer configuration to include such items as modems and plotters.

expansion slot   A place inside the computer, usually on the mother board, where the expansion board and accessory circuit cards are added.

expert systems   An operationalization of artificial intelligence that uses a computer to simulate human brain power.

extended industry standard architecture (EISA)   The alternative standard to the MCA architecture of IBM's PS/2 hardware.

extended memory   In a microcomputer, memory higher than 1M (megabyte).

extension   On the Internet, each network has a different extension in its name. It appears after the name and domain and is usually a period followed by two to three lower-case letters. For example, the extension .edu tells us that the network is an education network.

external modem   Connects to a microcomputer's serial interface.

fat bit editing   The ability to magnify a portion of a computer image and edit it pixel by pixel.

fat Mac   The common name given to the 512K Macintosh computer.

fax (facsimile transmission) machine   A device for transmitting or receiving text or images over telephone lines.

feasibility study   Defines a problem and determines whether a solution can be implemented within budget constraints.

feedback The process of sampling output to make certain that it is within established limits. Data are then sent back to the system as input. Audio feedback can cause "squeals." Video feedback (pointing the camera at the monitor) can produce interesting visual effects.

fiber optics A communication line made of hair-thin strands of material that conduct light, replacing copper wires as the dominant message-transmission medium for both telephone and computer network systems.

field Subdivision of a record that holds one piece of information about a transaction in records, such as names, dates, addresses. Or one-half of a video frame, each consisting of 262.5 lines, each field being scanned in 1/60th of a second. One field scans the even lines, and the second scans the odd ones. (See **interlace**.)

fifth-generation computer The next generation of computers—will be used for artificial intelligence applications.

field frequency The number of fields per second. The NTSC field frequency is 60 per second; PAL is 50 per second.

file A collection of related records.

film recorder Device for creating slides or film prints of a video or computer graphics image.

finder Macintosh software that manages files and disk directories.

FINGER Finger command allows user to search for other users in the Internet.

firmware Programs permanently stored in the computer, usually in read-only memory.

first-generation computer The first computers. They used vacuum tube technology.

fixed disk Also called a *hard disk*.

flat-bed plotter An output device equipped with moving pens that draw on a flat sheet of paper.

floppy Floppy disk. The mass storage device used primarily with microcomputers. The main sizes used are 5¼ inch and 3½ inch.

flowchart A graphical representation of the sequence of operations needed to complete a task. Uses circles, rectangles, diamonds, ovals, parallelograms, and arrows with words.

flutter Rapid change in frequency of a video or audio signal that is due to variations in tape or disk speed.

font A physical style of character display on a CRT, a printer, or a plotter.

format To initialize or organize a disk so information can be stored on it.

FORTH A high-level language used for application and system software development.

FORTRAN Formula translation. A high-level language used primarily for mathematical and scientific programming.

fourth-generation computer A contemporary computer that uses large-scale integration technology.

frame A complete video image containing two interlaced video fields; 525 horizontal lines written in ⅟₃₀ second.

frame animation An animation technique in which video images are recorded on film one frame at a time. The process is quite time-consuming but produces most of the high-quality video seen in commercial titles for television programs, etc.

frame grabber A device for capturing and storing a video frame from an external video source for display in a computer. Sometimes frame grabbers grab only one field.

frequency response The frequency range over which signals are reproduced within a specified amplitude range. The frequency response of the human ear, for example, is from about 20 to 20,000 hertz (Hz).

friction feed A paper-feed mechanism that feeds a single sheet of paper through the printer using pressure. Traditional typewriters use a friction-feed system.

front-screen projection An image projected on the audience side of a light-reflecting screen.

FTP File Transfer Protocol. A way to send and receive data across a network.

full duplex Simultaneous and independent transmission of data in two directions over one communications channel.

Full Internet Access A network service provider capable of entering different networks linked to the internet and using the information and services they may provide.

full-motion video Video sequences that have enough images (30 frames per second) to impart smooth motion.

function keys Keys on a keyboard that can be programmed to perform a certain task.

Gantt chart A chart used to document a schedule for each of the tasks in the development of a system.

general-purpose computer A digital computer—a Power Macintosh 6100 is a general-purpose computer.

genlock A device that synchronizes one video source with another (e.g., computer graphics and video) for mixing and recording.

GIF Graphics Interchange Format. A method of storing and receiving graphic images often used over the

Internet or with commercial information utilities such as America Online.

gigabyte   One billion bytes. A CD-ROM holds 0.65 gigabytes of data.

Gopher   A menu-based method of storing and displaying information on the Internet.

grab utility   A RAM- or ROM-resident program that allows the user to capture a screen image from any program and save it on disk or send it to a printer.

graphical user interface (GUI)   An alternative to character-based computer interfaces such as MS-DOS. The Macintosh Finder and Microsoft Windows are two popular examples of GUIs.

graphics tablet   An input device for creating graphics in a computer from a drawing or freehand.

gray scale   An even range of gray tones between black and white.

hacker   Individual who uses computers continuously, possibly to the point of obsession.

half duplex   Data transmission through a communication line in only one direction at a time—similar to a CB radio, push-to-talk, release-to-listen system.

handshake   An electrical signal used by a receiving device to stop transmission from the sending device until data already received can be processed. The handshake between printers and computers allows the printer to catch up with the characters coming from the computer.

hard copy   A permanent paper copy of computer output. Usually, the output of a printer or plotter. The image on the CRT is not hard copy.

hard disk   Once called a Winchester disk. A magnetic storage medium consisting of a rigid platter coated with magnetic emulsion. Memory capacity of hard disks is in the tens, hundreds, and thousands of megabytes.

hardware   The physical components, or machines, of a computer system.

hertz (Hz)   Electronic measure of cycles per second.

high-definition television (HDTV)   Any of several proposed standards for higher resolution television approaching the quality of 35mm slides.

high-level language   A humanlike language used to program a computer. BASIC is high-level language often used in microcomputers.

high-resolution graphics   Highly detailed images produced by programming each pixel, or picture element, of the CRT.

Hollerith   The standard 80-column punch card and the code used to represent information punched into it.

Developed by Herman Hollerith of the Census Bureau in the 1880s.

horizontal blanking interval   The time from the end of one horizontal scan to the start of the next. Other information can be sent during this time period.

horizontal resolution   The number of pixels available horizontally across the screen.

horizontal scan rate   The speed at which the electron beam scans across a CRT. It is usually measured in kilohertz and ranges between 15 and 40 Khz and higher.

host computer   Usually, the mainframe that terminals are attached to.

host   Maintains the access point to the Internet and determines how the connection is accomplished.

HTML (Hypertext Markup Language)   The command language used for creating pages on the World Wide Web.

HTTP (Hypertext Transfer Protocol)   The method (protocol) used to transfer HTML documents from a server computer to a client's computer.

hue   A single identifiable color, such as green.

hypertext   Text with links to other pages or elements. Think of a book, and how the footnotes and index link one page to another page, or a whole different source altogether.

icon   A little picture. A pictorial representation of a potential function the computer can perform.

IEEE (Institute of Electrical and Electronics Engineers)   An organization composed of engineers and computer scientists.

IIIR (Integrated Instructional Information Resource)   A part of EPIE that helps educators locate particular instructional materials related to specific objectives.

image processing   Using software to manipulate a scanned video image. It is used to add colors, increase contrast at boundaries, and produce other effects.

image recorder   A device that records digital signals and graphics to create, typically, 35-mm slides.

impact printing   Printing by which the image is transferred to paper by some type of printing mechanism striking the character, ribbon, and paper.

information superhighway   The information superhighway consists of millions of users and connects a variety of existing and new networks, making it possible to access any computer located anywhere in the system.

information utility   A service that provides access to data bases.

initialize   Preparation of a blank disk to receive information. Organizing it so data can be stored on it. Also called *formatting*.

ink-jet printer   A printer that squirts ink in precise, controlled streams on paper to form letters, numbers, and symbols.

in-point   The starting point of an edit. (Also see **out-point**.)

insert editing   A video editing technique in which audio or video is inserted seamlessly into already recorded material. This requires a time code or control track on both the source and master videotape.

integer   A whole number.

integrated circuit   A complete circuit. Made in a single process that replaces traditional circuits of transistors, resistors, and capacitors. Solid-state electronics device, etched on a chip of silicon.

integrated software   Software packages that combine several applications, such as word processing, record keeping, and spreadsheet.

interactive computing   Operating the computer from a terminal on-line—when the user is finished typing, the computer responds immediately.

interactive video   Instructional system that uses a computer and computer program and video device such as a laser disk player.

interface   To communicate with the computer. Also, the cables that connect computer components.

interlace   A method of scanning used in video transmission in which each frame is divided into two interlaced fields to reduce flicker.

internal memory   The storage locations in a computer system where data and programs are stored immediately before use. Usually the fastest memory. Also called *working memory*.

internal modem   A modem installed inside the computer.

Internet   A complex interconnection of networks which links millions of computers in thousands of networks on all continents. Networks connected through the Internet use a particular set of communications standards to communicate, known as TCP/IP.

interpret   To convert a program, one line at a time, from high-level language to machine language.

interpreter   A translation program that executes programs line by line, checks them for accuracy, and converts them to machine language.

I-O (Input–Output)   The sending of information to a computer or receiving it from the computer. Keyboards are input devices. Printers are output devices. Disk drives are input–output devices.

IOCS (Input–Output Control System)   A set of standard programs to handle the movement of data to and from input–output devices.

iteration   Repetition of one or more statements in a program.

jaggies   Jagged edges of shapes in computer graphics. Also called *aliasing*.

JCL (Job Control Language)   Controls the flow of work through a computer.

jitter   Instability of an image due to sync or tracking problems.

job   A complete unit of work done by the computer.

joystick   Hand-operated input device used in computer-based instruction and with computer games. Permits the up–down, left–right movement of the cursor.

jump cut   A jarring edit that creates a visual non sequitur, out of sync with the original.

K   One thousand. In computer terminology, K = 1,024 bytes of memory (2 to the 10th power).

key   A special effect accomplished by electronically cutting a hole in a video image and inserting another picture. Keys are most often used for titles but are also seen on television weather reports.

keyboard   A collection of keys or buttons used to enter information into a computer. Similar to a typewriter keyboard, but with additional keys. To keyboard is to enter data.

keypunch   A machine used to encode data by punching holes in a tape or card. Data are typed in at a keyboard.

kilobyte   (See **K**.)

kilohertz   1,000 hertz.

koala pad   An input device used to enter a variety of information into the computer, especially drawings.

label   A symbolic notation that identifies a location or address for a command.

language translator   Software that converts statements from one language into another language.

laser printer   A nonimpact printer that transfers information onto paper by using a ruby laser to charge the surface of the paper for print to form on. Laser light encodes an organic photo conductor with the data to be printed.

laser video disk   A video playback system that uses optical disk. Individual scenes or frames on a disk can be accessed directly or through computer control.

lavalier   A small microphone worn on the lapel or under clothing.

LCD　(See **liquid crystal display**.)

LD-ROM　A laser video disk (12-inch format) used to hold digital data.

learning style　Characteristics of learners that relate to how they process information during instruction. The way a person cognitively deals with information.

leased line　A point-to-point, permanent circuit used to connect two computers—often a telephone line. Many school LANS are connected to the Internet through leased lines.

ledger sheet　A worksheet for two-way data entry. Paper version of a computer spreadsheet used in accounting applications, originally, then transferred to computer.

left justify　To align a column so that the leftmost characters are all lined up evenly.

letter-quality print　Printing that is indistinguishable from that produced by a regular typewriter.

library functions　Special mathematical functions that occur within program statements.

light-emitting diode (LED)　A digital output display device that produces characters using electronic segments that produce light.

light pen　A light-sensitive device used to mark locations on a display screen or to read input data from some printed object, such as a bar code.

line level　Refers to signals that are at or near the nominal operating level of an audio system.

line number　An integer assigned to every line in BASIC programming. Between 1 and 32,767.

line printer　Printer capable of printing whole lines of output at once. Typical line printers will print 80 or 132 characters at a time.

liquid crystal display or **liquid crystal diode (LCD)**　Output display consisting of a liquid crystal deposited between two sheets of polarizing material that when exposed to an electrical signal creates an image. Often used in portable computers and also used for some video projectors.

liquid crystal display panel (LCD panel)　A video display designed to be set on a standard overhead projector for group viewing.

LISP　A high-level programming language used primarily for processing recursive data stored in a list. Frequently used in artificial intelligence systems.

Listservs　Mailing lists on the Internet. If you subscribe to a listserve, you will receive all of the messages that are sent (perhaps 100 a day).

load　To place a program in random-access memory.

local area network (LAN)　Communications network covering a limited geographical region. Privately owned—for the transfer of internal data within the school or business. Normally, in a single building or office.

logarithm　The exponent expressing the power to which a fixed number must be raised to produce a given number.

logic　A series of unambiguous steps that make up an algorithm. The path of reasoning for the solution to a problem.

logic gates　Electronic switches that are part of a computer.

logical operator　A key word such as *and* used to combine descriptors.

LOGO (Language-Optimizing, Graphically Oriented system)　A high-level programming language that has powerful list-processing capabilities similar to LISP. Uses turtle graphics.

log on　Entering a computer system correctly. Often, this involves the use of a password and special code.

long-term memory　A place where data are stored and not changed.

loop　A sequence of instructions of program code that are repeated a number of times.

low-level language　A computer or machine language.

low-resolution graphic　Apple graphics mode in which the display screen is divided into a grid of 40 by 40 blocks. Low-resolution graphics lack detail and fineness.

LSI (Large-Scale Integration)　An integrated circuit with a high density of components—a chip.

lumen　A measure of light emitted by a light source at the point of emission.

luminance　The range from black through gray to white in a video picture.

lux　A measure of light reflection. 1 lux is 1,076 foot candles.

machine language　The instructions that the computer directly executes—binary code.

Macintosh　A model of computer produced by Apple that features the use of a mouse, pull-down menus, icons, and desktop screen.

macro　A statement that can be used to replace several simpler statements—one command used to replace several commands.

magnetic disk　A long-term storage device. Information is stored in circular tracks that are divided into sectors.

magnetic tape　A traditional form of storage for computer data. Information is stored magnetically in a linear track on the tape.

main storage   Memory that is directly accessible by the central processing unit.

mainframe   The largest and most powerful of the three categories of computers—10 times more capable than a minicomputer and 100 times more capable than a microcomputer.

Mark 1   The first practical electromechanical computer developed by Aiken and co-workers at Harvard University in 1944.

mark reader   A device that reads pencil marks from special documents.

mass storage   Storage devices, such as floppy disks or magnetic tape, for storage of large amounts of information usable by computers.

matrix   The format of an array that is dimensioned in rows and columns.

matte   Method for creating composite pictures by placing a multicolored image from one video source over a background from a second source; a form of keying.

MCA   Microchannel architecture for IBM's OS/2 microcomputers.

MECC (Minnesota Educational Computer Consortium)   A cooperative effort in Minnesota to develop computer software. Originally, schools worked together to share programs developed locally. Now MECC is a major distributor of teacher-produced software at inexpensive rates.

megabyte   1,024 times 1,024 bytes, or one million bytes.

megaflop   One million operations per second in floating point. Floating point is the binary version of scientific notation.

memory   Storage locations in the computer, in RAM or ROM.

menu   A program written to give users easy access to programs or program segments. Used to allow users to select programs by merely selecting the option related to that program.

menu bar   A line with available menus at the top of the Macintosh and Windows screens. Also called *pull-down menus.*

mic level   Signals that are at the low levels produced by microphones. Mic-level signals can be amplified to become line-level signals.

MICR (Magnetic Ink Character Recognition)   System used by banks to code and read information from checks into computer memory.

microcomputer   The smallest of the three categories of computer. Approximately 1/10th the power, memory, cost, and difficulty of use, among other char-

acteristics, of the next largest category of computer, the minicomputer. Also called *personal computer.*

microprocessor   A type of LSI chip with the complete processor including the arithmetic, logic, and control units.

microsecond   One millionth of a second.

microworld   A simulated learning experience/environment that students control to explore relationships.

MIDI   (See **musical instrument digital interface**.)

millisecond   One thousandth of a second.

minicomputer   The middle category of computer, between the microcomputer and the mainframe. Approximately 1/10th the power, price, storage, and flexibility of the mainframe, and 10 times more powerful than the micro. Usually used in moderate-size schools or businesses.

MIPS (Millions of Instructions Per Second)   A measure of computer performance.

modeling   Translation of a real-world situation into an abstract or conceptual world.

modem   Modulator, demodulator. Attaches computer output to an audible tone that can be sent over standard telephone lines.

Modula-2   A programming language containing improvements and refinements to Pascal.

modular programming   An ordered approach to programming that emphasizes structure.

monitor   Control program of a computer. Also, an output device that converts the output of a computer into a visible image on a cathode ray tube. Basically, the picture tube of a television with composite or RGB video inputs. In audio, a personal amplifier and/or speaker system designed to emulate larger systems used in presentation or performance.

monochrome   Monitor–CRT screen in one color on a black background.

monophonic (mono)   An audio signal that has one channel of information.

Mosaic   A graphical interface to the Internet that allows images, sound, and movies to be played.

motherboard   The computer's main circuit board. Chips and other boards are plugged into it.

mouse   A desktop input device used as an alternative to a keyboard. Moving it on the desktop moves a pointer on the screen. Buttons on the mouse are pushed to activate some command designated on the screen.

MS-DOS (Microsoft Disk-Operating System)   The disk-operating system chosen for use on the IBM personal computers. Developed by Microsoft, it is the same as PC-DOS except that there is no ROM BASIC provision.

multi-image   A slide show that uses two or more slide projectors in a programmed presentation.

multimedia   Transmitting text, audio, and graphics in real time.

multiplexor   A device that routes the output from several terminals or computers into a single channel. This allows one telephone link to carry a transmission that normally would require several such links.

multiprocessing   The simultaneous running of two or more programs, or two or more instructions from a single program on a computer, or on a computer network.

multiprogramming   Simultaneously running of two or more programs on a computer system.

multiscan monitor   A video monitor that works at various scan frequencies, allowing it to be used with different graphics adapters.

multiscreen   Projecting images onto several image areas.

multitasking   An operating system that can run more than one program at a time.

multitrack   A recording method in which more than two tracks are used to record individual portions of an audio production.

multiuser system   A computer system accessible to more than one user.

musical instrument digital interface (MIDI)   A standard for communicating information between synthesizers, sequencers, percussion machines, computers, and other electronic musical equipment.

musical instrument digital interface time code   A portion of the MIDI standard that allows the SMPTE time code to be directly represented as MIDI messages that can be read by a computer or sequencer.

nanosecond   One billionth of a second.

Napier's rods   A calculating device invented by John Napier. Also called Napier's bones. Forerunner of the slide rule.

National Television Standard Committee (NTSC)   An advisory group to the Federal Communications Commission (FCC) that sets the standards for video hardware and broadcasting. The U.S. standard is 525 lines per frame, interlaced, with 30 frames per second.

natural language   Communicating with a computer in a human language, such as English.

nested expressions   Expressions, or program statements, that are contained within other statements, often inside parentheses.

network   Any system consisting of two or more computers of any category.

network topology   Pathways by which devices on a local area network are connected to one another.

NIC (Network Information Center)   As close as an Internet-style network gets to a hub; it's usually where you'll find information about that particular network.

nibble   One-half the bits used to represent one character. If 1 byte is 8 bits, then 1 nibble is 4 bits.

node   A computer or terminal capable of sending and receiving data from other computers or terminals on a network.

noise   In audio, it is electrical interference or unwanted sound. In video, this interference appears as "snow".

nonimpact printing   Printing by electrostatic or other means that do not rely on physical contact.

nonvolatile memory   Form of storage that does not lose its content when the system's power is turned off. It may take the form of bubble memory, or it may be powered by batteries.

NSF (National Science Foundation)   Organization that funds the NSFNet, a high-speed network that once formed the backbone of the Internet in the United States.

NTSC   (See **National Television Standard Committee**.)

numeric keyboard   A data entry device consisting of numbered keys.

numeric variable   A variable whose value must be a number.

object code   Machine language instructions generated from higher-level source language statements, created by the compiler and executed by the computer.

OCR (Optical Character Reader or **Recognizer)**   Device capable of reading typed information directly into the computer.

omnidirectional microphone   Accepts sound equally well from all directions.

on-line   A direct communication connection with the computer.

open-bus system   Contains expansion slots that let users expand the system as needed. A peripheral is added to the computer by plugging it into an expansion slot with an interface board.

operating system   Program that controls the operation of the computer.

operational decision making   Ensures that employees perform tasks efficiently by measuring their output against preset standards.

operational symbols Mathematical symbols used to represent operations that are to occur.

optical disks Devices that use a laser for reading and writing on an optical disk device to store large amounts of data.

optical fiber A long, thin strand of glass that carries information as modulated light beams.

optical mark recognition A system of input based on a scanning device that locates and interprets pencil or pen markings on a piece of paper, such as a multiple-choice questionnaire.

organization controls Controls that divide data processing operations among several users so that if fraud is perpetrated there must be collusion among several people.

OS/2 An IBM operating system used on 80286-chip computers and later machines. OS/2 allows more than one program to be in RAM at once.

OSF/MOTIF A graphical user interface that provides standards for a wide range of computing environments.

output Computer-generated data whose destination is the screen, disk, printer, or some other output device.

output controls Involve reconciling control totals from one job step to another and scanning the output to make certain that the data were processed correctly. They can also involve delivering output to the authorized individual.

output device A peripheral device that produces the results of the computer's effort. CRTs and printers are output devices.

outsourcing A business arrangement whereby one company sells its information systems functions to another company and then leases back computer and programming time.

overscan Computer screen mode that extends a computer graphics image to the limits of the visible TV screen.

paddles A pair of devices used to control objects such as the cursor on the screen. One paddle determines the position on the x axis and the other on the y axis.

page-control language (PCL) A language designed to load bit-mapped fonts and graphics into a printer.

page-description language (PDL) Creates characters using outline fonts developed from formulas.

page printers Printers that print more than 3,000 lines per minute. Also called *very high-speed printers*.

PageMaker A popular package for desktop publishing.

PAL (See **phase alternating line**.)

palette The selection of colors available in a computer graphics system.

pan A camera move that swings along the horizontal axis.

parallel Information that is sent one word, or one byte, at a time.

parallel interface Interface arrangement that transmits all bits of a character at one time.

parallel processing Multiple operations performed simultaneously by several related facilities. Often, several CPUs.

parallel transmission Sends data one byte at a time.

PASCAL A problem-solving high-level language, designed for teaching structured programming techniques.

Pascaline A calculating device based on a mechanical gear system. Invented by Blaise Pascal.

pasteboard The area around a document in desktop publishing.

patch Connecting video and audio equipment with cables or through a central panel.

PC-DOS The operating system for IBM personal computers (MS-DOS).

pen plotters A type of plotter that creates images on paper by the movement of one or more pens over the surface of the paper under the pens.

peripheral A device attached to the computer such as a modem or laser disk player that is not part of the main computer. Most peripherals are input and/or output devices.

personal computer (PC) A computer with the CPU on one chip. Equipped with memory, languages, and peripherals. Also called *microcomputer* or *home computer*.

phase alternating line (PAL) The video standard used in Western Europe, Latin America, Great Britain, South Africa, Australia; not compatible with NTSC.

phone plug/socket A two- or three-lead connector standard based on a ¼-inch diameter plug element found in the microphone inputs and headphones of most consumer-grade audio equipment. This connector also exists in mini and micro sizes.

phono plug/socket A two-lead connector system for shielded cables sometimes called RCA connectors. This connector is used for both video and audio signals on most consumer products.

physical view The exact manner in which data are stored to devices used in a data base.

picosecond One trillionth of a second. One thousandth of a nanosecond.

picture element   (See **pixel**.)

pie chart   Compares the proportional parts of a whole. Useful for comparing component shares with one another and with the combined total.

PILOT (Programmed-Inquiry Learning or Teaching)   Authoring language that permits the development of computer-based instruction such as drills, tutorials.

Ping   A program that can trace the route a message takes from your site to another site.

pitch   The number of letters printed per line inch, such as 10 pitch (pica), 12 pitch (elite), or 15 pitch (15 characters per inch).

pixel   Picture element. An addressable dot that can be illuminated on a CRT screen. The smallest dot a computer can generate.

pixelization   Using image processing software to break up a continuous image into rectangular blocks and give it a digitized look.

plasma screen   An output display consisting of a grid of conductors sealed between two flat plates of glass containing a gas that when excited creates an image.

PLATO (Programmed Logic for Automatic Teaching Operations)   Programming language developed at the University of Illinois and marketed by Control Data Corp. A computer-based education system.

PL/1 (Programming Language One)   Programming language devised by IBM in 1965 to support scientific and commercial work.

plotter   A mechanical device used to draw lines such as graphs or pictures under the control of a computer.

point   A printer's measurement, about $1/72$ of an inch.

Point to point protocol (PPP)   A method that allows a computer to connect directly to the Internet through a telephone line and high-speed modem (similar to a SLIP connection).

pointer   Reverse-video bar, sometimes referred to as the *cursor*. Its width depends on the width of the cell it is referencing. In a data base, it is the data item in a record that identifies the storage location of another record that is logically related. It may also indicate the current record being processed. The exact role of the pointer depends on the type of data base-structuring technique in use.

polling   The process of a computer checking to see if there are data at a node location ready for transmission.

port   A standard plug and socket with predefined connections, used to transmit serial streams of bits into and out of the computer.

portrait format   Text printed on a sheet of paper in 8½-inch-by-11-inch format.

post   To compose a message for a Usenet newsgroup and then send it out for others to see.

postmaster   The person to contact at a particular site to ask for information about the site or complain about one of his/her user's behavior.

postscript   The PDL language developed by Adobe systems for PageMaker.

predictive report   Used in the planning process to construct what–if scenarios.

presentation graphics   Turns numeric information and data relationships into graphics—charts and graphs.

presentation manager   A graphical user interface built into OS/2.

primary memory   Internal memory used by the computer for several different functions. It can contain data, program instructions, or intermediate results of calculations.

primitive   A term, or command, in the LOGO language that is used to create more complex commands.

printer   Device used to make a permanent copy of any output on paper.

print thimble   Device used by impact letter-quality printers to form characters on paper.

privacy   The claim of individuals, groups, or institutions to determine for themselves when, how, and to what extent personal information about them is communicated to others.

Privacy Act of 1974   Regulates how the federal government manages information collected on citizens.

procedural controls   Written instructions on operating and maintaining a computer system.

procedure   In LOGO, a short set of instructions that can be named and defined by the user and then used as if it were a primitive command. Also a special-purpose module within a program.

processing   Handling, manipulation, and storage of data or information.

processing controls   Provide evidence that data are being processed properly. A typical example is the control total.

productivity software   Packages that include such applications as desktop organizers and outline software.

program   A set of instructions that tells the computer what to do and in what order.

program controls   Verify that data are entered and processed properly and that the resulting information is correctly outputted.

programmer   A person who writes the instructions that direct the computer in the solution of a problem.

programming language A set of characters and prescribed syntax for combining these characters to produce communication between humans and computer systems, to instruct the computer to perform a certain task. BASIC, COBOL, PASCAL, and FORTRAN are examples of programming languages.

PROM (Programmable Read-Only Memory) Memory that can be programmed, or written to, by the user once.

prompt A symbol displayed on the screen to indicate that the computer is ready to accept instructions from the user. The LOGO prompt is a question mark, while the Applesoft prompt is a bracket.

protocol A formal set of rules governing the format and timing of messages exchanged between two communication devices.

prototyping The process of creating a new information system by first rapidly developing a scaled-down or functionally limited model. The prototype model is subsequently modified with the aid of fourth-generation languages.

pseudo-code An arbitrary code made up of instructions in mnemonic or symbolic language and used for designing and documenting the logic of a module.

public domain Something that is not protected by copyright and may be duplicated.

pull-down menu A menu that is pointed at with a mouse and when activated shows the user the options available. It pulls down like a window shade.

punched cards Cards containing holes that represent data or information. Hollerith/IBM punch card is the most famous.

query A request for information, asked of and processed by a data base management system.

query language A simple, easy-to-learn language used to interface with the data base that lets users quickly generate needed reports.

queue A temporary storage of information ready to be processed by the computer.

qwerty The standard keyboard arrangement for keys located above the "home" keys.

RAM (See **random-access memory**.)

RAM-resident program A program loaded into memory that stays there until either the machine is turned off or the user tells it to erase itself.

random-access memory (RAM) Temporary memory. If the computer is turned off, everything stored in RAM is lost. Random access means that information is both placed in RAM and taken out of RAM according to the programmer directions. Programs loaded into the computer are stored in RAM. RAM is the main memory of a computer. The acronym RAM can be used to refer either to the integrated circuits that make up this type of memory or to the memory itself. The computer can store values in distinct locations in RAM and then recall them, or it can alter and restore them.

raster graphics A graphics system in which the computer image is treated as a collection of dots.

raster scan CRT screen A type of CRT screen that uses a projected electron beam that strikes a phosphor-coated screen to form an image.

read-only memory (ROM) Memory that information can be taken out of but not placed into. ROM is permanent storage in the computer for information essential to the operation of the computer. Information in ROM is not lost when the computer is turned off; rather, it is only inactivated.

read process Transfers data into a computer from a secondary storage device.

read–write access hole Oval opening on a diskette that allows the read–write heads to record or access information.

real time Processing of data with the results immediately available.

real-time animation The ability to create and display animation at the final viewing speed.

real-time processing Updates each master file by processing each transaction as it is entered into a computer and transmits the resulting information back to the user.

rear screen projection Projection of an image onto a translucent screen material for viewing from the opposite side. The screen is between the projector and the viewer.

record A complete set of fields and a single unit of storage in a data base.

record key Data that identify one record from others. Student Social Security numbers serve as record keys in many colleges' sequential files. The file must be searched in sequence; if the desired record is passed, the operator must return to the start of the file and search again.

record structure The fields, data type, and field length.

recording density The number of bits of information that can be recorded on a disk in a 1-inch circumference of the innermost track.

reference black level (pedestal) Part of the video signal that provides a reference level for total video picture brightness.

refresh The process of scanning the CRT screen with an electron beam which causes the phosphors to remain lit.

relational structure Structural arrangement consisting of one or more tables. Data are stored in the form of relations in these tables.

release A version of a piece of software. The latest release of a software package typically has enhancements as well as corrections of errors found in prior releases.

remote Usually refers to a terminal or other input–output device at some distance from the CPU.

replace A word processing function that permits the replacing of a word throughout the entire document, such as replace "recieve" with "receive."

report generator Portion of the query language that lets a user quickly generate reports on paper or video medium.

resolution The clarity or graininess of a video or computer image as measured by lines or pixels; the smallest resolvable detail in an image.

reverse video Dark characters on a light background.

RGB (Red, Green, Blue) A video signal that consists of these three colors. RGB monitors receive three signals from the computer and use them to create the image seen on the CRT. RGB video keeps the intensity of each of these three colors on separate cables to produce higher quality images than available with composite video. RGB video output can be either analog or digital.

RGB monitor A type of color monitor with separate inputs for red, green, and blue. It is especially well suited for high-resolution color images.

right justify To align the text of numerical output of a computer so that the rightmost characters of each line are directly under each other.

Right to Financial Privacy Act of 1978 A Congressional act limiting government access to customer records of financial institutions.

rigid disks Magnetic disk packs. Also called *fixed disks*, which are not removable from the disk drive.

ring network A series of computers communicating with one another, joining each computer in the system to two other computers, in opposing directions, forming a ring without a centralized host computer.

ring topology Devices in a local area network connected by a single communication cable in the form of a circle.

robot An analog mechanical device with digital control that functions in a human-like way.

ROM (See **read-only memory**.)

Router A computer that, once dialed into, then acts as a switchboard to make a network connection.

routing The process of controlling the path taken by an audio signal.

RS-232C A widely used serial interface.

run A common DOS command that tells the CPU to execute the program in memory. When accompanied by the name of a program, such as "run hello," it directs the CPU to load the program from the disk in the disk drive and execute it.

sample A digitized version of a sound as processed by a sampler.

sampler An audio device that converts sound to digital information that can be manipulated by a computer. Many high-quality music synthesizers use sampled sounds from acoustic instruments as the basis for their signals.

sans serif A style of type without serifs.

saturation The intensity of a particular hue.

scan converter A device that changes the scan rate of a video signal and may also convert it from interlaced to noninterlaced mode. This allows computer graphics to be displayed on a standard video screen.

scan rate The speed with which the electron beam scans the picture tube.

scanner Converts text, photographs, and black-and-white graphics into computer-readable form and transfers the information to a computer.

scatter plot (or *x–y graph*) Two-dimensional graph of points whose coordinates represent values on the x (horizontal) and y (vertical) axes.

scheduled report Generated at set intervals and usually contains much detailed information.

schema How data are physically stored in the data base.

scientific notation Exponential form for numbers.

scrapbook In a Macintosh computer, a way to transfer text and pictures between files created with different programs.

screen capture A part of your communications software that opens a file on your computer and saves to it whatever scrolls past on the screen while connected to a host system.

screen dump A pixel-for-pixel screen image printed on paper rather than on the CRT.

screen printer A printer that accepts video input and produces a monochrome or color picture directly.

screen shot A photograph of the screen of a computer or video monitor.

scroll Move through text displayed on a video screen, usually one line or one page at a time.

second-generation computers Computers that used transistors to replace vacuum tubes.

secondary key Defining key used to order information within the primary key.

secondary storage Magnetic storage media with high capacity, usually external to the computer itself, and holding most of the data processed by a computer.

sector A portion of a track of magnetic information on a disk where data are stored. In Apple DOS 3.3, one sector can contain 256 bytes of information. There were 16 sectors and 35 tracks on each disk side. Other operating systems have sectors that hold larger numbers of bytes.

semiconductor A solid-state material midway between an insulator and a metal (conductor) in its ability to conduct electricity.

sequencer Software for controlling MIDI musical devices.

sequential-access method Stores records in a file in ascending or descending order by record key; data that identify one record from others.

serial Data sent 1 bit at a time. Serial communications devices permit the sending 1 bit of data at a time.

serial interface Transmits bytes, 1 bit at a time.

serial transmission Sends data 1 bit at a time.

serif A short ornamental stroke or line stemming out at an angle from the end of a printed character.

signal path The complete route followed by a signal in a recording system.

silicon chip A wafer of silicon, typically a fraction of an inch long, containing computer circuitry.

simplex A communication channel that always works in only one direction, such as radio or TV broadcast.

simplex transmission Data can be sent but not received or received but not sent.

single density Disks and drives that read approximately 2,768 bits per inch (360K).

single screen A presentation in which all the images are superimposed on the same screen area.

single-sided drives Disk drives designed so that data are recorded or retrieved from only one side.

slide-show option A feature offered by some presentation software products that allows slides to be shown on the computer screen in a predetermined order.

SLIP (Serial Line IP) A method that allows a computer to connect directly to the Internet through a telephone line and high speed modem (similar to *PPP*).

smart modems Modems that contain a microprocessor that controls many functions, allowing easier and more flexible use of data communications.

SMPT (Simple Mail Transfer Protocol) Alerts the computer that the message being sent is going to a person connected to the Internet by a different service provider.

Society of Motion Picture and Television Engineers (SMPTE) An organization that sets technical standards for film and video.

Society of Motion Picture and Television Engineers Time Code An eight-digit address code used to identify each videotape frame by hour, minute, second, and frame number for precise editing.

soft copy Output displayed on a CRT.

soft-sectored disk Has each track divided into sectors during the format process.

software Usually considered synonymous with *program*. Stored digital information on magnetic disks or tapes or as electronic information in the computer's memory. Software determines what a computer does. Software converts a general-purpose machine into a special-purpose machine. Word processing software converts a general-purpose computer into a word processor. Commands and directions are software, as are the media they are stored on.

software piracy Illicit duplication of software.

song position pointer A MIDI message that indicates the measure number and quarter-note beat location within a composition.

sort The process of physically rearranging records within a file.

source code Set of program instructions written in a high-level language.

source document The original paper document that holds information about a record or transaction.

special effects generator A device used to produce wipes, split screens, inserts, keys, and mattes.

speech synthesizers Mechanical devices capable of reproducing sounds similar to the human voice.

speller Software that checks the spelling of words in a document.

spelling checker A software package used with a word processor that checks the spelling of individual words in a document.

split screen The ability to divide a monitor screen in half and display a different document or graphic image on each half. Multiple-split screen shows images from several sources or different actions taking place in several windows in the screen area.

spreadsheet   An electronic ledger sheet used to enter numbers and words in rows and columns: x–y entry of information.

sprite   A graphic image in some animation packages that can be manipulated to produce animation, or movement.

stair-stepping   Discontinuous nature of a line drawn at any angle other than horizontal or vertical. Also called "jaggies."

stand-alone   presentation   graphics package   A software program through which text or graphic files can be used to create images for presentations.

star network   A single central host computer with one or more terminals or microcomputers connected to it, forming a star.

start-up disk   A disk that has been initialized or formatted with information to start computer operation.

still-frame storage unit   A digital device used to store individual video frames, any of which can be recalled for display.

still video   A camera that stores still images on magnetic disks rather than on film.

stored-program concept   Permits the reading of a program into a computer's memory and then executing the program instructions without rewiring the computer.

storyboard   A visual outline of the narrative of a video or film production.

strategic decision making   Includes setting objectives for an organization and devising long-range plans.

string testing   Verifies that interprogram control results in files being transferred properly from one program to the next.

structured decisions   Any decisions made via existing procedures.

structured English   Plain English with certain restrictions, which derive from its structural similarity to program code.

structured language   Languages based on a hierarchy of operations starting with the general and going to the specific.

structured walkthrough   Process of having several individuals review a program or worksheet and check it for accuracy, logic, and readability.

stub testing   Involves designing dummy modules, with a minimum of program code, that let a programmer verify that linkage between modules functions properly.

subcarrier   The portion of the composite video signal containing the color information.

subschema   How data are accessed by a user or an application.

supercomputer   The fastest, most expensive computers manufactured. They can run numerous different calculations simultaneously, thereby processing in 1 minute what would take a personal computer several weeks or months.

superimposition   Laying titles or graphics over a video image.

super-VHS (S-VHS)   Videotape format that provides better resolution and less noise than standard VHS tapes.

synchronous communication   Transmission of groups of characters over a communications line without start or stop bits.

synchronous protocol   Transmits data in groups of characters, called packets, at fixed quantities and intervals.

synergism   The concept that the whole is greater than the sum of its parts.

syntax   Set of grammatical rules that govern languages.

synthesizer (synth)   An electronic device for creating musical sounds and sound effects.

system   An integrated set of procedures to achieve a desired result. Also consists of hardware.

system analysis   Procedure of developing MISs that provide managers with the information they need to make decisions.

system analyst   A person responsible for examining an existing information system and suggesting improvements to the system.

system audit   A step in the system development life cycle (SDLC) in which it is verified that a system meets expectations and processes data appropriately.

system command   An instruction that directs the system, such as the disk-operating system, to perform some function.

system controls   Ensure the proper development of information systems.

system development life cycle (SDLC)   A series of formalized steps used in system analysis.

system disk   The disk with start-up and other utility information. In the Macintosh, it includes the finder.

System Query Language (SQL)   A standardized language through which queries are directed to data bases.

system testing   Verifies that the manual and computerized parts of the system function properly.

T1-Connection   A type of direct connection where your computer or computer network has a cable connecting you directly to the Internet.

tablet   A flat drawing surface and a pointing tool that functions like a pencil. The tablet turns the pointer's movements into digitized data that can be read by special computer programs. Tablets range from palm to desktop size.

tactical decision making   Implements strategic decisions by allocating an organization's resources (personnel, budgeting, production scheduling, and allocation of working capital).

tag image file format (TIFF)   The format used for transporting computerized versions of scanned images.

tape density   The number of characters or bytes that can be stored on an inch of tape.

tape drive   A hardware device that reads data from and writes data on magnetic tape.

tape format   Any of several tape widths and recording methods, such as ½-inch VHS and ¾-inch U-Matic, used in video recording.

TCP/IP (Transmission Control Protocol/Internet Protocol)   The rules (or protocols) for data transfer on the Internet.

telecommunications   Data communication using communications facilities, such as telephone, radio, or microwave.

teleconferencing   Creating a meeting by transmitting voice and visual images to and from physically remote individuals.

TELNET   A remote log-in tool used to connect your computer to other computers and networks. Once your computer is connected to a remote computer, it acts as though it is connected to the remote computer's network. For example, to connect to NASA's computer in Alabama, you would type: telnet spacelink. msfc.nasa.gov.

template   The organizational plan for a spreadsheet that contains the labels for columns and rows, the formula needed to perform calculations, and all other information except the data.

terminal   A device for passing information to a computer, generally consisting of a keyboard for entering data or instructions and a screen for displaying output.

terminal emulation   Enables a microcomputer to serve as a computer terminal for another system.

testing   The process of verifying that all processes and procedures work properly. This includes input, processing, output, and file-generation procedures.

thermal printer   Uses specially treated paper to "burn" in dots to form characters; it produces hard copy output on this type of heat-sensitive paper.

thesaurus   Software that allows the user to obtain synonyms.

third-generation computer   Computers that use integrated circuits instead of individual transistors— produced since 1964.

time base   The timing portion of a video signal, particularly the horizontal and vertical sync pulses.

time base corrector (TBC)   A device that corrects time-base signal instabilities caused by VCRs during playback, making it possible for two or more VCRs to be in sync.

time code   An electronic counter or indicator of videotape duration; the hours, minutes, seconds, and frames that the tape lasts. This is usually visible only with a special time code reader.

time sharing   Several users sharing the same computer central processor.

timing hole   Small hole to the right of the centering hole on a diskette. Used to synchronize disk speed.

token   A control signal passed from one node to the next, indicating which node is allowed to transmit.

token passing   The transmission of a token from one computer to the next in a bus or ring local area network that gives the receiving computer permission to transmit on the network.

toolbox   An icon-based menu with tools that can be used in desktop publishing.

top–down programming   A style where the programmer divides the problem into successively small procedures, then writes the program in these pieces or procedures.

touch pad   A computer pointing device that the user operates by moving a finger over a surface.

touch screen   Lets user enter instructions by touching a menu selection or indicating which text to include in an instruction by moving across the text with a finger.

track   Concentric circles of storage on a disk's read–write surface on which data are stored. On disks, tracks are circular and divided into sectors; on tapes, tracks are linear.

tractor feed   A printer that uses paper with holes (e.g., sprocket holes) that mesh with sprockets to pull the paper through the printer.

traditional approach   File-based processing.

transaction file   Contains data about some business action and is by nature transitory. After its information is inputted, the transaction file is discarded.

transaction log   Contains complete audit trail of all activity of a data base for a given time.

transaction-processing system   Another name for data processing.

transistor   A compact electronic device composed of semiconductor material that controls current flow, similar to a vacuum tube.

transmission speed   The speed at which data are transmitted across communications links.

turtle   Used by LOGO. A mechanical device that can be programmed to move around on the floor and to draw with a pen, or a triangle-shaped design that can be programmed to move around on the CRT and to draw with a pen.

tutorial   A form of CBI, or CAI, where the computer carries on a dialogue with the student, presenting new information and giving the student a chance to practice becoming proficient at the new skill or concept.

twisted pair wire   Common telephonelike wire.

UNIVAC (UNIVersal Automatic Computer)   First commercial electronic digital computer. Used by the U.S. Bureau of the Census to process the 1950 census.

UNIX   A widely used operating system developed by Bell Laboratories for use on minicomputers but which has been modified to run on personal computers.

uploading   Sends a file from a small remote computer to a large central computer.

URL (Uniform Resource Locator)   This is the standard system used to identify different types of servers and assign them Internet addresses on the World Wide Web.

Usenet   Message-based discussion groups. They operate as electronic bulletin boards where you can leave messages for entire groups. Numerous Usenet newsgroups are on the Internet for a variety of topics.

user friendly   Software designed to be easily used by nontechnically trained persons.

user memory   The amount of memory available to the user. Usually is an amount less than the total RAM because some of this memory is used for the computer's operating system and is not available to the user.

utilities   Programs that handle routine tasks and that can be inserted into other programs to avoid having to program them repeatedly.

vacuum tube   An electron tube from which most of the air has been removed that contains one or more wire grids. Used as a switching and memory device in first-generation computers.

variable   A symbolic name of an address where information that may change is stored.

VCR (Videocassette Recorder)   A device for recording video on cassettes.

VDA (Video Distribution Amplifier)   A device used to allow the connection of several monitors to one video source.

VDT (Video Display Tube)   The same as CRT, or cathode ray tube. The output device for computers that gives soft copy.

vector graphics   A display technology that builds images from the strokes of lines rather than from collections of individual pixels.

vectorscope   Video test equipment that displays information about the color portion of the video signal.

VERONICA (Very Easy Rodent-Oriented Net-Wide Index to Computerized Archies)   A search utility that allows you to type in a topic on which you want information. VERONICA will search through all of the gopher servers, world wide, for information on the topic.

vertical blanking interval   The time between fields from one vertical scan to the start of the next. Other information can be sent during this period.

vertical resolution   The number of pixels available vertically down the screen.

vertical scan rate   The speed at which the electron beam scans down the entire screen of a monitor.

very high speed printers   Printers that print in excess of 3000 lines per minute.

VHS (Video Home System)   The most popular ½-inch consumer videotape format.

video disk   A round plastic platter that contains tiny bumps (lands and valleys) that are coded digital information that are read into the computer's memory by a laser.

video graphics adapter (VGA)   High-quality graphics standard for MS-DOS computers compatible with EGA (enhanced graphics adapter).

video player   A device that only plays back, but does not record, videotapes or optical disks.

video signal   A wave form carrying video information.

video still camera   A camera generally shaped like a 35mm film camera that captures still images and saves them on magnetic disks in an analog video format. Consumer-grade devices capture single fields, and professional-grade cameras can capture fields and frames. This technology also allows for up to 10 seconds of audio to be captured along with each picture.

videoconferencing   The ability for groups at distant locations to participate, through audio and video, in the same meeting at the same time.

videospace   The sum total of all the visual elements that interact to create the visual counterpart to audiospace.

virtual reality   Highly realistic computer simulations that use three-dimensional displays to create the impression of being inside a place.

virus   A self-replicating piece of software that may or may not cause severe danger to a user's computer system.

virus vaccines   Special software packages designed to detect and remove viruses.

VisiCalc   First electronic spreadsheet program introduced for microcomputers, designed by Dan Bricklin and Bob Frankston.

VLSI (Very Large-Scale Integration)   Integrated circuits (IC) with a very large number (50,000 to 1,000,000) of electronic components built on one chip.

volatile memory   Memory that is erased when the electrical current to the computer is turned off. RAM is volatile memory.

VT100   Another terminal-emulation system. Supported by many communications programs. VT102 is a newer version.

warm boot   Rebooting a program without turning the computer's power off.

waveform monitor   Video test equipment that measures and displays the parameters of the video signal.

white space   The blank space left on a page to make it more readable.

Wide Area Information Server (WAIS)   A powerful system that enables people to search for information in databases and Internet libraries.

Winchester disk   A type of hard disk used with computers.

Windows   A graphic user interface developed by Microsoft for use by IBM and compatible computers.

wipe   A visual transition in which one image replaces another along a border that moves across the screen.

word   A byte, or a place where one alphanumeric character is stored in a computer's memory. A word is one byte.

word processing   Automated manipulation of text data via a software package that usually provides the ability to create, edit, store, and print documents easily.

word wrap   Feature that automatically places a word on the next line when it will not fit on the current line.

work stations   Personal computers connected into a local area network.

workspace   Another name for random-access memory (RAM).

World Wide Web (WWW)   Documents on the Internet that contain hyperlinks to other documents.

write process   Transfers data out of a computer back to secondary storage.

write-protect notch   Rectangular notch at upper right-hand edge of some disks. Prevents alteration of disk's information, but disk remains readable.

write-protected   Diskettes that have been protected from having information stored on them, being altered, or being deleted.

WYSIWYG (What You See Is What You Get)   Generally used with word processing and graphics applications to indicate that how an image appears on the screen is also how it will look in print.

WWW   (See **World Wide Web**.)

x (horizontal) axis   The left-to-right axis.

y (vertical) axis   The up-and-down axis.

zone portion of a byte   The leftmost 4 bits of an 8-bit byte.